The Eagles Encyclopedia

The photo collage on the title page represents all eight decades of Eagles football: quarterback Davey O'Brien (8) starred for the team in the 1930s; halfback Steve Van Buren (lower right) led the team to two world championships in the 1940s; Eagles play at Shibe Park (lower left), their home in the 1950s; linebacker Chuck Bednarik (upper right, number 60) starred for the 1960 world championship team; quarterback Ron Jaworski (7) set passing records in the 1970s; quarterback Randall Cunningham (12) was one of the most exciting players of the 1980s; Donovan McNabb (hoisting the NFC Championship trophy) joined the team in the 1990s and teamed with Freddie Mitchell (84) and Brian Westbrook (36) to win four consecutive Eastern Division titles, beginning in 2001.

The photo on the dedication page is Hall of Famer Chuck Bednarik in his final season, 1962.

A photo gallery of Eagles players through the years appears at the beginning of each chapter. Featured are (left to right) tackle Vic Sears (1941–53), Hall of Fame halfback Steve Van Buren (1944–51), end Jack Ferrante (1941, 1944–50), quarterback Bobby Thomason (1952–57), Hall of Fame quarterback Norm Van Brocklin (1958–60), Hall of Fame flanker Tommy McDonald (1957–63), Hall of Fame tackle Bob Brown (1964–68), defensive end–linebacker Tim Rossovich (1968–71), halfback Wilbert Montgomery (1977–84), kicker Tony Franklin (1979–83), and two current Eagles, defensive tackle Corey Simon and quarterback Donovan McNabb.

The *EAGLES* Encyclopedia

RAY DIDINGER and ROBERT S. LYONS

TEMPLE UNIVERSITY PRESS
Philadelphia

Temple University Press
1601 North Broad Street
Philadelphia PA 19122
www.temple.edu/tempress

Design by Lynne Frost

⊛ The paper used in this publication meets the requirements of the American
National Standard for Information Sciences—Permanence of Paper for Printed
Library Materials, ANSI Z39.48-1992

The authors and publisher wish to thank the following for permission to reprint the
photographs that appear in this volume: Philadelphia Eagles; Pro Football Hall of
Fame; *Philadelphia Daily News*; Temple University Urban Archives; Tom Briglia/NFL
Photos; Joseph V. Labolito; Ed Mahan; Michael Mercanti/*Philadelphia Daily News*;
J. Warren; personal collection of Ray Didinger; and *Sports Illustrated* and photogra-
phers Simon Bruty, Heinz Kluetmeier, Peter Read Miller, and John G. Zimmerman.

This book is not sanctioned by the NFL or its teams.

Library of Congress Cataloging-in-Publication Data

Didinger, Ray.
   The Eagles encyclopedia / Ray Didinger and Robert S. Lyons.
      p.   cm.
  ISBN 1-59213-449-1 (cloth : alk. paper)
    1. Philadelphia Eagles (Football team)—History.   I. Lyons, Robert S.,
1939– II. Title.
GV956.P44D53 2005
796.332'64'0974811—dc22   2005043935

2 4 6 8 9 7 5 3 1

*To my parents, Ray and Marie Didinger,
and to my grandparents, Ray and Margaret Didinger,
who taught me the joys of family and football.*

—Ray Didinger

*To my mother, Catharine M. Lyons, who instilled in me
a profound appreciation of the written word.*

—Robert S. Lyons

RAY DIDINGER has won four Emmy Awards as a writer and producer at NFL Films. Before that, he was a reporter covering the National Football League for *The Philadelphia Bulletin,* and later *The Philadelphia Daily News.* In 1995 he was enshrined in the Pro Football Hall of Fame as the recipient of the Dick McCann Memorial Award for long and distinguished reporting of pro football. He is also a weekly commentator and panelist on Comcast's *Post-Game Live* show during the football season.

ROBERT S. LYONS has covered professional and college sports for the Associated Press for more than thirty years, and has contributed to numerous national publications. The former director of the La Salle University News Bureau, editor of the university's alumni magazine, and an instructor of journalism at La Salle, he is now president of RSL Communications. He is the author of *Palestra Pandemonium: A History of the Big 5* (Temple).

Contents

Preface

THEY CAME in planes and buses, in Winnebagos and sedans, a caravan of green and silver rolling into Jacksonville, Florida. They were everywhere—on the streets, in the hotels, and, yes, in the bars—with their jerseys, their face paint and, most of all, their hope. With Eagles fans, there is always hope.

In the days leading up to Super Bowl XXXIX, they owned the city of Jacksonville. An estimated 40,000 Eagles fans made the trip, many of them without tickets to the game or a place to stay. They just felt they had to be there, even if it was in the parking lot or in a trailer watching on TV, but they had to be close enough to pour their own emotion onto the tribal fire.

They drove 15 hours through ice storms in the Carolinas and rain in Georgia. They slept in their cars; they scrounged for tickets. Why? One fan, Vince Boyle, told the *Florida Times-Union*: "We've cheered [the Eagles]. We've cried for them. This is the payoff."

Kevin Reilly was born in Delaware, attended Villanova, and was an Eagles fan even before he was a linebacker with the team in 1973 and '74. He, too, was in Jacksonville, and he was interviewed on a Florida radio station. He was asked to explain this phenomenon, how the Eagles fans outnumbered New England fans 10–1, according to the *Times-Union*.

"It's like trying to explain Mecca, why do the pilgrims go there?" Reilly said. "I told the guy, 'Unless you're from Philadelphia, you'll never understand.'"

The Eagles lost to New England in the Super Bowl, 24–21, but that result does not change the story. Indeed, it merely reinforces it. In a history that dates back to 1933, the Eagles have lost far more than they have won. Their overall record through the 2004 season is 458 wins, 511 losses, and 25 ties. They have won just three NFL championships, the last one in 1960. Yet the passion of the fans endures.

That is really the theme of this book. Like any encyclopedia, it is full of records and statistics, but they only form the framework for the real story. This is a book about a city and a team and the emotional tether that binds them. It is a book about frustration (remember the chants of "Joe Must Go"?), about heartbreak (three straight losses in the NFC championship game), and about jubilation (Wilbert Montgomery's off-tackle burst against Dallas), but mostly it is a book about devotion. It is a love story, pure and simple.

During the run to Super Bowl XXXIX, the Eagles adopted the theme "One City, One Team, One Dream." It was a fine slogan, and it fit the mood perfectly, but it could be applied to the whole history of the franchise. It was a sentiment Philadelphians—from blue blood to blue collar—felt long before the marketing department put it on a T-shirt. It was part of our civic identity, something that pulled this diverse region together in one heartbeat.

"There's passion everywhere you go," said defensive end Jevon Kearse, who was introduced to the Philadelphia football culture in 2004. "They're just die-hard fans. People were born Eagles fans around here. You go other places, people are made into fans. Here, they're born."

For most people in the Philadelphia region, the Eagles are family. For generations, they have been a Sunday ritual. Mom, Dad, the kids, everyone planned the day around the game. Maybe they had tickets, maybe they watched on TV, but it didn't matter. Come the fourth quarter, nobody was worrying about the pot roast or the book report that was due tomorrow. Everyone was too busy high-fiving after another big play.

Philadelphia is a great sports town, and the fans in the region support all the teams, but it is not the same. With the Phillies, the Sixers, and the Flyers, it is like you drop in on them once in a while. You catch them flipping around the dials. Oh yeah, there's a game tonight. But the Eagles are something you plan for, something you share. You watch the game with family and friends, and there is an investment of time and emotion that is unique.

The Eagles are a kind of heirloom that is handed down from one generation to the next. Many of the fans who were in Jacksonville in February had fathers who were at Veterans Stadium in 1981 when the Eagles beat Dallas, and grandfathers who were at the 1960 championship game at Franklin Field, and so on, back through time.

Rich Hofmann of the *Philadelphia Daily News* profiled such a family, the Clarks of Bucks County. Ernie, the 70-year-old patriarch, went to the 1948 NFL championship game with his father, attended the 1960 championship game with his wife-to-be Anne, went to the 1981 Dallas game with his son Chris, and suffered through the two most recent NFC championship game losses with his grandsons. The venues change, the players change, but it's always about family. The Clarks are typical of the Eagles fan base.

"Nothing is like Philly, I'll tell you," Donovan McNabb told Jim Corbett of *USA Today*. "The best thing about the fans here is that they are very supportive. They love their Eagles. They'll do whatever it takes to help us win. But they'll do whatever it takes to let you know when you're not winning, too."

Eagles fans are often identified with bad behavior. Yes, they threw snowballs at Santa Claus in 1968. And it is true, they threw snowballs at Dallas coach Jimmy Johnson. The court-room in the Vet with the adjoining cells? It is not a myth, it did exist—and did a brisk business, in fact.

No sense denying any of this. But put it in context. Think about all the losing seasons. Think about the bad ownership. Think about the stupid trades and lousy drafts. Still, the fans kept coming. Yes, they got angry. Sure, they got loud. And if their frustration boiled over from time to time—and once a generation some snowballs flew—well, it was almost under-standable. The point is, they never stopped caring.

The perfect profile of an Eagles fan would juxtapose two images: first, the TV news shot of the anguished man in the green jersey standing outside Lincoln Financial Field after the NFC Championship Game loss to Carolina, screaming, "You broke my heart again"; second, the sight of 25,000 fans turn-ing out for an Eagles training camp practice six months later, the largest crowd ever to attend an NFL summer workout. (And you just know the guy with the broken heart was some-where in that crowd, his hopes reborn.)

"You don't know what to expect with Philadelphia fans all the time," safety Brian Dawkins said. "But the one thing you do know is that they come and they come in bunches."

Prior to Super Bowl XXXIX, the Associated Press wrote about Kevin O'Donoghue, an Eagles fan from Glen Mills, who took out a second mortgage on his home to pay for his trip to Jacksonville. O'Donoghue was 11 when the Eagles went to their only other Super Bowl, and he vowed that if they ever went back, he would be there, no matter the cost. "I can't wait," he said. "It feels like Christmas Eve."

Psychologists talk about Philadelphia having an inferiority complex. Something about living in the dual shadows of New York and Washington, D.C. That is supposed to explain why Eagles fans are so devoted, why we see each Sunday as a chance to get even. Maybe at some level that explanation is true. But I think the people in this area just love football. They love it in a way that has nothing to do with demographics. They see the game as a reflection of who they are.

"Every city not named Los Angeles tries to portray itself as 'blue-collar' and its teams as 'throwbacks.' Few qualify," wrote Paul Daugherty of the *Cincinnati Enquirer.* "Pittsburgh loves its Steelers. Green Bay always will claim ownership of the Packers … But the Eagles are different. No town derives its identity from its football team the way Philadelphia does."

"Philadelphia, ever since I went there in 1985, has always had a lot of heart and character," said Randall Cunningham, who played 11 seasons with the Eagles. "They take it from the town. It's a hardworking place where the people have a lot of heart."

That feeling is what sustained the Eagles through more than 70 seasons, from the beginning when a former Penn quarterback named Bert Bell founded the team, through the lean years when the club moved around the city like a float-ing dice game, going from the Baker Bowl to Temple Stadium to Municipal Stadium. Bell believed that pro football and Philadelphia were a perfect marriage. It took a while, but he was proven right.

The history of the franchise can be found in this book. There are bleak stretches to be sure. The first decade, for exam-ple, did not produce a single winning season. And what about the 11 consecutive losses to Dallas from 1967 through 1972? The disappointment of Super Bowl XV followed by the burnout and resignation of coach Dick Vermeil. The finan-cial collapse of not one, but two owners: Jerry Wolman and Leonard Tose. It is all part of the story.

But so are the championship teams of 1948 and '49, the iron-man saga of Chuck Bednarik in 1960, the Miracle of the Meadowlands, Reggie White and the Body Bag Game, and now the unprecedented success of Andy Reid, winning four consec-utive division titles. Those highlights are here as well. But the real story is what's between the lines, the hard-to-define, impossible-to-measure, but we-all-can-feel-it emotion that defines the Eagles' hold on the city.

Over the 4th of July weekend, when one million people jammed the Benjamin Franklin Parkway for the Live 8 concert, the "E-A-G-L-E-S" chant could be heard. Whenever there was a lull between the musical acts, someone in the crowd would shout "E" and thousands would join in, spelling out the name of the football team—not the rock group—that cuts across all social lines. It went on for hours, in the middle of what *Phila-delphia Inquirer* columnist Phil Sheridan called "the most far-reaching single-day cultural event in the history of the planet," rolling down the parkway and echoing around the globe. "E-A-G-L-E-S, Eagles."

"There is nothing else like it," said Governor Edward G. Rendell, a season ticket holder who spent the past five seasons as an analyst on the Eagles postgame show on Comcast Sports-Net. "The Eagles affect everyone. Win or lose, they pull peo-ple together. I remember one day after a big win seeing a busi-nessman getting a shoeshine, and this guy in the three-piece suit and the guy shining his shoes were talking about the game. 'Yeah, how about this play? What about that play?' There was no [class] distinction, no rich and poor, no black and white, just two guys talking about the Eagles.

"When I hear people say, 'It's only a game,' I think of that scene and I realize, no, it's not. Not with the Eagles, it's not."

—Ray Didinger

Acknowledgments

WRITING *The Eagles Encyclopedia* was a labor of love, but it would not have been possible without the assistance of many good friends and colleagues.

Joe Horrigan, Pete Fierle, and Saleem Choudhry of the Pro Football Hall of Fame provided valuable material. T. J. Troup of the Professional Football Researchers Association offered insightful analysis. Jim Gallagher—who lived Eagles history for almost half a century as a team executive—was, as always, an unfailing source of wisdom and humor.

Derek Boyko, the director of football media services for the Eagles, and his staff, which includes Rich Burg, Bob Lange, Scott Horner, Chris Lundy, and Ryan Nissan, were always willing to open their archives. Mark Donovan, senior vice president for business operations, helped in gathering illustrations. Margaret Jerrido and her staff at Urban Archives at Temple University's Paley Library indulged us as we spent weeks poring over the photographs and clippings from the *Philadelphia Bulletin* and the *Inquirer*.

Ed Mahan, the Eagles photographer, has chronicled the team's history for more than 30 years, and his images, along with those of Joseph V. Labolito, helped to bring this book to life.

We thank Pat McLoone, assistant managing editor for sports at the *Philadelphia Daily News*; Josh Barnett, sports editor; and Paul Vigna, special projects editor for sports at the *Daily News*, for their help. We also thank Michael Panzer, library supervisor at the *Daily News* and *Inquirer* as well as Bob Vetrone, Jr., and Ed Barkowitz of the *Daily News* sports staff for their assistance.

Others who helped include Ernie Accorsi, Merrill Reese, Mark Eckel, Mike Adams, Chris Willis, Jim Campbell, Ralph Goldston, Al Wistert, Tommy McDonald, Leo Carlin, and Jim Murray, all of whom contributed to making this account as accurate and detailed as possible.

Among the books that provided valuable background were *Total Football*, by Bob Carroll, David Neft, Michael Gershman, and John Thorn; *The Pro Football Chronicle*, by Dan Daly and Bob O'Donnell; *Tales from the Eagles Sidelines*, by Gordon Forbes; *To Every Thing a Season: Shibe Park and Urban Philadelphia*, by Bruce Kuklich; *Confidence: How Winning Streaks and Losing Streaks Begin and End*, by Rosabeth Moss Kanter; *A History of Athletics in Pennsylvania*, by George W. Orton; *Pigskin: The Early Years of Pro Football*, by Robert W. Peterson; *The Phillies Encyclopedia*, by Rich Westcott and Frank Bilovsky; and *Iron Men*, by Stuart Leuthner.

We were fortunate to have a dedicated staff pushing this project along. Our editor at Temple University Press, Micah Kleit, and production director Charles Ault worked Dick Vermeil hours to keep the book on schedule. Peter Reinhart did a superb job checking the facts and polishing the copy, while Lynne Frost artfully designed the pages.

Bob offers a special note of appreciation to his wife Joan for her proofreading as well as for her understanding of the many hours he spent consumed in this book, and to his son Greg for his assistance in preparing the manuscript.

Ray thanks his wife Maria for interrupting her own writing night after night to proofread another chapter of Eagles history and ship it to the publisher. He also thanks NFL Films President Steve Sabol and coordinating producers Pat Kelleher and Ross Ketover for giving him the time to complete the project.

—Ray Didinger and Bob Lyons

Professional Football in Philadelphia: The Early Years

PROFESSIONAL FOOTBALL in Philadelphia owes its beginning to a war between the city's two major league baseball teams, the Phillies and the Athletics.

It happened in 1902—long before the Eagles and Frankford Yellow Jackets ever existed, and seven years after the first professional football game was played in Latrobe, Pennsylvania.

Major league baseball had waged bitter warfare for more than a year, ever since 1901 when the newly organized American League started raiding the more established National League for its better players.

The animosity became more intense when Phillies owner Colonel John I. Rogers decided to bankroll a professional football team and appointed his manager, Bill Shettsline, as its coach. Ben Shibe, the A's owner, quickly joined the fray and named *his* baseball manager, Connie Mack, the coach of the Athletics football squad.

The two Philadelphia baseball club owners rarely agreed on anything. But they did see the value of making some money from the new gridiron sport. So they looked across to the western part of the state, where football had become an even hotter attraction, and invited the powerful Pittsburgh Stars to join in a round-robin competition with the winner being declared "world champions."

Pittsburgh owner Dave Berry was elected the first president of the new organization. It was christened the *National Football League*—believed to be the first attempt to organize a professional football circuit. Teams from New York and Chicago declined invitations to join.

Connie Mack quickly caught the public's attention by signing future baseball Hall of Famer Rube Waddell to a football contract in a move that almost cost the "Grand Old Man of Baseball" his life. Another future baseball Hall of Famer, pitcher Christy Mathewson, joined Pittsburgh as a fullback.

In round-robin action, Pittsburgh and the Athletics each split their two games with the Phillies. The Athletics edged Pittsburgh, 11–10, in a tense game when the Stars missed two extra points. So the season came down to an A's-Stars rematch in Pittsburgh on Thanksgiving Day. A Philadelphia win would give the A's the title. A Pittsburgh victory would leave the three teams deadlocked with 2–2 records.

Mack prepared his team for the big showdown by traveling to Elmira, New York, and playing in what is believed to be the first night game, beating Kanaweola A.C., 39–0.

When the team got to Pittsburgh, according to the Professional Football Researchers Association, Mack discovered Waddell sneaking into the hotel lobby long after curfew. "Holding his temper, he gave Waddell a firm but kindly talking to that left Rube tearfully contrite and promising to behave forever. Then as the big pitcher turned to go quietly to do penance in his hotel room, a loaded pistol dropped out of his pocket and went off. The bullet missed Connie's head by inches."

When the Athletics arrived at the Pittsburgh Coliseum the next day, the stands were nearly empty. Berry had guaranteed Mack $2,000. With visions of being stranded and broke hundreds of miles from home, Mack ordered his team to stay on the buses. Unless he was paid first, Connie announced, there would be no game.

About an hour later, a distinguished looking gentleman walked up to Mack. It was William Corey, head of Carnegie Steel. After inquiring about the delay, Corey pulled out his checkbook and gave Mack his $2,000 guarantee.

The game ended in a scoreless tie, and the teams agreed to stage another "championship" two days later. This time, the Stars took advantage of two Philadelphia turnovers in the last two minutes to push across a pair of touchdowns for an 11–0 win.

At the end of the season, all three Pennsylvania teams claimed the professional championship. But Berry awarded the title to the Stars because they outscored their opponents, 39–22. The A's went home and beat the Phillies to clinch the city championship, but that game did not count in the final NFL standings.

Players from the Athletics and Phillies then teamed up to form a club called *New York* and entered the first World Series of Professional Football, a five-team tournament held at the old Madison Square Garden at the end of the 1902 season. The combined squad of Philadelphia players lost to Syracuse 6–0 in what is believed to be the first indoor football game ever played. Syracuse, with Glenn (Pop) Warner at guard, went on to win the tournament.

The first National Football League lasted just one season.

OVER THE NEXT few years, professional football was in complete disarray. Interest in the sport shifted west into Ohio, Indiana, and Illinois. In 1920 the American Professional Football Conference was formed, and within months the name of the league was changed to American Professional Football *Association.*

In 1922 the APFA changed its name to the National Football League. By 1924 the league had 18 franchises including

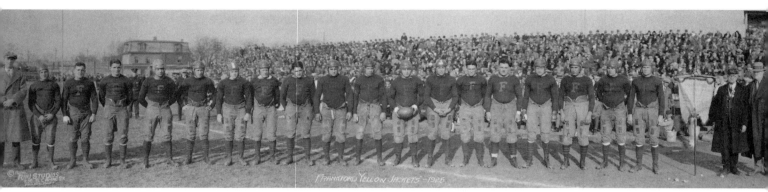

The Frankford Yellow Jackets, the National Football League's first franchise in Philadelphia, at Frankford Stadium in 1925.

a new team from the Frankford section of Philadelphia. In 1925, five new franchises were admitted, including the Pottsville Maroons, who had been the most successful independent semiprofessional team in the Anthracite League, comprised of teams from eastern Pennsylvania mining towns. Covering the team for the *Pottsville Republican* was John O'Hara, who would later become a world-famous novelist.

Late in the 1925 season, the NFL gained instant national recognition. Shortly after the University of Illinois season ended, All-America halfback Harold (Red) Grange, the first true football superstar, signed to play for the Chicago Bears. In December the Bears began two barnstorming tours, the first of which saw them play eight games in 12 days in the Midwest and East. The second tour—nine games in six weeks—took the "Galloping Ghost" through the southern and western states.

"It was like a coast-to-coast ticker-tape parade," said Dan Daly and Bob O'Donnell, in *The Pro Football Chronicle*. "Bands blaring, crowds cheering, cash registers ringing."

Grange was under contract to play a minimum of 25 minutes each game and rarely played more. In Philadelphia, the second stop on the first tour, 25,000 fans braved the rain and mud at Shibe Park to watch him lead the Bears to a 14–7 triumph over the Frankford Yellow Jackets. Grange scored both Chicago touchdowns. The largest crowd was in Los Angeles, where 75,000 fans saw the Bears defeat the Los Angeles Tigers, 17–7.

Pottsville and the Chicago Cardinals were the top contenders for the NFL title that year, with Pottsville believing it clinched the championship by winning a late-season showdown, 21–7, at Comiskey Park. Walter (Piggy) French, an outfielder with the Philadelphia Athletics during the summer, was the offensive and defensive star for the Maroons.

Pottsville then scheduled a game against a team of former Notre Dame stars, including the legendary Four Horsemen, at Philadelphia's Shibe Park. The Frankford Yellow Jackets immediately lodged a protest.

Not only was the game being played in Frankford's protected territory, but it was also scheduled at the same time as a Yellow Jacket home game. League Commissioner Joe Carr gave the Maroons three specific warnings not to play the game, but they played anyway, beating the Fighting Irish, 9–7, on a last-minute 30-yard field goal by Charley Berry, who would later become umpire in chief of the American League.

Watching the game was Knute Rockne, the famed Notre Dame coach, who didn't want his former players to know he was there. Rockne hid behind a pole in the press box. Pottsville's team was immediately suspended, had the final

game of its season against the Providence Steam Roller canceled, and had its franchise returned to the league.

Even more devastating, Carr took Pottsville's league title away, even though the Maroons finished with a 10–2 record, recorded seven shutouts, and outscored their opponents, 270–45.

Since then, numerous pleas have been made to the National Football League to restore the 1925 title to Pottsville. Even Pennsylvania Governor Ed Rendell got involved in 2003, lobbying NFL owners and state officials to put pressure on the league to act in time for the city's bicentennial in 2006. But the NFL owners rejected the request by a 30–2 vote, with only Pittsburgh's Dan Rooney and Philadelphia's Jeffrey Lurie supporting the Maroons.

In 1926, Pottsville was reinstated in the NFL and went on to play 18 games in 80 days. Its NFL record was 10–2–1. In one of its nonleague games, a 60–0 victory over Lancaster, ten players were injured. The Maroons trainer, Eddie Gillespie, was pressed into action and scored two touchdowns. After suffering through losing seasons for the next two years, the Pottsville franchise was moved to Boston before the 1929 campaign.

But the big news in 1926 focused on Red Grange's manager, C. C. Pyle, who formed a new league, the American Football League, because the Bears refused to meet his contract demands. The nine-team league—including Grange's New York Yankees—lasted one season. It folded after the AFL champion Philadelphia Quakers lost to the New York Giants, the NFL's seventh-best team, 31–0 in December. It was the first interleague game on record and preceded the modern Super Bowl by four decades.

The Philadelphia Quakers had been a barnstorming team without a league affiliation, with local standouts like Heinie Miller, Lou Little, Butch Spagna, Lud Wray, and Johnny Scott making appearances when they weren't playing for teams like the Buffalo All Americans, of the APFA and, later, Frankford.

Meanwhile, late in the 1926 season, the Frankford Yellow Jackets scored in the last two minutes to beat the Chicago Bears, 7–6, at Shibe Park and move into first place in the NFL.

"The Bears were the Dallas Cowboys–type team of that period," recalled Matt Goukas, in a *Philadelphia Bulletin* interview with Michael D. Schaffer. "Beating them was a major feat." Goukas, who was the Yellow Jackets' 11-year-old visiting-team water boy at the time, later starred in basketball with St. Joseph's College and the Philadelphia Warriors. He was the long-time public address announcer for the Eagles.

The Yellow Jackets didn't clinch the 1926 NFL title in the 21-team league until their final game of the season, a scoreless tie with the third-place Pottsville. A loss would have dropped Frankford into second place behind the Bears.

For the first time in history, Philadelphia had the best team in professional football!

In addition, with the Quakers' championship, it technically marked the only time in pro football history that the champions of rival leagues were based in the same city. But by the following year, the Quakers had disappeared from the professional landscape.

Playing to capacity crowds in a 9,000-seat stadium built on a converted horse track at Frankford Avenue and Devereaux Street, in the Northeast section of the city, the Yellow Jackets finished with a 14–1–1 record in 1926. It was the best mark in the club's eight years of existence. It took 46 years before another NFL team—the Miami Dolphins—equaled that win total en route to an unbeaten (14–0) season and a Super Bowl title.

Coached by Guy Chamberlin, the Yellow Jackets shut out 11 opponents in 1926. They blanked the Canton Bulldogs, with Jim Thorpe, 17–0. They beat Duluth, with Ernie Nevers, 10–0. They handed George Halas's Chicago Bears their only defeat of the season, 7–6. The Yellow Jackets "tackle like demons," said Halas afterward. Frankford's only loss, 7–6 to Providence, was avenged when they bounced back to shut out the Steam Roller twice, 6–0 and 24–0.

The National Football League in those days was a barnstorming circuit with schedules and rosters that were constantly changing. Some players wore baseball caps instead of helmets and used newspapers for hip pads. Teams formed and disappeared in a matter of weeks. A team called the Los Angeles Buccaneers never played a game west of Kansas City. Joe Carr just liked the idea of having a team with a Los Angeles label because he thought it added a touch of glamour.

Because of the Pennsylvania blue laws, the Yellow Jackets were forced to play their home games on Saturdays. Other NFL teams preferred to play their home games on Sunday. So Frankford often was forced to hop on a train after a Saturday game, ride all night, and play the next day in Duluth or Milwaukee.

Once, according to football historian Hugh Wyatt, the Yellow Jackets rode a train 12 hours to Buffalo, only to discover that the game had been canceled due to "wet grounds." Philadelphia sportswriters accompanying the team noted that the streets were dry and speculated that an earlier whipping put on the New York team by Frankford really prompted the cancellation. The writers also heard the Buffalo players weren't even in town—they had all gone to see the World Series.

Considering that the Yellow Jackets were often bruised and battered when they faced a well-rested team, it's remarkable that they finished with the third-best overall record in the NFL during the decade of the 1920s.

Chamberlin was hired as Frankford's player-coach in 1925 after guiding Canton and Cleveland to previous NFL championships. His blocked extra point was decisive in the Yellow Jacket's slim victory over the Bears. Chamberlin was elected to the Pro Football Hall of Fame in 1965, the only member of that team to be enshrined.

The 1926 Frankford Yellow Jackets, champions of the National Football League.

Frankford Yellow Jackets Fight Song

There's a team in Frankford here,
A team that can't be beat.
For them, we surely hold no fear
That they'll ever taste defeat.

• • • • •

Frankford Yellow Jackets in the NFL

Year	W	L	T	Position
1924	11	2	1	3
1925	13	7	0	6
1926	14	1	1	1
1927	6	9	3	7
1928	11	3	2	2
1929	9	4	5	3
1930	4	13	1	9
1931	1	6	1	10
Totals	69	45	14	

Other key Frankford players included quarterback Harry (Two Bits) Homan (Lebanon Valley), center Bill Springsteen (Lehigh), end Les Asplundh (Swarthmore), halfback Ed Weir (Nebraska), tackle Swede Youngstrum (Dartmouth), interior lineman Bill Hoffman (Lehigh), and triple-threat fullback Houston Stockton (Gonzaga), the grandfather of NBA great John Stockton. Most of the starters played both ways, often going the entire 60 minutes offensively and defensively.

Homan, the smallest player in the league at 5–5, 145, was, perhaps, the greatest punt returner in NFL history. Although no official records were kept in those days, *The Sports Encyclopedia: Pro Football* ranks him No. 1 all-time, ahead of George McAfee and Jack Christiansen, with a 13.59 yard-per-return average on 82 runbacks.

Homan–called "a manikin in moleskins" by sportswriters— also excelled as a pass receiver, blocking back, and defensive safety when he wasn't playing quarterback. According to unofficial statistics, he averaged 22.2 yards a catch during his six seasons. Defensively, he intercepted five passes in his first two years.

In 1926, Homan missed the first nine games of the regular season after having his ribs crushed in an exhibition game against the Atlantic City Roses. He came back against the Green Bay Packers on Thanksgiving Day. The Yellow Jackets had blown a 13–0 lead and were trailing 14–13 late in the game. Then Homan went to work. He took a short pass from Houston Stockton and raced 38 yards down the sideline to score the game-winning touchdown.

Homan's heroics triggered "a spectacle of joyful exuberance not witnessed in professional gridiron annals in this dear Quaker City of ours," said the *Philadelphia Inquirer*. "Oh, what a bedlam, as hats and other miscellaneous articles were tossed in the air, and the crowd threatened to break forth in its demonstration in true rabble fashion on the gridiron."

Frankford was a colorful neighborhood team with six young male cheerleaders, its own fight song, and a mascot. Its roster consisted mostly of area college stars who were funded by a group of Frankford businessmen, who kicked in $50 apiece to cover expenses. The average salary for a player was $150 a game. Stars like Thorpe and Nevers made considerably more—usually a percentage of the gate.

Most of the Frankford players lived together in boarding houses near the stadium. They ate at the local YMCA and played cards on the front porch. They socialized with the neighbors and played football with the kids in the street.

"The Yellow Jackets drew the community together, it was a wonderful thing to see," said Howard Barnes, the curator of the Historical Society of Frankford, years later in an interview. "We all felt a sense of pride in the team because it made Frankford famous. The [NFL] standings appeared in newspapers from Los Angeles to London. The spirit was contagious. Literally everyone in the community was caught up in it."

Frankford finished third or better four times in the NFL and actually had a better overall record than the Green Bay Packers (61–25–13) during the 1920s.

In 1930 the Yellow Jackets lost money and began losing most of their key players. The Great Depression of October 1929 had taken its toll, especially those who lost their jobs in the textile mills in Frankford and Kensington. Their original

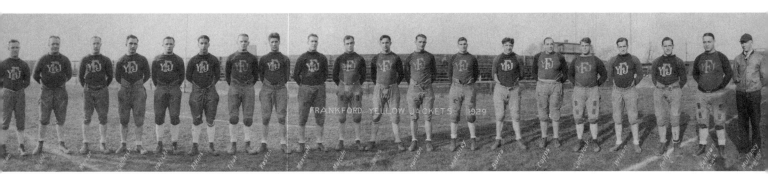

The 1929 Frankford Yellow Jackets at Frankford Stadium.

The first Eagles team reports to training camp, 1933.

stadium was damaged by a fire in 1929, and it would suffer the same fate again in 1931. It was vandalized several times, leaving it in disrepair. Frankford dropped all the way to ninth with a 4–13–1 record.

In 1931, Herb Joesting, the former Minnesota All-America considered by many to be the best player in Yellow Jacket history, was named head coach. The team moved most of its home games to the Phillies ballpark at Broad Street and Lehigh Avenue. But their support dwindled. Fans started calling them the *Philadelphia* Yellow Jackets.

Early in the 1931 season, the Yellow Jackets had the distinction of hosting the first professional night game in the league's—and city's—history. Some 2,000 fans watched Brooklyn blank Frankford, 20–0, at Municipal Stadium. But midway through the season, with only one victory in their first eight games, the Yellow Jackets folded their franchise. Their final game was a 13–0 loss to the New York Giants at the Polo Grounds.

Never again would future Pro Football Hall of Fame greats like Jim Thorpe, Ernie Nevers, George Halas, Red Grange, Curley Lambeau, Bronko Nagurski, Steve Owen, Kenneth Strong, and others display their talent on Frankford Yellow Jackets fields.

Two years later a pair of former University of Pennsylvania teammates, Bert Bell and Lud Wray, purchased the defunct franchise and renamed it the *Philadelphia Eagles*. They paid $2,500 to the league as a guarantee in case the club folded. They also assumed $11,000 in debts owed by the Frankford franchise to the Chicago Bears, New York Giants, and Green Bay Packers.

Bert Bell and the Birth of the Eagles

THE FASCINATING STORY of Bert Bell reads like the history of the early days of the Philadelphia Eagles.

It's also the chronicle of the beginning of the golden age of the National Football League.

And justifiably so, because no one did more to influence the early success of professional football in Philadelphia—and across the nation—than de Benneville (Bert) Bell, the founder of the Eagles and, later, one of the most powerful commissioners in the history of sport.

It was Bell who made some monumental decisions during his 14 years as head of the NFL, decisions that helped transform a struggling ten-team league awash in red ink into America's most popular professional sport.

"Bert Bell was a wonderful person," said Don Looney, who played for the Eagles in 1940. "He was so honest. If he told you something, you didn't have to worry about it. His word was his bond. He made the NFL what it is today."

"Dad took the NFL out of the dark ages and brought it into modern times," said his daughter, Jane, who later became a writer and producer in Hollywood.

- Bell, a charter member of the Pro Football Hall of Fame, created the player draft that has helped maintain parity in the NFL.
- He negotiated the merger between his league and the All-America Football Conference that probably saved the sport from bankruptcy.
- He settled the costly bidding war for players with the Canadian Football League.
- He negotiated the first national TV contracts and instituted the "blackout rule" that prohibited televising of home games, thereby bolstering attendance and keeping the weaker franchises afloat.
- He sided with the players when they formed their union, the NFL Players Association, and helped devise their first pension plan.
- He introduced the concept of "sudden-death" overtime, paving the way for the most exciting game in pro football history: the 1958 NFL championship between the Baltimore Colts and New York Giants. That game propelled the sport into the national consciousness.
- He coined the phrase "On Any Given Sunday"!

Many of these decisions were unpopular—Bert went head to head with everyone from the club owners to members of Congress—but his foresight paved the way for the immense success enjoyed by the NFL today.

When he was born in 1894, Bell was christened "de Benneville," in honor of his French grandmother. His family name was well known on Philadelphia's prestigious Main Line, but his given name was another matter. "If I can lick the name 'de Benneville,' I can handle anything," he frequently said.

Bell's father, John Cromwell Bell, was attorney general of Pennsylvania and a trustee at the University of Pennsylvania. Once when asked where his young son would attend college, the elder Bell said, "Bert will go to Penn or he'll go to hell." Bert's mother, Fleurette de Benneville Myers, was a prominent bridge player. His brother, John C. Bell, was a justice to the Pennsylvania Supreme Court who also served as the

Bert Bell founded the Eagles and served as NFL Commissioner from 1946 until his death in 1959.

commonwealth's attorney general and, briefly, as Pennsylvania's governor in 1947. At one time the Bell family owned the ground where Franklin Field stands today.

Bert Bell, a graduate of the Haverford School, did, indeed, attend the University of Pennsylvania (class of 1920), where he majored in English and captained the Quakers football team. In addition to excelling at quarterback, the 155-pound Bell punted, returned punts, kicked field goals, and played defense. His teammates included Lou Little, who coached at Columbia, and All-America Heinie Miller, who would later star locally with the Frankford Yellow Jackets.

After playing in the 1917 Rose Bowl (losing to Oregon), Bell served as a member of the University Ambulance Corps in France for 13 months during World War I, where he was cited for bravery.

Bell came back to finish his playing career at Penn. He coached football at Penn from 1920 to 1928, and later coached at Temple University in 1930 and 1931. He also managed Philadelphia's Ritz Carlton and St. James hotels, both owned by the family.

Despite his family's wealth, Bell always knew what he wanted to do in life. "All I ever wanted to be was a football man," he said. Larry Merchant of the *Philadelphia Daily News* called Bell "a red-blooded blue blood."

"Football was the biggest thing in his life," recalled Bell's son, Bert, Jr., who was business manager of the Baltimore Colts. "But here was a guy whose family had a tremendous amount of money. But he put on no airs. He was as much at home in the huddle as he was with Main Line society in Philadelphia. He treated them no differently. He just didn't operate like some genteel elitist."

In 1933, Bell formed a syndicate with Lud Wray, an old Penn teammate, and purchased the Frankford Yellow Jackets. The price was $2,500; Bell and Wray each paid half. Bell immediately renamed the team the *Philadelphia Eagles*, in honor of the bald eagle, the symbol of President Franklin D. Roosevelt's National Recovery Act.

A year earlier, Bell had recommended Wray for the coaching position with the new Boston Redskins franchise in the NFL, owned by Bell's friend George Preston Marshall. After the 1932 season, Wray returned to Philadelphia to join Bell for the first season.

Bell paid his players between $100 and $150 a game. Most games were played at the cavernous Municipal Stadium, usually before crowds of less than 5,000. Children were admitted for one cent when accompanied by an adult.

That season, Bell obtained the first Sunday license ever issued in the Commonwealth of Pennsylvania allowing the Eagles and the mighty Chicago Bears to battle to a 3–3 tie in the Baker Bowl. That license remained one of Bell's prized possessions.

In 1936, after absorbing losses of some $90,000, the club was offered for sale at a public auction at Samuel T. Freeman and Company, on Chestnut Street. Bell made the only bid—$4,500. He was the sole owner and, also, the coach, trainer, scout, business manager, janitor, publicist, and ticket seller. In those days, it wasn't unusual for the team to be rumbling across the country in a battered bus heading for a game when Bell would suddenly spot an empty field, stop the bus, and hold a practice.

In 1939 the Eagles played a scoreless tie with the Brooklyn Dodgers in a driving rainstorm at Municipal Stadium. Fewer

Bert Bell, shown here with Dave Smukler (13), was both owner and head coach of the Eagles from 1936 through 1940. In those five seasons, the team won just 10 games.

than 50 spectators attended, and Bell brought them all into the press box where he served them free coffee and hot dogs.

"It's days like that when it takes a very good sense of humor and an utter lack of regard for your bank balance to stay in professional football," Bell said. "I'm glad I had both."

Bell didn't have much success as a coach—his overall record was 10–44–2—but he brought in several stars during his tenure with the Eagles. The brightest was Davey O'Brien, the All-America quarterback from TCU, who played in 1939 and 1940 for $12,000 a year and a percentage of the gate. O'Brien set an NFL passing record with 1,324 yards in 1939.

"O'Brien was one of the greatest football players of all time," Bell said. "He played 299 minutes out of a possible 300 in his last five games for us, despite his 144 pounds. When I took him out of his final game at Washington with a minute to go, the entire Washington team escorted him to the sideline. He had set three league records for passing that afternoon, and the ovation those Washington fans gave him was something that Hitler and Mussolini always dreamed of."

Another of Bell's favorite players was Dave Smukler, the former Temple star who was called "the greatest fullback of all time" by the legendary Pop Warner. Once after the Eagles played before a very small crowd, Smukler stepped into Bell's office and said, "If you're going to have a hard time making out [financially] this week, Bert, just forget my check. I looked awful out there today, anyway."

Although Bell's teams noticeably lacked talent, the coach himself never lacked for enthusiasm. One time, a Chicago Bears end named Luke Johnsos tricked one of Bell's players into lateraling him the ball. Johnsos sprinted down the field with Bell running alongside, calling him a no-good cheater among other things.

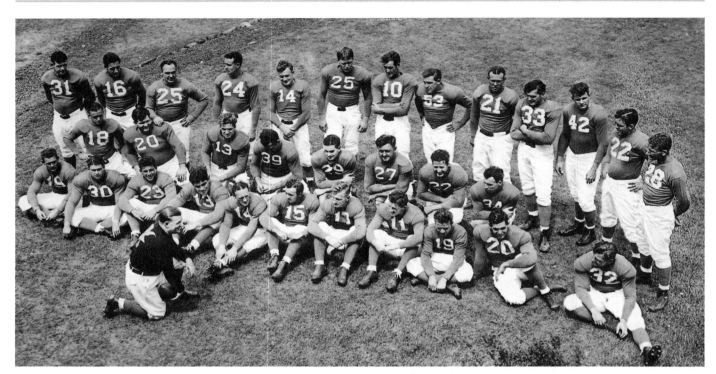

Bert Bell with the 1937 Eagles. "All I ever wanted to be," he said, "was a football man."

After the 1939 season, Bell relinquished his coaching duties with the Eagles and hired H. J. Miller, of St. Joseph's College, as his successor. But in 1940, before Miller ever coached a game, Art Rooney sold his Pittsburgh Steelers to Alexis Thompson and became Bell's partner in Philadelphia. Soon they negotiated an unprecedented switch, with the Rooney-Bell partnership moving to Pittsburgh and Thompson coming to Philadelphia. Eagles games were moved from Municipal Stadium to Shibe Park.

When World War II depleted the players' ranks, the Eagles and Steelers merged and became the *Steagles* for one season, 1943. They practiced at 54th and City Line on a shabby field littered with broken glass, tin cans, and oil from a nearby gas station. They also finished with a 5–4–1 record, the first winning season ever for the Eagles' franchise.

"My earliest memories are of large bodies sprawled asleep on the floors of our house and draped over the furniture," recalled Bell's son Upton, in a *Boston Magazine* article. "The bodies belonged to Eagles players who were making so little money that they lived with us."

In 1946, Bell agreed to succeed Elmer Layden, one of the Four Horseman of Notre Dame, as commissioner of the NFL on one condition—the league had to move its offices from Chicago to Philadelphia.

A chain-smoking chocoholic who napped every afternoon, Bell had a voice that sounded like "scraping sandpaper over an empty orange crate," according to his friends. Working 18-hour days, he had his hand in everything, from approving player contracts to assigning the game officials, negotiating TV contracts, and arranging schedules. He started with an office in center-city Philadelphia, then moved the league headquarters to Bala Cynwyd, Pennsylvania. But he did much of his work at home late at night.

Upton Bell, who later became general manager of the New England Patriots, remembers seeing his dad sitting at their kitchen table. "I'd say, 'What the hell is this?'" the younger Bell said. "It was a checkerboard with dominoes marked with the names of the teams. He'd be there until one or two in the morning with the cigarettes on the side. This is six months before the next season, and he'd be positioning these teams all over. He would come up with the schedule that I think saved the league."

Bell followed the same scheduling formula for many years: for the first six weeks of every season, he matched the strong teams against the strong teams and the weaker clubs against the other weak teams. It didn't matter if the teams had to travel from coast to coast on consecutive weekends; Bell wanted as many teams as possible still in contention at midseason. Such scheduling meant that more people would flock to the games and TV contracts would be worth more the following season.

When Bell took the commissioner's job, he signed a three-year contract at $20,000 a year. At the time of his death in 1959, Bell was working on a 12-year contract for $30,000 annually. The contract also included a deferred-payment bonus with $10,000 put in escrow for each additional year he served, to be paid at the termination of the contract.

Bell was regarded as the strongest commissioner since baseball's Judge Kenesaw Mountain Landis. His decisions were not always popular. For example, the club owners were livid when Bell recognized the formation of the NFL Players Association. "They said, 'If you recognize the Players Association, you're in deep trouble,'" recalled Upton Bell. "My dad said, 'I'll tell you what: If you don't recognize it, I'm quitting. These are the people that are building the game with us. We've got to begin to recognize in some way that they have the right to form an association.'"

The owners vested Bell with unprecedented power. All contracts had to be approved by him to be valid. He selected the game officials. He functioned as a one-man Supreme Court. If an issue could not be resolved by the 13 owners, Bell decided it.

One of Bell's primary concerns was protecting the integrity of the game. It was critical that pro football be seen as absolutely honest, avoiding even the slightest hint of scandal. In 1946 it was revealed that Frank Filchock and Merle Hapes, of the New York Giants, failed to report the offer of a bribe to throw the championship game. Bell barred only Hapes from the game because Filchock had not yet admitted being approached. After the gamblers and fixers were convicted and sent to prison, the commissioner suspended both players. Three months later, he barred them indefinitely from the league, although Filchock was reinstated in 1950.

Neither player had accepted the bribe, but Bell said, "The players must be not only absolutely honest; they must be above suspicion." Bell campaigned vigorously for federal and state laws making it illegal to offer a bribe to an athlete. By the end of 1948, all but one of the states in which the NFL had franchises had passed such legislation.

Bell hired Austin Gunsel, a former Federal Bureau of Investigation agent, to head the league's security. He appointed former FBI agents as watchdogs in each city to keep an eye on any suspicious activity.

Each summer, Bell traveled across the country, visiting the football training camps to deliver what his family called *The Sermon on the Mount*. He lectured the players on a variety of topics, including how to dress, how to act, and how to deal with the press. He ended every training camp session with the same lines: *"Don't forget boys, if you've got a problem, call me collect anytime night or day—MOHAWK 4-4400."* And many players took him up on it. "He talked to us like a father," said Chuck Bednarik. "He was strict but fair."

One day in the 1950s, Bell was walking through Memorial Stadium in Baltimore with his daughter, Jane, during a Colts-Eagles game. "The wife of one of the players sidled up to my dad like so many other strangers would do," she recalled. "She said, 'Excuse me, aren't you Commissioner Bell?' He said, 'Yes, I am.' She said, 'You're the man that's going to stop me from getting my fur coat for Christmas.' My father said, 'How did that happen?' She said, 'Well, you fined my husband, Bucko Kilroy, twice for infractions on the field.'

"My father said, 'I'll tell you what I'll do. If your husband doesn't get another infraction for the rest of the season,'—and by this time it was a little after Thanksgiving—'I'll send all the money back to you, and you can buy your fur coat.' And that's exactly what he did."

Bell had financial issues with team executives as well, including singer Kate Smith, who was part owner of the Boston Yanks football team in the 1940s. Upton Bell recalls that his dad's "upbeat expression would sag so he looked like a bulldog in mourning" whenever he talked to Smith on the telephone.

"How we doing up there in Boston, Kate? Your singing tour's going fine? That's great. Tell me, Kate, did you make the payroll this week? No? We gotta get the goddamned payroll paid, Kate." Then, to us, shaking his head, he would say, "Christ, I gotta get on a train to Boston again."

My mother, Frances Upton, would sigh. Before she married my father, she had been a Ziegfeld Follies star who had played in such shows as *Little Jesse James*, *Hold Your Horses*, and *Me and My Girl*, and starred in *Making Whoopee* with Eddie Cantor. "Oh, Bert," mother would say, "I just love Boston. I opened all my shows in Boston." My father would say, "Christ, Frances, you opened all your shows there? I gotta go up and close this show."

The NFL's TV code was constantly under attack. It withstood a federal court challenge in 1957, but finally in 1973 Congress adopted legislation requiring that any NFL game that had been declared a sellout 72 hours prior to kickoff would be made available to local TV.

By the mid-1950s, each club was receiving an unheard-of $1 million a year from a newly negotiated TV contract after Bell sold the club owners on the revolutionary concept of *revenue sharing*, which meant that every franchise received the same amount of revenue whether it was in one of the top markets like New York or Chicago or a small market like Green Bay or Baltimore.

Bell was the first commissioner to recognize the value of television as a vehicle to enhance the image of professional football. He kept a tight reign on TV producers and directors, never permitting shots of injured players or fights on the field. He also went of his way to assist the media in doing its job.

"At our annual meetings, Bert will walk out every 15–20 minutes to tell the press what's happening," Eagles vice president Joe Donoghue once told *The Saturday Evening Post*. "He doesn't believe in handouts, and he's always trying to make deadlines for newspapermen across the country."

"Outside of something personal like finances," explained Bell, "the fellas in our room know I'll talk. Why not? We got no secrets. The more the public knows, the better off we are."

Bell's most significant achievement—an innovation that revolutionized the NFL forever—came when he was serving as general manager of the Eagles. In 1935, concerned that the so-called "rich" teams would always outbid the "poorer" teams for college players, he persuaded club owners to accept a draft system based on the league standings. Last place meant first pick; first place meant the last pick; and so forth.

"That's the one thing that Bert Bell always should be remembered for," said his son Upton. "Bert always had the worst team. He did it out of self-interest. He saw that the Redskins and the Bears, who won every year, and the Giants were the only teams that had money. He got the owners to realize, no matter how much they squabbled, how much they cared about their own product, that unless they stuck together, they'd all perish together. The draft is still in effect 70 years later. Every court has tried to knock it down, and it's still there."

One day in 1955, after the lowly Pittsburgh Steelers upset the mighty Chicago Bears, a sportswriter asked Bell what he thought of the game. "It doesn't matter in the NFL how many games you win, what your score is, how well you do," the commissioner replied. "On any given Sunday, any team in the NFL can win." A half century later, that statement is still true.

Worried that a tie could diminish the impact of a championship game, Bell sold the club owners on the concept of *sudden death* in 1956. "If it ever happens, it's going to really call attention to pro football," he explained. He didn't realize that his prophecy would be fulfilled so quickly. Two years later, not only did it happen, but the drama hooked millions of fans on pro football. On December 28, 1958, at Yankee Stadium, Alan Ameche scored from the one-yard line to give the Baltimore

Colts a 23–17 sudden-death overtime win over the Giants for the National Football League championship. That was the spark that set off the pro football boom.

"When it ended, I remember looking over and seeing my father in tears," Upton Bell said. "He was a rough, gruff little guy. He wasn't very emotional, but he turned to his old friend Carroll Rosenbloom, the Colts owner, and said, 'I'm happy I lived to see this day.'"

It was the last NFL championship game Bert Bell ever saw. He died suddenly on October 12, 1959, at the age of 65. He was stricken with a heart attack in the final two minutes of an Eagles-Steelers game at Franklin Field, watching the game he loved, between two teams he once owned, at the stadium where he began his football career as a Penn quarterback in 1919.

"It was like Caruso dying in the second act of *Pagliacci*," wrote Phil Musick in *Pro* magazine.

Eagles' Hall of Famer Tommy McDonald had just scored a touchdown and looked toward the stands. "Half of the stadium was cheering, but the whole mob of people on the other side of the stadium were yelling and running the other way," he said. "I'll never forget it."

Hundreds attended Bell's funeral Mass at St. Margaret's Roman Catholic Church in Narberth. It was celebrated on a rainy October 14, 1959. Honorary pallbearers were the owners of the 12 NFL clubs: Carroll D. Rosenbloom, of the Baltimore Colts; George S. Halas, of the Chicago Bears; Walter H. S. Wolfner, of the Chicago Cardinals; David R. Jones, of the Cleveland Browns; Edwin J. Anderson, of the Detroit Lions; Dominic Olejnicak, of the Green Bay Packers; Daniel F. Reeves, of the Los Angeles Rams; John V. Mara, of the New York Giants; Frank L. McNamee, of the Philadelphia Eagles; Victor B. Morabito, of the San Francisco 49ers; George P. Marshall, of the Washington Redskins; and, of course, Arthur J. Rooney, his former partner from Pittsburgh.

The church was filled with such dignitaries as Anthony J. Drexel Biddle, Jr., former U.S. ambassador to Poland; Ned Irish, the president of Madison Square Garden; New York restaurateur Toots Shor; and Philadelphia contractor John B. Kelly.

If Bell had lived a few days longer, his children might own the Eagles today. "Three days later, he was supposed to go see Jim Clark [the club chairman]," Bert, Jr., said. "He was stepping down as commissioner, and he was going to buy the Eagles back for his kids. That was $180 million ago. That didn't happen."

"The deal was to be signed on Wednesday to buy the Eagles for $900,000," Upton Bell said. "I think my brother, Bert, was the only one who knew."

Three months later, Pete Rozelle, the 33-year-old general manager of the Los Angeles Rams, was named Bert Bell's successor as NFL commissioner.

In 1969, Upton Bell, who was then personnel manager of the Colts, was among the bidders when the Eagles went on the auction block following the bankruptcy of owner Jerry Wolman. Bell dropped out of the bidding, he claimed, because Leonard Tose's offer was at least $4.6 million more than what Upton and his partners were willing to pay.

3

Player Profiles

IN THEIR LONG and (sometimes) illustrious history, the Eagles have dressed more than 1,200 players. That's just for regular-season games. We aren't counting all the free agents who passed through training camp or made a cameo appearance in an exhibition game. We're talking about players who appeared in a league game and earned a line in the club's official roster.

They came from near and far, from a banana plantation in Honduras (Steve Van Buren) to a steel mill in upstate New York (Ron Jaworski), from small-town Mississippi (Wilbert Montgomery) to the sandlots of South Philadelphia (Jack Ferrante). There are players from big colleges and players who never went to college, players who were enshrined in the Hall of Fame and others who faded quietly away, but their footprints are all on the same trail from Baker Bowl to Lincoln Financial Field.

In this chapter, we profile more than 100 of the most interesting characters in Eagles history. The list was drawn more on stories attached to these players than any statistical formula. There are Pro Bowlers and no-bowlers, all-timers and part-timers, but they all made their mark on Eagles history.

DAVID AKERS
Kicker

Ht: 5–10 • **Wt:** 200 • **College:** Louisville • **Years with the Eagles:** 1999– • **Birthplace:** Lexington, Kentucky • **Born:** December 9, 1974

When David Akers walked into the Eagles locker room for the first time, having failed in tryouts with Atlanta, Carolina, and Washington, he looked like every other itinerant kicker. Here today, gone tomorrow. That's how it goes with kickers. Akers appeared to fit the profile. Instead, he defied it.

After six seasons, Akers is firmly established as the finest kicker in Eagles history and one of the most accurate kickers of all time. A three-time Pro Bowl selection, Akers owns the Eagles' record with 139 field goals, and his career field-goal percentage of 83.2 is second only to Mike Vanderjagt (87.0), who plays his home games in the cozy comfort of the Indianapolis dome. Akers had to contend with the cold, swirling winds at Veterans Stadium and Lincoln Financial Field.

Akers led the NFC in scoring with 122 points during the 2004 regular season, and he set a league record by kicking 17 field goals of 40 yards or longer. When you combine his accuracy (27 for 32, 84.4 percent) with the fact that his average field goal attempt was 40.8 yards (longest in the NFL), it adds up to the finest season in a stellar career.

"There is no money in betting against Akers, none," wrote Rich Hofmann in the *Philadelphia Daily News.* "You might as well bet against winter. Maybe the day will come when you're not sure anymore, when Akers runs out there for that 42-yarder and you really wonder, but it will almost certainly be because of an injury. Or because he's 50."

"He has become so compact and so consistent with his technique, and that has been developed through really hard work,"

David Akers

special-teams coach John Harbaugh said. "I think he's the best in the business [and] I think he has a chance to be the best kicker in NFL history, I really do."

Akers' journey was typical of most kickers. After finishing his college career at Louisville, he bounced around the pro circuit, looking for a job. He played one game in Washington in 1998, missed two field goal attempts, and was released. He spent a season with the Berlin Thunder in NFL Europe. In between, he waited tables at a Longhorn Steak House to pay the bills.

The Eagles signed Akers as a kickoff and long field goal specialist—their primary kicker was a fading 39-year-old Norm Johnson—and when Akers hit a 53-yard field goal against Miami (the fourth longest field goal in team history), the Eagles realized they had a keeper. He was successful on 29 of 33 field goal attempts the following season, 2000, and he was voted Most Valuable Player on the Eagles special teams. He has been as consistent as a metronome ever since.

Akers has kicked six game-winning field goals in overtime or with less than five minutes remaining in regulation time. He kicked a 50-yard field goal in overtime to defeat Cleveland, 34–31, in Week 7 of the 2004 season. It was the longest game-winning kick in franchise history. He set a club mark with 153 consecutive extra points, and he has the six longest streaks of consecutive field goals in team history, from 12 in a row (2002) to the record 17 in a row (2001).

"I feel very confident with my man Ake kicking," defensive tackle Darwin Walker told Ashley McGeachy Fox of the *Philadelphia Inquirer*. "He don't miss."

Akers has demonstrated physical toughness as well. He was a high school tailback, so he is not afraid to take a hit. He was credited with 28 special-teams tackles through the 2004 season, and several saved potential touchdowns. Akers is trained in jujitsu, which explains the martial arts bow he performs after each field goal.

Sometimes his physical play has repercussions. In the NFC Championship game, he shoved Atlanta's Siddeeq Shahazz to the ground on a kickoff return. Later in the game, Shahazz blindsided Akers with an elbow that bloodied his nose.

"I guess he was embarrassed because I put a legal hit on him and put him down," Akers told Bernard Fernandez of the *Daily News*. "Nobody wants to be knocked down by a kicker."

ERIC ALLEN
Cornerback

Ht: 5–10 • **Wt:** 180 • **College:** Arizona State • **Years with the Eagles:** 1988–94 • **Birthplace:** San Diego, California • **Born:** November 22, 1965

On NFL draft day, 1988, Eagles coach Buddy Ryan made a trade with Tampa Bay to move up nine spots in the second round and select Arizona State cornerback Eric Allen.

"He was my favorite of all the defensive backs," Ryan said. "When I first saw him on film, he just stood out. He plays the game all the way to the hilt."

Allen played seven seasons with the Eagles and appeared in five Pro Bowls. He tied the club record with 34 career interceptions and set the record for most interceptions returned for touchdowns in a career (five), most interceptions returned for touchdowns in a season (four in 1993), and most intercep-

Eric Allen

tions returned for touchdowns in a game (two against New Orleans on December 26, 1993).

Allen had great physical ability, combining 4.4 speed in the 40-yard dash with soft, sure hands. But he also had a studious approach to the game, watching film for hours and taking notes on every quarterback and receiver, charting their patterns, their moves, their tendencies. He also worked with a punching bag to develop fast hands and a hard jab to help him jam receivers at the line.

Put the physical and mental parts together in one player and you have a corner with virtually no weaknesses. "I'm not as flashy as Deion [Sanders]," Allen said. "I'm a blue-collar worker. When I'm on the job, I work hard to get it done."

Allen credited Roynell Young, the veteran cornerback, with educating him to the pro game.

"He emphasized that I had to fit into a game plan, but I also had to excel using my skills," Allen told Thomas George of the *New York Times* in 1993. "This is difficult because football is such a team-oriented game. But when you're running down the sideline in man coverage against an All-Pro receiver like Michael Irvin and the safeties are up and there is no one in the middle, there isn't much team play in that."

In the 1993 season, Allen intercepted six passes and returned four of them for touchdowns, tying the NFL single-season record set by Jim Kearney of Kansas City (1972) and Kenny Houston of Houston (1971). One of his returns was a twisting 94-yard run against the New York Jets that was selected for the NFL Films video "The 100 Greatest Touchdowns of All Time."

In the 1992 postseason, Allen had two interceptions in the NFC Wild Card playoff game against New Orleans, including an 18-yard return for a touchdown that secured the Eagles' 36–20 victory.

Allen missed only one regular-season start in his seven years with the Eagles. He signed a free-agent contract with New Orleans in 1995. He played three seasons with the Saints, then went to Oakland where he played another four years before retiring. In all, Allen played 14 seasons as a starting cornerback in the NFL, a testimony to his physical and mental toughness.

Allen once was asked how he'd like to be remembered. "I would like to have the respect of the young players," he said. "I'd like to have them say, 'Damn, that Eric Allen, he could play today.' To have the respect of the players, that's real important."

BILLY BARNES
Halfback

Ht: 5–11 • **Wt:** 205 • **College:** Wake Forest • **Years with the Eagles:** 1957–61 • **Birthplace:** Landis, North Carolina • **Born:** May 14, 1935

Billy Barnes averaged just 3.4 yards per carry in his nine-year NFL career, but he was a hard man to stop near the goal line.

"Whenever we get close," quarterback Norm Van Brocklin said, "I give it to the Boiler."

The Boiler, that's what Van Brocklin called Barnes because the stocky halfback's face would turn beet red during a game. It fit his fiery personality. Barnes was not the biggest or fastest back in the league, but he made himself into a three-time Pro Bowl selection on sheer determination.

Barnes scored 20 rushing touchdowns, which ranks seventh in Eagles history. In the 1960 season, Barnes averaged only 2.7 yards per rushing attempt, but he scored six touchdowns (four rushing, two receiving) as the Eagles won the world championship.

"I had a bad knee that year, but I kept playing," Barnes said. "We didn't run the ball too much. We had Van Brocklin and we had great receivers, so why not throw the ball?"

Barnes was a major league baseball prospect, but he decided to play football when the Eagles made him their second-round selection in the 1957 draft. He still recalls his initiation to Philadelphia.

"The Eagles were still playing at Connie Mack Stadium," Barnes said.

There was no heat in the meeting room. The locker room was the size of a closet. I thought, "This is pro football? Wake Forest was better than this."

After that season, we moved to Franklin Field and the team hired me to work in the ticket office. They had me calling people on the phone, asking if they wanted to renew their season tickets. We were coming off a bad year (4–8), and half the people cussed me out and slammed down the phone.

But the move to Franklin Field helped. It was like turning the page. That same year, they brought in [coach] Buck Shaw and Van Brocklin, and we could feel things were headed in the right direction. Van Brocklin was the key. He instilled that cockiness in our team. I might be prejudiced, but I'd take him over any quarterback who ever played. Montana, Namath, Unitas, any of them. The Dutchman was the best.

Billy Barnes

Barnes was traded to Washington in 1962 and finished his career with Minnesota in 1966, playing for Van Brocklin, who was then the Vikings coach. Barnes later served as offensive backfield coach under Van Brocklin in Atlanta from 1971 through 1974.

WALTER BARNES
Guard

Ht: 6–0 • **Wt:** 245 • **College:** LSU • **Years with the Eagles:** 1948–51 • **Birthplace:** Parkersburg, West Virginia • **Born:** January 26, 1918 • **Died:** January 6, 1998

His full name was Walter Lee Barnes, but he was better known as Piggy.

He had a round face, a stubby body, and almost always the dirtiest uniform on the field.

"We played side by side," said tackle Frank (Bucko) Kilroy. "He was like my running mate. On the field, he looked out for me; I looked out for him."

Once, Kilroy walked to the other end of the field during pregame warm-ups to challenge the entire Pittsburgh Steeler

Walter Barnes

team. "Piggy said, 'You're crazy, you know that,'" Kilroy recalled. "But then he said, 'Wait up, I'll go with you.'"

Barnes enrolled at LSU after serving in World War II and earned all-conference honors as a two-way lineman. He also was a collegiate weightlifting champion. After college, Barnes signed with the Eagles and was a starting guard on the championship teams of 1948 and '49.

"Piggy was a tough individual," said tackle Vic Sears. "I wouldn't say he had the best [blocking] technique, but he was a fighter. He'd stick his nose in a guy's chest and just knock him backward."

Barnes was one of five Eagles voted into the 1951 Pro Bowl. He retired one year later, and the Eagles did not send another offensive guard to the Pro Bowl until Jermane Mayberry went in January 2002.

After football, Barnes went into motion pictures. He had a successful career that lasted more than 30 years, starting with roles in the TV series "Gunsmoke" and "Rawhide." He became a familiar character actor, usually playing two-fisted lawmen, ranchers, and an occasional villain.

While filming "Rawhide," Barnes befriended a young actor named Clint Eastwood. In the 1970s, when Eastwood became a big-time movie star and director, he made Barnes part of his acting stable. Barnes appeared in *High Plains Drifter*, *Every Which Way but Loose*, and *Bronco Billy* among other films.

Barnes is best remembered for the role of Tank Murdock, the potbellied street fighter who squares off with Eastwood in the final scene of *Every Which Way but Loose*.

Barnes continued to work until 1989 when diabetes finally forced him to retire. He died in the Motion Picture and Television Retirement Home near Los Angeles in 1998, and at his request, his ashes were spread over the football field at LSU.

FRED BARNETT
Wide Receiver

Ht: 6–0 • **Wt:** 205 • **College:** Arkansas State • **Years with the Eagles:** 1990–95 • **Birthplace:** Shelby, Mississippi • **Born:** June 17, 1966

When Fred Barnett was a rookie, head coach Buddy Ryan called him "Arkansas Fred." The nickname stuck, even though it did not fit after a while.

Barnett arrived in Philadelphia in 1990 as a shy kid from a small town (Gunnison, Mississippi, population 702) and a small school (Arkansas State). On the football field, he was talented, but raw. Off the field, he was polite, but fearful of the big city.

By his second season, Barnett was living in center-city Philadelphia and hanging out on South Street. He was wearing stylish Italian-cut suits, going to the theater, and taking ballet lessons. "Arkansas Fred" had become "Uptown Fred."

"I liked the atmosphere in the city, I liked the energy," Barnett said. "When I got to know the people, they were really nice. I felt at home. I bought a bike and rode it everywhere. I rode it to and from the stadium rather than take my car."

Riding a bike, that's one thing, but ballet lessons? For a pro football player, that took some explaining.

"I saw a lot of parallels [between] football and dance," Barnett told Mark Bowden of the *Philadelphia Inquirer*. "The two are related in a number of ways: the dedication, the physical discipline. Both require athletes. [Dancers] have a lot of injuries just like we do. I was more tired in a dance class than I've ever been in a football game."

Barnett was a third-round pick in the 1990 draft despite running the 40-yard dash in 4.42 seconds. "It's a funny thing with Fred," said Larry Lacewell, who coached Barnett in college. "He runs on his heels, so it's kind of ugly looking, but he can fly. We ran the wishbone, so we hardly ever threw the ball, which hurt his stock, too. No one knew how good he was."

Barnett adapted quickly to the pro game, catching 36 passes for 721 yards and eight touchdowns in his rookie year. He increased his production each of the next two seasons with 62 catches for 948 yards in 1991 and 67 catches for 1,083 yards in 1992. He was selected for the Pro Bowl after the 1992 season.

Barnett's biggest game was the 1993 NFC Wild Card playoff in New Orleans when he caught two touchdown passes from Randall Cunningham in a 36–20 victory. It was the Eagles' first postseason win since the NFC title game in January 1981, and Barnett's leaping 35-yard touchdown catch in the fourth quarter sparked the comeback from a 20–7 deficit.

Barnett is best remembered for the 95-yard touchdown catch in Buffalo (December 2, 1990), the play in which Cunningham ducked away from a rush in his own end zone and threw a desperation pass to midfield. Barnett soared over a Buffalo defender to make the catch and galloped away for the score. He had envisioned himself making just that kind of play ever since he was a kid, watching football on TV.

"I would lay across my bed, visualizing that NFL ball coming at me in that perfect spiral you see on TV and me catching it," Barnett told Kevin Mulligan of the *Philadelphia Daily News.* "I kept visualizing it, and it became stronger as I kept working for it. I just felt that one day I'd be where I am right now, right here in the NFL."

MAXIE BAUGHAN
Linebacker

Ht: 6–1 • **Wt:** 230 • **College:** Georgia Tech • **Years with the Eagles:** 1960–65 • **Birthplace:** Forkland, Alabama • **Born:** August 3, 1938

Maxie Baughan was the only rookie to start every game for the 1960 Eagles championship team. He was the club's second-round draft pick that year. Their first pick, running back Ron Burton from Northwestern, signed with the Boston Patriots of the American Football League, so Baughan arrived to the scrutiny normally associated with a first-round selection.

"If there was pressure, I didn't feel it," Baughan said. "I felt like I was in hog heaven. I was only playing half the game compared to playing both ways in college. Plus, I was getting paid for it. I was doing pretty good for a country boy from Alabama.

Maxie Baughan

"My daddy worked in the steel mills all his life. That's where I would've wound up, too, if it wasn't for football. Only 15 kids from my high school class went to college, and most of us went on athletic scholarships. That was the only way out of town."

Baughan was paid $13,000 for his rookie season with a $2,000 signing bonus. He bought a new Chevy Impala and recalls thinking, "If I make the team and play two or three years, I'll have enough money to last me a lifetime."

The 1960 Eagles were a veteran team and viewed most rookies with suspicion. Baughan, however, earned their respect. In a preseason game against San Francisco, a brawl erupted when 49er halfback Hugh McElhenny kicked Eagles tackle Ed Khayat in the head. Baughan was the first one to rush to Khayat's defense.

"That Maxie is a real tough kid," coach Buck Shaw said. "I thought McElhenny was pretty rugged himself, but Baughan chased him about 40 yards, then yanked off his helmet and began letting him have it where it hurts."

Baughan was an All-America at Georgia Tech and set the school record for tackles as a senior. He had a keen instinct for reading plays and finding the football.

"You look at some rookies in the huddle and their eyes are like this [wide]," safety Don Burroughs said. "Maxie was never like that. He looked like a veteran from Day One."

Baughan was voted into the Pro Bowl five of his six seasons with the Eagles, nine of his 11 seasons overall. The Eagles traded him to Los Angeles in 1966 for a package of three mediocre players. Baughan played five seasons with the Rams. He was responsible for making the calls in coach George Allen's system, which had 250 different coverages and 180 audibles.

"Maxie was one of my favorites," Allen said. "He enjoyed the physical game. He had an abundance of ability, and he was smart enough to make the most of it. He never gave up on a play. No one loafed when Maxie was around."

ED (BIBBLES) BAWEL
Halfback

Ht: 6–1 • **Wt:** 185 • **College:** Evansville • **Years with the Eagles:** 1952, 1955–56 • **Birthplace:** Boonville, Indiana • **Born:** November 21, 1930

His last name is spelled Bawel, but it is pronounced "Bobble." So it was inevitable, once he began playing football, that someone would give him a nickname. For Edward Ray Bawel, that nickname was "Bibbles."

Bibbles Bawel. Anyone who followed the Eagles in the 1950s will remember him, and not just because of his name. He spent three seasons with the team, and he displayed a knack for making the big play.

As a rookie in 1952, he led the NFL with 34 punt returns, including one for a 52-yard touchdown against the New York Giants. He also intercepted eight passes that season and returned them for 121 yards, an average of 15.1 yards per return.

Bawel was called for military duty after his rookie year, and he missed the next two seasons. When he rejoined the team in 1955, he picked up where he left off, intercepting nine passes, finishing second to Willard Sherman of the Los Angeles Rams, who had 11. Bawel led the league in return yardage (168) and touchdown returns (two).

In his final season, 1956, Bawel had one interception, and he returned it for 33 yards. Bawel's career numbers are impressive: 18 interceptions in 36 games with an average return of 17.9 yards. His nine interceptions in 1955 stood as the club's single-season record until 1971.

Bawel played at a tiny school, Evansville (Indiana) State Teachers College, far off the NFL scouting radar. No pro teams knew about Bawel, so he was ignored in the 1951 draft. However, Evansville coach Don Ping was a friend of Jim Trimble, and Ping convinced the Eagles coach that Bawel was worth a tryout. Trimble brought Bawel to training camp, and he wound up making the team. He earned $4,500 for his rookie season.

"Bibbles could really run, especially in a broken field," said Tom Brookshier, who played in the secondary with Bawel in 1956. "He was an offensive end in college and that was his first love, but we were loaded at that position with [Pete] Pihos, [Bobby] Walston, and [Pete] Retzlaff, so the coaches put Bibbles on defense."

Trimble left for the Canadian Football League in 1956 and, one year later, Bawel followed. Bawel played both ways in the CFL, doubling as an offensive end and a defensive back, and helped Trimble's Hamilton Tiger-Cats win the Grey Cup.

When he retired from football, Bawel returned to Evansville, where he taught for several years before becoming involved in auto racing with Jasper Engines in Jasper, Indiana.

CHUCK BEDNARIK
Center-Linebacker

Ht: 6–3 • **Wt:** 235 • **College:** Pennsylvania • **Years with the Eagles:** 1949–62 • **Birthplace:** Bethlehem, Pennsylvania • **Born:** May 1, 1925

Chuck Bednarik and his wife Emma visited the former Soviet Union in 1994. One day they boarded a bus in Kiev, and before they could take a seat, a woman called out, "Chuck Bednarik."

Think about that for a moment …

Bednarik had retired from pro football 32 years earlier. Here he was, boarding a bus in Kiev, which is about as far from Franklin Field as you can get, and still someone recognized him.

That's fame.

The woman was a tourist from the Philadelphia area. She was stunned to see this Eagles great, the last of the 60-minute men, on her bus. No doubt it was one of the first things she talked about when she came home: "Guess who I met over there. No, not Gorbachev. Not Yeltsin. Someone more famous than that …"

Chuck Bednarik is a larger-than-life figure. In 1993, *Sports Illustrated* devoted nine pages to a Bednarik profile. A photograph of Bednarik's hands, gnarled by 14 seasons of pro football, dominates the office of NFL Films president Steve Sabol in Mount Laurel, New Jersey.

Bednarik is decades removed from the game, yet people still talk about him. Mostly, they remember two things. They remember his knockout hit on Frank Gifford in 1960. And they remember him playing both ways, offense and defense, in the championship game the same year as the Eagles defeated Green Bay, 17–13.

What Bednarik did that season is now legend. At age 35, playing his 12th pro season, Bednarik was forced to play almost every down in four games, including the title game. He played center on offense and outside linebacker on defense. He also snapped on punts, extra points, and field goals.

The only time Bednarik left the field in those games was on kickoffs. He played 58 minutes in the championship game against the Packers, and it was his tackle of fullback Jim Taylor in the closing seconds that saved the Eagles' victory.

"It was 20 years before it dawned on me what I did," Bednarik said. "I took it for granted. They told me to play, so I played. But as I got older, I thought about it. I said, 'Do you know what the hell you did?' No one will ever do it again, certainly not at the professional level. You don't even see two-way players in college anymore.

"I was the end of an era. No NFL player could do it today. These guys play three or four plays and come off sucking air. And they're making millions of dollars? It makes me sick."

Bednarik was hardened by his upbringing in the steel-mill town of Bethlehem. As a boy, he would scale the barbed-wire fence around the athletic fields at Lehigh University and play football. Most of the time, he did not even have a real ball. His family could not afford one, so Bednarik filled an old stocking with rags and played with that.

At 18, he was a waist-gunner on a B-24 bomber, flying combat missions over Europe. He earned an Air Medal with five oak leaf clusters and five battle stars. When he returned from the war, Bednarik enrolled at the University of Pennsylvania, where he was a two-time All-America who worked for his meals by waiting on tables in the school's dining hall.

The Eagles made Bednarik the first pick in the 1949 draft and signed him to a $10,000 contract with a $3,000 cash bonus. "I'd never seen that much money in my life," Bednarik said. "I went to Ellian Motors, bought a brand-new Pontiac for $2,200, and drove it all over Bethlehem. I thought, 'So this is what it's like to be rich.'"

Bednarik played 14 seasons with the Eagles, a team record. He missed only three games in his career, two of those in his rookie year. He played both ways, center and linebacker, throughout the 1950s. He was selected for eight Pro Bowls. His number 60 was retired by the Eagles, and in 1967 he was inducted into the Pro Football Hall of Fame.

"Chuck Bednarik was as great as any linebacker who ever lived," said Jim Brown, the Hall of Fame fullback of the Cleveland Browns. "I don't know how old he is, but I'll bet nobody can kick his butt today."

Bednarik actually retired in 1959. The Eagles had a ceremony honoring him before the final game of that season. Bednarik was the last player introduced that day at Franklin Field, and the team presented him with a color television and a check for $1,000. At 34, Bednarik had nothing left to prove. He was a certain first-ballot selection to the Hall of Fame. He had won an NFL championship as a rookie with the Eagles in 1949. He felt it was as good a time as any to walk away.

But when Emma gave birth to their fifth child early in 1960, Bednarik decided to come back. He needed money, and general manager Vince McNally was offering him $15,000 to play one more season. He also was encouraged by the team's 7–5 finish the previous season. They had a proven winner at quarterback in Norm Van Brocklin. Bednarik figured why not play one more year and see what happens.

"I was going to play center, which is the easiest position from a physical standpoint," Bednarik said. "It's not like linebacker where somebody is coming at you from an angle, hitting you on every play. I was 35, but I thought I could play maybe three or four more years at center. A guy like Jim Otto [in Oakland] was still playing at 40. So I was playing center and doing okay, then, boom, Bob Pellegrini gets hurt in Cleveland and everything changes."

Pellegrini was the starting left linebacker, and he went down with a broken leg early in that game. The Eagles had a backup linebacker, John Nocera, but he was young, and coach Buck Shaw did not feel he was ready. With the Eagles in title contention, Shaw called on Bednarik, the oldest player on the team, one year older than Van Brocklin, to play linebacker as well as center.

"Defenses weren't as sophisticated as they are now," Bednarik said. "I got tossed in cold, but Chuck Weber [middle linebacker] told me what to do on every down. It wasn't that hard. The game is half instinct anyway. I never got tired. It was late in the season and the weather was cool, so I stayed pretty fresh. Besides, when you're winning, you don't feel the aches and pains. You feel like you can play all day."

"Chuck wasn't made of the same material as the rest of us, I'm convinced of that," said cornerback Tom Brookshier. "One exhibition game, he got kicked in the arm and his biceps tore off the bone. The muscle fell from here [upper arm] to here [forearm]. Chuck pushed the muscle up and told the doctor, 'Put some tape around it,' and he went back in. That was an exhibition game, so you can imagine what he was like when we were going for the championship. He would've played every play. And he darn near did."

Time has a way of distorting things, enlarging them, expanding them, exaggerating fact into folklore. That is particularly true in sports where, upon closer examination, the 500-foot home runs of legend are likely to measure closer to 400 feet, and the breathtaking runs you read about are often less than that when finally discovered on old black-and-white newsreels.

But Bednarik's career—and in particular, his 1960 season—is the exact opposite. What he accomplished that season is actually greater than the legend that now surrounds it. Most football fans know he played both ways. What they may not realize is how brilliantly he played. The snarling old man they called "Concrete Charlie" made the plays that defined the Eagles' improbable run to the championship.

The enduring image of that season is Bednarik's thunderous hit on Gifford. It took place November 20 at Yankee Stadium. The Eagles were 6–1, the Giants were 5–1–1, so first place in the Eastern Conference was at stake. The Eagles were ahead 17–10 late in the game, but the Giants were driving. Gifford, their star halfback, caught a pass across the middle and was immediately hit by Bednarik coming full-speed in the opposite direction.

"It was like a truck hitting a Volkswagen," Bednarik said. "Frank never saw me coming."

The 6–1, 185-pound Gifford was slammed violently backward onto the frozen turf, where he lay unconscious, his arms and legs limp.

"I played football a long time, but I never heard anything like that collision," Brookshier said. "It wasn't the usual thud. This was a loud crack, like an axe splitting a piece of wood. I saw Frank on the ground, and he looked like a corpse. I thought he was dead."

As Gifford hit the ground, the ball rolled loose and Weber fell on it to seal the victory that lifted the Eagles to the confer-

Chuck Bednarik

ence title and the world championship. When Bednarik saw Weber recover the fumble, he did a fist-pumping victory dance over the motionless Gifford.

Bednarik insisted he did not see Gifford at his feet. He said he was simply reacting to the win, which was now assured. But a *Sports Illustrated* photograph snapped at that moment told a different story. In the photo, Bednarik appears to be staring at his fallen opponent and saying, well, something.

"I said, 'This f——ing game is over,'" Bednarik said. "I wasn't directing it to Frank or anyone else. I was just happy we won. If people think I was gloating over Frank, they're full of you-know-what."

Gifford suffered a severe concussion on the play and sat out the remainder of the 1960 season and all of the following season before returning to the Giants in 1962. Bednarik and the Eagles went on to complete a 10–2 regular season and defeat the Packers in the championship game with Bednarik again playing a key role.

In the first quarter, Bednarik hit Green Bay's Paul Hornung on an end sweep and knocked him out of the game. Hornung was the Packers top all-around threat—a runner, receiver, and placekicker—who set an NFL scoring record that season with 176 points. He left the game with a pinched nerve in his shoulder, and the Green Bay offense suffered the rest of the day.

"I don't remember it as anything dirty, just a good, hard shot by a great player," Hornung said. "But my whole right side went numb. It was a chronic thing the rest of my career. I'd take a hit and lose feeling."

"It was one of those things," Bednarik said. "I jammed his shoulder; it was the only shot I had. I didn't try to hurt him. I never did that. The New York people still think I was out to get Gifford but it's not true. I played hard, yeah, but clean."

Against the Packers, Bednarik was on the field for 139 of 142 plays. He protected Van Brocklin when the Eagles had the ball, and he tackled Hornung and Taylor when the Eagles were on defense. They were clinging to a 17–13 lead in the closing seconds, but the Packers had the ball at the Eagles 22-yard line with time for one more play. Bart Starr wanted to throw deep, but the Eagles had the end zone covered, so Starr dumped the ball to Taylor.

Taylor lowered his head and drove toward the goal line. Several Eagles bounced off him, but Bednarik was waiting at the nine-yard line. He stopped Taylor in his tracks and wrestled him to the ground, then held him down until the last few seconds rolled off the clock.

"[Taylor] was squirming like hell, trying to get up," Bednarik said. "He was saying, 'Get off me, you so-and-so.' When the second hand hit zero, I said, 'You can get up now, you so-and-so, this f——ing game is over.' That was the ultimate, winning that game. It was a great achievement because, man for man, we weren't that good. I still don't know how we won it, but we did."

Bednarik played two more seasons at center, then retired for good. His final game was a 45–35 loss in St. Louis. When it ended, the equipment managers shipped his uniform, with the mud and blood still caked on it, to the Pro Football Hall of Fame, where it was put on display. Five years later, Bednarik was enshrined as well.

In his book *Pro Football's 100 Greatest Players*, George Allen ranked Bednarik as his No. 1 linebacker ahead of Dick Butkus, Ray Nitschke, and Joe Schmidt. Allen wrote, "Chuck Bednarik not only was the best linebacker I ever saw, he also was the best offensive center of the past 30 years and would have ranked right up there with Mel Hein and Bulldog Turner among the offensive linemen had I chosen to put him on that list. He was the surest, strongest snapper I've ever seen and an absolutely brutal and unbeatable blocker. But his hits are what one remembers best about him."

After his retirement, Bednarik spent 20 years working as a salesman for the Warner Concrete Company, hence the nickname "Concrete Charlie." He later worked in sales for Mrs. Paul's Kitchens and the Regal Corrugated box company. He never pursued a full-time job in football. He was content to work 9 to 5 and play golf on weekends. He watched the Eagles on TV and attended the occasional alumni party, but for more than a decade, that was the extent of his involvement.

When Dick Vermeil was hired as coach in 1976, one of the first things he did was arrange a dinner meeting with Bednarik. They went to Bookbinder's, and over the second bottle of wine Vermeil asked Bednarik to be part of his rebuilding program. He wanted Bednarik around the team as a symbol of what the Eagles once were and what Vermeil hoped they would be again.

For the next seven seasons, Bednarik was at every game—his title was associate coach—standing behind Vermeil, charting plays and, with his craggy features and championship rings, looking every inch the football icon. Linebacker Bill Bergey gave Bednarik a hug before every game. "It made me feel good just seeing him there," Bergey said. "He didn't have to say a word. He had that aura, Mr. Eagle, the legend come to life."

When Vermeil stepped down following the 1982 season, Bednarik walked away as well. He went back to watching the games on TV. When Deion Sanders began playing both ways in Dallas, reporters called Bednarik for his assessment of the new 60-minute man. He scoffed. "Deion doesn't hit anybody," Bednarik said. "He runs around the whole game, scared stiff, ducking. He couldn't tackle my wife Emma."

Asked whether he could play in today's bigger, faster, and more sophisticated NFL, Bednarik replied, "I consider that [question] a complete insult. Could I play today? Hell, yes, I could play. I'd be a star today."

Anyone who saw Bednarik play—or better still, anyone who ever played against him—would surely agree.

In a 1961 interview, Bednarik summed up his approach to the game, saying, "I just want to play, that's all. I guess you can call it desire. That's the biggest asset I have. When I go out there, I want to be the greatest football player who ever lived. I realize I won't ever be, of course, but that's the attitude I play with."

BILL BERGEY
Linebacker

Ht: 6–2 • **Wt:** 245 • **College:** Arkansas State • **Years with the Eagles:** 1974–80 • **Birthplace:** South Dayton, New York • **Born:** February 9, 1945

Bill Bergey was a middle linebacker in the classic sense. He did not simply play the position; he *was* the position. There are a few men who are born to play the middle. Dick Butkus was one. Ray Nitschke was another. Bergey fits the mold. When he was in his prime, there were none better.

Physically, Bergey had everything. He had size combined with extraordinary quickness and agility. He weighed anywhere from 245 pounds to 260 during his career, yet he could do a front handspring, in full pads, and land on his feet. But what really set Bergey apart was his fire. He hit opposing ball carriers as if he caught them sneaking in his bedroom window.

"Bill reminds me of Rocky Marciano," said Walt Michaels, the Eagles defensive coordinator from 1973 through '75. "He knows how to gather himself. Some boxers are always on their toes, never in balance to deliver a blow. Bill delivers with his whole body. He explodes. Boom. You can't teach that. A guy has it or he doesn't."

Bergey had it, which is why he was voted into the Pro Bowl four times as an Eagle. Two of those years, he was the team's lone representative. It was unfortunate that Bergey spent his peak years playing on a defense that wasn't very good. Some weeks, it appeared number 66 was playing alone. But even in those losing seasons, Bergey played all out all the time.

One of Bergey's most memorable games was his regular-season debut at Veterans Stadium. The Eagles met their arch-rival, the Dallas Cowboys, in a Monday night game. The Philadelphia fans were anxious to see this new linebacker the Eagles

Bill Bergey

Bergey missed only two games in his first 10 NFL seasons, but in 1979 he suffered a serious knee injury when his foot caught on the artificial turf in the New Orleans Superdome. It was a sad twist of fate: Bergey going down with a devastating injury just at the time the Eagles were becoming a formidable team. He was on crutches as the team advanced to the NFC semifinals that season.

At 35, Bergey pushed his knee through a long, painful rehabilitation so that he could return to the field in 1980. He started every game, right through Super Bowl XV, and while he was not the same devastating force he once was, he still gave it everything he had. As it turned out, the Super Bowl was his final game. His knee simply would not allow him to play beyond that.

"I have no regrets," Bergey said in announcing his retirement. "My only complaint is the 12 years [in the NFL] went too darn fast."

BILL BRADLEY
Safety

Ht: 5–11 • **Wt:** 190 • **College:** Texas • **Years with the Eagles:** 1969–76 • **Birthplace:** Palestine, Texas • **Born:** January 24, 1947

The Eagles were a lifeless, dead-in-the-water football team when they went to Dallas to meet the Cowboys in October 1969. They were five weeks into a season headed nowhere. The

had acquired in a trade with Cincinnati at the expense of two first-round draft picks, plus a second-round choice.

"I had so much to prove," Bergey said. "I wanted to show the Bengals what a horrible mistake they made, letting me go. And I wanted to show the Eagles I was worth what they paid for me. I was absolutely gung-ho crazy that night."

The Cowboys led 7–0 in the third quarter and were threatening to put the game away. They had first and goal at the three. They handed off twice for no gain. Bergey made both tackles. On third down, Roger Staubach handed off to rookie Doug Dennison of Kutztown State. Dennison swept right end and was one step from the goal line when Bergey met him with the force of a tractor-trailer.

The ball popped loose, and cornerback Joe Lavender scooped it off the carpet. He raced down the sideline, 96 yards the other way, for the touchdown that swung the game in the Eagles' favor. They finally won it on a 45-yard field goal by Tom Dempsey with 25 seconds left on the clock. Bergey finished the night with 18 tackles and the Vet Stadium crowd chanting his name.

"I don't know if that was my best hit," Bergey said, "but it surely came at the best time."

The Eagles were 7–7 that season, but slipped to 4–10 the next year, which led to the firing of coach Mike McCormack. At first, Bergey was not thrilled with the hiring of Dick Vermeil. He saw the hard-driving young coach as a "Harry High School." But when he saw Vermeil's program taking shape, he became one of the coach's biggest supporters.

Bill Bradley

Cowboys dominated the Eagles through three quarters on a hot, sunny day in the Cotton Bowl.

Finally, a frustrated rookie named Bill Bradley approached defensive coordinator Jimmy Carr. Bradley tugged on Carr's sleeve and said, "C'mon, Coach, put me in. What have you got to lose?" Carr agreed and told Bradley to take over at free safety.

A little background: Bradley was a high school football legend in Texas—his nickname was "Super Bill"—and he was a quarterback and defensive back at the University of Texas. In his mind, there was only one thing worse than losing a game in the Cotton Bowl, and that was sitting on the bench in the Cotton Bowl.

"Once I got on the field, I was looking to make a big play," Bradley said. "Dallas put in a rookie quarterback who was just out of the Navy, a guy named [Roger] Staubach, and they put in a tight end they just picked up from the Eagles. His name was [Mike] Ditka. We called a blitz; I saw Staubach look for the quick throw to Ditka, and I stepped in front of him. The ball fell right into my lap."

Bradley returned the interception 56 yards for a touchdown. He slowed down the last few yards to wave the ball in the face of his pursuers, including Bob Hayes, the former Olympic sprinter. Hayes was so enraged, he hit Bradley after he crossed the goal line, drawing a penalty.

Watching Bradley that day—young, brash, and fearless—you had a feeling he was going to be fun, and he was, through eight colorful seasons. He wasn't big, he wasn't fast, but he had a radar bead on the football. He intercepted 34 passes to set a team record.

Bradley still holds club records for most interceptions in a season (11 in 1971), most interception return yardage in a season (248 in 1971), and most interception return yardage in a career (536). He was selected to the Pro Bowl three times.

Super Bill, or Soupy as his teammates called him, had a ton of personal accomplishments. He was the first NFL player to win interception titles in back-to-back seasons. He picked off 11 passes in 1971 and nine in 1972, but no matter how many plays he made, it was never enough to get the Eagles over the hump.

"The personal stuff was nice, winning the interception title and going to the Pro Bowls," Bradley said, "but when you get right down to it, this is a team game, and that's where the real satisfaction is. We just couldn't put it together."

Bradley came to the Eagles as a third-round pick in the 1969 draft. He saw spot duty as a rookie and missed most of the 1970 season with a knee injury. His first season as a regular was 1971, and he led the league in interceptions.

As a free safety, Bradley had two major assets: (1) great instincts that were developed as a do-it-all quarterback at Palestine High School and (2) sure hands. He used his instincts to get to the football, and his pickpocket hands did the rest.

The best description of Bradley was offered by Hall of Fame quarterback Sonny Jurgensen who said, "He's like a ghost. He's there but you don't see him until it is too late."

"One play sticks out in my mind," Bradley said. "We were playing the Cardinals, and a receiver named John Gilliam came across the middle. I saw the ball in the air and broke on it. We came together, Gilliam and me, and I just took the ball away. On the films, you could see one guy really wanted the ball and the other guy didn't. That's how I remember my career. I was the guy who wanted the ball."

TOM BROOKSHIER
Defensive Back

Ht: 6–0 • **Wt:** 196 • **College:** Colorado • **Years with the Eagles:** 1953, 1956–61 • **Birthplace:** Roswell, New Mexico • **Born:** December 16, 1931

The Eagles have retired very few uniform numbers, and Tom Brookshier's number 40 is one of them. It is a fitting tribute to a player who was a key member of the 1960 world championship team and for generations of Philadelphia fans was a pro football icon.

It is impossible for Brookshier to walk anywhere in the city without someone calling his name, shaking his hand, or reliving the championship game against Green Bay. Often, it is a thirty-something fan who says his or her grandfather was at Franklin Field that day when the Eagles beat Vince Lombardi's mighty Packers.

"It says something about the Philadelphia fans, but it says something about that team, too," Brookshier said. "We were the team nobody believed in, but we won the whole thing and we had fun doing it. I often say we only led the league in two categories: wins and curfews broken. I think the fans picked up on that."

Brookshier was an outstanding athlete at the University of Colorado. The Eagles selected him in the 10th round of the 1953 draft. As a rookie, he led the team with eight interceptions, but he spent the next two years in the Air Force. When he was discharged in 1956, he rejoined the Eagles and reclaimed his starting position.

Brookshier joked about his lack of speed, and it is true, he was no Olympic sprinter, but he made up for it with his toughness. The Eagles never had a more physical cornerback or better open-field tackler. He also brought a swagger to the defense that was contagious.

"When I think of Brookie, I think of a guy who was fearless," said linebacker Maxie Baughan. "I was a rookie thrown into the starting lineup [in 1960]. All of a sudden, we're on a roll and people are talking about going for the championship. I was wondering, 'Am I ready for this?' Being around a guy like Brookie made me feel better. I'd see the way he played, throwing his body around, taking on Jim Brown, and it would get me going."

"The fans identified with me because of the way I played," Brookshier said. "I wasn't a Philly guy, but I played like a Philly guy. I wasn't real talented, but I played to win. The [fans] remember that I hit Jim Brown hard and I hit Jim Taylor hard. I played against a lot of Hall of Famers, but they didn't make the Hall of Fame the days I played against them."

Brookshier credits secondary coach Jerry Williams with devising a system that allowed a group of defensive backs with average (or less) speed to win a championship. Williams had the Eagles playing combination zone defense in an era when most teams were playing man-to-man. Williams also employed a nickel package, with a fifth defensive back, although no one thought to call it a nickel back then.

"Jerry played to our strength, which was physical play," Brookshier said.

In the championship game, Gummy [Carr, the other cornerback] and I worked over [Boyd] Dowler and [Max] McGee pretty good. We hit them at the line, and the safeties

Tom Brookshier

said, 'Tom, this is a bad one.' I looked down and the bone was sticking through my sock."

Brookshier tried to come back the following season, but his leg would not allow it. He pursued a career in broadcasting, starting at WCAU radio in Philadelphia and working his way up to CBS, where he and ex-Giant Pat Summerall formed one of the most popular play-by-play and color commentary teams in TV history.

BOB BROWN
Tackle

Ht: 6–4 • **Wt:** 285 • **College:** Nebraska • **Years with the Eagles:** 1964–68 • **Birthplace:** Cleveland, Ohio • **Born:** December 8, 1941

"When Bob Brown pulls out to lead a sweep," Green Bay cornerback Herb Adderley once said, "there are two things a guy like me can do: Get out of the way or get hurt."

Brown played 10 seasons in the NFL, five with the Eagles, two with the Los Angeles Rams, three with Oakland. His size, strength, and mean streak made him one of the most feared offensive linemen in the game.

"Bob was the most aggressive offensive lineman that ever played," said John Madden, who coached Brown in Oakland. "Bob used to say that if he could get the right hit on a defensive end, hit him in the right place, like the solar plexus, that he could take a quarter out of him. And he would do it. He'd hit a guy in the first quarter and say, 'I won't see him again until the third quarter.'"

"Bob Brown had a cold-blooded mentality," said Rams defensive end Deacon Jones. "He'd kill a mosquito with an ax."

covered them downfield. We had them confused. They didn't do much [three catches, 24 yards].

There was no big civic celebration the next day. It was just a normal day. I went into Wanamaker's, and they were selling glasses with the headline: Eagles Win NFL Championship. The guy behind the counter said, "Hi, Tom. Good game." I said, "Thanks. How much for the glasses?" I bought a set, walked out, no big deal. Today, there would be parades, police escorts, trips to the White House. I think I like it better the old way.

Coach Buck Shaw and quarterback Norm Van Brocklin both retired after the 1960 season, but the Eagles kept on winning the following year. They were leading the Eastern Conference with a 7–1 record when Brookshier went down with a broken leg. That changed everything. The Eagles started two rookies, Glen Amerson and Irv Cross, in Brookshier's place the next two weeks and were blown out by the Giants (38–21) and Cleveland (45–24). They finished the season in second place, a half game behind the Giants.

"I really think if Tom had played the whole season, we would've been back in the championship game," safety Don Burroughs said. "Without him, we weren't the same."

"The injury was a freak thing," Brookshier said. "The Bears ran a reverse; I came up to make the tackle. The end, John Farrington, blocked me and our legs tangled. The runner came through and hit my lower leg. The bone snapped in half.

"I didn't realize how bad it was. I was saying, 'C'mon, help me up.' Then I saw Maxie's face. He was white as a sheet. He

Bob Brown

"I dislike every man I play," Brown said in a 1967 interview with Gordon Forbes of the *Philadelphia Inquirer*. "I may not even know the guy … but I dislike him because he is standing between me and all-pro, between me and my paycheck.

"Willie Davis once told me, 'Play on Sunday so you can live with yourself on Monday,'" Brown said, referring to the Green Bay Hall of Famer. "That's how I approached the game. I wasn't out there to make friends, shake hands, or pave the way for a TV career. I played as hard as I could every week. It didn't matter if we were 11–0 or 0–11."

Brown made six Pro Bowls and earned All-NFL honors five times during his career, which began in 1964 with the Eagles. He was the second overall pick in the draft following an All-America career at Nebraska. He played at 285 to 300 pounds at a time when most linemen weighed between 250 and 260. Brown was one of the first serious weight lifters in the NFL. He had a weight room built in his house, and in 1966 his military press was within 10 pounds of the American record.

"In college, I got by on my size," Brown said. "I was bigger than most of the other players. But in the pros, there are a lot of big men who are also very strong, very smart, and very quick. Opposing them, I have to have something more than mere size."

Brown looked ponderous in his oversized shoulder pads and size 13, triple E shoes, but he ran the 40-yard dash in 4.6 seconds at his first Eagles training camp. He polished his footwork by skipping rope and playing basketball. He had 20-inch biceps and 33-inch thighs. His neck was 18 and a half inches, and his chest, expanded, measured 57 inches.

Linebacker Maxie Baughan recalls Brown as "cut high," meaning he had a massive upper body and long legs that coiled behind him when he was in his three-point stance. At the snap, Brown shot forward with awesome force. The impact, it was said, sounded like an explosion. Hence his nickname: Boomer.

"Bob was an explosive drive blocker," said Dick Vermeil, who was an assistant coach with the Rams when Brown played there (1969–70). "When he fired out, he catapulted people off the line. Knocked 'em back five yards. You just don't see that in pro football. Bob was one of a kind."

"Bob was the most devastating blocker I ever played against," said Joe Robb, who played against Brown as a member of the St. Louis Cardinals. "I played against Jim Parker and Forrest Gregg, but Brown was bigger, stronger, and better than both of them."

Atlanta linebacker Tommy Nobis agreed. "Brown hit me and it felt like the world turned upside-down," Nobis said. "I've never been hit like that before. Bob Brown manhandled me."

"The job of an offensive lineman is an obscure living," Brown said. "A guy can be lost in the shuffle of tremendous rushers, tremendous passers, tremendous defensive effort. Those [players] tend to stick out in the layman's eyes. They have the stats to back them up. Me, I've got to work at it every day. If it required punching a clock, I'd gladly do that. This is a professional sport and I'm a professional. And I'm going to give my coach and my employer the best days I can."

Brown had the misfortune of joining the Eagles when they were one of the worst teams in football. He was with the team for five seasons, and only one of those produced a winning record. The franchise bottomed out in 1968 when the team finished 2–12 and the fans organized a campaign to oust coach Joe Kuharich.

Brown was one of the few people who remained loyal to Kuharich. He said the coach "was like a father to me. I thought he was a good coach and a good human being. I had such respect for him." When Kuharich was fired in 1969, Brown demanded a trade, so the Eagles dealt him to the Rams for three players: cornerback Irv Cross, guard Don Chuy, and tackle Joe Carollo.

Brown retired following the 1973 season. It took a long time, probably too long, but in 2004 he finally was voted into the Pro Football Hall of Fame. In his enshrinement speech, an emotional Brown explained his motivation on the field: "I could either go out there and be real good and be the beater, or I could go out there and be very mediocre and be the beatee. I liked the role of beater better."

JEROME BROWN
Defensive Tackle

Ht: 6–2 • **Wt:** 300 • **College:** Miami • **Years with the Eagles:** 1987–91 • **Birthplace:** Brooksville, Florida • **Born:** February 4, 1965 • **Died:** June 25, 1992

Jerome Brown was the fire that burned at the center of the Eagles defense from 1987 through 1991. He was boisterous, ferocious, irrepressible, and unforgettable. He described himself as "a big, old kid," yet he became a leader of men, playing

Defensive tackle Jerome Brown (99) was coming off his finest season when he was killed in a car crash in June 1992.

The late Jerome Brown's number 99 is retired by the Eagles at the 1992 regular season opener at Veterans Stadium. Taking part in the ceremony are Reggie White (92), Clyde Simmons (obscured), and Seth Joyner (59).

through pain and rallying the NFL's most intimidating defense week after week.

"Jerome was like a wild man on the field," said Mike Golic, who played alongside Brown. "Every play was a search-and-destroy mission."

Brown's image, built over an All-America career at the University of Miami and five seasons with the Eagles, was one of a brash and mouthy mauler, long on talent and short on discipline. He swaggered and swore, and he played the game with a fuse that burned hot and fast.

Off the field, he lived the same way. He once told an interviewer, "I'm not the type of person you dare to do anything. If you say, 'Don't do it,' it's done."

Brown had his best season in 1991 when he dropped 30 pounds and really dedicated himself to the game. He led all NFL tackles in solo stops (88) and ranked near the top in quarterback sacks (nine). He made the Pro Bowl for the second consecutive year and, at 27, he was acknowledged as the best run stuffer in the business.

"It took me four years to get my priorities in place," he said. "Now I realize how important it is to get in good shape and work at things. I don't take stuff for granted the way I used to. I guess I'm maturing. Either that or I'm just getting old, like Reggie [White]."

Five months after the close of the 1991 season, Brown was killed when the car he was driving flipped over on a rain-slicked road in his hometown of Brooksville, Florida. His 12-year-old nephew Gus also died in the accident. It was a devastating blow to the entire Eagles organization.

The team kept Brown's Veterans Stadium locker intact for the 1992 season. It was preserved just the way he left it, with his football shoes stacked in the bottom and his shoulder pads and helmet resting on the shelf. His number 99 jersey was

mounted in a silver frame and placed inside the stall. The players wore a patch with the initials "J. B." on their jerseys.

"Jerome might not be here, but his presence is still here," coach Rich Kotite said. "We all feel it in some way every day."

When the Eagles went to New Orleans for the NFC Wild Card playoff that season, the team's equipment managers packed Brown's gear and brought it to the Superdome. On the morning of the game, they set up Brown's locker along with the rest of the team. The players knew nothing about it until they arrived at the stadium and found Brown's number 99 waiting for them. The Eagles went out and won the game, 36–20, their first postseason victory since January 1981.

"It was an inspiration, definitely," safety Wes Hopkins said. "It was a reminder of what we were playing for. Jerome wanted to win a championship more than anything."

The Eagles retired Brown's number and inducted him into the team's honor roll in September 1996.

TIM BROWN
Halfback

Ht: 5–11 • **Wt:** 195 • **College:** Ball State • **Years with the Eagles:** 1960–67 • **Birthplace:** Knightstown, Indiana • **Born:** May 24, 1937

Tim Brown grew up in an Indiana orphanage and went to Ball State Teachers College, where he was a Little All-America in football and basketball. He was drafted by both the Green Bay Packers and the NBA Philadelphia Warriors.

At a shade under 6 feet tall, Brown thought he would have a better chance at success in pro football, and he was right, although for a while it did not appear that way. He was cut after playing just one game with the Packers ("Vince Lombardi and I didn't get along, plain and simple," he said), and he was claimed by the Eagles, but he did not get a chance to show what he could do for several years.

"I almost quit after the 1961 season, I was so frustrated," Brown said. "We won the championship in '60, and that was great. We just missed winning the division again the next year, fine. But I wasn't playing, except for kick returns. I felt like I was wasting my time.

"I really thought about not coming back in 1962, but I was living with a family on Pine Street, and the lady, she was like my mother, told me to give it another shot. She said things would break my way, and she was right. That season [coach Nick] Skorich finally gave me the ball."

In 1963, Brown set an NFL record with 2,425 combined yards (rushing, receiving, and kick returns), quite a feat in a 14-game regular season. Two years later, he became the first NFL player to rush for more than 850 yards (he had 861) and average five yards per carry (he averaged a league-high 5.4) while also catching 50 passes in the same season.

"Timmy was a Gale Sayers–type back," Pete Retzlaff, the Eagles All-Pro receiver, said. "He was very quick with a knack for finding daylight. He had great hands. He would be sensational in today's game. Spread the offense, throw him the ball, and watch him go."

"It was a slow process, convincing people I belonged in the NFL," Brown said. "When I finally got to show what I could do, their reaction was 'Gee, what a surprise.' That's the price you pay for coming out of a small college and going late in the draft. You get labeled as a fringe player.

"Buck Shaw sent me into one game, and [quarterback Norm] Van Brocklin waved me off the field. Van didn't have any confidence in me. Skorich was skeptical, too. He thought I was too small. I really believe the only reason Skorich gave me a chance to play was the fans at Franklin Field kept chanting, 'We Want Brown.' I think he finally got tired of hearing it and put me in."

Brown was the Eagles' top offensive threat through the mid-'60s. He led the team in rushing four of five years. He led the league in kickoff returns twice. In 1966, Brown became the first player in league history to return two kickoffs for touchdowns in the same game, a 24–23 upset of Dallas at Franklin Field.

Brown played eight seasons with the Eagles before he was traded to Baltimore in 1968 for Alvin Haymond. When he left, Brown was second only to Steve Van Buren in franchise history with 3,703 yards rushing. He still holds the club records for most kickoff returns (169), most kickoff return yards (4,483), most returns for touchdowns (five), and the longest return (105 yards against Cleveland in the 1961 regular-season opener).

"He gave us fits," Bob Lilly, the Cowboys' Hall of Fame defensive tackle, said. "In those years, the Eagles didn't have many players. We'd spend the whole week talking about how we had to stop Brown, and he'd still find a way to hurt us, either running the ball or returning a kick. I can't tell you how many times I thought I had him and wound up tackling nothing but air."

In a 1967 game, Dallas linebacker Lee Roy Jordan hit Brown with an elbow in the face, breaking his jaw and knocking out four teeth. It was a cheap shot delivered after an overthrown pass, and it is often cited as the blow that set off the Eagles-Cowboys rivalry.

The following year, Brown was traded to Baltimore where he finished his career. His final game was Super Bowl III, which the Colts lost to the New York Jets, 16–7. At 31, Brown retired from football and moved to Hollywood to pursue an acting career. He landed roles in several Robert Altman films including *M*A*S*H* and *Nashville*.

JOHN BUNTING
Linebacker

Ht: 6–1 • **Wt:** 220 • **College:** North Carolina • **Years with the Eagles:** 1972–82 • **Birthplace:** Silver Spring, Maryland • **Born:** July 15, 1950

John Bunting arrived at the Eagles training camp in 1972 in a style befitting a 10th-round draft choice. He was driving a used Volkswagen Squareback with 160,000 miles on it.

Bunting was, in his words, "the seventh-string right outside linebacker. I was 6–1 and 222 pounds and ran the 40 in 4.85 with a little tailwind." It was an indication of how little the team thought of him when they assigned him jersey number 95.

"Numbers in the 90s were definitely not cool at the time," Bunting said. When he made the team that season, and in future seasons, he had the opportunity to trade that number for a lower number, but he refused. He kept 95 as a reminder of where he started and how far he had come.

Bunting started three games as a rookie and won a full-time starting job in 1973, but his season was shortened to seven games when he broke his arm making a tackle on the Cowboys' Calvin Hill. He returned in 1974 and started 60 of the next 62 games before suffering a serious knee injury in 1978. Nine months of rehabilitation put Bunting back on the field, calling the signals for an Eagle defense that allowed the fewest points in the league from 1979 to 1981.

"John knew more about our defense than [coordinator] Marion Campbell, who was a defensive genius," Bill Bergey said. "More than once, Marion was challenged by John. Not in a threatening way, but in a 'Why don't we do this?' way. Marion would do it his way because he didn't want to be shown up by a player. But afterward you'd see them talking about it. Marion wanted to know what John thought."

Bunting watched hours of film to prepare for a game. He took notes on tendencies and habits of opposing players. Often, his attention to detail led to big plays. Example: In the NFC championship game against Dallas, Bunting spilled Rod Springs for a seven-yard loss on the second play from scrimmage. Dallas was forced to punt, the Eagles got the ball in excellent field position, and two plays later Wilbert Montgomery broke his 42-yard touchdown run, setting the tone for the Eagles 20–7 victory. But Bunting's tackle made all that possible.

On the play, Bunting anticipated the double screen. It was a favorite second-and-long play by the Cowboys; Bunting had noted that tendency. Quarterback Danny White tipped it by dropping back a little too fast; Bunting noted that fact, too. As the play unfolded, Bunting charged into the backfield to hit Springs just as he caught the ball.

"Best pure defensive play I saw in my 12 seasons," Bergey called it.

After working so hard to get to the Super Bowl, no one took the 27–10 defeat to Oakland harder than Bunting. After the game, he sat in the shower with tears in his eyes.

"I remember Roynell Young, our rookie cornerback, saying, 'Don't worry, J. B., we'll be back here next year,'" Bunting said. "I told him, 'Roynell, this is my ninth year. You have no idea how hard it is to get here.'"

Bunting finally did win a championship in 1984 with the Philadelphia Stars of the USFL. Later, he went into coaching and earned a Super Bowl ring as co–defensive coordinator for the St. Louis Rams under his former Eagles coach Dick Vermeil. In 2001 he was hired as head football coach at his alma mater, North Carolina.

ADRIAN BURK
Quarterback

Ht: 6–2 • **Wt:** 190 • **College:** Baylor • **Years with the Eagles:** 1951–56 • **Birthplace:** Mexia, Texas • **Born:** December 14, 1927 • **Died:** July 28, 2004

Adrian Burk has only one line in the Eagles record book, but it is a huge one: seven touchdown passes in one game versus Washington on October 17, 1954. That's not only a team record; it is a league record that Burk shares with Sid Luckman (Chicago), George Blanda (Houston), Y. A. Tittle (Giants), and Joe Kapp (Minnesota).

"I'm sure people see those names and say, 'I've heard of these other guys, but who's Adrian Burk?'" he said in a 1987 interview.

Burk was an All-America quarterback and punter at Baylor who was a first-round draft pick by Baltimore in 1950. He was traded to the Eagles the following year and split the quarterback duties with Bobby Thomason. His first season with the Eagles, Burk threw 14 touchdown passes and 23 interceptions.

"[Burk] had ability, but he didn't have confidence in himself," wrote John Webster in the *Philadelphia Inquirer.* "He was a mousy sort. His teammates did not seem to believe in him."

"Adrian was no sissy, but he was different in the sense he was like an Eagle scout," said Jim Trimble, who was the Eagles head coach from 1952 through 1955. "When he was throwing all those interceptions, I said, 'Look, if you don't have an open receiver, just throw the ball away.' He said, 'You mean on purpose? But Coach, that's not nice.'

"I finally convinced him to do it, but every time he did it, he would wipe his hands on his pants, pretending his hands were wet and the ball slipped. He was just a real straight arrow. The players didn't have a problem with him. They liked him just fine. We all could see his talent. He was a big kid with a strong arm and great form."

Burk was a bright, energetic guy with a vision that extended well beyond the playing field. He attended law school in the off-season and passed the Texas bar exam in 1956. He joined with two Cleveland Browns, Dante Lavelli and Abe Gibron, to create the first NFL Players Association.

"At that time, we were fighting for things like money for exhibition games and injury coverage, things the current players take for granted," Burk said. "Back then, you got nothing, not a penny, the whole preseason. You only got paid if you made the final roster."

Adrian Burk

Burk retired as a player following the 1956 season. He was 28 and healthy, but the Eagles were going nowhere under new head coach Hugh Devore, and Burk felt he had better things to do with his life than tag along with a 4–8 football team. He became a full-time attorney and quickly earned a reputation as one of the top trial lawyers in Houston.

When the American Football League was formed in 1960, he joined the Houston Oilers as assistant to team president Bud Adams. He was the in-house legal counsel during the years when suits and countersuits were flying back and forth between the rival leagues. Burk also recruited talent. He signed LSU's Heisman Trophy winner Billy Cannon on the field after the Sugar Bowl while an unsuspecting NFL representative waited in the locker room. It was the ultimate quarterback sneak.

Burk resigned from the Oilers in the mid-'60s to concentrate on his law practice. He kept his hand in the game by working as an official. He started by calling college games, then moved up to the NFL as a back judge. He was the official who made the call on Franco Harris's "Immaculate Reception" in the 1972 AFC playoffs. Burk ruled that the ball caromed off Oakland's Jack Tatum, so Harris's touchdown stood, and the Steelers won the game, 13–7.

In his later years, Burk and his wife, Neva Nelle, devoted their lives to the church as volunteer missionaries for the Southern Baptist Church.

"It's the best decision we ever made," Burk said. "If I had known how sweet full-time Christian service was, I would have been at it 15 years ago. I've never had so much peace of mind."

DON BURROUGHS
Safety

Ht: 6–4 • **Wt:** 185 • **College:** Colorado State • **Years with the Eagles:** 1960–64 • **Birthplace:** Los Angeles, California • **Born:** August 19, 1931

Norm Van Brocklin took one look at the rookie defensive back with the long, spindly frame and said, "You look like a damn blade." That was 1955 in Los Angeles. Don Burroughs was known as "the Blade" for the rest of his pro football career, which spanned a decade and ended in Philadelphia.

"Van Brocklin had a gift for that, coming up with names," Burroughs said. "I didn't mind. At the time, I was just glad someone noticed me. Besides, I was skinny. I was like a Blade."

As a rookie with the Rams, Burroughs intercepted nine passes in a 12-game season. He intercepted 21 passes in his first four seasons. When Van Brocklin came to the Eagles, he told general manager Vince McNally to trade for Burroughs, who was holding out for a new contract with the Rams. During the 1960 exhibition season, the Eagles acquired Burroughs for a future draft pick.

"The whole team was built through trades," Burroughs said. "The only people we didn't get were probably from Taiwan or Korea. There were almost no original Eagles. I told Van Brocklin, 'I feel like I'm in a bus terminal. I don't know any of these guys.' Norm said, 'Don't worry about it, Blade. We can win.'"

Burroughs was a big part of the 1960 team's success. The Eagles defense ranked ninth in yards allowed, but they won by making big plays at critical times. They led the NFL with 45 takeaways in the 10–2 regular season, and Burroughs, the free safety, led the team with nine interceptions and 124 return yards. His last interception came in the closing minutes of a 20–6 win in St. Louis that clinched the Eastern Conference title.

"I had too many interceptions that year; I cost myself money," Burroughs said. "Vince McNally said he'd give me $100 bonus for every interception, then he'd double it at a certain point. At midseason, he said, 'Blade, I can't do it. It's going to cost me too much.' Can you believe it?

"But I'm not complaining. I loved everything about Philadelphia. It was a totally different team than the Rams. In LA, we had all these stars, but we weren't a team. There was all this petty jealousy and Hollywood crap, and we never won. With the Eagles, it was 35 guys pulling together and that's how we did it.

"[Coach] Buck Shaw was a fine guy. He knew how to handle men. McNally was a solid football man. I've never played with a better bunch of guys. I look back on that year as the highlight of my career. I still get a warm feeling every time I look at this championship ring."

Burroughs played only five seasons with the Eagles, but when he retired in 1964, he held the team record with 29 pass interceptions.

KEITH BYARS
Running Back

Ht: 6–1 • **Wt:** 250 • **College:** Ohio State • **Years with the Eagles:** 1986–92 • **Birthplace:** Dayton, Ohio • **Born:** October 14, 1963

Keith Byars evolved into one of the NFL's most versatile players. He lined up at five—count 'em, five—different positions, moving around the various formations like an oversized pea in a carnival shell game.

Sometimes he was a halfback; sometimes he was a fullback. Sometimes he lined up in the slot; other times he split as a wide receiver. He also played tight end. Around and around he goes and where he stops, that's for the defense to figure out.

"People ask me what position I play and I say, 'Offense,'" Byars said. "I never wanted to be a one-dimensional player. I never wanted to be the guy who goes in the game and people say, 'Okay, now they're gonna run it because that's all he can do.' When I'm out there, I want the defense to worry about everything I can do."

With his size and speed (4.5 in the 40-yard dash), Byars was projected as a workhorse runner in the mold of Earl Campbell and John Riggins. However, two freakish injuries (a broken metatarsal bone in each foot) cost him his first two training camps. When he finally got a chance to carry the ball, he looked stiff and tentative. He had just 1,003 yards rushing in his first two seasons.

In 1988 the Eagles coaches reassessed the situation. They noticed that Byars was surprisingly fluid catching the football. He had soft hands and ran excellent patterns. Buddy Ryan, who selected Byars with his first pick in the 1986 draft, did not know he was a tight end his first two years at Roth High School in Dayton, Ohio.

These observations started the coaches thinking: Why keep running Byars up the middle when we can split him wide,

Don Burroughs

throw him the ball, and watch him overpower people? So the Eagles began to utilize Byars as a combination halfback and receiver with impressive results.

Over his last four seasons with the Eagles, he averaged 69 receptions a year. When he left the Eagles following the 1992 season, Byars ranked fourth on the team's all-time receiving list with 371 catches. He trailed only Harold Carmichael, Pete Retzlaff, and Pete Pihos.

Byars signed with Miami as a free agent. He played three seasons with the Dolphins, then signed with New England in 1996 and was part of the Patriots team that played in Super Bowl XXXI. His final season was 1998 with the New York Jets.

When he retired, Byars had more pass receptions (610) than any other running back in NFL history. He broke the record previously held by Hall of Famer Marcus Allen.

HAROLD CARMICHAEL
Wide Receiver

Ht: 6–8 • **Wt:** 225 • **College:** Southern • **Years with the Eagles:** 1971–83 • **Birthplace:** Jacksonville, Florida • **Born:** September 22, 1949

It was a routine 7-on-7 drill at the Eagles training camp in 1971. Quarterback Rick Arrington lofted a ball to the back of the end zone. Cornerback Nate Ramsey eased up when he saw the pass was overthrown. But the rookie running the pattern couldn't ease up, not if he hoped to make the team. He kept going back until he ran out of room, then he stuck up his right hand and plucked the football out of the drizzly sky. He didn't jump, he simply unfurled that fire hose of an arm until it met the ball.

"Damnedest catch I ever saw," said assistant coach Tom Fears, who once was a Hall of Fame receiver with the Los Angeles Rams.

"I think we may have found a new weapon," said head coach Jerry Williams.

At 6–8 and 225 pounds, Harold Carmichael was unlike anything the NFL ever had seen before. He could beat double coverage simply by reaching above it. The Eagles stole him in the seventh round of the draft because no one could believe a receiver with such a long, lean frame could survive in the NFL.

At first, Williams used Carmichael at tight end. His ninth game was in Dallas, and middle linebacker Lee Roy Jordan ripped out his knee. His career almost ended right there. Carmichael returned in 1972, but offensive coordinator John Rauch could not figure out what to do with him. He had one catch in the first three games, 11 catches after 11 games (none for touchdowns), playing for the NFL's worst offense.

"The kid needs work," Rauch said. "His stride is too long."

It wasn't until 1973 when coach Mike McCormack put Carmichael at wide receiver and Roman Gabriel took over at quarterback that the big guy came into his own. He teamed with 6–5 Charles Young and 6–4 Don Zimmerman to form the "Fire-High Gang," a flashy receiver corps that terrorized every secondary in the league.

"That Carmichael is amazing," Atlanta coach Norm Van Brocklin said. "He could stand flat-footed and eat the apples out of a tree."

Harold Carmichael

In the 1973 season Carmichael led the NFL with 67 receptions, a club record, and 1,116 yards. He scored nine touchdowns and was voted into his first Pro Bowl. In 13 seasons with the Eagles, Carmichael appeared in more games (180), caught more passes (589), and scored more touchdowns (79) than any other player in team history. He set an NFL record by catching at least one pass in 127 consecutive games, a streak that spanned eight seasons (1972–80).

In a 1981 interview Carmichael said:

I didn't expect any of this. I didn't think I was a good enough athlete to even get a scholarship to college. The first positive sign I got was from this scout who came to our high school [William M. Raines High School in Jacksonville, Florida] to check out Kenny Burrough [who later played for the Houston Oilers]. Kenny was one year ahead of me.

This scout talked to Kenny and me at the same time. When he left, he told me, "I'll be back to get you next year." That's when I first started thinking seriously about college ball. I was a late bloomer. It took me awhile to get my feet on the ground at every level, especially the NFL.

There is an amusing piece of footage in the NFL Films vault. It was shot during the first football game at Veterans Stadium, a 1971 preseason game with the Eagles and Buffalo. The NFL Films crew was on the Buffalo bench in the second half when Carmichael entered the game and made several big plays.

O. J. Simpson asks, "Who's that big rookie?" Then he asks, "What round was he drafted?" Told Carmichael was a seventh-round pick, Simpson blinks in disbelief.

"Can you believe that?" Simpson asks teammate J. D. Hill. "All those [scouting] computers and he's a seventh-round pick. Ain't that a trip?"

Carmichael went through some difficult seasons in Philadelphia. After his breakout year in 1973, his production slipped each of the next three seasons: 56 catches and eight touchdowns in 1974; 49 catches and seven touchdowns in 1975; 42 catches and five touchdowns in 1976. The same fans who cheered his colorful "roll-the-dice" end-zone celebrations in '73 were booing him for his drops the next three years.

"Nobody likes to be booed," Carmichael said. "I didn't like it; it hurt me. But I always tried my best. The best thing that could have happened was Dick [Vermeil] came in and built my confidence back up."

"When I got the job, Harold was beaten down emotionally," Vermeil said. "He was booed; he was maligned unfairly. What he needed was for someone to believe in him so he could believe in himself. We talked about the hot dog stigma he had. I said he was a leader on the team, it was important that he show class in everything he did, on and off the field. He said he only did the dice roll thing because he thought people expected it."

As the Eagles came of age under Vermeil, so did Carmichael. In 1978 he caught 55 passes for 1,072 yards, a 19.5-yard average, and eight touchdowns as the Eagles finished with their first winning record in 12 years. The following season, Carmichael had a career-high 11 touchdowns, including two in a 31–21 win over Dallas that helped the Eagles lock up a playoff berth.

Carmichael is remembered for catching alley-oop passes in the end zone, using his height to take the ball away from smaller defenders. But he could do a lot more than that, evidence his 15.2-yard career receiving average. He did not have great speed, but he was willing to catch the ball over the middle, and he was hard to tackle in the open field.

"Harold was never given credit for being the great athlete that he is," quarterback Ron Jaworski said. "People would say, 'He's 6–8. Just throw it up there, he gets it.' He did a lot more than that. He ran great patterns. He had good hands. He caught a lot of balls around his ankles. He blocked. I played with some great receivers—Harold Jackson, Lance Rentzel, Jack Snow—but Harold is head and shoulders above them. I mean that in every sense of the word."

"I didn't even like those [high] throws," Carmichael said. "I might catch it once or twice, but one of those times I'm gonna be up in the air and somebody's gonna get a good shot on me. They may not hit me hard, but the way I fall really could do some damage. And I want to play every game."

Carmichael set a club record by playing in 162 consecutive games from 1972 through 1983. After the '83 season, the Eagles released Carmichael and he signed with Dallas. He appeared in only two games with the Cowboys in the 1984 season; one of them was a Week 3 game against the Eagles at Texas Stadium. It was a strange sight: Harold Carmichael on the Dallas bench, wearing the silver helmet with the blue star, staring across the field at the Eagles.

"The truth is, I didn't even want to go down there," Carmichael said. "That Eagles-Cowboys rivalry runs deep. I never felt right in that uniform. I'll always be an Eagle."

In 1998, Carmichael rejoined the Eagles organization as director of player development and alumni relations.

JIMMY CARR
Defensive Back

Ht: 6–1 • **Wt:** 215 • **College:** Morris Harvey • **Years with the Eagles:** 1959–63 • **Birthplace:** Kayford, West Virginia • **Born:** March 25, 1933

When Jimmy Carr was 16, he was stricken with rheumatic fever, which caused him to lose most of his upper teeth. Little wonder he became known as "Gummy." It was a nickname that followed him through Morris Harvey College, the U.S. Army, and later a long career in pro football.

Carr was a single-wing tailback at Morris Harvey, a small school in Charleston, West Virginia. He signed with the Chicago Cardinals as a free agent in 1955 and played one season before going into the Army. Upon his discharge, he went back to the Cardinals, played one season, signed with Baltimore, then was traded to the Eagles for a 10th-round draft pick in 1959.

The Eagles were already well stocked with running backs, so they put Carr on defense where he found a home at left cornerback. With the stocky Carr at one corner and the aggressive Tom Brookshier at the other, the Eagles had two players who could knock opponents silly.

"Carr and Brookshier can curl the whiskers off any runner in the league," assistant coach Charlie Gauer said. "They're the best pair of tacklers I've seen."

"They might not be the fastest men at that position," head coach Buck Shaw said, "but they have a gift for smelling out plays. It's like a sixth sense that allows them to find the ball."

Carr overcame physical hardship to make it to the NFL. In addition to the rheumatic fever, which caused him to drop out of school for six months, he also was stricken with spinal meningitis. When he was eight years old, living with his seven brothers and sisters in the coal region of West Virginia, he suffered severe leg burns that required skin grafts and put him on crutches for almost a year.

"All that taught me," Carr said, "was that nothing in life comes easy. It was a valuable lesson."

Carr made one of the biggest plays of the 1960 season, catching a Mel Triplett fumble in midair and racing in for the touchdown that lifted the Eagles to a 17–10 win over the New York Giants. It was the only touchdown Carr scored in his nine NFL seasons, but it was a pivotal moment in the Eagles' drive to the championship.

In 1964, Carr was traded along with quarterback Sonny Jurgensen to Washington for quarterback Norm Snead and defensive back Claude Crabb. Carr would later say, "The deal was really me for Crabb. Jurgensen and Snead were just throw-ins."

Carr retired following the 1965 season and spent the next three decades as a defensive coordinator and secondary coach in the NFL, the USFL, the CFL, and the World League of American Football. He was an assistant coach with the Eagles from 1969 through 1972.

KEN CLARKE
Defensive Tackle

Ht: 6–2 • **Wt:** 275 • **College:** Syracuse • **Years with the Eagles:** 1978–87 • **Birthplace:** Savannah, Georgia • **Born:** August 28, 1956

Ken Clarke spent ten seasons with the Eagles playing a difficult position (nose tackle) without much fanfare. He was signed as an undrafted free agent out of Syracuse and spent his first four seasons as a backup to Pro Bowler Charlie Johnson. When Johnson was traded in 1982, Clarke took over the position and played it well.

He did not miss a game, other than strike games, in his ten seasons with the Eagles. His streak of 139 consecutive games ranks among the team's all-time leaders. He had 31 sacks, which ranks third among Eagles tackles.

Clarke was named NFC Defensive Player of the Week for his performance in a 16–7 win over Indianapolis in October 1984. He recorded nine tackles, added two sacks, and forced a fumble.

"I don't see any nose tackle in football playing better than Kenny," head coach Marion Campbell said.

"[Nose tackle] is a hard position to play because most of the time, you're going to get double-teamed," Clarke said. "A lot of times you get triple-teamed because the back picks you up, too. Consistently getting good pressure on the quarterback is new ground. I don't know too many nose tackles that do it well."

When Clarke first joined the Eagles, he platooned with Johnson in Campbell's three-man line. Johnson was the starter, but Clarke was quicker, so Campbell substituted Clarke for Johnson on passing downs. When Johnson was traded, Clarke was promoted to the first team, but there was some doubt about whether he could handle the heavier load.

Clarke answered all the questions by recording 85 tackles and four and a half sacks in the strike-shortened '82 season.

Jack Concannon still holds the Eagles record for most yards rushing by a quarterback in a single game, 129 against Pittsburgh in 1966.

In 1983 he had 110 tackles to lead the team's defensive linemen. In 1984 he posted career highs in sacks (10½) and tackles (123) and was voted the team's Most Valuable Defensive Player. In 1985 he finished with seven sacks and 112 tackles, including a 17-tackle game in a 23–17 win over Atlanta.

"As I play more and more, I'm getting better and better," Clarke said. "I'm just beginning to scratch the surface of my ability. I'm playing good, but I feel inside I have so much more to give."

Despite playing one of the game's most punishing positions, Clarke had a long career: 10 seasons with the Eagles, one season in Seattle, and three seasons in Minnesota. He credited his conditioning program, which included long hours of weight training (he could bench press 465 pounds) and aerobics to increase his flexibility.

After his playing career Clarke went into coaching, serving as an assistant with Tampa Bay and Washington. He spent the 2004 season as defensive line coach of the Rhein Fire in NFL Europe.

JACK CONCANNON
Quarterback

Ht: 6–3 • **Wt:** 205 • **College:** Boston College • **Years with the Eagles:** 1964–66 • **Birthplace:** Boston, Massachusetts • **Born:** February 25, 1943

Jack Concannon was a player who attracted a large fan following in Philadelphia, yet when you check the records, you see he did not accomplish very much.

In three seasons with the Eagles, Concannon appeared in 18 regular-season games, completed 43 percent of his passes, and threw twice as many interceptions (eight) as touchdowns (four). Yet there are fans who still remember his Eagle highlight reel, brief as it was.

Concannon defeated Dallas, 24–14, in his rookie season, 1964. He also put together a three-game winning streak at the end of 1966, lifting the Eagles to a 9–5 finish and a spot in the Playoff Bowl. After that season, he was traded to Chicago for tight end Mike Ditka.

Coach Joe Kuharich selected Concannon in the second round of the 1964 draft, but he never could decide how to use him. The former Boston College star played in four games as an Eagles rookie and only three games his second year. In 1966, Kuharich had Concannon returning punts and lining up at running back and wide receiver before finally playing him at quarterback the last month of the season.

Concannon's best game was a 27–23 win over Pittsburgh on December 4, 1966. In that game, he completed 13 of 25 passes for 131 yards, and he carried the ball 15 times for 129 yards, a single-game record for an Eagles quarterback.

"I ran around out there like a wild man," Concannon said.

"If Kuharich played either of the other two quarterbacks, [Norm] Snead or [King] Hill, our defense would've smothered them," said ex-Eagle center Ray Mansfield. "But Concannon was something different. He was just too nimble. You just don't expect to see a quarterback run for that kind of yardage."

Like most scrambling quarterbacks, Concannon was exciting but erratic. He could be brilliant one week, as he was against Pittsburgh, and dreadful the next, as he was in the Playoff Bowl against Baltimore when he threw four interceptions.

Concannon was with the Bears for five seasons and played out his option, signing with Dallas in 1972. He spent two years on the Cowboys inactive roster, then was traded to Green Bay, where he played 14 games in 1974. He finished his career as a backup with Detroit in 1975.

RUSS CRAFT
Halfback

Ht: 5–9 • **Wt:** 178 • **College:** Alabama • **Years with the Eagles:** 1946–53 • **Birthplace:** McEwan, Tennessee • **Born:** October 15, 1919

When NFL Films produced its ultimate highlight film, *Pro Football's 100 Greatest Touchdowns*, Russ Craft had a featured role. Craft scored only seven touchdowns in his nine-year pro career, but the one he scored against the Los Angeles Rams in 1947 was worth putting in a time capsule.

Rams quarterback Bob Waterfield threw a pass to Elroy (Crazylegs) Hirsch in the flat. Hirsch made the catch over his shoulder, and as he turned toward the goal line, Craft stole the ball and, without breaking stride, raced away to score the winning touchdown. It happened so quickly that on the film, Hirsch is seen taking several more steps before he realizes he no longer has the ball.

"That play got a lot of publicity," Craft said. "The next year, we went to Los Angeles to play the Rams, and when we got off the train, two policemen grabbed me and handcuffed me. Some lady came running up, screaming, 'He's the one. He's the one who stole the ball.' I didn't know what the heck was going on. Turns out it was a publicity stunt. There was a photographer there, and they put the picture of me in handcuffs on the front page of the LA papers."

Russ Craft

That may have been Craft's most memorable play, but it was not the only highlight in his career. On September 24, 1950, he intercepted four passes in a 45–7 win over the Chicago Cardinals. More than half a century later, that is still a team record, and it shares the NFL single-game interception mark.

"I had my share of interceptions, but I really played the game more conservatively," said Craft, who was twice selected to the Pro Bowl. "I could make the big play, but I was more concerned with not allowing touchdowns. There weren't many touchdowns caught on me. I took pride in being a good, sound player."

"Russ was one of those unsung heroes," tackle Vic Sears said. "He did a little of everything. He played some halfback, he returned kicks, and he was outstanding on defense. He was a little guy, but he was the last guy on our team that I'd want to fight. I don't think anybody could've whipped him, not even Bucko [Kilroy]. He was strong and he had unbelievably quick hands. Pound for pound, I think he was the toughest guy on the team."

Craft ran the 100-yard dash in 9.9 seconds at the University of Alabama, and he probably would have played offense if he was drafted by any team other than Philadelphia. But the Eagles had a full complement of running backs led by Steve Van Buren and Bosh Pritchard, so coach Greasy Neale moved Craft to defense, where he used his speed to cover the league's top receivers.

"I often thought the word 'crafty' originated with Russ Craft because that's what he was," Tom Brookshier said. "When I joined the team [1953], Russ was in his last season, so he knew all the tricks. I learned so much just by watching him. He was always in position. By the end of a game, he'd have even the great ones like [Cleveland's Dante] Lavelli talking to themselves."

"Hardly a night that goes by that I don't dream about playing with the Eagles," Craft said in a 1982 interview with the *Philadelphia Daily News*. "Some people worry about concentrating on the past, but I don't really do that. I'm glad to relive those days. Why shouldn't I? I had a grand time there."

IRV CROSS
Defensive Back

Ht: 6–2 • **Wt:** 195 • **College:** Northwestern • **Years with the Eagles:** 1961–65, 1969 • **Birthplace:** Hammond, Indiana • **Born:** July 27, 1939

Irv Cross had a rude introduction to professional football. As a rookie in the Eagles' 1961 training camp, he was assigned to cover veterans Tommy McDonald and Pete Retzlaff.

"Tommy came at me, faked to the inside, and whoosh, he was gone," Cross said. "I was 30 yards away from him when he caught the ball. They put me on the other side, and Pete ran a short pattern. I went for him, and whoosh, he was off in another direction catching the ball. I said to myself, 'If this is what I have to go through, I may as well quit.'"

Cross did not quit. Rather, he dedicated himself to learning the pro game, which he did well enough to become one of the league's top cornerbacks. He took over for Tom Brookshier when the veteran suffered a career-ending leg injury in 1961. He was a starter for four seasons until he was dealt to the Los Angeles Rams. The Eagles reacquired Cross in a 1969 trade that sent future Hall of Fame tackle Bob Brown to the Rams.

Cross was a track star at Northwestern, competing in the 100-yard dash, the low hurdles, the pole vault, and the broad jump. He was a running back and end in football, so he was not schooled in proper tackling technique. He learned the hard way at the NFL level. He launched himself at his opponent's knees, often leading with his head. Result: Three concussions in his rookie year.

Cross was knocked out so often that his teammates nicknamed him "Paper Head." One afternoon a light snow began to fall during practice. Jimmy Carr shouted, "Better get inside, Cross, before one of those flakes hits you in the head."

With practice, Cross improved his tackling. He also was fitted with a specially padded helmet that absorbed more of the impact. As a result, he was able to avoid further injury. He did not miss a game in his final eight seasons with the Eagles and Rams. He was named to the Pro Bowl three times.

Cross was a student of the game. He kept a file on every receiver in the league, noting their tendencies, their strengths and weaknesses. He brought film home to study every night. When the Eagles traded for Cross in 1969, they made him a player-coach for one season, and he stayed on as the secondary coach in 1970.

"I always enjoyed thinking about football, thinking about strategies, coming up with ways to break offenses and design defensive concepts," Cross told Jim Gehman of the *Eagles Digest*. "That's always been a real exciting thing for me to do. So with that [coaching] job, I was able to do that as well as do contracts with some of the guys who were lower-round draft choices. My hope was to be a general manager some place in the league, but that never developed."

When Cross quit football in 1971, CBS signed him as an NFL analyst. He was a regular on "The NFL Today," the show that pioneered the modern studio pregame show.

"I knew the teams well," Cross said. "Just going through the film breakdowns and everything, you could understand what people were trying to do. I think if you can convey that information to fans, they can better understand what's going on out on the field. That's what we tried to do with 'NFL Today.' We wanted to be entertaining, but more importantly, we wanted to be able to inform people."

In 1999, Cross accepted the post of athletic director at Macalester College in St. Paul, Minnesota, a Division III school.

"I like being on a college campus where you have this sea of free thought, great intellectual challenges, and a chance to grow and learn," he told Gehman. "We believe in high academic standards. We believe in multiculturalism and internationalism and community service as the core values of the college. We want to win every game we play, but if not, we want to be competitive and give our best effort."

RANDALL CUNNINGHAM
Quarterback

Ht: 6–4 • **Wt:** 200 • **College:** UNLV • **Years with the Eagles:** 1985–95 • **Birthplace:** Santa Barbara, California • **Born:** March 27, 1963

When most people think of Randall Cunningham, they think of one play, a play that ranks among the all-time highlights of ABC-TV's "Monday Night Football."

Randall Cunningham

The date was October 10, 1988. The Eagles were playing the New York Giants at Veterans Stadium. On third and goal from the four, Cunningham faked a handoff, rolled right, and found himself face-to-face with Giants linebacker Carl Banks. Banks dove at Cunningham and hit him just above the knees. Cunningham appeared to be going down, but he put one hand on the turf, somehow regained his balance, straightened up, and zipped a touchdown pass to tight end Jimmie Giles, sparking the Eagles to a 24–13 win.

The play was vintage Randall Cunningham. No other quarterback could have done it, or would have dared to try. There is no computer programmed to defense something like that. Said Cunningham, "It was a play a lot of people would have gone down on, but I didn't give up."

Another famous play occurred on December 2, 1990, when Cunningham eluded the clutches of Buffalo's Bruce Smith in the end zone and unfurled a majestic pass that Fred Barnett pulled down at midfield and raced away to complete a 95-yard touchdown, the second-longest pass play in team history. A play that, for most quarterbacks, would have resulted in a safety, Cunningham turned into an Eagles touchdown.

"Randall takes the game to another level," Washington cornerback Darrell Green said. "Even the other top quarterbacks, like [Phil] Simms and [Joe] Montana, have to stand in awe of what Randall can do. He comes as close as anyone in the league to being able to win a game by himself."

In 1989, *Sports Illustrated* put Cunningham on the cover of its Pro Football Preview issue, identifying him as "The Ultimate Weapon." He played 11 seasons with the Eagles and finished as the team's second leading all-time passer behind Ron Jaworski and third leading rusher, trailing only Wilbert Montgomery and Steve Van Buren. He was the Eagles' top rusher four years in a row (1987–90), an unheard-of feat for a modern-day quarterback.

"He is the best athlete ever to play the position," said Eagles coach Buddy Ryan. "He's got the best arm in the league. He's the best runner and the best punter. The only thing he can't do is play basketball."

"No one has the ability to bring a team back better than Cunningham," said Arizona linebacker E. J. Junior. "He's the quickest [runner] we face. When he gets going, it's like a track meet. He just runs by you."

Cunningham joined the Eagles as a second-round draft pick in 1985, the 37th player selected overall. He had a record-setting career at UNLV, where he led the Rebels to an 11–2 record as a senior and became only the third quarterback in NCAA history (Doug Flutie and John Elway were the others) to throw for more than 2,500 yards in three consecutive seasons.

Cunningham arrived in Philadelphia wearing rock-star shades and a T-shirt that read, "Questions? Ask My Agent." He had his hair in Jheri curls and flaunted a cooler-than-thou arrogance that turned off many veterans. On the field, the rookie struggled in four starts, throwing one touchdown pass and eight interceptions.

In 1986, Ryan took over as coach and created a rotating quarterback system, with the veteran Jaworski playing on first and second down and Cunningham, the scrambler, taking the ball on third down. Playing behind a makeshift line, Jaworski and Cunningham were sacked a combined 104 times that season, an NFL record, as the Eagles limped to a 5–10–1 finish.

In 1987, Ryan released Jaworski and made Cunningham the full-time starter. For the next eight seasons, Eagle fans were alternately dazzled, puzzled, thrilled, and frustrated by the player whom Stan Walters, the team's radio analyst, aptly nicknamed "Starship 12" for his mercurial personality. With Cunningham, there were long stretches of virtuoso brilliance followed by crushing letdowns, most often in the postseason.

In 1988, Cunningham led the Eagles to their first NFC East title in eight years as he passed for 3,808 yards and 24 touchdowns. In the divisional playoff, the Eagles faced Chicago at Soldier Field on a day when the fog made it almost impossible to see, yet Cunningham passed for 407 yards in a 20–12 Eagles loss. In 1990, Cunningham passed for 3,466 yards and 30 touchdowns (tops in the NFC) and also rushed for 942 yards, the second-highest single-season rushing total ever for an NFL quarterback.

"I think he's the most talented quarterback in the league," Chicago defensive coordinator Vince Tobin said. "The thing that concerns you is the way he improvises. If a play breaks down or he feels pressure, he steps out and runs the ball, and he's hard to tackle in the open field. Or he'll throw the ball on the run and throw it a long way. As a coach, that scares you because it takes it out of the defense's hands and puts it in the hands of individual talent."

Cunningham was capable of extraordinary moments, such as the 1989 game in Washington when he brought the Eagles back from a 20–0 deficit to win, 42–37, as he threw for 447 yards and five touchdowns. In 1990 he passed for four touchdowns and ran 52 yards for another in a 48–20 win over New England. On the flip side, there was Cunningham's postseason record with the Eagles: one win, five losses.

Ryan contributed to the problem by providing little in the way of direction to the young quarterback. Ryan was a defensive coach. His idea of an offensive game plan was to tell Cunningham to make three or four big plays and the defense would take care of the rest. With a mediocre line and no running game, the offense became a one-man trapeze act with Cunningham turning broken plays into touchdowns. It was exciting, it was even productive to a point, but it did not advance Cunningham as an NFL quarterback, and it proved his undoing in the postseason when he faced defenses that were more talented and disciplined.

Ryan also fed Cunningham's sense of privilege, which irritated his teammates. For example, the coach allowed Cunningham and tight end Keith Jackson to leave a preseason game at halftime so they could attend the birthday party of singer Whitney Houston. Cunningham wrapped himself in celebrity, hosting fashion shows and traveling in his own personal Lincoln limousine. He wore gold-tipped shoelaces on his cleats and hung out with TV host Arsenio Hall. He was a loner in the locker room, yet his teammates respected him for the courage he displayed on the field.

"People don't know how tough this guy is," coach Rich Kotite once said. "One time we were getting ready to play Green Bay. Randall was so beat up, he could hardly walk. He sat in meetings with ice bags taped to each knee. It took him forever to get out of the chair. I thought, 'No way he's able to play this week.' But he played. Not only did he play, but he jumped six feet in the air and hurdled four guys to score a touchdown."

There were two occasions in Cunningham's career with the Eagles when it appeared he was on track to a Super Bowl, and each time his season was cut short by injury. The first time was in 1991. Kotite had replaced Ryan as coach, and Cunningham was coming off his best preseason, but in the opener at Green Bay, Cunningham suffered a knee injury and was lost for the year. The second time was in 1993 when the Eagles were 4–0 and Cunningham was completing 69.1 percent of his passes. He broke his leg in a 35–30 win over the New York Jets and spent the rest of the season on crutches as the team faded to an 8–8 finish.

Cunningham's career with the Eagles trailed off from there. He was phased out in 1995 when Ray Rhodes came in as coach and hired Jon Gruden as offensive coordinator. Rhodes and Gruden saw Rodney Peete as a better fit for their West Coast offense. Peete led the Eagles to the playoffs, and while the team was preparing for a second-round game against Dallas, Cunningham flew to Las Vegas to be with his wife Felicity for the birth of their first child. The team gave him permission, but told him to return as soon as possible. Instead, he rejoined the team late Friday, more than 24 hours after the baby was born, and missed the Friday practice.

What would have been a minor annoyance turned into a major issue when Peete was knocked out of the game and Cunningham had to play the last three quarters. He looked lost, completing 11 of 26 pass attempts in a 30–11 loss.

The Eagles made no attempt to re-sign Cunningham. At 32, he drifted into the free-agent market where he was ignored for more than a year. In 1997, Minnesota signed him to back up Brad Johnson, but when Johnson was injured the following year, Cunningham stepped in and wrote a remarkable comeback story. He threw for a career-high 34 touchdowns as the Vikings finished the regular season 15–1 and scored more points (556) than any other team in NFL history.

Cunningham went from the scrap heap to MVP in two years. But even in his finest hour, Cunningham still fell short of the Super Bowl as the Vikings were upset by Atlanta, 30–27, in the NFC Championship game.

BRIAN DAWKINS
Safety

Ht: 6–0 • **Wt:** 210 • **College:** Clemson • **Years with the Eagles:** 1996– • **Birthplace:** Jacksonville, Florida • **Born:** October 13, 1973

To watch Brian Dawkins on the field—flying around, delivering head-snapping blows, all fire and rage—you would never imagine he prepares for the game by listening to gospel music.

"It relaxes me, it gets me ready," Dawkins said. "I'm laid-back, I'm praying. When I put my uniform on, every distraction, every burden is cleared from me so I can concentrate fully and totally on the game and the game plan."

But once Dawkins pulls on his helmet with the black visor, he becomes a different person. On the days when the Eagles introduce the defense, Dawkins comes onto the field bursting with emotion. Sometimes he does a somersault; other times he flexes his muscles, throws back his head, and lets out a primal scream. But there is no doubt that the man has come to play.

"This guy isn't just a player, but a ferocious state of mind," wrote Rich Hofmann of the *Philadelphia Daily News.*

"Dawk is the hardest hitter on the team," linebacker Jeremiah Trotter told Marcus Hayes of the *Daily News.* "He hits like a linebacker. He hurts people. He's knocked them out. He's knocked himself out. Shoot, he's knocked us out."

That's no exaggeration. Dawkins has twice knocked out defensive tackle Hollis Thomas and once staggered defensive end Hugh Douglas when he hit them while making a tackle. Pound for pound, Dawkins is one of the hardest hitters ever to wear an Eagles uniform and one of the best defensive players in franchise history.

"If I'm going to build a football team, Brian Dawkins is my free safety," defensive coordinator Jim Johnson said. "Brian could play strong safety, corner, free safety and not miss a beat. He is in the Jerry Rice mold in terms of self-sacrifice. He practices as hard as he plays. He has no regard for his body."

"Most people don't think of the safety as an important part of the defense," Dawkins said in a 2002 interview with *Pro Football Weekly.* "It's like the safety is the last line of defense and that's it. I want to redefine the safety position as one to be reckoned with."

In his nine seasons with the Eagles, since joining the team as a second-round draft pick in 1996, Dawkins has made free safety more of an attacking position. He can line up close to the line of scrimmage to shut down the run, he can blitz the quarterback as well as any linebacker (he has 13½ career sacks), he can cover a receiver one-on-one, and in a zone, his mere presence can discourage a receiver from going across the middle.

"When you play the Eagles, the first thing you have to do is find number 20," Oakland quarterback Kerry Collins said. "They have an aggressive scheme and good players, but it all revolves around Dawkins. You have to be aware of where he is at all times, because he can do so many things. He's always a threat to make the big play."

Brian Dawkins

In 2002, Dawkins demonstrated his versatility by becoming the first player in NFL history to record a sack, an interception, a fumble recovery, and a touchdown reception all in the same game. The Eagles defeated Houston that day, 35–17, as Dawkins capped his hat trick of big defensive plays by taking a pitch from Brian Mitchell on a fake punt and racing 57 yards for his fourth career touchdown.

Dawkins aggressive play has drawn the attention of the NFL office, which in the 2002 season fined him $50,000 for a hit on Giants wide receiver Ike Hilliard. The league ruled Dawkins hit Hilliard with his helmet. It fell under the league's definition of "an intent to injure" play. Dawkins insisted there was no such intent. He said the hit was one of those things that happen in the warp-speed blur of an NFL game.

"I can't push a button and change the way the collision is going to happen," Dawkins said. "I can't tell a receiver to turn left instead of right so I don't hit him head-on. The ball's in the air. As a defender, you do what you have to do. We're talking about split seconds. The rule says I'm supposed to lead with my shoulder, but my head is inches away from my shoulder. I'm not out there trying to hurt anyone. I would challenge anyone who calls me a dirty player. But I play hard, and sometimes things happen."

Dawkins suffered a Lisfranc foot sprain in 2003 that forced him to miss nine games. There was some question how effective Dawkins would be when he returned for the 2004 season. He was coming off a serious injury, and his age (he turned 31 in October) was a concern. But Dawkins had perhaps his finest season as he equaled his career high with four interceptions and finished second on the team with 95 tackles.

He took on even more responsibility in the 2004 season when the Eagles lost veteran cornerbacks Troy Vincent and Bobby Taylor, and youngsters Lito Sheppard and Sheldon Brown moved into those spots. Dawkins provided the leadership that helped the Eagles set a club record with 13 regular-season victories and win their first NFC championship since the 1980 season. His teammates voted him the Defensive MVP.

Dawkins saved a 17–14 win over Washington with an end-zone interception in the last two minutes. It was a typically instinctive play by Dawkins, who read the eyes of quarterback Patrick Ramsey and followed them to tight end Chris Cooley. Dawkins cut underneath both Cooley and Sheppard to take the ball away.

"That's why I'm here, to make plays to help this team win games," Dawkins told Reuben Frank of the *Burlington County Times*. "I want that ball coming my way with the game on the line. I want to be the guy my teammates are all counting on. Some guys can't handle it. Some guys don't want to be in a pressure situation. I love it."

TED DEAN
Fullback

Ht: 6–2 • **Wt:** 215 • **College:** Wichita State • **Years with the Eagles:** 1960–63 • **Birthplace:** Radnor, Pennsylvania • **Born:** March 24, 1938

Ted Dean

There is a fascinating footnote to Ted Dean's touchdown run in the 1960 NFL championship game, the play that lifted the Eagles to a 17–13 victory over Green Bay. It was the rookie fullback's first rushing touchdown. He had not scored in 113 carries in the regular season. He averaged just 2.7 yards per rushing attempt.

"In that situation, late in the game, so much on the line, I knew [quarterback Norm] Van Brocklin would want to go with Barnes," Dean said, referring to Billy Barnes, the veteran halfback. "And in the huddle, he called Billy's number. But as we walked to the line, he changed the play. He called an off-tackle play with me carrying the ball.

"I don't know why he did it. I guess he saw something in the defense. But I remember thinking, 'Ted, you've got something left. This is the time to use it.'"

It was second and goal at the Packer five-yard line. The Eagles trailed 13–10 with less than six minutes remaining. Dean took the handoff and followed the blocks of guard Gerry Huth and tight end Bobby Walston into the end zone for the game-winning score. Dean also set up the winning drive with a 58-yard kickoff return to the Green Bay 39-yard line.

"After the game, a man came up to me in the locker room and said I was selected the Most Valuable Player," Dean said. "I thought, 'Great, that's a new car.' Then he said, 'But since this is Van Brocklin's last game, we're giving the award to him.' I was a naive kid, I didn't know what to say. Besides, I was still high on winning the championship.

"The guy said they'd give me a color TV instead. I said okay. I'll never forget it. He said, 'You're young. You have a long career ahead of you. You'll win this [award] again.'"

As it turned out, Dean's career peaked that day. He played only four more seasons before he was involved in a near-fatal automobile accident that ended his career. We can only speculate how good the kid from Radnor might have been.

"I remember one preseason game in Hershey when Ted scored three touchdowns against Chicago," Tom Brookshier said. "He scored on a run, a pass, and a punt return; the shortest one was, like, 55 yards. Walking off the field, I heard [Bears coach George] Halas say, 'That kid is going to be the best ever.'"

Dean ran so smoothly that he did not appear particularly fast, but he easily outdistanced linebackers and defensive backs in the open field. He had soft, sure hands that Van Brocklin used to good advantage. It was a long touchdown pass from Van Brocklin to Dean that helped rally the Eagles from a 17–0 deficit to a 31–23 win over the New York Giants, a critical step in their drive to the 1960 championship.

Dean was a fourth-round draft pick in 1960. He was forced into the lineup as a rookie when fullback Clarence Peaks went down with a broken leg halfway through the season. After the championship season, Dean was hobbled by injuries, and in 1964 the Eagles traded him to Minnesota, where he was reunited with Van Brocklin, who was then coaching the Vikings.

Dean played only two games in Minnesota before he was involved in the accident that ended his career. He was riding with teammate Sandy Stephens when their car slammed into a tree. Dean's right leg was so badly mangled that he never played football again. At 26, his career was over. Dean returned to the Philadelphia area and became an elementary school teacher.

"I'm not bitter about the way things worked out," he said. "I could have wound up in a wheelchair or had brain damage. It's like the Lord took my hand and said, 'Ted, there are other things in life besides football.'"

TOM DEMPSEY
Kicker

Ht: 6–1 • **Wt:** 260 • **College:** Palomar (California) Junior College • **Years with the Eagles:** 1971–74 • **Birthplace:** Milwaukee, Wisconsin • **Born:** January 12, 1941

Tom Dempsey was famous long before he arrived in Philadelphia. In 1970, as a member of the New Orleans Saints, Dempsey kicked the longest field goal in NFL history, a 63-yarder, shattering the old record set by Baltimore's Bert Rechichar by seven yards.

For Dempsey, setting the record was a mixed blessing because the fame that came with it contributed to his reporting to training camp the following year out of shape, which led to his release. The Eagles claimed him midway through the 1971 season when they soured on their own kicker, Happy Feller. Dempsey was successful on 12 of 17 field goal attempts, including a club-record 54-yarder against St. Louis. His 70.6 field goal percentage led the league.

The following season, Dempsey set another club record by kicking six field goals in one game, an 18–17 win over Houston in the Astrodome. He accounted for all the Eagles scoring. Houston kicker Skip Butler missed a field goal that could have won the game for the Oilers. The *Philadelphia Bulletin*'s headline the next day read, "The Butler Didn't Do It—Tom Did."

Born with a two-fingered stub instead of a right hand and only half of a right foot, Dempsey overcame the odds to make it in pro football. He credits his father, Huey, a former all-state basketball player, for encouraging him. "He always told me, 'You can do anything you want to do,'" Dempsey said. "He'd tell me, 'You may have to do it differently, but you can do it.'"

In high school, Dempsey played offensive tackle. When he enrolled at Palomar Junior College, he started at defensive end. He did not start kicking until the coach, looking for someone who could kick off, asked for volunteers. Dempsey removed his shoe and, wearing only a sock, drilled the ball out of the end zone.

Dempsey spent that season kicking shoeless with his right sock wrapped in athletic tape. When San Diego coach Sid Gillman discovered him and signed him to his taxi squad in 1968, he had a special shoe designed with a flat, malletlike face made entirely of leather. It resembled the head of a sledgehammer, and when it struck the ball, it had the same effect.

The Chargers had a proven kicker in Dennis Partee, so Gillman released Dempsey in 1969. He signed with the Saints, and one year later he boomed the field goal heard around the football world.

When he joined the Eagles, Dempsey set a team record by kicking 20 field goals in the 1972 season. The following year, he kicked a 45-yard field goal to lift the Eagles to a 13–10 win over Dallas, their first "Monday Night Football" victory at Veterans Stadium.

"Tom inspired people," Eagles quarterback Roman Gabriel said. "No one talked about it. Tom certainly never talked about it. But you could feel it. You saw what he overcame to make it to the NFL, and it just said so much about him."

HUGH DOUGLAS
Defensive End

Ht: 6–2 • **Wt:** 280 • **College:** Central State (Ohio) • **Years with the Eagles:** 1998–2002; 2004– • **Birthplace:** Mansfield, Ohio • **Born:** August 23, 1971

In the 2000 NFC Wild Card game, the Eagles were trailing the Tampa Bay Buccaneers 3–0 in the second quarter. They needed a spark, and Hugh Douglas provided it, sacking quarterback Shaun King and forcing a fumble, which Mike Mamula recovered. Five plays later, Donovan McNabb scored a touchdown, and the Eagles were on their way to a 21–3 victory.

Douglas made many such big plays for the Eagles, each of them accompanied by a chorus of Philadelphia fans chanting, "Huuuuue." He ranks third on the team's all-time list for quarterback sacks with 54 and a half, trailing only Reggie White and Clyde Simmons. His 15 sacks in the 2000 season is the sixth-best single-season total in franchise history.

"Hugh is an effort guy," said Orlando Pace, the St. Louis Rams All-Pro tackle. "He's a smaller guy, but he plays with a lot of power."

Douglas refers to himself as "The Little Defensive End Who Could." He was 250 pounds when he came into the NFL as a first-round pick of the New York Jets in 1995. He packed on more than 30 pounds over the next decade, but he still was undersized by the standards of his position. For example, Douglas gave away five inches in height and 50 pounds in his matchup with Pace in the 2001 NFC Championship game.

"He's built so low to the ground and so strong that he gets great leverage," said Chris Samuels, Washington's 6–5,

Hugh Douglas

310-pound left tackle. "That's what separates him from the rest." Larry Allen of the Dallas Cowboys called Douglas "the all-around package."

Douglas learned the hard way, practicing against Erik Williams, the future Dallas All-Pro, while they were teammates at Central State. Williams outweighed Douglas, who was then a freshman, by 60 pounds.

"Erik almost drove me out of football," Douglas said. "He was a senior, getting ready for the NFL. I was a kid just out of high school. I'd never seen the game played the way Erik played it. It was like he wanted to kill me.

"He'd pick me up and head-butt me. He'd drive block me down the field, then put me on my back. This was every day. Finally, I couldn't take it anymore, so I left. I packed up and went home. I left like a thief in the night."

Douglas returned home to Mansfield, Ohio, where he lived with his father, a former steel worker disabled by a bad back. His father, also named Hugh, asked his son if he had any plans. Hugh, Jr., wasn't sure. Maybe he would enlist in the Marines, maybe he would get a job at the steel mill. His father looked him in the eye and asked, "Is that really want you want?" Of course, they both knew it wasn't.

A few days later, Douglas was back on the practice field at Central State, taking everything Erik Williams could dish out.

"It's like the saying 'Whatever doesn't kill you makes you stronger,'" Douglas said. "That's what Erik did for me. I made up my mind I'd never allow myself to be intimidated like that again."

Douglas became the intimidator in his final college season, recording 15 and a half sacks and earning NAIA All-America honors. An impressive showing at the Hula Bowl against the top Division I prospects solidified his position as a high draft pick. The Jets took Douglas with the 16th selection in the first round, and he set a franchise rookie record with 10 sacks.

When Bill Parcells replaced Rich Kotite as Jets head coach, he installed a 3–4 defense, which was not a good fit for a smaller lineman such as Douglas. The Eagles were able to acquire Douglas from the Jets for a second- and a fifth-round draft pick. It proved to be one of the best trades in franchise history.

Back in the 4–3 defense, Douglas had an outstanding 1998 season, tying a club record with four and a half sacks in one game against San Diego. He finished the season with 12 and a half sacks and 55 tackles, an indication that he was developing into a solid all-around player, equally adept at stopping the run and pressuring the quarterback.

"What good are you if you're a one-dimensional player?" Douglas said. "All you ever heard was 'Hugh Douglas, pass rusher.' I got sick of that."

Douglas was voted into three Pro Bowls in his five seasons with the Eagles. He left after the 2002 season to sign a five-year deal with a $6 million bonus in Jacksonville. However, Douglas never felt at home with the Jaguars and admitted he played "in a funk." The Jaguars released him in the 2004 preseason just when the Eagles were looking for someone to replace the injured N. D. Kalu.

The Eagles signed Douglas and gave him back his familiar number 53. He sacked Giants quarterback Kurt Warner in the league opener, and the chant of "Huuuue" rolled through Lincoln Financial Field. Douglas saw spot duty in the 2004 season, playing behind Derrick Burgess at right end. He appeared in every game and finished with 19 tackles and three sacks.

"It doesn't matter if I'm starting or coming off the bench," Douglas said. "I take the same approach for every game. I just strap on my blue collar and go to work."

OTIS DOUGLAS
Tackle

Ht: 6–1 • **Wt:** 225 • **College:** William & Mary • **Years with the Eagles:** 1946–49 • **Birthplace:** Reedville, Virginia • **Born:** July 25, 1911 • **Died:** March 21, 1989

Otis Douglas joined the Eagles as a 35-year-old rookie in 1946. He played at William & Mary, and following his graduation in 1931, he pursued a career in coaching. He was head coach at Akron when the Second World War broke out and he enlisted in the Navy.

Douglas was stationed at the Jacksonville (Florida) Naval Air Base and played on the football team under coach Jim Tatum, who later would lead the University of Maryland to a national championship. Although Douglas was already in his 30s, he played well enough to attract the interest of Eagles line coach John Kellison.

On Kellison's recommendation, the Eagles signed Douglas as a backup lineman and assistant trainer. He was schooled as a Navy medic and served as the trainer for the football team in Jacksonville. Douglas did not expect to play much for the Eagles, but when tackle Vic Sears was sidelined in 1947, Douglas started in his place and went both ways, averaging 55 minutes of playing time a game.

"It wasn't as bad as it sounds," Douglas said. "Everybody went two ways in those days. Usually by the fourth quarter, you had some tired boys out there. I was in better shape than most of them, so I was able to do okay."

The 1948 season, Douglas said, was more difficult because he played part of the year with three broken ribs. "Playing the games was tough," he said, "but you know what was tougher? Being the trainer, I had to tape my own ribs."

During that season, Douglas began stopping by the football practices at Drexel University. The campus was only a few blocks from his West Philadelphia apartment. The Drexel team had not won a game in almost three years, and the football program was on the verge of collapse. Douglas was offered the coaching job, and he accepted even though he had to juggle that responsibility with serving as both a player and trainer with the Eagles.

Somehow, Douglas led Drexel to a 3–3–1 finish in 1948. Eagles coach Greasy Neale was so impressed that he recommended Douglas to the University of Arkansas, which hired him in 1950. That was the start of a long, winding road that saw Douglas serve as head coach for Calgary in the Canadian Football League and assistant coach for three colleges and three NFL teams.

His final job in professional sports was head trainer of the Cincinnati Reds in 1961. He put the players through a rugged conditioning program, similar to his football training, and after a week the players were begging for mercy. Douglas refused to let up. The result: the Reds went through the entire season without a serious injury, and they won the National League pennant.

HERMAN EDWARDS
Cornerback

Ht: 6–0 • **Wt:** 195 • **College:** San Diego State • **Years with the Eagles:** 1977–85 • **Birthplace:** Fort Monmouth, New Jersey • **Born:** April 27, 1954

Before Herman Edwards could make the play known as the Miracle of the Meadowlands, he first had to make it onto an NFL roster, which was something of a miracle in itself.

Edwards possessed average size and below-average speed. He ran the 40-yard dash in 4.85 seconds, which took him off most NFL scouting boards. He also had a troubling college career, twice leaving the University of California (he did not get along with the coach) before finally finishing at San Diego State.

"I had a label as uncoachable and undisciplined," Edwards said. "I had long hair, too, which didn't help. Then [the scouts] timed me and decided I was too slow. But what they couldn't measure was how competitive I was."

Edwards was ignored in the 1977 NFL draft, but Eagles coach Dick Vermeil remembered him as a high school player in Monterey, California. Vermeil tried to recruit him when he was coaching at UCLA. He thought Edwards was worth signing as a free agent.

Edwards wound up starting every game at cornerback for the next nine seasons. He intercepted 33 passes, one short of the team record. And of course, there was the Miracle, the fumble that Edwards recovered and carried into the end zone to give the Eagles a 19–17 victory over the New York Giants in 1978.

How ironic that when Edwards became an NFL head coach in 2001, it was with the New York Jets and the Meadowlands became his home!

"That play proves what I've always believed: You have to finish every play," Edwards said. "It's a great lesson. I remind our [Jets] players of it every day."

"When I think of Herman Edwards," Vermeil said, "I think of a guy who was a student of fundamentals, who understood and perfected technique. He was a 4.85 guy, but what the stopwatch didn't tell you was what a great athlete he was. Smooth turns, no wasted motion. He could run with a much faster receiver because he didn't make fundamental mistakes. He was always in great position."

The son of a career army man, Edwards used the skepticism of the NFL scouts to his advantage. When he was passed over in the draft, it only made him more determined to succeed.

"That's always been my way," Edwards said. "When you say I can't do something, that's fine. I like hearing that because it motivates me. This goes all the way back to when I was eight years old. I told the other kids in the neighborhood, 'You're gonna see me on TV someday. I'm gonna play in the NFL.' They laughed. I said, 'Okay, just wait and see.'"

Edwards was competitive even in practice. Bill Bergey recalled Vermeil testing Edwards one day, calling four consecutive deep passes to his side. Edwards batted away each throw. After the fourth one, he shouted, "That's okay, keep throwing it my way. I'm right here. C'mon." Edwards made his point.

"It's like I always tell our players, it doesn't matter how big you are or how fast you are," Edwards said. "It's all about playing the game of football, and you play the game between the lines."

JACK FERRANTE
End

Ht: 6–1 • **Wt:** 197 • **College:** No college • **Years with the Eagles:** 1941–50 • **Birthplace:** Camden, New Jersey • **Born:** March 9, 1916

Jack Ferrante rose from the Philadelphia sandlots to a starting position on the greatest team in Eagles history, the 1947–49 club that went to three consecutive NFL title games and won back-to-back world championships.

"Not one out of five million boys could play in this league without college or high school experience," Eagles coach Earle (Greasy) Neale said. "Jack is the exception. He can catch the football as well as any receiver in the league, and he knows what to do with the ball once he has it."

Ferrante was born in Camden and grew up in South Philadelphia. Known as "Blackjack," he began playing sandlot football at age 14 with a club called the Rockne AA. Over the years, he played for other teams, including Seymour AC and the Wilmington Clippers.

A delivery boy named Jim Lewro helped Ferrante make the leap to the big time. Lewro brought groceries to the home of

Jack Ferrante

Bert Bell, the Eagles' owner and coach. As Bell was fumbling through his pockets for tip money, Lewro would say, "You should take a look at this receiver with the Seymour AC. His name is Ferrante. I know he could help your team"

This went on for months. Finally, Bell agreed to scout a Seymour game. He was impressed enough to sign Ferrante to a contract in 1939. Ferrante did not make the Eagles roster that season, so he returned to the sandlots for two more years. In 1941 he was back in the Eagles training camp, and this time he made the team.

Ferrante said:

People laugh when they hear the term "sandlot," but that was a good brand of football. With the depression, there were a lot of guys like myself who had to work instead of going to college, so there were guys playing sandlot ball who would've been playing for Penn or Villanova if times weren't so tough. You had to be pretty good to play for those clubs. It wasn't like they were a bunch of stumblebums.

With Wilmington, we played two games a week, one at home, one away. They paid us $75 for the home games and $50 for the road games because they deducted travel expenses. I didn't care. I felt like a millionaire with that $125 in my pocket.

Ferrante led the Eagles in receiving three times in five seasons from 1945 through 1949. He had three consecutive 100-yard receiving games in 1950. He finished his career with 169 receptions for an average of 17.1 yards per catch. His best game was a 1948 win over Detroit in which he had 184 yards receiving and scored three touchdowns.

Ferrante said:

No one on the team said anything about my background. We had guys from big schools like Michigan, Indiana, Stanford, places like that, but they didn't look down on me. I was accepted the same as everyone else. I was just another guy on the team doing my best to help them win. That's all anyone cared about.

At the home games, though, they would introduce the starters and give their position and college. For me, the [public address] announcer would say, "And from the sand-lots of South Philadelphia, Jack Ferrante." The crowd would give me a big cheer. I loved it. What Philly kid wouldn't?

Ferrante earned just $6,200 in 1949 when the Eagles rolled to an 11–1 regular-season record and won their second world championship. He told Dick Cresap of the *Philadelphia Bulletin* that he felt underpaid. He also was unhappy with the conditions at Shibe Park.

"For seven years I've had the same locker," he said, "and while I'm dressing a drop of water will hit me on the head every 20 seconds from a dripping pipe. It's worn a bald spot and it's making me goofy."

Cresap brought Ferrante's complaint to Neale, who was less than sympathetic. "That explains everything," the coach said. "He's either too lazy or too dumb to move over one foot."

Ferrante retired following the 1950 season. He became the first football coach at Monsignor Bonner High School in Drexel Hill and led the team to the city championship in 1959 and 1961.

IRVING FRYAR
Wide Receiver

Ht: 6–0 • **Wt:** 200 • **College:** Nebraska • **Years with the Eagles:** 1996–98 • **Birthplace:** Mount Holly, New Jersey • **Born:** September 28, 1962

Irving Fryar has the two most productive pass-catching seasons in Eagles history. In 1996, Fryar set the team record with 88 receptions, breaking Keith Byars' mark of 81 set in 1990. In 1997, Fryar had another big year with 86 catches, and his 1,316 yards was the second most receiving yards in Eagles history, topped only by Mike Quick's 1,409 yards in 1983.

For Fryar, it was another chapter in a comeback story that began in New England, where he was the first overall pick in the 1984 draft, continued through Miami, where he spent three seasons catching passes from Dan Marino, and peaked during his first two years with the Eagles when he was named to the NFC Pro Bowl team each season.

"I play every day with a chip on my shoulder," Fryar said. "When you ask somebody about good receivers—I don't even say great, but good—they won't mention my name. When I was young, [they said] I never reached my potential. Now [they say] I'm too old to play."

Early in his career, Fryar had numerous off-the-field issues, including drug use, marital problems, and an arrest on weapons charges. He was quoted in *Sports Illustrated* as saying, "I know I was dirty. I know I was filled with drugs, filled with lies, filled with alcohol."

But in 1996, Fryar had a spiritual awakening. He became a Pentecostal minister and began preaching in Pompano Beach, Florida. He turned his life around.

Fryar played eight disappointing seasons with the Patriots, then had three good years in Miami (averaging 66 catches per season) before signing with the Eagles as a free agent in 1996. In his first season, Fryar caught 11 touchdown passes, including a club-record four in one game against the Dolphins.

Over the next two seasons, the Eagles won a total of nine games. The 1998 season was particularly frustrating as the Eagles started a young quarterback, Bobby Hoying, and his struggles resulted in Fryar catching just 48 passes. Heading toward a 3–13 finish, with coach Ray Rhodes on his way out and another shakeup looming, Fryar announced his plans to retire at the end of the season.

His final game as an Eagle was on December 27, 1998, at a cold and gloomy Veterans Stadium. The South Jersey native was honored in a pregame ceremony. The Eagles presented Fryar with a motorcycle as a retirement gift. In the game, Fryar caught three passes for 36 yards as the Eagles lost to the New York Giants, 20–10.

"It felt like a funeral," Fryar said.

A month later, in an interview with the *Boston Globe*, Fryar was quoted as saying, "I didn't retire because I can't play anymore. Playing in Philadelphia was rough this year. Playing on a 3–13 team was hard on me. It did a lot of things to my mind and spirit. They were squashed and stomped on. But those things can be rejuvenated if I were in a different area in the right situation."

Fryar spent one year working as a sports reporter for WPVI-TV in Philadelphia, but in 2000 he came back and played another season with the Washington Redskins.

WILLIAM FULLER
Defensive End

Ht: 6–3 • **Wt:** 280 • **College:** North Carolina • **Years with the Eagles:** 1994–96 • **Birthplace:** Norfolk, Virginia • **Born:** March 8, 1962

The Eagles lost Reggie White and Clyde Simmons to free agency, so in March 1994 they responded by signing defensive end William Fuller from Houston. It was a difficult position for Fuller, coming in to replace the two leading sack artists in franchise history, but he met the challenge, giving the Eagles three consecutive Pro Bowl seasons.

"He is a different kind of player than Reggie and Clyde, but he's definitely comparable," defensive tackle Andy Harmon said. "He has a great work ethic. He's been real consistent, and he's always where he is supposed to be. That's what makes a great player."

"You can't replace Reggie White," Fuller told Kevin Mulligan of the *Philadelphia Daily News*. "I can come in here and be William Fuller. That's what I'm trying to do, be an effective player. I would hope and dream that I could be a Reggie White type of player. I give him the utmost respect. I feel I'm a good player in my own right, but I'm not Reggie White and I wouldn't dare try to be Reggie White."

Fuller had nine and a half sacks in 1994 and 13 sacks each of the next two seasons. He set an Eagles record by recording at least one full sack in seven consecutive games in 1994. Along the way, he picked up the nickname "The Fuller Rush Man."

"He has been a great addition for us," defensive coordinator Bud Carson said. "He's brought leadership, he's smart, he's got experience, he can rush the passer, and he's an excellent run player. He doesn't make mistakes. He's a very unselfish player, which says a lot in itself. He's a consummate pro."

There was some initial concern when Fuller, who signed a three-year, $8.4 million contract with the Eagles, had a sluggish preseason. Questions were raised about whether the 32-year-old Fuller was slowing down and, if so, whether the Eagles made a costly mistake in signing him. Fuller assured everyone that he would be ready to go when the regular season started.

"I can't get up for scrimmages and preseason games," Fuller told Jim Ducibella of the *Virginian Pilot*. "If your house was on fire and you ran in to get your mama, you'd kick that door down to get her. But if someone tells you to pretend the house is on fire, you can't do it."

Fuller's first big game was Week 4 of the 1994 season when he recorded two sacks and tackled Steve Young for his first career safety in the Eagles 40–8 rout of San Francisco. He also tipped a Young pass that fell into the arms of Harmon for an interception. It was the 49ers worst loss in 23 years at Candlestick Park.

Signing with the Eagles was like a homecoming for Fuller, who began his professional career with the Philadelphia Stars of the United States Football League. He helped the Stars to two USFL championships, and when the league disbanded in 1986, he signed with Houston. He played for the Oilers for eight seasons and led the AFC with 15 sacks in 1991. It was hard for Fuller to leave Houston after all those years, but the fact that he was going back to Philadelphia made it easier.

"I didn't get any sleep the night before I came to Philadelphia to sign my contract," Fuller told Sal Paolantonio of the *Philadelphia Inquirer*.

I told my wife, "Gee, I should be happy. This is the biggest deal of my life, financially. After this, we should be set for life." But it was tough to get on that plane. There were eight years of friendships and hard work in Houston. But I couldn't have asked for a smoother transition.

[Philadelphia] is a good town. People appreciate good football here. In Houston, everyone would be dressed to the nines, wearing high-heeled shoes. Here, everybody has on an old Randall jersey or anybody jersey. They're not dressed to impress. They're dressed to have fun … They have a beer and enjoy themselves. And they understand the game of football. They understand and appreciate good defense.

I'm glad everybody is saying, "The Eagles did right to get this guy" and "He's worth whatever they're paying him." That's great. That's what I was hoping they'd say.

After the 1996 season, Fuller left the Eagles and signed with San Diego, where he played two years before retiring. He could have continued, he had other offers, but he felt it was time to walk away.

"I played 15 years in a league where the average career is about three years," Fuller told Warner Hessler of the *Newport News Daily Press*. "I never had a major surgery, and I made more money than I ever dreamed of making. I've been blessed. I loved every minute I played football, and I believe it made me a better person."

ROMAN GABRIEL
Quarterback

Ht: 6–5 • **Wt:** 220 • **College:** North Carolina State • **Years with the Eagles:** 1973–77 • **Birthplace:** Wilmington, North Carolina • **Born:** August 5, 1940

On June 13, 1973, Roman Gabriel arrived in Philadelphia as the Eagles' newest starting quarterback. Unlike most of his predecessors, Gabriel had a résumé of genuine accomplishment. He played 11 seasons with the Los Angeles Rams, and just four years earlier, he was the NFL's Most Valuable Player.

When Gabriel met the press for the first time, he offered a startling prediction: "I feel that in two years, we'll have a world championship in Philadelphia." For a franchise that had not won a championship in more than a decade—and had won just 17 games in the previous five seasons—that was a bold vision, indeed.

Gabriel could not make his prediction come true. In his five seasons with the Eagles, the team never did finish with a winning record. But for at least one year, 1973, Gabriel brought welcome excitement back to the team.

In Gabriel's first season with the Eagles, they more than doubled their point total from the previous year (310 compared to 145), and they almost tripled their touchdown production (34 up from 12). Gabriel established career highs in pass completions (270), completion percentage (58.7), and yards passing (3,219). His yardage and his 23 touchdown passes led the NFL and earned him Comeback Player of the Year honors.

The Eagles won only five games that season as the defense collapsed, allowing 393 points, most in the NFC. But the offense, with Gabriel throwing to a talented fleet of receivers,

Roman Gabriel

led by Harold Carmichael and tight end Charles Young, was prolific.

"Mike [McCormack, coach] said that with such a young team, I'd feel like Moses," Gabriel said. "He said, 'With so many young players, we need your leadership and work ethic.' I said, 'That's fine because I don't have to do anything different than what I've been doing with the Rams. I'll come in and lead by example.'"

Gabriel developed a sore arm in his final season with the Rams; that was one reason why they were willing to trade him. But he began strenuous workouts with martial arts champion Gus Hoefling, who accompanied Gabriel to Philadelphia, and those training sessions restored Gabriel's strength and confidence. He also packed his arm in heated paraffin every day after practice, all of which helped put the zip back on his fastball.

"I'm not doing this [martial arts] so I can go around breaking concrete blocks with my head," Gabriel told Bill Lyon of the *Philadelphia Inquirer*. "It helps keep my body supple. I've taken some pretty good shots that might have slowed me down otherwise. But the big thing about kung fu is mind over matter. You really learn to concentrate."

Gabriel's finest hour was a 30–16 win over Dallas, snapping the Eagles' 11-game losing streak to the Cowboys and setting off a wild celebration at Veterans Stadium with fans pouring onto the field as the final seconds ticked away. Gabriel, who was called "The Messiah" by fans and media, led the victory by throwing two touchdown passes to Carmichael.

"This is the kind of day that makes you glad you can play football for a living," Gabriel said. "Some beautiful people were rewarded today. The coaches, the players, Mr. Tose, and the fans in this city. This is the most satisfying win of my career."

My teammates named me offensive captain on Friday. It's the first time I've been a captain in my pro career. That thrilled me more than anything I've received in athletics."

"The trade for Gabe made us a football team," McCormack said. "We thought we were trading for a leader. We got a super-leader instead."

But Gabriel's leadership was damaged the following summer when the NFL Players Association went on strike. Training camps opened, but veterans were urged to stay away while the union tried to negotiate a new contract with the owners. After three weeks of waiting, Gabriel broke ranks with his veteran teammates and joined the rookies and free agents in camp. The striking players felt betrayed.

Gabriel explained his decision by saying he felt he owed it to Leonard Tose, who had treated him so well. Gabriel said, "You don't kick somebody in the teeth who's been good to you. Particularly when you've been kicked in the teeth yourself. Mr. Tose brought me to Philadelphia when other people said I couldn't compete anymore."

When the strike ended, the chemistry that existed the previous season, when the younger Eagles rallied around Gabriel, was gone. The team started well enough, winning four of its first five games, but then lost six in a row with McCormack complaining about "the worst pass blocking I've ever seen." McCormack said he did not think the strike had anything to do with it, but clearly, it didn't help.

McCormack benched Gabriel in favor of rookie Mike Boryla for the final three games. The following year, McCormack opened the season with Gabriel, but with the Eagles floundering at 2–7, he switched to Boryla again. Gabriel slipped into a backup role when Dick Vermeil took over as coach, and in 1977, with Ron Jaworski entrenched as the starting quarterback, Gabriel attempted only three passes and completed one, a 15-yarder to Vince Papale.

His final appearance was in a mop-up role in the regular-season finale against the New York Jets. The Eagles were leading 20–0 when Gabriel came in and drove them down the field one last time, finishing it off with a pitchout to Wilbert Montgomery, who raced 27 yards to a touchdown. Gabriel ran to the end zone and gave the rookie a hug, then returned to the bench with a huge smile on his face.

After the game, Gabriel expressed a desire to return to the Eagles, but he knew at age 37 and with Vermeil building for the future, that was unlikely. However, he did make another prediction.

"This team is going to be a winning football team," Gabriel said.

This time, Gabriel was right. The next season, the Eagles finished 9–7, their first winning record in 12 years, and three years later, they won the NFC Championship and went to the Super Bowl.

JOHNNY GREEN
Defensive End

Ht: 6–1 • **Wt:** 190 • **College:** Tulsa • **Years with the Eagles:** 1947–51 • **Birthplace:** Hastings, Oklahoma • **Born:** October 14, 1921 • **Died:** March 6, 1989

Like many players of his generation, Johnny Green had his football career interrupted by World War II. He was a two-way end at Tulsa, but he was called to serve in the Navy before he could graduate to professional football.

When he was discharged from the service in 1946, Green had a choice of signing with Buffalo of the All-America Football Conference or the Eagles. Both teams owned his rights. The Eagles claimed him in the 14th round of the 1944 draft. Green signed with Buffalo, but he was released because the Bisons coaches felt he was too small to survive on the defensive line.

Green contacted the Eagles, but coach Greasy Neale's roster was set. Neale suggested Green play for the semipro team in Bethlehem (Pennsylvania). If he did well, Neale said, he would consider bringing him to Eagles camp the following year.

Green went to Bethlehem and was the best defensive player in the league. His next stop was Philadelphia.

Green still was considered a long shot to make the Eagles roster in 1947. Neale's team was on its way to the first of three consecutive Eastern Division titles, and the defense was deep in talented veterans. But Green played so well that he not only made the team, but he won the starting left end position.

"I didn't expect it, but he earned it," Neale said. "In the exhibition game against Chicago, he caught [Ken] McAfee from behind. McAfee was on his way to a touchdown that would've beat us, but Johnny pulled him down. The Bears ran a play we didn't expect, and Green used his own judgment and saved our hides."

Green was undersized, but he made plays with his quickness. He came out of his three-point stance like a trackman coming out of the blocks. That burst of speed may have been

Johnny Green

due, at least in part, to the $10 bonus Neale paid Green for every hit he put on the opposing quarterback.

Since Green was only earning $5,000 in salary, the chance to pick up an extra 50 or 60 bucks a week was a powerful incentive.

"Johnny was hungry, and Greasy kept him hungry," defensive back Russ Craft said. "Johnny could bring it hard and fast. At first, I think some teams overlooked him. He was small and wiry, but he was vicious. He went all-out, every snap."

CARL HAIRSTON
Defensive End

Ht: 6–3 • **Wt:** 275 • **College:** Maryland–Eastern Shore • **Years with the Eagles:** 1976–83 • **Birthplace:** Martinsville, Virginia • **Born:** December 15, 1952

Dick Vermeil had a special affection for Carl Hairston. Maybe it was because they came up the same way, picking dirt from under their fingernails. Vermeil grew up working in his father's garage. Hairston worked two jobs all through high school, driving a delivery truck and washing dishes in an all-night diner.

Vermeil and Hairston came to Philadelphia the same year, 1976. Vermeil was the rookie head coach; Hairston was a seventh-round draft choice from a small college, Maryland–Eastern Shore. They had much to prove: Vermeil, that he could turn around an Eagles franchise that had not won in a decade, and Hairston, that he could cut it in the big leagues. Together, they helped turn the Eagles into winners.

"Carl Hairston epitomizes our program," Vermeil said. "He puts 100 percent of himself into everything he touches. Watch the way he plays, all out on every snap. He'd be the same way, whether he was playing football, driving a truck, or raising a family. He's one of those rare guys. We have a few, but Carl is special."

Vermeil said he was often mesmerized by Hairston on game films. Six or seven plays would go by, and suddenly Vermeil would realize he didn't see the plays at all, he only saw number 78. He saw him pursue a runner clear across the field; he saw him hurdle two blockers, stumble, get up, and still make the play.

"Carl could win a game ball every week," Vermeil said.

"When I go on the field, I'm like a totally different person," Hairston said. "I'm hyper. I'm aggressive. You could say I'm mean. That's not my normal personality, but it's my game day personality. I watch myself on film and see some of those hits and I think, 'Who is that?' But if I ever lost that, I'm not sure I'd be able to play."

Hairston was the Eagles defensive captain four consecutive seasons (1979–83), and he missed only one game in eight years. He recorded more than 100 tackles five years in a row (1977–81), and he led the NFC with 15 sacks in 1979.

In 1983, after Vermeil stepped down as head coach, Hairston was phased out by Marion Campbell. Slowed by a knee injury, Hairston's sack total dropped to five that year, and the Eagles felt he was near the end of the line at age 31. They traded him to Cleveland for a ninth-round draft pick (center Dave Toub, who did not even make the team.)

"I didn't expect this," Hairston said. "It hurts. I don't want people saying Carl Hairston is old and can't play anymore. I'm not washed up, far from it. I guess it looked like I slowed down last year, but since the [knee] operation, I feel fine. I'm anxious to get back."

Hairston proved he could still play as he gave Cleveland six solid seasons, leading the team with nine sacks in 1986 and earning Defensive MVP honors in 1987. As the veteran leader on defense, Hairston was known as "Big Daddy."

It was no surprise that when Vermeil returned to coaching in 1997 with the St. Louis Rams, he hired Hairston as his defensive line coach. When Vermeil went to Kansas City in 2001, he brought Big Daddy with him.

THOMAS (SWEDE) HANSON
Halfback

Ht: 6–1 • **Wt:** 192 • **College:** Temple • **Years with the Eagles:** 1933–37 • **Birthplace:** Navesink, New Jersey • **Born:** November 10, 1907 • **Died:** August 5, 1970

Swede Hanson was the Eagles' leading rusher and best all-around player in their first four seasons. A former All-America selection at Temple, Hanson had his best season in 1934 when he led the NFL with 146 rushing attempts and averaged 5.5 yards per carry.

On November 6, 1934, Hanson rushed for 190 yards and three touchdowns in a 64–0 rout of the Cincinnati Reds. His three rushing touchdowns in one game still stands as an Eagles record, now tied by six other players including Steve Van Buren and Wilbert Montgomery.

Frank Brookhouser of the *Philadelphia Bulletin* described Hanson as a "rawboned, lantern-jawed, easygoing New Jersey farm boy who never cared much about anything except lugging a football past white lines."

Hanson was Temple's first football star, enrolling in 1927 and scoring 80 points as a freshman. He scored 29 points in one game, a 110–0 romp over Blue Ridge College. He added muscle to his lanky 6–1 frame by doing construction work in the summer.

After college, Hanson played two seasons of professional football with Brooklyn and Staten Island before signing with Bert Bell's newly formed Eagles in 1933. The Eagles were a dismal team in those early years, winning only 10 games in Hanson's four seasons, but he managed to provide a few highlights along the way.

The Eagles concluded their first season with a 20–14 loss to the New York Giants, but the next day in the *Philadelphia Bulletin*, Ray Hill wrote, "[Hanson] scored a brilliant touchdown with an open field run of 61 yards on an off-tackle slice. It was Hanson against the whole New York eleven for he had no interference and how he scampered down that icy field is still a thrill to think about."

Brookhouser wrote that Hanson "could run like a stag at bay, interference or not. He could do everything and sometimes he did it with a flourish worthy of Stokowski."

Eagles coach Lud Wray was most impressed by Hanson's toughness. Said Wray: "He has been suffering for weeks with an ankle injury that would keep most boys on the sidelines, yet he never once complained, and it was impossible for us to keep him out of action."

After retiring from football in 1938, Hanson went to work as a boat builder at the Philadelphia Navy Yard. He died in 1970.

ANDY HARMON
Defensive Tackle

Ht: 6–4 • **Wt:** 270 • **College:** Kent State • **Years with the Eagles:** 1991–97 • **Birthplace:** Centerville, Ohio • **Born:** April 6, 1969

Andy Harmon was a sixth-round draft pick in 1991, a little-known player from a small school (Kent State) hoping to find a job on a defensive line already stocked with Pro Bowlers Reggie White, Clyde Simmons, and Jerome Brown. He appeared to have as much chance as a garage musician trying to crack the E-Street Band.

Swede Hanson led the NFL with 146 rushing attempts in the 1934 season.

But when Simmons sat out the preseason in a contract dispute, Harmon was given the opportunity to start in his place, and he opened the coaches' eyes with three sacks in three exhibition games. Simmons came back for the regular season, but Harmon had shown enough to make the team as a backup end.

The following season, with the tragic death of Jerome Brown, the Eagles had a huge hole to fill at defensive tackle, so they moved Harmon inside, and he developed into a solid starter. Despite playing part of the season with his hand in a cast due to a broken bone, Harmon finished with 36 tackles and seven and a half quarterback sacks.

In 1993, Harmon played through a pulled hamstring and a sore Achilles tendon to record 60 tackles and 11 and a half sacks, breaking Brown's team record for sacks by a defensive tackle. He added 20 more sacks over the next two seasons and was voted second-team All-Pro by the Associated Press in 1995.

Harmon added some 30 pounds between his rookie year and his All-Pro year so he could withstand the punishment as a starting tackle. Even with the additional bulk, Harmon still was one of the NFL's lighter tackles, yet he could take on and defeat most double teams.

"I've heard people say Andy is a finesse player, but he's not a finesse player," assistant coach Emmitt Thomas said. "He has three or four different games. When they double-team him and he needs power, he uses power. When he needs quickness, he uses quickness. He plays the run well and is one of the best pass-rushing tackles I've seen in a long time."

"A lot of that has to do with timing and intelligence," line coach Mike Trgovac said. "Some [linemen] have the ability to punch, but they can't do anything with it. Andy does a great job of accelerating and getting to the corner off his punch."

"Beautiful kid," defensive coordinator Bud Carson said. "He busted his thumb and they didn't pin it and it just kind of wobbled around, but even with that he never thinks the play is over."

Harmon had 39 sacks in a four-year period (1992–95), but a series of leg injuries finally ended his career following the 1997 season.

BEN HAWKINS
Wide Receiver

Ht: 6–1 • **Wt:** 180 • **College:** Arizona State • **Years with the Eagles:** 1966–73 • **Birthplace:** Newark, New Jersey • **Born:** March 22, 1944

Ben Hawkins is best remembered for his trademark: the dangling chin strap. It was a habit he acquired practicing in the desert heat at Arizona State under coach Frank Kush.

"I felt like the air got to my face better," Hawkins said. "I left the strap unbuckled and I could just push the helmet back on my head whenever we took a break. Frank didn't let me do it in the games though, just in practice."

When Hawkins joined the Eagles as a third-round draft pick in 1966, the NFL did not have a rule requiring players to buckle up, so the Hawk, as he was called, left his chin strap unsnapped in games as well as practices. The sight of Hawkins exploding off the line and gliding downfield with his chin strap flapping in the breeze caught the attention of football fans everywhere.

Ben Hawkins with his trademark: the dangling chin strap.

"It was something different," Hawkins said. "People identified it with me, so I kept doing it. I didn't worry about [injury]. You get hurt anyway playing football, one way or the other. I never got hurt because of that."

The Hawk's unbuckled helmet actually contributed to a 78-yard touchdown in 1970. He caught a pass from rookie quarterback Rick Arrington, and a Green Bay defender went for his head. Hawkins turned and left the startled defender standing in the open field, holding a white Eagles helmet. Hawkins raced to the end zone, his stylish Afro resplendent in the autumn sunshine.

In 1973, NFL commissioner Pete Rozelle put in a rule that "all uniforms must be worn properly." Part of the edict was all players must have their chin straps buckled. The Hawk complied, although he admitted, "It won't seem the same."

That season, Hawkins suffered the first serious injury of his career, and it had nothing to do with his helmet. He sustained a broken leg in a 27–26 loss at Buffalo. He did not play again that season, and the Eagles traded him to Cleveland the following year. He played two games for the Browns and was released.

Few players in Eagles history improved as much from their rookie season to their second season as the Hawk. In his first year, Hawkins caught just 14 passes and dropped at least that many. He also fumbled three times. It was a difficult time for Hawkins, who played with such confidence at Arizona State. "I started pressing," he said, "which is the worst thing you can do."

Hawkins worked hard in the off-season and came to training camp with a renewed sense of determination. In 1967 he caught 59 passes for a league-high 1,265 yards and 10 touchdowns. He averaged a gaudy 21.4 yards per catch. The Hawk quickly became a crowd favorite, but his act did not play nearly as well with the league's defensive backs.

"He's a showboat," said Dallas cornerback Mel Renfro after Hawkins beat him for a touchdown, then bounced the ball off Renfro's helmet. "He's always trying to show you up."

Hawkins' career highlight was a four-touchdown receiving game against Pittsburgh in 1969. That still is an Eagles record, shared by Joe Carter (1934) and Irving Fryar (1996). The Hawk's flashy play combined with his bachelor lifestyle—he drove an Aston-Martin and owned a bar in Society Hill—earned him celebrity status in Philadelphia.

WES HOPKINS
Safety

Ht: 6–1 • **Wt:** 212 • **College:** SMU • **Years with the Eagles:** 1983–93 • **Birthplace:** Birmingham, Alabama • **Born:** September 26, 1961

"When other teams watch film of our defense," Reggie White once said, "I know what they're saying. They're saying, 'Watch out for number 48.'"

Number 48 was Wes Hopkins, and for 10 seasons, he hit everything that moved in the Eagles secondary. He played both safety positions, but he was at his best playing the deep middle, making receivers think twice about reaching for the football.

Hopkins had his best season in 1985 when he was voted Most Valuable Player on the Eagles defense. He led the team in tackles (136) and interceptions (six). He was named NFC Defensive Player of the Week for his performance in a 19–6 win over Washington when he had 16 tackles and set up the winning touchdown with a 42-yard fumble return.

His career almost ended the following year when he suffered a severe knee injury colliding with teammate Alonzo Johnson. Hopkins missed the rest of that season and spent the entire 1987 season on the injured reserve list. He returned in 1988 and played six more seasons.

Hopkins was a walk-on at SMU, but he finished his career as the school's all-time leader in interception return yardage (231). He was an All-Conference selection each of his last two seasons and was Defensive MVP in the Mustangs' 7–3 Cotton Bowl win over Pitt.

Hopkins was the Eagles' second-round draft pick in 1983, and he started 14 games as a rookie. He finished his Eagles career with 30 interceptions, fourth on the club's all-time list.

Hopkins' career had a strange final chapter. The Eagles released him prior to the 1993 season, and Kansas City claimed him. On cutdown day, the Chiefs tried to work a deal in which Hopkins was released, allowing them to get down to the 47-player limit, then they would re-sign him the next day when the rosters were expanded to 53. The Chiefs claimed Hopkins and his agent agreed, but went back on their word and re-signed with the Eagles for one last season.

"It was a very trying experience," Hopkins said, "but the bottom line is, given the choice, I'd rather be an Eagle."

CLAUDE HUMPHREY
Defensive End

Ht: 6–5 • **Wt:** 260 • **College:** Tennessee State • **Years with the Eagles:** 1979–81 • **Birthplace:** Memphis, Tennessee • **Born:** June 29, 1944

In March 1979 the Eagles made a move that struck many around the NFL as curious. They traded two future draft picks to Atlanta for the rights to Claude Humphrey, a 35-year-old defensive end who had retired four games into the 1978 season.

"You improve your football program by adding quality football players," coach Dick Vermeil said. "Claude Humphrey is a quality football player. I considered him the best pass rusher in professional football. Absolutely the best. No question."

Still, there was skepticism—about Humphrey's age, about his health (he missed all of the 1975 season with a knee injury), about his desire. He quit on the Falcons one month into the previous season. What made Vermeil think he still had the fire necessary to play at an All-Pro level?

There were no guarantees. But Vermeil felt at the price—a fourth-round pick in 1979 and a fourth-round pick in 1980—it was worth the gamble. He believed reuniting Humphrey with his former Atlanta coach Marion Campbell, who was the Eagles defensive coordinator, would rekindle his enthusiasm. He was right on all counts.

Campbell utilized Humphrey as a pass rush specialist. Even in the role of a part-time player, Humphrey led the Eagles with 14 and a half sacks in the 1980 season when the Eagles went to the Super Bowl.

"In all my years of football, rarely have I seen a player play that position with as much skill and determination on a consistent basis," Campbell said. "I mean, in practice, in game situations, every day of the week, every game of the season. If he's not getting to the quarterback three or four times a game, he's not enjoying himself."

Humphrey quit the Falcons because he was frustrated with their defensive system, which required their linemen to play a read-and-react game. It was too passive for Humphrey who went to six Pro Bowls as an aggressive, fire-off-the-ball, attacking force.

"I wasn't going out and kicking guys in the butt," Humphrey said. "But coming to Philadelphia and playing for Coach Campbell again will put some adrenalin back in my blood."

With the Eagles, Humphrey realized his goal of winning the NFC championship and going to a Super Bowl. Late in the NFC title game, with the Eagles running out the clock against Dallas, Vermeil hugged Humphrey in a scene captured by NFL Films.

"You know where you're going?" Vermeil asked, then turned to the other coaches and players on the sideline. "He's going to the Super Bowl, that's where he's going."

HAROLD JACKSON
Wide Receiver

Ht: 5–10 • **Wt:** 170 pounds • **College:** Jackson State • **Years with the Eagles:** 1969–72 • **Birthplace:** Hattiesburg, Mississippi • **Born:** January 6, 1946

When Irv Cross returned to the Eagles in a 1969 trade with the Los Angeles Rams, he brought a scouting report for general manager Pete Retzlaff. He saw a young receiver on the Rams taxi squad that he felt could be a star.

"I worked against him in practice, and I couldn't cover him," said Cross, a nine-year veteran with three Pro Bowls to his credit. "All he needs is a chance to play."

So Retzlaff traded fullback Izzy Lang to the Rams for the fleet Harold Jackson, who quickly became known as "The Roadrunner" because, like the cartoon character, he left his pursuers—beep, beep—in a cloud of dust.

Jackson played four seasons with the Eagles, and in two of those seasons he led the league in receiving yardage. In 1969 he caught 65 passes for 1,116 yards and nine touchdowns. In 1972 he caught 62 passes for 1,048 yards. He set the team record for most consecutive 100-yard receiving games: five, the last three games of the 1971 season and the first two games of 1972.

Jackson's career in Philadelphia consisted of 56 games, and he topped the 100-yard receiving mark 13 times. That's 23.2 percent of his starts, the highest ratio of any Eagles receiver prior to the arrival of Terrell Owens in 2004.

A shy, soft-spoken man, Jackson was driven by an inner fire.

"I want to prove some things to some people," he said.

He was referring to the college coaches who ignored him because they felt he was too small and the pro scouts who rated him a marginal prospect despite his success at Jackson State. The Rams selected Jackson in the 12th round of the 1968 draft and put him on the practice squad. One year later, he was starting for the Eagles and on his way to the Pro Bowl.

"My size was never a problem," Jackson said. "I was the most valuable player on my college team. I had confidence in my moves and my speed [he ran the 100-yard dash in 9.3 seconds]. I know I'm not much of a target, and if I use my moves and speed, I'm even less of a target.

"Running was the thing to do in my neighborhood," said Jackson, who was one of six children. "If Mama asked you to run an errand, we'd turn it into a game. Who can run those three or four blocks the fastest? By the time I was in sixth grade, I was the fastest."

Jackson weighed just 130 pounds as a ninth grader, so his parents would not allow him to sign up for football. He joined the band instead. But when the Rowan High School coaches saw Jackson playing touch football in gym class, they convinced him to trade in his trumpet for a set of shoulder pads.

"My parents didn't like the idea, but when the coach told them I might be good enough to get a [college] scholarship, they went along with it," Jackson said.

In 1973 the Eagles sent Jackson back to the Rams in the trade that brought quarterback Roman Gabriel to Philadelphia. Jackson played 16 seasons in the NFL, retiring in 1983 with 579 catches for 10,372 yards and 76 touchdowns.

KEITH JACKSON
Tight End

Ht: 6–2 • **Wt:** 250 • **College:** Oklahoma • **Years with the Eagles:** 1988–91 • **Birthplace:** Little Rock, Arkansas • **Born:** April 19, 1965

When Keith Jackson joined the Eagles as their first-round draft pick in 1988, he talked openly about making the Pro Bowl—not as a long-term goal, but something he fully expected to accomplish his rookie year. Then he went out and did it.

That year, Jackson caught 81 passes to set an Eagles single-season record that was later surpassed by Irving Fryar, but Jackson's total still stands as the most catches ever for an Eagles rookie and the most by an Eagles tight end.

"I didn't know how long it would take him to master the pro game," coach Buddy Ryan said. "It took him about 30 minutes, I think."

Ryan named Jackson his starting tight end the day he drafted him, putting him ahead of veterans John Spagnola and Jimmy Giles, who had a combined 21 years of NFL experience. Ryan had as much confidence in Jackson as Jackson had in himself.

"I looked at all the tight ends in the league, and I decided these guys aren't any better than I am," Jackson told Rich Hofmann of the *Philadelphia Daily News*. "I just felt I had that something special that would make me different. I never had any doubts. It's not that I'm conceited. It's just that I know what I can do."

"I can't think of another rookie who has had a greater impact on his team than this kid has had on the Eagles," said Bill Parcells, who was then coaching the New York Giants. "I don't even look at him as a rookie. He plays like a veteran already. With his size and hands, he can take over a game."

Jackson was an All-America at Oklahoma, despite playing in a wishbone offense where the quarterback rarely threw the ball. He had just 62 catches in his entire college career, but he averaged 23.7 yards per reception and scored 14 touchdowns. He also was an academic All-America and earned his communications degree in three and a half years.

The Eagles took Jackson with the 13th pick in the draft. Joe Wooley, the Eagles personnel director, explained, "You take a tight end this high when you get one like him or Kellen Winslow. They only come along once every 10 years or so. This guy [Jackson] is as fine an athlete as there is in this whole draft."

Jackson was a musician as well. He learned to play the cello in junior high school. He also wrote music and recorded a rap album under the name K-Jack. He said, "I don't see why an athlete should be one-dimensional."

Jackson went to the Pro Bowl each of his first three seasons with the Eagles. He never could match the numbers of his rookie year, but he still was among the leading tight ends in receptions and yards every year.

He had 12 catches and three touchdowns in a 42–37 win over Washington in 1989.

In 1992, Jackson joined the ranks of Eagle veterans leaving Philadelphia and the ownership of Norman Braman to sign for more money elsewhere. Jackson signed with Miami, where he made the Pro Bowl twice. He finished his career with two seasons in Green Bay.

MIKE JARMOLUK
Tackle

Ht: 6–5 • **Wt:** 255 • **College:** Temple • **Years with the Eagles:** 1949–55 • **Birthplace:** Philadelphia • **Born:** October 22, 1922 • **Died:** November 23, 2004

It took a while, but Mike Jarmoluk finally got his wish. In 1949, after three seasons with the Chicago Bears, Boston Yanks, and New York Bulldogs, Jarmoluk was traded to his hometown team, the Philadelphia Eagles. He arrived just in time to play for the best team in Eagles history, the team that went 11–1 in the regular season and shut out the Los Angeles Rams, 14–0, in the NFL championship game.

"I went from one extreme to another," Jarmoluk said. "I started with the Bears in 1946, and we won the championship. Then I got traded to the worst team in football [the Yanks] and was miserable. Then I wound up coming home to Philadelphia and playing for maybe the best team ever, the '49 Eagles. On the whole, I'd say I was pretty lucky."

Jarmoluk was a four-sport athlete at Frankford High School, competing in football, basketball, wrestling, and track. At the high school level, basketball may have been his best sport. As a senior, Jarmoluk led the Philadelphia Public League in scoring.

At Temple, Jarmoluk competed in basketball and track (he threw the shot put and discus) and excelled as a two-way football lineman. His dream was to play for the Eagles, but general manager Harry Thayer reportedly claimed he was "too busy" to make the trip to North Philadelphia to scout Jarmoluk. As a result, Detroit was able to select him in the fifth round of the 1945 draft.

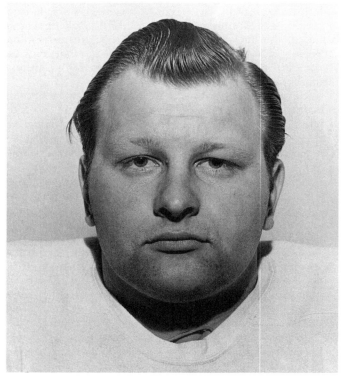

Mike Jarmoluk

Jarmoluk enlisted in the Army and fought in the Battle of the Bulge. While he was overseas, the Lions traded his rights to Chicago. When Big Mike joined the Bears in 1946, George Halas gave him a $300 bonus and a salary of $3,850. Jarmoluk tore a leg muscle in his second season with the Bears, and Halas traded him to the Boston Yanks, who were on the verge of financial collapse. In 1948 the Yanks went under, and Jarmoluk was claimed by the Bulldogs, who traded him to the Eagles. He played both ways for their championship team in 1949.

With his basketball background, Jarmoluk had surprising mobility for a big man. In his NFL career, he intercepted seven passes and scored three touchdowns: one on an interception, one on a fumble recovery, and the third on a pass reception.

"It takes a while, but you learn what you're doing," Jarmoluk said. "You develop what you might call the instinct to do the right thing. You instinctively know when to charge and when to avoid a trap. You even learn how to trap the trapper."

"They didn't wear facemasks back then," Jarmoluk's son, Mike III, told Ed Barkowitz of the *Philadelphia Daily News*. "I can remember in the early '50s when he came home and he had about four or five of his lower teeth in his hand because he had finally gotten a cleat to the face. Actually, in that game, he went to the bench and they sewed a facemask thing onto his leather helmet and he went back out and finished the game. He was just one of those old warrior-type guys."

"You've got to have it inside yourself if you want to play professional football," Jarmoluk said in the book *Iron Men*. "There was many a Monday morning when I would have black and blue marks all over my body and could hardly get out of bed. I didn't wear hip pads. Bucko [Kilroy] and I never wore pads because we wanted to be faster."

Jarmoluk announced his retirement following the 1954 season, but he changed his mind when the team went to training camp the following summer. Said Jarmoluk: "I was like an old fire horse. I kept reading about the players the Eagles were signing, and I started to get the feeling that maybe I had retired too soon."

Jarmoluk retired for good following the 1955 season. He went to work as a salesman for Ortlieb's Brewery. "They paid me $75 a week and all the beer I could drink," he said.

Big Mike spent his final years in Florida, where he enjoyed the warm weather but he never forgot his hometown. He told friends the worst thing about living in Florida was that he could not find a decent steak sandwich anywhere.

"Down here," he said in a 2002 interview, "they think putting meat in a roll with cheese is a cheese steak. They have no idea and they don't know how important the roll is. I say it's 40 percent of a good cheese steak."

Jarmoluk died on November 23, 2004, in Ocala, Florida. He was 82.

RON JAWORSKI
Quarterback

Ht: 6–2 • **Wt:** 195 • **College:** Youngstown State • **Years with the Eagles:** 1977–86 • **Birthplace:** Lackawanna, New York • **Born:** March 23, 1951

Ron Jaworski was the perfect quarterback for the Eagles of the Dick Vermeil era. He was a blue-collar guy who drank beer with the offensive linemen and wore his heart on his wristband every Sunday. He was tough and cocky. He had to be to live with the boos he heard at Veterans Stadium.

"I might not be the most revered athlete in Philadelphia history, but I think I earned the fans' respect," Jaworski once said. "I think they knew I gave it all I had every week. Win or lose, I was out there, busting my butt."

In ten seasons with the Eagles, Jaworski became the team's all-time leader in pass attempts (3,918), completions (2,088), passing yards (26,963), interceptions (151), and touchdowns (175). He set a durability record for NFL quarterbacks by starting 116 consecutive games, a streak that began with the 1977 league opener and continued until Jaworski went down with a broken leg in 1984.

"Jaworski is from the old school," New York linebacker Harry Carson said. "He takes a licking and keeps on ticking. He battles you for four quarters, regardless of the score. He's a tough guy; I respect that."

Jaworski grew up in Lackawanna, a steel mill town in upstate New York. He was a running back early in his high school career, but the coaches switched him to quarterback when they realized he had the strongest arm on the team. He was recruited by several major colleges, but he chose Youngstown State because he wanted his parents to be close enough to drive to his games.

As a senior, Jaworski was the fifth-leading passer in college football. The Los Angeles Rams selected him in the second round of the 1973 draft. The Rams quarterback situation was a mess with John Hadl, James Harris, Pat Haden, and Jaworski taking turns as the starter over a four-year period. Jaworski started nine games and won them all, including a 1975 NFC Divisional playoff game against St. Louis.

In 1976, Jaworski turned down a five-year, $700,000 contract and told the Rams he intended to play out his option. He wanted a fresh start somewhere else. Vermeil, who decided he could not win with the aging Roman Gabriel and inconsistent Mike Boryla, traded for Jaworski in 1977, sending tight end Charles Young to the Rams.

"I remember coming to Philadelphia to meet with Dick," Jaworski said. "The deal with the Rams wasn't even final yet, but I flew in and Dick met me at the airport. We talked for two hours. By the time we finished, I knew this was where I wanted to play. Dick said, 'We're going to turn this thing around. We're going to build a winner here.' I was young and eager. I wanted to be a part of that."

"I told him he was my quarterback," Vermeil said. "And I said, 'You're going to play on your bad days until they become your good days. It may cost us three bad games in a row, but you're going to start and play, no matter what.'"

Vermeil wore a wireless microphone for NFL Films during a 1977 game at Veterans Stadium, and the cameras captured a fascinating moment when the coach pulled the struggling Jaworski aside and said, "Listen to me. You never have to worry about me jerking you [from a game]."

NFL Films also recorded Vermeil's postgame press conference when he said, "Guys, you might as well write this: I'm not gonna let the [booing] fans substitute my quarterback for me. They've been doing that in this town for years and they've never won. I have a quarterback who can win for us, and the only way he's going to develop is if he stays in there and throws nine innings."

Vermeil started the Polish Rifle, as Jaworski was known, in every game for the remainder of his tenure with the Eagles.

Ron Jaworski

Vermeil molded Jaworski into an efficient and disciplined quarterback who led the Eagles to the playoffs four straight years, capped by an NFC Championship win over Dallas and trip to Super Bowl XV in January 1981.

"I didn't like the 18-hour workdays any better than anybody else," Jaworski said in a 1980 interview, "but I soon realized that I'd gotten all the way from high school and into the pros with very little more than a strong arm. I thought I could throw the ball right through defenders. I was just a gunner, a slinger. Dick opened my eyes and taught me how the game should be played. He taught me how to be patient, how to take something off [a throw], how to play smart, basically."

Jaworski had his finest season in 1980 as he led the NFC in passing with a career-high 27 touchdown passes and 91.0 efficiency rating. He was voted NFL Player of the Year by the Maxwell Football Club as he led the Eagles to a 12–4 regular-season mark and their first conference title in 20 years. From 1978 through 1981, Jaworski won 42 regular-season games, second only to Pittsburgh's Terry Bradshaw among NFL quarterbacks.

"We had a lot of good players, but Ron was the one who made things go," said Wilbert Montgomery, the club's all-time leading rusher. "He was our leader, on and off the field. He was a guy who would say something crazy to pick everybody up. He'd come up with the big play when we needed it."

"The thing I remember was his enthusiasm," tackle Stan Walters said. "You've gotta realize, the Eagles hadn't won in a long time before he got there. There were a lot of guys in that locker room who didn't know what it felt like to win. They were beaten down emotionally. Jaworski was like a breath of fresh air. He came in and said, 'We're gonna win; we've got what it takes, let's go.' He was so genuine, guys just responded."

Jaworski's teammates respected him for his toughness. He took many big hits in the pocket, but he always got up. He also

Ron Jaworski being inducted into the Eagles Honor Roll, December 27, 1992. Dick Vermeil, far left, stands with him.

played with no ego. He did not worry about his personal statistics. Most of the time, he had no idea how many passing yards he compiled or how many touchdown passes he threw. He cared about only one thing, and that was winning. It was because of that attitude that Vermeil traded for him in the first place.

"I liked his intensity," Vermeil said. "He was a competitor. I just couldn't picture him ever being a fathead."

By 1987, Buddy Ryan was coaching in Philadelphia, and a young Randall Cunningham was doing exciting things at quarterback, so the Eagles did not offer the 36-year-old Jaworski a new contract. He held a farewell press conference at the Eagles Nest, the golf course he owned in Sewell, New Jersey.

"Guess I'll just have to take my show on the road," he said.

Jaworski signed with Miami, and in August he returned to the Vet as a member of the Dolphins. The fans, many of whom no doubt booed Jaworski in the past, came to the preseason game with signs reading, "We Love Jaws" and "Bring Back Jaws." They gave Jaworski a standing ovation when he started the second half.

"I expected applause, but that [ovation] surprised me," Jaworski said. "I looked around and saw the people standing. Tears came to my eyes."

"It was very gratifying to hear the cheers," said Liz Jaworski, Ron's wife. "It helped mend the ulcer the fans gave me the last ten years."

Jaworski concluded his 17-year playing career with Kansas City in 1989. He became a successful businessman in the Philadelphia area with ownership in several hotels and golf courses. He also launched a career as a football analyst with ESPN. In 2003 he brought arena football to the city as president of the Philadelphia Soul.

SETH JOYNER
Linebacker

Ht: 6–2 • **Wt:** 240 • **College:** Texas–El Paso • **Years with the Eagles:** 1986–93 • **Birthplace:** Spring Valley, New York • **Born:** November 18, 1964

The scowl was Seth Joyner's trademark. Even when the Eagles were winning, even when he was being hailed as one of the NFL's best linebackers, Joyner was scowling.

"Every picture I'd ever seen of him looked like literally a mug shot," said Green Bay coach Mike Holmgren, who signed Joyner as a free agent in 1997 after he played 12 seasons with the Eagles and Arizona Cardinals. "I asked him: 'Do you ever smile about anything?' He said, 'I'll smile when we go to the Super Bowl.'"

Joyner smiled that season when Green Bay went to the Super Bowl, although the Packers lost to Denver. He smiled again the following season when he signed with Denver and went back to the Super Bowl, this time finally winning that elusive championship ring.

By then, Joyner was an aging part-time player. His best seasons were spent with the Eagles when he was the superb outside linebacker on the NFL's most intimidating defense. At a time when many linebackers, such as Derrick Thomas in Kansas City and Pat Swilling in New Orleans, were pure pass rushers, Joyner excelled in all phases of the game. He was strong against the run, he was effective in pass coverage, and, when called upon, he could chase down a quarterback with the best of them.

"Seth Joyner can do anything you ask of him," said Eagles defensive coordinator Bud Carson. "We ask him to do it all. I wouldn't trade him for another linebacker anywhere."

Through his first five seasons, Joyner's versatility was actually a liability in terms of attracting recognition. Sacks were the measuring stick for All-Pros at the linebacker position, and Joyner, who averaged 4.4 sacks per season from 1986 through '90, was overshadowed by the likes of Lawrence Taylor, Thomas, and Swilling. They went to the Pro Bowl most years while Joyner, because of his varied role, stayed home.

That situation changed, however, in a 1991 Monday night game in Houston when Joyner, who was playing with a 102-degree fever, had eight solo tackles, two forced fumbles, two fumble recoveries, and two sacks in a 13–6 win over the Oilers. That became known as the "House of Pain" game because the Eagles knocked out three Houston receivers and dismantled the Run-and-Shoot offense.

ABC-TV's Dan Dierdorf surveyed the wreckage and told the national viewing audience, "If there is a better linebacker in the NFL than Seth Joyner, I haven't seen him."

"I've been sick for a week," Joyner said after the game. "I got it bad last night. I was throwing up all day. My stomach was bubbling. It was hard to breathe. But you have to play."

Joyner was voted into his first Pro Bowl that season. He also was voted NFL Player of the Year by *Sports Illustrated*'s Paul Zimmerman, who called Joyner "the glue that holds the Philly defense together." The perpetually underrated linebacker finally was getting his due.

Joyner was originally an eighth-round draft pick in 1986. Buddy Ryan cut him during the preseason, then brought him back when another linebacker was injured. In Week 10 of the regular season, Ryan told Joyner, "Learn your stuff. You're starting this week." Joyner had 10 solo tackles and two assists in the game, a 17–14 loss to the New York Giants, and he was a fixture in the Eagles lineup for the next seven years.

Joyner had ideal size for a linebacker, combined with surprising speed. As a college senior, he anchored the Texas–El Paso 400-meter relay team. But his greatest attribute was his mental preparation. No player on the Eagle defense watched as much film as Joyner; no one had a more complete book on opposing teams.

"That's why, week in and week out, he is so consistent," Carson said. "You never see him confused out there. You never see him hesitate. He is so well prepared, he plays with complete confidence."

"I want people to know that if they come my way, it's not going to be easy yardage," Joyner said.

But what about that scowl?

"I'm an intense person," Joyner told Dave Spadaro of *Eagles Digest*. "Sometimes even too intense or too locked in on certain things. Football is supposed to be a fun game, and I try to have fun when I'm playing. But unfortunately, I only have fun when I'm winning."

The Eagles won 10 or more games in five consecutive seasons from 1988 through '92, but they fell short of Joyner's ultimate goal, the Super Bowl. The frustration boiled over, and Joyner often lashed out, particularly after Ryan was fired as coach and replaced by Rich Kotite.

Joyner blasted the play calling after a loss to Tampa Bay, he criticized the front office for not re-signing veterans such as Reggie White, and, in his most famous outburst, he described Kotite as "a puppet" of owner Norman Braman.

"People get pissed off at me, but I don't care if they like me or dislike me," Joyner said in a 1991 *Sport Magazine* interview. "I care that they do their jobs because I'm busting my behind to do mine. I know I can't expect everybody to have the same passion I have for the game, but it really pisses me off when guys say they're trying their hardest. That's not enough."

SONNY JURGENSEN
Quarterback

Ht: 6–0 • **Wt:** 205 • **College:** Duke • **Years with the Eagles:** 1957–63 • **Birthplace:** Wilmington, North Carolina • **Born:** August 23, 1934

His name is Christian Adolph Jurgensen, but everyone knew him as Sonny. He is best remembered as a Washington Redskin, but he began his professional career with seven seasons in Philadelphia.

Sonny Jurgensen

Jurgensen was a fourth-round selection in the 1957 draft. The Eagles took him largely on the recommendation of Duke's backfield coach, Hall of Famer Ace Parker, who called Jurgensen "the best pro prospect I've seen in years." He did not throw the ball much in college because the Blue Devils were a running team, but when he threw it, he threw it with stunning accuracy.

"Sonny was a unique talent, maybe the best pure passer I ever saw," said King Hill, who was Jurgensen's backup in Philadelphia. "He had a great release. Most quarterbacks are programmed into a five-step drop or a seven-step drop, set up and throw. Sonny could unload at any time. He'd be back-pedaling and just flick the ball when his receiver cleared."

Jurgensen started four games as a rookie, and among his victories was a 17–7 upset of Cleveland. When the Eagles traded for Norm Van Brocklin in 1958, Jurgensen went to the bench for three seasons. After leading the Eagles to the title in 1960, Van Brocklin retired and Jurgensen took over as the starting quarterback.

"I knew what people were saying, 'What will they do without Van Brocklin?'" Jurgensen said. "But I was pretty confident. People forget, I played quite a bit as a rookie, then I had the chance to sit and study Van Brocklin, so I learned a lot. That was my big chance [1961], and I felt ready."

Jurgensen had a spectacular 1961 season as he passed for a league-high 3,723 yards and 32 touchdowns, a club record that still stands. He passed for more than 300 yards in five different games. He passed for more than 400 yards twice. Those are impressive totals when you consider Van Brocklin had just one 300-yard game in three seasons with the Eagles.

However, Jurgensen suffered a shoulder separation in the Playoff Bowl against Detroit, and the injury hampered his play the next few seasons. When the Eagles fell to the bottom of the Eastern Conference in 1962 and '63, the fans turned their wrath on Jurgensen, blaming him for everything that went wrong. It did not matter if it was his fault or not.

"They look for faults when you lose," Jurgensen said in a 1965 *Sport Magazine* interview. "They try to lay their finger on it. That's natural. But look at the injuries we had. Four ends broke their arms in one year [1962], and one broke his leg. Who'd they expect me to throw the ball to, the guards and tackles?'"

"Jurgy's a very sensitive guy, even though he doesn't show it," halfback Tim Brown said. "He'd always act like the boos didn't hurt him. The crowd would start on him before the game, and he'd just grin and say, 'Well, here it is again, fellows.' It was really hurting him, but he acted like it wasn't. That takes a helluva guy, really."

In 1964, Joe Kuharich was hired as Eagles coach and general manager. One of his first acts was to trade Jurgensen and cornerback Jimmy Carr to Washington for Norm Snead and Claude Crabb. Jurgensen went on to play 11 more seasons with the Redskins, and in 1974, at age 40, he still completed 64 percent of his passes.

Jurgensen played for Vince Lombardi in 1969, the lone season Lombardi coached in Washington before his death. Lombardi's widow Marie once said it was the opportunity to coach Jurgensen that convinced Lombardi to take the job in Washington, such was his admiration of the talented redhead.

"He is a great performer," Lombardi said of Jurgensen. "He is perhaps the best [quarterback] the league has ever seen. He's all man. He stays in there under the most adverse conditions."

In 1983, Jurgensen was voted into the Pro Football Hall of Fame. In his induction speech, he said, "I didn't play on great football teams … but this honor more than makes up for all the frustrations and disappointments. I'm so proud, so humbled to be recognized as this kind of player."

FRANK (BUCKO) KILROY
Tackle

Ht: 6–2 • **Wt:** 250 • **College:** Temple • **Years with the Eagles:** 1943–55 • **Birthplace:** Philadelphia • **Born:** May 30, 1921

Frank (Bucko) Kilroy played in the middle of Greasy Neale's five-man defensive line and was a major factor in its success. Kilroy played in a down position and on most plays attacked the line of scrimmage. But he also dropped back in pass coverage on some plays and intercepted five passes in his career.

Kilroy was voted onto various All-Pro teams every season from 1948 through 1954. He was named to the NFL's All-Decade team for the 1940s. He had a reputation as a dirty player, which he did not totally dispute. "I was a bad boy," he said in a 1953 interview, "but only at times."

A Chicago writer described Kilroy as "a knuckle-duster in knee pants who gives our fellows that boyish grin while kicking their teeth loose in a pileup."

Kilroy was the central figure in a 1955 *Life* magazine article entitled "Savagery on Sunday," focusing on violence in pro

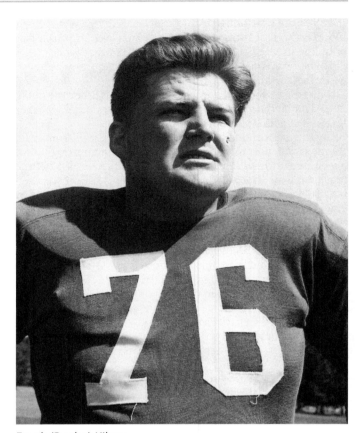

Frank (Bucko) Kilroy

football. In the article, Kilroy was described as "the toughest of the bad men" and "the orneriest of ornery critters." Kilroy sued the magazine for libel and won $11,600 in damages.

"I am elated that the jury saw fit to clear my reputation for sportsmanship," Kilroy said after the decision was handed down in federal court.

Kilroy's own teammates admit he was a nasty player. Chuck Bednarik never forgave Kilroy for what he claimed was an illegal shot to the face when they were opponents in an all-star game. In a 1999 interview, Bednarik said he "hated" Kilroy after that play and referred to him as "a so-called teammate." Russ Craft said:

Bucko didn't care what you thought about him. I saw him kick Charlie Trippi [Cardinals halfback] off the field one day. He could've tackled him or pushed him out; he took his right foot and kicked him. We got a big penalty, and Bucko got thrown out of the game. He just laughed. He said it's worth that in publicity … But Bucko was a very good player. He was so big and naturally strong, people just couldn't handle him. He'd put those two big paws out there and he'd stop anything that came his way. And if they were a little afraid of him besides, worried about what he might do, that just added to his advantage.

Kilroy is a Philadelphia native, a product of Northeast Catholic High School and Temple University. He signed with the Eagles in 1943, the year they merged with the Pittsburgh Steelers and played as "the Steagles."

"Because of my reputation, Greasy took me down to the cellar of the Eagles offices when he signed me," Kilroy told Hugh Brown of the *Philadelphia Bulletin*. "Greasy said, 'I know your kind. You make just one false move and I'll kick you right off the team on your fat Irish haunches, only he didn't say haunches."

Kilroy's original contract called for a $500 signing bonus and $150 a game. He became an invaluable two-way player, a powerful drive blocking tackle on offense and the middle guard on defense. He did not miss a start for eight consecutive seasons (1947–54), and he finished his career as a player-coach with the Eagles in 1955.

After he retired as a player, Kilroy began a long career as a coach, scout, and front office executive in the NFL. His longest affiliation was with the New England Patriots, joining the team as player personnel director in 1971 and working his way up to general manager (1979) and vice president (1983). Even after retiring from full-time duty in 1993, he stayed active as a scouting consultant and helped find the players that won three of four Super Bowls from 2002 to 2005.

KEITH KREPFLE
Tight End

Ht: 6–3 • **Wt:** 225 • **College:** Iowa State • **Years with the Eagles:** 1975–81 • **Birthplace:** Dubuque, Iowa • **Born:** February 4, 1952

On the wholesomeness scale, Keith Krepfle ranked right up there with homogenized milk, vanilla wafers, and Walt Disney movies. Boyish, well-scrubbed face. Floppy blond hair, not too long, not too short. Pepsodent smile.

"Keith looks like a choirboy," middle linebacker Bill Bergey said, "but he plays like the devil."

Bergey tested Krepfle in his first Eagles training camp, 1975. The young tight end, who joined the Eagles after one season with Jacksonville of the World Football League, came across the middle and Bergey welcomed him with an elbow to the jaw.

"He got up, shook his head, and walked back to the huddle," Bergey said. "I thought, 'Okay, now we'll see what this guy is made of.' Next play, he came across the middle again. Quarterback threw him the ball. Keith went up and caught it in a crowd. I knew right then he was a football player. Keith doesn't hear footsteps. He makes the other guy hear *his* footsteps."

Krepfle spent his first two NFL seasons playing on special teams. He was named special-teams captain in 1976, and his ferocious hitting on kick coverage earned him the nickname "Captain Crunch." He was the backup to Charles Young at tight end, but when the Eagles traded Young to Los Angeles for quarterback Ron Jaworski, Krepfle moved up to the first-team offense.

He was the starting tight end for five seasons. His best year was 1979 when he caught 41 passes for 760 yards, an average of 18.5 yards per catch, and three touchdowns. He was also a punishing blocker. He once drove Thomas (Hollywood) Henderson of Dallas 25 yards downfield while blocking on a run. Dick Vermeil reran the play a dozen times at the next squad meeting, noting, "This is what I call 'Eagle effort.'"

"I've been coaching since 1959," Vermeil told Frank Brady of the *Philadelphia Bulletin*, "and Keith Krepfle gives as much on every snap as any player I've ever coached, maybe more. An expression I use is 'He demonstrates what he is by what he does.' That describes his character. If I were ever in trouble downtown somewhere and needed somebody to help me fight my way out, he'd be one of the first guys I called."

Krepfle grew up in the small town of Potosi, Iowa (population 713), and received the very last football scholarship Iowa State had to offer in 1971. He played seven seasons with the Eagles, but never was voted into a Pro Bowl or onto an All-Pro team.

"To me, All-Pro doesn't mean very much," Krepfle said. "You want to talk about honors, the greatest one is to be voted captain by my teammates. I'm not sure making All-Pro is a good indication of your talents. But the guys who play alongside you know if you're doing the job. I'd rather have their respect than anything else."

Krepfle is the answer to the trivia question "Who scored the Eagles' only touchdown in Super Bowl XV?" He caught an eight-yard touchdown pass from Jaworski in the fourth quarter of the 27–10 loss to Oakland.

FRANK LeMASTER
Linebacker

Ht: 6–2 • **Wt:** 232 • **College:** Kentucky • **Years with the Eagles:** 1974–82 • **Birthplace:** Lexington, Kentucky • **Born:** March 12. 1952

Frank LeMaster joined the Eagles as a fourth-round draft pick in 1974, and after the first week of training camp coach Mike McCormack was calling him "a big Chris Hanburger."

For McCormack, formerly an assistant coach in Washington, to compare anyone to Chris Hanburger, the Redskins' All-Pro linebacker, was a supreme compliment. It was ironic, too, because LeMaster wore the same jersey number as Hanburger (55). A radio reporter actually began an interview with LeMaster by saying, "Tell me, Chris …"

"I don't mind," LeMaster said. "They say Hanburger is the best outside linebacker in the game. If you're gonna be compared to somebody, you might as well be compared to the best."

LeMaster broke into the starting defense his second season when Steve Zabel was traded to New England. He made a strong impression in a preseason game against the Patriots when he intercepted two passes and returned them both for touchdowns.

"I thought losing Zabel's experience at that spot would hurt us, but gaining the aggressiveness of LeMaster has helped," middle linebacker Bill Bergey said. "He buzzed a few of their receivers. I saw one [Patriot] drop a ball because he heard Frank coming."

In his early years, LeMaster played outside in a 4–3 defense. When Dick Vermeil became head coach, he brought in Marion Campbell as his defensive coordinator, and Campbell was a believer in the 3–4. It was not a problem for LeMaster, who shifted to an inside linebacker spot next to Bergey.

LeMaster was a star fullback at Bryan Station High School in Lexington, and he played his first two seasons at the

University of Kentucky paired in the same backfield as Doug Kotar, who later played for the New York Giants. LeMaster also played a season of basketball at Kentucky before devoting his full attention to football.

LeMaster's athletic ability was evident whenever he touched the football. He scored three touchdowns, including a return of an interception against the Giants in 1978, a play that clinched a 20–3 victory and gave the Eagles their first winning season in 12 years.

LeMaster also scored on an 89-yard interception return against Washington in the final game of the 1975 season. At the time, it was the third-longest interception return in Eagles history. In the 1981 season LeMaster led the team with 133 tackles and was voted into the Pro Bowl.

CHAD LEWIS
Tight End

Ht: 6–6 • **Wt:** 250 • **College:** Brigham Young • **Years with the Eagles:** 1997– • **Birthplace:** Fort Dix, New Jersey • **Born:** October 5, 1971

Chad Lewis helped put the Eagles in Super Bowl XXXIX, but he could not play once they got there. He suffered a Lisfranc ligament tear in his left foot while scoring his second touchdown in the 27–10 win over Atlanta in the NFC Championship game. He watched the Super Bowl loss to New England on crutches.

"You sure don't like to see that happen to a veteran player who waited his whole career to get to this thing," coach Andy Reid said.

Few players worked harder—or overcame more—than Lewis to play eight years in the pros. A walk-on at Brigham Young, he played four seasons and caught 111 passes for the Cougars. He was ignored in the 1997 NFL draft, in part because he was 25 and the pro scouts felt that was too old for a rookie tight end.

The Eagles signed him as a free agent, and he made the team, catching 12 passes in his first season, including a last-minute game winner against Dallas. He was released the next year and claimed by St. Louis. He played only six games with the Rams and was cut loose again. The Eagles re-signed him midway through the 1999 season, and he developed an immediate chemistry with Donovan McNabb, who was then a rookie.

Lewis caught McNabb's first NFL touchdown pass, a six-yard score against Indianapolis, and over the next six seasons McNabb completed more passes to Lewis (196) for more touchdowns (18) than any other receiver. Lewis was a big target, and his ability to work the middle of the field made him McNabb's go-to receiver, especially in 2000 when Lewis led all NFL tight ends with 69 catches for 735 yards.

His numbers declined over the next few years as the Eagles tried to stretch their offense with more throws to the wide receivers and as running backs, such as Duce Staley and Brian Westbrook, became more involved in the passing game. In 2003, Lewis split time with rookie L. J. Smith and finished the season with 23 catches. He did not score a touchdown until the final week of the regular season. Yet he never complained.

"I'd serve my team no good purpose if I'm going to be a crybaby, worrying about my own stats," Lewis told John Smallwood of the *Philadelphia Daily News.* "We're a team. That's

Chad Lewis

been our whole focus. There wasn't one time this season when I went into the locker room after a game thinking, 'Man, I'm not playing good football.' We're winning games, and that's the whole purpose of this business."

Former Dallas quarterback and current FOX football analyst Troy Aikman admired Lewis's "team-first" attitude. "[Lewis] epitomizes unselfishness," Aikman said. "He doesn't have near the receptions he is accustomed to having. He has been a great mentor for L. J. Smith and has done a great job putting his ego aside."

A former Eagle scout who learned to speak Chinese during a Mormon mission to Taiwan (the reason he was late coming to the NFL), Lewis brought maturity and a level head to the Eagles locker room. He missed only two games in five seasons (2000–2004), and he saved his best performance for the NFC final against Atlanta. It was his first two-touchdown game since December 2001.

His first touchdown was a fingertip catch in the corner of the end zone, balancing on his toes just inches inside the white stripe. "The wind was howling," Lewis said, "and the ball just sailed. I thought, 'Oh man, I've got to get that thing.'"

His second touchdown gave the Eagles a 27–10 lead with just 3:27 left, setting off the victory celebration in Lincoln Financial Field. Even as he listened to the fireworks and the roaring crowd, he knew his season was over. When Lewis returned to the bench, he told Andy Reid, "I think I broke my foot." An MRI confirmed his fears.

"Howie Long, I think, said, 'The thrill of the kill is second to the challenge of the chase,'" Lewis said. "Just having a small part in helping the Eagles win the NFC Championship game is gratification enough. I had a blast."

VIC LINDSKOG
Center-Linebacker

Ht: 6–1 • **Wt:** 210 • **College:** Stanford • **Years with the Eagles:** 1944–51 • **Birthplace:** Roundup, Montana • **Born:** December 3, 1914

Vic Lindskog chose a career in football, but he almost chose professional boxing. Prior to enrolling at Stanford, Lindskog was working out in the ring under George Blake, a noted boxing trainer in Los Angeles. Blake felt Lindskog had the strength and stamina to develop into a heavyweight contender.

"It came down to a matter of preference," Lindskog said, "and I preferred football."

Lindskog was a two-way player at Stanford and was part of the unbeaten 1941 team that won the Rose Bowl. He was selected in the second round of the 1942 draft by the Eagles, but military service kept him from joining the team until 1944.

Lindskog played center and linebacker his first four seasons with the Eagles. He intercepted four passes and returned one 65 yards for a touchdown in 1944. He concentrated on offense later in his career, and he was the starting center on the Eagles' world championship clubs in 1948 and '49.

"Vic has a lot of power," halfback Bosh Pritchard said. "He is not the biggest guy, but he knows how to deliver a blow. I can see where he must have been a pretty tough man in the ring."

Coach Greasy Neale considered Lindskog the best center in the league. It bothered Neale that Lindskog was named All-Pro only once (1951) while Clyde (Bulldog) Turner of Chicago was an All-Pro six times.

"If Turner is considered the leading center, it must be due to his defensive ability," Neale said. "He can't hold a candle to Lindskog on the offense. Vic is the greatest offensive center ever to play pro football. He's the only center I've ever seen who can block the halfback out of bounds on an end run. This is so unusual that I can count how many times I've seen it performed. Five—and all by Vic."

In 1949, when the Eagles drafted Chuck Bednarik from Penn, Neale put the rookie together with Lindskog on the practice field. The coach told Bednarik, "Here is the fellow who will teach you more about playing center than you ever dreamed was possible."

Lindskog, who already was thinking about retirement, welcomed the rookie. "I'll give it to you just as fast as you can absorb it," Lindskog told Bednarik. "You, Charlie, are my 'out' of pro football."

Lindskog was planning a career in coaching. He served as line coach at the Friends Central School while he still was playing for the Eagles. When he retired in 1952, Lindskog became an assistant coach with the Eagles. He later went into scouting, covering colleges on the West Coast.

RANDY LOGAN
Safety

Ht: 6–1 • **Wt:** 195 • **College:** Michigan • **Years with the Eagles:** 1973–83 • **Birthplace:** Detroit, Michigan • **Born:** May 1, 1951

The Eagles never had to worry about Randy Logan reporting late for training camp. In fact, the opposite was true. As a rookie in 1973, Logan came to camp two days before the scheduled check-in date. He was that eager to get started. And over the course of 11 seasons, he never lost that desire.

It would have been easy for Logan to become discouraged. He came from a highly successful Michigan program, where he lost only two games in three varsity seasons, to an Eagles team that was 25–44–1 in his first five years.

"It hurts to lose, but I'll never just give up and go through the motions," Logan said. "I approach every game with the attitude that this will be the one we win, this will be the one that turns it around. I remember what it was like at Michigan. We didn't know what losing was. Every time we went on the field, we knew we were going to win. It was the greatest feeling in the world. I want to be here when the Eagles are in the same position."

Logan had that opportunity as he was one of the few players Dick Vermeil retained when he took over as head coach in 1976. Logan was part of the nucleus Vermeil built around as he changed the Eagles from sad sacks to winners.

"Randy has two key ingredients," Vermeil said. "One, he's a damn good athlete. Two, he's a character individual. Playing well and giving 100 percent effort is important to him. Everybody knows what kind of hitter he is. He hits so hard, he scares me. He's only 190. The way he takes on those 260-pound blockers, I'm afraid he's going to get hurt."

Logan's durability was remarkable. He never missed a game in his 11 seasons. His streak of 159 consecutive games is the second longest in Eagles history, just three games short of Harold Carmichael's record. His career total of 23 interceptions ranks among the team's all-time leaders.

Coach Mike McCormack saw Logan on tape and made the decision to select him in the third round of the draft. Logan was the "Wolfman" on the Michigan defense, which meant he was part linebacker and part safety. McCormack was impressed with Logan's smarts and his physical toughness.

"I watched every [Michigan] game on tape, and I never saw the kid out of position," McCormack said. "And when he hit people, he made their heads snap."

Logan became interested in football as a youth, but the only organized team on his side of Detroit was at the Catholic school. Logan was told he could not play because he was not a member of the church, but, as he put it, "I kept hanging around, coming back every day."

Finally, a priest saw him and worked out a deal: He could play on the parish football team if he agreed to attend catechism class every Monday. Logan went on to star at Detroit Northern High School and earn the distinction as the first player from that school to win a football scholarship to a Big Ten college.

TOMMY McDONALD
Wide Receiver

Ht: 5–9 • **Wt:** 172 • **College:** Oklahoma • **Years with the Eagles:** 1957–63 • **Birthplace:** Roy, New Mexico • **Born:** July 26, 1934

Tommy McDonald is the smallest player in the Pro Football Hall of Fame, but he made the biggest splash during his induction ceremony on August 1, 1998. He bounced across the stage with the same exuberance that captivated the Philadelphia fans a generation earlier.

Tommy McDonald

"Do I look excited, like I just won the lottery?" he asked the estimated 10,000 spectators gathered under dazzling blue skies in Canton, Ohio. "I feel sooooooo good. I'm in the Hall of Fame, baby."

McDonald grabbed his bronze bust off its pedestal. "They said I had good hands," he said. With that, he tossed the 25-pound bust in the air—not once, but twice—and caught it on his fingertips as the Hall of Fame officials gasped. He also pulled out a boom box and danced to the Bee Gees disco hit "Stayin' Alive."

He concluded by chest-bumping the other four enshrinees: Chicago linebacker Mike Singletary, Cincinnati tackle Anthony Muñoz, Minnesota safety Paul Krause, and Miami center Dwight Stephenson. "Thank you, Canton," McDonald shouted. "I love it."

The crowd laughed and cheered, as did NFL Commissioner Paul Tagliabue and the 52 Hall of Fame members who returned for the induction weekend.

"It had to be the darnedest expression of unbridled, shared joy any Hall of Fame has ever seen," wrote Steve Doerschuk in the *Canton Repository.*

Longtime Eagle fans probably were not surprised that McDonald departed from the traditional acceptance speech. He defied convention throughout his NFL career, which spanned 12 seasons and five teams. He was the last player in the league to play without a face mask. He was among the first to celebrate a touchdown by heaving the ball into the stands. He was considered too small to play in the pros, yet he became a star.

He was, in every way, an original. He crossed the threshold in Canton the same way.

"I played with a lot of great receivers, including [Elroy] Hirsch and [Tom] Fears with the Rams," said Norm Van Brocklin, who quarterbacked the Eagles to the 1960 NFL Championship, "but if I had to pick one guy to throw the ball to with the game on the line, I'd pick McDonald. I know somehow the little bugger would get open and he'd catch the football."

In the 1960 season, McDonald scored 13 touchdowns on 39 receptions, that's one touchdown for every three catches. He also averaged 20.5 yards per reception. In the championship game, with the Eagles trailing 6–0, Van Brocklin hit McDonald with a 35-yard touchdown pass that helped lift them to the 17–13 victory over Green Bay. It was the only postseason game Vince Lombardi ever lost as a head coach.

Afterward, Lombardi said, "If I had 11 Tommy McDonalds, I'd win a championship every year." McDonald still considers it the greatest compliment he ever received.

"My memory of sports will be the words 'He's too small; we can't use him,'" McDonald said. "I always had to prove myself. It wasn't until we won the championship that I finally felt I could sit down with the other guys on the team and feel no shame. I didn't have to feel somebody else had placed a chair there for Tommy McDonald to sit on. I could finally feel like Tommy McDonald had set his own chair there."

Because he felt discriminated against due to his size, McDonald reacted strongly to any perceived slight. He used it as motivation. When Pittsburgh upset the Eagles in 1959, coach Buddy Parker asked, "How many touchdowns did McDonald score today?" Parker was gloating about cornerback Johnny Sample shutting out McDonald, who normally tormented the Steelers. The quote made all the papers.

McDonald clipped out the article and pasted it inside his helmet. "It's going to stay there for the rest of the season," he said. "Just as a reminder."

He played seven seasons with the Eagles and finished his career with stops in Dallas (1964), Los Angeles (1965–66), Atlanta (1967), and Cleveland (1968). When he retired, he was sixth on the NFL's all-time list in pass receptions (495), fourth in yardage (8,410), and second to Green Bay's Don Hutson in touchdown catches (84). Perhaps his most impressive statistic is his ratio of one touchdown for every 5.89 receptions, third best all-time behind Hutson and Paul Warfield, the former Cleveland and Miami star.

The numbers are gaudy, but they don't tell the whole story. Unless you were fortunate enough to see McDonald play, you cannot fully appreciate his greatness. He played the game with a bubbly daring that was part All-Pro and part little boy. He was a combination juggler and gymnast. He once hoisted himself on the shoulder pads of a taller defensive back, tipped the ball with one hand, and caught it with the other. It was like something out of a Saturday morning cartoon show.

For a small man, McDonald was remarkably durable. He missed only three games in his pro career. His jaw was broken in the 1959 league opener against San Francisco, but he played the next week with his mouth wired shut and scored four touchdowns in a 49–21 win over the New York Giants. In that game, McDonald set a club record with an 81-yard punt return.

McDonald chose not to wear a face mask because he said the bars made it difficult for him to see the ball. He said, "If I was a running back, darn right I would've worn one. Those linebackers and tackles come out of nowhere. But being outside [as a flanker], I could see everything. If anyone tried to throw a haymaker or give me a big forearm, I could see it coming."

In 1962, *Sports Illustrated* put McDonald on its cover with the title "Pro Football's Best Hands." McDonald actually had very small hands and lost the tip of his left thumb in a motorbike accident. He sandpapered his fingertips before every game, much like a safecracker. He said it made his fingers more sensitive and helped him feel the ball. He would scrape his fingers on the brick wall at Franklin Field just before kickoff to achieve the same effect.

McDonald developed his extraordinary hand-eye coordination as a youngster, growing up on the family farm in Roy, New Mexico (elevation 5,000 feet, population 300). He would bounce a tennis ball off the chicken coop. He threw the ball into the corners so it would carom in different directions. Right, left. High, low. He would do this for hours. He learned how to adjust to a ball in the air, which he did better than anyone else in the NFL.

"When I ran a deep route, I'd keep pumping my arms and reach for the ball at the last second," McDonald said. "You've got to be able to see the ball and adjust to it. You don't follow it all the way [with your eyes]. It's all timing, knowing where [the ball] is going to be and when."

In the years 1958 through '62, he scored 56 touchdowns in 63 games, including the championship game against Green Bay. He set a team record with 237 yards receiving in a 1961 game against the Giants at Franklin Field.

"The best thing you can do after you knock McDonald down is to sit on him and pin his arms to the ground," said Cardinals safety Jerry Norton. "Even then, he's liable to catch the ball between his feet."

Giants coach Allie Sherman said:

I don't think I ever saw McDonald play a bad game. He scared the hell out of me. He might only catch four balls in a game, but two of them would be big plays that usually swung the balance. He had what I call a great sense of pace. He would shift gears on a defender, turn him around, and get open anytime he wanted. He was like Fred Biletnikoff and Steve Largent, only more explosive.

We had a defensive back named Erich Barnes who was 6–3, about 200 pounds and very good at "man" coverage. But he had a heckuva time with McDonald. Erich could wear down other receivers, but he couldn't do that to McDonald. Tommy was too tough, too competitive. I've never seen anyone run the post [pattern] better. He was fearless coming across the middle.

"Tommy had more guts for a little guy, I can't say enough about him," Chuck Bednarik said. "He would catch the ball and he'd actually challenge guys. He'd run right at them. Big guys, linebackers, it didn't matter. That's like crashing into a wall. He'd take that big hit and he'd pop right up and flip the ball to the official as if to say, 'Look, you can't hurt me.'"

The big guys hurt McDonald a number of times, but he never let it show. Over the course of his career, he sustained cracked ribs, a shoulder separation, and two broken jaws, but he bounced up after each big hit, clapping his hands, looking for more.

In a 1964 interview with *Sports Illustrated*'s Tex Maule, McDonald said, "I don't like to let some guy on the other side think he can hurt me just because I'm small. If he gives me his best lick and doesn't cave me in, he gets a little discouraged. I just get a kick out of proving there's a place for a runt in pro football. I got so tired, my whole life, hearing, 'You're too small.' All that did was make me try that much harder."

It started when McDonald was a 5–3, 115-pound sophomore at Roy High. He had to plead with the coach to give him a uniform. He wound up setting the state scoring record with 26 touchdowns and 157 points. He also was the 100-yard and 220-yard sprint champion. His mother wanted him to attend Notre Dame, but when she wrote coach Frank Leahy, he suggested Tommy try a smaller school. Leahy wrote, "Your son would just sit on the bench here."

When McDonald blossomed into an All-America halfback at Oklahoma under coach Bud Wilkinson, his most satisfying moment was the 40–0 rout of Notre Dame in 1956. He was the leading scorer on the mighty Sooner team that compiled the longest winning streak in college football history (47 games). He played three varsity seasons at Oklahoma and never lost a game. In 1956 he won the Maxwell Award as the nation's top college player.

When the pro scouts evaluated McDonald, they, too, questioned his size. They did not feel he was big enough to play halfback in the NFL. They thought he might make it as a kick returner, but nothing more. He was ignored through the first two rounds of the 1957 draft. The Eagles finally selected him in the third round.

Tommy McDonald at his 1998 enshrinement in the Pro Football Hall of Fame. Ray Didinger (right) was his presenter. "There is only one place better than this and that's heaven," McDonald said.

Head coach Hugh Devore tried McDonald at halfback, then defensive back. Assistant coach Charlie Gauer felt McDonald would be most effective at flanker. Split him wide, throw him the ball, and let him use his quickness in the open field. It wasn't until the ninth week when the Eagles were 2–6 and playing out the string that Devore finally put McDonald at flanker. The result: two touchdowns, including a leaping grab between two defenders that Commissioner Bert Bell called "one of the greatest catches I've ever seen."

The next year, when Buck Shaw took over as head coach and Van Brocklin arrived in a trade from the Rams, everything came together. Van Brocklin was a great deep passer, and in McDonald he had a receiver with superb big-play ability. It was a perfect marriage, and in 1960 it helped the Eagles win an NFL championship.

"Most of the time, Tommy doesn't have to run a pattern against a defensive back," Van Brocklin said. "He just beats him."

When Van Brocklin retired after the 1960 season and Sonny Jurgensen replaced him, McDonald said, "What's everybody so worried about?" He turned to Jurgensen and said, "You just throw the ball. I'll make you just as great a passer as I made Van Brocklin."

McDonald was joking, but there was some truth to his words. In the 1961 season he caught 64 passes for a league-high 1,144 yards, a 17.9-yard average, and 13 touchdowns. The following year, McDonald caught 58 passes for 1,146 yards, a 19.8-yard average, and 10 touchdowns.

In 1964, Joe Kuharich was hired as head coach, and he dealt McDonald to Dallas for three players: kicker Sam Baker, defensive tackle John Meyers, and offensive lineman Lynn Hoyem. It was one of the most unpopular trades in Eagles history. Baker was a good kicker, but, well, he was a kicker. Meyers and Hoyem were journeymen who accomplished little.

The night the trade was announced, McDonald was playing with the Eagles basketball team in a charity game at Monsignor Bonner High School. McDonald scored 30 points against the Bonner faculty, stayed to sign autographs, then returned to his King of Prussia home, thinking everything was fine. It wasn't until Ben Callaway of the *Philadelphia Daily News* called that he learned he was no longer an Eagle.

"I'm flabbergasted," McDonald said. "I feel like I've been thrown away like an old shoe."

McDonald played only one season in Dallas, but he thrived following a trade to Los Angeles in 1965 when he teamed with quarterback Roman Gabriel and had his sixth Pro Bowl season, pulling down 67 passes for 1,036 yards and nine touchdowns. Gabriel said, "Heart alone set Tommy apart from other players. He was a complete player. He could run, catch, block and inspire his teammates. I can honestly say I never saw him have a bad practice or a bad day."

McDonald retired following the 1968 season and devoted his time to his oil portrait business. His staff of artists produced portraits for clients as varied as the Maxwell Football Club and the Miss America pageant. It was a happy life. There was only one thing missing, and that was a bust in the Pro Football Hall of Fame.

It took a long time—30 years to be exact—but McDonald finally was voted in with the class of 1998. He was overjoyed as he stood on the steps of the Hall for his enshrinement.

"There is only one place better than this," he said, "and that's heaven."

DONOVAN McNABB
Quarterback

Ht: 6–2 • **Wt:** 240 • **College:** Syracuse • **Years with the Eagles:** 1999– • **Birthplace:** Chicago, Illinois • **Born:** November 25, 1976

Donovan McNabb took his game—and his team—to a new level in the 2004 season. He set career highs in touchdown passes (31), passing yardage (3,875), completion percentage (64.0), and efficiency rating (104.7). He also became the first quarterback in NFL history to throw more than 30 touchdown passes and fewer than 10 interceptions (8) in the same season.

But in McNabb's mind, the bottom line to all those gaudy numbers is this: the Eagles finally won the NFC Championship after falling just short the previous three seasons. "To me, statistics are just numbers," McNabb said. "What matters is wins. Wins and losses."

In the Super Bowl era, only four quarterbacks who have played more than one full season have winning percentages higher than .700: Tom Brady of New England, Hall of Famers Roger Staubach and Joe Montana, and McNabb. His 56–23 regular-season record, a .709 percentage, is a testimony to how well he does his job. His interception rate (2.20) is the lowest among active quarterbacks, and his streak of five consecutive playoff seasons is the longest in Eagles history.

"I'm partial; I think he's the best quarterback in the game," said coach Andy Reid, who went against public opinion in selecting McNabb with the second overall pick in the 1999 draft. "He's playing great football right now, and, in my eyes, he's the MVP of the NFL."

McNabb played well each of the previous four seasons, but he improved on that performance in 2004. The one knock on him earlier in his career was his lack of pinpoint accuracy. His completion percentage (57.0) was low for a quarterback in the West Coast offense. Of course, he was not exactly working with a stellar cast of receivers in those years.

In 2004, with the addition of Terrell Owens and the emergence of Brian Westbrook as a full-time player, McNabb's numbers improved dramatically. His completion percentage jumped by seven full points, and he set an NFL record by completing 24 consecutive passes over two games against the New York Giants (10) and Green Bay (14). He broke the old mark of 22 consecutive completions set by Montana, generally considered the most accurate passer in league history.

"[McNabb] reminds me of Steve Young," said Carolina safety Mike Minter, comparing him to another Hall of Fame quarterback from the West Coast system. "I remember my rookie year playing against San Francisco on a Monday night. I don't think a pass ever touched the ground. That's how Donovan is getting. He understands the West Coast offense to a T."

McNabb set a team record with 464 passing yards in the 47–17 win over Green Bay. He could have broken the Eagles single-season record for touchdown passes (Sonny Jurgensen, 32, in 1961), but he sat out virtually all of the last two games as Reid rested his key players for the postseason. He finished as the second-rated passer in the NFC, trailing only Daunte Culpepper of Minnesota.

"McNabb is as close to a one-man gang as anyone in the NFL since John Elway," said ABC football analyst John Madden.

In 2004, McNabb scrambled less than in other years. He ran the ball a career-low 41 times. That's 30 fewer rushing attempts than the previous year and a 50 percent drop from the 2001 season. But he still could use his legs if necessary, an ability which he demonstrated on the most spectacular play of the season, when he scrambled away from a pack of Dallas defenders and threw a strike to Freddie Mitchell 60 yards down the field as the Eagles ripped the Cowboys, 49–21, on "Monday Night Football."

"This was the escape of all escapes, Houdini raised to a higher power," wrote Rich Hofmann in the *Philadelphia Daily News*, describing the play that McNabb kept alive for 14 mind-boggling seconds. "It wasn't merely an athletic play. This was a great, thinking football play. This is what McNabb does best now, using his mobility to buy time to hit the big one down-field. He does it multiple times every week, escaping and scheming and turning garbage into gold."

"It is more than natural ability," center Hank Fraley said. "People don't see how much time and work Donovan puts in. He studies film on his own, then with the coaches, then we study more film together. That's probably five hours a day. He is so prepared; that makes his confidence level really high, and he believes he can do anything on the field."

McNabb has come a long way from September 2003, when the Eagles were 0–2 after losses to Tampa Bay (17–0) and New England (31–10) and he was struggling with a bruised thumb that made it difficult for him to grip the football. He had no touchdown passes and three interceptions, prompting Rush Limbaugh to claim McNabb "wasn't that good from the get-go." Appearing on ESPN, Limbaugh said McNabb was over-rated by a media "desirous" to see a black quarterback succeed.

McNabb responded by calling Limbaugh's remarks "sad" and pointed out there were a number of African American quarterbacks already playing well in the NFL with more on the way. He did not lash out, nor did he ask for sympathy. He knew the best way to answer the charge was to play better, which he did. He led the Eagles to 11 wins in their next 12 games and improved his level of play every week. Over the last nine weeks of the regular season, he had 13 touchdown passes and just four interceptions as the Eagles won the NFC East for the third consecutive year.

"If beforehand you had said, 'I'm going to send this player through all this adversity to see how he handles it,' the way Donovan handled it was perfect," safety Brian Dawkins told Jim Corbett of *USA Today*. "He told us, 'Everything is going to work out.' He wasn't just saying it. He truly believed it."

"I'm not a quitter, and I never give up," McNabb said. "I've always said, 'I'll go out there with one arm or one leg.' It doesn't matter what kind of challenge I'm facing; I'm gonna fight through it."

In the 2004 season, McNabb had an efficiency rating over 100 in nine of his 15 regular-season starts. He threw for four touchdowns in a game on four different occasions, and he passed for five touchdowns against the Packers. Peter King of *Sports Illustrated* called McNabb "one of the best quarterbacks in football, playing at a virtuoso level."

McNabb's leadership was never more evident than after Owens went down with a leg injury in December and fans and media questioned whether the Eagles could win in the postseason without their big-play receiver. McNabb told a roomful of reporters, "You guys said T. O. took the pressure off me.

Donovan McNabb

Now I guess I have all that pressure again. That's fine. I love pressure. I love to step out there, and everybody is standing with their mouths open to find out what I'm going to do next. I'm sure that's how you guys are sitting there now, waiting to find out what we're going to do. Well, buckle your seat belts and enjoy the ride."

In the NFC Divisional playoff, McNabb completed 21 of 33 passes for 286 yards and two touchdowns in a 27–14 win over Minnesota. The next week, he played through the numbing cold and 35 mile-an-hour wind gusts at Lincoln Financial Field to complete 17 of 26 passes for 180 yards and two touchdowns as the Eagles defeated Atlanta, 27–10, in the NFC championship game.

After the game, McNabb savored the victory, saying, "It's definitely everything I thought it would be. Obviously, it took a couple years for it to happen, but we continue to stay patient. A lot of people turned their backs on us and didn't have the confidence that we'd be able to do it. I think we answered a lot of questions."

As McNabb waved to the cheering crowd, it was impossible not to think back to April 1999, when he was booed by several dozen Eagles fans on draft day. They wanted the team to select Ricky Williams, the Heisman Trophy winner from Texas, and they took a bus to New York, site of the draft, to make their feelings known. When McNabb was introduced as the Eagles pick, the group booed loudly from the balcony.

McNabb did his best to ignore it, donning an Eagles cap and smiling for the TV cameras, but he was hurt and embarrassed. "You dream of getting drafted in the NFL, and finally it happens," he told Mark Kram of the *Philadelphia Daily News.* "My name actually gets called, the dream comes true, then they start booing. It was a shock. You try to forget the bad things that happen, but that was something I'll always remember because I'd never been booed before."

It did not take McNabb long to turn those boos to cheers. He won his first start against Washington, 35–28, then came back from a knee injury to throw three touchdown passes against St. Louis to close out his rookie season. In 2000 he led the Eagles to an 11–5 finish and the first of five consecutive playoff appearances.

In 2002, McNabb suffered a fractured ankle but stayed in the game to throw four touchdown passes in a 38–14 win over Arizona. McNabb limped the entire game, but he refused to come out or allow the doctors to X-ray him. He insisted it was nothing, just a sprain.

"It told you everything about the kind of competitor he is," tackle Jon Runyan said. "There are times during the game when the [TV] camera catches him smiling and people think he's not serious, but he's real serious. He might have a little fun and keep it loose at times, but when it's time to lay it on the line, he does it. He's the captain of the ship, and this season when T. O. went down, he put the team on his back and carried it."

McNabb became just the third African American quarterback to start in a Super Bowl—following Doug Williams of Washington and Steve McNair of Tennessee—when he led the Eagles against New England in Super Bowl XXXIX. He passed for 357 yards and three touchdowns, but he also threw three interceptions as the Eagles lost to the Patriots, 24–21.

"As disappointed as we feel now," McNabb said, "I really believe we will be back."

WILBERT MONTGOMERY
Running Back

Ht: 5–10 • **Wt:** 195 • **College:** Abilene Christian • **Years with the Eagles:** 1977–84 • **Birthplace:** Greenville, Mississippi • **Born:** September 16, 1954

Wilbert Montgomery arrived in Philadelphia in 1977, his eyes fixed on his shoe tops, his voice turned down to a Sunday school whisper. For a while, no one could get his name right. He was called Wilbur and Wilver and a few other things his mother never dreamed of.

He was going to leave the Eagles training camp one night, but his roommate, Cleveland Franklin, talked him out of it. He was scared of the big city, scared of pro football, and, most of all, scared of Dick Vermeil, the coach whose voice was everywhere on the practice field. The rookie packed his bags the morning of every cutdown.

"That first year, Wilbert kept a towel under his door so they couldn't slide the pink slip into his room," quarterback Ron Jaworski said. "He didn't think he'd make the team. He was insecure, like most rookies, but everyone else in camp recognized his talent. He had that great vision, the ability to cut

Wilbert Montgomery

back and make something out of nothing. He ran hard, blocked, caught the ball well. He had everything it takes to make it in the NFL. The only thing he lacked was confidence."

Montgomery was a sixth-round draft pick, the 154th player chosen overall. He had scored 76 career touchdowns at Abilene Christian College, an NCAA record, but he missed 11 games his final two seasons due to various injuries. The pro scouts felt he was too small and too brittle to last in the NFL. The Eagles felt anyone who scored that many touchdowns was worth a look, so they dropped him into their shopping basket on day two of the draft without any fanfare or illusions.

"When I first came to the Eagles, what an adjustment it was," Montgomery told Stan Hochman of the *Philadelphia Daily News.* "I went to Abilene Christian, a religious school. I didn't hear any profane language. Everyone spoke in nice tones. Here, it stung me, the words I heard. I'd get cussed out by a coach, and it messed me up for the next couple series."

Montgomery spent his rookie year playing mostly on special teams, and he led the NFC with a 26.9-yard average on kickoff returns. In 1978 he became the team's featured running back and gained 1,220 yards on 259 carries, a 4.7-yard average, and scored 10 touchdowns. That was the beginning of a stellar four-year run in which Montgomery was the focal point of the Eagles offense and earned a permanent place in Philadelphia sports history by rushing for 194 yards in the NFC Championship game against Dallas, a game the Eagles won 20–7 in a frigid Veterans Stadium.

"When Wilbert is healthy, he is the finest player in the game," Jaworski said. "Some backs might run better, some might catch a little better, but no one does everything as well as he does."

Montgomery played a total of eight seasons with the Eagles and finished as the team's all-time leader in rushing attempts (1,465) and yards (6,538), surpassing the great Steve Van Buren. Montgomery also set the club record for most rushing yards in a season with 1,512 yards in 1979. He was the first player in team history to rush for more than 1,000 yards in three different seasons.

Montgomery broke Van Buren's career rushing record in a September 1984 game against Minnesota. At his request, the Eagles did not stop the game to acknowledge his accomplishment. They flashed the news on the PhanaVision scoreboard, and referee Jim Tunney handed Montgomery the football, but he quickly flipped it to the equipment manager and returned to the huddle. No curtain call, no prolonged ovation. That was not his style.

"The most important thing," he said, "was we won the game."

With Montgomery, the team always came first. He was shy, almost painfully so, early in his career. He actually hid from reporters after games, ducking into the trainer's room and not emerging for hours. He did not enjoy the limelight and avoided it as much as possible. He wasn't rude; he just didn't know what to say.

"I wasn't comfortable when everyone made me the center of attention, when I knew the guys opening the holes were just as responsible for what we were doing," Montgomery said. "I didn't feel right, getting all the glory. I'd rather not get any. It's a team game."

Montgomery was similar to Van Buren in his modesty. Neither man cared about individual statistics; they only cared about helping the team win. Both Montgomery and Van Buren played through injuries that would have sidelined other backs. That was especially true in the Dallas championship game, when Montgomery played despite a badly bruised hip and strained knee.

"I was sore all down my left side," Montgomery said, "but I just sucked it up. You come this far, you don't sit down for a little pain."

That day, playing in below-zero wind chill, against a Dallas defense that had not allowed an opponent to rush for more than 100 yards in 29 consecutive postseason games, Montgomery carried the ball 26 times for 194 yards, just two yards short of Van Buren's record for a championship game set in 1949 against the Los Angeles Rams.

The image is forever frozen in the minds of Eagles fans: Montgomery taking a handoff from Jaworski, starting left, then veering sharply to the right, cutting behind the blocks of center Guy Morriss, guard Woody Peoples, and tackle Jerry Sisemore, finding a crease in the Dallas defense and racing 42 yards to the end zone. It was the Eagles' second play from scrimmage, and it sparked them to the NFC title and a trip to Super Bowl XV.

"He's not well yet, but he really wanted to play," trainer Otho Davis told Tom Cushman of the *Philadelphia Daily News*. "He came in this morning and took about one and a half hours of treatment, mostly massage. All we did was sort of wind him up, turn him loose, and let him go. The final and most important ingredient was Wilbert himself, just him, a super young man."

"Sometimes I'm not smart," Montgomery said. "I like to hit up in there [between the tackles], and either I give or some-

body else is gonna give. It's not the best way to stay healthy. Tony [Dorsett of Dallas] is the kind of runner who, if he knows he's not gonna get anything, he lies down. That's smart, that doesn't usually lose you any yards, and it gets you a long career."

Taking that much punishment week after week, it was inevitable that Montgomery's body would finally break down. That process began in 1982 when he missed one game; then he was out for 11 games in 1983. He played all 16 games in 1984, but he had just 789 yards on 201 carries, and his average per attempt dropped below 4.0 for the first time.

After that season, the Eagles traded Montgomery to Detroit for linebacker Garry Cobb. He played just seven games with the Lions, then retired. In 1997, Dick Vermeil hired him as his backfield coach with the St. Louis Rams. Montgomery was on the Rams staff when they won the Super Bowl in January 2000.

GUY MORRISS
Center

Ht: 6–4 • **Wt:** 255 • **College:** TCU • **Years with the Eagles:** 1973–83 • **Birthplace:** Colorado City, Texas • **Born:** May 13, 1951

Guy Morriss has an Eagle tattooed on his left calf. It was a neat conversation piece in the locker room. Reporters always assumed it was a symbol of his devotion to the team, the city, the cause, whatever.

Actually, it was none of those things. He just liked the way it looked.

"You walk into a tattoo shop, and there's a million designs to pick from," Morriss told Stan Hochman of the *Philadelphia Daily News*. "The eagle looked best. And not because it's a majestic bird, or even because it's the national bird. I just liked it."

Morriss was that way—direct and uncomplicated. He was, in other words, the perfect offensive lineman. He wore jeans and flannel shirts. Kept an old brass spittoon in his locker. Didn't say a whole lot. He just strapped it on and went out to play every Sunday. He is fourth all-time in games played for the Eagles with 157, including 150 starts.

His first start came in the sixth week of the 1973 season. Veteran center Mike Evans was bedridden with the flu when the team went to Minnesota. Morriss, a rookie, was forced to start against the Vikings' Purple People Eaters with future Hall of Famers Alan Page and Carl Eller.

The Eagles lost, 28–21, but Morriss did a solid job blocking on Page, the panther-quick tackle, and he put middle linebacker Jeff Siemon flat on his back, opening a huge hole for running back Po James to gain 23 yards on a draw play.

"I spent the time from Friday through [Saturday] night just thinking about those guys," Morriss said, referring to the Minnesota front four. "Before the game, I had butterflies real bad. But once I got in there and popped those guys a few times, the nervousness started to go away. The longer the game went on, the better I felt. I thought, 'Well, these guys are supposed to be the best. Now I know what to expect the rest of the way.'"

Morriss remained the Eagles starting center for the next nine seasons, earning first-team All-NFC honors from UPI in 1981. It was quite a climb, considering Morriss never played center until he joined the Eagles as a second-round draft pick in 1973. He was a tight end in high school and played tackle and guard at TCU.

"My second or third week at training camp, coach [Mike] McCormack asked me if I'd mind trying out at center," Morriss said. "I was a scared rookie then, raw and green, and all I wanted to do was make the team. I was willing to play anyplace. Anyway, snapping the ball seemed to come easy. I didn't have to think much about it."

Morriss was not a naturally big man, so he had to spend extra time in the weight room building himself up to take on the defensive tackles who were lining up on his nose as more teams switched to the three-man line.

"Guy Morriss is playing better football than he's ever played," Dick Vermeil said during the 1980 Super Bowl season. "He's stronger, fundamentally sound, and more confident. He's getting out of his ability what he has. He's not an explosive-type guy. He's a stick-and-stay guy. Determined. He gets in a guy's chest and stays there."

"Guy is my security blanket," quarterback Ron Jaworski told Bill Lyon of the *Philadelphia Inquirer*. "Standing behind him is like being in a bullet-proof car. I like the ball centered a certain way, the same way, every time. With Guy, it always is. Those guys [the offensive linemen] are the ditch diggers. Without them, we're nothing. They'll announce over the PA system, 'Jaworski pass for a touchdown to Harold Carmichael.' They never say, 'That play made possible by Guy Morriss's great block.' But that's the truth."

Morriss finished his playing career with four seasons in New England. When he retired as a player in 1987, he went into coaching. He worked his way up to head coach at Kentucky, and in 2003 he was hired as head coach at Baylor.

JOE MUHA
Fullback-Linebacker

Ht: 6–1 • **Wt:** 205 • **College:** VMI • **Years with the Eagles:** 1946–50 • **Birthplace:** Central City, Pennsylvania • **Born:** April 28, 1921 • **Died:** March 31, 1993

Joe Muha was one of the unsung heroes of the Eagles 1948–49 championship teams. On offense, he was the fullback who did the lead blocking for Steve Van Buren and Bosh Pritchard. On defense, he was overshadowed by the team's other linebacker, future Hall of Famer Alex Wojciechowicz.

But the one area where Muha had no peer was punting. More than half a century after his retirement, he still was the Eagles all-time leader in career punting average (42.9 yards), and he had the highest single-season punting average (47.2 in 1948). He was an all-around weapon who contributed mightily to the Eagles' success.

Under coach Greasy Neale, the Eagles won with their running game and defense, and Muha was key in both areas: his blocking opened the holes for Van Buren and Pritchard, and his punts kept driving opponents back, making it easier for the defense to keep them in check.

Muha was a master of the quick kick. He would line up at fullback, take a direct snap from center, and punt the ball away. The idea was to catch the opponent by surprise, and with no safety back to field the punt, it could roll forever.

In 1947 the Eagles knocked off the powerful Los Angeles Rams, 14–7, thanks in part to two Muha quick kicks, one for

Joe Muha

72 yards, the other for 71. "Muha's kicking had as much to do with our victory as anything else," Neale said. "[Bob] Waterfield has been outkicking all his opponents this season, but he met his match today."

Muha set the record for the longest punt in Eagles history with an 82-yard quick kick against the New York Giants in 1948. That mark stood for 41 years until Randall Cunningham boomed his 91-yarder against the Giants at the Meadowlands in 1989.

Talking about the quick kick, Muha told Phil Jasner of the *Philadelphia Daily News*, "I was probably the best in the business. I had a rocker step that allowed me to maneuver. The ball was snapped directly through the quarterback's legs to me, and I could get it off before anyone realized what was coming. I never had one blocked."

Muha and Pritchard were teammates at VMI. During his college career, Muha was so versatile that Clark Shaugnessy, the coach who created the T formation, called him "the equal of any back I've ever seen." Muha was the Eagles' first-round draft pick in 1943, but he joined the Marine Corps and served with distinction in the Pacific, earning a battlefield commission.

Muha joined the Eagles in 1946 and played five seasons. Neale gave him high marks for his defense, saying, "If there is a better linebacker in the league than Muha, I have yet to see him. He must be part bloodhound, for he has an uncanny instinct where the opposition is going to send its plays."

As Muha was preparing for his final game in 1950, he told Dick Cresap of the *Philadelphia Bulletin*, "I've enjoyed it, made

Player Profiles **61**

a lot of friends in Philadelphia and around the league. But it's not getting any easier. I want to leave while I can still walk out of Shibe Park."

After football, Muha went back to school to earn his masters degree and doctorate. He became a college professor, teaching business administration at Pasadena (California) City College.

AL NELSON
Defensive Back

Ht: 5–11 • **Wt:** 185 • **College:** Cincinnati • **Years with the Eagles:** 1965–73 • **Birthplace:** Cincinnati, Ohio • **Born:** October 27, 1943

Al Nelson was a standout running back at the University of Cincinnati, but the Eagles converted him to defense when they selected him in the third round of the 1965 draft. He earned a starting cornerback position as a rookie and held it for nine seasons.

Nelson had two of the longest scoring plays in Eagles history: a 101-yard return of a missed field goal against Dallas (September 26, 1971) and a 100-yard return of a missed field goal against Cleveland (December 11, 1966). He also ranks third in club history for kickoff returns (101) and yards (2,625).

As a senior at Cincinnati, Nelson finished third in the nation in rushing and scoring. He also won the Missouri Valley Conference championships in the 100- and 220-yard dashes. That speed, combined with his shiftiness, made Nelson a threat to go all the way every time he touched the football.

"Pound for pound, [Nelson] has to be one of the most powerful runners in the country," said Chuck Studley, his college coach. "He's Mr. Inside and Mr. Outside rolled into one. He runs like a halfback to the outside and like a fullback to the inside."

Given those credentials, you might wonder why the Eagles played Nelson on defense. The College All-Star coaches put him there first when they were preparing for the annual exhibition against the NFL champions, the Cleveland Browns. Nelson was outstanding in the game, blanketing Browns star Paul Warfield and sending the future Hall of Famer to the sidelines with a broken collarbone.

When Nelson arrived at the Eagles camp, the veterans called him "Crusher" for the hit he put on Warfield.

One requirement for playing cornerback is confidence, and Nelson had it. In October 1965, Bill Gildea of the *Washington Post* asked the rookie Nelson for his assessment of NFL receivers. Said Nelson: "They're not as tough as I thought they'd be. I used to watch [the pros] on television and thought you had to be a God to play. Now I see them making mistakes, too."

Nelson was very good in his first two pro seasons, but he missed most of the 1967 season with a broken arm. He had another setback in 1969 when he was diagnosed with an irregular heartbeat. The team doctor told Nelson, "You have the heart of a 60-year-old man." Nelson feared his career might be over at age 25.

As it turned out, an abscessed tooth had infected Nelson's system and inflamed the lining of his heart. Nelson was given medication, and within a few days the symptoms were gone.

Nelson started at left cornerback through the 1972 season, but his playing time dwindled when Mike McCormack took over as coach and put the newly acquired Johnny Outlaw in that spot. With the team in a rebuilding mode, Nelson was released in 1974. He worked out for the Chicago Bears, but when they did not sign him, he quit football and took a job with the Delaware County division of parks and recreation as a special assistant in community affairs.

JERRY NORTON
Halfback

Ht: 5–11 • **Wt:** 195 • **College:** SMU • **Years with the Eagles:** 1954–58 • **Birthplace:** Gilmer, Texas • **Born:** May 16, 1931

Jerry Norton was a talented athlete who could play offense and defense as well as lead the NFL in punting (which he did in 1960). But Norton also could exasperate coaches and general managers by insisting on doing things his way.

Example: In 1957, Norton set an Eagles record with a 99-yard interception return against the New York Giants. He picked off a Charlie Conerly pass and ran through the entire Giants team, trotting the final 10 yards to the end zone. It was a brilliant play, except for one thing: He was out of position.

"I smelled something," Norton said. "I gambled."

Norton often played that way, trusting his instincts and disregarding his coach's instructions. Sometimes he would be in punt formation and decide, on his own, to run for the first down. Often he made it work. Against Detroit in 1957, he was back to punt and instead put the ball under his arm and galloped 61 yards.

"It was easy as pie," Norton said.

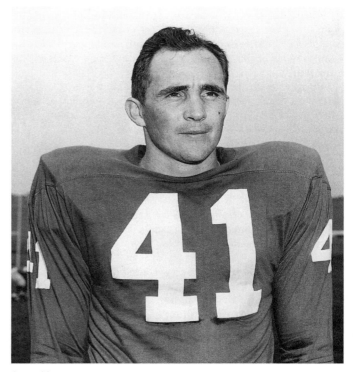

Jerry Norton

There were other occasions when it did not work. He tried it in a 1959 exhibition game against Green Bay and was stopped cold. Coach Buck Shaw was asked if he called for the fake. Shaw's curt reply: "I sure didn't."

One way or another, Norton made things happen. In 1957 he handled the ball six times on interceptions and fake punts and gained 228 yards, an average of 38 yards per touch. The team finished 4–8, but Hugh Brown of the *Philadelphia Bulletin* noted, "Without Norton, our Eagles would have moulted far worse than they did."

Norton began his football career as a 110-pound halfback and punter at Texarkana High School. He earned a scholarship to SMU, where he started on defense, then switched to offense as a senior and finished as the fourth-leading scorer in the nation. The Eagles selected him in the seventh round of the 1954 draft.

As a rookie, Norton played safety on defense and intercepted five passes, returning one for a touchdown. In his second season he was switched to offense to replace Jerry Williams, who retired to become head coach at Montana State. Norton had 36 carries for 144 yards, a 4.0 average. He also returned one kickoff for a touchdown.

In 1956, Norton went back to defense and established himself as one of the top safeties in the game. He took over the punting duties in 1957 and led the league in punts (68) and yardage (2,798). He was selected for the Pro Bowl in 1957 and again in 1958.

Norton informed the Eagles he wanted to play out his option in 1959. General manager Vince McNally was quoted as saying, "When he came to camp, I said, 'Let's talk. If it's a question of money, maybe we can get together.'"

According to McNally, Norton declined. The speculation was that Norton wanted to be a free agent so he could sign with the American Football League, which was about to get under way the following season.

Fearing he would lose Norton at the end of the season and get nothing in return, McNally traded him to the Chicago Cardinals for guard Bob Konovsky and end Jerry Wilson. Konovsky never played a game for the Eagles, and Wilson was gone within a year.

Norton never did sign with the AFL. He played three seasons with the Cardinals and one season with Dallas, and finished his 11-year pro career as a punting specialist for Vince Lombardi in Green Bay in 1963 and 1964.

DAVEY O'BRIEN
Quarterback

Ht: 5–7 • **Wt:** 150 • **College:** TCU • **Years with the Eagles:** 1939–40 • **Birthplace:** Dallas, Texas • **Born:** June 22, 1917 • **Died:** November 18, 1977

For a little man, Davey O'Brien was the biggest star in college football in 1938. He led TCU to an undefeated season and won the Heisman Trophy as the nation's top collegiate player. But not even a quarterback with his passing skills could make the woeful Eagles winners.

The Eagles won only two games in O'Brien's two seasons, both of those against the Pittsburgh Steelers. O'Brien completed 46 percent of his pass attempts and threw 11 touchdown passes with 34 interceptions. Coach Bert Bell, who paid O'Brien the hefty sum of $12,000 to sign, found himself defending that decision.

"When I drafted him, I wasn't thinking of buying a name," Bell told Ray Hill of the *Philadelphia Inquirer.* "I'm interested in building the Eagles into a championship team. I think he's the quarterback who can spark us ahead. Otherwise, I wouldn't be interested, no matter what his college reputation might be."

Later, Bell told Harry Robert of the *Philadelphia Bulletin,* "The trouble is that O'Brien was so built up by his play at TCU, the public expected a magician who would complete 99 of 100 passes. No rookie can come out of college and burn this league up. O'Brien is playing as well as any first year man could possibly be expected."

But the Eagles did not have enough good players to compete. Their only offensive threat was O'Brien passing to his former college teammate, end Don Looney. In 1940, the one season they played together as pros, O'Brien and Looney connected 58 times for 707 yards. That made them the most prolific pass-catch team in the league.

On December 1, 1940, O'Brien set an NFL record by throwing 60 passes and completing 33 in a game against Washington. Looney caught 14 of those passes to set the Eagles single-game reception mark. Yet, the Eagles lost the game 13–6, and when it was over, O'Brien announced he was retiring from football to pursue a career with the Federal Bureau of Investigation.

It was a big story: one of pro football's marquee players quitting after just two seasons to become a G-man. O'Brien said his decision had nothing to do with the Eagles' sorry record. He said he would have done the same thing if he were playing for a first-place team. Government service was something O'Brien wanted all along.

"Football has always been my first love, and it has been mighty nice to me," O'Brien said. "But for the sake of the future, it's time to quit. I'm fortunate to get this [FBI] job, and unless a man expects to stay in football, the longer he plays it, the longer he delays starting whatever work he's going to do afterwards."

Before his final game, O'Brien was presented with a silver plaque by Bert Bell. The inscription read, "Davey O'Brien, the greatest player of all time; retiring from pro football to serve his country. Small in stature with the heart of a lion. A living inspiration to the youth of America."

Redskins president George Preston Marshall said, "The National Football League, naturally, will miss Davey. However, he will become the property of all the people of the nation, and I feel sure he will be a credit to his country."

O'Brien spent ten years with the FBI as a field agent. When he left the bureau, he went into private industry in Texas. He and Looney formed a business partnership that proved very successful.

In a 1953 interview with Hugh Brown of the *Philadelphia Bulletin*, O'Brien admitted he may have erred in walking away from the NFL after just two seasons. Said O'Brien: "It's a wonderful game. Maybe I did leave it too soon."

O'Brien died in November 1977. His college coach Dutch Meyer offered a fitting tribute, saying, "He was everything. He was the best play selector, the greatest field general I ever saw. He had a brain, boy; he had a football brain. He made a darn good coach out of me."

TERRELL OWENS
Wide Receiver

Ht: 6–3 • **Wt:** 225 • **College:** Tennessee–Chattanooga •
Years with the Eagles: 2004– • **Birthplace:** Alexander City,
Alabama • **Born:** December 7, 1973

On December 20, 2004, Dr. Mark Myerson offered the grim prognosis on Terrell Owens, who suffered a high ankle sprain and fibula fracture in his right leg in the previous day's game against Dallas.

"To be fair to him and the team and its fans, it doesn't make sense to say that he could be back in time to play in the Super Bowl," Dr. Myerson said.

Dr. John Kelly, vice-chair of orthopedic surgery at Temple University Hospital, went even farther, saying, "The only way, in my estimation, that he could be back is that he goes to a faith-healing service."

Fast-forward to February 6, 2005. Owens catches nine passes in the Super Bowl for 122 yards, easily the best performance by any Eagles player in the 24–21 loss to New England. It is a valiant effort destined to go down in sports history alongside Curt Schilling's bloody sock, Kirk Gibson's limping home run trot, and Jack Youngblood gutting out Super Bowl XIV on a broken leg.

"To be able to do what he did, it's amazing," said Patriots safety Rodney Harrison. "You could tell that he was still hurting, but he played through it. He was tremendous."

Even in defeat, wrote Ian O'Connor in *USA Today*, "Owens was the biggest winner on the biggest stage, a picture of me-first action suddenly exposed as a portrait in team-first sacrifice."

Prior to the game some columnists suggested Owens was milking the "will-he-play-or-won't he?" angle. It was, they felt, more about T. O. grabbing the Super Bowl spotlight than catching the football. With his courageous performance, he proved them wrong.

"The media made it look like I was grandstanding," Owens said after the game. "In this situation, if it had been Brett Favre, they would have called him a warrior. They said I was selfish. If I'm selfish, I'm selfish because I want to help my team win."

Owens' performance in the Super Bowl was the culmination of a remarkable season in which the All-Pro receiver elevated his game and his image. His arrival in a March 2004 trade created an excitement in Philadelphia rivaled only by the Phillies' signing of Pete Rose and the Sixers' trade for Julius Erving, and those landmark events took place more than a quarter of a century before. Philadelphia was ready for T. O., and, as it turned out, he was ready for the fresh start that Philadelphia represented.

In eight seasons with San Francisco, Owens established himself as one of the most talented players in the NFL with 592 catches (including 20 in one game, a league record) and 83 touchdowns, second only to Jerry Rice in franchise history. He also earned a reputation as one of the most troublesome players in the game. His on-field antics—dancing on the Cowboys star at Texas Stadium, taking a Sharpie from his sock to autograph a football after scoring a touchdown—were only part of it. He also clashed with coaches and teammates and was called a cancer in the locker room.

"You get to the point where people accuse you of not being a good teammate, then you get the media criticizing you,"

Terrell Owens

Owens said. "All I ever wanted to do was win. People haven't always understood what I'm all about. But I knew with a new [team], I could play free. I wanted that opportunity."

After the 2003 season, when it was obvious the Eagles needed to add a blue-chip receiver, Donovan McNabb talked to Reid about acquiring Owens. The four-time Pro Bowler wanted out of San Francisco, in part because he had soured on quarterback Jeff Garcia. Owens felt he needed to play with a better quarterback to maximize his game. McNabb, he felt, was that quarterback.

Still, most people saw it as an unlikely marriage: The no-nonsense Reid and the volatile Owens. Would Reid risk bringing in a player who might disrupt the team chemistry? Assistant head coach Marty Mornhinweg, who coached Owens in San Francisco, convinced Reid it could work. Mornhinweg told Reid, "I know how the guy is wired. He just wants to win."

The Eagles tried to sign Owens as a free agent, but his attorney missed a filing deadline, resulting in the 49ers retaining his rights. They traded Owens to Baltimore, but he refused to play there. Catching passes from Kyle Boller, he felt, was no better than catching passes from Garcia. An arbitration hearing was held and a compromise reached: Owens would join the Eagles, and they would compensate the Ravens with a fifth-round draft pick and send defensive end Brandon Whiting to the 49ers.

It wasn't long before Owens was happily bouncing up the Art Museum steps and shaking hands at Pat's Steaks. "Eagle fans let me know what I meant to them, and they've been gracious," he said. "I know what they are feeling. They are hungry to win a Super Bowl. So am I."

Owens and Reid clashed the first day of minicamp. Owens wore black tights just as he had done for eight years in San Francisco. Reid informed him the dress code in Philadelphia was shorts, not tights. The media braced for the T. O. eruption. Instead, Owens and Reid negotiated a pact, an amusing one at that. Owens would wear the shorts, which he hated, but if he scored 15 touchdowns, he could switch back to tights and Reid would wear them, too.

Everyone laughed, but as it turned out, Reid almost had to be fitted for Spandex as Owens caught 14 touchdown passes, breaking the club record of 13 shared by Mike Quick (1983) and Hall of Famer Tommy McDonald (1960 and '61). He was well on his way to winning the bet, but the leg injury sidelined him for the final two weeks of the regular season and both NFC playoff games.

Owens started fast, scoring three touchdowns in the league opener against the New York Giants. He had a streak of five consecutive games with more than 100 receiving yards, a club record, and he finished the regular season with 77 catches for 1,200 yards. He supplied the big-play threat the Eagles previously lacked, and his presence helped McNabb establish career highs in completion percentage, yardage, and touchdowns.

What was equally significant—and perhaps more surprising—was the impact Owens had on the team. Rather than dividing the locker room, he energized it. He entertained the fans with his end-zone celebrations, which ranged from slam dunks over the crossbar to a devastating imitation of Baltimore linebacker Ray Lewis's hip-shaking dance. He did that one after scoring the decisive touchdown in a 15–10 win over the Ravens at Lincoln Financial Field.

"Everyone was a little worried at first; no one knew how he'd fit in," linebacker Ike Reese said. "We're kind of a laid-back ball club. But he's given us an edge, a different mental edge over everyone, and it's welcome."

"I like guys with a little spice," said Quick, who called the games on the Eagles radio network as Owens shattered his records. "Everyone can't be the same. That's boring. You don't want bland guys; then the soup is bland. You want different spices. T. O. is a spice. He's different."

How different? When tight end Chad Lewis met President George W. Bush during a campaign stop in South Jersey, Bush had one question: "What's T. O. really like?"

"That's when you know you're big time," Owens said.

VINCE PAPALE
Wide Receiver

Ht: 6–2 • **Wt:** 195 • **College:** St. Joseph's (Philadelphia) • **Years with the Eagles:** 1976–78 • **Birthplace:** Chester, Pennsylvania • **Born:** February 9, 1946

Vince Papale's story is part Rocky and part Rudy: a school-teacher who never played college football and spent three years playing in a two-hand touch league, yet fought his way onto the Eagles roster as a 30-year-old rookie. His is the ultimate story of dreams coming true.

There were many parallels between the story of Vince Papale and Rocky Balboa: two gutsy, street-tough Italian stallions taking their million-to-one shot at the big time. Papale made the Eagles roster in 1976, the same year that *Rocky* was released and won an Academy Award.

"Most people thought I was nuts," Papale said. "Fortunately for me, Dick Vermeil wasn't one of them. He promised me a

Vince Papale

fair shot at training camp, and he gave me one. How many coaches in the NFL would even bother to look at a 30-year-old rookie free agent? Dick Vermeil, maybe George Allen, and that's it."

Papale grew up in a housing project on the outskirts of Philadelphia. He was an outstanding high school athlete, but he was too small (5–6, 150) to attract college football recruiters. He went to St. Joseph's College to compete in track as a pole-vaulter and decathlete. After graduation, he became a high school teacher and coach while playing in a touch football league on weekends.

Papale had grown to 6–2, 190 pounds, so he decided to move up to tackle football. He played for a local semipro team, the Aston Knights. In 1974, when the World Football League was born, Papale went to an open tryout for the Philadelphia Bell. He not only made the team; he made the starting lineup as a wide receiver.

When the WFL folded, Papale contacted the Eagles. Vermeil had just come aboard as coach, and he was looking for, in his words, "character players," men who were tough enough and hungry enough to change the atmosphere in the Eagles locker room where the team had not managed a winning season in a decade.

Papale lacked football experience, but he did not lack for hunger. He won a job on the team with an impressive training camp, and he stayed on the roster for three seasons as an aggressive, hard-hitting special-teams player. He was a fan favorite in Philadelphia, even after his retirement in 1979.

"The blue-collar guys in the upper deck love it when I hit a first-round draft pick," Papale said. "They feel like they got a piece of that rich so-and-so, too."

"Vince is every fan's dream," general manager Jim Murray said. "He is Walter Mitty. He went from being a season-ticket holder to now he's on the field. He is emotion to the ninth power. He's a blue-collar guy wearing green and white."

FLOYD PETERS
Defensive Tackle

Ht: 6–4 • **Wt:** 255 • **College:** San Francisco State • **Years with the Eagles:** 1964–69 • **Birthplace:** Council Bluffs, Iowa • **Born:** May 21, 1936

The Eagles were flying home from a 1966 exhibition game, and the stewardess was serving meals in the main cabin. She handed a tray to defensive tackle Don Hultz, but she ignored Floyd Peters who was in the next seat. When Peters asked why he did not receive a meal, the stewardess answered, "I was told to serve the players first."

The other Eagles roared with laughter. Peters was 30, but with his bald head and weathered face, he looked much older. Too old, the stewardess thought, to be one of the players. Yet Peters was the best defensive player on the team, one of only two Eagles who would be selected for the Pro Bowl that season. (Offensive tackle Bob Brown, the future Hall of Famer, was the other.)

Peters played 12 seasons in the NFL with four different teams, but he played his best football in Philadelphia. He was acquired by Eagles coach Joe Kuharich in a 1964 trade with Detroit, a deal in which Kuharich sent offensive tackle J. D. Smith to the Lions in exchange for Peters and running back Ollie Matson. It was one of the few Kuharich trades that actually worked out for the Eagles. Matson gave them three good years. Peters was voted into two Pro Bowls and was named Most Valuable Lineman in the 1967 game.

Originally, Peters was drafted by Baltimore in 1958, but the Colts were loaded with defensive linemen, including Gino Marchetti, Art Donovan, and Big Daddy Lipscomb. There was no room for a raw 220-pounder from San Francisco State. Peters was cut and returned to California, where he played semipro football for the Salinas Packers.

Peters made only $100 a game with the Packers, but he caught the eye of a scout who recommended him to Cleveland coach Paul Brown. Peters was signed for $7,500 and played four seasons with the Browns. He was traded to Detroit in 1963, and he replaced Alex Karras when the All-Pro tackle was suspended by the NFL for betting on games. The following year, with Karras coming back, the Lions were willing to deal Peters, so they swapped him to the Eagles.

Peters performed well for the Eagles, but the team struggled through most of those six seasons. As Peters saw his career winding down, he felt frustrated. In 1969 he told William Speers of the *Philadelphia Inquirer*, "There's a saying around the league that you haven't really played this game if you don't have the scars and championship ring to prove it. Well, I have the scars. The championship is important because the day you win it, you know you're the greatest in the world."

Peters never did win a championship. At the end of the 1969 season, he asked for—and was granted—his release from the Eagles. He signed with Washington, hoping he might finally win a championship there with Vince Lombardi as the coach. Lombardi died that year, however, and the Redskins sank to a 6–8 finish. Peters retired as a player after the season, but he went into coaching and spent the next three decades as a line coach and defensive coordinator in the NFL.

PETE PIHOS
End

Ht: 6–1 • **Wt:** 215 • **College:** Indiana • **Years with the Eagles:** 1947–55 • **Birthplace:** Orlando, Florida • **Born:** October 22, 1923

Pete Pihos, "The Golden Greek," was one of the best all-around players in Eagles history. He was an All-Pro selection on offense (six times) and defense (once). He led the league in receiving three consecutive years (1953–55) and was voted into the Pro Football Hall of Fame in 1970.

"Pete was the greatest third-down receiver I've ever seen," said Vince McNally, the Eagles general manager during Pihos's career. "He also was a great blocker. But greatest of all his assets was the fact that every week he came to play."

Pihos was the rugged son of a Florida sponge diver. He attended the University of Indiana, where he became only the second player in college football (Bronko Nagurski was the first) to earn All-America honors at two different positions. Pihos played both fullback and end for the Hoosiers and finished his career with 138 points, a school record.

Pete Pihos

Pihos served 14 months in the European theater during World War II, earning five combat medals and a battlefield commission. "I served under General Patton," Pihos said. "We went from Normany [D-Day] right through the Battle of the Bulge. All you could do was say, 'I hope I live through today, and I hope I take care of my men the same way.' It made you grow up in a hurry."

The Eagles drafted Pihos in 1945 even though they knew he could not join them until he completed his military service. "I can wait for a player like Pihos," coach Greasy Neale explained.

Pihos joined the team in 1947, and in his first two seasons he caught 69 passes and scored 18 touchdowns. He added another touchdown in 1947 when he blocked a punt by Washington's Sammy Baugh. Later that season, Pihos blocked another punt to set up the first touchdown in the Eastern Division playoff game against Pittsburgh, a 21–0 Eagles victory.

In the 1949 NFL championship game, Pihos scored the first touchdown on a 31-yard pass from quarterback Tommy Thompson as the Eagles defeated the Los Angeles Rams 14–0 at the Los Angeles Coliseum. That was typical of Pihos: He always played his best in the big games.

In his book *Pro Football's 100 Greatest Players*, Hall of Fame coach George Allen called Pihos "the first great tight end." Allen wrote, "[Pihos] was no giant, but he was big enough. He was no sprinter, but he was fast enough. He was extremely tough and durable and he seemed to me an exceptionally smart player. He never gave an opponent anything."

Allen concluded, "Everyone wants to win, but few will sacrifice everything to do it. I got the impression Pete would do almost anything to win and I really respected him for that."

Pihos missed only one game in nine seasons. He led the Eagles in pass receptions eight of those nine seasons. The lone exception was 1952 when coach Jim Trimble, his former Indiana teammate, used him on defense. Pihos was named to the All-Pro team as a defensive end, but when Bud Grant jumped to the Canadian League in 1953, Pihos was switched back to offense and led the league with 63 catches for 1,049 yards (both career highs) and 10 touchdowns. Pihos led the NFL in receptions each of the next two seasons as well.

"Pihos is the best all-around end in the league," Trimble said. "I wish I had half a dozen like him."

"Pete could do everything," said Russ Craft, a defensive back on those Eagles teams. "He had those big paws, and he could catch a ball in a crowd better than anyone I've ever seen. Because he was a fullback in college, he knew how to run with the ball once he had it. He wasn't the fastest guy, but he was so strong, he'd just knock people over in the open field."

"Any defender who battles Pihos for a pass is bound to get the worst of it," said NFL Commissioner Bert Bell. "He plays it clean but very hard, and after he catches the pass, you would think he was a bulldozing fullback."

Neale put in a special play for Pihos: the middle screen, which some NFL teams still use today. On the play, Pihos would slide down from his end position and catch the screen pass from Thompson while the offensive line formed a wall in front of him. It was a risky play for Pihos, who had to make the catch with his back to the defense, but he was fearless enough to run it successfully.

Wrote Hugh Brown in the *Philadelphia Bulletin*: "For nine years, the followers of the Eagles have been watching the solid, confident, determined figure detach himself from a phalanx of opposing gladiators, whirl, cut, fake, then clutch to his broad bosom one of the most elusive of all objects: the prolate spheroid known as a football. Many of the catches bordered on the miraculous, or the incredible, the kind that only the Golden Greek could make."

Pihos played in six consecutive Pro Bowl games from 1951 through 1956. In Eagles history, only Chuck Bednarik (eight) and Reggie White (seven) have more Pro Bowls to their credit.

Pihos shocked the Eagles by retiring following the 1955 season. He still was at the top of his game at age 32, but the Eagles were coming off a discouraging 4–7–1 season, his first losing season as a professional, and his good friend Jim Trimble had been replaced as head coach by Hugh Devore. Several promising business opportunities beckoned, so Pihos decided it was a good time to hang up the pads.

"It wasn't my age that made me quit," Pihos said. "I've always kept in top condition, and I have never smoked or drank. I know I have a couple of years of football left, but I have reached that stage in life when a man cannot serve two masters. I think I've found myself in the business world. I can no longer afford to give five months to football. And I can no longer be a stranger to my family. Just the other day, my little girl asked me, 'Daddy, when are you going to stay home?'"

In a 1981 interview with Bill Fidati of the *Philadelphia Bulletin*, Pihos told a fascinating story about a chance meeting with baseball great Joe DiMaggio and how that influenced his decision to retire. Pihos told Fidati, "I ran into Joe DiMaggio once in Atlantic City. He said, 'Pete, when you retire, make sure you retire on top. Things will be better for you. Don't retire as a has-been.' I always remembered that. I could've played longer, but I chose to retire on top."

Fifty years after his retirement, Pihos still ranked third on the Eagles all-time list for pass receptions (373) and touchdown catches (61), and he was fourth in receiving yardage (5,619) and total touchdowns (63). It is quite a record when you consider he played in an era of 12-game regular seasons.

In a 1999 interview, Pihos talked about the modern NFL receivers and how frustrating it was for him to watch these millionaire athletes drop so many passes. Said Pihos: "I never dropped a pass, period. A few might have gone over my head or something like that. But if the ball hit my hands, it was caught. I wasn't the fastest guy in the world, but I was quick and I could get open. The big thing was, I caught the ball. If you can't do that, you shouldn't be out there."

BOSH PRITCHARD
Halfback

Ht: 5–11 • **Wt:** 165 • **College:** VMI • **Years with the Eagles:** 1942–51 • **Birthplace:** Windsor, North Carolina • **Born:** September 10, 1919 • **Died:** November 7, 1996

His name was Abisha Pritchard, but Eagles fans remember him as "Bosh." He was the jackrabbit-quick halfback who played alongside Steve Van Buren when the Eagles won their back-to-back NFL championships in 1948–49.

Pritchard's speed was the perfect complement to Van Buren's power. When opposing defenses stacked the line to stop Van Buren, quarterback Tommy Thompson would simply pitch the ball to Pritchard going wide, and the result was usually a big gain. Pritchard had a 77-yard touchdown run

Bosh Pritchard

Pritchard graduated from VMI in 1942 and signed with the Cleveland Rams for $225 a game. The Rams traded him to the Eagles, where he played only six games before joining the Navy. During his service hitch, Pritchard played football for the semi-pro San Francisco Bombers. At halftime, he sang with the band. "The Crooning Halfback," that was his billing.

Pritchard rejoined the Eagles in 1946. Coach Greasy Neale would not let him sing at halftime in Philadelphia, so Pritchard did most of his performing after the games. He didn't care where. Anyplace that had a microphone and an audience would do. And if they didn't have a microphone, well, that was okay, too.

"We'd go into a club and we'd take bets on how long it would be before Bosh was up on the bandstand," halfback Russ Craft said. "Actually, he was a pretty good singer, but we needled him something awful."

"I was the team funny man," Pritchard said. "Today, I guess they'd call me a flake. But Greasy encouraged it, particularly before games. He said I kept the boys loose. I'd get on the team bus and I'd say, 'All right, all together now …' And I'd start singing the VMI fight song. All the guys would laugh and boo. That's how we'd get ready to play."

Pritchard was traded to the New York Giants midway through the 1951 season, but he played only five games with the Giants and retired. He became the color analyst on the Eagles TV network.

About his given name: Abisha (pronounced a-BY-sha) is a name from the Bible. It also was the name of Pritchard's uncle. "He told my mother that if she named me after him, he'd buy me my first pair of long pants," Pritchard said. "He never did buy me those pants."

MIKE QUICK
Wide Receiver

Ht: 6–2 • **Wt:** 190 • **College:** North Carolina State • **Years with the Eagles:** 1982–90 • **Birthplace:** Hamlet, North Carolina • **Born:** May 14, 1959

In the 1982 draft, the Eagles had their eyes on a wide receiver, but it was not Mike Quick. The Eagles wanted Clemson's Perry Tuttle, who ran the 40-yard dash in 4.4 seconds. But the Buffalo Bills wanted Tuttle, too, so they traded up in the first round to take him with the 19th overall selection.

The Eagles, who had the 20th pick, were blindsided by the Bills and left scrambling for a Plan B. They still wanted a receiver, so they went with their second choice, Mike Quick of North Carolina State. As it turned out, the Bills did the Eagles a huge favor. Tuttle was a bust, catching just 25 passes in a three-year NFL career, while Quick became one of the best players in Eagles history.

"Perry was a step faster than me," said Quick, who ran the 40 in 4.6 seconds, "and Clemson threw the ball a lot more than we did, so he had better numbers. But I wasn't worried. The scouts are smart. They look at individuals. I knew I'd get my shot. The Eagles may have liked Perry better, but they liked me enough to take me in the first round. It all worked out."

Quick played nine seasons for the Eagles and was voted into five consecutive Pro Bowls (1984–88). In those five seasons, Quick led all NFL players in touchdown catches (53), and he was third in receiving yardage (5,437) behind only future Hall

against Washington in 1949, and that stood as the team's longest run from scrimmage until Leroy Harris broke off an 80-yard run in Green Bay in November 1979.

"I was small, but I wasn't afraid of being tackled, and I was never hurt being tackled," said Pritchard, who grew up in Hopewell, Virginia, and was nicknamed "The Hopewell Hurricane." "I was really only hurt one time, and that was when I went out of bounds and fell over one of my teammates."

In the Eagles' two championship seasons, Pritchard had 201 rushing attempts for 1,023 yards, an average of five yards per carry. He scored 13 touchdowns in the two seasons.

"Even though players are bigger and faster today, I feel Steve and I could run with anybody today," Pritchard said in a 1980 interview. "But because I was so small, they probably wouldn't let me play … I used to cut back against the grain, a lot like Wilbert Montgomery does now. You'll find most of your backs who are able to pull off the long runs are able to cut back.

"It's such a different game now. Our tackles averaged 220 pounds. Today, they've got fullbacks who weigh 250. These players work out with weights all year. Our coaches wouldn't let us lift weights. They said the weights made you muscle-bound. Of course, no one ever said that about me."

Pritchard was a dangerous kick returner. In 1947 the Eagles and Pittsburgh Steelers finished the regular season with identical 8–4 records. They had a playoff to decide which team would win the Eastern Division title and play for the NFL championship. Pritchard made the big play, breaking a 79-yard punt return for a touchdown as the Eagles defeated the Steelers, 21–0.

Mike Quick

of Famers James Lofton and Steve Largent. Buddy Ryan, the Eagles coach, said, "I wouldn't trade Quick for any of those guys. For my money, he's the best receiver in football."

Quick's rookie season, 1982, was interrupted by the players' strike, so he played nine games and caught just 10 passes. But the following year he led the league with 1,409 receiving yards, which also established a single-season team record. That same year, Quick tied Tommy McDonald's club record with 13 touchdown catches and averaged 20.4 yards on his 69 receptions.

"Mike has deceptive speed," said cornerback Herman Edwards, who covered Quick every day in practice. "He's very smooth, and he runs with those long strides that lull you to sleep. You don't realize how fast he's moving until he is right on top of you. Then it's too late, because with the next step, he's past you."

"I run with the same motion at full speed as I do when I'm just starting, and guys say it's hard to key on me," Quick told Jim Kaplan of *Sports Illustrated*. "What's important are good, disciplined routes and a knack for catching the ball. A lot of guys aren't burners, but they can catch in traffic. Look at Fred Biletnikoff."

Quick's only fault was his timing. He joined the Eagles as the Dick Vermeil era was winding down, and his prime years ended just as the team was bouncing back under Buddy Ryan. The Eagles finished with a losing record in each of his five Pro Bowl seasons, leaving Quick with a fistful of team records but little else.

"When you first come into the league, it's important that you make a name for yourself," Quick told Dave Spadaro of *Eagles Digest* in 1989. "But even then, in my younger days, winning was the most important thing. You're always part of a team effort to win. That's the bottom line. Without that, there isn't total satisfaction."

In 1988 things were coming together. The Eagles were on their way to the playoffs for the first time in Quick's career, and he was peaking at age 29. In Week 5, Quick made a spectacular one-handed catch against Houston, but when he hit the artificial turf, two Oilers landed on his left leg. Quick suffered a fractured fibula and was lost for the season.

The next year Quick played just six games before going down with a knee injury. In 1990 he lasted four games before he was sidelined again. He was forced to retire after that season, having played just 18 games in his final three seasons. Prior to sustaining those injuries, Quick was on a Hall of Fame pace, averaging 62 catches, 1,087 yards, and 10.3 touchdowns in his five Pro Bowl seasons, one of which was shortened by the players strike in 1987.

At the time of his retirement, Quick ranked fourth on the Eagles all-time reception list (363), third in receiving yards (6,464) and touchdown catches (61). He had the most consecutive 100-yard receiving games in one season (four in 1983), and he was the first player in club history to have more than 1,000 yards receiving in three consecutive years.

Quick is perhaps best remembered for his 99-yard touchdown in overtime that gave the Eagles a 23–17 win over Atlanta in 1985. Quick ran a quick slant, caught the Ron Jaworski pass, split two Falcon defenders, and raced away to tie the record for longest pass play in NFL history.

For all of his accomplishments, Quick kept a low profile. He was a bachelor throughout his career and enjoyed his privacy. In many ways, he was still the quiet kid from tiny Hamlet, North Carolina, who, as a teenager, worked in the fields, picking tobacco and peaches to help support his mother and nine siblings.

In a 1983 interview Quick said:

I'm not playing football to be famous. I never approached it that way. When I came out [of college], I thought if I played one year, that means I'd have enough money to buy a home and then go to work like a normal person. I could have done fine. I'm pretty simple in my thinking sometimes.

[Pro football] has worked out far beyond my wildest dreams. I make a lot of money, a great living, and sometimes I feel like I'm stealing from the world. But I would never tell anybody to try to be a football player. Just have fun. If you're good enough, somebody will want you. In the meantime, remember, football is a game.

PETE RETZLAFF
Tight End–Wide Receiver

Ht: 6–1 • **Wt:** 215 • **College:** South Dakota State • **Years with the Eagles:** 1956–66 • **Birthplace:** Ellendale, North Dakota • **Born:** August 21, 1931

Pete Retzlaff is the greatest bargain in Eagles history. In 1956 general manager Vince McNally claimed Retzlaff on waivers when he was cut by the Detroit Lions. The Eagles paid $100 for Retzlaff's rights.

All he did was play 11 seasons in Philadelphia, earn five trips to the Pro Bowl, and help the Eagles win the NFL championship in 1960. That's a pretty nice return on such a modest investment.

"He is the best tight end in the league," Washington coach Bill McPeak once said. "No, make that the world."

Retzlaff was originally drafted by the Lions as a fullback, a 22nd-round pick from South Dakota State. The Eagles switched him to split end, and he blossomed into one of the game's finest receivers. Bill Campbell, the radio voice of the Eagles, described him as "a quiet, unassuming guy who possesses the body of a weight-lifter and the intense desire of a starving man."

"The best thing that happened to me was the trade for Norm Van Brocklin," Retzlaff said, referring to the 1958 deal that brought the future Hall of Fame quarterback to Philadelphia from the Los Angeles Rams. "The first year he was in camp, he was watching the receivers, and he said, 'You know, that Retzlaff runs patterns a lot like Elroy Hirsch.'

"That boosted my confidence tremendously. Elroy Hirsch was one of my idols. I loved to watch him play, and I knew he had tremendous success playing with Van Brocklin in Los Angeles. I thought, 'If the Dutchman said that, I guess I must be okay.'"

In his first two seasons with the Eagles, playing a part-time role, Retzlaff caught just 22 passes, but once Van Brocklin arrived, Retzlaff's career took off. In 1958 he caught 56 passes to tie Baltimore's Raymond Berry for the league lead. In 1960 he led the Eagles with 46 catches for 826 yards, an 18.0-yard average, as they rode their passing attack to the world championship.

"Pete was a great technician," said Tom Brookshier, the former Eagles cornerback. "He worked for hours on running patterns, getting every step exactly right. When you watched Pete on the field, it was like watching the [play] diagram come to life. He was so disciplined in his routes; that's why quarterbacks loved to throw to him."

It was Brookshier who nicknamed Retzlaff "the Baron." The origin: Several players, including Brookshier and Retzlaff, visited a military base to meet the troops and sign autographs. During the visit a rifle instructor asked the players if they would like to test their skill on the firing range. Retzlaff, who was an Army first lieutenant before playing in the NFL, accepted the offer. He fired nine bull's-eyes on nine shots.

The blond hair, the rifle, the bull's-eyes: Brookshier decided Retzlaff looked like a German marksman, a "Baron Von Somebody." Hence, the Baron. Today, almost half a century later, the name still resonates among Philadelphia's sports fans.

In 1964, Retzlaff switched from split end to tight end and helped redefine the position. Along with Mike Ditka in Chicago and John Mackey in Baltimore, Retzlaff was one of the new wave at tight end, skilled players who could put up big receiving numbers as well as block.

In 1965, Retzlaff caught 66 passes for 1,190 yards, an average of 18 yards per reception. He also scored a career-high 10 touchdowns. He was named NFL Player of the Year by the Maxwell Football Club and the Washington Touchdown Club. He also won the Wanamaker Award that year as the outstanding athlete in Philadelphia.

Berry called Retzlaff's 1965 season "arguably the best season a tight end ever had." Berry made a film reel of Retzlaff's '65 season so he could study his moves. Berry was stunned

Pete Retzlaff

when Retzlaff said he played hurt most of that season. He had a heel injury that kept him from practicing. Retzlaff would rest the foot all week, then take three shots of novocaine on Sunday so he could play the game.

"I ended up with 21 holes in my heel," Retzlaff said. "It wasn't fun. After the season, I thought about resigning. I guess most players my age do."

"Nobody questioned that Retzlaff was the best tight end in the business," wrote Sandy Grady in the *Philadelphia Bulletin*. "He had the muscle to block the 260-pound tackle … but it was really the defensive back on a Retzlaff pass pattern who stayed goggle-eyed. The comment was always the same from the 25-year-old sprinter assigned to handle Retzlaff: 'He's the toughest in the league to cover. He's invented moves I don't understand yet.'"

Off the field, Retzlaff helped establish the NFL Players Association and was twice elected president. He carried the players' battle for benefits, such as improved health and accident insurance, more pay for exhibition games, and a better retirement plan. Retzlaff stood up to the owners at a time when it was still considered risky business to do so.

Retzlaff retired following the 1966 season after catching 40 passes for 653 yards, a 16.3-yard average. At the time, he held virtually every Eagles receiving record, including most catches (452), most yards (7,412), most catches in a season (66), and most yards in a season (1,190). The team honored him by retiring his number 44, and he walked away as one of the most popular players in Eagles history.

"In 11 years, I can only remember being booed once," Retzlaff said. "That was in 1958 when I dropped three passes in a row, all in the end zone. Van Brocklin had to settle for three points, and I got the boos.

"Actually, the great relationship and great acceptance given to me by the fans had something to do with my retirement. At this point, I'd hate to let them down, and if I continued to play, sooner or later, I'd reach the point where I couldn't get the job done. I couldn't let that happen."

Retzlaff told coach Joe Kuharich prior to the final game of the 1966 season, the Playoff Bowl against Baltimore, that it was likely his last game. But Retzlaff said it did not sink in until a month later, when he was driving through Philadelphia and stopped at a traffic light near Franklin Field.

"I just looked at Franklin Field and I had a strange feeling," he told Gordon Forbes of the *Philadelphia Inquirer.* "I knew I was through then. I knew that Franklin Field would be no more than a memory."

Sandy Grady wrote a glowing tribute to Retzlaff upon his retirement. In part, it reads: "The mind's lens sees Retzlaff crouching, then fighting out of the linebacker's grasp, then the No. 44 shirt tilting downfield, shoulders bulldog-low. There is a head bob, a foot planted to the outside, freezing a cornerback for an instant and Pete careening into the middle, snatching a ball in the mob's flurry, then knocking down people like bowling pins."

After hanging up his uniform, Retzlaff spent two years as a full-time sportscaster for WIP radio and WCAU television. In 1969, when Leonard Tose bought the Eagles from Jerry Wolman, he hired Retzlaff as his general manager. Retzlaff's career in the front office was less successful than his career on the field. After four losing seasons, Retzlaff resigned as general manager in December 1972 and went into private business.

JESS RICHARDSON
Defensive Tackle

Ht: 6–2 • **Wt:** 265 • **College:** Alabama • **Years with the Eagles:** 1953–61 • **Birthplace:** Philadelphia • **Born:** August 18, 1930 • **Died:** June 17, 1975

The Eagles' 1960 championship season had special meaning for Jess Richardson because he was the only Philadelphia high school product on the team. The man they called "the Roxborough Rock" grew up in the East Falls section of the city, just a few blocks from the Kellys. He knew Grace well enough to call her by her first name, even after she became an Oscar-winning actress and the princess of Monaco.

So being a defensive stalwart on the Eagles team that rolled through a 10–2 regular season and then defeated Green Bay 17–13 for the NFL championship was the biggest thrill of Richardson's career.

"You don't know how much all this excitement, this winning means to me," Richardson told Sandy Grady of the *Philadelphia Bulletin.* "I was an Eagles fan when I was just a kid and used to sneak into the park to see Van Buren and Bednarik play. One of my biggest thrills was when Al Wistert, the old Eagle tackle, came to our Roxborough High School banquet and presented me with a little gold trophy. I still have it."

Richardson started his career as a fullback at Roxborough High, but when he went the wrong way on his first rushing

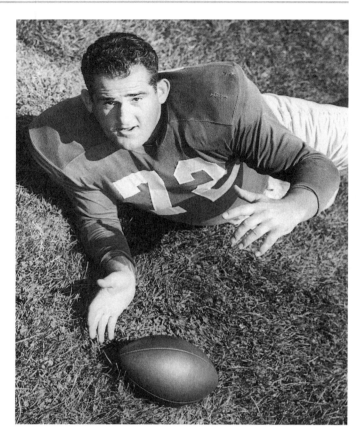

Jess Richardson

attempt, coach Moe Weinstein wisely moved him to the line. Richardson played well enough to earn a scholarship to Alabama, where he starred on a Crimson Tide team that routed Syracuse, 61–6, in the 1953 Orange Bowl.

The Eagles selected him in the eighth round of the '53 draft. At the time, the team still had Bucko Kilroy, Vic Sears, and Mike Jarmoluk in the middle of the defensive line, but their careers were winding down. Coach Jim Trimble saw Big Jess as the cornerstone of the line that would take the Eagles into the future.

"He's one of those big, jovial, awkward-appearing guys," Trimble said, "but on the field, he's mean, and that's what it takes in this league."

"Jess was mean, and he'd really bust guys," said Ed Khayat, who played alongside Richardson. "But off the field, he was a gentle guy. He loved the theater and poetry. Boy, he could quote you Longfellow all day. It seems like a contradiction, doesn't it? Someone that big and tough, but inside he was kind and gentle."

Richardson missed only one game in nine seasons with the Eagles. He was not, as Tom Brookshier once noted, "a pretty player." He was more of a mauler than a technician, but he was hard to move, especially in short yardage or near the goal line.

"A team might run against us for a while and he'd look horrible," Brookshier said. "But then it came to third and seven and he'd leapfrog over his man and tackle somebody for a two-yard loss. He'd grab the guy by the shirt or inhale him or swallow him up. We called him Captain Easy. He had a face that looked like a car coming down Broad Street with both fenders dented. But he was one of the best big-play tackles I ever saw."

Richardson never wore a face mask. His nose took a pounding, but as he once pointed out, "I was never what you'd call handsome anyway."

Following the 1961 season, Richardson was released, and he signed with the Boston Patriots of the American Football League. He played three seasons with the Patriots, then stayed on as an assistant coach. When Khayat became head coach of the Eagles, he hired Richardson to coach the defensive line. When the Eagles collapsed in 1972, finishing 2–11–1, Richardson was fired along with the rest of the coaching staff.

Tragically, Richardson died just three years later of kidney disease. He was ill for more than a year, taking daily dialysis treatments at Temple Hospital. Attempts to find a kidney donor failed, and Richardson died at his parents' home in East Falls in June 1975. He was 44 years old.

"When I heard the news, I was shocked," said Norm Van Brocklin, who quarterbacked the Eagles to the championship in 1960. "What will I remember about him? His great sense of humor, he was the kind of guy who was easy to like, comfortable to be around.

"I'll tell you, with ol' Jess, every day was Christmas and every night was New Year's Eve."

JERRY ROBINSON
Linebacker

Ht: 6–2 • **Wt:** 225 • **College:** UCLA • **Years with the Eagles:** 1979–84 • **Birthplace:** San Francisco, California • **Born:** December 18, 1956

In 1979 the Eagles had a first-round pick in the college draft for the first time in six years. Head coach Dick Vermeil knew he could not afford to make a mistake, so he was thrilled to find Jerry Robinson still on the board when the Eagles' turn finally came, 21 picks into the draft.

"As much as there can be a sure thing [in a draft], Jerry Robinson is a sure thing," Vermeil said.

He knew Robinson well, having recruited him for UCLA four years earlier. He was so sure Robinson would be a top-10 pick, he did not even bother to work him out prior to the draft. Vermeil said, "We'd love to get you, but I don't think we'll have a chance. It would take a miracle." Robinson replied, "Well, coach, miracles do happen." So it did for Robinson and the Eagles.

Vermeil originally recruited Robinson for UCLA as a wide receiver, but switched him to defense midway through his freshman year. Vermeil left UCLA for the Eagles after that season, but Robinson blossomed as a linebacker. He became the first three-time All-America since Doak Walker (1947–49). He set the school record for tackles and returned three of his four interceptions for touchdowns. He is one of only six players in UCLA football history to have his number (84) retired.

"When Coach Vermeil went to the Eagles, I thought, 'That's where I want to play my pro ball,'" Robinson said. "I was recruited by a lot of coaches, but I went to UCLA because of Coach Vermeil. He talked to me directly. He didn't try to fill my mind with a lot of hogwash. When I was looking ahead to this [draft], I kept thinking: 'Let it be Philadelphia.'"

"Jerry has such tremendous quickness, he goes from sideline to sideline with ease," Vermeil said. "Once he spots the football, he has outstanding acceleration to the point of attack.

And when he gets to the ball, he makes things happen. He'll fit right in with [Bill] Bergey and those guys."

A hamstring pull slowed Robinson in his first training camp, so he opened the 1979 season as a backup. But when Bergey went down with a knee injury in Week 10, Robinson slipped into that inside linebacker spot the way Christie Brinkley slips into designer jeans. The fit was perfect, the effect lovely to behold. He was all over the field, making tackles and earning NFL Defensive Rookie of the Year honors.

The following year, when Bergey came back, Robinson moved to outside linebacker where he made 99 tackles and two interceptions and returned a fumble 59 yards for a touchdown against Washington. He was named first-team All-NFC by UPI as he helped the Eagles win the conference title and a trip to Super Bowl XV.

Tackle Stan Walters recalled one play that epitomized Robinson's talents: "Tony Dorsett was running away from Jerry's side. I saw number 78 (Carl Hairston) and number 55 (Frank LeMaster) pursuing, then this flash of green went by. It was so fast, I couldn't even see the number. He nailed Dorsett, and then I saw it was number 56. That's what Jerry will be to me from now on, The Green Flash."

"There are two different kinds of linebackers, reckless ones and ones who play under control," Robinson said. "I like to think I'm one of the second ones. I get reckless sometimes, but most of the time, I like to react to what's going on in front of me. It used to be that linebackers were big, mean, and aggressive. Now the league is going to smaller, quicker people at that position. I'm not very big, but I do think I'm aggressive."

Robinson was shifted to inside linebacker in 1982 and stayed there for the next three seasons, leading the team in tackles every year. In 1985, with the club in a rebuilding mode under new owner Norman Braman, Robinson was traded to the Los Angeles Raiders for a second-round draft pick. Robinson played seven more seasons with the Raiders, finally retiring in 1992.

TIM ROSSOVICH
Defensive End–Linebacker

Ht: 6–4 • **Wt:** 240 • **College:** Southern California • **Years with the Eagles:** 1968–71 • **Birthplace:** Palo Alto, California • **Born:** March 14, 1946

Tim Rossovich is best remembered as the wild-eyed, bushy-haired free spirit who ate glass and livened up parties by setting himself on fire. What is sometimes forgotten is the fact that he was a first-round draft pick in 1968 who displayed real promise as a defensive end and linebacker before a training-camp holdout ended his Eagles career in 1972.

"Tim was tremendously quick for a big man," said Gary Pettigrew, who played alongside Rossovich on the Eagles defense and shared an apartment with him. "I recall him playing against Bob Brown [then with the Rams] who was one of the best linemen ever, and Tim was beating him inside, beating him outside; it was amazing. Tim had a lot of talent, and that was sometimes overshadowed by his off-the-field antics."

In many ways, Rossovich was a product of his time, the psychedelic '60s, the age of long hair, acid rock, and rebellion. He balked when Eagles coach Ed Khayat ordered all players to shave their mustaches and cut their hair during the 1971 season. "He's wrong," Rossovich said. "He says it will help discipline. It will hurt discipline. Instead of talking about football, we're talking about mustaches and sideburns."

Rossovich went along with the policy, as did all the other players, but he resented it. The following summer, he and safety Bill Bradley refused to report to training camp in a contract dispute. General manager Pete Retzlaff, frustrated with Rossovich's attitude, ended the holdout by trading Rossovich to San Diego for a first-round pick in the 1973 draft. Bradley got the message and reported to camp.

Rossovich had excellent ability, which he demonstrated playing for the College All-Stars against the world champion Green Bay Packers in August 1968. In that game, Rossovich went against tackle Forrest Gregg, a future Hall of Famer, a man Vince Lombardi called the finest football player he ever coached, and Rossovich won the battle.

However, Rossovich joined the Eagles in a turbulent period as the team was losing, the ownership was changing, and there was no sense of direction. He was with the Eagles for four seasons, and in that time he played for three different head coaches. He was switched from defensive end to middle linebacker, where he never was quite as effective. He was more comfortable chasing down quarterbacks than he was dropping into zones and playing pass defense.

Off the field, however, Rossovich enjoyed himself thoroughly. Many of his stunts were a carryover from his days at Southern Cal, where he first set himself ablaze during a fraternity party. The secret, he said, was to wear two T-shirts. The outer one would burn, but the other would not. "But people are so amazed, they don't even see that," he explained. "All they see is the fire."

Rossovich had a haunting stare which, combined with his long hair, gave him the appearance of a football Rasputin. He was the subject of a 1971 *Sports Illustrated* cover story in which he told writer John Underwood, "I live my life to enjoy myself. I can't explain things I do much beyond that. I have more energy than I know what to do with. I can't sit around. I get bored. A lot of what I do is silly, trying to cheer other people up, to cheer myself up. To be funny. To get attention. That's probably the best reason, to get attention."

"We knew Tim was not some savage human being, but the opponents didn't know that," Pettigrew said. "People heard about him and all these things he did. I think it served as a way for him to become this feared athlete, but at the same time, have a good time."

Rossovich played two seasons with the Chargers and was released. He signed with the Philadelphia Bell of the World Football League, but when the WFL folded in 1975, Rossovich caught on briefly with the Houston Oilers before returning to California to launch a new career in Hollywood as an actor and stunt man.

JON RUNYAN
Offensive Tackle

Ht: 6–7 • **Wt:** 330 • **College:** Michigan • **Years with the Eagles:** 2000– • **Birthplace:** Flint, Michigan • **Born:** November 27, 1973

Jon Runyan was the first big-money free agent signed by Eagles head coach Andy Reid. The massive tackle had just played in

Super Bowl XXXIV for Tennessee, and Reid felt he was worth the investment of $30 million over six years.

"In addition to being a very fine player, Jon brings an attitude to an offensive line," Reid said. Asked to describe that attitude, Reid smiled and said, "Toughness. Jon is an aggressive guy, and that tends to rub off on the other guys."

Runyan took over at right tackle and did not miss a start in his first six seasons with the Eagles. By the end of the 2004 season, Runyan had extended his streak of consecutive games to 144 (including postseason) dating back to his days with the Titans and Houston Oilers. It was the fourth-longest consecutive-game streak among active players.

Runyan played through nagging injuries in 2004, including a pulled groin muscle that had him listed as "questionable" for the Baltimore game in Week 8. But Runyan took the field for that game, just as he did for every game in his first nine seasons in the NFL.

"That's why they pay me the big bucks," Runyan said.

When Reid brought Runyan to Philadelphia prior to signing him in 2000, he took him to dinner at a downtown restaurant. Seated at the next table was John Chaney, the Hall of Fame basketball coach from Temple University. Reid asked Chaney if he would stop by the table and say hello to Runyan, who was an all-state high school basketball player in Flint, Michigan. Runyan turned down a basketball scholarship to Michigan State to play football at Michigan.

"I walked over to the table," Chaney recalled, "and when [Runyan] stood up, I couldn't believe it. I thought, 'This is the biggest man I've ever seen.' He looked as big as Shaq [O'Neal]. When we shook hands, his fingers wrapped all the way up my arm. I thought, 'I should be recruiting this young man for my team instead of Andy recruiting him for his.'"

At 6–7 and 330 pounds, Runyan has the size for basketball, but his temperament is better suited for football. He enjoys hitting people and knocking them to the ground, which he did well enough to earn a trip to the Pro Bowl following the 2002 season.

Runyan told Shannon Ryan of the *Philadelphia Inquirer*:

That's all about being physical. The more you push on somebody, the more they're worried about you. The more they're worried about you, the less they're thinking about what they have to do … Not that you're going to try to hurt them, but you're trying to rough them up like a bully would do.

There's a point of blocking people and a point of finishing people. If you're always finishing people, that guy—whether he's going to make the tackle or he's the second or third guy in on a tackle—he's peeking out of the side of his helmet to find you. Sooner or later, they're going to start missing those tackles because they're not concentrating on what they're supposed to be doing.

Coming to the Eagles forced Runyan to change his game. His size and strength were ideally suited for the Tennessee offense, which was built around the power running of Eddie George. With the Eagles, Runyan had to adapt to the West Coast offense, which meant less run blocking and more pass protection, less brute force and more finesse. It frustrated Runyan at times—he openly admits he wishes Reid called more running plays—but he has performed well week after week.

"It's all about winning games," Runyan said, "and we've won a lot of games."

JOE SCARPATI
Safety

Ht: 5–10 • **Wt:** 185 • **College:** North Carolina State • **Years with the Eagles:** 1964–69, 1971 • **Birthplace:** Brooklyn, New York • **Born:** March 5, 1943

Vince Lombardi did not make many mistakes as coach of the Green Bay Packers, but he made one in 1964 when he cut a rookie free agent named Joe Scarpati. Lombardi liked Scarpati's spirit, but he looked at the kid's small frame and wobbly knee and decided he would never last in the NFL.

As it turned out, Scarpati lasted seven seasons, the first six with the Eagles, who claimed him on waivers after he was released in Green Bay and later in Minnesota. Tight end Pete Retzlaff recalled seeing Scarpati come onto the practice field for the first time.

"When I took a look at his size, my first reaction was 'This will be easy,'" Retzlaff said. "Then when I ran against him, I found out that I couldn't get rid of him."

"It came down to the last spot on the roster," coach Joe Kuharich said. "Who would be the 40th guy? I spent two hours in a hotel room, debating it with the staff: 'Do we keep Scarpati, or do we let him go?' He wasn't that big or fast, but everything we asked him to do, he did it. In the end, we just decided he had earned the chance to show us what he could do in the regular season. It was one of the best decisions we ever made."

Scarpati worked his way into the starting lineup at free safety, easing out veteran Don Burroughs, who retired following the 1964 season. It was quite a contrast, going from the 6–4 Burroughs to the undersized Scarpati, but the two men had one thing in common, and that was a nose for the football. By the time Scarpati completed his first six seasons with the Eagles, he ranked second to Burroughs on the club's all-time interception list.

Scarpati had 24 interceptions, and his 182 return yards (on eight interceptions) led the NFL in 1966. But he is best remembered for a fumble recovery—an outright theft is more accurate—that saved a 24–23 win over Dallas at Franklin Field. On the play, Scarpati stole the football from the Cowboys' Dan Reeves after he caught a pass at the Eagles 13-yard line with Dallas in position to win the game with an easy field goal.

In addition to his ball-hawking skills, Scarpati also was an active, aggressive tackler. Line coach Brad Ecklund once said that in doing his scouting reports, he only bothered to put numbers on two defensive backs: Cardinals safety Larry Wilson, a future Hall of Famer, and Scarpati.

"They were the only backs I listed as primary tackling threats," Ecklund said. "They made as many tackles in a game as anyone on the field."

"I get a kick out of tackling a guy hard or breaking up a pass or intercepting one," Scarpati said. "I consider myself the most fortunate guy in the world just to be playing. When I was let go twice, I was back at my parents' house, thinking my football career was over. Then Mr. Kuharich called and asked if I was interested in going to the Eagles camp. Interested? I almost jumped through the phone.

"I just have a love to play this game," he said. "I know that sounds corny, but I get a great deal of satisfaction just practicing."

In 1970 the Eagles traded Scarpati to New Orleans for guard Norman Davis and safety Bo Burris. Scarpati played only one season with the Saints, but he became a part of football history that year as the holder on Tom Dempsey's NFL-record 63-yard field goal. "That was a great experience," Scarpati said. "I could never regret having gone to New Orleans just for that one moment alone."

Scarpati re-signed with the Eagles for a brief return in 1971.

VIC SEARS
Tackle

Ht: 6–3 • **Wt:** 230 • **College:** Oregon State • **Years with the Eagles:** 1941–53 • **Birthplace:** Ashwood, Oregon • **Born:** March 4, 1918

Vic Sears played 13 seasons for the Eagles, and, since he played both ways for most of his 131 regular-season games, it is believed he logged more actual minutes on the field than any other player in franchise history.

Sears was a rugged lineman who played offensive and defensive tackle and earned All-Pro mention four times. As the Eagles were going for their second consecutive NFL championship in 1949, coach Greasy Neale called Sears the team's most valuable defensive lineman.

"Sears has done the best job of all the last two years," Neale told Dick Cresap of the *Philadelphia Bulletin*. "He's not as spectacular as [Al] Wistert, but then Wistert is an open tackle. That is, he can be handled when the play is run straight at him. He's

Vic Sears

not as big as Sears. But Sears is just as tough when the play heads directly at him as he is when they're trying to go around. There's never any doubt on plays into our left side. We know Sears will make the tackle."

Sears' durability was remarkable. In 1952, when he was in his 12th NFL season, only one player in the league had more years of service, and that was Washington's Sammy Baugh, who was in his 13th season. Baugh played quarterback and defensive back as well as punting, but he was not taking the same physical pounding as Sears, who played 60 minutes on the line each week.

Sears only missed a handful of games in his career. He was sidelined by a broken leg in 1944 and hospitalized in 1947 with stomach ulcers. But over his final six seasons with the Eagles, he started 71 of a possible 72 games.

On an Eagle defense that was known for its rough play (dirty, in the view of some opposing coaches), Sears was admired as a skillful athlete who played within the rules. Only once was he accused of dirty play, and that was when New York coach Steve Owens accused him of kneeing Giants quarterback Arnold Galiffa. However, Joe King of the *New York World Telegram* checked the films and absolved Sears of blame. It was Bucko Kilroy who landed on Galiffa, King wrote, and it did not appear deliberate in any way.

"The tall, quiet lineman [Sears] is emphatically not that type of football player," wrote Hugh Brown in the *Philadelphia Bulletin*. "He has never been known to foul out, not even under the bitterest provocation."

Sears announced his retirement following the 1952 season, but he was talked into coming back the following summer when the Eagles lost several of their younger linemen to military service. He took a leave of absence from his sales job and returned for one more year in the trenches.

"You'll have to pull me down out of the clouds," coach Jim Trimble said when informed that Sears agreed to come back. "Vic is one of the all-time greats in my book."

CLYDE SIMMONS
Defensive End

Ht: 6–6 • **Wt:** 280 • **College:** Western Carolina • **Years with the Eagles:** 1986–93 • **Birthplace:** Lanes, South Carolina • **Born:** August 4, 1964

Clyde Simmons played in the shadow of Reggie White, the dominant defensive end of his era and a future Hall of Famer. Reggie got most of the attention, while Clyde was generally overlooked. And that was fine with him.

"I prefer it that way," Simmons said. "I don't need to bother with that mess. I like my privacy."

Simmons was a brooding presence in the Eagles locker room. He seldom spoke or smiled. He often answered reporters' questions with a shrug. He was not rude or hostile; he just preferred to keep his distance. Most of the time, he let his play speak for him.

In eight seasons with the Eagles, Simmons had 76 and a half sacks. Only White, with 124 sacks, ranks ahead of Simmons in the years since 1982 when sacks became an official statistic. Simmons led the NFL with 19 sacks in the 1992 season. That was just two sacks shy of the Eagles' single-season record set by White in 1987.

Clyde Simmons

"It's a shame; Clyde should be an All-Pro, but he's a victim of playing on a line with Reggie White," said Eagles defensive coordinator Bud Carson. "He's the smartest defensive end I've ever been around. You don't fool him. You run a bootleg to his side and you earn it because he's not going to make a mistake."

Simmons set an Eagles record with four and a half sacks in one game, a 24–0 rout of Dallas on September 15, 1991. The Eagles set a team record with 11 sacks of quarterback Troy Aikman in that game. That season, Simmons was one of three Eagles defensive linemen in the Pro Bowl, joining White and tackle Jerome Brown.

Simmons was a ninth-round pick in the 1986 draft. He was passed over by many pro scouts because he played at a small school (Western Carolina) and was rather small himself. He weighed only 240 pounds as a senior, but he still recorded 97 tackles and eight sacks to earn Division 1-A All-America honors.

Eagles coach Buddy Ryan found Simmons while studying tape prior to the draft. "We knew we weren't gonna draft a lineman high," Ryan said, "so we were looking for a guy we might be able to get late. I was looking for a guy with some tools. I saw Clyde's speed and knew we had something."

Simmons spent most of his rookie season on special teams and in the weight room. He added 20 pounds of muscle with 10 more to follow. In 1987, Ryan dealt veteran defensive end Greg Brown to Atlanta and promoted Simmons to the first unit. Simmons started every game, other than the 1987 strike games, for the next seven seasons.

In 1989, Simmons was named the Eagles' Most Valuable Defensive Player. He led the club with 15 and a half sacks, and he led all linemen with 135 tackles. In Week 13, Simmons intercepted a Phil Simms pass and returned it 60 yards for a touchdown in a 24–17 win.

In 1991, Simmons missed the entire training camp in a contract dispute. He did not join the team until the eve of the league opener, yet he had another impressive season, recording 13 sacks and 115 tackles. He was voted into his first Pro Bowl.

"Clyde is on a par with anybody in the league, he's come that far," Reggie White said. "The first time I saw him, he was this tall, skinny kid. Now he's bulked up, and that made the difference in his game."

Rather than resent White for getting so much of the acclaim, Simmons used him as a source of inspiration.

"Reggie is still the best," Simmons said. "We've worked with each other and pushed each other so much that we expect a lot out of each other. Without him, I don't know where I'd be."

JERRY SISEMORE
Tackle

Ht: 6–4 • **Wt:** 265 • **College:** Texas • **Years with the Eagles:** 1973–84 • **Birthplace:** Olton, Texas • **Born:** July 16, 1951

Jerry Sisemore is the classic laconic Texan. Big and strong, quiet as a summer night on the Panhandle.

"I was always told if you keep your mouth shut, people will never know how stupid you are," Sisemore told Stan Hochman of the *Philadelphia Daily News* in 1980. "Actually, I just feel nothing can be gained from opening your mouth in my position. Some times the other team will use the stories against you.

"But mostly I've never seen where publicity would help a situation. Not even at contract time. I honestly believe you get paid strictly on your performance."

Sisemore was a superb lineman: strong and smooth. He was not a massive tackle in the mold of a Bob Brown or Art Shell, but he had excellent technique. He would get inside on a bigger defensive end, such as Ed (Too Tall) Jones of Dallas, and control him with his arms and shoulders. He was rarely off his feet.

Eagles tight end Keith Krepfle, who played next to Sisemore for seven seasons, called him "the best blocker I've ever seen."

Defensive end John Matuszak played with Sisemore in the 1973 College All-Star Game and played against him in Super Bowl XV as a member of the Oakland Raiders. Matuszak did not shower praise on many people, but he spoke highly of Sisemore.

"The first time I ever saw Jerry," Matuszak said, "I was watching film of a Texas-Miami game. There was a 70-yard run and [Sisemore] was right downfield next to the guy carrying the ball. That's why he's the kind of player I like, because he never gives up."

Sisemore was an All-America tackle at the University of Texas. The Eagles selected him with the third overall pick in the 1973 draft. He was the starting right tackle as a rookie, and he went on to start 127 consecutive games, most of them at tackle, although he did spend two seasons at guard (1976–77).

Sisemore regularly scored the highest grades among Eagle linemen when coaches reviewed the films. According to head coach Dick Vermeil, Sisemore did not allow a sack for two full seasons. He was voted into the Pro Bowl in 1980 and '82, but his coaches and teammates felt he should have gone every year. His cause was harmed by the fact that he seldom spoke to the press and, as a result, received little publicity.

"I don't care about the Pro Bowl or individual awards," Sisemore once said. "If my teammates think I did a good job, that gives me all the satisfaction I need. If the coaches approve of my work, I'll probably keep my job and get paid. And if we win, I'm a happy man."

DAVE SMUKLER
Fullback

Ht: 6–1 • **Wt:** 225 • **College:** Temple • **Years with the Eagles:** 1936–39 • **Birthplace:** Gloversville, New York • **Born:** May 28, 1914 • **Died:** February 22, 1971

Dave Smukler was known as "Dynamite Dave," a powerful fullback who was bigger (6–1, 225) and stronger than many linemen of his era. He started his college career at Missouri but transferred to Temple, where he played three years under coach Glenn (Pop) Warner. Warner coached Jim Thorpe at Carlisle, and he considered Smukler the equal of Thorpe as a running back.

Following a 22–0 win over Villanova in 1934, Warner said, "Dave Smukler played as good a game as I ever saw in my 40 years of coaching. Jim Thorpe and Ernie Nevers never looked better than Smukler did on Saturday. If he develops in the next two years as he has this season, the football public will soon forget about Thorpe, Nevers, [Red] Grange, George Gipp, and other great backs."

While Smukler's career never reached those heights, he played well enough at Temple to attract the interest of the Eagles, who signed him in 1936. Smukler was the team's leading rusher in 1938 (96 carries, 313 yards) and 1939 (45 carries, 218 yards). He was the first Eagle to score on a kickoff return, 101 yards against Brooklyn in 1938. He also was the team's leading passer for three years, although he never had a season in which he threw more touchdown passes than interceptions.

The Eagles were the worst team in the league in those years, winning nine games in Smukler's four seasons. Frustrated with the losing and his salary, which was just $3,000 for the season, Smukler quit after four games in 1939.

"I'm fed up with the whole thing," Smukler was quoted as saying. He went back to his hometown of Gloversville, New York, to work for his brother Louis, cutting leather gloves. (What else would someone do in a town called Gloversville?)

The Eagles traded Smukler's rights to Detroit in 1940, just about the time Smukler enlisted in the Army. After he completed his military service, Smukler played two games with the Boston Yanks in 1944, carrying the ball twice for seven yards.

NORM SNEAD
Quarterback

Ht: 6–4 • **Wt:** 215 • **College:** Wake Forest • **Years with the Eagles:** 1964–70 • **Birthplace:** Halifax County, Virginia • **Born:** July 31, 1939

Norm Snead may have taken more verbal abuse than any player in Eagles history, but he holds no grudges. He played seven seasons in Philadelphia, most of it as the starting quarterback, and he was booed, often viciously, but he insists he never took it personally.

Norm Snead was not a fan favorite in Philadelphia.

"I thought the Philly fans were great," Snead said. "They were a lot like fans anywhere. If you played badly and the team lost, they booed. But if you played well, they let you know they appreciated it. Philadelphia is a passionate sports city. As an athlete, you have to be prepared to deal with both sides of that passion. It can be real good or real bad.

"Nobody likes to be booed, but it's not personal. At least, I never viewed it as personal. It's part of the business."

Snead did not have the best introduction to the Philadelphia fans, considering he arrived in an unpopular 1964 trade that saw the Eagles send Sonny Jurgensen, a future Hall of Fame quarterback, and cornerback Jimmy Carr to Washington for Snead and cornerback Claude Crabb. It was part of Joe Kuharich's makeover for the Eagles in his first year as head coach.

Though Jurgensen was coming off two poor seasons and was hampered by injuries, the Eagles fans still saw him as the better quarterback. As a result, they were quick to criticize Snead.

"I have always felt that Norman has never been in a situation where he was allowed to do all the things he could do," said Charley Johnson, who quarterbacked 15 seasons in the NFL and played against Snead dozens of times. "He can throw the ball anywhere on the field, and he has a sharp mind. He's never had the supporting cast, but you can't blame him for that."

Snead was Washington's No. 1 draft choice in 1961 after an All-America career at Wake Forest. The Redskins put him in the starting lineup as a rookie, and he took a terrible beating. The team won only one game, and Snead threw twice as many interceptions (22) as touchdown passes (11). Things were not much better the next two seasons as Snead threw 22 interceptions in 1962 and 27 in '63 before the trade to Philadelphia.

The Eagles had only one winning season during Snead's seven years, and that was 1966 when Kuharich rotated three quarterbacks: Snead, King Hill, and Jack Concannon. The Eagles won seven of their last nine games to finish 9–5 and qualify for the Playoff Bowl, a game between the second-place finishers in the Eastern and Western Conferences. The Eagles lost to Baltimore, 20–14, with Snead watching Hill and Concannon take turns running the offense. When the Eagles got the ball at the end with time for just one play, Kuharich told Snead, "Go in there and throw it as far as you can."

Snead was furious, but he did as he was told, heaving a desperation pass that fell incomplete.

After that season, Kuharich traded Concannon to Chicago for tight end Mike Ditka, and he installed Snead as the starter ahead of Hill. In 1967, Snead responded with his best season, completing 55 percent of his passes for 3,399 yards and 29 touchdowns, both career highs. But he suffered a broken leg in the first exhibition game in 1968, and things went downhill from there.

Following the 1970 season, the Eagles traded Snead to Minnesota for three draft picks and a journeyman tackle, Steve Smith. Snead was the Eagles' all-time leader in pass attempts (2,236), completions (1,154), passing yards (15,672), touchdown passes (111), and interceptions (124), but most people agreed it was time for a change.

"The fans' [negative] attitude toward Norman played a role in our decision," coach Jerry Williams said. "Hopefully, this move will prove beneficial for everyone."

Snead played seven games for Minnesota in 1971, but lost the starting job to a younger quarterback, Bob Lee, who led the Vikings to the playoffs. Snead was traded to the New York Giants the following year, then moved on to San Francisco in 1974, and finally back to the Giants for his last season, 1976. He played a total of 16 seasons, and he did reach the 30,000-yard passing plateau (30,797), which put him ahead of several Hall of Famers, including Norm Van Brocklin, Bart Starr, and Y. A. Tittle.

"It's a shame we never put it together in Philadelphia," Snead said. "It seemed like we were right on the verge a few times, then one or two key guys would go down with injuries. I enjoyed my time there, though. I remember playing at Franklin Field and riding the bus to River Field for practice. You'd have to say those were my prime years. I made a few stops after Philadelphia, but most of my memories are there."

JOHN SPAGNOLA
Tight End

Ht: 6–4 • **Wt:** 240 • **College:** Yale • **Years with the Eagles:** 1979–87 • **Birthplace:** Bethlehem, Pennsylvania • **Born:** August 1, 1957

When John Spagnola was a senior at Bethlehem Catholic High School, Chuck Bednarik was the guest speaker at the sports banquet.

"I was so impressed," Spagnola said. "Here was this legend, telling us about his life in pro football. It was really inspiring. It made me think how great it would be to do that someday."

Spagnola followed in Bednarik's footsteps: a Bethlehem boy who attended an Ivy League school (Yale) and starred for the Eagles. They were together at Super Bowl XV: Bednarik as an associate coach charting plays for Dick Vermeil and Spagnola as a second-year tight end, splitting time with Keith Krepfle.

"The years I played for the Eagles were wonderful," Spagnola said. "I look back on those days as a time when life could not have been any better. I played with a great bunch of guys, for a tremendous coach, and shared in some great moments. The win over Dallas [NFC championship game] and the joy of the fans, the whole city, is something I'll never forget."

Spagnola played eight seasons with the Eagles. He missed the entire 1983 season following neck surgery, but he came back to catch 65 passes the following year and 64 the next. He had 12 catches in one game against New Orleans (October 6, 1985), just two short of Don Looney's team record.

Spagnola formed an effective pairing with Mike Quick, who was an All-Pro deep threat. In 1985, Spagnola and Quick combined to set two club records: most receptions by two players (137) and most combined receiving yards (2,019, breaking a record previously shared by Hall of Famer Tommy McDonald and Timmy Brown).

Spagnola set the all-time receiving record at Yale (88 catches) and was a ninth-round pick by New England in the 1979 draft. However, the Patriots already had two good tight ends, Russ Francis and Don Hasselbeck.

"The head coach, Ron Erhardt, told me I was the best rookie in camp, then he said, 'But unless somebody gets hurt you're probably not going to make the team,'" Spagnola said. "It hurt my pride, and I could've quit right then, but I kept working to make myself the best player I could be. I thought if it didn't work out there, maybe I could play somewhere else."

The Patriots released Spagnola in the last cut of the preseason. The Eagles claimed him and activated him for the home opener. An hour before the game, Spagnola went onto the Veterans Stadium turf to warm up.

"There was a guy leaning over the railing, yelling at me," Spagnola recalled. "He was shouting, 'Spagnola, you're a bum. You're no good.' I thought, 'Geez, I haven't even played a down, and already they're booing me.' It wasn't the best of starts."

But Spagnola won over the fans with his knack for making tough catches in clutch situations. He developed an excellent chemistry with quarterback Ron Jaworski, who relied on Spagnola to make the right read and run the right route.

In 1987, when the NFL Players Association went on strike, Spagnola was the Eagles player representative. He was the voice of the veterans when they walked out and the owners signed replacements to play for three weeks during the regular season. It was a difficult time in which Spagnola became the lightning rod for the frustration of fans and management.

When the strike was settled and the veterans returned to play Week 6 against Dallas, Spagnola knew how he would be received.

"The fans identify this strike with two people: [owner] Norman Braman and me," Spagnola said. "Norman Braman won't be on the field Sunday, but I will be. That means I'll bear the brunt of the bad feeling."

Spagnola put that to rest in the best way possible: He caught two touchdown passes as the Eagles defeated the Cowboys, 37–20. "The first time I got in the end zone," he said, "all was forgiven."

DUCE STALEY
Running Back

Ht: 5–11 • **Wt:** 220 • **College:** South Carolina • **Years with the Eagles:** 1997–2003 • **Birthplace:** Tampa, Florida • **Born:** February 27, 1975

Duce Staley finished his career in Philadelphia as the third-leading rusher in Eagles history with 4,807 yards. Only Wilbert Montgomery (6,538) and Hall of Famer Steve Van Buren (5,860) have more yardage than Staley, who worked his way up from special teams to stardom.

"I'm proud of the fact that I overcame a lot," Staley said. "I work hard; I run hard. I think that's why the fans relate to me. I'm a blue-collar guy like them."

Staley was a third-round draft pick in 1997 and spent his rookie season as a backup to Ricky Watters. Staley carried the ball only seven times, but he led the team in kickoff returns (24.2 average) and special-teams tackles (15). In 1998, Staley became a starter and led the team in rushing (1,065 yards) and receiving (57 catches) despite playing half the season with a painful hernia.

In 1999, Andy Reid took over as head coach, and he ignored the public clamor to draft Ricky Williams, the Heisman Trophy–winning tailback, and used his first pick on quarterback Donovan McNabb. One reason Reid felt comfortable with the choice was his confidence in Staley. He felt Staley was a better

Duce Staley

fit for the West Coast offense than a power runner like Williams.

"Duce is so versatile," Reid said. "He can catch the football as well as run it. And he can run inside and outside. You don't see many backs his size running inside as well as he does."

That year, Staley rushed for 1,273 yards, the fourth-best rushing season in team history. Adding in his receiving totals (41 catches for 294 yards), Staley had 1,567 total yards, which was 40.9 percent of the Eagles total offense, the highest percentage for any individual player in the league. He became a crowd favorite in Philadelphia. Each time Staley lowered his shoulder and ran over a would-be tackler, the fans would call out, "Duuuuuuu-ce."

"Everybody thinks only big backs, guys like Jerome Bettis and Bam Morris, can dish out punishment," Staley said. "But when someone tries to tackle me, I try to take their head off. That's been my mentality since I came into the league. Why should the guy with the ball take the blows? If there's a collision, I'm gonna give as good as I get."

Staley opened the 2000 season with a career game, rushing for 201 yards on 26 carries in a 41–14 rout of Dallas. It was only the second time in team history that a back reached the 200-yard plateau. The other time it was done by Van Buren, who set the club record with 205 yards in a 1949 game against Pittsburgh.

But Staley's season ended just four weeks later when he suffered a severe injury that threatened his career. It was called a Lisfranc sprain, a dislocation of two bones in the right foot. It was named after Jacques Lisfranc, a surgeon attached to Napoleon's cavalry. He was the first to diagnose the injury, which most often occurred when riders were thrown from their horses and their feet stuck in the stirrups.

It is a serious injury for an athlete because it weakens the foot at the critical spot where the toes and foot come together. That is the area that takes the stress whenever a runner cuts, plants his foot, or pushes off. It ended the careers of some athletes and greatly reduced the effectiveness of others. It was feared Staley might never be the same.

But he pushed himself through a long rehabilitation and came back in 2001 as determined as ever. He led the team with 604 yards rushing and tied for the lead with 63 receptions as he won the Ed Block Courage Award presented by the NFL Players Association for his remarkable comeback. In 2002, Staley again led the team with 1,029 yards rushing, and he added 51 receptions.

In the 2003 season Reid went to a rotation system using three running backs: Staley, Brian Westbrook, and Correll Buckhalter. As a result, Staley's rushing attempts went down (96), but his production remained high. He finished the season with career highs in rushing average (4.8) and receiving average (10.6), and he ranked first among NFL backs in average yards per touch (6.4).

"Duce has really taken on his leadership role on this football team," Reid said. "He could've taken a very selfish approach toward this rotation that we have, but it's just the contrary. He's so supportive of those young guys, and he's doing a great job."

While Staley did not complain about the three-back setup, he didn't like it much either. He also was frustrated with Reid's play calling, which favored the pass over the run. After the Eagles lost the NFC Championship game to Carolina—a game in which Staley played very well, rushing for 79 yards—he indicated it probably was time to move on.

He said he had two regrets: one, the Eagles never made it to a Super Bowl in his seven seasons, and two, he had to leave the Philadelphia fans who treated him so warmly.

Staley signed a free-agent contract with Pittsburgh, and, as it turned out, the Steelers third preseason game was against the Eagles at Lincoln Financial Field. In the first quarter, Staley scored on a 14-yard run. As he crossed the goal line, he ran to the stands and handed the football to a youngster in the front row.

"Just my way of saying 'thanks,'" Staley explained.

ERNIE STEELE
Halfback

Ht: 6–0 • **Wt:** 185 • **College:** Washington • **Years with the Eagles:** 1942–48 • **Birthplace:** Bothell, Washington • **Born:** November 2, 1917

Ernie Steele was a swift, elusive player who excelled in all phase of the game: offense, defense, and special teams. In his seven NFL seasons, Steele averaged 9.6 yards every time he touched the ball.

He was particularly dangerous on punt returns. In his rookie season Steele led the NFL with a 26.4-yard average on punt returns. He was the first player in Eagles history to have more than 100 yards on punt returns in a single game. (He had 106 yards on two returns in a game against the world champion Chicago Bears.)

"As a boy, I used to run from my house to the store, which was four blocks away, and get some milk and have my mother time me," Steele told Dale Raley of the *Seattle Post-Intelligencer.* "When I was in grade school, I did something and the principal said he was going to give me the paddle. I said, 'If you can catch me, you can hit me.'"

Steele was a football, basketball, and track star at Highline High School in Seattle. He went to the University of Washington on a football scholarship, but he also worked as a laborer at a Seattle shipyard to help support his family. He led the Pacific Coast Conference in punt returns and was named second-team All-America. He was ranked in the nation's top ten for kick returns each of his final two seasons at Washington.

Steele was drafted by Pittsburgh, who traded his rights to the Eagles. As a rookie, he averaged 5.2 yards per rushing attempt, 16.3 yards on each pass reception, 26.4 yards on punt returns, 22.9 yards on kickoff returns, and 24.1 yards on interception returns. That is an average of 14.2 yards per touch.

What is surprising about that season is that Steele had 264 yards on 10 punt returns in the first seven games and did not return another punt for the rest of the year. The Eagles acquired halfback Bosh Pritchard in a midseason trade, and he took over the kick-return duties while Steele concentrated on defense.

Steele's 24 interceptions put him in the top five for the decade. Eight of those interceptions, one out of three, came against Washington's Sammy Baugh, the greatest passer of that era. Steele preserved the Eagles' 7–0 win in the 1948 NFL championship game, intercepting a pass by Chicago's Charlie Eikenberg on the final play.

Steele was en route to training camp the following summer, but he got as far as Montana, made a U-turn, and drove back to his home in Seattle. He had a family and a new restaurant and decided they needed him more than the Eagles, so he retired from football at age 31.

TOM SULLIVAN
Running Back

Ht: 6–0 • **Wt:** 190 • **College:** Miami • **Years with the Eagles:** 1972–77 • **Birthplace:** Jacksonville, Florida • **Born:** March 5, 1950 • **Died:** October 10, 2004

Tom Sullivan was elusive, on the field and off. He was a running back with obvious physical ability, but he had interests outside the game, such as painting and meditation, that set him apart.

"I try not to give an outright impression of what I'm doing," Sullivan once said. "In a lot of ways, I'm still trying to find myself."

Sullivan studied the paintings of Toulouse-Lautrec and the teachings of Mahara Ji, whom he called "the perfect master." As a rookie, he left Eagles training camp and drove to Stafford Springs, Massachusetts, where he spent a week living in his camper and eating the fish from a nearby lake. He did not tell the team he was leaving. The coaches assumed he quit, as rookies—especially late-round draft picks such as Sullivan—often do.

One week later he was back on the practice field, explaining, "I just needed to think things over."

Sullivan made the team as a 15th-round draft pick because the coaches recognized his talent, but they never did forgive him for walking out of camp. He spent most of the 1972 season on special teams. He had just 13 carries for a team that had only two rushing touchdowns all season.

The following year, when Mike McCormack took over as head coach, he saw number 25 on the practice field and asked, "Where was that guy last season?" He could not believe the NFL's worst rushing team could have kept such a gifted player on the bench. McCormack gave Sullivan a nickname ("Silky") and put him in the starting lineup, where he quickly flourished.

In the 1973 season Sullivan rushed for 968 yards, the most by an Eagles player since Steve Van Buren led the league with 1,146 yards in 1949. Sullivan had three 100-yard rushing games that season, quite a feat considering it had been four years since any Eagle had cracked 100 yards in a game.

Sullivan's most impressive performance that season was a 26-carry, 155-yard effort against Buffalo. It was the biggest day for an Eagles back since Timmy Brown rushed for 180 yards against St. Louis in 1965. After the game, the Bills' O. J. Simpson asked, "Who's that number 25? He sure can dance."

Sullivan's yardage totals declined each season after that, although in 1974 he rushed for 11 touchdowns, which at the time was the most rushing touchdowns in one season by any Eagle other than the great Van Buren.

Sullivan was phased out with the arrival of Wilbert Montgomery in 1977. He finished his career in Cleveland, playing just four games in 1978 before he was released. He was killed in an automobile accident in his native Florida on October 10, 2004.

BOBBY TAYLOR
Cornerback

Ht: 6–3 • **Wt:** 215 • **College:** Notre Dame • **Years with the Eagles:** 1995–2003 • **Birthplace:** Houston, Texas • **Born:** December 28, 1973

In the 1995 draft, the Eagles traded up in the second round to acquire Bobby Taylor, the All-America cornerback from Notre Dame. After years of watching Michael Irvin outmuscle and outjump their smaller cornerbacks, the Eagles felt they needed a player like Taylor, who had both the size and speed to match up with the 6–2, 205-pound Dallas receiver.

"This is the way the league is going," said Eagles coach Ray Rhodes, a former cornerback himself, who drafted Taylor. "You're seeing more and more receivers like [Irvin], big guys who know how to use their size. The only way to deal with it is to get your own big guys, but there aren't that many. We're lucky to get this kid."

Rhodes did not rush Taylor onto the field. He did not start him until the fifth week of his rookie season. But when Taylor did get on the field, he got everyone's attention. Fox TV analyst Jerry Glanville said, "[Taylor] has a great future. In three years, I haven't seen a rookie corner look this good."

Taylor's official coming-of-age moment was the 20–17 win over Dallas at Veterans Stadium on December 10. Most fans

Bobby Taylor

remember the Eagles defense stopping Emmitt Smith twice on fourth and one. But another highlight was the rookie Taylor covering the All-Pro Irvin and basically shutting him out. Irvin finished the game with three meaningless catches, and Taylor was named NFC Defensive Player of the Week.

When the Eagles went to the playoffs that season, they drew Detroit as their first-round opponent. The Lions had one of the NFL's most prolific passing attacks. Their top receiver, Herman Moore, led the league with 123 catches for 1,686 yards and 14 touchdowns. Rhodes assigned Taylor to cover the 6–4 Moore as the Eagles routed the Lions, 58–37. Again, Taylor was named NFC Defensive Player of the Week.

"I didn't look at it as a personal thing," Taylor said. "I was just happy we put a nice butt-whipping on the Lions. It was exciting to be in the playoffs my first year. I remember the veterans saying, 'You need to appreciate this because you don't get this opportunity every year.'"

Taylor learned the truth of that statement as the Eagles suffered through three consecutive losing seasons from 1997 through '99. If the team had one area of strength during that period, it was the defensive backfield, specifically the play of the cornerbacks, Taylor and Troy Vincent. And it was their talents that became the foundation of the defense that eventually turned the Eagles around.

Jim Johnson was hired as defensive coordinator under Andy Reid, and his scheme was built around the blitz. However, to make the blitz work, a team must have cornerbacks who can cover one-on-one. That frees up the linebackers and safeties to rush the quarterback. In Taylor and Vincent, the Eagles had a pair of corners who could handle that responsibility, and from 2000 through 2003, their defense allowed the fewest points in the NFL, an average of 15.5 per game.

Taylor was not a physical player, and fans sometimes criticized him for missing tackles, but he had superb coverage skills. With his rangy frame and long arms, he could blanket a receiver. In the 2002 divisional playoff, Taylor sparked the Eagles' 20–6 victory over Atlanta by intercepting a Michael Vick pass and returning it 39 yards for the game's first touchdown. That season, Taylor was voted into his first Pro Bowl.

The 2003 season was Taylor's ninth as an Eagle, giving him more consecutive years of service than anyone else on the roster. He missed nine games with a foot injury, but he returned for the postseason. The loss to Carolina in the NFC championship game marked the end of an era because it was the last game Taylor and Vincent would play for the Eagles. Both left in the off-season to sign free-agent contracts elsewhere, with Taylor signing in Seattle and Vincent in Buffalo.

HOLLIS THOMAS
Defensive Tackle

Ht: 6–0 • **Wt:** 305 • **College:** Northern Illinois • **Years with the Eagles:** 1996– • **Birthplace:** Abilene, Texas • **Born:** January 10, 1974

Hollis Thomas won All–Big West Conference honors at Northern Illinois, but he was passed over in the 1996 NFL draft. The scouts thought Thomas lacked the height to play defensive tackle at the pro level. Thomas felt all he needed was a chance to prove himself, so he made his own highlight film (set to rap music) and sent it to every NFL team.

The Eagles were interested enough to sign Thomas as a free agent, and he wound up cracking the starting lineup and earning a spot on the NFL's All-Rookie Team. Since then, Thomas has battled through injuries to play nine seasons with the Eagles, mostly as a wide-bodied run stuffer.

"Hollis is the key in stopping big runs and controlling the middle," Jim Johnson, the Eagles defensive coordinator said. "He's very smart; he really understands the game. He reads things well. He helps the other [linemen], too. Plus, it helps that he's a big body in there."

The big body was too big earlier in his career, a fact which contributed to two foot injuries that sidelined Thomas for the 2001 postseason and the entire 2002 season. But he hired a nutritionist and changed his eating habits—bye-bye cheeseburgers, hello low-fat tuna salad—and lost 55 pounds. At 305, Thomas still was big enough to take on blockers, but at the lighter weight, he had more quickness.

In 2003, Thomas was playing well until a biceps tear sidelined him after seven games. In 2004, he was part of a four-man tackle rotation with Corey Simon, Sam Rayburn, and Darwin Walker, which allowed them to share playing time and made the line more effective. Thomas missed the final three regular-season games with a dislocated elbow but returned for the playoffs and recorded a key sack of Atlanta's Michael Vick in the NFC championship game.

"It's a long road back," Thomas said. "Like with the [broken] foot. You start out on crutches, then walking, then jogging, then running straight, then cutting. When you go through it twice, it gets kind of tedious and you get frustrated. But it helps you develop patience, and patience is a virtue."

Nicknamed "Tank," Thomas is a collector of everything from DVDs (he has more than one thousand) to automobiles (he has ten, ranging from a 1969 Chevrolet Impala to a 2004 Porsche Cayenne). He also has more than 20 tattoos and wears diamond studs in his ears and under his lip. He is quick to laugh, but not on game day.

"When it comes down to business, Hollis is all business," Rayburn told Shannon Ryan of the *Philadelphia Inquirer*. "He can get you back to where you're supposed to be."

TRA THOMAS
Tackle

Ht: 6–7 • **Wt:** 350 • **College:** Florida State • **Years with the Eagles:** 1998– • **Birthplace:** Deland, Florida • **Born:** November 20, 1974

The Eagles had the 11th pick in the 1998 NFL draft, and many fans wanted them to select wide receiver Randy Moss. When the team chose Tra Thomas, the talk radio shows were flooded with angry callers.

"We chose the player we felt was the best player on the board," coach Ray Rhodes said. "Tra Thomas was the best pass blocker in college football last season. We expect him to come in here and play for a long time."

Rhodes' track record on first-round picks was not terrific—remember Jon Harris?—but he was right about Thomas, who won the starting left tackle position as a rookie and held it for seven seasons. In the fourth game of his rookie year, Thomas went up against Kansas City's Derrick Thomas, and he dominated the Chiefs' All-Pro, holding him without a tackle or a

Tra Thomas

sack. After that, no one questioned whether he was worth the 11th pick in the draft. The proof was there for all to see.

In seven seasons Thomas missed only four starts, and he was entrusted with protecting quarterback Donovan McNabb's blind side. His play tailed off in 2003, but he rebounded with a strong 2004 season that earned him a third trip to the Pro Bowl.

A massive figure, Thomas has a 36½-inch sleeve ("arms that hang down to his knees," read one scouting report) to go along with his 6–7, 350-pound frame. He set the Florida State record with a 550-pound bench press and a 1,200-pound leg lift. Yet he is a surprisingly fluid athlete with good footwork.

"He has very good technique and lateral movement," said Carolina head coach John Fox. "Most guys that big don't move that well. He has real good feet, almost like a basketball player. He has that big body and those long arms, it's hard to get around him."

"He is as good as any tackle in the National Football League," coach Andy Reid said.

Thomas credited his development as a pass blocker to practicing against the likes of Andre Wadsworth, Peter Boulware, and Reinard Wilson in college. Similarly, Hugh Douglas said he improved by working against Thomas every day in practice. "To be a great fighter, you have to have a great sparring partner," Douglas said. "Tra is the best."

"I want to be the league MVP as an offensive lineman," Thomas said. "I want to get nine or 10 Pro Bowls under my belt. When people talk about the greatest linemen of all time, they talk about Anthony Muñoz and Art Shell and Bob Brown. I want my name in there, too."

WILLIAM THOMAS
Linebacker

Ht: 6–2 • **Wt:** 223 • **College:** Texas A&M • **Years with the Eagles:** 1991–99 • **Birthplace:** Amarillo, Texas • **Born:** August 13, 1968

William Thomas, or "Willie T" as he was called, was a weakside linebacker with the Eagles for nine seasons. His teammates selected him as the Eagles' Most Valuable Defensive Player three years in a row (1995–97), and he was voted into two Pro Bowls.

"He's an impact-type guy who makes plays," coach Ray Rhodes said. "From the pass coverage game, he's outstanding. He's going from sideline to sideline on the running game, making plays all over the field."

Thomas was versatile enough to play the run, cover receivers man-to-man, and also blitz the quarterback. He had a knack for making big plays. Example: A 1996 game against the New York Giants. The Eagles were clinging to a 12–10 lead when Thomas sacked quarterback Dave Brown, forced a fumble, recovered it, and returned it 23 yards for a touchdown. He was named NFC Defensive Player of the Week for that performance.

He had a similar game in 1995 against Arizona when he intercepted a Dave Kreig pass in the end zone with 33 seconds left to preserve a 21–20 victory that clinched a playoff berth for the Eagles. That year, Thomas intercepted seven passes, the most in one season by an NFL linebacker since the Jets' Lance Mehl had seven in 1993.

"I know I'm not a household name like some linebackers, like Greg Lloyd [Pittsburgh] and Derrick Thomas [Kansas City]," Thomas said. "I'm just doing my job, whatever it happens to be that week."

Thomas was a defensive back early in his career at Texas A&M, but he grew into a linebacker. As a senior he had 13 sacks to earn Defensive Player of the Year honors in the Southwest Conference. The Eagles selected him in the fourth round of the draft, and he broke into the starting lineup (on a defense that was ranked No. 1 in the NFL) in Week 9. He missed only three games in the next eight seasons.

When Thomas finished his nine-year career with the Eagles, he ranked ninth in club history with 33 sacks. He was released in March 2000, when the team decided to sign a younger linebacker, Carlos Emmons from Pittsburgh. Thomas signed with Oakland, where he finished his career.

TOMMY THOMPSON
Quarterback

Ht: 6–1 • **Wt:** 190 • **College:** Tulsa • **Years with the Eagles:** 1941–42, 1945–50 • **Birthplace:** Hutchinson, Kansas • **Born:** August 15, 1916 • **Died:** April 21, 1989

When people talk about the great quarterbacks of the 1940s, they mention Sammy Baugh, Sid Luckman, Bob Waterfield, and Otto Graham. Rarely does anyone put the Eagles' Tommy Thompson in that category. It's too bad no one does because he belongs.

Thompson directed the Eagles offense for most of the decade, and while the team is best known for its powerful running attack led by Steve Van Buren, Thompson's accurate arm

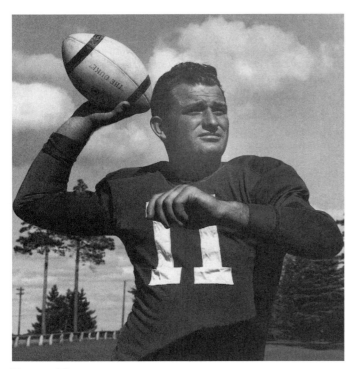

Tommy Thompson

and keen football mind contributed greatly to the 1948 and '49 championship seasons.

As T. J. Troup of the Professional Football Researchers Association wrote in 2001, "Tommy Thompson has been somewhat overlooked. From 1947–1949, Thompson threw 661 passes and had only 37 intercepted, 5.59 percent. The league average for the decade of the 1940s is 9.06 percent."

In the same three-year period, when the Eagles went to the championship game each season, Thompson averaged 8.22 yards per pass attempt while completing 55 percent of his throws. In 1948, a 12-game regular season, Thompson led the league with 25 touchdown passes. Baugh was second with 22. No other quarterback in the league had more than 14.

Thompson was a perfect fit for coach Greasy Neale's T formation. He was a slick ball handler, adept at faking a handoff, hiding the ball on his hip, then lofting a long throw downfield. The Eagles were one of the first teams to use this play on short-yardage situations, such as third and one. Thompson knew the defense expected Van Buren to get the ball, so the fake worked every time, and usually his receiver was wide open for a big gain, even a touchdown.

"And if we missed [the pass], I'd just give the ball to Steve on the next play, and he'd get the first [down] anyhow," Thompson said. "People said it was a gamble, but when you have Steve, nothing's a gamble."

Thompson went both ways (he was a safety on defense and intercepted 12 passes) and also returned kicks, but after he returned from missing two years due to military service in World War II, he was a full-time quarterback.

"The thing I remember is his confidence," said center Chuck Bednarik. "I was a rookie in 1949, Tommy was a lot older (33). He'd say to me, 'Who are we playing this week?' I'd tell him, the Bears, the Giants, whoever it was. He'd say, 'Ahh, we'll beat the bums.' It always made me feel good. A great

quarterback should have that cockiness. It's part of what makes them great."

Thompson was born in Kansas, the son of a railroad worker. The family moved to Fort Worth, Texas, when Thompson was a boy. He was struck in the eye by rock thrown by a classmate, and he lost the central vision in the eye. "It never affected me in sports," he said. "I had some peripheral vision. I could see well enough."

"Tommy had a good arm and a nice touch on his long throws," said end Jack Ferrante. "If I had one step on a defender, Tommy would drop the ball right in my arms."

"We knew we had a tremendous team," Thompson said. "Most of the guys had been together four or five years. We knew we were going to win the championship sooner or later. Finally, things came together, and we won it twice."

Thompson wore the same set of shoulder pads through high school, college, and the pros. After the 1948 season Eagles equipment manager Fred Schubach sent all the gear away to a leather factory for repairs. Thompson's shoulder pads were returned with a note that read, "Rejected. This article is too far gone to justify the expense of reconditioning it."

Schubach put the pads in Thompson's locker with the tag still attached. Thompson saw the note and became indignant. "These pads are the best in the world," he said. "They get better every year."

He continued to wear them until he retired following the 1950 season. He went into coaching at the University of Arkansas and later went to the Canadian League before returning to the NFL with the Chicago Cardinals as backfield coach. In 1960, Thompson was forced to retire due to severe arthritis.

He lived in a quiet cabin in Calico Rock, Arkansas, where he spent his days fishing and watching football on TV. "Calico Rock is a great place, but you'll never find it on any map," Thompson once said. "It's about 150 miles from everywhere."

JEREMIAH TROTTER
Linebacker

Ht: 6–1 • **Wt:** 262 • **College:** Stephen F. Austin • **Years with the Eagles:** 1998–2001, 2004– • **Birthplace:** Texarkana, Texas • **Born:** January 20, 1977

When Jeremiah Trotter left the Eagles in a contract dispute following the 2001 season, he thought he was leaving for good. It was a messy divorce, with Trotter ripping coach Andy Reid on his way out the door. The Eagles front office wasn't exactly thrilled with Trotter either. The bridge between Trotter and the Eagles was so badly burned, Phil Sheridan wrote in the *Philadelphia Inquirer*, "the Army Corps of Engineers couldn't have fixed it."

Trotter signed a fat free-agent contract with Washington, but his two seasons with the Redskins were a disaster. The team collapsed under coach Steve Spurrier, and Trotter blew out his knee. When Joe Gibbs came out of retirement to coach the Redskins in 2004, he released Trotter. At 27, Trotter feared his career was over.

Trotter called Reid, who was on vacation with his family. He apologized for his angry exit and said he wanted to rejoin the Eagles. He was willing to sign for the veteran minimum ($660,000) and accept the role of backup linebacker and

Jeremiah Trotter

special-teams player. Most people would consider that a major comedown for a five-year starter and two-time Pro Bowl player, but for Trotter, this wasn't about pride. It was about opportunity.

"I'm just looking forward to coming in and helping out wherever I can," Trotter said. "I went through two years [in Washington] where I didn't enjoy the game. Even though the money was there, I didn't enjoy the game. I just want to enjoy the game again."

Trotter accepted his supporting role with an enthusiasm that impressed his teammates. "He didn't gripe about playing special teams," linebacker Ike Reese said. "He busted his tail. You can't help but root for somebody like that." Trotter led the Eagles kick coverage teams with five tackles in the Week 3 win over Detroit, 30–13.

After the Eagles were pounded by Pittsburgh, 27–3, in Week 9, Reid and defensive coordinator Jim Johnson made Trotter the starting middle linebacker and moved Mark Simoneau from the middle to the weak side. Immediately, the defense improved, in particular, the defense against the run. The Eagles had allowed an average of 172 yards per game on the ground, but with Trotter in the middle, they cut that total by more than half (83.5) over the next six weeks.

"From day one, he told you what he was going to do," safety Brian Dawkins said. "He's been making big plays for us. He's coming in with an attitude and with an aggressive mentality, helping us plug that thing up."

"Inserting Trotter was huge," safety Michael Lewis told Sheridan. "He is a proven leader. Trotter came into the huddle, and he was that voice, that voice that we were missing, that leader that we needed in there."

Trotter started the last nine regular-season games and finished fifth on the team with 80 tackles. He led the Eagles with 10 tackles behind the line of scrimmage, and he celebrated each one with a simulated ax chop, a tribute to his late father, Myra, who chopped wood for a living.

Trotter's impact did not go unnoticed. He was voted into the Pro Bowl, even though he did not crack the starting lineup until mid-November. Gibbs, the Hall of Fame coach who released Trotter, admitted he made a mistake.

"I'd say right now watching [Trotter] play, he'd fit into anybody's plans," Gibbs said in a conference call with the Philadelphia press. "Sometimes you make decisions, sometimes they're good, sometimes they're bad. What he's doing right now, Jeremiah is being very aggressive. He's pounding centers off the ball. We made an evaluation off what we thought, watching film [on Trotter]. Sometimes you make bad decisions. In this case, we made a bad one."

Trotter also played well in the postseason, sacking Daunte Culpepper and intercepting one of his passes in the 27–14 divisional playoff win over Minnesota. The following week, he accounted for a team-high eight tackles in the 27–10 win over Atlanta in the NFC championship game.

"I'm a better player now than I've ever been," Trotter said. "I'm more disciplined; I'm smarter; I'm playing more within the system. I'm trusting myself, and I'm trusting the guys around me."

NORM VAN BROCKLIN
Quarterback

Ht: 6–1 • **Wt:** 195 • **College:** Oregon • **Years with the Eagles:** 1958–60 • **Birthplace:** Eagle Butte, South Dakota • **Born:** March 15, 1926 • **Died:** May 2, 1983

Norm Van Brocklin was one of the most complex and fascinating personalities to ever flash across the pro football horizon. He was a man of consummate talent and temper, a man who could ooze charm one moment, spew volcanic ash the next.

He was a man whose emotions tilted like a seesaw, a man who would play catch with the kids in the Eagles locker room, then curse out their fathers on the practice field. He would invite a sportswriter out for a friendly dinner, then challenge him to a fight between the appetizer and the entrée.

One ex-teammate called Van Brocklin "a father figure"; another called him "a cantankerous old SOB." Women who met him at parties said he was sweet; men who served under him called him cold and sadistic.

"Dutch was at least three people—and they were all perfectionists," said Pete Retzlaff, who flourished as a receiver under Van Brocklin's direction.

"The Dutchman was the most unforgettable man I met in my football career," said Tommy McDonald, who caught 13 touchdown passes from Van Brocklin during the Eagles' 1960 championship season. "He was tough, yet he was soft-hearted. He was demanding, yet he was the first one to offer help if you needed it. There wasn't a guy on our team who didn't think the world of him. He was a man's man."

Van Brocklin's career was the stuff of legend. He broke in with the Los Angeles Rams in 1949, following an All-America career at the University of Oregon. He played nine seasons in Los Angeles, led the Rams to an NFL championship in 1951, and set a league record by passing for 554 yards in one game against the New York Yanks. But the Rams played rotating quarterbacks, which meant Van Brocklin split time with Bob Waterfield and later Billy Wade. He detested the arrangement, so following the 1957 season he told coach Sid Gillman to trade him.

"Anywhere but Pittsburgh and Philadelphia," Van Brocklin said.

When Gillman traded Van Brocklin to the Eagles (in exchange for tackle Buck Lansford, halfback Jimmy Harris, and a first-round draft pick), the Dutchman was furious. He threatened to quit rather than report. Commissioner Bert Bell interceded and, according to Van Brocklin, made a promise: if the Dutchman accepted the trade and joined the Eagles, Bell would see to it that he took over as head coach when Buck Shaw stepped down. Shaw, 58, already had indicated he did not intend to coach much longer.

So Van Brocklin came to Philadelphia, and in just three seasons he turned a last-place team into a world champion. His finest moment was the 1960 season when he led the Eagles to a 10–2 regular season and a 17–13 win over Green Bay in the championship game. Van Brocklin announced his retirement immediately after the game. When a reporter asked if he intended to keep his number 11 jersey as a souvenir, Van Brocklin said, "I never want to see the damn thing again."

"This is a young man's game," Van Brocklin said. "I'll admit, a quarterback doesn't work too hard and, theoretically, I could play as long as I can lift my arm and throw. But at my age, it simply isn't the same anymore. Something is missing, so I figure I better get out while I can."

Shaw also retired, and it was generally assumed Van Brocklin would succeed him as coach. However, Bell, the man who Van Brocklin claimed promised him the job, had died the previous year, and there was nothing in writing to prove that such a deal existed. It was only Van Brocklin's word, and when he clashed with Eagles management over his plans for the team, which included a shakeup of the front office, any chance he had of landing the job was lost.

"They asked if he'd consider being a player-coach, knowing full well he'd reject it," said Jack McKinney, who covered the Eagles for the *Philadelphia Daily News.* "Dutch said, 'Player-coach? That stuff went out with Johnny Blood.'"

Feeling betrayed, the Dutchman accepted an offer to become the first head coach of the Minnesota Vikings. He coached the Vikings for six years, then coached the Atlanta Falcons for seven seasons, but his record as a coach (66–100–7) never approached his record as a player. His genius served him better in the huddle than on the sidelines.

As a player, Van Brocklin was a triumph of attitude over ability, of fire over logic. He won as many games with the gravel in his belly as he did with his strong right arm. He was cranky and vulgar, maybe the worst loser the league ever saw, but in his own earthy way, he embodied the spirit of pro football. And in a career of towering accomplishments, his 1960 season—which earned him the NFL's Most Valuable Player Award and insured his selection to the Pro Football Hall of Fame—surely ranks at the top.

"What Van Brocklin did with that Eagles team was unbelievable," said Sam Huff, the New York Giants linebacker. "They were strictly an average club. They had no running game; their offensive line was lousy; their defense was mediocre. Van Brocklin carried them to the championship. With any other quarterback, that team would've been lucky to break even."

In the 1960 season, Van Brocklin passed for 24 touchdowns, a career high, and he averaged a gaudy 8.70 yards per attempt, which meant he was throwing the ball deep. His numbers are even more impressive when you consider the Eagles had no running threat—Billy Barnes and Ted Dean averaged less than three yards a carry—so defenses were designed to stop Van Brocklin, and they still couldn't do it.

"Van Brocklin is, without question, the best quarterback the Eagles ever had," said Chuck Bednarik. "I remember Tommy Thompson, Adrian Burk, Sonny [Jurgensen], all those guys right through Ron Jaworski, and they couldn't touch Van Brocklin. I rate quarterbacks in classes from A to Triple A. I have five quarterbacks in my Triple A class: Otto Graham, Johnny Unitas, Bobby Layne, Y. A. Tittle, and Van Brocklin. That was the cream of the crop, and, in a big game, I'd take Van Brocklin over any of them."

In 1960, the Eagles lost their opener to Cleveland, 41–24. They won their next nine games in a row, with Van Brocklin bringing them from behind almost every week.

"He was uncanny," McDonald said. "He kept probing the defense until he found a weakness. Once he did, it was all over."

A classic example came in the second meeting between the Eagles and Giants, a tense, late-season showdown at Franklin Field with the conference title on the line. The Giants took an early 17–0 lead, and they were stuffing the Eagles running

Norm Van Brocklin

game. Van Brocklin correctly deduced that Huff was picking up his audibles.

"This one play," Bednarik recalled, "Dutch called, 'One-twenty-one' [an audible], and Huff shot the gap and hit Barnes as soon as he touched the ball. Dutch said, 'Okay, that baits the trap.' None of us knew what he was talking about.

"The next series, Dutch got into the huddle and said, 'Look, I'm gonna call an audible, but ignore it. It's just a fake for old Sammy boy.' So we lined up, Dutch called out, 'One-twenty-one.' Sure enough, Huff came crashing through and almost took Barnes' head off. Except this time Barnes didn't have the ball."

Van Brocklin faked the handoff, and while Huff was tackling Barnes, Dean slipped unnoticed across the middle. Van Brocklin hit him with a short pass, and Dean ran 64 yards to the touchdown that sparked the Eagles to a 31–23 victory.

"I had tremendous respect for Van Brocklin because he was such a competitor," Huff said. "He'd spit in your eye, call you every name in the book, then run your butt off the field. We used to hit him some wicked shots, and he'd say, 'Is that the best you can do, sweetie?'"

Van Brocklin's toughness rubbed off on his Eagle teammates, and they surprised everyone by winning their first conference title in 11 years. On December 26 they met Vince Lombardi's Packers for the NFL championship, and once again Van Brocklin brought the Eagles from behind in the fourth quarter to win, 17–13, as he was voted the game's Most Valuable Player.

"In that game, I told Dutch I could beat the cornerback deep if I went to the post, then broke back to the outside," McDonald said. "He said, 'Okay, do it.' I ran the pattern, made my cut, and when I looked back, the ball was already in the air. It was a perfect throw, right in my hands. I caught it and tumbled into the end zone. People ask, 'What was your greatest thrill in football?' That was it, right there. It helped us win a world championship. What can be bigger than that?"

"Buck Shaw was our coach, but by God, Dutch was our leader," Billy Barnes said. "He was the greatest leader of any quarterback who ever lived. He didn't make us feel like we might win; with Dutch, we felt like we couldn't lose."

Sandy Grady of the *Philadelphia Bulletin* wrote:

[As] a sportswriter, 1,000 games become a blur, the arenas and the noise and sweat and faces tumble together like bright colors in a washing machine. But Van Brocklin was the pure, hard metal that stays with you. I think there was a reason. He had the gift of drama. He always dominated the stage in the last act. What the mind's eye sees is this slightly pouchy, scowling man in the green No. 11 shirt. It is always dusk in a cold ballyard and the scoreboard lights are running against him. He shuffles on stubby legs, throwing with the classic overhead motion, picking his way against the clock and the crowd's roar. With Van Brocklin, you were always watching a man playing a 100-yard chess game, terribly alone in his decisions, desperate for the kill.

Eagles radio broadcaster Bill Campbell said of Van Brocklin, "Never in the history of football in Philadelphia has there been such an artist at throwing the football. And rarely has there been such a competitor."

For all his on-the-field toughness, Van Brocklin could be a charming, generous man. Friends claim the Dutchman melted around children. He once described himself as happiest "sitting around the Christmas tree, putting toys together."

In 1959, when Dr. Tom Dowd, the Eagles team physician, died suddenly, Van Brocklin became the family's unofficial guardian. He looked after Dowd's son and daughters and made sure they completed their educations. He even painted the smaller house to which the family moved.

Van Brocklin had little use for the press, yet he launched a campaign to raise money for the widow and children of an upstate Pennsylvania sportswriter. He sponsored several benefits in the area and finally reached into his own pocket to help the family through.

Once while visiting the home of Bill Campbell, Van Brocklin heard Campbell's young daughter talk about wanting a dog. "When's your birthday?" Van Brocklin asked. She mentioned a date that was months away. When that day arrived, there was a knock at the Campbells' door. It was Van Brocklin, holding a birthday card and a puppy.

The best example of Van Brocklin's compassion was his adoption of three youngsters, ages 5 through 8, whose parents were killed in an automobile accident. The family lived near the Van Brocklins in Georgia, and the Dutchman could not bear the thought of the three kids growing up in an orphanage. His three daughters were away at college, so he took the youngsters into his home. Asked why he would assume the responsibilities of parenthood all over again, he replied, "It gives me a good feeling to know there are little feet under the table."

"There has to be something special in a man to make him do that," McDonald said. "I've always contended the Dutchman was a misunderstood person. He had a heart of gold."

After his firing by the Falcons in 1974, Van Brocklin retired to his 70-acre pecan farm in Social Circle, Georgia. He worked briefly as a part-time assistant coach to Pepper Rogers at Georgia Tech, but he developed health problems in his early 50s. In 1979 he underwent surgery to relieve a blood clot near his brain. A fall at his home necessitated a second operation a few weeks later. He finally succumbed to a heart attack on May 2, 1983. He was 57 years old.

"You go through so much with a man and you share something as special as an NFL championship, there's always an emotional bond," McDonald said. "When I heard the Dutchman had died, it was like a little piece of me died, too."

STEVE VAN BUREN
Halfback

Ht: 6–1 • **Wt:** 210 • **College:** LSU • **Years with the Eagles:** 1944–51 • **Birthplace:** La Ceiba, Honduras • **Born:** December 28, 1920

Steve Van Buren carried the Eagles to three consecutive division titles and back-to-back world championships in 1948 and '49. He led the NFL in rushing four times, and he twice went over the 1,000-yard mark in an era, with 12-game seasons and seven-man lines, when such a feat was unheard of.

"Steve was as good as any running back who ever played," said Pete Pihos, the Hall of Fame end. "He was as good as Jimmy Brown, in my opinion. We had a good team, but it was Van Buren who made us great."

"Steve was our paycheck," said Frank (Bucko) Kilroy, the All-Pro guard. "He could do everything. He was the best

Steve Van Buren

blocking back in the league. He could catch the ball. He could return punts and kickoffs. And there was no one better running with the ball. Steve was the prototype [back] that every team has been looking for ever since."

Van Buren was a player ahead of his time. He was 6–1 and 210 pounds, yet he could beat teammate Clyde Scott, a world-class hurdler, in the 40-yard dash. Van Buren's combination of power and explosive speed was more than the defenses of the '40s could handle. Teammates nicknamed him "Wham-Bam" because, they said, that was the sound they heard when number 15 hit the line.

"When Steve carried the ball, he struck fear in the heart of the defense," said Russ Craft, an Eagles halfback. "He leaned forward so much and ran so hard, you could actually see the dirt flying off his cleats. When he hit the line, he looked like a bulldozer going through a picket fence. I saw him knock off more headgears than you could count. I saw him bust up a lot of faces, too. [This was the era before mandatory face masks.] Thank God he seldom got mad. He might have killed somebody."

Van Buren was the first Eagle player elected to the Pro Football Hall of Fame (1965), but the real measure of his greatness is the fact that a half century after his retirement, he still held nine team records, including most touchdowns in a season (18), most yards rushing in a game (205), most touchdowns rushing (69), most consecutive games with a rushing touchdown (8), and highest career kickoff return average (26.7 yards).

Earle (Greasy) Neale, who coached the Eagles from 1941 through 1950, called Van Buren the greatest runner he ever saw, better than Jim Thorpe and Red Grange. Said Neale: "Grange had the same ability to sidestep, but he didn't have Van Buren's power to go with it."

In 1994, when the NFL selected its 75th anniversary all-time team, Van Buren was one of seven running backs selected, along with Jim Brown and Marion Motley of Cleveland, Bronko Nagurski, Walter Payton, and Gale Sayers of Chicago, and O. J. Simpson of Buffalo.

You never would know any of this if you visited Van Buren's modest apartment in Northeast Philadelphia. A widower, he lived alone with just a few photographs (mostly of his 10 grandchildren) on display. There were no trophies, no game balls, no football portraits anywhere. Most, he gave away to friends. Others, he said, he lost or threw away.

"I never cared about that stuff, just like I never cared about records," Van Buren said. "The only thing that mattered to me was winning. If we won, I figured I did my job. Basically, I'm a shy person. I almost didn't go to my Hall of Fame induction. My family made me go. Once I got there, I was glad. But I don't like a lot of attention. I never did."

Van Buren was born in Spanish Honduras, the son of a fruit inspector. The family moved to Louisiana where Steve worked in a steel mill as a teenager. He went to LSU on a football scholarship and spent two seasons as a single-wing blocking back, opening holes for Alvin Dark, who later was an All-Star infielder with the New York and San Francisco Giants.

It wasn't until Dark graduated that Van Buren, then a senior, got to carry the ball. That season he broke the Southeastern Conference rushing record and was named to every All-America team. Coach Bernie Moore apologized to Van Buren for not recognizing his talents sooner.

"He said he had done me a terrible injustice," Van Buren recalled. "I told him not to think twice about it. Everything turned out all right."

The Eagles made Van Buren their first-round selection in the 1944 college draft. Van Buren told general manager Harry Thayer he wanted $10,000 to sign. Thayer said that was ridiculous, no rookies were earning five figures in those days. A week later, Van Buren went to the College All-Star game, where he was stricken with appendicitis.

"I was in the hospital feeling awful, and guess who showed up? Harry Thayer," Van Buren said. "Harry said, 'Well, Steve, we're prepared to offer you $4,000.' The way I felt, I thought I was done for the year, maybe forever. I figured if I didn't take the four thousand, I was liable to wind up with nothing. So I signed the contract, and I was grateful to have it."

The Eagles fitted Van Buren with a special corset, and he was practicing in 10 days. That summer, the rookie gave new meaning to the expression "surviving the cut."

"I had this incision seven inches long where they removed my appendix," Van Buren said, "and here I was, running with the football, getting banged around. It sounds crazy, I know. We played an exhibition game in Green Bay, and I took a hit on the incision. It began oozing blood right through the padding. I had to take myself out, and Greasy gave me hell for not being in shape. That's when I knew pro football was gonna be tough."

Yet Van Buren made it look easy. As a rookie, he averaged 5.6 yards per carry and led the NFL in punt returns as the Eagles finished 7–1–2, placing second to the New York Giants in the Eastern Conference. The following year Van Buren won the first of his rushing titles, gaining 832 yards and scoring

18 touchdowns in just 12 games. His yards-per-carry average was a stunning 5.8.

"I'll never forget the first time I hit Steve in a scrimmage," said Leo Skladany, an Eagles defensive end. "I thought I was run over by a tractor trailer. I hit him as hard as I could, and he just kept going. I'll never forget it. My goodness, it was really awesome."

His teammates held Van Buren in awe, as much for his character as his talent. He was the most unassuming member of the team, without the slightest hint of ego. He would receive gift certificates for free clothes and free dinners and hand them over to teammates, saying, "Here, I don't need this."

"He was a superstar, but he never acted like one," Pihos said.

He was embarrassed when people asked for his autograph. Photographers would come to practice to take his picture, and he'd call three or four other [players] to get in the picture with him. He was a total team man.

He set his own [practice] schedule, and Greasy understood it. He took such a pounding in the games that he would just run on the side for two or three days while the rest of us were hitting. He'd be in sweats, stretching and running. By Friday, he'd be back on the field, then Sunday he was ready to go again.

Every so often some [opponents] would say, "We're ready for Van Buren. He's not gonna run over us." I'd just laugh because I knew before the first quarter was over, those same guys would be ducking and trying to get out of his way.

In 1947, Van Buren went over the 1,000-yard mark for the first time, finishing with 1,008 yards, and the Eagles went to their first NFL championship game. They lost to the Chicago Cardinals, 28–21, on a frozen field at Comiskey Park. The following year, the same two teams met in the title game, this time in a blizzard at Philadelphia's Shibe Park, and the Eagles won, 7–0, as Van Buren scored the lone touchdown on a five-yard run.

There is a fascinating footnote to that game: Van Buren almost missed it. He awoke in his suburban home that morning, saw the heavy snow, and went back to bed, assuming the game would be postponed. An hour passed and Van Buren decided he probably should go, just in case. So he made the trek using public transit, taking a bus to Philadelphia, then a trolley car, and finally the subway to Lehigh Avenue, where he trudged seven blocks through the knee-deep snow to the ballpark.

After scoring the touchdown that brought the Eagles their first NFL championship, Van Buren again walked alone through the snow to the subway and repeated the long ride home.

The next year, the Eagles had their greatest team, with the addition of the rookie Bednarik, another future Hall of Famer. They were 11–1 in the regular season and went to their third consecutive NFL championship game. Playing in a driving rain that flooded the Los Angeles Coliseum, Van Buren enjoyed his finest hour. He carried the ball 31 times for 196 yards, an NFL championship-game record, as the Eagles defeated the Rams, 14–0.

Afterward, several Hollywood celebrities visited the locker room. Among them was Clark Gable, the most famous leading man of the day. Gable shook Van Buren's hand and said, "You're the greatest athlete I've ever seen." Van Buren thanked him. Later, Van Buren said to teammate George Savitsky, "He seemed like a nice guy. Who is he?"

"I told him, 'Steve, you ought to get out more,'" Savitsky said.

"Steve was the best runner in the game," said Bosh Pritchard, who played next to Van Buren in the Eagles backfield. "People thought I was fast, but Steve could outrun me. He could run away from people, but he liked running over them better. I never saw anyone bring Steve down one-on-one. He'd lower his shoulder and run right through them."

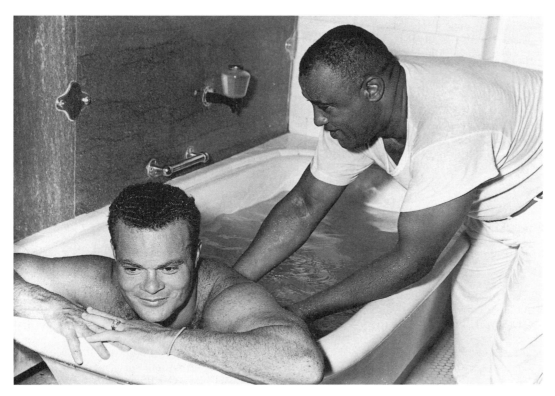

Steve Van Buren eases his aches and pains with a warm bath and massage. Van Buren had the heaviest workload of any running back in the 1940s. He led the NFL in rushing attempts five times in a six-year period from 1945 through 1950.

In 1950, Van Buren was slowed by injuries. A broken toe, torn ankle ligaments, and cracked ribs, all on his right side, made him an easy target for opposing defenses. He took six painkilling shots before every game and six more at halftime, but he refused to come out of the lineup. He still led the NFL with 188 carries, but his yardage slipped to 629 (from 1,146 in 1949), and he had only four touchdowns. Not surprisingly, the Eagles' reign as world champions ended with Van Buren's decline.

"We had a great team, but take away Van Buren and we were like a bull without its horns," tackle Al Wistert said. "Our whole personality changed. That's why they went to such lengths to keep Steve playing even after he was hurt. If Steve had as many needles sticking out of him as he had stuck in him those last few years, he would've looked like a porcupine. He was in pain, but he kept on playing. He never said a word."

In 1951, Van Buren was again slowed by injuries. He carried the ball 112 times for 327 yards, a 2.9-yard average. He worked out harder than ever that off-season, hoping to regain his form. The following summer, the 31-year-old Van Buren reported to the team's training camp in Hershey, Pennsylvania, in great shape, looking forward to a big season. But one day in practice he made a cut and fell to the ground. Ernie Accorsi, the New York Giants general manager, was a youngster living in Hershey at the time. He was watching from the sidelines.

"I remember it like it was yesterday," Accorsi said. "The offense was moving right to left. Van Buren was running and tried to cut upfield. No one touched him; he just went down. I can still remember his brother Ebert [an Eagles halfback] running across the field screaming, 'Don't touch him, don't touch him.' It was really sad. The way it happened, the reaction of the other players, you just had the feeling this was it."

Bednarik recalls looking down and seeing Van Buren's leg bent into the shape of an L. Said Bednarik: "I wanted to throw up. I was sick. We all were, because we loved the guy so much."

The ligaments in Van Buren's knee were so badly torn that there was no possibility he would ever play again. He retired as the league's all-time leading rusher with 5,860 yards. He also held the league records for rushing yards in a season (1,146) and touchdowns in a season (18). For his career, Van Buren averaged one touchdown for every 19.1 rushing attempts. Only one player in history, Lenny Moore of the Baltimore Colts, had a better touchdown-to-carry ratio (17.0).

Van Buren stayed with the Eagles for a while as a scout, but he didn't like the traveling. He coached some semipro football—Bristol (Pennsylvania) Saints, Franklin Miners, Newark Bears—but he was not interested in coaching at the NFL level. Too many hours, too many egos. He did not want the headaches.

He dabbled in the used car business, the insurance business, the roofing business. He never struck it rich, but he got by. In 1988 he suffered a major stroke and almost died. Doctors told his family that if he lived, he probably would be paralyzed. Van Buren refused to accept it.

Three months after the stroke, Van Buren walked unassisted onto the field at Veterans Stadium to join his former teammates at a 40th anniversary of the Eagles' first championship team. Wearing his familiar number 15, Van Buren waved to the fans who greeted his introduction with a standing ovation.

"There were a lot of guys with tears in their eyes," Al Wistert said later. "He was the heart and soul of our team, and he was our heart and soul today."

TROY VINCENT
Cornerback

Ht: 6–1 • **Wt:** 200 • **College:** Wisconsin • **Years with the Eagles:** 1996–2003 • **Birthplace:** Trenton, New Jersey • **Born:** June 8, 1971

Troy Vincent never imagined he would play professional football. Growing up in Trenton, he wanted to play basketball. He never played organized football until his senior year at Pennsbury High School when coach Jim Dundala convinced him to try out.

Vincent played so well in that one season that the University of Wisconsin offered him a full scholarship. Four years later, the Miami Dolphins made him the seventh overall pick in the NFL draft. In 1996 he signed with the Eagles as a free agent, and he became the first defensive back in franchise history to earn Pro Bowl honors five consecutive years.

"I look at it as a miracle," Vincent told Dave Caldwell of the *Philadelphia Inquirer*. "I never thought this would happen to me on a gridiron. I always grew up with a basketball in my hand, with a tank-top T-shirt and with high-top sneakers. Never spikes. God works in mysterious ways, I guess."

Vincent was the prototype cornerback: he had ideal size, a strong upper body that allowed him to jam receivers at the line, and excellent speed (he was timed in 4.29 seconds for the 40-yard dash). He was very intelligent and rarely made a mistake in coverage.

Vincent, fellow cornerback Bobby Taylor, and safety Brian Dawkins formed three-quarters of the Eagles secondary for eight seasons. They combined for nine Pro Bowls and 58 interceptions as they helped the Eagles rank among the league's top defensive teams.

"What's made it special is we did it over time," Vincent said. "It wasn't one year or two years. We contributed consistently for eight years. That's a long time to dominate. We won a lot of football games because of our play on the back end."

It was the ability of Vincent and Taylor to cover receivers man-to-man and shut them down that allowed defensive coordinator Jim Johnson to run such a high percentage of blitzes. He could send his linebackers and safeties after the quarterback because he felt confident in Vincent and Taylor's ability to cover one-on-one.

When Vincent finished his eight seasons with the Eagles, he ranked sixth in team history with 28 interceptions. He also had a share of the longest interception return in NFL history, a 104-yard return against Dallas with linebacker James Willis picking off a Troy Aikman pass and lateraling to Vincent, who ran the last 90 yards for the touchdown that locked up a 31–21 win on November 3, 1996.

"Troy is the model of a professional player," Bobby Taylor said. "He has such high standards. He is always looking at film, studying receivers' moves, picking up little things. I've learned so much, just being around the guy."

Vincent's high standards extend off the field, as well. He was named NFL Man of the Year in 2002 for his work in the community. He also was presented with the Byron (Whizzer) White Humanitarian Award. *The Sporting News* put him first in its list of "100 Good Guys in Sports."

Vincent and his wife Tommi created "Love Thy Neighbor," a nonprofit community development corporation in Trenton. They began a program to improve literacy and provide medical care for families that cannot afford it. They distribute gift certificates outside Trenton-area supermarkets at Thanksgiving and donate clothing and blankets to homeless shelters at Christmas.

"Troy Vincent is Trenton's treasure," Mayor Douglas Palmer told Paul Attner of *The Sporting News.* "He doesn't have to be here, getting his hands dirty. He could be like a lot of athletes who have made it and forgotten where they came from. But Troy remembers. And he is giving back."

Following the 2003 season, the Eagles made the decision to let the 32-year-old Vincent leave rather than sign him to a new contract. He signed with Buffalo, but he had no hard feelings for the Eagles as he left.

"It's strictly business," he told Marcus Hayes of the *Philadelphia Daily News.* "When Jeremiah [Trotter] left, we all said, 'Red flag. One day that's all of us. It might be one at a time, it might be all at one time, but that's us.'"

HERSCHEL WALKER
Running Back

Ht: 6–1 • **Wt:** 225 • **College:** Georgia • **Years with the Eagles:** 1992–94 • **Birthplace:** Wrightsville, Georgia • **Born:** March 3, 1962

Herschel Walker was the national high school player of the year, a Heisman Trophy winner, the Most Valuable Player of the USFL, and a two-time Pro Bowler with the Dallas Cowboys. He was destined to be, experts said, the most dominating runner to hit pro football since Jim Brown.

But Walker's career took a downward turn when the Cowboys traded him to Minnesota in 1989. The Vikings gave Dallas seven draft picks and six players for Walker, predicting he would carry them to their first Super Bowl championship. But when it did not happen, the same people who cast Walker as the Vikings' savior blamed him for the team's failure.

In 1992 the Vikings tried to trade Walker but found no takers. "We couldn't get a warm six-pack for him," one team official told Jill Lieber of *Sports Illustrated.* So the Vikings simply released him. Other teams were reluctant to sign him. He had acquired a reputation as an oddball who was more interested in his exotic hobbies, such as ballet and bobsledding, than playing football.

The Eagles, who finished 21st in rushing the previous season, signed Walker, and he proved to be a solid addition. In his first season he rushed for 1,070 yards and scored 10 touchdowns. His 1,348 combined yards, rushing and receiving, was the most for an Eagles back in more than a decade.

What was most surprising about Walker was his attitude. In Minnesota he was labeled soft and selfish, a player who would not pay the price to win and only cared about his own statistics. With the Eagles he was just the opposite. He did whatever was asked of him and at times went above and beyond the call of duty, including volunteering for special teams.

"Just give me some roles and I'll do whatever it takes," Walker said. "I never understood when people said I couldn't fit into an offense or that I needed to have the offense patterned around what I did. I've always felt I could do anything anybody asked of me."

The Eagles used Walker mostly as a power runner in his first season, but they experimented with him in other roles after that. He continued to play in the backfield, but he also played tight end and occasionally lined up as a wide receiver, where defenses had to respect his world-class speed.

"I saw in Herschel an exceptional athlete who gave us tremendous versatility," coach Rich Kotite said. "He allows us to use different formations, move the ball around, and show defenses different things. Maybe some teams didn't know how to use him. I just know that with Herschel Walker, we have a weapon not many teams can match."

Walker carried the ball less from scrimmage in 1993 and '94, but he still maintained a good rushing average (4.3 one year, 4.7 the next). He was most effective as a receiver, catching 125 passes in the two seasons combined.

In 1994, Walker became the first player in NFL history to have a 90-yard, or longer, running play, pass reception, and kickoff return all in the same season. His 91-yard touchdown run against Atlanta (November 27) was the longest run from scrimmage in team history. His 93-yard reception against the Giants (September 4) was the longest in Eagles history by a running back. His 94-yard kickoff return came in the season finale at Cincinnati (December 24).

"I'm not hard to figure out," Walker said. "I'm a football player. I'll do anything the team wants me to as long as it helps us win. I think Philadelphia has appreciated me more than any place I've played."

Following the 1994 season, Ray Rhodes was hired to replace Kotite as coach, and when Rhodes signed Ricky Watters, Walker was released. He signed with the Giants and played one season there, then returned to Dallas where he played his final two seasons.

BOBBY WALSTON
End-Kicker

Ht: 6–0 • **Wt:** 190 • **College:** Georgia • **Years with the Eagles:** 1951–62 • **Birthplace:** Columbus, Ohio • **Born:** October 17, 1928 • **Died:** October 7, 1987

Bobby Walston is probably the most underrated Eagle. He is the team's all-time leading scorer with 881 points. He is the last Eagle to lead the league in scoring, piling up 114 points in just 12 games in 1954. He set the team record for most points in a game: 25 against Washington in 1954. Yet the rugged pass catcher and kicker is seldom mentioned when people discuss the great players in franchise history.

Too bad because the former University of Georgia star was something special, a 14th-round draft pick who became NFL Rookie of the Year in 1951, a fierce competitor who was the league's No. 2 all-time scorer (behind Hall of Famer Lou Groza) when he retired after the 1962 season.

Walston was cool and crafty, blessed with superb hands and deceptive speed. He was a chain smoker, but he had such amazing stamina that quarterback Norm Van Brocklin predicted, "Bobby will play until he's 60."

Walston missed just one football game dating back to high school. He started all 148 games with the Eagles, not counting preseason and playoffs. He broke his jaw in 1954 and had his mouth wired shut. The doctor told him to rest for at least three weeks. Walston refused. He borrowed a pair of pliers and removed the wires himself so he could play against the New York Giants the following Sunday.

Jack McKinney of the *Philadelphia Daily News* described the scene: "[Walston] fashioned his own makeshift brace out of gauze and tape. He looked like Lon Chaney, Jr., in *The Mummy's Curse*. His voice was so muffled under all that swathing, his teammates took to calling him 'Mumbles.'"

In his final season, Walston broke his left arm. That finished him as a pass receiver, but he continued to kick extra points and field goals with his arm in a harness. His toughness was legendary. He was a former collegiate boxing champion who spent his off-seasons working as a deputy sheriff in Georgia, chasing down moonshiners in the hills of Tattnall County. He also was a certified deepwater diver.

"Bobby was the best draft pick I ever made," said general manager Vince McNally, who selected more than 400 players in his 15 years with the Eagles. "I remember scouting him at a Georgia-Maryland game. He played halfback and safety and kicked like hell. We drafted him more for his kicking than anything else. Cliff Patton [a veteran kicker] was gone, and we needed somebody. The fact that Bobby blossomed into a great receiver was a bonus."

Walston was known as "Cheewah," a nickname given to him by Van Brocklin. According to McKinney, when Van Brocklin joined the Eagles, he noted Walston's high cheekbones and swarthy features and—crossing his arms, Indian fashion—introduced himself by saying, "How. Me, Dutch. You, Cheewah."

Walston caught 311 passes for 5,363 yards, and his career average of 17.2 yards per reception is among the best in team history. His 46 touchdown catches still ranks with the Eagles' all-time leaders. He was the smallest tight end in the league, but he ran excellent routes and seldom dropped a ball. He also was an effective blocker and helped clear the path for Ted Dean to score the winning touchdown against Green Bay in the 1960 championship game.

"Cheewah isn't big enough to be a textbook blocker," coach Buck Shaw said. "But he'll bite, claw, kick, and just plain out-nasty anyone he's up against."

"Bobby was the best all-around athlete on our team," flanker Tommy McDonald said. "He could do anything: basketball, baseball, boxing. If we stayed at a hotel with a pool, he'd put on a diving exhibition. You'd think he was in the Olympics, he was that good. He had unbelievable body control. He was a great pass receiver and a clutch kicker. We never worried about him in a pressure situation."

Walston is best remembered for his 38-yard field goal that won a critical game in Cleveland, 31–29, during the drive to the 1960 championship. Most Eagles players point to that victory—and Walston's kick—as the moment their championship vision came into focus.

"Bobby didn't have the world's strongest leg," McNally said. "He was accurate, but anything outside 35 [yards] and you held your breath. I didn't think he would make this kick. The field was all torn up, so it was hard to get a decent spot. The wind was blowing in off the lake. Bobby had been running pass patterns all day, so his leg had to be tired. Remember, he was no youngster by then. But he got the strength from somewhere. It barely cleared the crossbar, but it got there. It was the greatest clutch kick I ever saw."

Walston stayed in football after his retirement. He worked in scouting with the Chicago Bears and the United States Football League. He returned to Philadelphia in 1985 for the silver anniversary of the title season. At the team dinner, Walston rose and offered a toast: "Here's to 1960. To the champions."

STAN WALTERS
Tackle

Ht: 6–6 • **Wt:** 275 • **College:** Syracuse • **Years with the Eagles:** 1975–83 • **Birthplace:** Rutherford, New Jersey • **Born:** May 27, 1948

Stan Walters was in his fifth NFL season, his second with the Eagles, when Dick Vermeil was hired as head coach. Early in the 1976 training camp, Vermeil called Walters into his office for the meeting Walters recalls as the turning point of his career.

"Dick said, 'I expect you to be a better player, or you'll be out of here,'" Walters said. "I don't know if he would've cut me or not, but that's what I got out of it. Here's this young coach and I'm a five-year veteran, and he's telling me I have to play better or I'll be gone. It shook me up. It definitely made a difference."

Walters had played fairly well to that point. He was a part-time starter in Cincinnati for three years before being traded to the Eagles in 1975. He started all 14 games for the Eagles that season, but the team finished 4–10, and coach Mike McCormack was fired. At the time, Walters was seen as a fair-to-good offensive tackle, but too passive to be an All-Pro.

Watching the tapes, Vermeil came to the same conclusion, so he lit a fire under Walters, who accepted the challenge. He worked harder in the weight room and on the practice field, and, pretty soon, he was a Pro Bowler and the Eagles were NFC champions. He started 122 consecutive regular-season and postseason games at left tackle.

"Now I'm trying to be the best player I can possibly be," Walters said in a 1979 interview. "Before, I'd just go out and try to play a decent game. I was happy with that. But I don't feel that way now. I guess I'm striving for the perfect game. I've changed my whole attitude."

Harvey Martin, the Dallas Cowboys' All-Pro defensive end, said Walters was his toughest opponent. "He's not the most physical [tackle], but he's the smartest," Martin said. "He never makes a mistake, he never loses his cool. He just keeps that big body between you and the quarterback."

"I just go out there and do my job," Walters told Danny Robbins of the *Philadelphia Inquirer*. "Fortunately, I've been doing a pretty good one lately. The violence, I think that's blown out of proportion. I can think of sometimes, preseason especially, when coach Vermeil has said, 'Let's go get 'em,' and the rookies yell, 'Yeah, kill, kill.' I just laugh. You don't kill anybody out there, and if you think that's what you have to do, you've got a lot to learn."

Walters was a different breed. Even in the clannish fraternity of offensive linemen, he stood apart. For one thing, he was a chain smoker. The ceiling tiles above his Veterans Stadium locker were yellow from the cigarette smoke. Walters also loved to talk about books, about the theater, about life in general. He was reflective, often talking about "the real world," meaning the world outside of football.

But on game day, Walters was a tough competitor. He proved that in January 1981 when the Eagles played Dallas for the NFC championship. Walters pulled a muscle in his back in the first half. He went to the locker room, took a shot of painkiller, and returned to action, playing Martin to a standstill on the bitterly cold afternoon. The Eagles rushed for 263 yards in that game, due in large part to Walters' tenacious blocking.

When it was over and the Eagles had won, Walters stood at his locker, quietly surveying the celebration. "I'm very melancholy right now," he said. "All those years of sweating, it's nice to savor this. I'm feeling very satisfied. Not jubilant or anything. Just very content, I guess, is the feeling right now."

Walters played through the 1982 season and retired, but when the team lost several players with injuries the following summer, he agreed to play another season. When he did finally retire, he became the color commentator on the Eagles radio broadcasts, teaming with veteran play-by-play man Merrill Reese for 14 years.

ANDRE WATERS
Safety

Ht: 5–11 • **Wt:** 200 • **College:** Cheyney State • **Years with the Eagles:** 1984–93 • **Birthplace:** Belle Glade, Florida • **Born:** March 10, 1962

Andre Waters once was asked what drove him on the football field. He said it was knowing that somewhere there was a young player who was as hungry as he once was and now was after his job.

"The way I see it, I have to earn my spot every day," Waters said. "If I let down at all, I leave the door open [for the competition]. I'm not gonna do that."

That attitude explains how a player with average size and speed, a free agent from Cheyney State, lasted 12 seasons in the NFL. It also explains the ferocity that, for better or worse, characterized his play. If he hit people hard, if he made them angry, he did not feel the need to apologize. He was doing what he had to do to survive among the richer and more gifted athletes in the league.

"It was a million-to-one shot that I'd ever play professional football," Waters said. "If someone came to my hometown when I was in high school and said I was going to play pro ball, people would have laughed in their face and then run them out of town. But I knew in my heart, I could do it. I just needed a chance."

He was given the nickname "Dirty" Waters after highly publicized hits on quarterbacks David Archer (out of bounds) and Jim Everett and Rich Gannon (diving at their knees). The hit on Gannon, which occurred on "Monday Night Football" and drew a $10,000 fine from NFL commissioner Paul Tagliabue, was the one that put a permanent stain on Waters' reputation, even though Gannon was not injured on the play.

"I don't want to be known around the league as a cheap shot artist," Waters said. "I'm not trying to hurt anybody. I tackle everybody low: running backs, receivers, quarterbacks. If you go at a running back low, nothing is said about it. If a quarterback can't be hit, you shouldn't put them out on the field.

"I'm labeled a nasty player, so I guess that makes people take notice. It seems like every time I do something, everybody points it out."

Waters made the Eagles as a special-teams player in 1984. As a rookie, he returned a kickoff 89 yards for a touchdown in a 16–10 win over Washington. His big break came in 1986 when Buddy Ryan took over as head coach. Waters, with his all-out, aggressive style of play, was an ideal fit for Ryan's 46 defense.

"He is the kind of player who turns people upside-down and laughs at them," Ryan said.

With Waters at strong safety and Wes Hopkins at free safety, the Eagles put fear in the heart of receivers who ventured across the middle. Waters led the team in tackles for three consecutive seasons (1986–88). In 1986 he was named NFC Defensive Player of the Week in a 33–27 win over the Los Angeles Raiders. In that game Waters had 14 tackles, intercepted a pass, and returned a Marcus Allen fumble 81 yards to set up the winning touchdown.

Waters' physical brand of football took a toll on his body as well as the opposition. He played through knee and back injuries in 1990, missed 10 games after suffering a broken leg in 1992, and lost half a season to a toe injury in 1993. He was released the following year and reunited with Ryan in Phoenix, where he played his final two seasons.

RICKY WATTERS
Running Back

Ht: 6–1 • **Wt:** 220 • **College:** Notre Dame • **Years with the Eagles:** 1995–97 • **Birthplace:** Harrisburg, Pennsylvania • **Born:** April 7, 1969

"For who? For what?"

Those were the rhetorical questions Ricky Watters asked after his first game as an Eagle when he lost two fumbles and short-armed two passes over the middle in a 21–6 loss to Tampa Bay. Watters wondered aloud why he should extend for two high throws and risk taking a big hit when the game was already lost.

"For who? For what?" that was what Watters said to the assembled media. And those words created a firestorm in the newspapers and talk radio. Watters, who signed a three-year deal with the Eagles that season for $6.9 million, was vilified as a selfish player who cared only about himself.

Two days later, Watters held a press conference to apologize to the fans, his coaches, and his teammates. He said his comments were "totally out of character."

Ricky Watters

"That's not me," Watters said. "I came in here talking the talk. And when you talk the talk, you have to walk the walk, and that's what I'm going to do."

Watters won back the support of the fans with his play over the next three seasons. He carried a tremendous load, breaking the club record for most rushing attempts in a season (353 in 1996) and putting up two of the five biggest rushing years in team history: 1,411 yards in 1996 and 1,273 in 1995. He also had 13 rushing touchdowns in 1996, just two short of the club record set by Steve Van Buren in 1945.

Watters, who earlier wore out his welcome in San Francisco with his bratty behavior, remained a volatile personality in Philadelphia. He had several clashes with offensive coordinator Jon Gruden, and he irritated his teammates with sideline tantrums when he felt he wasn't getting the ball enough. But Watters earned their respect with the way he played.

In his three seasons with the Eagles, Watters had 1,136 touches (combined rushing attempts and receptions) and gained 5,112 yards. He led the NFL with 1,855 total yards in 1996. The Eagles played five different quarterbacks in those three seasons. Watters was the one thing they could count on, week in and week out.

"There are a lot of negative clouds around Ricky sometimes because of his emotions," Gruden said. "But he certainly backs it up on Sunday. When he's on the field, he doesn't think anybody can tackle him. He's beautiful that way."

"If you want to say I'm an emotional player, that's true," Watters said. "That I'm a fiery competitor, that's true. Do I want to win every game? Yes. Do I want to do well? Do I want my team to do well? Yes. If that's where the criticism comes from and the fact that I get on myself at times and get fired up, then I don't know. Some people are different. Everybody's wound differently. If that's what makes me bad, then I'm bad."

The Eagles made the playoffs in Watters' first two seasons, but in his third year the team slipped to 6–9–1, and Watters' relationship with the front office and coaches deteriorated, so the Eagles decided not to offer him a new contract. He signed with Seattle.

"It was time for Ricky to move on; I think it was best for everyone," coach Ray Rhodes said.

"We'll miss his production, but I don't think we'll miss the way he acts on the sidelines," safety Mike Zordich said.

Troy Vincent, however, felt Watters would be missed. "On Sunday at 1 o'clock, the man showed up," Vincent said. "You need a few guys to put some hot sauce in the pot."

CHUCK WEBER
Linebacker

Ht: 6–1 • **Wt:** 230 • **College:** West Chester • **Years with the Eagles:** 1959–61 • **Birthplace:** Philadelphia • **Born:** March 25, 1930

Walk into any sports bar in Philadelphia and ask, "Who was the middle linebacker on the 1960 Eagles?" The first response almost surely will be "Chuck Bednarik."

Wrong. Bednarik played the left side when he replaced the injured Bob Pellegrini in the fifth week of that season. Chuck Weber started every game in the middle and intercepted six passes, most among NFL linebackers. Yet …

"I'm a trivia question," Weber said. "That's okay. That other Chuck you're talking about, he was pretty good."

Weber was pretty good, too. He was a Philadelphia native who attended Abington High School and played his college football at West Chester. He always wanted to play for the Eagles, but he was signed by Cleveland and traded to the Chicago Cardinals. He was acquired by the Eagles in 1959.

He was a smart player with a nose for the football. It was no surprise he went into coaching after hanging up his pads. He coached at Abington for two years (1962–63) and worked his way up the ladder to the NFL, where he worked as a linebacker coach and defensive coordinator with Cincinnati and San Diego.

That was typical of the 1960 championship team. Of the 22 starters, 12 wound up as NFL coaches or executives. Others, like cornerback Tom Brookshier and quarterback Sonny Jurgensen, became broadcasters.

"We weren't the most physically talented group, but we had a high football IQ," Weber said. "A lot of the plays we made, we made on our instincts. The big thing was we didn't make mistakes."

Weber played most of the 1960 season with two broken ribs. The trainer, Tom McCoy, strapped him up every Sunday, and Weber never missed a down. "Every time I got hit," he said, "it felt like I was cut in half."

The pain did not prevent Weber from making a number of big plays. He had three interceptions in the 27–25 win over Dallas, and he fell on the loose ball when Chuck Bednarik knocked out New York's Frank Gifford in the pivotal 17–10 win at Yankee Stadium.

Another case of being overshadowed by the legend: When people see the classic photo of Bednarik dancing over the unconscious Gifford, they rarely notice Weber off to the left, clutching the ball to his stomach.

"I was just glad I didn't get in the way," Weber said. "When Chuck hit Frank, it sounded like an explosion. I'll never forget it."

Chuck Weber

BRIAN WESTBROOK
Running Back

Ht: 5–10 • **Wt:** 205 • **College:** Villanova • **Years with the Eagles:** 2002– • **Birthplace:** Washington, D.C. • **Born:** September 2, 1979

In the week leading up to Super Bowl XXXIX, New England linebacker Willie McGinest was asked about Eagles running back Brian Westbrook. "It's like playing against Marshall Faulk," McGinest said.

Villanova football coach Andy Talley must have smiled when he read those words. He was making the same comparison when Westbrook was setting records for the Wildcats, but no one would listen. "Everyone laughed," Talley said. "But they're not laughing now."

At the time, the comparison did seem like a stretch. Faulk was leading the St. Louis Rams to the Super Bowl, and Westbrook was playing for Division 1-AA Villanova. But after the 2004 season, when Westbrook rushed for 812 yards and led all NFL backs with 73 receptions while helping the Eagles to the Super Bowl, the comparison with Faulk was certainly valid.

"There are very few players who can dominate a football game," guard Jermane Mayberry said. "Brian is one of them."

"He changes the speed of the game," said linebacker Jeremiah Trotter.

During Westbrook's senior season at Villanova, Talley approached Eagles coach Andy Reid at a football banquet. Talley told Reid, "You should take a look at our number 20 [Westbrook]. He's a very, very special player." When the NFL draft rolled around the following spring, Reid selected Westbrook in the third round.

"Everyone on this team knew what Brian was capable of," Reid said. "I don't think anybody's surprised. He's a very good football player. For the first ten yards, there are not a lot of players who are as explosive as he is."

Westbrook may have played at a small college, but he put up big numbers. In 1998, as a sophomore, he became the first college player at any level to gain 1,000 yards rushing and 1,000 yards receiving in the same season. After missing the 1999 season with a knee injury, Westbrook came back to score 29 touchdowns as a senior. He finished his career on the Main Line with 9,885 all-purpose yards, an NCAA record.

When Westbrook was drafted, he was projected as a third-down back and kick returner, but Reid felt Westbrook could play a bigger role. He is not very big (he is actually a shade under his listed height of 5–10), but he is elusive enough to avoid a lot of hits. As a rookie, he played a supporting role behind Duce Staley, carrying the ball 46 times for 193 yards, a 4.2-yard average.

In 2003, Westbrook blossomed in the "Three-Headed Monster" backfield with Staley and Correll Buckhalter. Westbrook led the team with 613 yards rushing (a 5.2-yard average) and scored 13 touchdowns. At the time, only two players in Eagles history—Steve Van Buren and Wilbert Montgomery—had scored more touchdowns in a single season.

Westbrook made the biggest play of the 2003 season when he scored on an 84-yard punt return to lift the Eagles to a 14–10 victory over the New York Giants. The Eagles were a struggling 2–3 at the time, and they were less than two minutes away from losing again. With one electrifying burst, West-

Brian Westbrook

brook turned around the entire season. The Eagles went on to win their next eight games and advance to the NFC final for the third straight year.

When they arrived at the championship game, however, they did not have Westbrook, who suffered a torn triceps tendon in the last regular-season game against Washington. Ironically, he was injured on a tackle by Trotter, who was playing his final game for the Redskins. Without Westbrook, the offense fell flat in the 14–3 loss to Carolina.

When Staley bolted for free agency and Buckhalter went down with a knee injury in the 2004 preseason, Westbrook became the Eagles' No. 1 back. The question was, Could he carry the heavier workload? He proved he could as he finished fourth in the NFC in total yards from scrimmage (1,515). He led the entire league in yards per touch (combined runs and pass receptions) with a 6.1 average. He could have added to those numbers, but Reid rested him, along with several other regulars, in the final two weeks of the regular season.

Reid and offensive coordinator Brad Childress moved Westbrook around the formation from running back to slot receiver and wide receiver. In the 47–17 rout of Green Bay, Westbrook caught 11 passes for 156 yards and three touchdowns. The receiving yardage was most for an Eagles running back in one game since Jerry Williams had 163 yards against Washington in 1954.

"It feels good," Westbrook said, "because people are counting on you and they know that you can handle it and they know that you can do it. And I feel as though Coach [Reid] realizes that I'm mature enough. I'm ready to handle what he's going to throw at me."

With Owens sidelined by an injury, Westbrook keyed the Eagles offense in the NFC playoffs. He had 117 total yards and one touchdown in the 27–14 first-round win over Minnesota. He had 135 total yards, including a game-high 96 yards rushing, in the 27–10 win over Atlanta for the NFC championship. In the Super Bowl loss to the Patriots, Westbrook had 44 yards rushing (on 15 carries) and six catches for 60 yards. He scored the Eagles second touchdown on a 10-yard reception from Donovan McNabb.

Westbrook was a late addition to the Pro Bowl team, and he scored a touchdown there, too, on a 12-yard run.

"Because of the work I had to do to get this [success] and the work I have to do to stay here, it becomes harder to appreciate," Westbrook told Mark Kram of the *Philadelphia Daily News.* "I never take the time out to say, 'You know what, Brian? You had a great season.'"

REGGIE WHITE
Defensive End

Ht: 6–5 • **Wt:** 295 • **College:** Tennessee • **Years with the Eagles:** 1985–92 • **Birthplace:** Chattanooga, Tennessee • **Born:** December 19, 1961 • **Died:** December 26, 2004

Reggie White is the greatest defensive lineman ever to wear an Eagles uniform. He set a club record with 124 career sacks, he never missed a game in eight years with the team, and he was voted into seven consecutive Pro Bowls, the longest such streak in Eagles history.

He was the cornerstone around which Buddy Ryan built one of the NFL's most feared defenses. When he left the team following the 1992 season, he was the only player in the league to have more sacks than games played (121). He is a lock for first-ballot election to the Pro Football Hall of Fame when he becomes eligible in 2006.

"Reggie is the most gifted defensive player I've ever been around," Ryan said, high praise considering he coached Chicago's Super Bowl defense in 1985 (with Hall of Famers Dan Hampton and Mike Singletary) and the fabled Minnesota defense of the 1970s (with Hall of Famers Alan Page, Carl Eller, and Paul Krause). "Reggie is almost 300 pounds and runs a 4.6 40. Eller couldn't run 4.6 and he only weighed 245, and he was a great player. If you wanted to make the perfect defensive lineman, you'd take Reggie's ingredients and then you'd have him."

White joined the Eagles in September 1985, jumping from the sinking ship known as the United States Football League to sign a four-year, $1.85 million contract in Philadelphia. He was an unproven commodity in the minds of most Eagles veterans. Okay, so he made All-USFL playing for the Memphis Showboats, big deal. What would he do in the NFL? White joined the team in Week 4 of the regular season after completing a full spring schedule in the USFL. In his first game, White had 10 tackles and two and a half sacks against the New York Giants. He also tipped a pass that cornerback Herman Edwards intercepted and returned for a touchdown. By the fourth quarter, the Veterans Stadium crowd was chanting his name: "Reggie, Reg-gie." A new era in Eagles football was born.

"We were all taken aback by just how dominant Reggie was," said tight end John Spagnola. "We had heard his name and read good things about him, but most of us took a wait-and-

Reggie White

see attitude. Once he stepped on the field, though, it was clear he was something special. I remember standing on the sidelines, thinking, 'Boy, I'm glad this guy is on our side.'"

White finished that season with 13 sacks and was named Defensive Rookie of the Year. And that was only the beginning. The next season, Ryan came to town, and that's when White's career really took off. He led the league in sacks in back-to-back seasons (21 in 1987, 18 in 1988) as the Eagles climbed from the depths of the NFC East to a division title in 1988.

At the time, the league record for sacks in a season was 22 set by Mark Gastineau of the New York Jets in 1984. White had 21 sacks in just 12 games in 1987 and would have broken the record easily had it not been for the four games he lost during the players' strike. He never had fewer than 11 sacks in any season with the Eagles. Some people felt he was slowing down in 1992 when he had just five sacks through 10 games, but he had nine sacks in the next seven games, including a safety in a 36–20 playoff win against New Orleans.

"I had the opportunity to watch Reggie play," said Dick Vermeil, who was out of football and living in Chester County during White's time with the Eagles. "I don't believe I've ever seen a better defensive lineman. He was the total package. Explosive power and quickness equaled by no one who has ever played. Every offensive game plan has to start with 'How do you handle Reggie White?' In most cases, the answer is 'Poorly.'"

Offensive teams assigned two, sometimes three men to block him. They held him, they tripped him, they chopped at his knees. Still, they could not keep him from punishing their quarterbacks and stuffing their ground game. That was a source of pride for White: He played the run as well as the pass. He got his sacks the old fashioned way, reading his keys and carrying out his assignment. He was a complete player, who averaged more than 100 tackles in his eight seasons with the Eagles.

White was voted NFL Defensive Player of the Year twice, 1987 and 1991. He was named to at least one All-Pro team each of last seven seasons with the Eagles.

If there was one quintessential Reggie White play, it occurred in the 1987 league opener at Washington. White sacked Redskins quarterback Jay Schroeder on the first series, sending him to the bench with a sprained shoulder. Doug Williams came in, and late in the game White grabbed Williams, wrestled the ball from his arms, and rumbled 70 yards to a touchdown. He resembled a bear making off with a picnic basket in Yellowstone Park. After the game, White said, "I saw the end zone and I was determined to get there. Praise Jesus, I got there." He instructed reporters, "Be sure to put that in there. Praise Jesus."

White was known as "The Minister of Defense," and he was, indeed, a licensed Baptist minister. He was raised by his grandmother, a deeply religious woman. He believed his athletic talent was a gift from God for the purpose of using his superstar status to make a strong Christian statement.

In a 1988 interview White said:

In the Bible, Jesus told the apostles to go and preach the gospel. That's what I'm doing. I'm sharing my faith the best way I know how. That's through football. My goal is to be the best defensive lineman who ever played the game. That's not cockiness; that's just part of my mission. If I'm the best, then I'll have a platform to preach, and more people will hear what I have to say. People who might not listen ordinarily will listen because of who I am.

Our society is crying out for role models. That's what I'm doing now, I'm trying to be the best role model I can be, on and off the field. I'm pleased with what I've done so far, but I know I can do better.

Football and religion is a curious crossbreeding, White acknowledged that. Critics call football violent and un-Christian. White disagreed. He said the game itself is fine; it is just certain players who act in an un-Christian way. There is no need for that. White was proof that a player can be just as intimidating playing within the rules.

"A lot of people think that being a Christian, you've got to be a wimp," White told Rich Hofmann of the *Philadelphia Daily News* in 1987. "Then they look at me as a Christian and say, 'You play this game, and you're trying to hurt people.' Well, I don't go out and try to hurt anybody. I try to go out and play the game the way it's supposed to be played."

White was a man of principle and dogmatic beliefs. As Spagnola once said, "With Reggie, there is right and wrong. He doesn't compromise or rationalize." Ultimately, that unwillingness to compromise brought him into conflict with Eagles management. First, he filed a $1.5 million civil suit against Patrick Forte, his former agent who went to work for the Eagles as assistant to team president Harry Gamble. White charged that Forte "pursued his employment with the Eagles at the same time that he was ostensibly representing the best interests of White." The suit was eventually dropped, but it was the first crack in the relationship between the All-Pro defensive end and the front office.

By the end of the 1992 season, White was an outspoken critic of Norman Braman, claiming the owner was not committed to building a championship team in Philadelphia.

White pointed to the large number of talented veterans who were allowed to leave as free agents. In March 1993, White joined the list of defectors, signing a four-year, $17 million contract with Green Bay.

The Philadelphia fans did their best to convince White to stay. They staged a "Keep Reggie" rally at City Hall with thousands of fans carrying signs that read, "Please Don't Go," and, "We Love You, 92." It was a noble effort and heartfelt, but also futile. White had made up his mind to leave the Eagles and Norman Braman.

"Philadelphia will remain a big part of my life," White said. "We met too many great people to forget. The time I spent with the Eagles, I'll always cherish. All my teammates, the coaches, and the fans, that's what I'll remember. But I want to win a championship, and I think we can do that in Green Bay. The Packers have made a commitment to improving the football team. I'm excited about it."

White's signing was a watershed event for the Packers, who were 19–29 in the three seasons prior to that. When White signed, it sent a powerful message to other players that maybe Green Bay wasn't such a bad place. Four years later, with White leading the defense, the Packers went to Super Bowl XXXI and defeated New England, 35–21. White set a Super Bowl record with three sacks and hurried Patriots quarterback Drew Bledsoe into four interceptions.

One month after the championship game, White was honored with a parade in his hometown of Chattanooga. Addressing the huge crowd that turned out on a cold, rainy day, White said: "One day [football] is not going to matter. What really matters is what I did with the life God gave me."

On December 26, 2004, White died suddenly at his home outside Charlotte, North Carolina. The cause of death was listed as respiratory failure. The news broke on a Sunday morning just as millions of fans were tuning in the NFL pregame shows. The shock and sense of loss was felt across the nation, but especially in Philadelphia and Green Bay.

The Eagles marked the passing of Reggie White by wearing his number 92 on their helmets for the final game of the 2004 regular season.

"Reggie meant so much in so many different ways," said Seth Joyner, his former Eagles teammate. "It's hard to hang one tag on him and say, 'This is what he really meant to me or anyone else.' He was a tremendous teammate, a tremendous spiritual leader, and more than anything, just a great person."

"Reggie White was a gentle warrior who will be remembered as one of the greatest defensive players in NFL history," Commissioner Paul Tagliabue said. "Equally as impressive as his achievements on the field was the positive impact he made off the field and the way he served as a positive influence on so many young people."

NORM WILLEY
Defensive End

Ht: 6-2 • **Wt:** 225 • **College:** Marshall • **Years with the Eagles:** 1950–57 • **Birthplace:** Hastings, West Virginia • **Born:** August 22, 1927

Norm Willey earned his nickname at his first Eagles training camp in 1950. Drafted as a fullback, Willey was riding the bench behind veterans Joe Muha and Jack Meyers. But coach Greasy Neale liked the strong country boy from Hastings, West Virginia (population 700), so he told Willey to line up at defensive end.

On the next three plays, Willey flew across the line and knocked quarterback Tommy Thompson to the ground. Finally, Thompson pointed at the rookie and said, "Somebody block that wildman."

Norm Willey

That's how he became Wildman Willey.

It was a fitting name for one of the Eagles' first great pass rushers. It is hard to document Willey's career because the NFL was not recording quarterback sacks in the 1950s (it did not become an official statistic until 1982), but Willey estimates he averaged 20 sacks per season, and no one who saw him play disputes that figure.

"He was a terror; he was in our backfield on every play," Detroit halfback Doak Walker said in a 1997 interview. "I remember Bobby [Layne, quarterback] telling our linemen, 'If you can't block the SOB, tackle him, do something.' It's a shame the Eagles weren't a better team because he didn't get the recognition he deserved. He should be in the Hall of Fame."

Willey should have made the Hall of Fame for one game alone: a 14–10 win over the New York Giants in 1952, a game in which Willey, according to press accounts, tackled quarterback Charlie Conerly 17 times while he was attempting to pass. Today, those would be counted as sacks, shattering the NFL record for sacks in one game (seven by Derrick Thomas of Kansas City).

"Wildman was a good description of how he played," said tackle Vic Sears. "He went full-speed all the time. He didn't always carry out his assignment. He'd just go. He played on instinct a lot, but he was so quick and so aggressive, he was always around the ball. The coaches knew it, and they let him be."

Actually, coach Jim Trimble did try to harness the Wildman. In 1952, his first year as head coach, Trimble kept Willey after practice to polish his technique. Trimble wanted Willey to read the split in the offensive line. If the guard and tackle were three yards apart, Willey was to take his normal outside rush. But if they were split wider, Trimble told Willey to rush inside.

The next game, Willey tried to follow Trimble's instructions, but he could not make a play. He was so concerned with calculating the distance between the blockers that he was slow coming off the ball.

"I had enough common sense at halftime to say, 'Norm, forget anything I ever told you. Just play like you played before,'" Trimble told Ron Pollack of *Pro Football Weekly*. "He was a spontaneous pass rusher. You just had to tell him, 'Sic 'em.'"

Willey did adopt one bit of coaching from a woman who taught lipreading. Willey studied with her so he could read the lips of opposing quarterbacks as they called the plays in the huddle. "It worked with some guys, not others," he said. "Once in awhile I'd see something and get a jump."

In the final week of the 1953 season, Cleveland came into Shibe Park with an 11–0 record, seeking to become the first NFL team to complete an unbeaten, untied season. Willey led the defensive charge on quarterback Otto Graham as the Eagles (7–4–1) won easily, 42–27.

"I was beating Lou Groza [Browns Hall of Fame tackle] all day," Willey said. "He was trying everything: holding, tripping, chopping. I was going right past him. I don't know how many times I dropped Otto, but it must have been eight or nine.

"After the game, who comes in our dressing room but Otto Graham. He walks up to me and says, 'Brother, am I glad I won't have to see you for another whole year.' They put that story on the back of my bubble gum card. I have it framed at home."

"Norm is one of those great forgotten players," said Tom Brookshier, who was Willey's teammate for three seasons. "He played before [network] TV, before the media caught on to pro football. If he played today, they'd have a camera isolated on him every play. He was so quick off the ball, he ran some blockers right out of the stadium. Even the great ones like Rosey Brown [Giants Hall of Fame tackle] couldn't lay a glove on him."

Willey's career was cut short by a compound fracture of his right leg in 1956. He came back the following year, but his leg was so painfully swollen that it robbed him of his speed. He retired after the season to become a teacher and coach at Pennsville (New Jersey) High School.

Willey stayed close to the game, working with field security at Eagles home games for 20 years. He wore a green blazer and patrolled the sidelines, checking media credentials and lining up the visiting team for pregame introductions.

"Sometimes these [players] act like they're bigger than God," Willey said. "I remember one time the Raiders gave me some guff. When I told them to line up, they got a little mouthy. I said, 'Look, someday you'll be like me, an ex-player standing on the sidelines. Show a little respect. Act like professionals.' They settled down after that."

AL WISTERT
Tackle

Ht: 6–1 • **Wt:** 215 • **College:** Michigan • **Years with the Eagles:** 1943–51 • **Birthplace:** Chicago, Illinois • **Born:** December 28, 1920

In his 1988 book *The Hidden Game of Football*, Bob Carroll wrote that of all the players who were not yet in the Pro Football Hall of Fame, the one who was most deserving of that honor was Al Wistert, the captain of the Eagles' 1948–49 championship teams.

Carroll used a simple formula to arrive at that conclusion. He tallied the consensus All-Pro seasons for each player (five for Wistert), the first-team All-Pro selections (two), and second-team selections (one) and awarded points for each. Wistert had the most points among the two-way tackles, including eight already in the Hall of Fame.

Carroll wrote, "We never met Al Wistert; maybe there's something awful about him that we don't know. But, golly! He was the top lineman, among several excellent guards and tackles, on one of the NFL's dynasties, the postwar Eagles." In other words, why doesn't this man have a bust in Canton, Ohio?

There is nothing awful, or hidden, in Wistert's résumé. He was a splendid player who was admired by teammates and opponents alike. But for some reason, he has been overlooked by the same Hall of Fame voters who enshrined his coach (Greasy Neale) and four of his teammates (Pete Pihos, Steve Van Buren, Chuck Bednarik, and Alex Wojciechowicz).

In a 1993 letter to the board of selectors, George Savitsky, a tackle on the Eagles 1948–49 teams, wrote, "[Wistert] certainly has all the credentials. He should have been inducted many years ago. A man of his stature and past performance, how could he be overlooked? Get him in!!"

In his book *Pro Football's 100 Greatest Players*, George Allen selected Wistert as one of his top-10 defensive linemen. Wistert is the only one of the 10 who is not in the Hall of Fame.

Allen wrote, "Wistert seemed to be born with perfect balance. He always played in perfect position and seldom was off

Al Wistert

his feet. He was a superb pursuit man and seemed somehow to get in on every play. He was a sure tackler. He maybe was best against the run, but he was among the good early pass rushers. He was as fine a blocker as you could want. He didn't have the size to overpower people on the pass block, but he was a master of every kind of block."

Wistert was a fierce player, who served as the Eagles captain from 1947 until his retirement following the 1951 season. He earned All-Pro mention every season except his rookie year, 1943.

Wistert was called "Big Ox," but he was only 6–1 and 215 pounds. He was a great trap blocker, opening holes for Steve Van Buren and Bosh Pritchard. On defense, Greasy Neale took advantage of Wistert's speed by sometimes assigning him to shadow a back in motion. He played every play, 60 minutes, almost every week.

"He was always first down the field on kickoffs and punts," Pritchard said. "He was very fast pulling out of the line on offense. He was an excellent downfield blocker. He did it all. Al was the greatest offensive tackle I have ever seen or played with."

"I played the game to the hilt," Wistert said. "I gave it everything I had on that football field. That's the only way I knew how to play the game."

Wistert was one of three brothers—Al, Francis, and Alvin—who were All-America tackles at Michigan, but he was the only one to play professionally. His father was a Chicago policeman who was killed in the line of duty.

Wistert retired following the 1951 season at the relatively young age of 31. He still was playing well enough to earn All-Pro mention, but he felt his skills were declining and chose to walk away.

"Pro football is a great game as long as you're able to give more than you receive," Wistert told Ralph Bernstein of the Associated Press. "In the past few years, I've reached the point where the receiving is getting the edge. Therefore, it's time to quit."

The Eagles honored Wistert by retiring his number 70. However, the uniform was mistakenly reissued in 1963 to guard Jim Skaggs. When the team realized its mistake, it allowed Skaggs to continue wearing the number until his career ended in 1972, then the number 70 was retired for good.

"Al was the glue that kept our team together," said quarterback Bill Mackrides. "His blocking was the mainstay of our offensive line. On many occasions, he bailed out the other linemen with last-second adjustments. Don't let his smaller-than-today stature fool you. Given the opportunity, Al could play in any era."

ALEX WOJCIECHOWICZ
Linebacker

Ht: 5–11 • **Wt:** 225 • **College:** Fordham • **Years with the Eagles:** 1946–50 • **Birthplace:** South River, New Jersey • **Born:** August 12, 1915 • **Died:** July 13, 1992

One month into the 1946 season, the Detroit Lions traded Alex Wojciechowicz to the Eagles. The Lions felt the 31-year-old Wojciechowicz was slipping, but Eagles coach Greasy Neale had a different role in mind for the former Fordham All-America.

Instead of asking him to play both center and linebacker, which Wojciechowicz had done throughout his career, starting as one of Fordham's famed "Seven Blocks of Granite," Neale made him a defensive specialist. He put Wojciechowicz at linebacker in his 5–2–4 defense, and "Wojie" responded by playing some of his best football.

"I had a lot of motivation because we'd never won a championship in my time with the Lions," Wojciechowicz said in a 1988 interview. "When I came to the Eagles, I saw immediately we had the makings of a championship club. Defensively, we were way ahead of the other teams and [Steve] Van Buren was the best running back in the league. Playing with those guys, I felt like a kid again."

Wojciechowicz was an excellent tackler whose physical play discouraged teams from running wide, and he made receivers think twice about coming across the middle. Wojciechowicz intercepted 19 passes in his career, including seven in one season with the Lions.

"Washington had a receiver named Bones Taylor," Neale said, "and in 1947, he caught five touchdown passes in one game. [Actually, it was three.] The next time we played them, I put Wojie on Bones. He never caught a pass that day, and he never caught a pass against us the next three years. Wojie made sure of that."

"I get a thrill out of playing on defense," Wojciechowicz said in a 1948 interview. "I get a kick out of the body contact. That's my game."

"Wojie was a very tough individual," said Al Wistert. "Receivers were always looking over their shoulder for him because he'd catch 'em with a forearm under the chin and send them flying. Wojie was a sweet guy, but on the field, he was one tough son of a gun.

"I'll never forget the time we were warming up before a practice, playing two-hand touch, and Wojie ran into the wall, full-speed. His head went 'Crack,' right into the wall. He stepped back, shook his head, and laughed. If that was me, they would've taken me away on a stretcher."

Wojciechowicz played a major role on the Eagles defense that won three consecutive Eastern Division titles and back-to-back NFL Championships in 1948 and '49. He retired following the 1950 season, completing 13 years in the NFL. At that point, only Washington's Sammy Baugh had played longer.

He was inducted into the Pro Football Hall of Fame in 1968.

TOM WOODESHICK
Fullback

Ht: 6–0 • **Wt:** 225 • **College:** West Virginia • **Years with the Eagles:** 1963–71 • **Birthplace:** Wilkes-Barre, Pennsylvania • **Born:** December 3, 1941

The final game of the 1968 regular season is best remembered as the day the Eagles fans threw snowballs at Santa Claus. Tom Woodeshick remembers it for another reason. That was the day he lost his best chance for a 1,000-yard season.

Unlike today, the 1,000-yard season was a major accomplishment in 1968 when teams played just 14 regular-season games. That year, only Leroy Kelly of Cleveland rushed for more than 1,000 yards. But in the final week Woodeshick had a shot. He was just 53 yards short in the third quarter against Minnesota when he suffered a gruesome eye injury that knocked him out of the game.

"I got straightened up by two guys, and [linebacker] Lonnie Warwick cracked me with the top of his helmet," Woodeshick said. "He hit my face mask and broke it. The jagged piece cut me at the top of my eyelid. I went down in a pool of blood. I was begging the doctor to stitch me up so I could back in. He said, 'Are you crazy? You can't play in your condition. Do you want to lose your eye?'

"I didn't care. I wanted those 1,000 yards. I worked so hard to get to that point. I knew there was a good chance I'd never get that close again. As it turned out, I was right."

Woodeshick did not return to the game, and although he finished the season with 947 yards, the most for an Eagles back since Steve Van Buren led the league with 1,146 yards in 1949, it was no consolation. He rushed for 831 yards the next year, then a knee injury in 1970 wrecked his career. He had 254 yards in 1970 and just 188 yards in 1971, his final year with the Eagles. He finished playing four games for St. Louis in 1972.

Woodeshick never reached the 1,000-yard plateau, but he earned the admiration of his peers. They respected him as a player who made it the hard way, an eighth-round draft pick who worked his way up from special teams to Pro Bowl status as a fullback.

"Woody was a football player's football player," said Bob Brown, the Hall of Fame tackle who blocked for Woodeshick for five seasons. "Our play was 34 cross buck. That was 'Woody, follow me.' I loved it because I knew Woody was coming through that hole like a man on a mission.

"There wasn't a fullback around who was tougher than Woody, and this was the era of Jim Brown, so you know what I'm saying. Some guys talk tough and act tough. Other guys play tough and are tough. That was Woody. It really hurt him to miss that 1,000-yard season. He would've run on hot rocks from here to Tokyo to get those 1,000 yards. We all felt bad when he didn't get it."

The injury in the final game wasn't the only thing that kept Woodeshick from reaching his milestone. He was ejected from a game in Dallas when he shoved cornerback Mike Gaechter during a sideline altercation. Both players were tossed out, so Woodeshick lost perhaps a dozen carries that day.

Woodeshick was fiercely competitive. He had so much trouble holding onto the ball as a rookie that the other players nicknamed him "Wooden Hands." But he kept working at it until he became a capable receiver.

Woodeshick told Gordon Forbes of the *Philadelphia Inquirer*, "When I run, I put my guts and everything else into it. I'm like a man with a circulatory system speeded up five times. What I love most about football is quite simply the contact and the violence. I don't mean to sound sadistic, but it's one of the few forms left in our society where we can go out and enjoy legalized brutality. Let's face it, once you put on that uniform and go on the field, it's no place for anyone but madmen."

The Philadelphia fans loved Woodeshick's blood-and-guts approach. He was a fan favorite even in his first few seasons when he played mostly on special teams. He was one of the first Eagles downfield on every kickoff, throwing himself full-speed into the wall of blockers.

"Who wants to play in San Francisco or New York, someplace like that?" Woodeshick said. "This is where I belong. They cheered me as a rookie and I only carried the ball five times. They love me and I love them."

CHARLES YOUNG
Tight End

Ht: 6–4 • **Wt:** 240 • **College:** Southern California • **Years with the Eagles:** 1973–76 • **Birthplace:** Fresno, California • **Born:** February 5, 1951

Charles Young was never a rookie. He was a first-year player with the Eagles in 1973, but he was not a rookie.

"What's this 'rookie' stuff?" he asked. "I'm doing everything a veteran could do and more than most veterans are doing around the league. If you can play, you can play."

There was never any doubt Young could play. He was an All-America tight end at Southern Cal, and the Eagles made him the sixth overall pick in the '73 draft. As a rookie—rather, a first-year player—he caught 55 passes for 854 yards, an average of 15.5 yards per reception.

In his second season, Young was even better as he led the NFC with 63 receptions for 696 yards. His combined total of 118 catches was the most for any NFL tight end in his first two seasons. And the cocky Young talked an even better game than he played.

He started talking the day he was drafted. In a conference call with the Philadelphia media, Young said, "I've got the best catching hands in the world." Asked if there were any NFL tight ends he admired, he replied, "I can't say who's the best because when I get to the pros, I'll be the best."

Later Young said:

I knew what I was doing the whole time. I knew I was a quality product, so all I was doing was advertising. Sony advertises. General Motors advertises. What was wrong with me advertising?

The average playing career lasts four and a half years. What was I supposed to do, wait three years to make a name for myself? That way I'd only have a year and a half to cash in.

So I talked a lot. I think people misunderstood me in the beginning. They called me arrogant and braggadocious. I could tell some of the veterans didn't like me. But I didn't care. I knew I could back up everything I said.

Young was named NFC Rookie of the Year by UPI. He also was voted into the first of three consecutive Pro Bowls. He teamed with quarterback Roman Gabriel and wide receiver Harold Carmichael to form an explosive passing attack.

"The Eagle image was suffering when I got there," Young said. "The Eagle is supposed to be a big, majestic bird. Powerful wings, sharp claws. A bird that soars to the heights. A bird that will rip your face off if you mess with it. But the Philadelphia Eagles weren't anything like that when I got there. They were more like some little flabby chicken that was getting kicked all over the barnyard. I said, 'This isn't for me,' so I set out to change it."

Young also changed the spelling of his name. He arrived as Charles, then became Charlie. In his second season, he decided to drop the *e* so he became Charli. Then he dropped the *i* and became Charle. Anything to be different.

In 1977, Young and his agent, Howard Slusher, became involved in a bitter contract negotiation with the Eagles. With the talks going nowhere, the Eagles traded Young's rights to the Los Angeles Rams in exchange for quarterback Ron Jaworski.

Young spent three frustrating seasons with the Rams, where his receiving skills were lost in a run-oriented offense. In 1980, Bill Walsh brought him to San Francisco where he fit perfectly into the West Coast offense. In 1981, Young caught 37 passes and scored five touchdowns as he helped the 49ers win their first Super Bowl.

He finished his career with three seasons in Seattle (1983–85). He played a total of 13 seasons in the NFL and retired with 418 receptions for 5,106 yards, and 27 touchdowns.

4

The Coaches

THE EAGLES have had 21 head coaches. Only nine have winning records, and two of those—Bo McMillin (2–0) and Fred Bruney (1–0)—held the job so briefly, they hardly count.

Fourteen of the 21 had no previous head coaching experience at the NFL level. You might say that lack of experience explains why the Eagles had so many losing seasons, except for one thing: the most successful coaches were the ones who were new to the job. Andy Reid, Greasy Neale, Dick Vermeil, and Buddy Ryan.

Twelve of the 21 played in the NFL, and two were Hall of Famers—Wayne Millner (Washington) and Mike McCormack (Cleveland)—yet that fact did not translate into coaching success. Millner coached the Eagles for one year (1951), McCormack for three (1973–75), and neither man produced a winning season. Reid, Vermeil, and Ryan never played a down in the NFL, yet they were winning head coaches. Neale played more baseball than football, yet he led the Eagles to back-to-back world championships.

Three of the head coaches played for the Eagles—Jerry Williams, Ed Khayat, and Marion Campbell—and all were part of the 1960 world championship team. Williams was an assistant coach that season; Khayat and Campbell were starters on the defensive line. As Eagles head coaches, however, the three men had a combined record of 32–66–5.

Nineteen of the 21 head coaches are profiled in this chapter. Bert Bell is not included because his story is told in Chapter 2, and, in truth, coaching was the least of his contributions to the franchise. He was the team's founder and president and performed those duties splendidly. In five seasons as head coach, however, Bell won a grand total of 10 games. There isn't much to say, in other words.

Walt Kiesling spent most of his career with the Pittsburgh Steelers. In 1943, when the Eagles and Steelers merged to form one team, "the Steagles," Kiesling and Neale were named co-coaches and spent most of the season bickering. The Eagles and Steelers went their separate ways the next year, and Kiesling remained with the Steelers. He is a footnote in Eagles history, nothing more, so he is not profiled in this chapter.

But the rest of the Eagles coaching history is here, from the lone Hall of Famer (Neale) to the three interim head coaches (Millner, Khayat, and Bruney) to the first African American coach (Ray Rhodes) to the winningest coach (Reid).

LUD WRAY

College: Pennsylvania • **Years as Eagles Coach:** 1933–35 • **Record:** 9–21–1

James R. Ludlow (Lud) Wray and Bert Bell were long-time friends. They grew up together in the Philadelphia area and were classmates at the University of Pennsylvania. They left school to serve in World War I, then returned to the Quakers football team in 1919. When Bell bought the Eagles franchise, it was no surprise that he named Wray head coach.

"You couldn't pick a more sincere guy nor anyone who knows more football than Ludlow," Bell said.

"Like brothers, they have argued and belted each other around, but each has turned on anyone else who dared voice an adverse opinion of the other," wrote Ed Pollock in the *Philadelphia Bulletin.* "It was a case of 'I can say what I please about him, but you can't.' For all their disputes, they've had a barrel of fun with each other, not only laugh-provoking fun, but the keen enjoyment of watching their strategy win football games."

Wray and Bell had great success at Penn, but they did not win many games with the Eagles. They were the entire front office and coaching staff. Bell was the president, which meant he answered the phones and sold tickets. Wray was the coach, so he diagramed the plays and ran practice.

The 6–0, 185-pound Wray played two years of pro football with the Buffalo Bisons (1920–21), and he coached the Boston Braves (1932), so he knew the challenge he faced with the Eagles. They dropped their first three league games, then recorded their first win over the Cincinnati Reds, 6–0, and actually got on a roll, tying the Chicago Bears, 3–3, and posting back-to-back wins over Pittsburgh, 25–6, and the Reds, 20–3. They lost their final two games to Green Bay, 10–0, and the Giants, 20–14, but they played respectably, and the future appeared bright.

After the season, Wray addressed the Penn Athletic Club and said, "We are building a great team for next year." However, the Eagles started slowly in 1934, losing five of their first six games, and finished 4–7. They slipped to 2–9 the next year, and Wray quit rather than accept a 66 percent pay cut ordered by the team's stockholders, who tired of losing money. Bell assumed the role of head coach for the next five seasons.

"It is with regret that I am forced to sever my connections with the Eagles," Wray said. "I had great hopes for the future of professional football in Philadelphia, even though the first few years were rocky. It is a wonderful game, and I may associate myself with another club in the National Football League or take a coaching job with a college."

Wray became an assistant coach at St. Joseph's Prep in Philadelphia, Manhattan College, Holy Cross, and Villanova. He returned to the NFL as line coach of the Steelers in 1945. He was a stern man who drove his players hard. His favorite expression was "Wear 'em down."

Wrote Pollock: "Wray dealt strictly in frank opinions and pulled no punches. Lud was told so often that he should use a little diplomacy that every time he heard the word, it kindled fire his eyes."

Wray was head coach at Penn in 1930, but he was dismissed after one season because so many players complained about his methods. "Football is the only sport I ever liked," said Warren Gette, one of several players who quit the team, "but I certainly did not like it this year. It was drudgery." Gette predicted, "If Lud Wray is the coach at Penn next season, there won't be three [lettermen] report for practice in the fall."

The Quakers were 5–4 in Wray's one season as head coach, but they were routed by Wisconsin (27–0), Notre Dame (60–20), and Navy (26–0). The student newspaper, *The Daily Pennsylvanian*, called for his firing. Wray tried to ignore the talk. Addressing a banquet in Audubon, New Jersey, Wray said, "[Reports] that many of the squad have turned against me [are] an exaggeration."

One week later, Wray was gone. He was so devastated by his firing that a month later, he collapsed during a dinner at the Union League. Doctors said he was the victim of "frayed nerves."

Wray was rocked again when he was forced out as the Eagles coach. He was angry at Bell for not fighting harder to save his job. Wrote Ed Pollock: "For many months, they were separated with a frigid silence between them."

During that time, Wray was in a serious automobile accident. He was in a coma for days. The doctors asked Bell to visit, hoping the sound of his gravelly voice would awaken Wray, and it did. As Pollock described it, "Lud opened his eyes and for the first time registered interest. Lud smiled and said, 'Where the hell have you been?'"

EARLE (GREASY) NEALE

College: West Virginia Wesleyan • **Years as Eagles Coach:** 1941–50 • **Record:** 66–44–5

Earle (Greasy) Neale was inducted into the Pro Football Hall of Fame in 1969. He was presented by another Hall of Famer, Chuck Bednarik, who broke into the NFL under Neale in 1949. "Greasy was my first coach," Bednarik said, "and he was the best coach I ever played for."

That opinion was shared by many who played under Neale during his ten seasons with the Eagles. Not only did Neale lead the team to world championships in 1948 and '49, but he also introduced new ideas on strategy and scouting that had a major impact throughout the National Football League.

On offense, Neale ran a T formation with occasional glimpses of what later became known as "the shotgun." On defense, he created his own alignment, a 5–2–4 that was known as "the Eagle defense," with the nose tackle sometimes

Hall of Famer Earle (Greasy) Neale coached the Eagles to seven consecutive winning seasons, the longest streak in franchise history.

dropping into pass coverage. It later evolved into the standard 4–3 defense with a middle linebacker.

Neale also was the first coach to bring detailed notebooks and scouting reports to the college draft. One year, he had 64 binders, jammed with statistics and evaluations of various players. "The other clubs laughed at me," Neale said. "They picked players out of magazines. But they stopped laughing when we started beating them. Now they all have their Blue Books."

"Greasy was the smartest football man I ever met," Tommy Thompson, the former Eagles quarterback, said in a 1983 interview. "His memory was fantastic. I remember sitting with him at a Brooklyn-Giants game. Pug Manders took the ball and ran up the middle. It looked like any other play to me. But Greasy said, 'I remember that play. Brown used it against Yale in 1933. Third play of the second quarter.'

"He'd do the same thing preparing for our games. He'd say, 'Remember what this team did against us last time?' Then he'd rattle off our last game, play by play. We didn't need films. Greasy had it all in his head."

Neale acquired his nickname as a boy in Parkersburg, West Virginia. One day in a name-calling session with a classmate, Neale said, "You're dirty," to which the other boy replied, "Well, you're Greasy." The name stuck.

He quit school in the ninth grade and took a job in a steel mill. He worked 16 hours a day and earned $12.50 a week. He toiled in the mill for two miserable years. "If I have to do this all my life, I might as well cut my throat," he said.

He returned to high school and earned a football scholarship to West Virginia Wesleyan. At the same time, he was playing for the Canton Bulldogs under the name "Foster." He could not use his real name because he would lose his college eligibility for playing with a professional team.

A swift 6–0, 170-pounder, Neale was a superb all-around athlete who starred in football, baseball, and basketball. He was confident to the point of cockiness, and when he became a coach, he looked for the same qualities in his players. He once said, "If a player doesn't think he's the best man on the field, I don't want him on my team."

When he finished college, Neale signed a professional baseball contract. He was an outfielder with the Cincinnati Reds in 1916 and batted .262 in 138 games. Three years later, he helped the Reds win the 1919 World Series. He hit .357 in the series, the highest average of any player with seven or more at bats, but most people remember it as the series in which the Chicago White Sox, better known as the Black Sox, took a dive.

Neale never believed the allegations. "There may have been shenanigans going on in the first game," he said in a 1950 interview. "But after the White Sox found out they were being duped, you'll never convince me they didn't play the rest of the series on the level. I've played ball too long to be fooled. Eddie Cicotte, Joe Jackson, Swede Risberg, Chick Gandil, Happy Felsch all played marvelous ball, hit the apple on the nose, and made great catches. We simply had better pitching, and pitching decides the World Series."

Years later, the Eagles would tease Neale about that World Series. "Steve [Van Buren] told him, 'Greasy, that's how they knew the fix was in. When you hit .357, they knew it couldn't be on the level,'" Al Wistert said.

Neale played eight seasons in the major leagues, including a brief stint with the Phillies. He coached college football at the same time, and in 1921 he attracted national attention for leading Washington and Jefferson College to a perfect season and a berth in the Rose Bowl. His team was a huge underdog to the University of California, but Neale's boys held the Golden Bears to a scoreless tie.

He later coached at the University of Virginia, West Virginia, and Yale. In 1941, Eagles owner Lex Thompson hired

Earle (Greasy) Neale with the team after defeating the Chicago Cardinals in the 1948 NFL championship game. Linebacker Alex Wojciechowicz said of Neale, "He devoted his life to teaching his men not only sports, but also an understanding and appreciation of life itself."

Neale to replace Bert Bell as coach of the flightless Birds. In five years under Bell, the Eagles had won only 10 games. Neale knew he had a lot of work to do.

One of the first things he did was study the Chicago Bears' 73–0 win over Washington in the 1940 NFL championship game. He purchased the game film from a newsreel company. It cost Neale $156, but it was worth it. He took the Bears' T formation offense apart, piece by piece, and examined it. Rather than simply copy it, Neale improved on it, creating deception with the quarterback hiding the ball and the halfbacks running reverses.

Neale had the plan, but he needed players to make it work. The Eagles were 2–8–1 in his first season and 2–9 the next. In 1943, Neale finally produced a winning record of 5–4–1 as the Eagles and Pittsburgh Steelers merged to form the "Steagles." Neale shared the coaching duties with Walt Kiesling, an arrangement that irritated both men. The teams went their separate ways the following year, and when the Eagles drafted halfback Steve Van Buren in 1944, they became a power.

Over the next six years, the Eagles won 51 games and lost 17, including postseason. They won back-to-back world championships, and in those two seasons, they outscored their opponents 740 points to 290. Neale was a superstitious man, so when the Eagles won, he insisted on wearing the same clothes, eating the same foods, and following the same pregame routine.

"His power of concentration is terrific," wrote Stan Baumgartner of the *Philadelphia Inquirer* in 1950. "He stood in a driving rain during one whole game and did not know it had rained until he looked at his suit afterwards."

"Greasy was always thinking about a new play, a new gimmick, something," Russ Craft, the former halfback, said. "I'll bet he saw football in his dreams. He'd come out to practice and say, 'Let's try this,' and it would be something brand new. We never knew what to expect, but neither did the teams we were playing, and that was to our advantage."

Neale's explosive temper intimidated some players, including Al Wistert, who developed into one of the game's outstanding tackles and captained the two championship teams. Wistert recalled:

My first impression of Greasy was he was the most uncouth man I ever met. He cussed and swore something awful. Foul language bothered me back then. I wasn't used to it. I was raised by my mother and three sisters. I never heard that kind of language around the house. I never heard it playing ball in high school or college. My coaches didn't believe in it.

At Michigan, I was coached by Fritz Crisler, who played his college ball under Amos Alonzo Stagg. Stagg studied to be a preacher, so he never swore. Neither did Fritz. But I joined the Eagles and here was Greasy calling us every name in the book. He'd say things like "You couldn't knock a whore off a s——pot." And "You're standing there like a statue of s——." It bothered me so much it hurt my play.

One day he asked what was wrong. I said, "I can't play for you. You don't know how to handle men." We didn't speak for the rest of the year. But eventually I realized the language didn't mean anything. The way he grew up, working in the steel mill as a boy, he was around a lot of roughnecks and it rubbed off on him. But he was really a gentle soul who cared for his players. I loved the guy.

Neale's coaching career ended abruptly in 1950, just one year after the Eagles' second world championship. The team was crippled by injuries and limped to a 6–6 finish that included four consecutive losses at the end of the season. During that slide, the Eagles dropped a 7–3 game to the New York Giants in the Polo Grounds, and team president James Clark burst into the locker room and berated Neale.

"Imagine this," Neale said in a 1968 interview, "the president of the ball club standing in the middle of the dressing room after you've been beaten 7–3, popping off in front of your players, telling me you can't win with three points. Anybody knew that. It didn't take a genius."

Neale and Clark stood nose to nose in the dressing room, cursing and poking each other in the chest. Finally, they were separated. Two days later, Clark came to practice and apologized for his outburst. According to Neale, Clark told him, "You can coach this team forever for me."

When the season ended, Neale went to Florida for a vacation. While he was there, he received a telegram from Clark reading, "You will be paid for the one year remaining on your contract, but you are no longer the coach of the Philadelphia Eagles."

"It was a complete surprise," Neale said. "After that blowup in New York, Clark told me I could coach the Eagles as long as he had the club. [The firing] liked to kill my wife. She died two months later."

Neale was invited to the Philadelphia Sports Writers Association banquet that year and received a standing ovation when he was called to the microphone. "I had a reputation for being a great handler of men," Neale said. "The only one I couldn't handle was Jim Clark."

"That [firing] was a tragedy," Bednarik said. "That was the worst thing that ever happened to me with the Eagles. We went 6–6, lost a lot of close games, and they fired the guy. That's stupid. Greasy was a football genius. Nobody I played for came close to him."

"I believe that Greasy Neale, in his time, was the greatest coach in football," said Alex Wojciechowicz, the Hall of Fame linebacker who played for Neale from 1946 through 1950. "He was the greatest teacher of fair play, a real player's coach. He devoted his life to teaching his men not only sports, but also an understanding and appreciation of life itself. Every player who ever has been coached by him retains an abiding feeling of thankfulness to him."

Neale's 66 victories stood as the record for an Eagles' head coach until Andy Reid surpassed it in 2004. After his firing by Clark, Neale never coached again. He retired to Florida where he played golf and pinochle. He died on November 2, 1973, three days short of his 82nd birthday.

BO McMILLIN

College: Centre (Kentucky) College • **Years as Eagles Coach:** 1951 • **Record:** 2–0

Alvin (Bo) McMillin's coaching career in Philadelphia was tragically short. A highly successful college coach, McMillin was hired to succeed Greasy Neale in 1951, but he was forced to retire after coaching just two games when he was diagnosed with cancer. He died less than a year later.

Under McMillin's direction, the Eagles defeated the Chicago Cardinals, 17–14, and San Francisco, 21–14. But the feeling of optimism created by the 2–0 start was dashed by McMillin's stunning announcement. Assistant coach Wayne Millner took over for McMillin, and the team lost eight of its final 10 games.

Pete Pihos, the Eagles' All-Pro end, was particularly devastated. In 1940, McMillin was head coach at the University of Indiana, and he spoke at a sports banquet in Chicago. Pihos was in the audience that night, and he was so impressed that he enrolled at Indiana, where he played for McMillin and earned All-America honors.

"He captivated me," Pihos said of McMillin. "He captivated a lot of guys. He was the only reason any [football] player wanted to go to Indiana, because prior to his arrival, Indiana was one of the poorest programs in the Big Ten. But he was the kind of coach you wanted to play for."

Indiana did not have a winning football season from 1920 until McMillin's arrival in 1934. In 14 seasons at the school, McMillin's teams went 63–48–11 and won their first Big Ten championship in 1945. Prior to Indiana, McMillin posted a 26–3 record at Centenary College, a 22–5–2 record at Geneva College, and a 29–21–1 mark at Kansas State.

After rebuilding the Indiana program, McMillin was hired as head coach of the Detroit Lions in 1948, but in three seasons with the Lions, he won only 12 games and lost 24. He resigned after the 1950 season, and the Eagles signed him to replace Neale. It was a difficult situation for McMillin, replacing a coach who had won two NFL championships. But McMillin earned the respect of the Eagles veterans, and they were shocked and saddened when he was forced to resign just two games into the season.

At 5–9 and 170 pounds, McMillin was a slight man, but he was very tough. As a teenager in Fort Worth, Texas, he was a successful amateur boxer and hoped to make a career in the professional prize ring until the high school football coach convinced him he would make a better quarterback than a middleweight.

McMillin attended Centre College, a tiny Presbyterian school in Danville, Kentucky, and scored the only touchdown in a 6–0 win over Harvard on October 29, 1921. It was Harvard's first loss in five years, and the *New York Times* hailed it as "the upset of the century." It was such a dramatic victory that Ralph D. Paine wrote a novel, "First Down, Kentucky," with a hero based on McMillin.

WAYNE MILLNER

College: Notre Dame • **Years as Eagles Coach:** 1951 • **Record:** 2–8

Wayne Millner assumed the head coaching duties when Bo McMillin stepped down two weeks into the 1951 season. Millner was only 39 years old and was in his first season as an assistant coach with the Eagles.

"It is a keen disappointment that we will lose Bo's services for this year," team president James Clark said in announcing the change. "But we are all confident that the team will give Wayne its best in cooperation and effort."

Millner was well liked by the players. Team captain Al Wistert said of Millner, "If we can't win for him, we can't win for anybody."

But as it turned out, the Eagles could not win for Millner. After winning their first two games under McMillin, they lost eight of ten under Millner. It was not entirely his fault. He inherited an aging team whose best players, notably halfbacks Steve Van Buren and Bosh Pritchard and linemen Vic Sears and Vic Lindskog, were at the end of their careers. Millner also was breaking in a new quarterback: Adrian Burk, who replaced the retired Tommy Thompson. Burk threw a league-high 23 interceptions.

Four of the first six losses were by four points or fewer. The strain weighed heavily on Millner, who was new to the role of head coach. He finished the 1951 season, but he resigned the following September. Millner stepped down just two weeks before the start of the regular season on the advice of his physician.

"Wayne was having attacks of nausea before and after every game," general manager Vince McNally said. "When he left camp [after resigning], he looked happier than he has been for some time."

The news shocked football fans who remembered Millner as a fearless All-America end at Notre Dame who caught the game-winning touchdown pass in a storied 18–13 upset of Ohio State in 1935. Millner also had a brilliant career with the Boston/Washington Redskins, catching passes from the great Sammy Baugh and ultimately joining him in the Pro Football Hall of Fame.

Baugh and Millner combined for two touchdown passes in Washington's 28–21 win over Chicago in the 1937 NFL Championship game. Redskin coach Ray Flaherty said afterward, "I'd have to resign if we didn't win a championship with that big Yankee playing end."

"Millner catches everything," Baugh said of the rangy 6–0, 190-pound Roxbury, Massachusetts, native. "He's got hands like buckets."

When Millner resigned the Eagles job, the *Philadelphia Bulletin*'s Ed Pollock wrote:

Like thousands of others, I didn't believe what I read in the papers about Wayne Millner quitting as Eagles coach because of ill health, but it is a fact that [it] was his own idea.

The concentrated pressures of games, even exhibitions, were too much for Millner's stomach. He lost his appetite and his weight dropped by 20 pounds, although he wasn't carrying any soft flesh around when the training season began. He suffered similarly last season after he succeeded Bo McMillin as head coach, but sold himself on the idea that it would be different this year when he would start as chief of staff from the beginning of training. It wasn't. If anything, his condition became worse.

Millner returned to the Redskins as an assistant coach in 1954, working with the receivers, but he never again served as a head coach. He died November 19, 1976, in Arlington, Virginia.

JIM TRIMBLE

College: Indiana • **Years as Eagles Coach:** 1952–55 • **Record:** 25–20–3

Jim Trimble was only 34 when he was named head coach of the Eagles. No one could have predicted his meteoric rise to the position. Certainly, Trimble never expected it. He joined

Jim Trimble (front row, second from left) with the Eagles in 1954. Trimble once said, "I'd rather be a successful football coach than President of the United States."

the Eagles as an assistant coach in 1951, but when Bo McMillin was diagnosed with cancer early that season and Wayne Millner, his successor, resigned one year later, also due to poor health, the job fell into Trimble's lap.

As it turned out, Trimble was up to the challenge. At 6–2 and 250 pounds, Trimble was an imposing figure who projected an air of strength and confidence. On his first day as head coach, several players were late for a team meeting. It was only a matter of minutes, but Trimble let them know it would not be tolerated.

"Gentlemen, this is a very bad start," Trimble said. "It is an insult to the entire team. Hereafter, everyone will be on time. There will be no exceptions."

Trimble played for McMillin at Indiana, where he was a teammate of Pete Pihos. He was a no-nonsense football man who once said, "I'd rather be a successful football coach than President of the United States." Early in his first season as head coach, the Eagles were routed by the New York Giants (31–7) and Cleveland (49–7). Hugh Brown of the *Philadelphia Bulletin* wrote a scathing assessment of the team, concluding, "The Eagles of 1952 are probably the worst football team ever to wear the Kelly green."

After the story appeared, Brown said, the players greeted him with "icy glares" and "clammy silence." Only Trimble was unfazed. The coach told Brown, "We had it coming to us." Trimble posted the article in the locker room. Brown felt it was no coincidence the Eagles went to New York that Sunday and upset the Giants, 14–10.

The Eagles finished the 1952 season with a 7–5 record, good for a second-place tie in the Eastern Conference. It was a sig-

nificant improvement over the 4–8 mark of the previous year and an impressive showing for Trimble, the rookie head coach who was thrust into the position just two weeks prior to the league opener.

After the season, a friend congratulated Trimble on his success. Trimble replied: "What do you mean, success? What success? We haven't won a championship yet, have we?"

Brown wrote, "It's true that Jim Trimble hasn't won the professional football championship yet, but he will." Brown noted that Trimble was new to the coaching profession, but he claimed, "Already Big Jim is regarded as a model of professional football sagacity and adaptability."

Trimble never did lead the Eagles to a championship, but he coached them to three winning seasons in four years. They won seven games each season from 1952 through '54. but they finished second to the powerful Browns all three years.

Trimble demanded a lot of his players, but he also demanded a great deal of himself. He took personal responsibility for a 6–0 loss to Cleveland in 1954, a game in which the Eagles had first-and-goal at the one-yard line and failed to score, due in part to a delay-of-game penalty that pushed them back five yards. Trimble blamed himself for sending in a late substitution that confused the team at the line of scrimmage.

"I'm taking full blame for this one," said Trimble, who apologized to the squad. "The team played its head off for me. They did everything I asked of them. I let them down."

The following season, the Eagles fell to 4–7–1, and Trimble was gone, off to the Hamilton Tiger-Cats of the Canadian Football League. When he took over the Tiger-Cats in 1956, the *Canadian Press* wrote, "Trimble arrived in Hamilton with a larger-than-life reputation and a tongue that never rested."

Trimble was quoted as saying, "I don't know if I'm the highest paid coach [in the Canadian League], but I ought to be. I'm the best coach in the country. I'm the best damned coach in North America." A writer in Hamilton described Trimble as "tough" and "touched by vanity."

Trimble had a successful run in the CFL, winning the Grey Cup in 1957 and posting an 88–71–2 mark in ten seasons with Hamilton and Montreal. Trimble's Tiger-Cats lost in the Grey Cup finals four times from 1958 through '62, each time falling to the Winnipeg Blue Bombers, coached by Bud Grant. Trimble coached Grant during his brief playing career with the Eagles in 1951–52.

Trimble returned to the NFL as an offensive-line coach with the Giants in 1967. Two years later, he moved to the front office as director of pro personnel. Trimble continued to work in the Giants personnel department through their Super Bowl victories in 1987 and 1991.

HUGH DEVORE

College: Notre Dame • **Years as Eagles Coach:** 1956–57 • **Record:** 7–16–1

Hugh Devore earned a reputation for toughness as a player at Notre Dame under Knute Rockne, but as a coach, Devore was just the opposite. He was a soft-spoken, kindly man who was reluctant to discipline players. That reluctance proved to be his downfall in two seasons as head coach of the Eagles.

Devore was fired following the 1957 season in which the Eagles posted a 4–8 record. In reporting Devore's dismissal, Hugh Brown of the *Philadelphia Bulletin* wrote, "He went out of his way to be nice to the players and they liked him, but unfortunately, that didn't win ball games."

In the *Philadelphia Daily News*, Jack Orr quoted an unnamed Eagles player as saying, "He is too nice a man for the pros. You have to be a [blankety-blank] to work in this league."

Even when Devore tried to get tough with his players, he could not quite pull it off. Example: During training camp, a player was late for a team meal. Devore informed him that he would be fined. The player left, visibly upset. Devore followed and returned a few minutes later with his arm around the player and guided him to his table.

"A generous act, indeed," Hugh Brown wrote, "but too generous for the likes of such coaches as Cleveland's Paul Brown, whose success has been built on strict discipline and split-second organization." The *Bulletin* columnist concluded: "[Devore] is too good for his own good."

A native of Newark, New Jersey, Devore was an outstanding end at Notre Dame from 1932 through '34. The highlight of his career was the 1932 game against Army. Devore played with a broken right hand, yet he still caught the winning touchdown pass. The same year, he took out three Pittsburgh defenders with one ferocious block, freeing Charlie Jaskwhich for a long touchdown run. "Some press box observers think that was the finest block ever thrown on any gridiron," wrote Arthur Daley of the *New York Times*.

What the 5–10, 175-pound Devore lacked in size, Daley wrote, "he more than compensated in fighting fury."

But when Devore took off the shoulder pads and picked up a coach's whistle, he exhibited none of that fire. After four years as an assistant at Notre Dame and Fordham, where he coached the legendary "Seven Blocks of Granite," Devore landed his first head coaching job at Providence. In four seasons, his teams won 12 games, lost 19, and tied 2.

Hugh Devore (second from right) with his coaching staff at the 1956 training camp in Hershey, Pennsylvania. From left, Frank (Bucko) Kilroy, Steve Owen and Charlie Gauer.

He returned to the role of assistant coach at Holy Cross in 1942, then went back to Notre Dame the following year as assistant to coach Frank Leahy. When Leahy was called to military duty in 1945, Devore filled in as head coach and led the Irish to a 7–2–1 mark. The next year, he was named head coach at Saint Bonaventure, where he had four winning seasons before going to NYU, where his teams won just four games in three years.

Devore was head coach at Dayton when the Eagles hired him to replace Jim Trimble in 1956. The decision reportedly was made by club president Frank McNamee without consulting general manager Vince McNally. At the time of Devore's hiring, McNally was interviewing Wally Butts, the University of Georgia coach, for the Eagles job. McNally was irritated, but when the news was announced, he swallowed hard and echoed the party line.

"[Devore] is honest, he's sincere, and he's a great coach," McNally told Ray Kelly of the *Philadelphia Bulletin.* "Some of his passing patterns with the Dayton team were so good that I know for sure that more than a few of the pro teams copied them."

The Devore era was a failure from the start. The Eagles were 3–8–1 in his first year, and when the team lost seven consecutive exhibition games the following summer, management considered firing him then. McNamee decided against it, fearing that another coaching change—this would have been the fifth in eight years—would make the organization look foolish. But when the Eagles lost their first three league games—and six of the first eight—it was clear Devore would be gone at the end of the season.

What clinched it was Devore's handling of Tommy McDonald, the Eagles' third-round draft pick. Devore wasted half the season playing the 5–9, 170-pound McDonald at running back and safety where his size worked against him. All the while, assistant coach Charlie Gauer tried to convince Devore to put McDonald at flanker where the rookie could use his speed and elusiveness in the open field.

When Devore finally gave in and put McDonald at flanker, the former Oklahoma All-America caught two touchdown passes to spark a 21–12 win over Washington. After the game, Devore was asked why he had not used McDonald as a receiver before. "He didn't know the pass patterns," Devore replied.

"Then why in tarnation didn't somebody take him aside and teach him the pass patterns?" asked Hugh Brown in the *Bulletin.*

When even the victories reflect badly on the coach, clearly, it is time for a change. On the Wednesday prior to the final game, the *Philadelphia Inquirer* reported the decision was made: Devore would be fired after the game against the Chicago Cardinals. There were the usual denials—the club said nothing was decided, Devore said he knew nothing about it—but everyone knew it was true. The players, who liked Devore, were angered when the news leaked out.

"He is one hell of a guy, he deserved better than this," an unnamed player told Jack Orr. "We're going to win one for him this week, you wait and see."

It proved to be a hollow promise. The Eagles lost to the Cardinals, 31–27, and Devore was fired with one year left on his contract. He returned to Notre Dame as an assistant coach the following year. In 1963 he served as interim head coach, filling the gap between the resignation of Joe Kuharich and the arrival of Ara Parseghian.

Devore died on December 8, 1992, at the age of 82.

BUCK SHAW

College: Notre Dame • **Years as Eagles Coach:** 1958–60 • **Record:** 20–16–1

One story will tell you everything you need to know about Lawrence Timothy (Buck) Shaw. In 1948 he was coaching the San Francisco 49ers in a critical late-season game against Cleveland. Otto Graham, the Browns' All-Pro quarterback, was playing on a bad knee. Addressing his players before the game, Shaw said he did not want anyone going after Graham with the intention of injuring him.

"I want you to rush him hard but fair," Shaw told his players. "No one is to twist his leg or rough him up. I want to win this game as much as you do, but there would be no pleasure in victory if we had to cripple Graham in order to win."

The 49ers followed Shaw's instructions. They played a clean game, but lost to Graham and the Browns, 31–28. Afterward, Shaw had no regrets. "If we had injured Graham and won, it would have been an empty victory," he said. "I don't believe in that kind of football."

"That's Buck, he was a gentleman in the truest sense of the word," said Tom Brookshier, who played for Shaw with the Eagles from 1958 through 1960.

"I played for lots of coaches in the NFL," Tommy McDonald said, "but Buck Shaw is the man at the top of the ladder. For me, he was the best of them all."

Shaw was a man of uncommon decency. Born on a farm in Iowa, he played football for Knute Rockne at Notre Dame. He was a 175-pound tackle on the Fighting Irish teams with the legendary George Gipp. It was Rockne who launched Shaw's coaching career, recommending him for a job as assistant coach at the University of Nevada in 1922. He climbed the ladder from there.

Shaw achieved national prominence as head coach at Santa Clara, where he led his teams to back-to-back wins in the Sugar Bowl (1938–39). He moved to the professional ranks with the 49ers of the All-America Football Conference in 1946. He coached the 49ers for nine seasons and compiled a 71–39–4 record. His career winning percentage of 63.8 is second only to George Seifert (75.5) in 49ers history.

Shaw was a consistent winner in San Francisco, but he never won a championship, so owner Tony Morabito fired him in 1955. Shaw returned to the college ranks as the first head coach at the Air Force Academy. He expected to finish his coaching career there, but in 1958 he received a call from Eagles general manager Vince McNally, an old friend from Notre Dame.

McNally wanted Shaw to succeed Hugh Devore as head coach of the Eagles. Shaw was 58 at the time. In his mind, his career was winding down. He did not want to devote 12 months a year to football. He was hoping to spend at least part of the year with his family in Northern California. He also was part owner of a corrugated box company in the Bay Area.

"I had just made up my mind, I'd never again coach year-round," Shaw said. "I explained that to Vince, and he was willing to go along with me, so I took the job on that basis."

Shaw was hired as the Eagles head coach with the understanding he would only be in the office from June through December. Once the season ended, he was gone. Pro football in the 1950s was not a year-round operation as it is today, but this arrangement—the head coach living half the year on the

Buck Shaw (second from left) with assistant coaches Nick Skorich, Jerry Williams, and Frank (Bucko) Kilroy. "[Buck] never screamed or raised his voice," Tommy McDonald said. "That just wasn't his way."

opposite coast—was unusual, even by those standards. Shaw, however, made it work.

The first season was a disaster. Even with the acquisition of quarterback Norm Van Brocklin, the Eagles were 2–9–1 in 1958. They finished the season with a 20–0 loss in Washington. On the train ride home, Shaw told the players, "Take a good look around, gentlemen, because it's the last time most of you will see each other."

Shaw and McNally stripped the team down to a handful of hungry, talented players. They added some draft picks, such as fullback Ted Dean and linebacker Maxie Baughan, and traded for a few veterans, such as cornerback Jimmy Carr and safety Don Burroughs. Two years later, they were world champions.

"What Buck did was fantastic," Van Brocklin said in a 1972 interview. "The Eagles in 1958 were a ragtag operation. Turning that thing around and winning a championship in just two years was a miracle. Buck never got enough credit, in my opinion. I think people overlooked him somewhat because he was so soft-spoken. He never raised his voice, lost his composure, or used profanity. He left it to guys like me."

Although he played for Rockne, who was the master of the pep talk, Shaw seldom gave locker-room speeches. He did not think the words had much effect, especially when a coach was dealing with professional football players who were older and more cynical.

"That stuff doesn't go anymore," Shaw told John Dell of the *Philadelphia Inquirer*. "Nowadays everything you say [to players] has to make sense. They'll laugh in your face if you try anything else."

"Some guys misunderstood Buck," end Pete Retzlaff said. "They saw how soft-spoken he was and thought he was easy. That wasn't so. Buck was no pushover. Look at his record. You don't win that many games being a pushover. Buck knew what he wanted done and it got done, one way or the other."

Shaw was a slender man with the silver hair and easy smile of a benevolent grandfather, but he had rules and expected his players to follow them. He had a curfew and fined players $200 for violating it. He once cut a veteran who talked back to him on the field. Wrote Hugh Brown in the *Philadelphia Bulletin*, "Shaw is kind, but no kidder."

Because Shaw was an older man, fully aware this was his last coaching job, he was not concerned with public perception. He did not feel the need to run the whole show. He had an excellent offensive coach in Charlie Gauer and an innovative defensive coach in Jerry Williams, so Shaw was content to function as a CEO. If in the end he did not get as much acclaim as other winning head coaches, it was fine with him. He cared only about the outcome.

"Buck reminded me of Bud Wilkinson, the man I played for at Oklahoma," McDonald told Phil Jasner of the *Philadelphia Daily News*. "He never screamed or raised his voice. I can't ever remember him chewing out a player in front of the other guys. That just wasn't his way.

"He would have a program rolled up in his hand during the game. He'd drum that program against the palm of his hand the whole game. His greatest asset was the psychology he used. If practice was going badly, he might end it instead of threatening us with extra sprints. His thought was maybe practice is bad because the players are tired. I'll give them a break. As a player, you'd do anything for a guy like that."

In 1959, Shaw's second season, the Eagles finished with a 7–5 record and tied for second place in the Eastern Conference. It was a dramatic improvement over the year before, and Shaw saw even better times ahead. "The Eagles," he said, "are a championship team in the making. When you get so close to the top, you don't want to quit until you reach it."

The following year, the Eagles reached the top, winning the Eastern Conference with a 10–2 regular season mark, then defeating Green Bay 17–13 in the championship game. Shaw was named Coach of the Year by United Press International, finishing well ahead of the Packers' Vince Lombardi in the voting.

Shaw informed Eagles management prior to the season that he would be retiring at the end of the year. He was 61, it was his 39th year of coaching, and he was ready to step down. It was only fitting that in his final game, he was able to claim the one prize he always wanted: a world championship.

"I feel I have a reasonable degree of good health and would like to keep it as long as I can," Shaw said, announcing his retirement the day after the title game. "Then, too, I can't think of a better time to bow out. I can't soar any higher than being head coach of a world championship professional football team. It was a distinct pleasure coaching the Eagles, and I can't pay too high a tribute to this 1960 team. It was a team of tremendous desire, a team that just would not accept defeat."

"All of us are sorry to see Buck Shaw go," said club president Frank McNamee. "We hate to lose a man of his high caliber. He is every inch a gentleman, a championship coach, and tremendous inspiration and influence to all of us. He leaves his mark on all who were fortunate enough to be associated with him in any way."

Arthur Daley in the *New York Times* wrote, "Long acknowledged as an imaginative coach with exceptional skills, the popular Buck has been a leader in his profession both on and off the field. He has the appearance of an aristocrat and he is one."

Shaw retired to his home in Menlo Park, California. He died on March 19, 1977, at the age of 77.

NICK SKORICH

College: Cincinnati • **Years as Eagles Coach:** 1961–63 • **Record:** 15–24–3

Nick Skorich succeeded Buck Shaw as head coach in 1961, and he had a tough act to follow. Under Shaw, the Eagles won the NFL championship the previous year. After the season, Shaw and quarterback Norm Van Brocklin, who was the league's Most Valuable Player, both retired.

As a result, Skorich, in his first season as a head coach, had to defend the world championship with an unproven quarterback, Sonny Jurgensen, who spent the previous three years on the bench. To the surprise of most experts, Skorich almost led the Eagles back to the championship game in 1961. They finished 10–4, just one-half game behind the New York Giants in the Eastern Conference.

"Nick was kind of low-key, but very precise," said Irv Cross, a rookie cornerback on the 1961 team. "He treated the men like men. There was a great deal of respect there."

"Nick had been the line coach for three years under Buck," said cornerback Tom Brookshier, whose career was ended by a broken leg midway through that season. "He knew the players, and we all knew him. We were a pretty savvy bunch, and we'd won it all in '60, so Nick didn't change the formula much. He was a good man, very fair. He didn't have a lot of rules, but the ones he set out for us, we followed."

Skorich had a hard life, growing up during the depression in Bellaire, Ohio. His father was disabled in an accident in a coal mine, so Skorich, as the second of nine children, had to support the family. He worked construction, painted bridges, and even tended bar while still in high school. He earned a football scholarship to the University of Cincinnati, where he starred as a two-way lineman, despite his 5–9, 195-pound frame.

"I never allowed my size to hold me back," Skorich said. "I never thought there was a team where I couldn't earn a place. There are 11 men on a football team. I always thought I could do better than at least one of the 11 men.

"In my time, there was what you might call a macho feeling," Skorich said in the book *Ironmen*. "We thought that it was sissy to wear a face mask. 'You afraid to stick your nose out and get it broken?' So you'd stick your nose out and get it broken. I never wore a face mask, and I broke my nose seven times. Two operations later, I still don't breathe very well."

Skorich graduated from college in 1943 and was drafted by the Pittsburgh Steelers, but he enlisted in the Navy and rose to the rank of lieutenant. He served in the D-Day invasion, shuttling a landing craft to the Normandy beach under heavy fire.

After the war, Skorich joined the Steelers, where he played three seasons before an injury ended his career. Coach Jock Sutherland, a stern man who rarely praised a player, was highly complimentary of Skorich. He was quoted as saying, "Someday this young man will be a great coach."

Skorich worked his way up the coaching ladder, starting at Central Catholic High School in Pittsburgh. He led the team to four undefeated seasons while studying for his doctorate at the University of Pittsburgh. He broke into professional coaching as an assistant under Walt Kiesling with the Steelers in 1955. Four years later, Shaw brought Skorich to Philadelphia as his offensive line coach.

"Nick was very smart," center Chuck Bednarik said. "Not a big rah-rah guy, but he got you prepared. Before the '60 championship game, he kept talking about how we'd have trouble with Henry Jordan [Green Bay tackle]. Gerry Huth, who was matched up with Jordan, was a pretty even-tempered guy, but he got so fired up, he played the best game of his life. I'm sure Nick planned the whole thing."

On game days, Skorich was so nervous that he could not eat a full meal. He would try to eat a bowl of cereal, but most of the time he could not keep it down.

"I've never been satisfied with just doing things; I want to do them well," he said. "I try to learn something new every day. The day I stop learning is the day they will bury me."

The Eagles crashed to earth in 1962, due in part to injuries to Jurgensen and other key veterans. They won three games that season and two games the next. Skorich was fired after the 1963 season. The Eagles were winless in their final nine games that year and closed out the season with a 34–13 loss to Minnesota.

Frank Dolson of the *Philadelphia Inquirer* described the scene at the end of the game: "Icy winds whipped across Franklin Field. The temperature was in the 20s. The losing coach walked off the field, head down, the boos bouncing off his frozen ears."

"It would bother any man," Nick Skorich said. "When a man does the best he can under the circumstances, he doesn't like to be ridiculed. We just lost too many key people at the times when it hurt. When a team loses, it's the coach's fault. Such are the fortunes of war."

Skorich was hired as an assistant coach in Cleveland, where he served for seven years under Blanton Collier. When Collier stepped down in 1971, Skorich succeeded him. He had three consecutive winning seasons and led the Browns to the AFC playoffs twice, but he was fired after a 4–10 season in 1974.

The next year Skorich went to work in the National Football League office as supervisor of officials, a position he held for 26 years until his retirement at age 80. He died October 2, 2004, at his home in Mansfield Township, New Jersey.

JOE KUHARICH

College: Notre Dame • **Years as Eagles Coach:** 1964–68 • **Record:** 28–41–1

Joe Kuharich coached the Eagles for five years, and in that time, he managed only one winning season, yet he occupies a prominent place in the team's history. He was the most reviled coach ever to walk the sidelines in Philadelphia. Indeed, he brought out the worst in the city's sports fans. It was during his final game as Eagles head coach that the fans at Franklin Field pelted Santa Claus with snowballs. It was a fitting way for the Kuharich era to end.

"A lot of people don't like Joe Kuharich," wrote Joe McGinniss in the *Philadelphia Inquirer*. "He's a stupid coach, they say, because who else but a stupid coach would make trades like he does? And he's a double-talker, he never levels with you. In short, they cry, he is a first-rate boob."

"Joe Kuharich," wrote Sandy Grady in the *Philadelphia Bulletin*, "couldn't sell iced tea to a Tasmanian at a dried-up water hole."

Kuharich was an unpopular choice from the day owner Jerry Wolman hired him in 1964. At the time, Kuharich was best known for being the only coach to have a losing career record at Notre Dame. His teams were 17–23 from 1959 through 1962. Kuharich had some success before that, coaching an undefeated team at the University of San Francisco (1951) and earning NFL Coach of the Year honors for guiding the Washington Redskins to an 8–4 finish in 1955. But his inability to produce a single winning season at Notre Dame made other college and pro teams reluctant to hire him.

Kuharich spent the 1963 season working for the National Football League as the supervisor of officials. He was hired by Commissioner Pete Rozelle, who was the public relations director at USF when Kuharich coached there from 1947 through '51. Rozelle and Kuharich were friends, and it was widely speculated that Rozelle pressured Wolman into hiring Kuharich as his coach when Wolman bought the Eagles in 1964. All parties denied it, but that perception hung over the franchise for five stormy seasons.

Shortly after his arrival, Kuharich began tearing apart the roster. He traded star players, such as Sonny Jurgensen, Tommy McDonald, Irv Cross, and Maxie Baughan and got almost nothing in return. When the Philadelphia fans and media criticized the moves, Kuharich scoffed. He said he would be proven right.

"Coaching takes a particular breed," Kuharich said. "A coach has to have a strong mental approach, a thick hide, and determination. As for booing, who don't they boo in Philadelphia?"

Kuharich assembled faceless teams with journeyman players who took orders and kept quiet. Players with strong personalities did not last long. "To play for this team," Kuharich told McGinniss, "a player must show he wants to be part of the organization."

Kuharich often talked in baffling circles. Explaining the Jurgensen-for-Norm-Snead deal, he said, "Trading quarterbacks is rare but not unusual." Asked about the status of an injured player, he said, "It's not probable he will have surgery, but I wouldn't rule out the possibility." During a long losing streak, he said, "This team has all the facets of a winner, but we just haven't won." When the team followed a good first half with a poor second half, he said, "That [half] was a horse of a different fire department."

Fans sometimes felt Kuharich insulted their intelligence. For example, he explained a 56–7 loss to Dallas by saying, "A missed block here, a missed assignment there, it adds up." He also said, "When the gods of the gridiron don't smile on you, you're in trouble." His nervous habit of going for a drink of water during every stoppage of play earned him the nickname "Water Bucket Joe." Quarterback King Hill and tight end Pete Retzlaff once hid the bucket just to see Kuharich's reaction.

"He panicked," Retzlaff recalled. "He didn't know what to do."

The Eagles won only six games in Kuharich's first season, but the week before the final game, Wolman made a stunning announcement: He signed Kuharich to a 15-year contract for $50,000 per year. It was the longest contract in professional

Joe Kuharich (left) with owner Jerry Wolman, who signed him to a 15-year contract in 1964.

sports, and it was given to a coach who had exactly one winning season in 13 years since leaving USF in 1952.

"I feel with the [personnel] changes Joe has made and with the leadership he has provided, he has this team going in the right direction," Wolman said.

The Eagles went 5–9 in 1965 and appeared headed for another miserable season in 1966 when they lost three of their first five games, including back-to-back routs by St. Louis (41–10) and Dallas. But they turned the season around with Kuharich using three quarterbacks—Snead, Hill, and Jack Concannon—in a rotation only he seemed to understand. All three started at various times. Sometimes one started and another came off the bench. It was odd to say the least, but it worked well enough for the Eagles to win seven of their last nine games and finish 9–5. They qualified for the Playoff Bowl, a game between the second-place finishers in the two conferences. The Eagles lost to Baltimore, 20–14, in Miami.

It was downhill from there as the team slipped back into its losing ways and the fans turned their wrath on Kuharich. In 1968, when the Eagles opened the season 0–11, the public organized in an attempt to oust the coach. They urged fans to wear "Joe Must Go" buttons. They hired planes to fly over Franklin Field, trailing banners that read, "Joe Must Go." Mayor James H. J. Tate expressed concern over what he called the team's "tarnished image." He feared that if the Eagles alienated their fan base, it would threaten the construction of the new stadium proposed for South Philadelphia.

Most Philadelphia sportswriters were hammering Kuharich, and the *Philadelphia Inquirer* editorial page joined the chorus. On November 22, the *Inquirer* ran an editorial that began, "All right, we've had enough. Joe must go." Characterizing the coach's tenure as "calamitous," the editorial said, "If Kuharich has any class, he would step out of the job he has so obviously botched."

The criticism peaked when Kuharich suspended veterans Mike Ditka and Gary Ballman for making negative comments about the team. Considering the Eagles were 0–10 at the time, it would have been hard to say anything positive. Actually, the comments were relatively mild. Ballman was quoted as saying the Eagles' offense was predictable. Ditka told a banquet audience the team lacked discipline. Kuharich read the quotes and suspended the two players. He reinstated them one day later.

Grady wrote a column comparing Kuharich to Captain Queeg, the paranoid character played by Humphrey Bogart in the film *The Caine Mutiny*. Wrote Grady: "The suspension caper has shown Kuharich at his peak, petty arrogance gone off its flywheel. His handling of the Ditka-Ballman incident puts a clear focus on the dime-store egomania that has helped make the Philadelphia franchise the biggest national laugh since the House of David team cut its beards."

Sandy Padwe of the *Philadelphia Inquirer* called for Kuharich to step down: "The object here is not to criticize Joe Kuharich's technical knowledge of football. But technical knowledge is only part of the game. It is obvious from the Ballman-Ditka incident and many other incidents in the past that Kuharich has a problem handling and making the best use of his personnel. If a [coaching] change isn't made, the situation can only grow worse. And it is at the very bottom now."

Padwe described a painful scene following a 29–16 loss to Chicago: Kuharich being grilled by the press while his 15-year-old son Billy sat nearby, staring at the floor. "[Billy] heard the whole demeaning exchange," Padwe wrote. "[He] heard his father trying to defend a record which is almost indefensible."

Kuharich's final game was a 24–17 loss to Minnesota on a frigid day at Franklin Field. The fans' anger boiled over, and they pelted Santa Claus with snowballs during a halftime show. Kuharich also was hit with snowballs as he left the field following the game, which concluded a 2–12 season, the team's worst since 1940.

Bob Brown, the All-Pro tackle, was seething after the game. He liked Kuharich. He said the coach was like a father to him. Brown called the fans "creeps" and expressed disgust at how they treated Kuharich. After the season, when Wolman lost the team to creditors and the new owner, Leonard Tose, fired Kuharich, Brown demanded a trade. He felt the team and the city had wronged Kuharich. Brown was dealt to the Los Angeles Rams.

When Kuharich was fired, Hugh Brown wrote in the *Philadelphia Bulletin*: "Flaws in his personality were the principal reason for Kuharich being a loser more than he was a winner, for disposing of players that would not bend to his will, and for his low boiling point. Ego isn't necessarily a flaw in a man's personality, but an overdose of it is. Joe had too much ego for his own good. Because of his ego, Joe deluded himself about players, particularly those players he had obtained from other teams in a trade."

A year after his firing, Kuharich was diagnosed with cancer. He was given less than a year to live, but he actually lived another 10 years. He maintained his home in Penn Valley, Montgomery County, and in 1977, Dick Vermeil brought him back into the Eagles family as a scout. He broke down film and filed reports on upcoming opponents.

In January 1981, when the Eagles won the NFC Championship, Kuharich was losing his battle against cancer. General manager Jim Murray visited him in the hospital, and Kuharich told Murray he was rooting for the Eagles to win the title.

"The man is lying there devastated by that disease, he's just come out of chemotherapy, and you know he's in agony and all he can do is wish us luck," Murray told Bill Lyon of the *Philadelphia Inquirer*. "The team that fired him, the city that crucified him, he's wishing them nothing but success. There are more records in this life than wins and losses. And I'd love to have his report card."

Kuharich died on January 25 while the Eagles were playing Oakland in Super Bowl XV. He was 63 years old.

JERRY WILLIAMS

College: Washington State • **Years as Eagles Coach:** 1969–71 • **Record:** 7–22–2

Jerry Williams was the mastermind behind the defense that helped the Eagles win the 1960 NFL Championship. That year, the Eagles led the league with 30 pass interceptions, and Tom Brookshier credits Williams, the assistant coach, for their success.

"Jerry was the first coach to disguise his coverages," said Brookshier, who played cornerback on that team. "He was the first one to use the bump-and-run. He was the first one to use the nickel [a fifth defensive back]. George Allen gets credit for it, but that's only because he came up with the name. Really, it was Jerry's idea."

Jerry Williams was a winning coach in the Canadian Football League, but he could not duplicate that success with the Eagles.

"Jerry was ahead of his time in terms of defensive strategy. He had to be because we didn't have great talent. It was me and Gummy [Carr] on the corners and Bobby Freeman and the Blade [Don Burroughs] at safety. We didn't have any speed, but we were successful because Jerry kept the other teams guessing."

As a coach, Williams seldom raised his voice. He was a thinker, not a shouter. He attended law school in the off-season and earned his Juris Doctor degree from Temple. He had an outstanding career as a head coach with Calgary of the Canadian Football League, winning coach of the year honors in 1967 and leading his team to the Grey Cup finals in 1968. But Williams found the victories harder to come by when Eagles owner Leonard Tose brought him back to Philadelphia as head coach in 1969.

Williams was the first former Eagles player to serve as head coach. A speedy halfback, he played two seasons under Jim Trimble and led the team with 1,151 yards of total offense in 1953. He had 163 yards receiving in a 1954 game against Washington, the third-highest single-game total for an Eagles running back.

Williams retired after that season to begin his coaching career at Montana State. He got his first NFL coaching job as an assistant under Buck Shaw with the Eagles in 1958. He stayed with the team until 1964 when he went to Calgary.

As Eagles head coach, Williams won four games in his first season and three games the next year. His teams started slowly each season—1–4 in 1969, 0–7 in 1970—and they won back-to-back games only once. When they opened the 1971 season with three embarrassing losses, Tose fired Williams and replaced him with assistant coach Ed Khayat. Despite the poor record, Williams had defenders who argued he was not given sufficient time to clean up the mess he inherited from Joe Kuharich.

"His biggest problem was that he is a slow builder, much the same as Tom Landry of the Dallas Cowboys," wrote Jack McKinney of the *Philadelphia Daily News*. "For a long stretch, it seemed Landry was never going to get it together either, but the Dallas management didn't panic, and Landry got all the time he needed to deliver a championship team. It is a pity Williams wasn't able to get it together in the short time that was allotted him. It certainly didn't help to be working for a dilettante owner."

Williams' dismissal was a bizarre scene that featured three press conferences over a period of four days. Tose went first, announcing the firing. Later that day, the players held their own press conference and called the firing "a grave injustice." Williams did not comment until three days later when he called the media to respond to statements made by Tose.

"It was the most absurd thing I've ever read," Williams said, "and I will respond, point by point."

First, Tose said the Eagles were "near the bottom in almost every statistic."

"When we had good statistics last year, [Tose] said they didn't matter," Williams said. "He said what matters is wins and losses. Suddenly, this year the statistics matter. It seems very convenient."

Williams characterized other Tose statements as outright lies.

"Like the [incident] where [Tose] said he talked to me before a game," Williams said. "He claimed that I said, 'I'm so nervous, I don't even know what I'm doing.' That's absolutely false. What happened was he came to the locker room before a game and asked me if I was nervous. Naturally, I was nervous. Everyone is nervous before a game. All I said was 'Yes.' That was all, the end of the conversation."

Williams concluded by addressing Tose directly, even though the owner was not in the room. Williams said, "I can only say that your lack of integrity has been firmly, unequivocally, and publicly established, and for me to now or in the future bother to deny your accusations would be a redundancy and an insult to the intelligence of the reading and listening public."

Williams died December 31, 1998, in Chandler, Arizona. He was 75 years old.

ED KHAYAT

College: Tulane • **Years as Eagles Coach:** 1971–72 • **Record:** 8–15–2

Ed Khayat is best remembered as the coach who patterned himself after General George S. Patton, the World War II tank commander known as "Old Blood and Guts." Like Patton, Khayat believed in discipline, dress codes, and short hair. Unlike Patton, Khayat could not turn those rules into victories.

His predecessor Jerry Williams had no rules about grooming or attire. It was 1971, a time when long hair and bell-bottom jeans were in fashion. Williams allowed each player to cultivate his own look. Mustaches, sideburns, and long hair were common. One of the first things Khayat did when he

Ed Khayat (left) and the freshly shaven Tim Rossovich. "Good grooming is one of many facets of good discipline," Khayat said.

took over as head coach was order all players to shave and cut their hair. He installed a dress code: coats and ties on road trips. Players had to wear slacks, not jeans.

Grudgingly, the players complied.

"Good grooming is one of many facets of good discipline," Khayat said, "and good discipline is conducive to good play. I know we live in a time when people talk about 'doing your own thing,' but when doing your own thing is more important than doing the Philadelphia Eagles thing, then doing your own thing won't do."

Khayat's philosophy was consistent with his reputation as a player. He spent 10 seasons in the NFL as a 6–3, 240-pound defensive tackle known as "the Hatchet." A native of Moss Point, Mississippi, Khayat came up the hard way. He played at Tulane, but no pro team felt he was worth drafting. He signed with Washington as a free agent in 1957, but was cut after one year. The Eagles claimed him, and he wound up starting for the 1960 championship team. Khayat was not known for his finesse as a player, and he was the same way as a coach.

Khayat was an assistant coach in New England and New Orleans for six years before Williams hired him to coach the Eagles defensive line in 1971. He never had been a head coach until Tose fired Williams three games into that season and handed him the job. Asked how he would handle the responsibility, Khayat, in his Mississippi drawl, replied: "I can only do it one way and that's my way."

While there was much debate about Khayat's rules—"Win One for the Clipper" was suggested as the team's new motto—the Eagles did play better, at least initially. The team that started the season 0–5 won six of its last nine games to finish with a 6–7–1 record. Tose was so delighted, he climbed atop an equipment trunk after the final game—a 41–28 rout of the New York Giants—and announced Khayat would be back as head coach in 1972.

"The reason I chose Eddie Khayat in the first place is I thought he displayed the type of leadership we needed," Tose said. "I think I've been proven right. I place most of the emphasis on the team's improvement on his ability to lead, to motivate and get this team together."

Tose took a long drag on his cigarette and declared, "I think we can bring a title to Philadelphia next season."

The players were less convinced. Even those who accepted Khayat's drill sergeant approach felt he should lighten up. All-Pro safety Bill Bradley, who led the league with 11 interceptions and 248 return yards in 1971, hoped Khayat would relax his rules. Bradley talked about finding "a middle ground" that would be acceptable to the coach and players alike.

"We have something real good going here," Bradley said. "The guys are fired up and they're enthusiastic, but maybe [Khayat] ought to think about some of his ideas. Like what difference does it make if a guy wants to wear his hair a little long or grow a mustache?

"Coach Khayat set the rule this year, and we complied. He earned our respect. But I think he'd be making a mistake to insist on the same rules starting again in July. He won't have to use discipline to bring this team together next year. The winning has done that already. The big thing now is not to mess it up."

Tim Rossovich, the free-spirited middle linebacker, sacrificed his mustache and bushy tangle of curls to Khayat's grooming edict. He was, in fact, the last player to comply. Khayat ordered all personnel to shave by noon on a given date.

At 11:55 A.M., Rossovich was still unshaven. Two minutes before the deadline, he shaved his mustache, but he let everyone know he did not agree with the policy.

"I don't know if this is the right way to coach," Rossovich said. "I don't know if it is required at the professional level. By the time you're a professional, you don't need a father or a general. If a man can produce on the field and not hurt the team off the field, I don't see the need to go as far as [Khayat] wanted to go. I respect him as a coach, but I think he could do a truly great job if he were able to compromise a little."

After the win over the Giants, while Tose and other team executives were celebrating the strong finish, Rossovich was conspicuous by his detachment. He dressed quickly, far removed from the laughter and the backslapping. It was clear in his words that day that the success the Eagles enjoyed in the final weeks of the season was a fragile thing, just as likely to collapse as continue.

"I respect Ed Khayat very much as a football coach," Rossovich said. "When I'm on the field, I do everything he says. But off the field, I'm going to try to get away with everything I can again."

The following summer, Rossovich and Bradley staged a dual holdout. The impasse dragged on for weeks. Finally, the team ended the stalemate by trading Rossovich to San Diego for a first-round draft pick. The other players saw the move as heavy-handed and spiteful, so while it ended the holdout and brought Bradley into camp, it hurt morale. Khayat's refusal to budge off his military school rules only made matters worse.

"We all felt like we were obeying rules we didn't understand," said wide receiver Harold Jackson. "It was like everything was collapsing around us, but all the coach could think about was who needed a haircut."

The Eagles opened the 1972 season with five consecutive losses, but unlike the previous year, there was no coming back. They stumbled to a 2–11–1 finish and scored the embarrassing total of 12 touchdowns. The day after the final game, Tose fired Khayat and his coaching staff. Khayat returned to the ranks of NFL assistant coaches, where he served for the next two decades with Detroit, Atlanta, New England, and Tampa Bay.

In 1991, Khayat became a head coach again, this time with the New Orleans Night of the Arena Football League. He later became head coach and general manager of the AFL's Nashville Kats and Carolina Cobras.

MIKE McCORMACK

College: Kansas • **Years as Eagles Coach:** 1973–75 • **Record:** 16–25–1

Mike McCormack came to Philadelphia with an impeccable résumé. A Hall of Fame lineman with the Cleveland Browns from 1954 to 1962. Played for Paul Brown. Coached under Vince Lombardi and George Allen. He had been around winners his entire career. Surely, he would bring some of that championship know-how to the Eagles.

McCormack was 42 when Leonard Tose hired him as head coach on January 17, 1973. It was a new role for McCormack, who previously served as an assistant coach with the Washington Redskins, but Tose was confident the 6–4, 250-pound McCormack was the man for the job.

"I spent six weeks investigating coaching possibilities, but Mike was No. 1 from the start," Tose said. "I wanted a man with class. I wanted a man associated with winning football. I wanted a knowledgeable man who could get along with players. Mike is all of these things and more."

McCormack spoke optimistically about the team he inherited, despite the fact that it won just two games the previous season, went winless at home (0–6–1) for the first time since 1942, and scored the pitiful total of 145 points, the lowest total in NFL history for a 14-game schedule.

"I feel very familiar with the Eagles personnel because we [the Redskins] played them three times last year," McCormack said, referring to two games in the regular season and one in the preseason. "They played us very tough. Until the Super Bowl, the Eagles defense held the Redskins to the fewest points they scored in any game last season [a 14–0 Washington win]."

"I don't see any reason why the Eagles can't win this season. I've been around George Allen long enough that I agree with his motto, 'The Future Is Now.' The day of the gradual building program is in the past."

McCormack knew he faced a real challenge. He was working for an impatient owner—Tose had fired two head coaches in as many years—in an impatient city. The Philadelphia fans were tired of losing. The Eagles had one winning season in the previous 11 years. The season ticket holders did not want to hear about a five-year rebuilding plan. They wanted to win and win now.

McCormack saw Allen turn the hapless Redskins around in one year by trading draft picks for veterans who could step in and play right away. The Skins were 6–8 the year before Allen arrived; he improved them to 9–4–1 his first year, and he led them to the Super Bowl the next. McCormack brought Allen's blueprint to Philadelphia. He traded away draft picks to acquire veterans such as quarterback Roman Gabriel, linebacker Bill Bergey, running back Norm Bulaich, defensive tackle Jerry Patton, and offensive guards John Niland and Bill Lueck.

In the first year under McCormack, the Eagles more than doubled their win total (five) and scoring output (310 points) from the previous season. The highlight of the year was a 30–16 win over Dallas at the Vet, the Eagles' first victory over their division rivals in 11 tries dating back to 1967. When the game ended, the jubilant fans mobbed McCormack and his players.

"This game could represent a turnaround for the fans," McCormack said. "They've waited for a team they could be proud of for too many years. They deserve a winner. The way they're supporting us [they gave the Eagles five standing ovations that day] makes me think they believe in us."

The Eagles had high hopes going into the 1974 season with Gabriel coming off a big year and Bergey added to the defense. They opened the regular season with four wins in their first five games, and they were beating Dallas until rookie Marion Reeves fumbled a punt, allowing the Cowboys to rally for a 31–24 win. It was a heartbreaking loss that sent the Eagles into a tailspin. They lost six games in a row, and McCormack benched Gabriel in favor of rookie Mike Boryla. They finished the season 7–7.

In 1975 the Eagles lost their first two games to the mediocre New York Giants (23–14) and Chicago Bears (15–13). McCormack was furious with the effort and said as much in his press conference. Tom Brookshier, the former Eagle who was working in TV, asked bluntly, "Mike, how many dogs do you have on your roster?"

It is the kind of question that football coaches typically deflect. The reporters expected McCormack to respond with a vague generality. He was old school: he never singled out players for public criticism. But this time McCormack was angry enough to take the bait. "You mean real mutts?" he said. "I'd say two."

McCormack refused to name the players, so the "mutt" label was attached to the entire team. The players were upset, and the relationship between the coaching staff and the squad never recovered. The season hit bottom with a 42–3 loss to the Los Angeles Rams on Monday Night Football. During the game, the Veterans Stadium crowd chanted, "Al-Po, Al-Po" loud enough to be heard on the national TV broadcast. Some fans carried a giant dog bone with the message "Hey Beagles, here's your dinner." When they tossed the bone onto the field, it drew the loudest cheer of the night.

Tose was seething. At halftime, he was interviewed on the Mutual Radio Network. He made no attempt to hide his frustration. "In seven years, we haven't made any progress at all in my opinion," he said, going back to the 1969 season when he purchased the team.

Tose considered firing McCormack immediately after the game, but decided against it. He would let the coach finish the season, but he was determined to clean house after that. The Eagles won their final game, 26–3 in Washington, to finish with a 4–10 record. The next morning, Tose fired McCormack and his entire staff.

So where did McCormack fail? In part, he failed because he was too nice. He did not scream or threaten players. He treated them like men, and they took advantage. "Players today are pampered, babied, and coddled," said Niland, who played for Tom Landry in Dallas before joining the Eagles. "Our losing is not the fault of the coaches. We just have players who aren't willing to pay the price."

Also, while McCormack tried to follow the Allen "Win Now" formula, there was a significant difference. In Washington, Allen inherited a nucleus of good players, including Sonny Jurgensen, Larry Brown, Charlie Taylor, Jerry Smith, and Pat Fischer, a dozen Pro Bowlers in all. When Allen traded draft picks for veterans, such as Diron Talbert, Jack Pardee, and Ron McDole, he used them to fill specific holes. By contrast, McCormack started with almost nothing, so although he acquired some good players, he did not have enough talent elsewhere to make it work.

After his firing, McCormack was hired by Paul Brown to serve as offensive line coach in Cincinnati. In 1980 he was named head coach of the Baltimore Colts. Two years later, he was head coach of the Seattle Seahawks and won four of seven games in the strike-shortened season. McCormack later served as president of the Carolina Panthers.

DICK VERMEIL

College: San Jose State • **Years as Eagles Coach:** 1976–82 • **Record:** 57–51–0

New Year's Day, 1976. Eagles owner Leonard Tose was watching the college bowl games on TV with Jim Murray, the team's

Dick Vermeil drove his players—and himself—harder than any other coach in football.

general manager. Tose had just fired his third head coach in five years, and he was shopping around for a new man.

He had interviewed Norm Van Brocklin, Hank Stram, Allie Sherman, Frank Kush, and Harvard coach Joe Restic, but he wasn't sold on any of them. Tose wanted to be sure his next hire was the right one. He had owned the Eagles for seven years and never had a winning season.

Flipping around the dial, Tose stopped at the Rose Bowl where UCLA was upsetting No. 1 ranked Ohio State, 23–10. The TV camera zoomed in for a close-up of the Bruins head coach, a fiery young guy named Dick Vermeil.

"He lit up the screen," Murray recalled. "You could just feel his intensity. You knew right away, this guy is going places."

Tose never had heard of Vermeil, but he liked what he saw. "Let's talk to that guy," Tose said. One week later, they did. And that's how it all began.

On February 8, 1976, after considerable soul-searching, the 39-year-old Vermeil signed a five-year contract to coach the Eagles. He took over a woeful 4–10 team that had not managed a winning season in nine years. To make matters worse, the previous regime had mortgaged the future, trading away the top three draft choices for the next two years and the top two picks the year after that. The task of turning the franchise around seemed insurmountable.

"I don't know if any coach in any sport ever took on a tougher challenge," Murray said. "I think that's what appealed to him. He loved the challenge."

Vermeil believed there were different ways to rebuild. There was rebuilding with high draft picks, which is the conventional way. Then there was rebuilding with plain old hard work, sacrifice, and something called "character." It was a word Eagles fans would hear quite often during the next seven years.

"A team with character can beat a team with better talent," Vermeil said, and, in Philadelphia, he proved it to be true.

The first season was tough. The Eagles won four, lost 10. The second season was not much better. Five and nine. If Vermeil was discouraged, he never let it show. He simply worked harder. The cot in his Veterans Stadium office became the symbol of his administration. He didn't like the constant harping on his work habits—he claimed to abhor the word "workaholic"—yet he did nothing to discourage the image. He once took a reporter aside and showed him, with considerable pride, a pass play he draw up one morning at 5:30.

"It just came to me," Vermeil said. "We're gonna use it inside the 20-yard line."

Vermeil put the play in the game plan. The result: an Eagles touchdown. Given the choice between six hours of sleep and six points, Vermeil would take the six points every time. He inherited his work ethic from his father, Louie, who owned a garage in Calistoga, California. It was named the "Owl Garage" because Louie worked around the clock, and Dick was right there working alongside his father.

"When Dick was in college, he would get up for an 8 o'clock class, be in school until 4, work from 4 to midnight in Dad's mechanic shop, study from 12 to 3, then go to bed and get up at 7 and start over again," said Al Vermeil, Dick's younger brother. "He developed a mental toughness, the ability to push on. There are so many of us who can find reasons not to excel. Dick never thinks 'can't.' Dad wouldn't let him."

Vermeil also was influenced by the one season he spent working for George Allen with the Los Angeles Rams. Allen made Vermeil the NFL's first full-time special teams coach in 1969. "George felt you hadn't seen a game film until you saw it three times," Vermeil said. "I learned that from him."

Vermeil was a stickler for details, which caused frustration in his early years with the Eagles. Like most losing teams, the Eagles went about things in a clumsy way. Stan Walters, the Pro Bowl tackle, recalled a rainy afternoon when the team was bused to Widener College, 30 minutes away, for an indoor practice. However, 10 minutes into the workout, the women's field hockey team came onto the floor and told the Eagles they had to leave. When the team went outside, the buses were gone and the coaches and players were left standing in the rain.

"Dick was leaning against the wall, shaking his head," Walters said. "I'll never forget the look on his face. It was like, 'What is this, the minor leagues?' I felt like saying, 'It's okay, coach. It's not your fault. We know you're trying hard.' But Dick changed things for the better. He put a real organization in place. We could all see the difference."

"I always had a sense that we were moving in the right direction," said Bill Bergey, the All-Pro linebacker. "Even in the early years when the wins were few and far between, we could see the intensity of the play picking up. Dick's personality rubbed off on us. He talked so much about character and paying the price, and he defined it better than anyone with his actions. No one worked harder than Dick."

There was another side to Vermeil, and that was the emotional bond he developed with his players. He drove them harder than any coach in the league, yet he treated them with affection. During pregame warm-ups, he walked among the players, embracing them, wishing them luck. When he addressed the squad before a game, his eyes often filled with tears. At first, the players were taken aback. Some wondered if it was an act. But they soon realized the heart Vermeil wore on his sleeve was the real thing.

"What Dick projects is a genuine caring for the people around him," said Ron Jaworski, who matured both as a quarterback and a man in six seasons of playing under Vermeil. "You see Dick hugging his players, tears streaming down his face. There is real love there. We all felt that. Just the fact that he would let his emotions show that way said a lot about the kind of person he was."

"I don't coach football players, I coach people to play football," Vermeil said. "To me, the person comes first. If he's a good person with some ability, then it's just a matter of giving him the opportunity to succeed. That's the best part of coaching."

The final game of the 1977 season was a turning point for the Vermeil program. The Eagles were coming to the close of another losing season. Only 19,241 fans turned out to see the game against the New York Jets. On that day, Jaworski completed his first season in Philadelphia, and a rookie named Wilbert Montgomery rushed for 103 yards in his first NFL

"I don't coach football players," Dick Vermeil said. "I coach people to play football. To me, the person comes first."

start. The Eagles romped to a 27–0 victory, and the foundation for a championship team was put into place.

From there, it was a steady progression: 9 wins and a playoff berth in 1978; 11 wins and a playoff victory in 1979; 12 wins and an NFC championship in 1980. Vermeil was named NFL Coach of the Year twice. In a tough sports town, with a throaty fan base that devoured dozens of coaches and managers, Vermeil was revered. Blue-collar Philadelphia admired him for his hard work and honesty. When he arrived in 1976, Vermeil said he had a five-year plan to build a championship team. In his fifth year, he took the Eagles to Super Bowl XV. Every coach promises success, but Vermeil was one of the few who delivered. The fans loved him for it.

"If Dick wanted to run for mayor of Philadelphia, or even governor of the state, I believe he would win in a landslide," said Edward G. Rendell, who has held both offices. "Ask anyone about Dick, and the first thing they say is, 'He's believable. He doesn't B.S. you.'"

But after the loss in Super Bowl XV, the combination of the long hours and the mounting pressure began to show. As the Eagles skidded from a 6–0 start to a 10–6 finish in 1981, the emotional strain was evident on Vermeil's face. Walters recalled seeing the coach in his car, clutching the steering wheel, staring straight ahead for what seemed an eternity.

"We [the players] could see him," Walters said, "and guys were saying, 'What's he doing? What's going on?'" Vermeil later said he was "frozen with fear." He did not realize it at the time, but it was the first stage of burnout.

"I'd sit there watching more film on the projector, and my neck would go stiff, just quivering from the intensity," Vermeil said. "I'd have to run the film over again because I found myself shaking, quivering. All those years of coaching with the same personality finally caught up with me."

In 1982 the NFL players went on strike, shutting down the season for two months. For the first time in his adult life, Vermeil had the chance to experience an autumn without football. He took long drives through the countryside with his wife, Carol. He was amazed to see the leaves change color. Said Carol, "All these years, he thought the world was green with white stripes."

When the season finally resumed, the Eagles lost four consecutive games and sank to the bottom of the NFC East. It was almost the same team that went to the Super Bowl two years earlier, but the overachieving collection of late-round draft picks and free-agent castoffs was simply worn out. All those grueling training camps, all those three-hour practices took their toll. Vermeil had squeezed the players dry and done the same to himself.

The Eagles closed the 1982 regular season with a 26–24 loss to the New York Giants. One week later, after hours of discussion with his family, Vermeil resigned as head coach. It was Carol, Vermeil said, who made the final call. "I said, 'I can't make this decision,'" Vermeil recalled. "Carol said, 'Well, if you can't, I can. We're getting out.'"

On January 10, Vermeil announced his resignation.

"I'm just burned out," Vermeil said.

I'm my own worst enemy. I'm far too intense, far too emotional, probably invested far too much time in trying to do something to win. Those things combined just catch up with you. Sid Gillman, Marion Campbell, my other coaches, my wife, they all tried to talk to me. They said, "Hey, slow down. How important is it to look at film at 6 o'clock in the morning?" But I didn't listen.

I wish I had a [Don] Shula personality or a [Tom] Landry personality. They seem to be able to turn the highs and lows off. My problem is the highs don't last very long and the lows linger for days. It gnaws at your insides. It's a drain and it's a deterrent in being as good a coach as I should be.

"Coaching was taking a tremendous toll on him," son David Vermeil said. "It seemed to build up more over the years. He always felt the harder you worked, the better you'd do. So he worked more and more hours, and it took so much out of him. It became harder and harder for him to control his emotions. I didn't like seeing that happen. I think this [resignation] was the right decision."

Vermeil spent the next decade working as a TV football analyst. Atlanta and Tampa Bay each tried to coax him back to the sidelines without success. But in 1995, Jeffrey Lurie talked to Vermeil about returning to coach the Eagles. It did not work out—Lurie hired Ray Rhodes instead—but the talks rekindled Vermeil's competitive fire.

Two years later, Vermeil accepted the head coaching position with the St. Louis Rams, a dispirited team that lost more games in the 1990s than any other club in the NFL. Energized by his 14-year break from coaching, Vermeil went to work rebuilding the Rams. In just three years, he led the team to Super Bowl XXXIV and a 23–16 win over Tennessee. At 63, Vermeil was the oldest coach to win a Super Bowl.

Two days after the championship game, Vermeil retired from the Rams. He returned to his home in Chester County and spent the next year delivering motivational speeches. But in 2001, Carl Peterson and Lynn Stiles, who worked with Vermeil at UCLA and Philadelphia, convinced him to come back one more time and join them in Kansas City. In his third season with the Chiefs, Vermeil led the team to a 13–3 record and the AFC Western Division title. He was named NFL Coach of the Year by the Maxwell Football Club.

"Why did I come back?" Vermeil said. "I missed the people, I missed the competition, I missed the game. As I've gotten older, I've learned to handle [the stress] better. I'm a coach, that's what I am. Football gets in your system, in your blood, and it's hard to get out."

MARION CAMPBELL

College: Georgia • **Years as Eagles Coach:** 1983–85 • **Record:** 17–29–1

Marion Campbell was an outstanding player in the National Football League, an All-Pro defensive end who helped the Eagles win the world championship in 1960. He was a highly regarded assistant coach who built superb defenses in Minnesota, Los Angeles, Atlanta, and Philadelphia. He was defensive coordinator for the Eagles in 1980 when they won the NFC championship.

Campbell was a success at every level except one, and that was head coach. He held the top job for all or part of nine different seasons in Atlanta and Philadelphia, and he never

As a player, Marion Campbell helped the Eagles win an NFL championship in 1960, but he had three losing seasons as head coach (1983–85).

produced a winning record. His career mark of 34–80–1 is one of the worst in NFL history.

Some players who served under Campbell felt he was more comfortable as an assistant coach and better suited to that role. That belief may be true. But to be fair, he was head coach of the Eagles during one of the most tumultuous periods in their history, a time when owner Leonard Tose was in financial ruin and plotting to move the franchise to Phoenix. The organization was in turmoil. The roster was aging, and cornerstones of the '80 championship team, such as Wilbert Montgomery and Harold Carmichael, were breaking down.

For three seasons, Campbell did his best to hold things together. However, his record—5–11 in 1983, 6–9–1 in 1984, and 6–9 in 1985—did little to inspire confidence, so he was fired by the new owner Norman Braman.

"Did Marion Campbell ever really have a chance?" asked columnist Rich Hofmann in the *Philadelphia Daily News.*

It is a valid question.

The sad irony is that the game that led directly to Campbell's firing was a 28–23 loss to Minnesota in December 1985, a loss that occurred the day the Eagles honored the 25th anniversary of the 1960 championship team. Campbell's finest hour and his worst were joined in one emotional afternoon. Eighteen players from the championship team watched from the stands as the Eagles blew a 23–0 lead in the final eight minutes. Tommy McDonald, the Hall of Fame receiver, had tears in his eyes.

"I feel so bad for the Swamp Fox," McDonald said, referring to Campbell by his nickname. "You lose a game like this, it breaks your heart."

"Any loss is bitter," Campbell said, "but that was probably the toughest loss I've been involved in since I've been in this business. I'm still numb."

The Eagles were 6–6 prior to that game, and they had a chance to sneak into the playoffs with a strong finish. However, the Viking loss crushed those hopes. They lost the next two weeks to Washington (17–12) and San Diego (20–14), and Braman fired Campbell with one game left on the schedule. The Minnesota game—"a total breakdown," Braman called it—convinced him a change was necessary.

Campbell had walked a tightrope for seven months, ever since Braman bought the club from Tose and appeared at his first press conference with a T-shirt that read: "Eagles, Super Bowl '86." Campbell smiled, but he must have wondered what would happen next. The man who brought him to Philadelphia, Dick Vermeil, was long gone. So was Jim Murray, the general manager who helped select him as Vermeil's successor. Now Tose was gone as well, replaced by a rookie owner with delusions of grandeur.

It was a difficult situation that was only made worse by Braman's hard-line stance on contract negotiations. Eleven players held out at the start of training camp. Several were traded or released; the others returned grudgingly, and the hard feelings contributed to the team's 1–4 start. Campbell replaced veteran quarterback Ron Jaworski with rookie Randall Cunningham, but after Cunningham struggled through four starts, Campbell went back to Jaworski, and that was when the team found its stride, winning five of six games before the fateful collapse against Minnesota.

As the team was flying home from San Diego, Campbell asked club president Harry Gamble if a decision had been reached about his future. Campbell did not know it, but Braman already had met with Miami assistant coach David Shula, the 26-year-old son of Don, for what were described as "exploratory talks" regarding the Eagles coaching position. Campbell told Gamble he would appreciate a quick verdict. That night, Gamble called Braman, and they agreed to announce Campbell's firing the next day.

Campbell left behind a prepared statement, which read, "I feel at peace with myself because I know that my coaching staff and I put every ounce of effort we had into making the Eagles a better team. And I feel we succeeded. There's no question in my mind that this year's team is considerably better than the one I inherited three years ago."

The players honored Campbell in the final game of the season by writing "Fox 78" on their shoes. "Fox" was short for Swamp Fox, and 78 was the number he wore for the Eagles from 1956 through 1961. They also won the game, 37–35 over Minnesota, avenging the devastating loss three weeks earlier.

While Campbell will not be remembered as a great head coach, his contributions to the championship teams of 1960 and '80 were enormous. As a player, the 6–3, 250–pound former Georgia All-America was the strongest man on the team. Sonny Jurgensen recalls Campbell "pinching me and [Tom] Brookshier on the wrist and putting us on our knees. We'd be crying, 'Uncle.'"

"Swamp Fox was the guy nobody messed with," Brookshier said. "Big guy, never said a word. You couldn't see his eyeballs.

His eyes were just slits. Even Chuck [Bednarik] was careful around him. I remember Chuck saying, 'That's one tough cookie.' And Chuck didn't say that about many people."

Campbell played most of the 1960 season on torn ankle ligaments. He took painkilling shots before every game and again at halftime. At night, while his teammates celebrated, Campbell was home with his foot propped up on pillows. By the time the Eagles met Green Bay for the NFL championship, Campbell's ankle was swollen to the size of a grapefruit. He had taken so many shots that the painkiller was no longer effective. He had to grit his teeth and play, which he did.

Jack McKinney of the *Philadelphia Daily News* wrote, "I can state this with certainty: If Marion Campbell hadn't been willing to pay that price, the 1960 Eagles would not have won their championship."

Campbell got his first coaching break in 1964 when Norm Van Brocklin, his former Eagles teammate, hired him in Minnesota. In 1977, Vermeil brought Campbell back to Philadelphia, naming him defensive coordinator. Over the next six years, with Campbell directing the defense, the Eagles allowed the fewest points in the NFL. He taught the 3–4 defense, and his success helped popularize that scheme around the league.

About his nickname: His full name is Francis Marion Campbell. People assumed he was named after Francis Marion, the Revolutionary War hero known as "the Swamp Fox" for his guerrilla campaigns against the British in South Carolina. Since Campbell was born in Chester, South Carolina, it made sense. Except for one thing: It wasn't true. Campbell was named after his father.

"The publicity man at the University of Georgia put that story out there," Campbell said. "He said to me, 'You were named for the general, right?' I said, no, I was named for my father. He said, 'Well, you've just been named for the general, and if you don't believe me, check the afternoon paper.'"

FRED BRUNEY

College: Ohio State • **Years as Eagles Coach:** 1985 • **Record:** 1–0

Fred Bruney spent more than 40 years in professional football, starting as a player in the 1950s and finishing up as an assistant coach in the 1990s. He got the chance to be a head coach for one game with the Eagles in 1985.

Bruney took over the team when his good friend Marion Campbell was fired with one week left in the season. Clearly, he was the interim head coach, but he hoped that if he won the game impressively, team owner Norman Braman might allow him to stay on. Bruney was 53 and felt this was his best—and perhaps last—chance to be an NFL head coach.

"There's a lot of things I'd like to do as head coach," said Bruney, who was a star halfback and MVP at Ohio State in 1952, then a defensive back in the NFL for nine seasons. "I think I can bring a winner here."

Bruney pulled out all the stops in the final game, defeating Minnesota, 37–35, in the Metrodome. Bruney was a defensive coach throughout his career, but he knew that Braman, who was completing his first season as owner, was bored with the conservative approach of Campbell. Braman wanted his next coach to pump excitement back into the team while also winning some games.

Bruney did his best to provide that, beating the Vikings with a wide-open offense that included a double reverse and halfback option pass and a blitzing defense that recorded eight sacks. Bruney also put in a fake punt that kept alive the Eagles' drive to the winning touchdown. The 37 points was the most the Eagles had scored in a game since 1981.

"That would happen again if I were head coach," Bruney said, doing his best to answer the question of whether he was too "old school" to suit Braman. "You think Tom Landry and Don Shula aren't inventive? Sure, I can do it. I've got a file of plays I'd love to run. Being a defensive coach all these years, I've come up with a lot of ideas [for offense]. I know I could succeed."

In his heart, however, Bruney knew he was a long shot. Braman wanted to make a complete change in the organization. Even with the win over Minnesota, the Eagles still finished with a 7–9 record, their fourth consecutive losing season. Bruney was on the staff the whole time as an assistant coach under Dick Vermeil and assistant head coach under Campbell. The hot rumor was that Braman wanted to hire Miami assistant David Shula, the 26-year-old son of Don Shula.

As it turned out, Braman hired Buddy Ryan, whose coaching star rose with the Chicago Bears' win in Super Bowl XX. Ryan offered Bruney the opportunity to stay on as the linebacker coach, but he chose to rejoin Campbell in Atlanta.

"I thought I had an outside shot," Bruney said as he cleaned out his office at Veterans Stadium. "I thought if they didn't get the guy they wanted, they might come back to me. I never did get my hopes up."

Asked about his chances of ever becoming a head coach, Bruney replied: "It probably won't happen for me now."

BUDDY RYAN

College: Oklahoma State • **Years as Eagles Coach:** 1986–90 • **Record:** 43–38–1

James (Buddy) Ryan was a brash and blustery character who believed in doing things his way. He was 51 years old when Norman Braman hired him to be the Eagles' head coach in 1986. He spent 25 years paying his dues as an assistant coach in the college and pro ranks, so when he finally was given the opportunity to run his own show, he took full advantage. He swaggered, he talked tough, and if some folks were offended, too bad.

"Some people go out of their way to public relate, to say the right things, to sooth people," Ryan once said. "I know the mealymouthed way to do things. I could whine and cry and all that, but that's not my style."

Sports Illustrated's Leigh Montville described Ryan as "the NFL's master of bombast. He is Roseanne Barr's father. He is Archie Bunker's next-door neighbor in Queens. He has demeaned opponents, feuded with their coaches, and cut a player he said was worth 'about two beers and they don't have to be cold ones.'"

A native of Frederick, Oklahoma, Ryan served in the Korean War as an 18-year-old master sergeant. Said Ryan, "I'd say, 'Who wants to go on patrol with me?' Ten guys would raise their hands. Another [sergeant] would ask, no one would go. It's something in your personality. You either have it [leadership] or you don't."

Buddy Ryan and Reggie White celebrate the Eagles' 1988 NFC Eastern Division championship.

Braman hired Ryan after reading a *New York Times* article detailing his role in Chicago's 1985 championship season. Ryan was the defensive coordinator and the architect of the blitzing "46" defense that dominated the NFL as the Bears rolled to their first Super Bowl championship. If Ryan could build half a championship team, Braman thought, why not let him try to build a whole one?

While Ryan improved the Eagles, he never did build a whole team. He built a ferocious defense, similar to the one in Chicago, but he made the mistake of believing his defense complimented by a few playmakers on offense, such as quarterback Randall Cunningham and tight end Keith Jackson, was enough to win a championship. It was not. Under Ryan, the Eagles went to the playoffs three consecutive seasons, but they lost in the first round each time, scoring just one touchdown in the three games.

Still, the five-year run of "Buddyball" was a colorful chapter in Eagles history. It was a dramatic change from the three previous seasons under coach Marion Campbell when the team lost and was boring in the process. There was nothing boring about the Ryan years, beginning with his first training camp when he announced the Eagles would win the NFC East.

"Anybody who knew a damn thing about football knew we didn't have a chance in 1986," Ryan said later. "But I knew what would happen. [After the prediction,] the fans and media would put all the heat on me, and that was okay because I knew I could handle it. It took the heat off the players. I knew what I was doing. You've just gotta have the guts to do it."

The Eagles won only five games that season, two fewer than they had won the year before, but most of the fans supported Ryan. They recognized that this was a team in transition—there were 20 new faces on the 1986 roster, including 14 rookies—and they knew it would take time for Ryan to put his system in place. They saw the young talent, such as Cunningham, Reggie White, Keith Byars, Seth Joyner, and Clyde Simmons, and felt the team was on the right track.

But more than that, the Philadelphia fans liked Buddy Ryan. They liked his earthiness and bravado. They liked the way he thumbed his nose at management. Ryan called Braman "the guy in France," a reference to the owner's villa on the Mediterranean. He called team president Harry Gamble "Braman's illegitimate son." Each time Ryan dissed his millionaire boss, the Eagles' blue-collar fans clutched him tighter to their chest. Buddy was their kind of guy. He did not concern himself with being tactful. He said and did what he damn well pleased.

That was certainly true in 1987 when the NFL players went on strike and the owners chose to continue the season with "replacement" players. Ryan treated the walk-ons with distain. "Dumb jerks," he called them. Ryan would stand off to one side during practice, twirling his whistle and saying nothing. He told his veterans to stick together. He did not want any of them crossing the picket line.

Ryan lost all three games with his replacement players, and while it infuriated Braman, it won Ryan the undying loyalty of his veterans.

"Buddy was the only coach who publicly spoke out for the players [during the strike]," Reggie White said. "He showed us that he was behind us and he was willing to put himself on the line for us. When someone treats you with respect and honesty, how can you not be loyal to him?"

During the strike, the Eagles replacements played a Dallas team reinforced by several veteran stars, including future Hall of Famers Randy White and Tony Dorsett, who crossed the picket line. On the very first play, the Cowboys ran a reverse for a 62-yard touchdown and rolled to a 41–22 victory. Ryan seethed, feeling Dallas coach Tom Landry took advantage of his sorry band of replacements. Two weeks later, the strike was settled, the veterans were back, and Ryan got his revenge, battering the Cowboys 37–20 at Veterans Stadium. Ryan ordered Cunningham to throw a pass in the closing seconds so the Eagles could score one more touchdown and add to the Cowboys' humiliation.

"It's always good to take it and shove it," Ryan said afterward.

The Eagles veterans were 7–5 that season, but the 0–3 record turned in by the replacements cost the team any chance of making the playoffs. After the final game, Ryan presented "scab" rings to George Azar, Gamble's assistant, and Joe Woolley, the personnel director, for assembling the hapless replacement team. Braman was furious. He saw the ring "ceremony" as one more Ryan cheap shot at the front office.

In 1988, the Eagles finished 10–6 and won their first NFC Eastern Division title in eight years. Late in the season, Ryan almost choked to death when a piece of pork chop became lodged in his throat. He was dining with his coaching staff, and offensive assistant Ted Plumb used the Heimlich maneuver to clear the air passage and save Ryan's life. He spent the night in the hospital, but he was back on the practice field the following day.

The Eagles ended that season losing to Chicago, 20–12, in the "Fog Bowl" at Soldier Field. Although the team lost that playoff game, there was a feeling of optimism, that the Eagles with all their young players would grow from that experience and become a world champion. Ryan told Stan Hochman of the *Philadelphia Daily News*, "We bring young kids in here who are cocky, arrogant. They don't stare at the ground and kick rocks when they talk to you. They believe in themselves, they believe in our team, and that's why we're gonna have a helluva football team."

But instead of moving forward, the Eagles slipped from first place to second in the NFC East the next two seasons. They made the playoffs each year as a wild card, but they were beaten at home by the Los Angeles Rams, 21–7, and Washington, 20–6. There was more controversy as Ryan was accused of putting a cash bounty on Dallas kicker Luis Zendejas, an ex-Eagle who criticized Ryan after his release. Rookie linebacker Jessie Small did flatten Zendejas with a blind-side block, but he insisted there was no bounty.

Jimmy Johnson, who was in his first season as the Dallas head coach, was furious. He wanted to confront Ryan, but Ryan followed his custom of leaving the field immediately after the game rather than shaking hands with the opposing coach. "I wanted to say something to Buddy," Johnson said, "but he wouldn't stay on the field long enough. He took his big, fat rear end up the tunnel."

The Eagles image grew steadily darker. Skip Bayless of the *Dallas Times Herald* called Ryan "an embittered bullfrog of a man with an inferiority complex." Gordon Forbes of *USA Today* criticized the team for its "borderline football, taunting, and juvenile showboating." Forbes called the Eagles "a team out of control, endangering careers and embarrassing the league office."

The Eagles set team records for penalties (120) and penalty yardage (981) in 1990. Ryan reveled in the team's outlaw image, but it made Braman uncomfortable. Given the difference in their personalities and Ryan's dismissive attitude toward the front office, he had to win and win big to keep his job. When the Eagles faltered for the third time in the playoffs, Braman had all the reason he needed to fire Ryan.

"I've been fired before for losing," Ryan said, "but I've never been fired for winning." He added, "It's their loss and my gain."

In a 1994 interview with the *New York Times*, Ryan said, "When the guy [Braman] fired me in Philly, that was ridiculous. There was nothing to prepare me for that owner. He didn't understand the people business at all. That's what the NFL is, a people business."

Ryan spent two years out of football, living on his horse farm in Lawrenceburg, Kentucky. In 1993, Houston hired him as defensive coordinator, and late in the season, he took a punch at offensive coordinator Kevin Gilbride during a sideline dispute. Hub Arkush of *Pro Football Weekly* wrote, "[Ryan] has done more damage to the concept of team sports, the idea of sportsmanship, and simple human decency than Woody Hayes, George Steinbrenner, and Bobby Knight have throughout their careers. The only difference between Ryan and them is that they, at one time, were winners."

Some people predicted Ryan would never get another football job after the Gilbride incident, but the very next season, he was hired as head coach of the Arizona Cardinals. He opened his first press conference in typical fashion, announcing, "You've got a winner in town." Ryan did not deliver on his boast. The Cardinals were 8–8 in 1994 and 4–12 the following year. Ryan was fired after the 1995 season.

RICH KOTITE

College: Wagner • **Years as Eagles Coach:** 1991–94 •
Record: 37–29

Norman Braman gave Rich Kotite a dual mandate when he named him head coach in January 1991. Braman wanted Kotite to (1) "take the Eagles to the next level," in other words, win in the postseason, which they never did under Buddy Ryan, and (2) clean up the team's bad boy image, an image Ryan cultivated and Braman despised.

"You can win in the NFL without being a bad boy," the owner said.

"There's not a tougher team in the league than the 49ers," Kotite said. "They've got class. They've got style. They play with good judgment. They don't beat themselves. They don't lose games they're not supposed to lose. They're not on an emotional roller coaster. That's the type of thing I'm looking for."

Kotite banished the black shoes and black towels that were the team's trademark under Ryan. He banned food, drink, and video games from the meeting rooms. He ordered the players to stand at attention and line up by uniform number for the national anthem. He closed his practices to the fans and media. It was all designed to create a more disciplined environment.

"Focus is the key word," said Kotite, a native of Brooklyn, who was a collegiate boxing champion and once sparred with Muhammad Ali. At 6–3 and 230 pounds, he was a tight end with the Giants and Pittsburgh Steelers for six seasons. He was an assistant coach with New Orleans and the Jets before Ryan hired him as offensive coordinator with the Eagles in 1990.

Nicknamed "Bullhorn" for his booming voice, Kotite did a fine job in his first season as the Eagles led the NFC in points scored (396) and quarterback Randall Cunningham threw a career-high 30 touchdown passes.

"I liked Rich; he did a good job," wide receiver Mike Quick said, referring to Kotite's season as offensive coordinator. "He put in the game plan, and he'd be pumping his fist, saying, 'We're gonna do this, we're gonna do that.' I know he got me fired up. I'd leave the meeting room on Wednesday ready to play the game."

When the Eagles lost in the playoffs that season, bowing out in the first round for the third straight year, Braman fired Ryan and promoted the 48-year-old Kotite to head coach.

The Eagles did manage to win a playoff game under Kotite, defeating New Orleans 36–20 in the NFC Wild Card round in his second season, and they did cut down on the penalties and trash talking. But from a high-water mark of 11–5 in 1992, the team slipped to 8–8 in 1993 and 7–9 in 1994. The Eagles finished the latter season with seven consecutive losses, a collapse that prompted Jeffrey Lurie, the team's new owner, to fire Kotite. It was the first time in NFL history a team started a season 7–2 and finished below .500.

"Our record over the second half of the season points to a downward spiral," Lurie said. "I felt that a change was necessary to give ourselves the best possibility to reach the Super Bowl."

Kotite left Philadelphia with a winning record overall, no small accomplishment considering the adversity he faced. In his first game as head coach, he lost Cunningham for the season with a knee injury. The Eagles started five different quarterbacks that year and still won 10 games. In 1992, Pro Bowl defensive tackle Jerome Brown died in a car crash. In 1993, Reggie White and 11 other veterans left the team as free agents, part of an ongoing war between the players and Braman over salaries, a war that eroded team morale and put Kotite in the difficult position of straddling the two sides.

In 1994, Lurie bought the team from Braman, and speculation began about a coaching change. Rumors about former Dallas coach Jimmy Johnson coming to the Eagles were rampant. Kotite coached the whole season under a cloud. "[The talk] was always there," center David Alexander said. "Even when we were 7–2 and [the front office] said there would be no talk about it, it was 'Jimmy Johnson this' or 'Somebody else' that."

In Week 8, Lurie was interviewed during a Monday night game, and despite the Eagles' 5–2 record, he hedged when asked if Kotite would be back in 1995. Lurie said he would evaluate the situation after the season. Two weeks later, when the Eagles defeated Arizona and Buddy Ryan, 17–7, to extend their record to 7–2, Kotite said he, too, would "evaluate" his position after the season. In other words, he might leave for a better offer elsewhere. With a 37–22 record as head coach, Kotite felt he had that kind of leverage.

However, the Eagles lost to Cleveland the next week, 26–7, and did not win another game the rest of the year. In the final game, the Eagles blew a 17-point lead to lose to Cincinnati, 33–30. Kotite was gone two days later.

Even when he was winning, Kotite was not a popular figure. He was not as colorful or quotable as Ryan. He was seen

Rich Kotite led the Eagles to their first postseason win in a decade.

as a yes-man who did what the front office told him to do, in contrast to Ryan, who delighted in shooting spitballs at management. Seth Joyner, the Pro Bowl linebacker, told the *New York Times*: "Braman wanted a puppet and that's what he got."

Kotite did not help himself with game-day gaffes, such as the loss in Dallas where he claimed the rain smeared the ink on his two-point conversion chart. But his most glaring mistakes came in the draft, where he missed on a number of high picks including Antone Davis, Jesse Campbell, Siran Stacy, Leonard Renfro, and Bernard Williams. In four years, Kotite drafted 41 players. Only 20 were still with the team at the end of the 1994 season, and less than half that number made any real contribution.

When running back Keith Byars left the Eagles to sign with Miami in 1993, he offered this assessment: "I know when Rich took over he wanted to change everything that had anything to do with Buddy [Ryan]. That was his choice, but when you erase one identity, you have to give it another. I don't know if that's been done yet. After Buddy left, [Kotite] took us out of black shoes. He wanted us to be a kinder, gentler team. From what I see, they haven't actually identified what their identity should be."

Shortly after his firing in Philadelphia, Kotite was hired to succeed Pete Carroll as head coach of the Jets. Kotite spent two seasons with the Jets, finishing 3–13 in 1995 and 1–15 the following year. He was fired after the 1996 season.

RAY RHODES

College: Tulsa • **Years as Eagles Coach:** 1995–98 • **Record:** 30–36–1

Ray Rhodes is unique among Eagles coaches. No other coach in franchise history enjoyed such immediate success and popularity. No other coach fell as quickly or crashed as painfully. As Bill Lyon wrote in the *Philadelphia Inquirer*, "Ray went from toast of the town to just plain toast in not much more than a finger snap."

It happened so quickly, it was almost dizzying. Jeffrey Lurie hired Rhodes in 1995, and in his first season as head coach, he led the Eagles to a 10–6 regular-season mark and a 58–37 blowout of Detroit in the NFC Wild Card game. For that, Rhodes was named Coach of the Year by the Associated Press. In his second season, he had the Eagles at 7–2 in November, and coming off an impressive 31–21 win over Dallas, they appeared ready to unseat the Cowboys as the dominant team in the NFC East.

Then with stunning swiftness, it all unraveled. The Eagles lost four of the next seven games to finish the regular season at 10–6. They limped into the playoffs and were quickly dispatched by San Francisco, 14–0. In 1997 the Eagles sputtered to a 6–9–1 mark, and the following year they collapsed altogether, finishing 3–13. By the end, Rhodes was a burned-out shell of the coach who offered so much promise just four years earlier.

"I don't think we got the best of Ray Rhodes the last few months," Lurie said when he fired the coach following the 1998 season. "We lost so many games the last year and a half, it probably has an effect on you. It's just a question of being human. As you continue to lose, you just get beaten down."

Ray Rhodes won NFL Coach of the Year honors in his first season with the Eagles.

Such was the trajectory of Rhodes' career in Philadelphia. He was like a stunt pilot: he went straight up, then flipped over and came straight down. He won 17 of his first 25 regular-season games culminating with the big win in Dallas, then he lost 27 of the next 40. In his final season, the Eagles weren't even competitive. They lost to Dallas 34–0 on a Monday night at Veterans Stadium, and the fans were so disgusted, most of them left at halftime.

"This year was a total embarrassment to me," Lurie said. "The way the team played, you just wanted to turn off the TV or walk out."

Where did it all go wrong? Instability in the personnel department was part of the problem. The Eagles had three different scouting directors in Rhodes' four seasons as head coach. After the playoff loss to San Francisco, Rhodes demanded and received control of personnel decisions, saying, "You don't want to go to war with somebody else's soldiers." But Rhodes wasted a first-round pick on defensive end Jon Harris and signed free-agent busts such as Steve Everitt and Chris Boniol.

When the Eagles went to training camp in 1997, Rhodes boasted it was the "most talented" team in his three years as coach. But as the season unfolded and the losses piled up, Rhodes seemed to lose his grip. He could not sleep. His blood pressure shot up. He lived on black coffee and antacid tablets. He carried ammonia capsules in his pocket and sniffed them to keep going.

As the situation deteriorated, Rhodes began blaming the front office, saying, "You know I don't control the money." When Rhodes' comments filtered back to Lurie and Joe Banner, the trust that once existed between coach and management broke down. It did not help that Rhodes had no previous experience as a head coach and Lurie and Banner were still new to the NFL themselves. When adversity hit, they did not know where to turn.

In his first two seasons as head coach, Rhodes strength was his ability to inspire his players. He used metaphors that were profane and even offensive—he compared losing a home game to burglars sodomizing a man's family—but the team responded. The players credited Rhodes' passionate speech for their 20–17 win over Dallas in 1995. That was the game in which the Eagles defense stuffed Emmitt Smith twice on fourth-and-one plays.

By 1997, however, the speeches were no longer working. After a particularly discouraging 31–21 loss to Arizona, Rhodes said, "The thing that shows up in a game like this is overall character and toughness. Those are the things that I think are missing in a lot of areas. It definitely looks like I've been shut out of the door [by the players]. It's like I'm on the outside, talking in."

The following year, offensive coordinator Jon Gruden left to become head coach in Oakland, and Rhodes replaced him with Stanford assistant Dana Bible. Quarterback Bobby Hoying, who had shown promise under Gruden, regressed under Bible. He finished the season with no touchdown passes and nine interceptions. The Eagles opened the season with five consecutive losses, including a 38–0 rout against Seattle and a 41–16 whipping in Denver.

After a while, it appeared Rhodes simply gave up. The fiery coach who once told cornerback Bobby Taylor, "Every day I want you to think you've got a loaded .38 pointed at your head," seldom raised his voice the last month of the season.

"The man who stood before us," Bill Lyon wrote in describing Rhodes, "in the midnight green all-weather sweat suit and white turtleneck was more stooped, more lined, and far more subdued than the eager fire-starter who flamed into town four seasons ago."

Rhodes did bring in some talent. His free-agent signings included running back Ricky Watters and cornerback Troy Vincent. His draft picks included Bobby Taylor, Jermane Mayberry, Brian Dawkins, Duce Staley, Tra Thomas, and Jeremiah Trotter. That nucleus helped the Eagles win four consecutive division titles under Andy Reid. But it was an overall breakdown in the organization, combined with Rhodes inability to develop a quarterback, that finally brought the whole thing crashing down.

As miserably as the Rhodes era ended, with the Eagles setting a franchise record with 13 losses in 1998, it was hard to remember how auspiciously it began. When Lurie met Rhodes for the first time, he believed he had found something special. He interviewed former Eagles coach Dick Vermeil and former Dallas coach Jimmy Johnson, both of whom were out of football, and he was disappointed when he could not strike a deal with either man. But when Lurie met Rhodes, he felt he had found the perfect guy.

Rhodes was young (46) and hungry with a résumé of success that included five Super Bowl rings earned as an assistant coach with the 49ers. He fought his way into the NFL as a 10th-round draft pick and played seven seasons as a receiver and cornerback with the New York Giants and 49ers. He was a fierce competitor who intimidated opponents despite his 5–10, 180-pound frame.

"Ray played a thuggery style of football," said former Giants teammate Beasley Reece. "He was like a bullet, a cannonball. He'd come flying at a guy and hurl his body out of control. Ray went through life with his fists balled up. He'd never back down."

The players in San Francisco loved him. All-Pro cornerback Ronnie Lott told Phil Sheridan of the *Philadelphia Inquirer*, "Ray coaches exactly the way he played. He played like he was desperate and he coaches like he's desperate. This is a man who could convince the pope to make a tackle."

With his appointment, Rhodes became the third African American head coach in modern NFL history, following Oakland's Art Shell and Minnesota's Dennis Green. A native of Mexia, Texas, Rhodes vowed to bring a Super Bowl championship to Philadelphia.

"I'm going to bring a winning attitude," Rhodes said. "It's easier for me to bring this because I've been a part of five world championships. I've been there. It's not hearsay. It's something I've been a part of. I didn't come here to lose. Ray Rhodes is not about losing, man."

After he was fired by the Eagles, Rhodes was hired to replace Mike Holmgren as head coach in Green Bay. Rhodes lasted only one season as the Packers finished 8–8. Since 2000, Rhodes has worked as defensive coordinator in Washington, Denver, and Seattle.

ANDY REID

College: Brigham Young • **Years as Eagles Coach:** 1999– • **Record:** 71–36

When the Eagles were searching for a head coach in 1999, there were several hot prospects on the market. Mike Holmgren was ready to leave Green Bay after two Super Bowls. Brian Billick had orchestrated the highest scoring offense in NFL history in Minnesota. Jim Haslett was a highly regarded defensive coordinator in Pittsburgh.

So when Eagles owner Jeffrey Lurie hired Andy Reid, the reaction in Philadelphia was a slack-jawed "Huh?" Reid was a positions coach with the Packers. He coached the quarterbacks in 1998. Before that, he coached the offensive line and tight ends. He never held the rank of coordinator, and he had no head coaching experience at any level. At age 40, he was a complete unknown.

Bill Lyon of the *Philadelphia Inquirer* described the new coach as "a large, lumbering, slightly rumpled man with a walrus mustache." At his first press conference, Reid said he had a plan for rebuilding the Eagles, but he offered little in the way of details.

"You have to trust me," he said.

Based on what, exactly, the fans and media wondered.

When Reid went against popular opinion to select Donovan McNabb instead of Ricky Williams in the draft, the criticism intensified. When the Eagles lost seven of their first nine games, with McNabb watching from the sidelines while journeyman Doug Pederson started at quarterback, the fans were ready to run both Reid and Lurie out of town.

Andy Reid surpassed Greasy Neale to become the winningest head coach in Eagles history.

But Reid did, indeed, have a plan and he stuck with it, and by his second season, the Eagles were a much-improved team. They went from a 5–11 record in 1999 to 11–5 in 2000, the biggest one-season improvement in franchise history. Over the next four seasons, the Eagles won 48 games, captured four division titles, and advanced to the NFC championship game each year. McNabb developed into one of the game's best quarterbacks, and in the 2004 season he led the Eagles to the Super Bowl for the first time in 24 years.

Along the way, Reid became the winningest coach in Eagles history, surpassing the 66 career victories of Greasy Neale, the Hall of Famer who led the team to back-to-back world championships in 1948 and '49. With a 71–36 record through the 2004 season, Reid also had the highest winning percentage of any active NFL coach (.664). Bottom line: Lurie's biggest gamble turned out to be his best.

"I don't care who you're hiring, you're always taking a risk," Lurie said. "But when you find somebody with [Reid's] reputation, presence, leadership, integrity, you cut down the risk dramatically. Andy values intelligence, loyalty, integrity. Those are the things he lives by."

Reid impressed Lurie and Joe Banner, showing up at his job interview with a six-inch-thick binder full of detailed notes on everything from how to organize a training camp to what players should wear on team charters. Reid collected the notes over

his 16 years as a coach, starting in 1982 as a graduate assistant at Brigham Young under LaVell Edwards and continuing through his seven seasons in Green Bay, where he worked under Holmgren. Everything those coaches did well, Reid wrote down and studied, hoping one day he would have a chance to run his own show. When Lurie called, Reid was ready.

"He had a clear vision of where he wanted to go," Banner told Marc Narducci of the Philadelphia Inquirer. "Nobody will follow you unless there is a plan. He convinced us with his vision and detail orientation that people would follow him."

Lurie and Banner had so much confidence in Reid that in May 2001 they fired Tom Modrak, the director of football operations, and promoted Reid, making him vice president in charge of football operations as well as head coach. At the time, some NFL people questioned the move, asking why the Eagles would make such a change, since the team was winning with the other arrangement, and wondering if Reid could handle all that responsibility. After all, he was a mere position coach just four years earlier.

Four seasons and four division titles answers that question. Reid did not merely cope in his new role; he thrived. Behind his desk at the NovaCare Center is a quote from the aviator Charles Lindbergh that reads, "The important thing is to lay a plan and then follow it step by step, no matter how small or large each one by itself may seem."

Reid goes about his work exactly that way, meticulously planning a strategy, then executing it. If times get tough, if public opinion is against him, Reid does not change. He stays the course. It is an approach that serves him well in a city like Philadelphia, where the blood runs hot and patience is short, especially among sports fans.

Reid's ability to stay calm and not overreact is critical in times such as the 2003 season when the Eagles opened with home losses to Tampa Bay (17–0) and New England (31–10), and the talk shows were flooded with callers who wanted Reid to bench McNabb and play A. J. Feeley. Reid never blinked. He stayed with McNabb, and the Eagles won 11 of their next 12 games en route to a 12–4 finish, tied with St. Louis for the best record in the NFC.

In the book Winning the NFL Way, Reid says, "You can't change during the tough times. You can't suddenly be a different person or present things differently to your people. You've got to stay consistent. Stick to your convictions. When players see you have that conviction and stick to them in spite of a lot of criticism, it makes them believe in you, too."

Along the same lines, Reid told Narducci, "Players will look at you to see how you react to different situations. If you are a mess, there is a big chance they will be. So you want to make sure you hang onto that iron rod and keep going forward."

"Andy is so flat-lined, that's the great thing about him," said offensive coordinator Brad Childress, who also worked with Reid at the University of Northern Arizona when they were both climbing the coaching ladder. "The highs aren't too high and the lows aren't too low. I had no doubt when he came here that he would turn things around. I remember telling my wife that when they hired him. He has a plan and he sticks to the plan."

Reid credits his stoic, steady-as-she-goes approach to his background as an offensive lineman. A native of Los Angeles, whose father was a studio set designer and mother was a doctor of radiology, he attended Brigham Young, where he blocked for a record-setting quarterback named Jim McMahon. Reid said the key to surviving on the offensive line was careful preparation and patience rather than emotion.

"As an offensive lineman, you are outmanned physically every week," Reid once said. "You are playing a better athlete every week. You know that. So what you do is you take that little 3 × 3 box that you're in and you master that box." Applying that philosophy to a whole team, Reid said, "Each guy doesn't have to be an all-star, they just have to be able to master their little box on the field. Then you can master that big box, which is the actual football field."

Reid did not intend to spend his life in football. He planned to follow in his mother's footsteps and attend medical school. But LaVell Edwards told Reid he thought he would make a good coach and offered him a job as a graduate assistant when he was through playing. Reid accepted, and the whole course of his life changed. In a 10-year period, he worked in five different college programs, usually as an offensive-line coach.

His big break came in 1992 when Holmgren was hired as head coach in Green Bay. Holmgren met Reid while he was at BYU as an assistant coach, and the two had an immediate rapport. Holmgren told Reid if he ever became a head coach, he would hire him, which he did, along with other talented assistants, including Steve Mariucci, Jon Gruden, Dick Jauron and Mike Sherman.

"Of all the guys that I worked with, [Reid] might have been the closest thing to a slam-dunk [to succeed as a head coach]," Holmgren told Gordon Forbes of USA Today. "He had a tremendous work ethic. He was very, very bright. And he was great with people. Those are the three things you've got to have to become a head coach."

Reid's first job in Green Bay was coaching the tight ends and assisting with the offensive line. In 1997 he was elevated to quarterback coach, which meant working with the gifted but reckless Brett Favre. Often Reid's duties consisted of serving as the sideline buffer between Holmgren and Favre.

NFL Films captured several instances in which Favre returned to the bench after a costly mistake and Holmgren came over, angrily demanding an explanation. Typically, Reid would take the blame, saying he sent in the wrong formation or called the wrong play. Holmgren would stalk away grumbling as Favre tried to stifle a laugh.

As a head coach, Reid is similarly protective of his players. He never criticizes them publicly, regardless of the circumstances. After a poor performance, his standard reply to any question is "Put the blame on me." The players are fiercely loyal to him as a result.

"I think Joe Gibbs was one of the best coaches ever, and I would compare Andy to Joe Gibbs," said kick returner Brian Mitchell, who won two Super Bowls with Gibbs in Washington before playing two seasons with Reid in Philadelphia. "Andy has gotten every guy on this team to believe in what he believes, and in this game, that's half the battle.

"Andy is not a rah-rah guy. He's quiet in demeanor, but he'll say something when it needs to be said and that gets everyone's respect. You see a lot of coaches who yell and scream and cuss all the time and get the players' attention by intimidating them. Joe wasn't like that and neither is Andy. They command respect because, as a player, you know they know what they're doing."

Reid coaches what is commonly called the West Coast offense, based on the high-percentage, short-passing principles employed by Bill Walsh with the San Francisco 49ers. Unlike other head coaches who delegate play-calling responsibility, Reid calls the plays on game day. Wrote Larry Weisman in USA Today: "With his list of plays shielding his mouth as he orchestrates from the sideline, Reid looks like an oversized geisha attempting modesty."

Reid admits he is not very vocal, which is something of an understatement. His postgame press conferences are almost sleep inducing. He begins by reading off a list of the day's injuries, then gives a brief overview of the team's performance before opening the floor to questions ("Time's yours"). His answers are usually short and dry as sawdust.

Bob Ryan of the Boston Globe referred to Reid as "the Bard of Blandness." Ryan noted New England coach Bill Belichick also answers questions in a monotone, but "Reid takes things a step further. He has both a monotone and a face right off Mount Rushmore."

In Reid's view, he is helping the media. "They don't want a comedian up there," said the coach, who wrote a sports column for the Provo (Utah) Daily Herald while he was in college. "They want someone to give them an answer. Most [reporters] are on deadline and they don't have time to waste."

Those who know Reid best—his wife, Tammy, his five children, and his players—claim he does have a personality. They point to his willingness to dress up like Benjamin Franklin and pose for the cover of Philadelphia Magazine as evidence there is a giggle or two lurking inside that plus-sized body.

"Andy has a personality just like we all do," quarterback Donovan McNabb said. "He knows when to get serious, and he knows how to enjoy himself and then click it back on when it's time to get serious again. But he's a cool guy. You can talk with him about a lot of things, even stuff outside of football. There's a lot of warmth there. He's the kind of coach you want to play for."

Reid downplays his individual accomplishments, such as breaking the Eagles record for wins by a head coach. When he passed Neale with his 67th win, the 47–17 rout of Green Bay on December 5, 2004, Reid said the record merely reflected the work of the entire organization. "It's not about one person," he said.

But that's not to say Reid is unaware of what he has accomplished. Peter King of Sports Illustrated interviewed Reid in 2002 and mentioned that there were people who thought the coach would "get eaten alive" by the Philadelphia fans and media.

"I know people thought that," Reid told King. "Instead, I'm eating the city alive."

5

The Front Office

OVER THE YEARS, the men in the Eagles front office have been as colorful—and controversial—as the men on the field. The owners have included an Olympic athlete (Lex Thompson), a self-made millionaire (Jerry Wolman), a world-class playboy (Leonard Tose), and a Hollywood producer (Jeffrey Lurie). The team presidents and general managers have included a Philadelphia political leader (James Clark), a Villanova sports publicist (Jim Murray), and a one-time WCAU radio producer (Joe Banner). Of course, it all began with Bert Bell, the team's founder and original owner, but his story is told in Chapter Two. This chapter is devoted to the men who carried on what Bell started more than 70 years ago.

THE OWNERS

ALEXIS (LEX) THOMPSON
1941–49

Alexis (Lex) Thompson, a millionaire playboy who once competed on the U.S. Olympic field hockey squad, owned the first Eagles team to win an NFL championship. Thompson purchased the franchise for $165,000 in 1940. Within a few years, he built the team into a winner.

Thompson, who was named after his grandfather, the founder of the Republic Steel Corporation, inherited more than $3.5 million when he was 15 years old. A Yale graduate, he launched a profitable wholesale company that distributed eye solution for hay fever victims. But sports were his first love.

Thompson was involved in a wide variety of athletic activities, including bobsledding, lacrosse, and hockey. He was a member of the 1936 U.S. Olympic field hockey team that competed in Berlin, lost all four of its games, and finished last in an 11-team field. A decade later, Thompson tried to make the Olympics in a second sport, bobsledding, but during the 1948 trials at Lake Placid his four-man sled went off the track at 90 miles per hour. He was thrown almost 200 feet and suffered a fractured ankle.

As owner of the Eagles, Thompson was not content to stay on the sidelines. He was injured playing touch football with the team at training camp in 1941. According to Arthur Daley of the *New York Times*, tackle Vic Sears, then a rookie, "shouted to Thompson to go out for a pass, pointed in one direction and impishly pegged the ball in a slightly different direction—behind Alexis's back. That certainly was no way to treat the

boss. As Thompson twisted to try for the catch, he stumbled over a clump of turf. The result: one broken ankle."

A "hobby," that's what Thompson called his purchase of the Eagles. He spent several years considering various sports investments. He thought about buying a National Hockey League franchise, but changed his mind after seeing two amateur teams outdraw the New York Rangers at Madison Square Garden.

He turned to pro football and purchased the Pittsburgh Steelers from Art Rooney in December 1940, renaming the team the "Ironmen." Rooney then purchased half interest in the Eagles from his good friend Bert Bell. But neither Thompson nor Rooney was happy with his situation in Pittsburgh or Philadelphia. Thompson tried to move his franchise to Boston, but the other owners blocked him. Rooney, meanwhile, was anxious to get back to his roots in Pittsburgh. So in March 1941, Thompson proposed a trade: He would take over the Eagles franchise, while Rooney and Bell took control of the Pittsburgh team.

"The deal was made and everything was cleared up in four days," Thompson said. Before his teams ever played a game, the 26-year-old entrepreneur had become an owner of two NFL franchises in less than four months.

"We will keep the players we selected and take them to Pittsburgh," Bell said, "and all the men on the Pittsburgh roster will be transferred to Philadelphia. In other words, this is strictly an exchange of territories." Once back in Pittsburgh, Rooney and Bell immediately changed the name of the team back to "Steelers."

Bell coached the Eagles the previous five seasons, so Thompson had to hire a coach of his own. He brought in Earle (Greasy) Neale, who was an assistant coach at Yale, Thompson's alma mater. The hiring of Neale, together with the drafting of Steve Van Buren three years later, was the foundation of two world championships.

"Lex was a great guy for saying, 'It only costs a little more to go first class,'" said Al Ennis, the team's publicity director. "The Eagles players always went first class, and it didn't cost any of them a dime. Lex wanted the players to travel in style and dress like big leaguers, so he bought sports coats for all of them. They were wonderful coats of the best material. Each coat cost Lex $75."

One of Thompson's great regrets was that he never got to see his team win its first NFL title in 1948. While the Eagles were beating the Chicago Cardinals, 7–0, at Shibe Park,

Thompson was in a New York hospital undergoing surgery for appendicitis.

Earlier that year Thompson had created a controversy by telling the guests at the New York Football Writers dinner that he favored a common draft of college talent with the NFL and the rival All-America Football Conference. It was the first public acknowledgement of the "other" league by an NFL executive.

Despite the opposition of owners such as George Preston Marshall in Washington, Thompson campaigned vigorously for a merger between the NFL and the AAFC. The Eagles, he claimed, lost $32,000 in 1947 despite winning the Eastern Division title. The losses were a result of the bidding war for players that was driving up salaries in the NFL.

"I'd be a fool if I didn't try to solve a situation in which most of us are losing money," Thompson said.

One year later, Thompson completely reversed his position and vowed a "war to the death" with the rival league. He said, "Any conciliation between the leagues now is impossible." By the time the NFL draft was held two months later, Thompson had changed his mind again and urged the two leagues to get together. He had lost $88,000 in the 1948 season while winning a world championship. He was so strapped for cash that he could not meet the players' payroll the final week of the season and the NFL had to bail him out.

Lex Thompson was a dashing young millionaire who enjoyed the high life and the company of Hollywood stars, such as Clark Gable (right). Thompson was the Eagles' owner when they won their first NFL championship in 1948.

Discouraged, Thompson sold the Eagles on January 15, 1949, for $250,000 to a group of investors known as the "100 Brothers." Three weeks before the sale, however, Thompson scored a major coup. In his last draft as owner, the Eagles made Penn's All-America center-linebacker Chuck Bednarik the No. 1 overall pick. It was the first time a lineman ever was taken with the top pick, and Bednarik went on to become one of the greatest players in NFL history.

Thompson stayed active in sports, promoting midget auto races on the West Coast and launching a tennis tour with world-class players such as Bobby Riggs and Don Budge. The tennis venture lost $100,000 in one year before he shut it down. Thompson, who was married three times, was found dead of a heart attack in his Englewood, New Jersey, apartment in 1954. He was 40 years old.

JAMES P. CLARK
Majority Owner
1949–62

James P. Clark, who built Highway Express Line into one of the nation's largest trucking empires, organized a syndicate of 100 Philadelphia businessmen to invest $3,000 apiece and purchase the Eagles for $250,000 on January 15, 1949. Eleven months later, the Eagles won their second straight NFL championship. It was the first of two titles that the "100 Brothers" would win before selling the club to Jerry Wolman in 1963.

Clark was a broad-shouldered, wavy-haired Philadelphian who claimed he often was mistaken for boxing champion Jack Dempsey. He started his company with one truck delivering film from distributing houses to movie theaters. By the time he took over the Eagles at age 49, his company had 480 vehicles traveling across eight states.

Over the years, Clark was involved in many endeavors. He was one of the major stockholders in the Liberty Bell harness racing track. He almost purchased the Philadelphia Athletics baseball team before it moved to Kansas City in 1954. He was active in Democratic Party politics and was an influential player in John F. Kennedy's successful run for the White House in 1960.

Clark was a forceful man who spoke his mind, and his assertive personality put him on a collision course with the head coach he inherited with the Eagles—Greasy Neale. Since taking over a losing team in 1941, Neale had turned the club around, guiding the Eagles to three division titles and back-to-back world championships. Even though Neale was twice named NFL coach of the year, he and Clark never saw eye to eye.

Their stormy relationship exploded late in the disappointing 1950 season when Clark burst into the Eagles locker room following a 7–3 loss to the New York Giants. Clark told Neale, "The team made plenty of mistakes, and you made mistakes." Neale responded with a string of profanities. Although Clark later apologized, it was clear the two men had reached the end of the road. Clark fired Neale two months later.

"Jim is a wonderful businessman, but he interfered with me," Neale told Jack Wilson of the *Philadelphia Bulletin*. Before the 1950 draft, Neale said, "I had to go before the 'brothers' with Clark sitting on the throne like a king and explain the whys and wherefores of every pick I was going to make. I felt like I was on trial. If they had suggestions, why didn't they make them informally without being so pompous?"

Clark was the kind of executive who made decisions and did not worry about how they would be received. For example, one of his first moves after taking over the team was to announce that the home games would not be televised in 1949. He pointed out that the best team in franchise history, the 1948 world champions, lost money. He said, "Attendance at each game was on the average of 5,500 less than in 1947."

Team officials contacted season-ticket holders who had not renewed their seats in 1949. According to Clark, more than 40 percent of the fans polled said they had purchased TV sets since the end of the 1948 season. Clark said, "They frankly told us that they were not going to buy tickets for 1949, but instead were going to watch us on television."

So Clark blacked out the home games, and the move caused an uproar among the fans. However, Clark said, over the next few months the team "noticed a definite increase in our sale of season tickets from among our old fans as well as from new ones." His policy, while unpopular, was effective.

The Eagles showed a profit the next two seasons, but then lost a reported $75,000 in 1951 and '52. At the end of the 1952 season, Clark again angered the fans by questioning whether they really deserved to have a team.

"Our 1952 season was an exciting and winning season," Clark said, referring to the 7–5 record the team posted in its first year under coach Jim Trimble. "Yet we lost money on the Shibe Park operations. We fielded a good, sound team, enterprising and exciting, backed by a smart, youthful coaching staff. The weather on each of the six home dates was ideal. So what is the answer to the lack of support by the fans? Frankly, we don't know."

Clark set a goal: 15,000 season tickets sold in 1953. "If Philadelphia wants professional football, it can prove it by buying season tickets," he said. "If it doesn't, then we shall have to take some drastic steps."

Clark's message was clear: If ticket sales did not improve, the Eagles might look for another home. Indeed, Clark and his partners met with a group of potential buyers from Louisville, Kentucky, and while nothing ever materialized, the meeting was reported in the papers. Whether that news spurred the fans to action is open to debate, but the fact is that ticket sales did pick up. By 1955 the Eagles were averaging more than 30,500 fans per game, and when the team moved to Franklin Field in 1958, attendance almost doubled.

Poor health plagued Clark throughout his tenure with the Eagles. In 1952 he took a one-year leave of absence from his duties as club president. A year later he stepped down from the position and accepted the role of vice president. Clark was succeeded as president by Frank McNamee, who in addition to being an Eagles executive also served as the fire commissioner of Philadelphia.

Clark died following a stroke on April 17, 1962, at age 62. At the time, he owned 20 percent of the team, and the original investment group of "100 Brothers" had dwindled to 65. In their book *The Pro Football Chronicle*, authors Dan Daly and Bob O'Donnell reported that President Kennedy expressed an interest in purchasing the Eagles following the death of Clark, who was an old friend of the Kennedy family.

An avid football fan, Kennedy was thinking about what he might do after completing his second term in office. He still would be a young man (51), and the thought of owning a pro football team intrigued him, so he authorized his brother Ted, then a freshman senator, to meet with McNamee and the other partners to discuss a possible deal. However, before the meeting could take place, Kennedy was confronted with the Cuban missile crisis, and all other business went on hold. He never pursued the matter after that.

In December 1963, when the Eagles were sold to Wolman, the remaining "Brothers" did very well. Their original $3,000 investment returned a handsome $60,000.

JERRY WOLMAN
1963–69

As a boy, Jerry Wolman hitchhiked 100 miles from his home in Shenandoah in upstate Pennsylvania to watch the Eagles play. In December 1963, Wolman bought the team for $5,505,000. It was a classic, only-in-America, rags-to-riches story. The only thing it lacked was a feel-good ending.

Wolman was 36 when he bought the Eagles, the youngest owner in the National Football League. On the day the sale was announced, Frank McNamee introduced Wolman as "a young man who has made a million dollars for every year of his age." It was true. The energetic construction magnate had amassed a fortune estimated at $36 million by the time he took control of the Eagles. But in just six years, he was forced to sell the team to avoid bankruptcy.

Jerry Wolman threw himself—literally—into the role of team owner. Here he is on the practice field in Hershey, Pennsylvania, as head coach Joe Kuharich looks on.

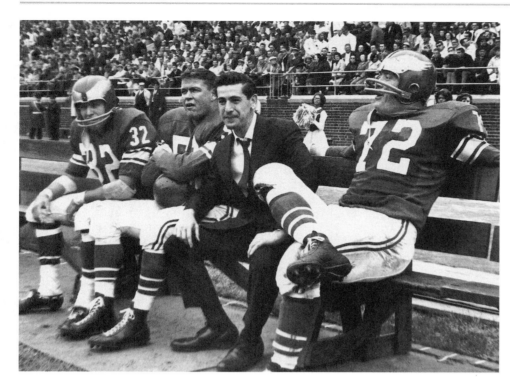

Jerry Wolman joined the players on the bench during his first game as Eagles owner, a 38–7 win over the New York Giants on September 13, 1964. "I had the feeling I was getting a new toy," Wolman said.

Wolman's journey began in 1952 when he and his wife Anne loaded everything they owned into one car and left Shenandoah. Wolman had dropped out of high school in his senior year to help his ailing father in the family's wholesale fruit business. At 24, he was ready for a new start.

Jerry wanted to relocate to Philadelphia. Anne preferred New York. They agreed to settle the issue by picking up the first hitchhiker they saw and going wherever that person was headed. The hitchhiker turned out to be a college student bound for Washington, D.C. So Washington it was.

Living in a $6-a-week room and cooking meals on a hot plate, Anne worked as an insurance clerk, and Jerry took a job in a paint store. He borrowed money to buy a piece of ground, where he built one duplex apartment, then another. He made money on his first two properties, but he lost everything—about $150,000—on a group of 60 ranch houses in Fairfax, Virginia. Rather than give up, Wolman begged his creditors to give him another chance. They agreed, and, working tirelessly, Wolman built a construction and real estate empire.

By the time he purchased the Eagles, Wolman owned 5,000 apartment units of the estimated 20,000 units he had built. He also owned a dozen office buildings. He was a man of wealth and influence, yet when he was around his football team, he was like a little kid at recess.

At his first training camp as owner in 1964, Wolman ran around the practice field in low-cut football shoes, catching passes with the receivers. He was so gung ho that he charged into a pack of jeering Redskins fans at an Eagles-Washington scrimmage and had to be rescued by assistant coach Fred Bruney.

He paid a small fortune to recruit and outfit the Philadelphia Eagles Sound of Brass, a 220-member marching band, complete with baton twirlers and drill team. Living in Washington, he was familiar with the Washington Redskins marching band, and he was determined to have an even bigger, better band for

his team. (Leonard Tose disbanded the Sound of Brass when he bought the team in 1969.)

Calling himself "a babe in the woods," Wolman told Hugh Brown of the *Philadelphia Bulletin* that his first visit to the annual NFL meeting was a "liberal education for me." Wolman admitted he knew nothing about the inner workings of the NFL. Said Wolman: "It is a far cry from the construction business."

"At first, I had the feeling I was getting a new toy," Wolman said. "But that feeling is definitely behind me. Suddenly, it dawned on me that I owe a tremendous obligation to the thousands of people who follow the Eagles. I owe it to them to put a winning team on the field, and a winning team I am going to put on the field. Therefore, I cannot make the mistake of picking the wrong man as head coach."

Wolman hired Joe Kuharich, who previously coached at his alma mater Notre Dame as well as Washington and the Chicago Cardinals in the NFL. The Eagles won their first regular-season game under Kuharich, routing the New York Giants 38–7, and they went on to win six games, a significant improvement over the 2–10–2 finish of the previous year.

Wolman was so elated with the team's progress that even though Kuharich still had three years left on his four-year coaching contract, Wolman signed him to a 15-year deal for $900,000 as the team's coach *and* general manager. It was the longest contract in professional sports, and it meant Kuharich could continue to coach as long as GM Kuharich so desired.

"This must be the way Sutter felt when he found all that gold in 1849," Kuharich said when the deal was announced. The *Philadelphia Daily News* ran a picture of a beaming Kuharich sitting in Franklin Field, holding his contract aloft and giving the "OK" sign.

Wolman appointed Ed Snider vice president and treasurer in charge of all Eagles operations. Snider was an old friend from Washington who served as Wolman's business adviser.

Snider and Kuharich did not get along, and their animosity led to an internal power struggle. Wrote Sandy Grady in the *Philadelphia Bulletin*: "The two are dissimilar as a Boston Bull and a Dalmatian, Joe K., heavy-handed and dominating, Snider elegant and sensitive." Kuharich was to run the football team, Snider the business operation, but they were at odds the whole time.

James Smart in the *Bulletin* wrote, "Snider felt that Wolman was favoring Kuharich to the detriment of the team." According to Smart, Snider told Wolman to make a choice: Kuharich or him. Wolman said, "Let's talk about it in a day or so." Smart wrote: "[Snider] adds bitterly: 'He took Kuharich.'" Ultimately, Wolman fired Snider from his position with the football team.

The Eagles had only one winning season under Kuharich, and that was 1966 when they finished 9–5 and went to the Playoff Bowl, a meaningless game matching the second-place teams from each conference, which the Eagles lost to Baltimore, 20–14. From there, the team went into a steep decline, winning just six games in 1967 and two games in 1968.

By 1967 reports began circulating that Wolman was having financial difficulties. Two years earlier he and Snider had acquired a National Hockey League franchise for Philadelphia. The deal was contingent on the building of a suitable arena, the Spectrum, which Wolman financed at an estimated cost of $12 million, roughly twice the original projection. Snider took over management of the hockey team, the Flyers.

Meanwhile, the economy was tightening, and Wolman was caught in the pinch. When construction delays stalled his biggest project—the $50 million, 103-story John Hancock Center in Chicago—Wolman's nightmare began. He estimated that he lost $20 million on that building alone. He had other holdings, including Yellow Cab Company, the Spectrum, and Connie Mack Stadium, but it was not enough to absorb the losses he suffered in Chicago.

Sources close to the beleaguered Wolman told Rem Reider of the *Philadelphia Inquirer* that many top people in the Wolman organization felt his financial position was hopeless. Still, he rejected advice from his attorneys that he should go into voluntary bankruptcy. He was clinging to the hope that he could arrange a major loan and satisfy a growing list of creditors.

Wolman made a number of frantic attempts to salvage his team. Former Philadelphia Mayor Richardson Dilworth traveled to New York in a futile effort to persuade the Morgan Guaranty Trust Company not to take over the Eagles stock because of Wolman's failure to make payments on several outstanding loans. Wolman flew to London in an unsuccessful attempt to swing a $36 million loan from a German bank.

In March 1969 the Eagles were put on the auction block by Joseph O. Kaiser, U.S. referee in bankruptcy, who was overseer of Wolman's financial affairs. For Wolman, the end came on May 1 when he drove to the team's offices at 30th and Market streets to officially sell the club to Leonard Tose.

Jack Morrison of the *Philadelphia Bulletin* described the scene: "[Wolman] pushed open the glass doors to the reception room and was greeted by Joseph A. Donoghue, an Eagles vice president and veteran of 20 years service with the club. Wolman shook hands with Donoghue, who was seated in a chair. Tears welled up in Donoghue's eyes. 'Take it easy, Joe, everything will be all right,' Wolman said, putting his arm around Donoghue's shoulders."

"I've been fighting this thing for some time," Wolman told Morrison. "This is a day I never thought for a second would come. But I had no choice. It's here."

Wolman, Tose, and their attorneys were in session for 14 hours working out the details of the sale. Wolman was granted a 90-day window that would allow him to buy back the team if he could somehow secure a loan, but even he knew this last-ditch bid was certain to fail, as it did.

When he met the press that night, Wolman was described as "pale and nervous with the hint of a 5 o'clock shadow." But he remained gracious, saying, "When I saw the expression on Leonard's face tonight, I remembered how I felt when I bought the Eagles."

Grady wrote a column tallying up Wolman's six years in the Philadelphia sports arena. He wrote, "Without Wolman, there would be no Spectrum. Without Wolman, there would be no NHL hockey team. And without Wolman, there would have been no Joe Kuharich and his disastrous regime. So do your own arithmetic. It seems here that Wolman left a helluva lot more in this town than he took out."

The love Wolman felt for his football team never died. In January 1981, when the Eagles went to their first Super Bowl, Wolman, who was then back on his feet financially, attended the game. "It hurts not being involved in the team," he told Bill Fidati of the *Bulletin*. Wolman also defended Kuharich, who died the day of the Super Bowl following a long illness.

"I don't think I've ever said it before, but a lot of people don't realize that many of the problems with the team were my fault, not his," Wolman said. "We made the Playoff Bowl in 1966, then I had those financial problems the next year, and they affected everything. They affected Joe and the players on the team as well as me. Joe never had an even shot because of those problems. It wasn't his fault that things didn't work out."

Over the next two decades, Wolman rebuilt his finances to the point where he was in position to once again bid for an NFL team. In 1998 he was one of eight finalists attempting to buy the Washington Redskins, but he lost out to Daniel Snyder, who purchased the club for $800 million.

LEONARD TOSE
1969–85

Leonard Tose, the dapper, impeccably dressed, free-spending owner of Philadelphia's first Super Bowl team, had a well-deserved reputation for going first-class. But his gambling and extravagant lifestyle eventually cost him not only his fortune, but his beloved Eagles as well.

Born in Bridgeport, a suburb of Philadelphia, in 1915, Tose developed his love of football while attending Notre Dame University (class of 1937). He was one of the "100 Brothers" who bought shares in the Eagles in 1949. He tried to buy the team in 1963, but lost out in the bidding to Jerry Wolman.

Tose bought the Eagles from Wolman in 1969 for $16,155,000, a record amount for an NFL franchise. Tose estimated his net worth at $20 million. Most of it came from the family trucking business, started by his father Mike, a Russian Jewish immigrant, with one horse and one wagon at the turn of the century.

When Tose took over the team, he fired Joe Kuharich, even though it meant paying off the remaining ten years of his outrageous contract. He hired Pete Retzlaff, the popular former

Eagles All-Pro, as general manager, and Jerry Williams, a former Eagles player and assistant coach, as his first head coach. Over the next four seasons, the team won only 15 games, and the fans became so frustrated that they surrounded his limousine and almost turned it over following a 1972 game at Veterans Stadium.

By 1976, Tose had gone through three head coaches—Williams, Ed Khayat, and Mike McCormack—and replaced Retzlaff as general manager with Jim Murray. In January of that year, Tose and Murray embarked on a lengthy search for a new coach. After interviewing Joe Paterno, Hank Stram, Norm Van Brocklin, Allie Sherman, and others, they went to California to talk with Dick Vermeil, who had just guided UCLA to a Rose Bowl upset of Ohio State.

When Tose contacted Vermeil, the coach told him he was not interested. But Tose and Murray refused to take no for an answer. Finally, after three days of persuasion, Vermeil accepted the job.

"Leonard was a salesman, no question," Vermeil said. "Plus the way he presented his product: 'You take over the football team, and I won't interfere. All I'll do is everything I can to help you. It'll be your football team to rebuild.' He said he had some frustrating experiences as an owner and he wanted to be a winner. He thought I was the guy. He would do whatever he could possibly do to make it happen."

"Leonard was the consummate owner," quarterback Ron Jaworski said. "He allowed the coaches to coach and the players to play. He'd come into a team meeting after the final ros-ter was set and say, 'Guys, my door is always open. But don't come to me and talk about football. We'll talk about anything but football. You want to talk football, go to your coaches.' He made that very clear, he was there for us."

Wide receiver Harold Carmichael recalls flying home from a game after injuring his knee as a rookie. He was frightened because at that time teams could drop injured players to the taxi squad and cut their pay. Tose sat next to Carmichael and assured him everything would be all right. "He said, 'Don't worry, you'll be okay, I'll see to it,'" Carmichael said. Tose was true to his word, and Carmichael went on to become the club's all-time leader in pass receptions and touchdowns.

Tose's spending habits were legendary. He traveled in a private helicopter adorned with green-and-white Eagles wings. He served filet mignon and lobster in the press box. He handed out $100 bills as tips to waiters and bartenders. He flew more than 700 friends to Super Bowl XV, including Philadelphia Archbishop John Cardinal Krol and comedian Don Rickles. Each year, Tose vacationed for eight weeks in a $1,000-a-day private residence in Acapulco, taking along dozens of friends and picking up their tabs.

Once, in St. Louis, Tose ordered a fleet of limousines to take his entourage to the game, even though the hotel was just one block from the stadium. Tose walked outside, took a deep breath of the crisp fall air and announced, "What a beautiful day. Let's walk." He proceeded to lead his well-tailored posse down the street, trailed by a procession of empty limos, all with their meters running.

Leonard Tose (foreground) presents a check to Audrey Evans of Children's Hospital of Philadelphia at the dedication of the first Ronald McDonald House. Taking part in the ceremony are Tom Brookshier (behind Evans), Randy Logan (41), Tom Sullivan (25), Bill Bergey (66), and Harold Carmichael (17).

Leonard Tose (left) and head coach Dick Vermeil. "Leonard was the consummate owner," Ron Jaworski said. "He allowed the coaches to coach and the players to play."

But if Tose was extravagant, he was also generous. In 1970 he donated $79,000 to keep extracurricular activities, including sports, going in Philadelphia's public schools. He wrote a $25,000 check to buy bulletproof vests for the police department. He established the Philadelphia City All-Star Football Game, which showcases the talents of local high school players for college coaches and scouts.

He pledged $1 million to launch the Eagles Fly for Leukemia, which has continued into its fourth decade. A bone-marrow-transplant laboratory at Children's Hospital of Philadelphia is dedicated to Tose and the Eagles. There were countless acts of individual kindness when Tose would see an item in the newspaper—a story about a family losing its home or a child in need of a medical procedure—and he would hand the clipping along with a check to someone on his staff and say, "Here, take care of this." It happened all the time.

"Mr. Tose did a lot of nice things for me and my family," Vermeil said. "He helped me when I got in over my head rebuilding my parent's home in California. I was making $75,000 a year. All of a sudden, it went from a $35,000 project to a $135,000 project. I couldn't make the payments because I was doing that with [public] speaking money. Mr. Tose settled the whole thing. He never asked for anything in return."

Tose and Vermeil developed a unique relationship, almost like father and son. Vermeil said, "Leonard and I became close friends because we had mutual respect. We trusted each other.

We had fun together. I was always included. My wife Carol was included. My kids were included. Trips to Acapulco, everything was paid for. You couldn't help but appreciate his sincerity in wanting to rebuild the organization."

"They had very little in common in terms of how they conducted their day-to-day affairs, but they certainly had the common mission of winning and doing it at all costs," tight end John Spagnola said. "With Leonard, all costs meant whatever he had to pay. With Dick, the cost side of the equation was whatever time or effort he had to put in. But they were two guys meant for one another."

Tose gave Vermeil an open checkbook to spend freely on veteran players, but the coach chose to rebuild with a mix of younger players and holdovers such as Carmichael and linebacker Bill Bergey. The Eagles won just four games in Vermeil's first season and five the next, but they had their breakthrough in 1978.

That year, the Eagles were 9–7, their first winning season since 1966, and they earned a wild-card berth in the playoffs. The turning point came November 19 when cornerback Herman Edwards picked up a fumble and raced into the end zone to lift the Eagles to a last-second 19–17 win over the New York Giants. The play became known as the "Miracle of the Meadowlands," and Tose listened to it unfold from a hospital suite in Houston. Two days earlier, he underwent open-heart surgery performed by Dr. Denton Cooley, one of the pioneers of the procedure.

"Surviving that [game] was the real test," Tose said. "If my heart didn't explode then, it never will. When Edwards picked up that ball, I started screaming, and all the doctors and nurses came running into the room. They thought I was dying. Vermeil called me from the locker room. We were all in tears. It was one of the great days of my life."

Four weeks later, the Eagles defeated the Giants again, 20–3, to clinch a winning record and a trip to the playoffs. In the locker room, Vermeil hugged Tose and, with tears streaming down his face, said, "That one was for you."

The Eagles flew upward from there, winning 11 games in 1979 and setting a franchise record with 12 regular-season wins in 1980 as they captured the NFC East Division title. They defeated Minnesota, 31–16, in the Divisional playoff and rolled over Dallas, 20–7, at the Vet to win the conference championship and earn a trip to Super Bowl XV. Tose was named pro football's Man of the Year by *The Football News*. It was a wonderful ride, which included a December wedding for the 65-year-old Tose, but it ended with a 27–10 loss to Oakland in the Super Bowl.

"The loss in the Super Bowl hurt us all, but I think I got over it much quicker than Leonard did," Vermeil said. "I don't know if he ever got over it. He took it personally. There's no question the Super Bowl was a real negative in Leonard's life and maybe a percentage of his downfall."

In 1982 the NFL was shut down for more than two months by a players' strike. It was a strain on all the team owners, but especially Tose, who was losing heavily at the Atlantic City casinos. There were issues raised about the Eagles' finances in other years—in 1977, First Pennsylvania Bank appointed a "financial consultant" to oversee the team's spending—but Tose always worked his way, or borrowed his way, out of trouble. But it was different in 1982. Tose was spinning out of control, and with no football revenue coming in, he was becoming desperate.

When the strike was settled and play resumed, the Eagles lost their first game to Cincinnati, 18–14. Afterward, Tose stormed into the locker room and blasted the players. "Why don't you go back out on strike?" he said.

"That wasn't Leonard," Vermeil said. "He was under so much stress at that time, he said things I know he didn't mean. That was the most depressed I've ever seen him."

"Things had built up inside him long enough that he just felt he had to lay into us," Spagnola said. "My immediate reaction was to go after him because I felt that his comments were totally out of line. I remember guys holding me back. Dick, of course, tried to pull everything back together, but all of us were looking at one another saying, 'What's going on?' You could feel the fiber of the team pulling apart. That was the end of the Vermeil era and the team as I knew it."

"It was a very ugly time," Jaworski said. "The battle lines were drawn. Leonard took a hard-line stance. We, the players, took a hard-line stance. Dick and the coaching staff were left in limbo. When the strike was finally over, we were never the same."

On May 19, 1983, Tose fired Murray and put his daughter, Susan Fletcher, in charge of the front office. Given the title of vice president, Fletcher was brought in to clean house and keep her father from drowning in a sea of red ink. She knew it would take drastic measures.

In December 1984 the *Arizona Republic* broke the story that the Eagles were in negotiations to move the franchise to Phoenix. The newspaper reported that people from the Eagles front office had visited Phoenix to check out available office space. The Philadelphia fans were shocked and angry. Death threats were phoned to the team offices. Fans called on city officials to get involved and block all the exit routes out of town.

The deal involved Tose selling 25 percent of the team to Arizona real estate developer James Monaghan and moving the club to Phoenix once the season ended. Tose would have pocketed enough cash to wipe out his debts and he still would have maintained control of the team. In the end, however, he decided against the move. Philadelphia Mayor Wilson Goode stepped in with some last-minute concessions that included restructuring the Veterans Stadium lease and the promise to build 50 luxury skyboxes with the team receiving 100 percent of that revenue. (Unfortunately for Tose, the skyboxes were not completed until 1987, long after he sold the team.)

"Susan, who is a lawyer, recognized maybe the only way they could save the Eagles for her dad was to take them to a new city," Vermeil said. "Arizona presented a tremendous package. But when it came right down to it, Leonard backed out because he could not take the Eagles out of Philadelphia. In making the decision not to do it, I think he knew eventually he was going to lose the football team."

Tose was crushed by a mountain of debt, estimated at some $42 million. In 1985, faced with the prospect of bankruptcy, he made the painful decision to sell the Eagles to Norman Braman for $65 million. After his corporate and personal obligations were settled and taxes paid, Tose netted $10 million from the sale. Within five years, he had lost virtually all of it.

In 1992, after the Sands Hotel and Casino in Atlantic City sued him to recover $1.23 million in gambling debts, he countersued, claiming the casino encouraged him to drink excessively and gamble away his fortune. He lost the suit. Later, he testified before a congressional hearing on compulsive gambling that his losses totaled between $40 and $50 million.

"I made every mistake you can make," he said.

Tose admitted to losing as much as $1.5 million in a single night of gambling, yet he spent years in denial. At one point, Murray arranged for Dr. Robert Custer of the National Institute for Pathological Gambling to meet with Tose. As Custer told Murray, "I met Leonard in a bar. He had a scotch in one hand and a cigarette in the other. He said, 'What are you here for?' I said, 'I'm here to help you with your compulsive gambling.' Leonard said, 'Hell, I beat smoking and drinking; what makes you think I can't beat gambling?'"

On his 81st birthday, Tose was evicted from his Villanova mansion after losing the estate in a U.S. marshal's sale. Divorced for the fourth time, he spent his final years living alone in a center-city hotel room. Vermeil stayed in touch with Tose and sent him whatever money he needed to get by. Said Vermeil: "I feel like I owe him so much. He gave me the opportunity to coach in the NFL. He changed my life."

Tose died on April 15, 2003, at St. Agnes Medical Center in Philadelphia, less than a mile from Veterans Stadium. At his bedside were his daughter Susan, Bill Bergey, and Murray, who had long since forgiven Tose for firing him.

Vermeil delivered the eulogy at Tose's memorial service. He brought a smile to everyone in the room when he opened his remarks by saying, "Leonard Tose was an original piece of work."

NORMAN BRAMAN
1985–93

He could be seen dining at an elegant French restaurant one day and eating off a paper plate in a food court the next. He was a staunch political conservative, but he lobbied for minority rights and the Equal Rights Amendment. He owned the Philadelphia Eagles, but he spent most of his time in South Florida and the French Riviera.

That is the profile of Norman Braman, a complex man who rose from water boy to owner of the Eagles. When he purchased the team in 1985, Braman and his wife Irma owned one of the world's most extensive private collections of modern art as well as one of the nation's premier wine cellars with more than 4,000 bottles of vintage brands stored at their home on Miami's Intracoastal Waterway.

When Philadelphia fans reflect on Braman's nine years as owner of the Eagles, they may not remember that the team twice won 11 games and went to the playoffs four times. They are more likely to remember Braman as the man who hired—and fired—Buddy Ryan, the most colorful and controversial coach in franchise history, and as the owner whose hard-line stance on free agency led to the departure of numerous star players, including Reggie White, Clyde Simmons, and Seth Joyner.

Braman was born in 1932 in West Chester, Pennsylvania, and grew up in the Cobbs Creek section of Philadelphia where his father Harry, a Polish immigrant, owned a barbershop. The younger Braman was a water boy at the Eagles training camp, which was then in West Chester. During the season he would sneak into Shibe Park to watch the team play. He attended West Philadelphia High School and graduated from Temple University in 1955 with a degree in business administration.

After spending four years in marketing and sales for the Seagram's Company, Braman joined his father in opening a self-service discount clothing store. Later he operated a chain of 46 drug stores. Braman cofounded the Philadelphia Pharmaceuticals and Cosmetics Company and remained with the firm until 1969. Three years later Braman opened his first automobile dealership, a Cadillac agency in Tampa, Florida.

When he purchased the Eagles in 1985, Braman owned almost two dozen luxury car dealerships in South Florida and Colorado, including Rolls Royce, Maserati, and Porsche-Audi. His company was selling more than 25,000 cars annually.

"It's the ultimate fulfillment of every red-blooded American boy's fantasy," Braman said after purchasing the Eagles from Leonard Tose for $65 million.

The Eagles lost a total of $4 million under Tose in 1983–84. Braman immediately turned the franchise into a financial winner, generating operating profits of $48.5 million from 1985 to 1990. But this financial success came at a price as players and fans accused Braman of being more concerned with making money than winning football games.

Stan Hochman of the *Philadelphia Daily News* gave him the nickname "Bottom Line Braman," a label he disliked but never denied. "I was accused of running the Eagles like a business," he said. "I plead guilty to that."

Braman raised the Eagles' season-ticket base from 40,000 to more than 55,000, but he increased ticket prices three times in his first five years. Under Braman, the team employed only three or four college scouts, while other teams had as many as a dozen. The operating budget was slashed dramatically.

Norman Braman was a successful automobile dealer in Florida and, as Eagles owner, he brought a new and aggressive marketing approach to the NFL.

Braman made an immediate impact in NFL circles. When he called for a more aggressive marketing approach by NFL Properties, the other owners put him in charge of the league's licensing department. During his tenure, revenue from NFL Properties to each of the member clubs grew from $100,000 to more than $2 million annually. As a member of the NFL's Super Bowl Site Selection Committee, Braman called for competitive bidding from cities anxious to host the big game. He was an astute businessman, and he knew how to cut a deal, so when he spoke, other owners took notes.

Eagles fans did not begrudge Braman his lifestyle—he spent part of the year at his villa in the south of France and flew to the home games in his private jet—but they resented it when he pinched pennies with the team. Every year, the Eagles led the league in contract disputes and training camp holdouts. When free agency came into the NFL, Braman refused to pay the big money necessary to retain his star players; as a result, many of them signed with other teams.

Yet Braman could also be generous. When Steve Van Buren, the Hall of Fame halfback, was hospitalized following a stroke in 1988, Braman picked up all his medical bills and paid for a special TV hookup so Van Buren could see the games. Marion Campbell, the coach Braman inherited when he bought the team, credited the owner with making the deal to sign White from Memphis of the United States Football League.

"We had starters holding out of training camp, and everywhere you turned [Braman] was being criticized," Campbell told Kevin Mulligan of the *Philadelphia Daily News*. "But when we finally got permission to pursue Reggie, Braman said to me, 'Is this guy good enough to go out and get?' I said, 'He was the best coming out of college, and he's still the best.' He said, 'It's going to cost me some big money to do this, you know?' And as much as I wanted my veterans in camp, I said, 'Whatever it costs you, it'll be worth it.'"

Braman wrote the check—a $1.38 million contract buyout plus a four-year deal worth another $1.65 million—and Reggie White was an Eagle. And Campbell was right: He was worth it. But in 1993, after 124 sacks and seven consecutive Pro Bowl appearances (both club records), White left the Eagles to sign with Green Bay. Braman never made him an offer. He just let him walk.

Braman and his second coach, Buddy Ryan, never got along. In part, it was a clash of personalities. Braman was an aristocrat; Ryan was a Kentucky horse farmer. Braman felt he should command respect; Ryan gave him none. On the rare occasions when Ryan referred to Braman, he called him "the guy in France."

The Eagles had three consecutive winning seasons under Ryan, but each year they lost in the first round of the playoffs. That record, combined with the bad-boy image the team cultivated under Ryan, was enough to make Braman decide to fire Ryan after the 1990 season and replace him with offensive coordinator Rich Kotite.

By 1992, Braman was almost completely detached from the team's operation. He put general manager Harry Gamble in charge and gave him the title of president and chief operating officer. Later that year, Stanford University economics professor Roger Noll testified at an NFL antitrust trial that Braman paid himself a $7.5 million salary as Eagles owner in 1990. It also was shown that Ryan and Gamble were among the lowest paid people in their respective positions in the entire league that same season.

Norman Braman (right) fired coach Buddy Ryan after the Eagles lost in the first round of the playoffs for the third consecutive year. "There was nothing to prepare me for that owner," Ryan said, referring to Braman. "He didn't understand the people business at all."

This revelation led to a new wave of public outrage which, combined with the team's declining fortunes on the field, began to wear on Braman. The value of the team was high—Fox had just paid $1.6 billion for the NFL TV rights; the expansion teams in Carolina and Jacksonville were kicking in big money to join the league—so Braman decided to put the franchise on the block. He sold the team to Jeffrey Lurie for an announced $185 million, a record amount for a professional sports franchise.

JEFFREY LURIE
1994–

When Jeffrey Lurie purchased the Eagles on May 6, 1994, the *Wall Street Journal* reported that he paid even more than the announced price of $185 million. The *Journal* claimed the total package was more like $198 million, a staggering sum. But for Lurie, it was the fulfillment of a dream, and how do you put a price tag on a dream?

He promised to do "absolutely everything possible to build championship football teams." In the first decade of his ownership, the Eagles began turning his vision into reality while becoming one of the NFL's marquee attractions. In 2003 their three national television appearances on "Monday Night Football" were the highest-rated games of the season. By 2004 the waiting list for Eagles season tickets had grown to more than 60,000.

At the end of the 2004 season, Lurie had the highest winning percentage of any Eagles owner with a 93–66–1 regular-season record. Under Lurie the team set a franchise mark by winning four consecutive division titles and qualifying for the

postseason five years in a row. With the team capturing the conference championship in 2004 and advancing to Super Bowl XXXIX, people were no longer snickering at Lurie's characterization of the Eagles as "the gold standard" of the NFL.

"I thought the challenge was to make people see the franchise differently, to treat it as a state-of-the-art franchise even before it was one," Lurie told Phil Sheridan of the *Philadelphia Inquirer.*

Two key elements in his effort to build the Eagles into an elite franchise were the construction of the $37 million NovaCare Complex and $512 million Lincoln Financial Field. The 108,000-square-foot NovaCare Complex, which houses the Eagles' indoor and outdoor practice fields, medical and training facilities, and executive offices, opened in March 2001.

The construction of Lincoln Financial Field began in 2001, with the city picking up nearly $200 million of the cost. On September 8, 2003, the gleaming structure with a seating capacity of 68,532 opened. It hosted its first regular-season game when the Eagles met Tampa Bay on "Monday Night Football." But the actual planning took five years and spanned the terms of two Philadelphia mayors.

Lurie is heir to the Harcourt General publishing and movie theater empire. He and his mother, Nancy Lurie Marks, the only daughter of the conglomerate's founder, Philip Smith, borrowed a reported $190 million from the bank of Boston to purchase the Eagles. They used their personal stock as equity capital and pledged stock in the family trust as collateral.

Lurie was born in Boston in 1951 and grew up in suburban West Newton as a passionate sports fan. He camped out at Boston Gardens to buy tickets to Bruins playoff games and cheered on the Celtics to the NBA championship. He attended the first game played by the Boston Patriots in 1960, and he spent so much time at Fenway Park watching the Red Sox that he believes he could find his way around the old stadium with his eyes closed.

At one time in the 1940s, Lurie's grandfather owned nine of the nation's 15 drive-in movie theaters. Later, he opened the first movie theater in a suburban shopping mall in Framingham, Massachusetts. His company, General Cinema Corporation, also became the largest independent bottler of Pepsi Cola. Later, it evolved into Harcourt General, Inc., a corporation that includes one of the nation's largest chains of movie theaters, three insurance companies, several publishing houses, and the Neiman Marcus department stores.

Lurie earned a bachelor's degree from Clark University, a master's degree in psychology from Boston University, and a doctorate in social policy from Brandeis University, where he wrote his thesis on the depiction of women in contemporary film.

In 1985, Lurie founded Chestnut Hill Productions, a Los Angeles–based film company. His five movie productions included *Sweet Hearts Dance* with Don Johnson and Susan Sarandon, *V. I. Warshawski*, starring Kathleen Turner, and *I Love You to Death*, with Kevin Kline and Tracey Ullman. It was on the set of the last film that Lurie met his future wife, Lori Christina Weiss, who was an associate producer. They were married in Gstaad, Switzerland, in 1992.

In 1993, the year before he bought the Eagles, Lurie was in a bidding war with Boston businessman Robert Kraft to purchase the Patriots. Lurie dropped out of the bidding when the price reached $150 million. At the time, he doubted that the Patriots—who were near bankruptcy under their previous

Owner Jeffrey Lurie shares the thrill of victory with the fans at Lincoln Financial Field after the NFC divisional playoff win over Minnesota.

ownership—would be able to generate the revenue needed to build a championship-caliber team.

Lurie also joined forces with Maryland Governor William Donald Schaefer in a bid to bring an expansion franchise to Baltimore, but the NFL chose instead to place the new teams in Jacksonville and Carolina.

Lurie finally got his big break in 1994 when Rams president John Shaw alerted him that Norman Braman might be putting the Eagles on the block. This time, Lurie jumped to the head of the line and stayed there, paying what was then a record price for the Philadelphia franchise. Eagles fans, tired of Braman's tightfisted ownership, welcomed Lurie with open arms.

In one of his first public appearances, Lurie competed in a celebrity batting contest against Eagles cornerback Eric Allen and 76ers center Shawn Bradley. Lurie won the event with five solid line drives and left the field to a standing ovation.

The new owner wasted no time immersing himself in the football operation. He set up an office in the dormitory at the Eagles training camp in West Chester. He often slept over if he worked late. "One hundred and eighty five million for the team and he's staying with us in the dorm," quarterback Randall Cunningham said. "That's what you call down to earth."

Lurie also demonstrated an appreciation for the team's history. On the first day of practice, he noticed a rookie wearing number 92, the number once worn by Reggie White. Lurie felt that a player of White's stature deserved more respect than that. He took the equipment manager aside and said, "Never again do I want to see anybody wearing number 92 without speaking to me first. That's not the way I want to run this team."

The story made the newspapers, and the next day, White, who was with Green Bay, called Lurie, whom he never had met, to say thank you. That was the beginning of a warm friendship. They would hug whenever their paths crossed. White told Lurie, "If you'd only bought the team a year earlier." In other words, he might have finished his career in Philadelphia.

Lurie is unlike any other Eagles owner. He has a Ph.D., for one thing. He also projects a world view that is unique. According to *BusinessWeek* magazine, Lurie "sometimes behaves more like a Peace Corps volunteer than a football owner." Said NFL Commissioner Paul Tagliabue: "Jeffrey is different and distinct." In the lobby of the NovaCare Complex, Lurie created a "Hall of Heroes" photo display honoring Martin Luther King, Jr., Mother Teresa, and Jonas Salk.

"I feel like everyone should walk in every day with a perspective on life and the values of caring about other people," Lurie told Gordon Forbes, author of *Tales from the Eagles Sidelines.* "The commonality with Dr. King, Mother Teresa, and Dr. Salk was that they cared for less fortunate people. I want that value to be on exhibit throughout our organization at all times."

In 1994, Lurie skipped a press conference introducing safety Greg Jackson, the first free-agent acquisition under his ownership, to attend the dedication of a new playground at a children's welfare home near Veterans Stadium. "That's my values," he said. "I always want that."

In addition to serving on the NFL's Finance Committee and Broadcast Committee, Lurie also serves on the Diversity in the Workplace Committee and is on the board of directors for NFL Charities. Along with Christina, he founded the Eagles Youth Partnership, the team's nonprofit charity operation that provides health and educational assistance to needy families throughout the Greater Philadelphia region. He wants the team's reach to extend beyond the playing field, but he also knows the team ultimately will be judged by what it does on the field. He strives each day to find that balance.

"When you buy a football team, you have no idea what to expect," Christina Lurie told Rich Hofmann of the *Philadelphia Daily News.* "So it takes a few years to realize all the intricacies, whether it's managing the salary cap or picking the right coach or creating a team that looks for the future and not short-term, then having to figure out how to finance the building of a new stadium. So it has been a learning experience for all of us."

In his early days as an owner, Lurie sought out the advice of people such as Bill Walsh, who built a dynasty in San Francisco, and Jimmy Johnson, who won two Super Bowls in Dallas. Lurie rebuilt the personnel department and hired more scouts. But he also knew he had much to overcome, starting with the facilities at Veterans Stadium.

Lurie was shocked when he toured the facilities for the first time. He told author Rosabeth Moss Cantor all he could think was "This is an NFL franchise? Every image I had was completely put into disarray. The offices were in an old stadium.

I saw no windows, lighting that could put you to sleep, rats walking across offices, and a lot of unenergetic expressions."

He made building a new stadium and practice facility a priority. Working with club president Joe Banner, he was able to get it done. After 70 years of being a tenant at every stadium from Baker Bowl to the Vet, the Eagles finally had a home of their own. It was a tribute to Lurie, who spent his early years in Philadelphia knocking down persistent rumors that he planned to move the team to Los Angeles.

"That was never going to happen," he said. "The Eagles belong in Philadelphia, and they will stay in Philadelphia."

Lurie went through growing pains as a rookie owner. Prior to the final cutdown before the 1994 opener, he instructed his coaches to keep the best 53 players, even if it meant putting the team flush against the $34.6 million salary cap. Knowing the team might need flexibility to add players in case of injury, Lurie asked six veterans—including starting offensive tackle Broderick Thompson—to take a 30 percent salary cut. He did not think morale would suffer because, as he put it, "the best players still were on the team."

He was wrong. The six players filed a grievance through the Players Association that resulted in the team restoring most of their pay. According to Thompson, the pay cuts were on the players' minds when they took the field for the opener against the Giants. The Eagles fell behind 14–0 early and lost, 28–23.

"I'll admit it, I made a mistake," Lurie said. "But I just wanted to make sure we started the season with our best players. I'm going to make mistakes, but I think the people will respect a well-intentioned owner."

It was a strange first season for Lurie as the Eagles came back from their opening-day defeat to win seven of their next eight games, then lost seven in a row to finish 7–9. Lurie fired coach Rich Kotite, and after interviewing—and almost hiring—Dick Vermeil, he brought in Ray Rhodes, who won five Super Bowl rings as an assistant coach with the 49ers.

Rhodes took the Eagles to the playoffs each of his first two seasons, but then the team collapsed, winning six games in 1997 and setting a franchise record with 13 losses in 1998. A disconsolate Lurie said, "We're pitiful. To say anything less wouldn't be appropriate. You'd rather see paint dry than watch our team play. We're pitiful, just pitiful."

Around the NFL, people were dismissing Lurie and Banner as clueless amateurs who were in over their heads. Brad Brink, an agent, told the *Philadelphia Inquirer* that Lurie and Banner were ridiculed as "camp buddies who went around with stopwatches and whistles like it was fantasy football."

But all that changed in 1999 when they hired Green Bay assistant Andy Reid as head coach. It was not a popular decision at the time—few people knew who Reid was—but Lurie and Banner trusted their instincts. They felt Reid was the right guy, and they were proven correct.

The first season did not begin well. The team lost its first four games under Reid and seven of its first nine. There was an embarrassing 44–17 home loss to Indianapolis, but that weekend Lurie introduced Reid to the members of the 1949 Eagles championship team who returned to Philadelphia for a 50-year reunion. "This is a great coach," Lurie said, "and one day he will take us back to the championship."

It sounded like wishful thinking at the time, but Lurie insists he believed every word. In a 2002 interview with *ESPN, the Magazine*, Lurie said, "We're still quite proud about not being struck by the same blind spots as everyone else [in hiring Reid]. And as far as great moments or difference-makers in team history, the hiring of Andy Reid forever changed this franchise."

Lurie still has strong feelings for his native Boston. He was at Fenway Park for the 2004 baseball postseason and celebrated along with the rest of the Red Sox fans when the team finally won the World Series. But it is also clear that Lurie has adopted Philadelphia. When he held aloft the George S. Halas Trophy after the NFC Championship Game victory over Atlanta, one of the first things he did was thank the fans for their support.

"It's always about the fans," Lurie said. "These fans are the most passionate, most deserving fans you can imagine. I'm just so happy we were able to win this for them."

OTHER KEY EXECUTIVES

JOE BANNER
President
1994–

Joe Banner joined the team as executive vice president and chief operating officer when Jeffrey Lurie purchased the club in 1994, and he was promoted to president in 2001.

"Joe plays a crucial role in most everything we accomplish," Lurie said. "His determination, intelligence, and desire for success are invaluable assets."

Lurie had a "gut feeling" that Banner, his boyhood friend, would be the ideal choice to help him run the franchise.

"Joe was dedicated, smart, a good person; we think alike about sports," Lurie said. "We were both newcomers, but we would think outside the box. I didn't want someone just like everyone else; that was not the way to get a great turnaround. I'm sure that a lot of people thought I didn't know what I was doing, and why bring in someone else like that? But I had confidence in myself and Joe that we could turn it around."

Banner, who was born in 1953, is a graduate of Denison University. His only previous experience in sports was working as a reporter and producer at WCAU radio in the 1970s. He also worked in the retail clothing business with his father, Ralph, with four stores in Boston and two in Chicago. After he sold the clothing business, Banner spent two years working at City Year, a nonprofit organization similar to the Peace Corps, encouraging young adults to participate in public service projects that promote social change in urban areas.

Lurie and Banner were friends from their days in Boston, where they often attended Red Sox and Patriots games together, so when Lurie bought the Eagles, he brought along Banner, who quickly demonstrated an ability to get things done.

In addition to creating a partnership with the City of Philadelphia to build Lincoln Financial Field, Banner put together the 25-year, $65 million partnership with NovaCare that led to the construction of the NovaCare Complex in 2001. It was the first naming-rights deal for a team headquarters in any professional sport.

Banner also handled the delicate three-year negotiations that led to the construction of the new stadium and the 21-year, $140 million naming-rights deal with the Lincoln Financial Group. No one was more thrilled than Banner when the players walked into the stadium for their first practice before the 2003 season. He called it "the fruition of a dream."

"We've spent three years working on getting a deal done and almost three years building a stadium," he said. "To actually be here and see the team and see their reactions and actually just look around, it's as good as it gets."

Banner is best known for his ability to master the NFL salary cap, which has been the ruin of many other teams. The *New York Times* called him "the Joe Montana of the salary cap. He's simply the best." The *Dallas Morning News* said that his salary cap strategy is "the blueprint for financial success in the NFL: Draft well, play them young, extend them early."

The salary cap, which is designed to ensure competitive balance, became part of the NFL in 1994, the same year Banner joined the Eagles organization. With his business background, he saw managing the cap as the quickest way for him to help the team.

"That's why I started learning the cap," Banner told Paul Domowitch of the *Philadelphia Daily News*. "Because I figured I've got to be able to do a couple things that can make this organization better. I studied the collective bargaining agreement and the cap, and I felt here was an area I should be able to bring an understanding to. I could create a real value and place for myself."

"With all the recent success of the team, most of the credit usually goes to the players and coaches," coach Andy Reid said. "But without the support and hard work of the front office, we would not have that success. Joe Banner is a big part of that support. Joe is the best as far as managing that salary cap."

Banner first employed his salary-cap strategy in 1998, when the Eagles were struggling through a 3–13 season. He signed safety Brian Dawkins, who was then a still-unproven third-year player, to a five-year extension that included a $2.5 million bonus. The move was widely second-guessed, but it turned out to be a great signing as Dawkins blossomed into a Pro Bowl player the next season and the Eagles had him locked him at a bargain rate. They have done the same thing with numerous players since then.

Banner's careful planning put the Eagles millions of dollars under the salary cap following the 2003 season and allowed them to sign Jevon Kearse, Tennessee's Pro Bowl defensive end, to an eight-year, $66 million deal on the first day of the NFL free-agency period. They had Kearse's name on a contract before other clubs had time to react.

Banner explained that the key to success with the salary cap is for everyone in the organization to be correct in recognizing a player's long-term potential.

"We haven't been right every time," he said. "This is a risk/reward situation, but overall the strategy has served us really well. Our batting average is pretty impressive."

VINCE McNALLY
General Manager
1949–64

Philadelphia native Vince McNally was the architect of the Eagles' 1960 NFL championship team. He was general manager in 1957 when the team had perhaps the best draft in its history, selecting halfback Billy Barnes in the second round, flanker Tommy McDonald in the third round, and quarterback Sonny Jurgensen in the fourth round. And when you consider what *might* have been …

Going into the draft, McNally had his sights set on Jim Brown, the All-America fullback from Syracuse. The Eagles had the seventh overall selection, and McNally was all set to take Brown, but the Cleveland Browns were drafting one spot ahead of them, and they chose Brown. McNally settled for his second choice: Clarence Peaks, a fullback from Michigan State who was hampered by injuries for most of his seven seasons with the Eagles.

"Vince was a smart guy," said cornerback Tom Brookshier. "He was one of those guys who could watch a team practice and pick out who could play and who couldn't, almost at a glance. He had that kind of eye. [Players] who were cut from other teams, Vince would sign them and they'd turn into All-Pros."

McNally did that with split end Pete Retzlaff and halfback Timmy Brown, both of whom were on waivers—Retzlaff was cut by Detroit, Brown by Green Bay—and he signed them for $100 apiece. They turned into two of the most productive players in team history.

But McNally's real masterstroke was making the trade for quarterback Norm Van Brocklin. The Eagles general manager had heard Van Brocklin was unhappy in Los Angeles, where he was sharing playing time with Billy Wade. He offered the Rams a package of tackle Buck Lansford, halfback Jimmy Harris, and a first-round draft pick for Van Brocklin. The Rams general manager—a young fellow named Pete Rozelle—accepted the deal.

Acquiring Van Brocklin also enabled McNally to hire Buck Shaw as head coach. McNally knew Shaw—they both coached in the Bay Area for a time—and respected him, but he could not convince him to come to Philadelphia. The Eagles were 4–8 in 1957, so it was not a very attractive situation for a coach.

"I offered Buck the job three times, but he kept turning it down," McNally said. "Once I was flying to Washington to sign a player, and I had a layover in San Francisco. I knew Buck lived only 15 minutes away, so I called and asked if he'd stop by and discuss the offer. He said, 'I can't. It's raining too hard.'"

Finally, McNally asked Shaw straight out why he didn't want the job. His reply was equally direct: "You don't have a quarterback, and you can't win without a quarterback." At that point, Jurgensen had played just a few games and still was unproven. But when McNally made the trade for Van Brocklin, he called Shaw. "I said, 'Okay, we've got a quarterback,'" McNally said. Shaw replied, "In that case, you've got a coach, too."

Three years later, the Eagles won the league championship.

McNally was a football and basketball standout at Roman Catholic High School in Philadelphia. He attended Notre Dame University, where he played for coach Knute Rockne. He was a college coach for years, then a personnel man for several pro teams before joining the Eagles as assistant general manager in 1949. He was promoted to GM two years later.

McNally was known as a tough negotiator. In 1963, Jurgensen and King Hill walked out of training camp in a contract dispute. They felt that walking out together and leaving the team with no veteran quarterback would put more pressure on the front office. Their tactic worked—they signed new contracts the next day—but not before McNally pulled the arm off the chair he was sitting in and flung it across the room.

After the papers were signed, McNally stalked out of the room and told the waiting reporters, "They're all yours."

McNally's influence waned after Jerry Wolman bought the team in 1964 and hired Joe Kuharich as coach. Within a year,

General manager Vince McNally (right) takes roll as the Eagles prepare to leave for their Hershey, Pennsylvania, training camp in 1956. Quarterback Bobby Thomason is first in line. Defensive end Norm Willey (white shoes) waits his turn.

Wolman had expanded Kuharich's duties to include those of general manager. McNally was still in the front office, but he was not being consulted on personnel matters. He told friends he was doing little more than "signing $6 per diem training tabs."

McNally was not consulted when Kuharich traded Jurgensen to Washington and Tommy McDonald to Dallas. By September he was fed up. Three days before the regular-season opener, he walked into Wolman's office and resigned—by "mutual agreement," according to both men. The owner agreed to honor the terms of McNally's contract, which still had three years left to run with an option for another five years.

JIM MURRAY
General Manager
1969–83

He never played the game and freely admits he would not know how to diagram an off-tackle slant, but Jim Murray delivered the prize no Philadelphia Eagles general manager had done before—a trip to the Super Bowl.

Murray fooled the critics who scoffed at his lack of football experience by persuading a skeptical Dick Vermeil to leave UCLA and accept the job as head coach. He also made the trades that brought All-Pro linebacker Bill Bergey and quarterback Ron Jaworski to the Eagles, setting the stage for four consecutive postseason appearances.

A 1960 graduate of Villanova University, where he also served as sports information director, Murray joined the Eagles as a public relations assistant in 1969. Two years later, he was named administrative assistant to general manager Pete Retzlaff. When Retzlaff resigned after the 1972 season, Murray assumed the administrative chores for the new head coach, Mike McCormack.

On December 16, 1974, the day after the Eagles completed a 7–7 season with a three-game winning streak, Eagles owner Leonard Tose stepped before a roomful of reporters and announced that Murray was being promoted to general manager. McCormack was as shocked as everyone else. Tose did not even tell the coach of his plans.

"My appointment not only was second-guessed; it was laughed at," said Murray, whose only professional sports experience prior to joining the Eagles was two summers spent in the front office of two minor league baseball teams. "It upset a lot of people. They didn't think I was qualified. They didn't have any faith in Leonard Tose's decision-making ability."

For the next nine years, Tose and Murray were inseparable. An engaging, self-described "neighborhood guy" from West Philadelphia, Murray understood the city and the fans. He set the tone for one of the most civic-minded organizations in professional sports, and in the process he rehabilitated the image of Tose, who was seen previously as a colorful but shallow playboy.

Murray and Tose were so close that Tose at one time wrote a clause in his will that Murray would assume control of the team in the event of his death. "One of the best things I ever did was to hire Jimmy," Tose said. "He had two things that count: brains and a sincere concern for people. And what a friend."

In addition to his football duties, Murray devoted himself to the Eagles Fly for Leukemia campaign, which started in

Jim Murray was the general manager when the Eagles went to their first Super Bowl. "Those were glory days," Murray said. "We made a difference in people's lives."

1969 when Kim Hill, three-year-old daughter of Eagles tight end Fred Hill, was diagnosed with acute lymphatic leukemia. While she was being treated at St. Christopher's Hospital for Children, she was given a 1 percent chance to live for six months. Hill asked Tose for financial support. Tose pledged $1 million and put Murray in charge of raising the funds.

Murray organized fashion shows with the players and their wives as well as a four-day radiothon. He also held a collection at the stadium during a home game that raised $20,000. He presented a check for $125,000 to Dr. Audrey Evans, the head of pediatric oncology at Children's Hospital in Philadelphia, one of the nation's leading cancer research centers.

Dr. Evans said, "Wouldn't it be great if we had a house where parents could stay while the children were receiving treatment?" Murray went to the McDonald's Corporation with an idea: selling green milk shakes, Shamrock Shakes, with all the profits going toward the creation of just such a house.

The drive was an enormous success, and the first Ronald McDonald House opened in West Philadelphia in 1974. By 2004 some 235 houses were operating in 24 countries—and

Kim Hill was a mother and housewife, living with her family in Southern California. Eagles Fly for Leukemia was the largest charitable endeavor of any professional sports franchise, and Murray still served on the International Advisory Board, although he no longer had any connection to the football team.

The highlight of Murray's time with the Eagles was the 20–7 win over Dallas in the 1980 NFC Championship game and the joyful ride to Super Bowl XV. The low point was his firing by Tose in 1983 at a time when the owner was losing control of his team to a gambling addiction. He fired Murray and replaced him with his daughter, Susan Fletcher, saying, "Instead of an adopted son, I have a real daughter."

It was a hurtful blow, but Murray stayed loyal to Tose even after that. Years later, after Tose had sold the team and lost his fortune at the gambling tables, he sued the casinos, and Murray was there supporting him every day in court. When Tose needed a place to live, Murray helped arrange it. Whenever there was a dinner recognizing Fly for Leukemia, Murray made sure to remind everyone it all started with the generosity of Leonard Tose.

"Those were glory days with the Eagles," Murray said. "We won a lot of games, we went to a Super Bowl, and we made a difference in people's lives. We're still making a difference through Eagles Fly and the Ronald McDonald House. To have been a part of that, even a small part, is a great thing."

JIM GALLAGHER
Public Relations Director
1949–95

Jim Gallagher spent 46 years working for the Eagles. That is an NFL record. No employee in the league has served the same team for such a long time, and no one has filled as many roles. He started as an office clerk, worked his way up to scout, then personnel director, public relations director, traveling secretary, and alumni relations director.

From the time he joined the Eagles as a $50-a-week stenographer in 1949 until he finally retired in 1995, Gallagher worked for five owners, seven general managers, and 17 head coaches. The only time he was not with the Eagles was the two years he spent in the Army, serving in the Korean War.

He is the only member of the front office who was with the team for the 1949 NFL championship season, the 1960 championship season, and Super Bowl XV. He is also the only staffer who worked games at Municipal Stadium, Shibe Park/Connie Mack Stadium, Franklin Field, and Veterans Stadium.

"Forty-six years, that's unbelievable," owner Jeffrey Lurie said when he was introduced to Gallagher after purchasing the team in 1994. "Jimmy began working for the Eagles before I was even born."

When Gallagher, a Philadelphia native, joined the Eagles, their offices were in a center-city storefront. The team shared the space with a dental lab where they made false teeth. "We used to hear the grinding all the time," he said. "The dust would come flying in, and we'd be coughing. We'd have to yell at each other over the noise."

Gallagher also helped out in the ticket office, and he even ran the switchboard some days. He moved to the scouting department and handled the preparation for the draft, compiling statistics and whatever information he could find on college players.

"Scouting wasn't as sophisticated as it is now," he said. "Back then, we'd pay [college] coaches $50 to send us a list of the top players they saw that season. Some teams drafted players out of magazines. If a guy looked good in a picture, they'd take him."

In the 1957 draft, Gallagher convinced general manager Vince McNally to draft Tommy McDonald in the third round. McDonald was an All-America halfback at Oklahoma, but he was only 5–9. McNally was not sure McDonald could compete with the big boys in the NFL.

"I said, 'I've seen him on film, and all he does is score touchdowns,'" Gallagher said. "It was one of the few times I spoke up. I'm glad I did."

In 1958, Gallagher used a 21st-round draft pick to select John Madden, an unknown tackle from Cal Poly. Madden later coached Oakland to a Super Bowl and became a national TV celebrity. But in those days he was just a rookie whose career ended with a knee injury at the Eagles training camp in Hershey. Feeling sorry for Madden, who was lonely and far from home, Gallagher took a bus from Hershey to Philadelphia and visited him in the hospital, bringing a stack of magazines and candy bars.

Later, as the team's public relations director, Gallagher made countless friends throughout the NFL with his warmth and wit. He agonized when the fans and media vented their wrath on coach Joe Kuharich with the "Joe Must Go" campaign in 1968. He was there for all the losing seasons—14 of 15 years in one stretch—and watched helplessly as the fans threw snowballs at Santa Claus.

"I had no idea what to do in those [losing] days," he said. "I just drank Maalox morning, noon, and night."

"Jimmy Gal never scored a touchdown for the Iggles or made a tackle or caught a pass," wrote Bill Lyon in the *Philadelphia Inquirer*. "But nobody—player or coach or front office—ever was more valuable, ever meant more, did more for them. He was the ultimate behind-the-scenes player. He made friends for a franchise that always was in desperate need of them. He rebuilt bridges, repaired rifts, created fans who stayed Iggles fans for their lifetime and the next generation's lifetime."

For Gallagher, it is no exaggeration to say the Eagles are family. His wife, Betty, is the daughter of the late Joseph A. Donoghue, who worked for the team for 20 years and served as executive vice president from 1955 through 1963.

LEO CARLIN
Ticket Manager
1964–77; 1980–

Leo Carlin went to work in the Eagles ticket office on a part-time basis prior to the 1960 NFL championship game. Four years later, he was the team's ticket manager. Forty years later, he has survived the moves from Franklin Field to Veterans Stadium to Lincoln Financial Field.

"Changing stadiums is a nightmare," he said.

The Eagles were scheduled to move to the Vet for the 1970 season, and they sold 50,000 season tickets with all the ticket holders assigned to new seats. But three months before the first game, the stadium was unfinished, and the field was littered with construction equipment. The team had no choice but to return to Franklin Field for the 1970 season, a move that Carlin estimates cost the team approximately $560,000.

Carlin had to order all new tickets and draw up a whole new seating plan in a matter of weeks. One year later, he had to do it all over again as the Eagles actually did make the move to the Vet with its circular design, which was a whole different configuration from the classic football stadium that is Franklin Field.

Some fans who had seats in the east stands (end zone) at Franklin Field were pleased when they were assigned end-zone seats at Veterans Stadium and found themselves much closer to the field. However, other fans who had sideline seats at Franklin Field were upset with the sideline seats at the Vet because they were farther away from the action. It was all due to the circular design of the new stadium. Carlin had no control over that, but he still caught all the grief.

"That was a brutal couple years of my life," he said. "That was a horror show. It was brutal because everyone pictured themselves in a better seat."

When Veterans Stadium finally opened in 1971, team officials were upset because the Eagles were forced to use two 90-by-13 foot auxiliary scoreboards. The three major firms supporting the high-tech scoreboard system elected not to show their messages during Eagles games. In addition, the stadium was built without a football clock, a case of "city negligence or forgetfulness," Carlin said.

Although each of the stadiums had its own difficulties, the formula was actually more complex moving into Lincoln Financial Field because of the seat license restrictions.

"At Lincoln Financial, we also had to be governed not just by the seat location but by the seat license that was purchased," Carlin said. "So we had to develop some priorities concerning where people were going to sit."

During the final year of the Vet, a man walked up to Carlin and asked, "You're going to the new stadium?" Carlin said he was.

The man said, "You know what, Carlin? When we moved from Franklin Field to the Vet, you really screwed me. You know what? You're going to get a chance to do it again."

Although Carlin gave numerous personal tours and tried to talk to as many people as he could during the transition from one stadium to the next, he found it impossible to satisfy everyone. His unanswered phone messages averaged 2,000 a week. "And I'm on the phone all day long," he said. When the Eagles went to Super Bowl XXXIX, his official title was director of ticket/client relations.

Carlin has been in the ticket business most of his life. Before he went to work for the Eagles, he was treasurer and ticket manager of the Walnut Street Theater in Philadelphia. He has been with the Eagles ever since, except for a brief stint with the Philadelphia Stars of the United States Football League.

His son, Leo, Jr., was a wide receiver at Holy Cross and signed a free-agent contract with the Eagles in 1986. He played in all the preseason games and was released just before the league opener.

"I remember Dick Vermeil was broadcasting our [preseason] games on television," the elder Carlin said. "He mentioned that Leo was coming into the game, and he said, 'Well, I certainly hope he's faster than his old man because I used to jog with him.'"

6

The Golden Years: 1948–49, 1960, 1980

THE DUFFEL BAG DYNASTY

The 1948–49 World Champions

The years immediately after World War II were a time of pride and prosperity in America. Fifty-three million Americans had jobs, and unemployment was less than 2 percent. The national income tripled, and the economy swelled with $150 billion in postwar money.

They were the years of convenience and leisure, the years of the first drive-in banks, frozen food, and television. Americans were building new lives, new families, and new dreams. In many ways, the Philadelphia Eagles were a metaphor for the time.

They were a diverse and cocky bunch, unpolished and ragged around the edges, cast together not so much by planning as by fate. They came from college campuses and foxholes, from the sandlots and the steel mills. One by one, they straggled into Philadelphia and became the champions of professional football, the Duffel Bag Dynasty.

"There were a lot of guys like me just back from the war," said Pete Pihos, the Hall of Fame end. "I was in the 35th Infantry. I went in as a private and came out a lieutenant. We were at Normandy. We were in the Battle of the Bulge. I served under General Patton, so you know I was in the front lines, I wasn't in the backfield. I know when I got out, I was happy to be alive."

"You come back a changed person," said Chuck Bednarik, the Hall of Fame center and linebacker who survived 30 combat missions as a waist gunner on a B-24 bomber. "I was 17 when I went in the service, a nice, easygoing kid who didn't know anything. Then all of a sudden, I'm in the middle of a war. You develop a killer instinct and it stays with you."

"It was a different time, that's for sure," said Al Wistert, the team captain. "I wasn't in the war. I was in college and joined the Eagles in 1943. But I know when the veterans came back, there was a real sense of joy, just being home and playing football again. We didn't have any jealousy, none of the bickering you see today. No one was making a million dollars, so there wasn't that resentment. Most guys were playing for the love of the game."

By any measure, the 1948–49 Eagles were a dominant team. They are one of four teams in NFL history—the 1941–42 Bears, the 1967–68 Raiders, and 1975–76 Steelers are the others—to outscore their opponents by more than 200 points in two consecutive seasons. But the Eagles are the only one to win the league championship in each of those seasons. The Eagles blanked the Chicago Cardinals, 7–0, and Los Angeles Rams, 14–0, in the two title games. No NFL team before or since has posted consecutive shutouts in championship play.

"All these other defenses have come along—the Fearsome Foursome, the Steel Curtain, the Bears under [Buddy] Ryan—but none of them could do what we did," said Bednarik, who joined the Eagles as a 24-year-old rookie in 1949. "I don't know where other people rank us, but I think we belong with the best teams ever."

After World War II, veterans Tommy Thompson (seated, left) and Fred Meyer (standing) rejoined the Eagles.

Halfback Steve Van Buren led the league in rushing four times. He became the first man in NFL history to rush for 1,000 yards in a season more than once. Pihos was the league's top pass receiver three straight years. Quarterback Tommy Thompson led the NFL in completion percentage one year, touchdown passes another.

Coach Earle (Greasy) Neale created a state-of-the-art defense that employed a five-man line, two linebackers, and four backs. It was a multiple defense with the middle guard occasionally dropping off like a modern middle linebacker. It frustrated the best offenses in the league as the Eagles won 22 of 26 games, including postseason, in 1948 and '49.

"We had two real strengths: Van Buren and our defense," said Pihos, who played both ways and was selected for six Pro Bowls. "I don't believe any team in the league could match us in those areas."

"We were the first [Eagles] team to enjoy any success, and the city really got behind us," Wistert said. "Bookbinder's, the fancy seafood restaurant, made us a deal: every time we got a shutout, we ate for free. Not just the players, but our wives, our kids, everybody. You don't think that was motivation? At half-time if we had a shutout working, guys would be talking about those lobster tails. Back in those days, we weren't making much money, so a free dinner really meant something."

In the three championship seasons, the Eagles had a total of 12 shutouts, counting the two title games. That's a lot of snapper soup and lobster tail.

Van Buren was their best player, but he didn't act the part. He was a modest man who cared little about money and even less about fame. Jack Hinkle, an Eagles halfback, saw a cereal company executive offer Van Buren several thousand dollars to endorse his product. Van Buren tasted the cereal and said, "I wouldn't feed this to my dog." The man left in a huff. Hinkle told Van Buren he had cost himself a lot of money. Van Buren shrugged.

"Why would I say I like something when I don't?" he asked.

Coach Greasy Neale was willing to get down in the dirt with the players. Here he demonstrates blocking technique for end Jack Ferrante.

In 1945, the fledgling All-America Football Conference was trying to steal marquee players away from the NFL, and there was no bigger name than Van Buren. The president of the Los Angeles Dons, Ben Lindheimer, sent a scout named Vince McNally, who later would become general manager of the Eagles, to sign Van Buren for the AAFC.

Van Buren was making $10,000 a year. McNally told him the Dons were prepared to pay him $25,000. Van Buren said he was not interested. Then McNally handed him a blank

The backfield that won two NFL championships: Bosh Pritchard, Joe Muha, Steve Van Buren, and Tommy Thompson.

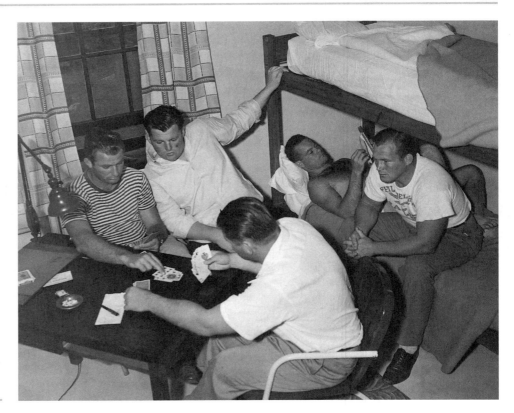

Tommy Thompson (left) and Alex Wojciechowicz playing cards at the Eagles training camp in August 1949. Frank (Bucko) Kilroy and Walter (Piggy) Barnes look on. Steve Van Buren relaxes in his bunk.

contract and told him to fill in whatever dollar amount he wanted.

"Steve wouldn't take the contract and didn't even seem tempted," McNally later told Ed Pollock of the *Philadelphia Bulletin.* "He said, 'You tell Lindheimer they don't have enough money in his league to get me away from the Eagles.'" Said McNally: "That's loyalty, isn't it?"

"That's the biggest difference between the NFL today and the NFL of that era," said Frank [Bucko] Kilroy, an All-Pro tackle with the Eagles who later served as general manager of the New England Patriots. "There is so much money and, of course, free agency. Every year, you lose players to other teams. Guys move around. You don't have the same loyalty. [Players] are more loyal to themselves than they are to their teams. In our day, it was like a big fraternity. We were like brothers."

That bond existed among all players in the league, not just teammates. In 1948, Stan Mauldin, the Chicago Cardinals tackle, collapsed and died in the locker room after playing against the Eagles. When the Eagles won the world championship that season, defeating the Cardinals in the title game, the players voted to give Mauldin's widow a full share of their championship money.

The Eagles were a rich mix of personalities. For every strong, silent type such as Van Buren, there was a free spirit such as halfback Bosh Pritchard, who moonlighted as a big band singer. There were young players, such as Bednarik and fullback Joe Muha, and old pros, such as linebacker Alex Wojciechowicz and tackle Vic Sears. Neale brought the whole thing together.

A former major league outfielder with Cincinnati and the Phillies, Neale was gruff and profane. His image was that of a strict disciplinarian, but Neale understood that those players

were a different breed: older, harder, many of them just back from the war with a chestful of ribbons. They did not need to be coached like schoolboys, so Neale did not impose a lot of petty rules. He felt if they could survive four years of combat, they did not need a football coach telling them what time to be in bed.

"When I joined the team, I was amazed," said Leo Skladany, an end who blocked a punt for a touchdown in the 1949 championship game.

I couldn't get over the way the players talked to Greasy. First of all, they called him "Greasy." No one called him "Coach" except me. And they did things just to irritate him.

One day we were loosening up before practice. We were rotating our arms like this. But Wojie [Wojciechowicz] was just wiggling his fingers. Greasy said, "Wojie, you'd better play a good game this week or else." Wojie just laughed. Another time, a couple guys caught this big, ugly fish and hid it under Greasy's bed. It stayed there for days stinking up the room until Greasy found it and threw it away.

I thought, "Who treats a coach like this? Where's the respect?" But after I was there awhile, I understood. The guys had tremendous respect for Greasy. On the things that really mattered—like preparing for games and getting the team motivated—he was the boss. He spoke and everyone listened. The other stuff was just for fun and I think, deep down, Greasy enjoyed it more than anyone.

One day Van Buren straggled onto the practice field a few minutes late. Neale said, "I won't stand for this, Van Buren. It's either you or me. One of us has to go." Said Wistert, "At that point, the whole team shouted, 'So long, Greasy.'" Neale laughed along with everyone else.

Neale was a brilliant coach, but he was not above taking suggestions from his players. Said Neale: "I have 32 coaches, not just 32 football players. With one or two exceptions, they are all college men. Why shouldn't I listen to what they have to say? They may have better ideas than I have."

"Greasy and his wife had no children," Wistert said, "so in effect, we were their children. We would go to the hotel where they lived for team meetings. Greasy would play golf with Tommy Thompson. He'd play cards on the train with Bucko and Jack Ferrante. Pinochle, that was his game. Penny a point. He'd be dealing the cards, telling jokes, we'd all be laughing. I never saw a team so totally together."

That feeling of closeness was enhanced by the transportation of the times. When the Eagles went to Los Angeles for the 1949 NFL championship game, they went by train because Neale was afraid to fly.

"It took three days; it was terrible," Bednarik said. "Once a day, they'd stop the train and we'd get off and practice in an open field somewhere. We'd practice for an hour, and the other passengers had to wait until we were done, then we'd get back on and the train would start again. That's how we prepared for a world championship game. Can you believe it?"

"Some of the guys played cards; Greasy was always in the middle of that," Wistert said. "Other guys read books or sat around telling stories. We couldn't sleep with the way the train was rocking and bouncing. When we got to LA, we were a tired team. But when it came time to play, we were ready."

The Eagles played their three championship games in horrific conditions. In 1947 they played the Cardinals on a frozen field at Chicago's Comiskey Park and lost 28–21. The following year, they played the Cardinals in a raging snowstorm at Shibe Park and won 7–0 on a Van Buren touchdown. The third championship game was the one in Los Angeles, which was played in a driving rain. The Eagles won, 14–0, as Van Buren slogged through the ankle-deep mud for 196 yards, setting an

Leo Skladany was a rookie who joined the Eagles late in the 1949 season and scored a touchdown in the NFL championship game against the Los Angeles Rams.

NFL postseason rushing record that stood for almost 40 years. Pihos and Skladany scored the two touchdowns.

"That was the nature of our team, we accepted the challenge," Pihos said. "A lot of us played both ways, we were out there every snap, but we knew that was required. There were only 32 [players] on the roster, so you had to carry the load. But it was something we took pride in."

The Eagles championship run ended in 1950 when a new power, the Cleveland Browns, came over from the All-America

After traveling three days on a train from Philadelphia to Los Angeles, the Eagles played the Rams in the 1949 NFL championship game. A heavy rain turned the field into a mud bath, but Steve Van Buren carried the ball 31 times for 196 yards as the Eagles defeated the Rams, 14–0.

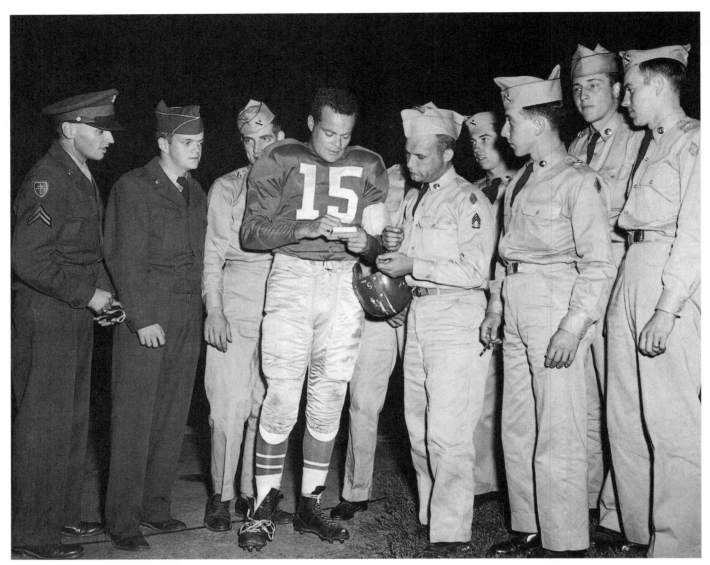

Steve Van Buren was pro football's biggest star in the 1940s.

Football Conference. Knee injuries struck down Van Buren and Pritchard. Age caught up with other veterans. Neale clashed with the new team president, James Clark, culminating with a shouting match in the locker room after a 7–3 loss to the Giants. Clark fired Neale after the season, and the nucleus of the championship team began to crumble. The feeling those Eagles had for each other, however, never changed.

"I stayed in contact with Greasy over the years," Wistert told Mark Kram of the *Philadelphia Daily News*. "I still have his letters. He would always say, 'You fellows made my life.'"

"People ask if I resent the money the players make today. The answer is no," Sears said. "If these guys make $2 million or $10 million, I don't care. I didn't play for the money. I played for the enjoyment, and I can't imagine anyone having a better time than I did in the years I played for the Eagles. I met and married a Philadelphia girl. I got a start in business. The game doesn't owe me a thing, not a penny.

"Everywhere we go in Philadelphia, we're still remembered as champions. What could be better than that?"

THE TEAM THAT HAD NOTHING BUT A TITLE

The 1960 World Champions

Chuck Bednarik still can't explain what happened in 1960. He remembers it, he can discuss it at length, but explain it? No way.

How was it that the 1960 Philadelphia Eagles won the National Football League championship? How did a team with virtually no running game and a patchwork defense finish the regular season 10–2 and defeat Green Bay 17–13 for the world title? How?

"It beats the hell out of me," said Bednarik, the only link between the championship teams of 1949 and 1960. "I look at our roster and I say, 'You mean this team beat Vince Lombardi's Packers? In a championship game? It's unbelievable, really.

"I'm not saying we were a bad team. We were better than average, but we weren't anything like the '49 team, which was a powerhouse. In '60 we didn't have the talent to compare with Green Bay, Cleveland, or the Giants. We won, though. We found a way. We have the [championship] rings to prove it."

The 1960 Eagles brought Philadelphia its last NFL championship. What's more, they sold the game of professional football in the Philadelphia area. Home attendance at Franklin Field more than doubled between 1958 and 1961. Season tickets, priced at $18 and $30 for six games, suddenly became a hot commodity.

It wasn't just the winning; it was how the 1960 Eagles won that captured the imagination. Every week was a new adventure. Every game was decided in the final minute, or so it seemed. The Eagles were behind six times going into the fourth quarter. They were outgained in 11 of their 13 games, including the championship game. They won two games by two points, two games by four points, and two games by a touchdown. Nothing came easily.

General manager Vince McNally watched the home games from a fire escape outside Penn's Weightman Hall. "I was too damn nervous to sit around other people," he explained. The Eagles were that kind of team, and it was that kind of season.

Twelve of the 22 starters were castoffs from other NFL clubs. The leading rusher, fullback Clarence Peaks, broke his leg at midseason. The oldest player, the 35-year-old Bednarik, was forced to play almost 60 minutes a game down the stretch. Yet somehow the Eagles kept winning. They were like a genie that appeared one autumn from a magic lantern, granted Philadelphia its every football wish, then—poof— just disappeared.

Quarterback Norm Van Brocklin, who was named the league's Most Valuable Player, retired after the championship game. Head coach Buck Shaw did likewise. Within two years, the roster was gutted, and the Eagles fell to last place. But nothing could take away the memory of that championship season or diminish the spirit of the 1960 team.

Even now, although 11 of its members are deceased and the rest are scattered across the country, that team feeling remains very much alive. The former players still talk about

Chuck Bednarik, the last of the 60-minute men. At age 35, he was on the field for virtually every play of the 1960 championship game against Green Bay. "We found a way [to win]," he said. "We have the rings to prove it."

each other as family, just as they did more than 40 years ago. Maybe that's how they won the title in the first place, by caring more than the other teams. About winning. About each other. About everything.

"We had what coaches today would call great chemistry," said Tommy McDonald, the Hall of Fame receiver who caught 14 touchdown passes that season, including a tumbling 35-yarder in the championship game. "People say we didn't have great talent, but that's overrated. What's important is how you play, and we played great.

"Teams would get us down, but they couldn't keep us down. We'd keep scratching and clawing until we found a way to win. Van Brocklin was the key. He'd get on one knee in the huddle, look you straight in the eye, and say, 'This is what we're gonna

The 1960 Eagles defense ranked ninth in the NFL in yards allowed, but it led the league with 45 takeaways, including this juggling interception by linebacker Maxie Baughan (55). Safety Don Burroughs (45) set a team record with nine interceptions that season.

Coach Buck Shaw (second from right) with his championship backfield. From left, halfback Billy Barnes, fullback Ted Dean, quarterback Norm Van Brocklin, and flanker Tommy McDonald. "I really think the reason we won is Van Brocklin scared the hell out of them," said general manager Vince McNally.

do.' And we believed him. He was like General Patton. He had that kind of presence."

Better known as "the Dutchman" or just plain "Dutch," Van Brocklin was the unquestioned leader of the team. He was 34 in 1960, and he had played in four championship games with the Los Angeles Rams. He was traded to the Eagles in 1958, and he turned a ragged 2–9–1 team into a world champion in just three years.

Van Brocklin was a fiery man with a bullwhip for a tongue. Like Patton, he demanded total commitment from his troops. Said halfback Billy Barnes, "If you didn't give 100 percent, Dutch's foot would be up your butt in a second." That applied to everyone, including defensive players, special teamers, coaches, and ball boys.

"I really think the reason we won is Van Brocklin scared the hell out of them," McNally said, referring to the other players. "They loved him, but they were afraid of him at the same time. The last thing in the world they wanted to do was let him down."

Therefore, Van Brocklin's obsession—winning the 1960 championship and going out on top—became the team's obsession. By midseason, the entire squad had taken on its quarterback's belligerent personality.

"It was an attitude; we weren't gonna lose," said Tom Brookshier, the Pro Bowl cornerback. "We didn't look like much on paper or films, but we knew how to win. It drove the other teams crazy. We'd be walking off the field, and one of their guys would say, 'We'd love to play you [blankety-blanks] again.' I'd say, 'Sorry, but we can't. We're on our way to the championship.' Some writer called us 'The Team That Had Nothing but a Title.' Fine, I'll take it."

"We were better than the stats showed," Barnes said. "Hell, we won nine games in a row and 11 overall. How many did the next team win?"

Green Bay and Cleveland each won eight games that season, Barnes was told.

"We won 11 and they won eight, but we're a fluke?" he said. "That's bull——. They all had their shots to beat us. Cleveland, New York, Green Bay, we played 'em all and we beat 'em all."

To understand the 1960 Eagles, it helps to understand the times. The pro football boom was just beginning. The 1958 title game between Baltimore and New York, won by the Colts in a dramatic overtime, had whetted the public's appetite for the NFL. In 1960 a rookie commissioner named Pete Rozelle, who succeeded the late Bert Bell, was selling the networks on a $4.5 million TV package.

The American Football League was born that year, resulting in a bidding war and higher salaries for players coming out of college. But for the veterans who were under NFL contract, there wasn't any leverage or players association (the NFLPA was created in 1965), and, consequently, there wasn't much money.

The average salary on the 1960 Eagles was $13,000 a year. Van Brocklin was the highest-paid player at $25,000. Tim Brown, a rookie halfback claimed on waivers from Green Bay, had the lowest salary at $7,500. Jimmy Carr, the starting right cornerback, earned $8,250. Bednarik was a 12-year veteran and seven-time Pro Bowl selection. He earned $15,000 for the championship season, which might not seem like much until you realize he was the highest-paid lineman in the league.

Because of the modest salaries, many Eagles were forced to share living quarters. Nine players, almost one-third of the roster, lived in an apartment building near 40th and Walnut streets. Several other players shared a flat around the corner on Chestnut Street. The players rode to and from practice together, went to the movies together, did the laundry together. They became, in the down-home words of defensive tackle Ed Khayat, "like kin."

Even married players with homes in the suburbs hung out with the guys. Their meeting place was Donoghue's, a small tap-room on Walnut Street. Each Monday morning, Van Brocklin would drop his two daughters at school, then head for the bar, where he would crank up the jukebox, light a Camel cigarette, and wait for the gang to arrive.

Barnes usually was first, followed by safety Don Burroughs, Brookshier, and guard Stan Campbell. By noon, half the team was there, talking over the previous day's game. If someone had a gripe, he aired it. If someone needed a kick in the tail, he got it. Tempers flared occasionally, but nothing serious.

"We'd get on each other, but, hell, there's nothing wrong with that," Barnes said. "I'd rather have someone criticize me to my face than talk behind my back. That's what tears teams apart. On our team, everything was right out front, and that's good. That's how it should be."

Not every player was a regular at Donoghue's. Pete Retzlaff, a nondrinker, did not go. Neither did Bednarik, who preferred to go his own way off the field. Rookie linebacker Maxie Baughan dropped in a few times, then begged off. "I was still a little intimidated by Dutch," he said.

The three black players—Peaks, Brown, and rookie fullback Ted Dean—didn't make it either. Said Peaks: "It wasn't that we were told not to go. We just didn't feel it was a good idea. You've got to remember how things were in 1960."

America was still a segregated society. There were fewer than 50 black players in the NFL. The Washington Redskins were lily white until 1962. Blacks faced prejudice on and off the field. In the 1960 preseason, the Eagles played the Redskins in Roanoke, Virginia, and the hotel manager said the black players would have to use the kitchen entrance and ride the freight elevator. Barnes, himself a native southerner, told the manager, "No way, we're all together." So the entire team—whites and blacks, coaches and players—rode the freight elevator that weekend.

"We stuck together as a team," Peaks said, "but there were certain things we [blacks] could see that the other guys couldn't see. There was a bar in Hershey where the team hung

Six members of the Eagles 1960 world championship team revisit the site of their triumph, Franklin Field. Left to right: Pete Retzlaff, Bob Pellegrini, Chuck Bednarik, Dick Lucas, Tommy McDonald, and Tom Brookshier.

out during training camp. When we [blacks] walked in there, it was like a scene out of a Western movie. You know, where the music stops and everybody turns around. You could cut the tension with a knife.

"As long as we stayed with the white players, we were okay. But if we had tried to go in there alone, it would've been a different story. That wears on you after a while. That's why we tended to do our own thing, just to avoid those negative vibrations."

Peaks was married and living in Mount Airy. Brown, a bachelor, moved in with a family in West Philadelphia. Dean, a Radnor High School graduate, lived at home with his parents in Bryn Mawr. Dean did not have a car, so Brown picked him up for practice each day.

The Eagles practiced at Penn's River Field, a lumpy patch of dirt and cinders next to the Schuylkill Expressway. "Today, coaches worry about opponents spying on their practices," said Marion Campbell, a defensive end on the 1960 team. "At River Field, anybody with a driver's license could spy on us, but we never gave it a thought. It was a fun atmosphere, truck drivers roaring by, blowing their horns, shouting things."

Buck Shaw was a quiet, silver-haired gentleman who did not believe in overworking the troops. Practices were a brisk 90 minutes. Sometimes they were shorter than that. Brookshier recalls one afternoon when Shaw announced, "We're knocking off early today, fellows. I have to go antique shopping with my wife."

McDonald, the bubbly 5–9, 170-pound flanker, kept everyone loose. Once he was riding in a car with several teammates. Tight end Bobby Walston was driving. McDonald slid out the back window, crawled across the roof, and made faces through the windshield at the startled Walston. Another time, McDonald jumped off a fourth-floor hotel balcony and caught the railing with one hand, a move worthy of a circus acrobat.

"We were a loosey-goosey bunch," Brookshier said, "but we strapped it on every Sunday."

The Eagles opened the 1960 season with a jolting 41–24 loss to Cleveland at Franklin Field. The next week, they barely squeaked past the expansion Dallas Cowboys, 27–25. But they built momentum, winning nine games in a row (a team record tied in 2003) to lock up the Eastern Conference championship.

With Peaks sidelined, Barnes and Dean averaged just 2.7 yards per rushing attempt. Van Brocklin carried the offense, passing for 2,471 yards and 24 touchdowns.

McDonald caught only 39 passes in the regular season, but 13 were for touchdowns. The defense allowed more than 4,000 yards, but led the league with 30 interceptions (nine by free safety Burroughs) and 45 takeaways, a stunning total for a 12-game season.

The key victory was a 31–29 thriller against the Browns in Cleveland. The Eagles trailed 22–7 in the third quarter, but Van Brocklin rallied them with three second-half touchdown passes. The Eagles won it on Walston's 38-yard field goal in the closing seconds.

Former Chicago Bears quarterback Johnny Lujack, who did color commentary on the network telecast, called it "the greatest pro game I've ever seen, and that includes the Colts sudden-death championship game against the Giants. That one had a great climax. This one was great throughout."

The dramatic victory did more than spark the Eagles' drive to the championship; it launched the sport of pro football in Philadelphia. One week earlier, the Eagles drew 38,065 for a home game against Detroit. After the win in Cleveland, they drew 58,324 for a game against Pittsburgh. That's a difference of more than 20,000 in just two weeks. The morning of the Pittsburgh game, the line outside the Franklin Field box office extended halfway to Market Street. Almost overnight, the Eagles had become the hottest ticket in town.

The Eagles buried the Giants with back-to-back November wins, then they clinched the conference title with a 20–6 win in St. Louis. In the championship game against Green Bay, they were once again outgained, 401 yards to 296, and they trailed in the fourth quarter, 13–10, but they fought back to win on Dean's five-yard touchdown run in the closing minutes.

It was the only postseason game Lombardi ever lost as a head coach. His Packers won five NFL championships in the next seven years, including lopsided victories in the first two Super Bowls. Green Bay was the team of the decade, but in 1960, the Eagles were the team of the moment. Maybe that's why the feeling surrounding that particular group is so special.

If a team stays on top for six or seven years, the cast changes and the highlights tend to blur. But if a team has just one season, it narrows the focus. It makes every game and every character stand out. It makes every emotion glow and endure. So it is with the 1960 Eagles.

When the former players gathered in Philadelphia for the silver anniversary reunion in 1985, they embraced like long-lost brothers. Barnes hugged Peaks and said, "Clarence, I love you." McDonald wept as he spoke about Van Brocklin, who died of a heart attack two years earlier. They had built new lives, raised children and grandchildren, found other careers, and drifted apart, yet the old bond remained.

"I played on a lot of teams, but none like that," Barnes said. "Normally, you put 35 guys together and you're lucky if half of them get along. I didn't think it was possible to have a team where everybody liked everybody else, but that's what we had. It was the best bunch of guys I've ever been around."

THE CITY OF WINNERS

The 1980 NFC Champions

It was a heady time, 1980 in Philadelphia. The Phillies had just won their first World Series. The Flyers and 76ers were on their way to the championship finals. And the Eagles, reborn under coach Dick Vermeil, were bound for the Super Bowl.

Like the 1960 world champions, the 1980 Eagles were an unlikely collection of misfits with almost half of the roster gathered from the discards of other teams. Fourteen players were free agents. Ten more were acquired through trades or waivers. Of the 21 draft picks on the team, only three were selected in the first round. The rest Vermeil found in the discount aisle. Running back Wilbert Montgomery was a sixth-round pick. Defensive linemen Carl Hairston and Charlie Johnson were seventh-rounders. It was a blue-collar, not a blue-chip, team.

Vermeil built the club that way out of necessity. The previous coach, Mike McCormack, traded away most of the premium draft picks, so Vermeil did not have a selection until the fourth round in 1976, the fifth round in 1977, and the third round in 1978. Vermeil had to cobble together a team out of players other clubs considered too old, too slow, or too fragile. Somehow, he turned that scrap into championship steel.

The 1980 Eagles were more spit than polish, more grit than glitter, but they won 12 games in the regular season and defeated Minnesota, 31–16, in the Divisional playoff before rolling over Dallas, 20–7, in the NFC championship game. They lost Super Bowl XV to Oakland, 27–10, but it is the emotional win over the Cowboys and the celebration that followed that lingers in the hearts and minds of most Philadelphians.

"When players say, 'I don't hear the crowd, I block it out,' that's bull," said Bill Bergey, the All-Pro linebacker who played his final home game that frigid day at Veterans Stadium. "There were 70,000 people in the Vet, and I heard every one of them. The emotion was like a million volts of electricity, and every player on our team had his finger in the socket. I still get a tingle when I think about it."

Hard work and discipline was the foundation of Vermeil's program. It irritated him when interviewers asked, "What's the secret of your success?" There was no secret. There were three-hour practices and coaches' meetings that lasted until dawn. There were players who pushed themselves to the point of exhaustion and beyond. Those were the things that made Vermeil's Eagles successful. Anyone who thought there was a secret or a shortcut of some kind missed the point entirely.

"Too often people talk about doing things, but that's all they do—talk," Vermeil said. "We talk about the goals we want to achieve, then we work toward achieving them. We work hard because that's what I believe in. They don't train Marines by sending them to the beach and putting an ice cream in their hands. We're preparing [players] for 11 individual wars every Sunday. I'm tough on them because I feel it's necessary."

"I'll never forget my first training camp," said tight end John Spagnola, who was signed by the Eagles in 1979 after he was released by New England. "We practiced twice a day every day. It was like being in a time warp. You practiced, you got chewed out, you saw film. You practiced, you got chewed out, you saw film. Over and over. It was brutal.

"But in a strange way, it brought us together. You'd lean over to the guy next to you and say, 'This coach is killing me.' He'd say, 'Yeah. Me, too.' But Dick saw things in each of us that we didn't see in ourselves. He knew we could be better than we were, and he was pushing us to bring out that [ability]. That's the mark of a great coach, someone who can reach down and pull something out of you that you don't even know is there."

"My first impression was that Dick was a crazy little guy who didn't know what he was doing," Bergey said. "He had all these rules. We had to wear our helmets at all times during practice. We had to keep the chinstraps buckled. Harry High School stuff like that. And he was killing us every day in practice. But I realized later it was all a test. He was getting rid of the whiners and losers and finding guys who were tough enough to play his brand of football."

When Vermeil was hired by owner Leonard Tose in 1976, he detailed a five-year plan to build the Eagles into a championship team. It was a long climb, but Vermeil made it right on schedule. By Year Five, he had the NFC's leading passer in Ron Jaworski, whom he acquired in a trade with the Los

Dick Vermeil used hard work and discipline to build a winning team. "Dick saw things in each of us that we didn't see in ourselves," said tight end John Spagnola.

Angeles Rams, a tough, dual-purpose running back in Montgomery, who led the team in rushing (778 yards) and receiving (50 catches for 407 yards), and a rugged 3–4 defense that allowed the fewest points in the NFL (222) during the regular season.

The defense, coordinated by Marion Campbell, was anchored by Bergey and Frank LeMaster, the inside linebackers, with John Bunting and Jerry Robinson, the former UCLA All-America, playing outside. Claude Humphrey, the 36-year-old former Pro Bowl end acquired in a trade with Atlanta, led the team with 14 sacks. Safety Randy Logan and cornerback Herman Edwards were the veteran leaders in the secondary.

The league average for quarterback efficiency in 1980 was 74.07, but the rating for quarterbacks playing against the Eagles was 57.8.

"We had a lot of confidence as a team," said Jaworski, who threw 27 touchdown passes that season and was voted the NFL's Most Valuable Player. "We felt whatever we needed to do to win, we could do it. The offense was solid, the defense was consistent, we had good special teams. It was just a great bunch of guys who understood their roles, loved to play, and loved being Eagles."

Louie Giammona, the 5–9, 180-pound running back, was one of those role players. In addition to his contributions on offense and special teams, Giammona was a character. As Rich Hofmann wrote in the *Philadelphia Daily News,* Giammona was "a guy with a touch of lunacy, just the thing to lighten up what occasionally can be a deadly serious locker room." He was Vermeil's nephew, but a totally different personality. He was irreverent and profane with a quick, cutting wit.

One day, the squad was reviewing a game film, and Vermeil pointed out a mistake by Giammona. "How do you explain that?" Vermeil asked. "Genetics," Giammona replied, cracking up the room.

Another time, the Eagles were preparing for a game, and to ease the tension Jaworski, Spagnola, and Giammona were talking about golf. They were debating the best way to hit a buried sand shot. Jaworski and Spagnola said it was to close the club face and hit down on the ball. Giammona said it was better to open the club face and hit under the ball. The debate went back and forth. As if on cue, Tose walked into the locker room with Arnold Palmer, who just happened to be his guest that day.

"We yelled, 'Hey, Arnie, come over here,'" Spagnola recalled. "We said, 'Settle this argument.' We asked him how to play the shot. He said, 'You close the club face and hit down on the ball.' Jaworski and I high-fived each other. Louie walked over to Arnold Palmer, poked him in the chest, and said, 'What do you know about golf anyway?'"

Giammona's uncle, the head coach, made the whole thing work. He put together the game plan, he ran the practices, and the night before the game, he lit the emotional fire.

"Dick was the master motivator," John Bunting said. "He'd address the whole squad and tell us exactly how we were going to win. He'd turn to a player like Claude and say, 'What are you going to do to help us win?' Claude would say, 'I'll rip the quarterback's head off.' Dick would say, 'Good, I hope you do.' Sometimes I was so fired up, I couldn't get to sleep."

The Eagles went to the playoffs and lost in 1978 (wild-card round) and '79 (divisional round), so they were a hungry team going into the 1980 season. They won 11 of their first 12 games with routs of Denver (27–6), Minnesota (42–7), the Giants (35–3), and Washington (27–0). Montgomery missed four weeks with injuries, but Giammona stepped in, and the team won all four games. Jaworski was injured against Chicago, but Joe Pisarcik came off the bench and completed 7 of 11 passes, and the Eagles won again. Vermeil's team appeared unstoppable.

However, the Eagles lost close games to San Diego (22–21) and Atlanta (20–17) in consecutive weeks and struggled to defeat St. Louis (17–3). They were 12–3, but sagging, as they traveled to Dallas for the final regular-season game. The Cowboys were 11–4, one game behind the Eagles in the NFC East. Due to various tiebreakers, the only way the Cowboys could win the division was to defeat the Eagles by 25 points or more. It seemed impossible; the Eagles had not allowed more than 24 points in any game all season.

Shockingly, the Cowboys jumped to a 21–0 lead and increased the margin to 35–10 in the fourth quarter. Jaworski recalls looking up at the Texas Stadium scoreboard, seeing the 25-point spread, and thinking, "This can't be happening. We can't blow this." To make matters worse, the Eagles lost wide receiver Harold Carmichael with a back injury. He was flipped out of bounds by Dallas safety Dennis Thurman, and his NFL-record streak of 127 consecutive games with at least one reception was snapped.

Jaworski pulled the Eagles back from the brink with three late scoring drives, the first culminating with a touchdown

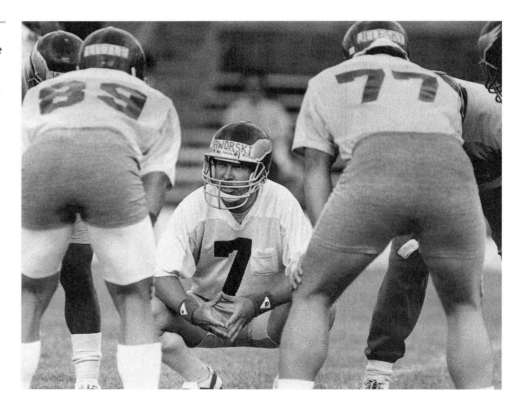

Quarterback Ron Jaworski had his finest season in 1980 as he led the Eagles to the NFC championship. "It was just a great bunch of guys who understood their roles, loved to play, and loved being Eagles," he said.

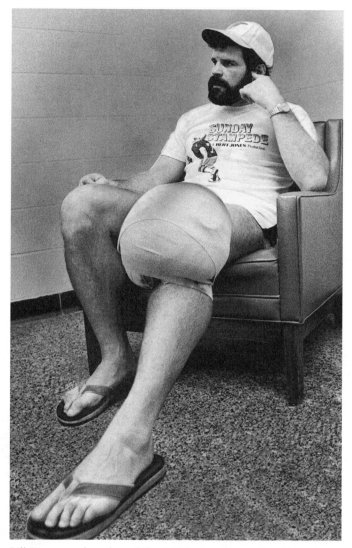

Bill Bergey, who played the 1980 season on a bad knee, was one of only 11 players to survive the five-year climb from last place to a Super Bowl under coach Dick Vermeil.

pass to Rodney Parker, the second setting up a Tony Franklin field goal, and the third finishing with a Montgomery touchdown run. The Eagles lost the game, 35–27, but won the division. It was the first time in NFL history that a team celebrated a defeat with Dom Perignon champagne in the locker room.

Vermeil delivered an emotional speech, expressing pride in what the players had accomplished, especially the 11 hearty survivors who were with him from the beginning. Vermeil singled out each of those players by name and said, "To be able to call you a 'champion' is the greatest thrill I've ever had in sports." Vermeil also raised his glass of champagne and offered

a toast to Tose, who was married in a private ceremony at Le Bec-Fin just two days earlier.

"To Mr. Tose and his new bride," Vermeil said. "You are now a champion."

"This is one helluva wedding present," Tose said, beaming.

In the Divisional playoff, the Eagles fell behind the Vikings, 14–0, but fought back to win 31–16 as Montgomery ran for two touchdowns and the defense intercepted five passes, two each by Edwards and rookie cornerback Roynell Young.

With an arctic cold front moving into the Philadelphia area, the Eagles flew to Tampa to prepare for the NFC Championship game. The biggest question surrounding the team was Montgomery's health. The team's leading rusher had a deep thigh bruise and sprained knee that limited his work in practice. No one knew if he would be ready for the showdown with the Cowboys.

"I knew he'd try to go because of the magnitude of the game," Spagnola said. "But I wasn't sure how effective he'd be. He was just so battered. It hurt just to look at him."

On the Eagles second play from scrimmage, Montgomery broke away on a 42-yard touchdown run that ignited the Veterans Stadium crowd and sent Vermeil's team on its way to a 20–7 victory. That night, Tose threw a victory party at Bookbinder's. Don Rickles was there along with Patti LaBelle. Dom Perignon flowed like tap water. Jaworski recalls riding in a car with several teammates, all of them singing, "We're going … we're going … we're going to the Super Bowl."

The 27–10 loss to Oakland was a bitter disappointment, which stayed with Vermeil and many of the players for years. However, when Vermeil returned to coaching in St. Louis and won a Super Bowl with the Rams in 2000, it helped to heal that old wound. After the game, Vermeil was interviewed while holding the Vince Lombardi trophy, and he spoke of his 1980 Eagles team. He said, "I hope this [victory] helps them because in my mind, they're a part of it."

"I was watching on TV when he said that," Spagnola said, "and I thought, 'Wow, at a moment like this, he's thinking of us.' I had tears in my eyes. It was moving beyond words, but it was what you'd expect from Dick Vermeil."

Several weeks later, Spagnola wrote Vermeil a letter that read in part:

You have no idea what a profound influence you have been and continue to be on the lives of the many men you have coached. Thank you for teaching me that dedication, hard work, teamwork, and devotion to family are the true keys to success and happiness … Long after the glow of this Super Bowl has faded, these principles will be passed on by your players to their children and to their children's children. I truly believe there can be no greater legacy for you than to inspire generations of people as you have and as you will. Of this, above all else, you should be most proud. Thank you for allowing me, in some small way, to share in your victory. I don't know if I'll ever be able to fully describe what it meant to me or to express my gratitude.

7

The Super Century: 2000–2005

IT WAS ONLY a generation, but for many Eagles fans the span between the Golden Years and the 21st century—the agonizing wait for another Super Bowl—seemed like a lifetime.

In many ways, it was.

When the Eagles played in Super Bowl XV in 1981, people hadn't begun to watch DVDs, drive SUVs, or listen to iPods. The laptop had just been invented, and cell phones cost $3,500. Postage stamps were 15 cents, and the minimum wage was $3.35. Average household income for Americans was a little over $19,000, and the prime rate was 21.5 percent, the highest since the Civil War.

By the time the Eagles returned to Super Bowl XXXIX in 2005, coaches were carrying computers instead of clipboards. They were scouting with videotape, challenging the officials with instant replay, communicating via satellite, and devising their game plans with the help of digital photography. It cost 37 cents to mail a letter and the minimum wage was up to $5.15. The average household income was a little over $43,000, and the prime rate had dropped to 5.5 percent.

For the Eagles and other National Football League teams, it was an entirely new world revolving around *free agency*, focusing on the *salary cap*, and depending on such medical breakthroughs as arthroscopic surgery and MRIs.

Professional football continued to enjoy unprecedented popularity. Capacity crowds were commonplace. Each team received $80 million a year from the league's network TV package. Super Bowl tickets sold for $500 apiece, *if* you could find one.

By the turn of the 21st century, the NFL had become the dominant entertainment package, especially in Philadelphia where the Eagles attracted an enormous following and generated an estimated $16.4 million in revenue for the city just from the 2005 NFC Championship Game.

As team officials unveiled their new battle cry during the 2004 season: "One City, One Team, One Dream," the value of the Eagles franchise had skyrocketed from $518 million to $833 million in only two years, according to *Forbes Magazine*. When you consider that Leonard Tose, the owner of the Eagles 1980 Super Bowl team, bought the club for a little over $16 million in 1969, the growth has been astounding.

THE EAGLES' SUPER CENTURY didn't actually start in the year 2000. It really began a full year earlier—in January 1999.

That's when Eagles owner Jeff Lurie and club president Joe Banner made a bold decision. They selected Andy Reid, a little-known assistant coach, to succeed Ray Rhodes, the first head coach they hired back in 1995. Rhodes was fired after the Eagles went into a tailspin and dropped 19 of their last 24 games.

Reid was the quarterbacks coach at Green Bay under Mike Holmgren. He never had been a NFL coordinator or a head coach at any level. Lurie's football operations chief, Tom Modrak, favored the other finalist, Pittsburgh Steelers defensive coordinator Jim Haslett, for the job.

Andy Reid had no head coaching experience when the Eagles hired him in 1999, yet he is the only coach to lead the team to the playoffs five years in a row. "Everyone who works with him and plays for him knows exactly where he's coming from," Joe Banner said.

Eagles fans saw their team host at least one playoff game in each of five consecutive seasons from 2000 through 2004. "The Eagles are the standard right now," said Giants head coach Tom Coughlin.

Most teams at the time would only consider hiring a head coach from a major college or someone with experience as an NFL offensive or defensive coordinator. "Not only had no one ever hired a position coach, no one, to our knowledge, had even *interviewed* one," said Banner to Paul Domowitch, of the *Philadelphia Daily News.* Banner explained that Green Bay general manager Ron Wolf—"maybe the smartest guy in football at the time"—had elected *not* to hire Reid as the Packers' head coach after Holmgren left for Seattle because *that* was the conventional wisdom.

It turned out to be a great decision for Lurie and Banner—and for Lurie's wife, Christina, who helped with the decision.

"Jeffrey really, really studies," Christina told *Philadelphia Daily News* columnist Rich Hofmann. "He wanted, absolutely, an offensive head coach and the West Coast offense. Having spent time with different people, I think he really had a sense of what Andy was going to bring, and the unbelievable work ethic that Andy brings with him. I've never seen anybody as prepared as Andy."

Before hiring Reid, Lurie and Banner carefully analyzed the qualities of every coach that had won two or more Super Bowls in the previous 25 years. They discovered there was nothing consistent about their coaching philosophies, how they ran their offense and defense, or which facet of the game they preferred. But they did discover that every one of the successful coaches had similar qualities.

"Every one of them had tremendous leadership skills," Banner told Nolan Nawrocki of *Pro Football Weekly.* "Every one of them was extraordinarily detail oriented. And we identified eight or nine characteristics that we felt were consistent with all of these multiple Super Bowl–winning head coaches."

After studying all these key qualities and reviewing a short list of candidates, "Andy fit phenomenally well," said Banner. "We really didn't care about experience at that point because after we did our study, we didn't feel like that was a key criteria."

Still the media and the fans were skeptical. The day he was introduced in January 1999, Reid stood at the podium in front of a jam-packed news conference and repeated what he said in his interview with Eagles officials.

"The thing I told Jeff Lurie was, this is not a quick-fix situation," Reid explained. "I'm not here to quick-fix the Philadelphia Eagles. I'm here to supply them with a tremendous, solid organization that is going to win football games. Now that doesn't happen overnight. We didn't do that in Green Bay. We built. And then, we eventually ended up in the Super Bowl."

Reid was correct. It didn't happen overnight.

The Eagles won only five of 16 games in Reid's first year in 1999, but the rookie head coach made it clear he was in complete charge.

Early in training camp, veteran offensive lineman George Hegamin stalked off the field after rookie Doug Brzezinski replaced him in the starting unit. Hegamin returned later in the day, only to be ordered by Reid to push a blocking sled up and down the football field in the blazing sun in front of his wide-eyed teammates and media members. Hegamin was later released, as were other veterans like defensive tackle Bill Johnson, linebacker William Thomas, and center Steve Everitt.

"He [Reid] got rid of lazy players, players he knew would give up," veteran defensive end Hugh Douglas told *Philadelphia Daily News* sportswriter Marcus Hayes. "It was like he was a gang leader. In order to get respect, you've got to do things from the jump to gain respect."

"It was a shock, but that's how you've got to run a team," defensive tackle Hollis Thomas said. "Steve and Bill were good guys, but Bill was outspoken and Steve was carefree. You've got to know there's one boss, and if you don't like it, there's no place for you here. There's no place for rebels without a cause."

"Practices got crisper, sharper," recalled John Harbaugh, who had been retained by Reid after serving as special teams coach under Rhodes. "Meetings went smoother. More people started showing up on time."

The other part of the equation was the drafting of Donovan McNabb. Again, the Eagles went against popular opinion. Most fans, including then–Philadelphia Mayor Ed Rendell, wanted the Eagles to use the second overall pick in the 1999 draft on running back Ricky Williams, the Heisman Trophy winner from Texas. But Andy Reid wanted a quarterback to run his offense, and he was sold on McNabb, the mobile, strong-armed All-America from Syracuse.

Reid took his time with McNabb, allowing him to watch the first half of the regular season from the sidelines while veteran Doug Pederson played and lost seven of the first nine games. McNabb did not start until Week 10, but once he stepped on the field, the team's future came into focus. The Eagles won their last two games over New England and eventual Super Bowl winner St. Louis, which provided the momentum for the team to reverse its record the following season, from 5–11 and last place in 1999 to 11–5 and a playoff berth in 2000.

"The last two games of 1999 were big, sending us into the off-season with a couple of wins," Reid said. "It was easier for guys to listen to you with those positives. That's probably where we had our biggest impact as a staff. And it was nice to have a couple of veterans in there saying, 'Hey, this isn't a bad thing that's going on here. We're going in the right direction. Let's go with it and run with it.' Guys like Troy Vincent."

"In 1999, when we beat St. Louis, you had a good feeling about where we could go," said McNabb. "In 1999, people expected so much, and they didn't know what kind of quarterback I'd be. In 2000, we opened some eyes. By the end of that season, people knew what we had. Getting to the play-offs—that said a lot."

Reid's first major free-agent signing came in 2000. It was 6–7, 325-pound right tackle Jon Runyan, who provided the offensive line with a solid foundation to build around as well as a winning attitude. By the end of the 2004 season, Runyan had started 128 consecutive regular-season games and 16 post-season games. His playoff streak was longer than that of any other NFL player.

In 2000, Reid picked up a few Coach of the Year awards after the Eagles fashioned the greatest turnaround in the franchise's history with an 11–5 record and a second-place finish in the NFC East. The Eagles won 10 of their last 13 games and clinched the top Wild Card spot. They beat Tampa Bay, for

Donovan McNabb was Andy Reid's first draft pick in 1999, and he already has appeared in more Pro Bowls (five) than any quarterback in Eagles history.

their first playoff win in five years, before losing to the eventual NFC champion, the New York Giants. McNabb had a brilliant season, accounting for almost 75 percent of the team's total net yards.

IN MAY 2001, Reid was promoted to executive vice president of football operations—giving him complete control over all the Eagles' personnel decisions at a time when most NFL teams were splitting these responsibilities among a coach and a general manager.

Over the years, Reid had surrounded himself with people who were considered among the best in the game—offensive coordinator Brad Childress, defensive coordinator Jim Johnson, the club's vice president of player personnel, Tom Heckert, and Harbaugh.

Childress, formerly an assistant coach at Wisconsin, was one of Reid's first hires. Credited with teaching McNabb the intricacies of the West Coast offense, Childress was promoted from quarterbacks coach to offensive coordinator in 2002.

In 2002, Childress's group set a club scoring record with 415 points despite starting three different quarterbacks. After McNabb and Koy Detmer went out with injuries, the Eagles turned to A. J. Feeley, who won four of five games down the stretch.

In 2003, Childress's offense set a team record for fewest turnovers in a season (22) with a versatile group that employed three running backs—Brian Westbrook, Correll Buckhalter, and Duce Staley—who combined for 27 rushing and receiving touchdowns.

"There are a lot of different ways to win a football game," Childress said, explaining his offensive philosophy. "You have to be open-minded. Innovate and adjust, play to the tools you have. We've done that here. We've had different personalities now than we had in the past. You need to utilize what you have."

Johnson joined the Eagles in 1999. That year, his unit forced a NFL-best 46 turnovers and set an Eagles team record with five interceptions returned for touchdowns.

Between 2000 and 2004, Johnson's defense was the stingiest in the NFL, allowing fewer than 16 points per game. During that period, Johnson's defensive unit led the league in sacks, red-zone touchdown percentage, and third-down efficiency.

In 2001, Johnson's unit became only the fourth defense in NFL history to go an entire season without allowing more than 21 points in any game. That streak eventually reached 34 straight games, the second longest ever.

"He's the mad scientist," defensive end N. D. Kalu once said in describing the team's affection for Johnson. "We could all be hurt and he'd have the cheerleaders out there blitzing."

Between 2000 and 2003, Harbaugh's special teams twice finished first in the NFL according to an intricate rankings system formulated by *Dallas Morning News* columnist Rick Gosselin.

From 1998 when Harbaugh joined the Eagles until 2004, his units produced 14 NFC Special Teams Players of the Week—David Akers (6), Brian Mitchell (3), Sean Landeta (2), Westbrook, Jevon Kearse, and Allen Rossum (1 each).

"I've said time and time again that John is the best in the business at what he does, and the statistics back it up," said Reid. "He spends so much time and effort preparing his guys each and every week. Special teams are such an integral part of this game today."

In his first 14 seasons in the NFL, including ten with the Miami Dolphins, Heckert never worked with a losing team. He displayed his player evaluation skills in his very first draft in 2002. The first four players selected that year—cornerbacks Lito Sheppard and Sheldon Brown, safety Michael Lewis, and running back Westbrook—all became valuable starters long before the Eagles went to the Super Bowl. So did offensive guard Artis Hicks, an undrafted free agent in 2002.

"This is a great organization," said Heckert after signing a three-year contract extension on the eve of the 2004 NFC Playoffs. "And the relationship I have with Andy, Jeffrey, and Joe and the fact that we're a good football team and we're going to be for a while—that's a big part of my decision."

ONE OF THE major factors in the Eagles' success was Banner's management of the salary cap, designed to ensure competitive balance in the league, which became an NFL requirement in 1994, the same year that Joe joined the Eagles' organization. Effective salary-cap management was recognized as the blueprint for financial success.

Banner mastered it so well that he turned it into a blueprint for success *on* the field. By drafting intelligently, fielding a young team, and extending contracts effectively, Joe earned a reputation as one of the NFL's most creative and innovative executives.

In an interview with *Pro Football Weekly*, Banner explained how he sat down with Reid and Heckert in the off-season,

studied the team's depth charts, and planned two years ahead. "We'll kind of plot out what our priorities are," he explained. "We never want to run out of money and still have some thing that we really need unfilled. So we literally have identified position priorities."

Banner explained that Reid always emphasized that "the key to building a successful team is having strong lines on both sides—that old cliché that it begins up front. So that's been an important part of our whole cap strategy."

At first, Banner's salary-cap strategy was roundly criticized by other NFL executives. But by the time the Eagles started winning, his philosophy was widely acclaimed, especially when opposing teams realized the Eagles were consistently among the league leaders in salary-cap space.

"I've had people tell me that Ray Rhodes has looked at the team we have and the cap situation we have and is totally dumbfounded," Banner once told Domowitch. "He said, 'I didn't think they knew what the hell they were doing.'"

Banner's first success with the salary cap involved a young free safety, Brian Dawkins, who was struggling on the field in

The Eagles' skillful handling of the salary cap allowed them to sign free-agent defensive end Jevon Kearse, who led the team in sacks in 2004.

Terrell Owens and Donovan McNabb were double trouble for opposing defenses in 2004 as they combined for 14 touchdowns.

1998. But Banner saw the potential in the third-year player and convinced the organization to sign him to a five-year extension with a $2.5 million bonus. A year later, when Dawkins made the Pro Bowl, he would have commanded much more money. Since then, he has returned to the Pro Bowl three times, has been the Eagles' defensive MVP, and has become one of the league's top bargains.

Of the top 32 players on the Eagles roster for the 2001 NFC Championship Game, Banner's salary-cap management enabled the organization to sign 25 of them through 2003. All but two of the 22 starters on that 2001 team were locked in for the following season.

That same strategy allowed the club to quickly sign Pro Bowl defensive end Jevon Kearse to an eight-year, $66 million deal on the first day of the NFL's free-agent signing period in 2004—before other teams had time to react.

With the salary cap under control, the Eagles brain trust made a number of excellent player transactions over the years. Some of them were questioned by the fans, especially when they did not re-sign popular high-priced veterans like Staley and defensive standouts Troy Vincent and Bobby Taylor, and replaced them with younger, less expensive players like Westbrook, Sheppard, and Brown. But the three youngsters played major roles when the Eagles finally reached the Super Bowl.

Staley was the workhorse of the Eagles running attack for seven seasons, rushing for more than 1,000 yards three times. After holding out in the 2003 preseason, Staley divided the ball-carrying duties with Westbrook and Buckhalter when he returned to the team. At the end of the year he signed a free-agent contract with the Pittsburgh Steelers.

Vincent, one of the most popular players in franchise history, was one of the NFL's top cornerbacks for most of his eight-year career in Philadelphia. A five-time Pro Bowl participant, Vincent signed with the Buffalo Bills before the 2004 season.

Taylor, who was often overshadowed by Dawkins and Vincent in one of the NFL's best defensive backfields, spent nine years with the Eagles before signing with the Seattle Seahawks after the 2003 season. He was named to the Pro Bowl in 2002.

As every Eagles fan knows, it was a maddening, frustrating journey to the Super Bowl. In 2001 the Eagles captured their first NFC East title in 13 years and surprised everyone by making it to the NFC Championship Game for the first time since 1980, only to lose to the St. Louis Rams, 29–24. The Eagles battled back from a 12-point deficit in the fourth quarter and were driving to take the lead when McNabb threw a last-minute interception on fourth down. Vincent, the Eagles' best cornerback, was forced to leave the game early with a groin injury.

In 2002, this time heavily favored, the Eagles were shocked by the Tampa Bay Buccaneers, 27–10, in the NFC title game, the last contest ever played at Veterans Stadium. With less than four minutes left, Ronde Barber shattered the Eagles' dreams of a comeback by intercepting a McNabb pass and returning it 92 yards for a touchdown.

In 2003 it was the Carolina Panthers who upset the Eagles, 14–3, in the first NFC Championship Game ever played at Lincoln Financial Field. The Eagles missed the multifaceted offensive skills of Westbrook, who was sidelined with a torn tendon in his left arm. McNabb completed only 10 of 22 passes for 100 yards and threw three interceptions before leaving the game with a rib injury.

The sting of dropping three straight NFC Championship Games was extremely painful. Asked how long it would take to get over the third one, the loss to Carolina, wide receiver James Thrash said, "Probably forever."

Still, after each championship game loss, Reid refused to make excuses. He didn't blame the injuries. He didn't blame his players. He blamed himself, saying, "I didn't do a good enough job. I have to do better."

That 2003 season started terribly as the Eagles dropped their first two games to Tampa Bay and New England. Fans were booing McNabb and calling for Feeley, the backup quarterback. The turning point of the season came in Game 6 when Westbrook ran a punt back 84 yards for a touchdown with 94 seconds left against the New York Giants. Westbrook's heroics turned an apparent 10–7 loss into a miraculous 14–10 victory. Instead of staggering out of the Meadowlands with a 2–4 record, the rejuvenated Eagles went on to win nine straight games and take the Eastern Division crown for the third consecutive season.

Finally, after the 2004 season, six years after Reid was named head coach, the Eagles were in the Super Bowl following the most successful regular season in their history. No Eagles team before had won 13 games. No NFC East team had swept all six regular-season division games as the Eagles did in 2004. The team also finished with the best record in the conference for the third straight year.

"The Philadelphia Eagles are the standard right now," said New York Giants coach Tom Coughlin after the Eagles clinched their fourth straight Eastern Division title. "And teams are constantly trying to look at the Eagles in the off-season and trying to find ways to become more competitive and to close that gap."

BY THE END of the 2004 regular season, Reid had passed Hall of Famer Greasy Neale and established himself as the most successful coach in the club's history. He had more wins than any other NFL coach over that span and had become the first coach ever to lead the Eagles to four straight NFC Championship Games.

"God knows what would have happened if we were wrong," Lurie told *Philadelphia Daily News* sportswriter Mark Kram. Lurie thought back to the days immediately following Reid's hiring when the Eagles were roundly criticized for being cheap and clueless. "I remember someone saying, 'How is he going to address the whole team when he has never even addressed the whole offense?'"

"Andy's a perfect fit for the city of Philadelphia," said TV analyst Troy Aikman, the former Dallas Cowboys quarterback. "He has the right demeanor for the job and doesn't let things affect him. He has strong convictions, believes in what he's doing, and doesn't waver."

Before the 2004 season, the Eagles resolved their most glaring offensive and defensive weaknesses by obtaining two of the NFL's top players. On March 3, Kearse, the All-Pro defensive end from the Tennessee Titans, signed an eight-year contract. Then, on March 16, All-Pro wide receiver Terrell Owens

was acquired in a complicated three-team trade involving the Baltimore Ravens and San Francisco 49ers.

Kearse, one of the league's most disruptive pass rushers, improved the Eagles defensive unit considerably.

Owens scored three touchdowns in his first regular-season game with the Eagles and provided the big-play dimension that the team had missed for years. He was tied for the NFL lead with 14 touchdowns when he suffered a severe high ankle sprain and fractured fibula during a Week 15 contest against Dallas.

Owens made a miraculous recovery in time for the Super Bowl, where he put on one of the most courageous performances in NFL history. Playing against doctor's advice, with two surgical screws in his right ankle, T. O. caught nine passes for 122 yards—all in a losing cause as the Eagles came up short against the New England Patriots.

Afterward, Owens insisted he didn't feel any pain. "I just feel bad that we lost the game," T. O. explained. "Nobody in this room thought I could play this game, but nobody knew but me. I tried to tell people from day one that I would play, but nobody wanted to listen."

In Super Bowl XXXIX, Terrell Owens returned to action after missing six weeks with a fractured fibula, and he caught nine passes for 122 yards. "I tried to tell people that I would play," he said, "but nobody wanted to listen."

By the time the Eagles made their run to the Super Bowl in 2004, 14 players had been on their roster for all four NFC Championship Games: Akers, the placekicker; long snapper Mike Bartrum, free safety Dawkins, quarterbacks Detmer and McNabb, center Hank Fraley, defensive end Kalu (who was on injured reserve in 2004), tight end Chad Lewis, wide receivers Freddie Mitchell and Todd Pinkston, defensive tackles Corey Simon and Darwin Walker, and offensive tackles Tra Thomas and Runyan.

Another six players were on the Eagles roster all four seasons but missed one or more NFC Championship Games because of injuries—running back Buckhalter, defensive end Derrick Burgess, defensive tackle Paul Grasmanis, offensive guard Jermane Mayberry, linebacker Ike Reese, and defensive tackle Hollis Thomas.

The Eagles finally reached the Super Bowl with McNabb, Westbrook, and Owens leading an offense that led the NFC in red-zone scoring, producing a touchdown 63.8 percent of the time in the regular season.

With Buckhalter out for the season with a knee injury, Westbrook, who played Division I-AA football at Villanova, did an outstanding job as featured back, leading all NFL running backs with 73 receptions and 703 yards.

"He creates more mismatch problems than any other player on the field," said Fox TV analyst Cris Collinsworth during the 2004 season. "For a quarterback, what greater luxury is there than to have a guy like Brian Westbrook, who can catch the football, make somebody miss, and add 10 yards to your stats?"

Linebacker Jeremiah Trotter (hugging owner Jeffrey Lurie) was welcomed back to the team in 2004 after two seasons in Washington. Trotter regained his starting position at mid-season and earned his third trip to the Pro Bowl.

Before going down with the broken leg, Owens had already set Eagles club records with those 14 touchdown catches as well as club records for seven games of 100 or more receiving yards and five consecutive 100-yard efforts.

Other major contributors to the offense in 2004 were running back Dorsey Levens, an 11-year veteran who led the Eagles with four rushing touchdowns; wide receiver Pinkston, the club leader with 575 receiving yards and 16 yards per catch in 2003; and wideout Mitchell, who had kept the 2003 season alive for the Eagles by catching a 28-yard pass from McNabb on a fourth-and-26 play against Green Bay in the NFC playoffs.

They reached the Super Bowl with a tight end tandem of Lewis, second-year player L. J. Smith, and Bartrum, the long snapper. Lewis suffered a foot injury while catching a fourth-quarter touchdown pass against the Atlanta Falcons in the NFC Championship Game and missed the Super Bowl. Smith led all NFL rookie tight ends in receiving yardage in 2003. Bartrum had the good fortune of playing on teams that made the postseason playoffs in 10 of his first 11 NFL seasons.

They finally reached the Big Game with an offensive line that protected McNabb well, allowing only 37 sacks during the regular season—Fraley, the center; guards Hicks and Mayberry; and tackles Runyan and Thomas. Mayberry was shifted from left guard to right guard after Shawn Andrews, the first-round draft choice, suffered a broken leg on opening day.

They finally did it with a defensive line, spearheaded by Kearse, that allowed the club to rotate fresh linemen into the game. Other starters included right end Burgess, who returned after two injury-plagued seasons to shine in the NFC playoffs, and veteran tackles Simon, who emerged as one of the team's all-time career sack leaders, and Walker, who was a valuable waiver pickup in 2000.

"We always said that we like to throw fastballs at the offense," said Reid of Kearse and his defensive line before the 2004 season. "Now we have Nolan Ryan."

Back in the rotation was Douglas, the defensive end who spent five years with the Eagles before signing with Jacksonville in 2003. After an unhappy season with the Jaguars, Douglas jumped at the chance to rejoin his former teammates in Philadelphia—even in a part-time role.

The Eagles reached the Super Bowl with a veteran linebacker corps headed by Trotter, who was named to the Pro Bowl even though he didn't start until Game 9. Mark Simoneau, who moved to the weak side to make room for Trotter, led the Eagles in tackles with 149 in 2003. Dhani Jones, one of the team leaders in tackles and hurries, started at the strong side, with Reese, a Pro Bowl selection, playing in the nickel package.

They did it with the second-youngest secondary in the NFL: the average age of the Eagles' nine defensive backs is 24.1 years. Dawkins, the team's defensive MVP, is the oldest at 31. Every other defensive player is 25 or younger, including Sheppard and Brown, who exhibited excellent play-making ability as full-time starters, and strong safety Michael Lewis, who led the team with 129 tackles.

And, finally, they did it with outstanding special teams. Akers, who led the NFC in scoring in 2004 with 122 points, including an NFL-record 17 field goals of 40 yards or more, shared club special-team MVP honors with Reese. Punter Dirk Johnson contributed two exceptional punts of 40 and 39 yards into the wind to help keep the Atlanta Falcons on their heels in the NFC Championship Game.

Owner Jeffrey Lurie is awash in confetti as he talks with Terry Bradshaw after the 2004 NFC Championship win over Atlanta.

The makeup of the roster in 2004 was another indication of the Eagles' outstanding personnel management—28 players obtained through drafts, 28 signed as free agents, five picked up off the waiver wire, and two acquired through trades.

If there was a defining moment to the 2004 season, it occurred after the Eagles fell from the unbeaten ranks with a 27–3 loss at Pittsburgh. After the Steelers scored on their first three drives and trampled the Eagles with 252 rushing yards, Jim Johnson inserted Trotter into the lineup at middle linebacker. Trotter had started only one other game, at Cleveland two weeks earlier when he replaced the injured Simoneau.

Trotter had left the team after a bitter contract dispute following the 2001 season. After two unproductive years in Washington, he was cast adrift by the Redskins. Trotter picked up the phone and called Reid before 2004 training camp. The two mended fences, and Trotter worked his way up from special teams into the first defensive unit.

Before Trotter's promotion to the starting lineup, the Eagles' previous four opponents had averaged 172 yards on the ground. In the next six weeks, the team went unbeaten and allowed only 83.5 yards a game and seven touchdowns. Their run defense improved from 27th to 11th. Even though he didn't start until the second half of the season, Trotter was one of ten Eagles named to the Pro Bowl, in Hawaii. He was joined by Akers (3rd Pro Bowl), Dawkins (4th), Michael Lewis (1st), McNabb (5th), Reese (1st), Sheppard (1st), Tra Thomas (3rd), Westbrook (1st), and Owens (5th), who did not play because of his injury.

By the time the Eagles reached the 2004 NFC playoffs, they were prepared and confident. They outscored their two opponents, the Minnesota Vikings and Atlanta Falcons, by a combined 54–24 score, and Reid finally had something to celebrate.

"It was a great feeling," Reid said after his players were showered with green, silver, and white confetti as they paraded the George S. Halas Trophy around Lincoln Financial Field following the 27–10 triumph over the Falcons in the NFC Championship Game.

"Really, with about two minutes left, the place erupted. The players felt it. I think it even makes it more worthwhile that we had to do it four times to get over the hump."

If anyone had the right to gloat or to feel vindicated, it was Lurie, who endured so much criticism in the early years. But Lurie told *Philadelphia Inquirer* sportswriter Shannon Ryan he didn't really get any extra gratification from finally making it to the Super Bowl.

"Honestly, I'm very confident in our strategies and the people around us," Lurie explained. "Our strategies never related to what was meant to be popular. I always felt that our decisions had to be best for the franchise, and they often were very unpopular. If you want to succeed in the NFL with this salary cap, you have to make unpopular decisions."

When he took over the club in 1994, Lurie was appalled by the decaying conditions of Veterans Stadium, the lack of first-class training and practice facilities, just about everything about the franchise he had inherited.

Early on, Lurie and Banner were ridiculed for almost every decision they made. The two boyhood friends from New England were accused of running the franchise like a fantasy football team. Some of their own staff accused them of meddling and interfering with football decisions.

When they gave Rhodes complete control over player personnel, the club was torn by dissension and finger-pointing, and the team won only nine games the following two seasons. The media scoffed when Lurie proclaimed the Eagles franchise would become the "gold standard" of the NFL.

One of their first priorities was to erase the perception that the Eagles organization was unwilling to spend the money required to win. They chartered bigger and better planes. They put the team up in better hotels, and they upgraded the quality of food at pregame meals.

"We believed that we had to do things in a first-class manner," Banner told Rosabeth Moss-Kanter, author of *Confidence: How Winning Streaks and Losing Streaks Begin and End*. "We went overboard in size and quality in the beginning."

Shortly after assuming control, Lurie and Banner flew to San Francisco to consult with 49ers coach Bill Walsh and other officials of the league's top franchise at the time—a team headed to its third Super Bowl championship in the previous seven years. Lurie told sportswriter Paul Domowitch that the 49ers had impressed him more than any other NFL franchise. "They made outside-the-box decisions," Lurie explained. "They consistently went into every season with the intention of winning the championship. They did things first-class in

every way. I just liked the way they operated. It was an upbeat, dynamic, high-energy organization with expectations to be the best every year."

Then came the two key components vital to transforming the Eagles into an elite NFL franchise: the $37 million NovaCare Complex opened in March 2001, and the $512 million Lincoln Financial Field was completed two years later.

The ultramodern, 108,000-square-foot NovaCare Complex houses the Eagles' indoor and outdoor practice areas, state-of-the-art medical and training facilities, and the club's executive offices. It is considered one of the finest facilities of its kind in professional sports.

The construction of Lincoln Financial Field began in 2001. On September 8, 2003, about 28 months later, the magnificent stadium with a seating capacity of 68,532 opened. Just 17 months later, it hosted the NFC Championship party.

The Eagles lost to New England, 24–21, in Super Bowl XXXIX, but they went into the 2005 season a healthy $16 million under the NFL's salary cap, putting them in good position to bid for some of the league's top free agents. In addition, they had 53 players under contract, a bundle of upcoming draft choices, and a record that no other NFL team could match—five straight trips to the postseason.

Vindication: Donovan McNabb basks in the glow of his first NFC Championship. "It's just a great feeling for the city of Philadelphia," he said. "We know what happened in the last three years."

8

The Postseason

THE EAGLES enjoy the distinction of being the only NFL team to qualify for the postseason each year since 2000. It is a remarkable streak, especially in the era of salary caps and free agency, and it is unprecedented in Eagles history. The longest previous streak of consecutive postseason appearances was four under Dick Vermeil, which included a trip to Super Bowl XV.

Over the years, the Eagles had long stretches without postseason appearances. For example, they did not play a postseason game until 1947, the 14th year of their existence. They were shutout for 10 years from 1950 until 1960, then they missed for another 18 years until Vermeil brought them back in 1978.

This chapter chronicles the Eagles' postseason history, game by game. We did not include the "Playoff Bowls" of the '60s because those matchups between the second-place finishers in the Eastern and Western Conferences were glorified exhibition games. There was nothing at stake other than the difference in the winner's and loser's paychecks. For the record, the Eagles lost both of those so-called "Runner-up Bowls": 38–10 to Detroit in January 1962 and 20–14 to Baltimore in January 1967.

EASTERN DIVISION PLAYOFF
December 21, 1947
Forbes Field, Pittsburgh, Pennsylvania
Eagles 21, Pittsburgh 0

The Eagles and Pittsburgh Steelers finished the 1947 regular season with identical 8–4 records, so a playoff was scheduled at Forbes Field to decide which team would be the Eastern Division champion and play the Chicago Cardinals for the NFL title.

The Eagles dominated the game from start to finish, winning 21–0. Quarterback Tommy Thompson threw two touchdown passes, one to Steve Van Buren, the other to Jack Ferrante to give the Eagles a 14–0 halftime lead. Bosh Pritchard sealed the victory with a 79-yard punt return for a touchdown in the third quarter.

The win was a team effort as end Pete Pihos blocked a Bob Ceifers punt to set up the first touchdown and Pat McHugh and Ben Kish threw key blocks to free Pritchard on his punt return.

When the two teams met earlier in the season, Pittsburgh won 35–24 as the Eagles could not contain the single-wing offense designed by coach Jock Sutherland. The Steelers were the last team in the league running the single wing, so they were a challenge for most defenses. However, coach Greasy Neale devised a plan to shut them down in the regular-season rematch, 21–0, and he did it again in the playoff game.

"Want to know where the game was won?" asked captain Al Wistert. "It was won yesterday in Philadelphia, where every man gave a short speech, telling how he thought the game would be won. We knew right then we wouldn't be beaten."

"They're a great team," Sutherland said of the Eagles. "I don't know if they're better than us without Van Buren, but he's just too much ball player for anyone to handle for a whole game."

The Eagles were in a festive mood after the game, shouting, "Bring on the beer."

Neale told the players there would be no victory party. The coach said they were in training for the championship game against the Cardinals the following week.

"Please, Coach, can't we have just one beer?" asked linebacker Alex Wojciechowicz.

"All right," Neale said, "but on your word of honor, not more than two bottles each."

Orlo Robertson of the *Philadelphia Inquirer* wrote, "At the request of Wojie, every man on the team raised his hand in a pledge that he would not drink more than two bottles of beer."

NFL CHAMPIONSHIP
December 28, 1947
Comiskey Park, Chicago, Illinois
Chicago Cardinals 28, Eagles 21

When the Eagles arrived at Comiskey Park the day before the 1947 championship game, they found the playing field covered by a tarpaulin and warmed by a layer of straw. Coach Greasy Neale put the team through a light workout, using the uncovered area behind the bench.

As the Eagles were practicing, team captain Al Wistert noticed the grounds crew removing the tarp from the field. Wistert could not understand it, since the weather forecast called for freezing temperatures and sleet overnight.

"I asked the crew chief what was going on," Wistert said. The guy said, 'We have to take it off now because we won't be here tomorrow.' I said, 'What do you mean you won't be here? This is the championship game.' He said, 'Tomorrow is Sunday. We'd have to pay double time and a half.' I was so angry, I couldn't see straight."

The next day when the Eagles returned to play the Chicago Cardinals, the field was frozen solid. "It was a sheet of ice," Jack Ferrante said. "It looked like a skating rink." In the locker room, Neale told the players to sharpen their cleats for better traction.

"One of the officials came into the room to give us the 10-minute warning," Wistert said, "and he saw Bosh Pritchard filing his cleats. He said, 'Hey, you're not allowed to do that.' Then he looked around and he saw we were *all* doing it."

The Cardinals came out wearing custom-made sneakers with cork cleats. They complained that the Eagles' sharpened spikes were illegal and unsafe. Shorty Ray, the league's supervisor of officials, agreed and ordered the Eagles to change shoes. They switched to flat-soled sneakers, but they could not handle the icy surface as well as the home team's cleated shoes.

"It was the worst footing ever," Van Buren said. "I slipped and fell twice just coming out of the huddle."

The Cardinals hit several big plays—a 44-yard touchdown run by Charlie Trippi, a 70-yard run by Elmer Angsman, and a 75-yard punt return by Trippi—to open a 21–7 lead, and they held on for a 28–21 win.

The Eagles finished with more yards (357 to 336) and more than twice as many first downs (22 to 10), but they still lost the game. Van Buren, who led the league in rushing that season, had just 26 yards on 18 carries.

"If we'd have been able to keep our regular football shoes on, we'd have won," guard Duke Maronic said. "But the [cleats] really were illegal, just a little too sharp. What I couldn't figure out was why Steve [Van Buren] couldn't run in the basketball shoes. We opened nice holes for him, but he was like a guy on roller skates for the first time. He just kept slipping every time he made the slightest move."

Quarterback Tommy Thompson completed 27 of 44 passes for 259 yards with one touchdown, a 53-yard pass to Pat McHugh. His attempts and completions were championship-game records, breaking the marks set by Washington's Sammy Baugh ten years earlier.

Thompon's performance vindicated coach Greasy Neale, who had to convince owner Lex Thompson that Tommy was the right quarterback for the Eagles offense. The owner and many of the fans preferred Roy Zimmerman. Neale stuck with Thompson and dealt Zimmerman to Detroit prior to the 1947 season. With a firm grip on the starting job, Thompson led the Eagles to three consecutive championship games.

"I'd take Thompson over any quarterback, including Baugh and Sid Luckman," Neale said. "He can stand up under pressure, and he thinks clearly when the going is the toughest. You can knock him down a hundred times and he still comes back for more. He has more courage on a football field than any man I know."

Neale was asked about the Cardinals, who had soundly defeated the Eagles, 45–21, three weeks earlier, and finished the regular season with a 9–3 record.

"They're a great team, and more power to them," Neale said, adding, "I hope they win the Western title next year, too, so that we can have the pleasure of knocking them off in Philadelphia."

NFL CHAMPIONSHIP GAME
December 19, 1948
Shibe Park, Philadelphia
Eagles 7, Chicago Cardinals 0

Greasy Neale got his wish. The Chicago Cardinals won the Western Division in 1948 with an 11–1 record, which brought them to Philadelphia for the NFL Championship game. The Eagles had dominated the rest of the league for two seasons, winning 18 games and losing only seven, but they were 0–3 against the Cardinals including the title-game loss the previous year.

"It was a pride thing with Greasy; he wanted to beat the Cardinals," team captain Al Wistert said. "He wanted to win the championship, yes, but if we beat another team [in the title game] it would not have been the same. Greasy wanted to prove we were the best team in football, and he felt we had to beat the Cardinals to do that."

The Cardinals had virtually the same cast that defeated the Eagles for the championship in 1947. They compiled the best record in the league in 1948 and handed the Eagles a 21–14 loss in the opener. Steve Van Buren won the rushing title with 945 yards, but Charlie Trippi (690) and Elmer Angsman (638) finished second and third. Pete Pihos had 46 receptions and 11 touchdowns, but Mal Kutner of the Cardinals had 41 catches and 14 touchdowns.

Although the game was scheduled for Shibe Park, the Cardinals were a five-point favorite. Neale used that as a motivational tool, telling the Eagles no one believed in them, no one gave them a chance—the old "no respect" routine that coaches have been using for generations. Neale rarely had the opportunity to use it with the Eagles, who were a great team themselves, but when he had the chance, as he did before this game, Neale made the most of it.

"Greasy had us keyed up," Wistert said. "We respected the Cardinals, they were a great team, but we felt confident we could beat them. We worked on a play called '81 Special,' a deep pass to Ferrante. Greasy and Tommy [Thompson] decided to throw it on the very first play. The Cardinals wouldn't be expecting it, and if we hit it, it would put them behind the eight ball."

But on the morning of the game, a winter storm rolled into Philadelphia. The snow began falling around dawn and continued all day. Eagles linemen Duke Maronic and Mario Giannelli went to breakfast, and in the time it took them to finish their pancakes a foot of snow fell. Heavy winds and drifting snow made many streets impassable.

Syndicated columnist Jimmy Cannon rode the train from New York to Philadelphia that morning. He walked from North Philadelphia station to Shibe Park and later described the scene: "The majority of [the fans] walked through the narrow streets in the storm. It was not like a football crowd at all. A lot of the guys were dressed as though they were going hunting. They wore plaid caps and earmuffs, high-laced boots, and the women carried blankets and used them as capes for the long slippery pilgrimage to the ballpark. Outside the park, guys were giving away tickets. The people would accept these and compare them with the tickets they had to see if they gave them better protection from the storm."

Neale wanted to postpone the game. He had bitter memories of the previous year's loss on the frozen field in Comiskey

Park, and he did not want to risk a repeat. Bert Bell, the commissioner, wanted to play. The game was a sellout, the network radio rights were sold, and, besides, it was football. You postpone baseball games; you don't postpone football games, especially championship games.

Neale felt the decision should be left up to the two teams, so he went to the visitors' dressing room to confer with Chicago coach Jimmy Conzelman. While Neale was gone, the Eagles took a vote, and the overwhelming majority were in favor of playing.

"Greasy came back and said, 'Can you believe it? They [the Cardinals] want to play. Let's go beat the hell out of them,'" Wistert said. "He didn't know we had already decided we wanted to play, too. We were at our peak, emotionally. I was afraid if we didn't play that day, it would be a real letdown."

There was one major concern, however. An hour before kickoff, Van Buren, the team's franchise player, was nowhere to be found. Backup quarterback Bill Mackrides was the first one to notice. He saw Van Buren's jersey and pants hanging in his locker. "I said, 'Anybody seen Steve?'" Mackrides said. "No one had. It was, like, 'Uh oh.'"

At that moment, Van Buren was on a trolley car somewhere between 69th Street and City Hall. He saw the heavy snow falling outside his suburban home that morning and went back to bed, assuming the game would be postponed. After dozing for another hour, Van Buren decided he probably

should make his way to Shibe Park, just in case. He took a bus, then a trolley, and finally the Broad Street Subway to Lehigh Avenue. From there, he walked seven blocks through the blinding snow to the stadium, arriving less than a half hour before the scheduled 1:30 start.

"I couldn't believe it when I got there and saw they were going to play," Van Buren said. "It was snowing so hard, you couldn't see."

Unlike Comiskey Park, the Shibe Park field was covered, but there was so much snow on the tarpaulin, the grounds crew could not remove it. They tried to shovel off the snow, but it was accumulating too fast. The workers had to call the two teams from their locker rooms, and with the aid of that additional muscle, they finally were able to drag the tarp off the field. With all the delays, the kickoff was pushed back 30 minutes.

"Can you imagine telling the two Super Bowl teams, 'Hey, fellas, give us a hand, will you?'" Wistert said. "It would never happen today, but we didn't think anything of it. We felt like the sooner we got the [tarp] off the field, the sooner we could play."

Once the tarp was removed, the snow quickly blanketed the field, so the officials used ropes to mark the sidelines. Cannon described the playing surface as "a big drift." With no visible yard lines, referee Ron Gibbs was responsible for all matters of down and distance. The two teams agreed not to question his

Steve Van Buren (left) scores the winning touchdown in the 1948 NFL championship game at snowy Shibe Park. "I knew I was close," he said, "so I just dove for it."

Coach Earle (Greasy) Neale presents Steve Van Buren (15) with the game ball after the Eagles' 1948 championship game win over the Chicago Cardinals at Shibe Park. Joining in the celebration are Pete Pihos (far left), Al Wistert (next to Van Buren), and Alex Wojciechowicz (between Van Buren and Neale).

judgment. There were no measurements. If Gibbs said it was a first down, it was a first down. "A parody of a football game," Cannon called it.

The blizzard did not change the Eagles' strategy. Thompson still called for the 81 Special on the first play, and it caught the Cardinals flat-footed. Thompson threw a perfect pass, Ferrante plucked the football out of the snowflakes, and the Eagles had a 65-yard touchdown, or so it appeared. However, the play was nullified by an offsides penalty.

"I was steaming," Ferrante said. "I went to the official and said, 'Who was offsides?' He said, 'You were.' I could've cried."

Ferrante's teammates felt it was a bad call. "With all the snow, you couldn't see the line of scrimmage," Wistert said. "When the ball was snapped, the linemen dropped back to [pass] protect. Jack was the only one moving forward, so it looked like he was offsides, but I don't think he was."

That could have been a demoralizing blow for the Eagles, losing a quick-strike touchdown on a day when scoring was sure to be difficult. But the Eagles shook it off and went back to their strengths: Van Buren and the defense. Van Buren carried the ball 26 times for 98 yards, while the defense held Trippi and Angsman to a combined 59 yards.

"You look at the pictures and the field looks terrible, but the footing wasn't that bad," Van Buren said. "It was a lot better than the field in Chicago the year before. The only problem was seeing. It was snowing so hard, I couldn't see their safety [Marshall Goldberg]."

The game was scoreless after three quarters, but Frank (Bucko) Kilroy and Alex Wojciechowicz hit Cardinals quarterback Ray Mallouf and forced a fumble, which Kilroy recovered at the Chicago 17-yard line. Four plays later, Thompson handed off to Van Buren, who followed the blocks of Kilroy, Wistert, and fullback Joe Muha into the end zone for the game's first and only touchdown.

"I ended up with my head down in the snow, but it was one of the easiest touchdowns I ever scored," Van Buren said. "They opened a big hole; I think only one guy touched me. I knew I was close [to the goal line], so I just dove for it."

Cliff Patton kicked the extra point, and the Eagles defense made that seven-point lead stand up. Chicago finished the game with just five first downs and 131 total yards. When the final gun sounded, many of the 28,864 fans who braved the elements poured onto the field and carried Van Buren off on their shoulders.

"That was the ultimate; the feeling in the locker room was just tremendous," Van Buren said. "We had worked so hard, and finally the reward was there. Even old Greasy was choked up."

"A lot of us went straight into the hot showers," Maronic told Jim Campbell in a *Pro Magazine* interview. "We didn't take off our uniforms or anything, just our headgear. We stood under the hot water just to thaw out."

Jimmy Cannon ripped Bert Bell for his decision to play the championship game in those conditions. In his column, Cannon wrote, "They should have postponed yesterday's game, and their alibi that people journeyed from Chicago to see it doesn't hold. Not even fight promoters, the greediest of them all, would try to get away with anything like that which was pulled off yesterday in Philadelphia. It is my opinion that nothing since the Alvin Paris scandal [Paris was a gambler who attempted to fix the 1946 NFL championship game] harmed football more than yesterday's game. It proved that anyone who buys a ticket before the day of a football game played in December must be classed with guys who think they can beat the races."

Cannon's outrage was not shared by most Philadelphia fans. They were only too happy to celebrate the Eagles' first world championship, and for years afterward they reveled in telling stories about how they made it to Shibe Park that day and sat shivering in the snow to watch their team make history.

NFL CHAMPIONSHIP GAME
December 18, 1949
Los Angeles Memorial Coliseum,
Los Angeles, California
Eagles 14, Los Angeles 0

When the Eagles reported to training camp in 1949, preparing to defend their NFL championship, coach Greasy Neale wanted to make sure there was no complacency, so he greeted the players with a line he had rehearsed the entire off-season.

"A team does not prove it is great," Neale said, "until it can repeat."

Since the creation of the first official championship game in 1933, only one team—the 1940–41 Chicago Bears—had won back-to-back NFL titles. Neale felt his club was capable of matching that accomplishment. All the key veterans were back, and the team added a rookie named Chuck Bednarik, an All-America center and linebacker from the University of Pennsylvania.

"We were an awesome team, really," captain Al Wistert said. "I don't use that term often, but it's the only way to describe that team."

Lex Thompson sold the club to a group of 100 investors who paid $3,000 each for the privilege of owning a piece of an NFL champion. James P. Clark was named team president, and Vince McNally was hired as general manager, but otherwise nothing changed. It was Neale's show, at least for the time being, and he ran it expertly.

The Eagles rolled through the regular season, winning 11 games and losing only one, a 38–21 decision to the Chicago Bears. They outscored their opponents 364 to 134. That is a 230-point differential amassed in just 12 games. Steve Van Buren had his best season, gaining 1,146 yards to win his fourth rushing title. The defense allowed opposing quarterbacks to complete just 39 percent of their passes. The efficiency rating for passers against the Eagles that season was an abysmal 29.9.

They had no real challenger in the Eastern Division—Pittsburgh finished in second place with a 6–5–1 record—so a return to the NFL championship game was a foregone conclusion. The only question was which Western Division team the Eagles would face in the big game. It turned out to be the Los Angeles Rams, who compiled an 8–2–2 mark to finish ahead of both the Bears (9–3) and the Chicago Cardinals (6–5–1).

That was good news for the Eagles, who had a history of tough games with the Cardinals and had no success at all against the Bears, winning just one of 13 games in that series. But under Neale, the Eagles owned the Rams and were unbeaten in their last six meetings (5–0–1), including a 38–14 win at Shibe Park earlier that season.

For the Eagles, the hardest part figured to be the trip to Los Angeles. Neale was afraid to fly, so the Eagles traveled primarily by train. It took three days to travel by rail from Philadelphia to Los Angeles. Each day, the train would stop to allow the Eagles to get off and practice for an hour. After the workout, the players would return, and the train would start again.

The Eagles passed the time by reading and playing cards, but mostly they discussed how much money they would make from the title game. The Los Angeles Coliseum had a seating capacity of 100,000, and they expected more than 75,000 to attend the first NFL championship game played west of Chicago. The bigger the gate, the fatter the purse, which meant more money for each player.

"They were talking about the biggest live gate in league history," halfback Bosh Pritchard said. "We were thinking, 'Oh boy, we could get five or six thousand [dollars] apiece for this.' We each made fifteen hundred the year before [the winner's share in 1948 was $1,540]. Some [players] weren't even making five thousand dollars for an entire season, so this was like hitting the lottery."

But shortly after the Eagles arrived in Los Angeles, it began raining and never stopped. It poured all day Saturday and continued Sunday. For the second year in a row, Commissioner Bert Bell was forced to consider a postponement. For the second year in a row, Bell ordered the teams to play.

"This time *we* didn't want to play," Wistert said. "We were thinking about the gate. We knew the weather would kill the crowd. We saw all that money going down the drain. But we were staying at the Bel Air Hotel, and I know that cost a lot of money. I'm sure they didn't want to keep us there for another whole week. I was pretty sure they'd make us play, and they did."

Instead of 75,000 paying customers, only 27,980 turned out. That was the official figure, but the actual attendance may have been less. Dick Cresap of the *Philadelphia Bulletin* did a head count 30 minutes before kickoff and reported there were 176 people in the stands. No doubt there were more people huddled below out of the rain, but Cresap's story painted a vivid picture of how deserted the Coliseum looked that day.

The field was a swamp with puddles the size of small lakes along the sidelines. The mud was ankle-deep in some places. Steve Van Buren ran through all of it, play after play, finishing with 31 carries for 196 yards, an NFL championship-game

Steve Van Buren carries the Eagles past the Los Angeles Rams in the 1949 NFL championship game. "One of their guys said, 'We're gonna kill you, Steve,'" Van Buren said. "It made me mad."

record that stood for 38 years until Washington's Timmy Smith gained 204 yards in Super Bowl XXII.

"Early in the game, I got knocked out of bounds near their bench," Van Buren said. "One of their guys said, 'We're gonna kill you, Steve.' It made me mad. I told [quarterback Tommy] Thompson, 'Give me the ball.' So he did. He just kept giving it to me."

"Steve was hell on a leash that day," end Pete Pihos said. "His stamina was unbelievable. How he kept going in those conditions, I'll never know. It was like running in glue."

Van Buren dominated the game, but he never reached the end zone. The Eagles touchdowns came on a 31-yard pass from Thompson to Pihos and a blocked punt by Leo Skladany, a rookie who started the season playing for a semipro team in Patterson, New Jersey. He signed with the Eagles in December when veteran end Johnny Green was injured. Skladany blocked a Bob Waterfield punt and recovered the loose ball in the end zone for his first, and last, NFL touchdown.

"You don't expect a rookie to make that kind of play in a championship game," tackle Vic Sears said. "Waterfield was a great punter, one of the best in the league, and Leo almost took the ball off his foot. It gave us a tremendous lift. We knew there was no way the Rams were going to come back from 14 points down."

The Rams were an explosive team, averaging 30 points a game during the regular season with two Hall of Fame quarterbacks, Waterfield and Norm Van Brocklin, and two Hall of Fame receivers, Tom Fears and Elroy (Crazy Legs) Hirsch, but their passing attack was useless in the monsoon rain, and their running game could not dent the Eagles defense. The Rams finished with just seven first downs, and Waterfield and Van Brocklin completed 10 of 27 passes for 98 yards.

Van Buren had no idea he set a postseason rushing record until Cresap informed him in the locker room. "I got 196 yards?" he said. "I thought I was doing pretty good but figured it was only a little over 100. Boy, that's what you can do with blocking."

"Van Buren was the greatest runner today that I've ever seen," Neale said. "No one has ever run like he did in that mud."

"We didn't have a chance in that weather," Rams coach Clark Shaughnessy said. "It was suicide for us to play in that mud. But don't take anything away from the Eagles. They were really a great team with power, speed, punting, and passing, everything a good team needs."

The Eagles had their back-to-back world titles, and they still are the only team in NFL history to win consecutive championship games by shutout. There was only one disappointment: the windfall turned out to be a waterfall. Due to the rain—and the disappointing live gate—the winner's share was just $1,094 per player, which was less than the Eagles made the previous year in Philadelphia.

"If you think we were mad, you should've seen our wives," Pritchard said. "They had their fur coats on order. They had that money spent already."

The Eagles' new owners threw a victory party at the Bel Air Hotel. Each player was given a memento to mark the second world championship: a cigarette lighter. "It wasn't even engraved," Wistert said. "It was a plain Zippo lighter. I thought, 'Isn't that wonderful? A cigarette lighter, for two world championships. I didn't even take mine."

Van Buren did not remember the Zippo lighters. He only remembered meeting Johnny Weissmuller, the Olympic swimmer who starred as Tarzan in the movies. Weissmuller was at the party along with other Hollywood stars, including Bob Hope and Clark Gable.

"When I met Weissmuller, he had a drink in each hand," Van Buren said. "I couldn't get over it. I never pictured Tarzan drinking."

NFL CHAMPIONSHIP GAME
December 26, 1960
Franklin Field, Philadelphia
Eagles 17, Green Bay 13

There were many great moments in that championship season, but it is the final play that stands out. It is a play that, in eight seconds and 13 yards, told us all we ever would need to know about the 1960 Eagles. It was their last stand, and their best.

They were two-point underdogs at home to Vince Lombardi's Green Bay Packers, a young, bruising team that would dominate pro football for a decade. The Packers had five future Hall of Famers on offense—quarterback Bart Starr, fullback Jim Taylor, halfback Paul Hornung, center Jim Ringo, and tackle Forrest Gregg—yet they only could manage one touchdown that day at Franklin Field.

Green Bay got the ball back one last time with 1:20 left, trailing 17–13, and started driving. If you read the play-by-play sheet today, you can feel the tension building between the mimeographed lines:

"Starr passes to Taylor for 5 yards … Starr passes to [Tom] Moore for 4 yards … Taylor wide left, 9 yards and a first down … Starr passes complete to [Gary] Knafelc for 17 yards and a first down."

Head coach Buck Shaw (second from right) discusses the 1960 roster with, left to right, assistant coaches Jerry Williams and Nick Skorich, general manager Vince McNally, and assistant coach Frank (Bucko) Kilroy.

That put the Packers at the Eagles 30-yard line. On first down, Starr threw incomplete to Boyd Dowler. On second down, he hit Knafelc, the tight end, for eight yards and used his last time-out to stop the clock.

It was third and two at the 22. There was time for one more play. Starr wanted to throw long to either Dowler or Max McGee, but the Eagles had the deep zones covered. Starr had no choice but to dump the ball to Taylor, his rugged 220-pound fullback.

Pulitzer Prize–winning columnist Red Smith described the scene: "That wonderful runner [Taylor] ducked his head like a charging bull and bolted like an enraged beer truck into Philadelphia's congested secondary."

Every man who was on the field remembers in vivid detail what took place in those next few seconds. Even greats like Taylor and Gregg, who went on to win five NFL titles, remember that final play and can reconstruct it, grunt by grunt.

"I guess that's the definition of a big play, one you still remember after 26 years," Taylor said in a 1986 interview. "Hell, there were some plays I'd forget by the time I walked back to the huddle. Not that one. That play was the difference between being a world champion and a loser."

As soon as Taylor caught the ball, he was surrounded by green jerseys. Don Burroughs hit him first, but Taylor shoved the spindly 185-pound safety aside. Maxie Baughan hit him next, but the rookie linebacker bounced off the fullback like a possum hitting a rhino.

"Jim was stronger than I was," Baughan said, "and I know he was meaner. He might have been the toughest runner I ever went up against, and, in that situation, he was ready to run through a brick wall. I got a shoulder into him, but I didn't even slow him down."

Taylor was at full speed when he crossed the 10-yard line, but there he ran into Bobby Jackson and Chuck Bednarik. Jackson, a slight 180-pounder, was in the game as a fifth defensive back. He hit Taylor low and Bednarik, the 6–3, 235-pound linebacker, hit him high. The impact was so great that it snapped the strap on Jackson's shoulder pads. Bednarik wrapped Taylor in a bear hug and wrestled him to the ground.

The play-by-play sheet notes that Taylor went down at the nine-yard line, but it was really closer to the eight. No matter. Bednarik pinned him to the turf as the last few seconds rolled off the clock. When time expired, Bednarik told Taylor, "You can get up now, you SOB; this f——ing game is over." With that, Bednarik jumped with joy as 67,325 fans, the largest crowd ever to see the Eagles at Franklin Field, began the celebration.

"That was the biggest tackle I ever made," Bednarik said. "A great runner, a world championship on the line, the last play. More people talk about the hit on Frank Gifford, the shot where I knocked him out in Yankee Stadium. That was more spectacular, but this was more meaningful. It won us a championship."

The game was played on Monday, the day after Christmas, and it was not televised locally. A tape of the game was shown that night on one of the Philadelphia stations, but unless you were lucky enough to have a ticket, the only way to follow the action live was to listen to Bill Campbell's radio call on WCAU.

In many ways, the game was typical of the Eagles' storybook season. They were outgained by the Packers, 401 yards to 296. They trailed in the fourth quarter, yet came back to win, some-

Tommy McDonald is helped to his feet after scoring the first touchdown in the 1960 NFL championship game against Green Bay.

thing they had done all season. Quarterback Norm Van Brocklin was named Most Valuable Player, as he was for his brilliant play during the regular season, but in the championship game, the decision was open to debate.

Van Brocklin was 9-for-20 passing with one interception and an errant lateral that Green Bay recovered on the very first play from scrimmage. He threw one touchdown pass, a 35-yard strike to Tommy McDonald, to give the Eagles their first lead at 7–6, but overall it was not the Dutchman's best effort.

The voters were no doubt influenced by the fact that the championship game was Van Brocklin's swan song. He already had announced he was retiring after the season.

A case could have been made for rookie fullback Ted Dean as MVP of the title game. The Radnor High School graduate broke a 58-yard kickoff return to set up the final scoring drive, and he punched over the winning touchdown on a five-yard end sweep with 5:21 remaining.

Bednarik probably was the most deserving Eagle of all, considering he played the entire game (except for punt returns and kickoffs) at center and outside linebacker and delivered the two biggest hits: the clinching tackle on Taylor and a jarring shot on Hornung that sidelined the NFL's leading scorer with a pinched nerve in his shoulder.

"Chuck was an explosive hitter," cornerback Tom Brookshier said. "I remember Paul saying later, he felt like his arm was ripped out of its socket. And it wasn't a dirty play. It was just Chuck playing his game. When I think back on it, I'm glad they didn't have Hornung on that final drive."

Bednarik was on the field for 139 of the 142 plays in the championship game, a remarkable feat for anyone, but especially a 35-year-old man who was the oldest player on either team. On every change of possession, 21 players would leave the field and 21 players would come on. One man, Bednarik, stayed. He stood alone at center stage, his hands on his hips, a virtuoso performer waiting for the rest of the cast to take its place around him.

"People still ask if I got tired playing the whole way," Bednarik said. "I didn't. At least I didn't feel it. Once the game started, my adrenaline was pumping pretty good. It was a nice day, 40 degrees, just cold enough. The fourth quarter, I was still coming on. It's all mind over matter anyway. When you play for a championship, you do things you couldn't ordinarily do."

A *Philadelphia Daily News* story the day after the game quoted Eagles defensive end Joe Robb as saying, "Bednarik kept me going. He kept saying we were going to win and the defense was going to win it for us. He's an inspirational player. All the things people say about him are true."

The coaching staff also deserves credit. Defensive assistant Jerry Williams designed the zone coverages that shackled Dowler and McGee. Offensive assistant Charlie Gauer drew up the kick return that set up the winning touchdown. In film study, Gauer spotted a weakness in Green Bay's special teams. On one side, they had a slow player flanked by two fast players, creating a natural seam. Gauer felt the Eagles could hit that gap and, with one or two well-timed blocks, get Dean into the open field, and that is exactly what happened.

Dean's game-winning touchdown was the first rushing touchdown of his NFL career. Van Brocklin had called an off-tackle play to halfback Billy Barnes, but when the Eagles broke the huddle, Van Brocklin saw something in the Green Bay defense and changed the play. Dean took the handoff and followed blocks by tight end Bobby Walston and pulling guard Gerry Huth into the end zone.

Then it was just a matter of the Eagles defense hanging on in the final minute, as it did, with Bednarik applying the final stop on Jim Taylor.

"That last drive had me worried," Bednarik said. "They were picking up yardage in chunks. If we had lost that game in the last few seconds, that would have stuck in my mind forever. As great as it felt to win that game, that's how bad it would've felt to lose."

In the winning locker room, head coach Buck Shaw and Van Brocklin confirmed their retirements. The silver-haired coach planned to move back to San Francisco as vice president of a paper box manufacturing company. "There can't be anything greater than this in the cards for me," Shaw said.

Van Brocklin was equally jubilant, saying, "This is by far the greatest season I've ever had with this title coming in my last game, at my age [34]." Most people assumed he would succeed Shaw as head coach, but it never happened. The prospect of giving the strong-willed Dutchman that much power frightened some Eagles executives, so they never offered him the job. They asked if he would consider staying on as a player-coach and, of course, he said no. Instead, he became head coach of the expansion Minnesota Vikings.

"I don't know how it would've worked out if Dutch had stayed on as coach," end Pete Retzlaff said. "Dutch was like a coach on the field, but his leadership was more effective inside the huddle [as a player]. I think it would've been awkward, having a guy who was your teammate and now he's your head coach. But I know Dutch was bitter about what happened. He felt betrayed [by Eagles management]."

"My lasting memory of that season," Brookshier said, "was heading for the shower after the championship game. I could hardly move, I was so drained. Bednarik was standing there with this big smile on his face, smoking a cigar. He had just played the whole game, practically, so I asked him how he was feeling. He said, 'I feel f——ing great.' His voice was like this lion's roar, it shook the walls. Concrete Charlie, he's one of a kind."

Ted Dean (35) follows tight end Bobby Walston (blocking far left) and guard Gerry Huth (65) to score the winning touchdown in the 1960 championship game against Green Bay.

Head coach Dick Vermeil and quarterback Ron Jaworski led the Eagles to the NFC playoffs four years in a row. "We know he's our quarterback and we're going to win with him," Harold Carmichael said.

NFC WILD CARD PLAYOFF
December 24, 1978
Fulton County Stadium, Atlanta, Georgia
Atlanta 14, Eagles 13

The 1978 season was a breakthrough for the Eagles, who posted their first winning record (9–7) in a dozen years and were in the postseason mix for the first time since 1960. Facing Atlanta in the NFC Wild Card game, the Eagles appeared on their way to a victory, leading 13–0 on touchdowns by Harold Carmichael and Wilbert Montgomery.

Late in the third quarter, the Eagles were driving for another score that would have iced the game, but fullback Mike Hogan fumbled at the Atlanta 15-yard line. The Falcons recovered, and the momentum shifted. The Falcons scored a touchdown with quarterback Steve Bartkowski passing to tight end Jim Mitchell, and in the fourth quarter, they scored again on a Bartkowski pass to Wallace Francis to take a 14–13 lead.

The Eagles had a chance to win in the final minutes as quarterback Ron Jaworski drove them from their own 34-yard line to the Atlanta 16. He hit rookie Oren Middlebrook with a pass in the end zone, but Middlebrook, who had not caught a pass all season and was only playing because of injuries to the other receivers, dropped the ball.

With 17 seconds remaining, Mike Michel came on to attempt a 34-yard field goal. Michel was the team's punter, but he assumed the placekicking duties after Nick Mike-Mayer was injured in Week 12. Michel was a mediocre punter (35.8 yard average) and a worse placekicker. He missed three of 12 extrapoint attempts in the final four regular-season games.

Most people assumed coach Dick Vermeil would sign a veteran placekicker with the Eagles fighting for a playoff berth. Vermeil did bring in a few candidates for tryouts, but he said Michel outkicked them all.

The Year of Kicking Dangerously finally caught up with Vermeil in the Wild Card game. Michel missed his first extrapoint attempt against the Falcons, and his second wobbled through the uprights after deflecting off the arm of an Atlanta defender.

Michel did not attempt a field goal in the regular season. His first NFL field goal try would come in the playoffs. Wrote Gary Smith in the *Philadelphia Daily News*: "This was like taking a driver's ed course at the Indy 500." His first attempt, a 42-yarder, was short. His second attempt was the 34-yarder with the game—and season—on the line. He missed it, wide right.

The lasting image is that of Michel after the miss, flat on his back in the mud, holding his head in despair while Atlanta's Wilson Faumuina stood over him, his arms raised in celebration.

Linebacker Frank LeMaster said, "I would have been more upset at him if it [placekicking] was his job. But that's not his job."

Asked if Vermeil made a mistake by entrusting him with that responsibility, Michel said, "I only missed five field goals in all the days of practice. I kicked well in practice. [Vermeil] had confidence in me, and that's the sad part, I let him down."

In the off-season, the Eagles used a third-round draft pick on a placekicker, Tony Franklin of Texas A&M, and an eighthround pick on a punter, Max Runager of South Carolina. Michel was released and never played another NFL game.

NFC WILD CARD GAME
December 23, 1979
Veterans Stadium, Philadelphia
Eagles 27, Chicago 17

It was a ritual Harold Carmichael followed for every Eagles home game. During warm-ups, he would look into the 400 level of Veterans Stadium and find Jim Solano, his agent and friend. Solano would hold up two hands. So many fingers on one hand, that was Solano's prediction for how many passes Carmichael would catch. So many fingers on the other hand, that was the number of touchdowns.

When the Eagles met Chicago in their first postseason game at the Vet, Carmichael looked up and saw Solano signaling five and two. Five catches, two touchdowns. Carmichael pointed back at Solano and nodded. Message delivered, message received.

The 6–8 receiver actually exceeded Solano's prediction, finishing with six catches and two touchdowns as the Eagles defeated the Bears, 27–17. He also set up the third touchdown, blocking linebacker Jerry Muckensturm and allowing halfback Billy Campfield to turn a short pass into a 63-yard dash to the end zone.

The Eagles struggled early in the game, fumbling four times and falling behind 17–10 at halftime. The fans booed quarterback Ron Jaworski, who fumbled a snap and threw an interception before pulling out the win in the fourth quarter.

"These fans expect so much of me, it puts a lot of pressure on me," Jaworski said. "I think this is the greatest sports town in the country. I just wish they'd be a little more patient with me. Like today, I think it's the first time I've been booed for throwing three touchdown passes."

Dick Vermeil created several new formations with Carmichael lined up as a slot receiver. The Bears were forced to play "man" coverage, and Carmichael was too tall for safety Doug Plank and Campfield was too fast for a linebacker such as Muckensturm.

"Harold Carmichael is a big, graceful basketball player playing football," said Dick Coury, the Eagles receiver coach. "You talk about all the things that go into being a superstar, he's got them. When we can get him one-on-one with anyone, we have a chance to make a big play."

"All the guys are behind Ron," Carmichael said. "A couple [negative] things happened, and maybe the fans got a little panicky. They thought something else was going to go wrong, but we weren't worried. We know he's our quarterback and we're gonna win with him. We have that confidence."

Walter Payton scored twice for the Bears, but the Eagles defense came up with a big stop late in the third quarter. With the score tied 17–17, cornerback Bobby Howard, playing with a painfully swollen knee, picked off a Mike Phipps pass in the end zone. A few plays later, Jaworski hit Campfield with the touchdown pass that broke the game open. A 34-yard field goal by Tony Franklin sealed the win.

Vermeil announced he was presenting the game ball to the fans of Philadelphia, a tribute to the city's first postseason win in a generation. "Maybe they can put this in City Hall," he said, "for all the people who supported us so loyally." He added a postscript, directed at the fans who were booing Jaworski early in the game.

"My sincere feeling was that these fans had been losers for so long and that they had better not turn back into losers before the game was over," Vermeil said. "Sometimes a team is a loser because its fans are losers."

NFC DIVISIONAL PLAYOFF
December 29, 1979
Tampa Stadium, Tampa, Florida
Tampa Bay 24, Eagles 17

On a warm, sunny day at Tampa Stadium, the Eagles were beaten, 24–17, in their most listless—and puzzling—performance of the 1979 season. The team that won 11 games in the regular season and held a dozen opponents to 20 points or fewer was manhandled by the Tampa Bay Buccaneers.

The home team took control on its first possession, driving 80 yards, taking 9:34 off the clock and finishing the march with a four-yard touchdown run by Ricky Bell. The Buccaneers extended their lead to 17–0, with Bell scoring another touchdown, and the Eagles were in a hole they could not escape.

The Eagles, wrote Gary Smith in the *Philadelphia Daily News,* "came out dead and stayed that way. The score was a mathematical lie. The Eagles should have lost by three touchdowns."

"We didn't play with all our enthusiasm," coach Dick Vermeil said, although he was at a loss to explain why. No one

said the Eagles lost to a better team, because no one outside of Tampa believed that. The Buccaneers won a mediocre Central Division with a 10–6 record, and they would lose to the Los Angeles Rams, 9–0, in the NFC championship game the following week.

So what went wrong? Did the Eagles underestimate the Buccaneers, who were just three years removed from being the worst expansion team in history? Possibly, although it is more likely that the long season—which under Vermeil meant three-hour practices and endless meetings—drained the team, and the needle finally had settled on "Empty." The Eagles looked like a tired team, and the Bucs, in their first-ever playoff appearance, were inspired.

Also, the one thing the Eagles needed to do—that is, run the football—was one thing the Buccaneers could take away. Their defense, led by future Hall of Fame end Lee Roy Selmon, held Wilbert Montgomery to 35 yards on 13 carries. The Bucs outrushed the Eagles 186 yards to 48.

The Eagles closed the gap to seven points twice, 17–10 in the third quarter and 24–17 on a Ron Jaworski to Harold Carmichael pass with 3:36 left. Kicker Tony Franklin ad-libbed an onsides kick after the last touchdown, but with none of his teammates expecting it, the Buccaneers were able to recover the ball and run out the clock.

"I was trying for a big play, and it just blew up in my face," Franklin said. "I was trying to pop it over their front line of players because I figured our guys could run forward faster than their guys could backward. It was just a screw-up on my part."

Vermeil was furious with the rookie kicker, saying, "That's one check on the board toward him leaving Philadelphia. He let me and the whole team down."

Defensive end Lem Burnham agreed, saying, "Tony had no respect for authority. When he pulled that stunt in Tampa, we just wanted to make him disappear."

NFC DIVISIONAL PLAYOFF
January 3, 1981
Veterans Stadium, Philadelphia
Eagles 31, Minnesota 16

Marion Campbell seldom raised his voice. The Eagles defensive coordinator spoke in a low, slow Southern drawl and measured his words. He wasn't one for speeches or pep talks.

Which is why the Eagles were so surprised when Campbell tore into them during the Divisional playoff against Minnesota. No question, they deserved it. They had allowed the Vikings to build a 14–0 lead, and they were allowing Tommy Kramer to pick them apart with passes to Sammy White and Ricky Young.

Campbell called the defense together, and NFL Films was there when the coach went off, saying, "I'm watching you, and you're walkin' around out there with your head up your ass, and you ain't hittin' a damn soul. The name of the game, men, is hit."

"For Marion to be that fired up, it definitely got our attention," linebacker Bill Bergey said. "And he was right, we weren't physical, we weren't knocking people around, we weren't doing all the things we had done during the season. Once we starting doing that, the whole game turned around."

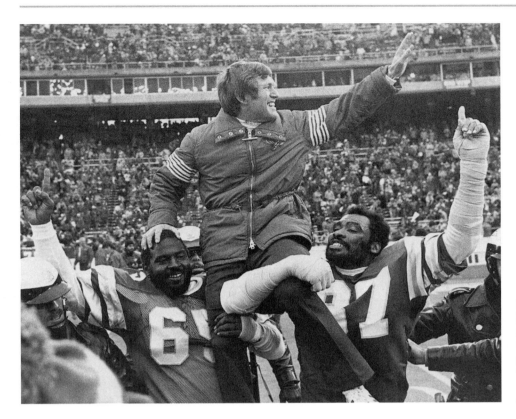

Dick Vermeil is carried off the field by Charlie Johnson (left) and Claude Humphrey after the NFC Divisional playoff win over Minnesota. "This wasn't a pretty win," Vermeil said, "but it was one we needed."

The Eagles allowed a league-low 222 points during the regular season. They pummeled the Vikings, 42–7, earlier in the year. There was no reason why they should struggle to win this game at home. Yet there it was on the Veterans Stadium scoreboard: Minnesota 14, Eagles 0.

The Eagles offense was in trouble. Wilbert Montgomery limped off the field four times during the game with various injuries. There were so many wide receivers out of action that tight end Keith Krepfle was playing flanker. Bergey and the defense realized it was up to them to save the day.

"One thing Marion said stuck with me," Bergey said. "At halftime, he told us, 'You're a great defense. Now, damn it, play like one.'"

In the second half, the defense took over the game, forcing eight turnovers—three fumbles and five interceptions—as the Eagles fought back to win, 31–16. Cornerbacks Herman Edwards and Roynell Young each had two interceptions, and linebacker Frank LeMaster had one. The Eagles also sacked Kramer three times.

"This wasn't a pretty win, but it was one we needed," said coach Dick Vermeil, who rode off the field on the shoulders of defensive linemen Charlie Johnson and Claude Humphrey. "We have a lot of people hurt, we're playing shorthanded in quite a few areas, but in this league, no one is going to feel sorry for you. You just have to find a way to win."

Montgomery scored two touchdowns, Perry Harrington scored one, and Harold Carmichael added another on a nine-yard pass from Ron Jaworski. For Carmichael, it was his fourth touchdown catch in as many postseason games.

"The Eagles are a good ball club," Viking coach Bud Grant said, "and good ball clubs are second-half ball clubs. They've got a lot of talent, they displayed it today, and they certainly played well enough to win. No fluke involved at all."

NFC CHAMPIONSHIP GAME
January 11, 1981
Veterans Stadium, Philadelphia
Eagles 20, Dallas 7

When Wilbert Montgomery looks back over the landscape of the 1980 season, he will see little bits of himself scattered here and there, like parts that have fallen from a broken-down jalopy. There is the hip he dented in St. Louis, the groin muscle he popped against Washington, the knee he wrenched in Dallas, and the thigh he bruised against Minnesota.

By the time the Eagles made it to the playoffs, Montgomery looked like somebody just scraped him off the brick wall at Indy. The checkered flag was just a few wins away, but Montgomery could hardly see it with all that smoke pouring out from beneath his hood.

The 5–10, 195-pound running back spent the week leading up to the NFC Championship game in trainer Otho Davis's body shop, having a season's worth of damage hammered out and refinished. When people asked Montgomery if he would be ready for Dallas—and they asked every five minutes—he said not to worry, he would be there.

"We're one win away from the Super Bowl," Montgomery said. "It's time to suck it up."

No one could suck it up like Wilbert Montgomery. Give him a straw and he could drain your swimming pool. He sat out seven games during the regular season, yet he still led the team in rushing (778 yards), receiving (50 catches), and touchdowns (10).

Linebacker John Bunting walked into the training room before the championship game and saw Montgomery stretched out on the table, the pain of a long, hard season etched on his face. Yet Bunting had no doubt Montgomery would play and play well against the Cowboys. "Wilbert," Bunting said, "has the heart of a lion."

Davis massaged Montgomery's thigh for 90 minutes and taped it for support. Then the Eagles all-time leading rusher pulled on his uniform, went out in the biting cold (minus-20-degree wind chill), and carried his team past Dallas, 20–7, and into its first Super Bowl.

Montgomery rushed for 194 yards, two short of the NFL postseason record set by Steve Van Buren in the 1949 championship game against the Los Angeles Rams. It was a magnificent performance, one that typified the 1980 Eagles, a team that bled and willed its way to the top.

"The knee felt pretty good," Montgomery said. "Not 100 percent, but good enough. I knew once I got the adrenaline flowing, it could overcome a lot of things."

Asked if he considered himself heroic, Montgomery said no. "Every guy in this room has some kind of pain, but we know we have a job to do," he said. "If you can go, you go, especially in a game like this."

Middle linebacker Bill Bergey had a bad knee, but at age 35, he knew this probably was his last shot at a Super Bowl, so he suited up and threw everything he had left at the hated Cowboys.

The Eagles limited Dallas to 11 first downs and held the explosive Tony Dorsett to 41 yards rushing. Unnerved by the swarming Eagles defense, the bone-chilling cold, and 70,696 screaming Philadelphia fans, the Cowboys turned the ball over four times and were outhit from beginning to end.

"The final score was not indicative of how dominant we were," Bergey said. "In terms of physical play, the hitting part

of the game, it was more like 42–0. The offensive line kicked the hell out of them, and we did the same on defense. We could've played 20 more quarters and the Cowboys would not have scored another touchdown."

Everything broke the Eagles' way that season. They tied Dallas in the NFC East with a 12–4 regular-season mark, but they finished first on the basis of tiebreakers. As a result, they had an easier first-round playoff opponent (9–7 Minnesota) plus home-field advantage.

Also, the Eagles wanted to play Dallas in the NFC championship game, not Atlanta. The Falcons gave Vermeil's team fits. They had beaten the Eagles each of the previous three seasons, twice at Veterans Stadium. When Dallas met Atlanta in the Divisional playoff, the Eagles were rooting for the Cowboys. An odd feeling, to be sure.

Playing at home, the Falcons took a 24–10 lead in the third quarter, but Danny White, who succeeded Roger Staubach at quarterback that season, led Dallas on two late scoring drives to pull out a 30–27 victory.

So the Eagles had the matchup they wanted: Dallas at the Vet (a place the Cowboys hated) in the bitter cold (weather they dreaded). Also, the Eagles used their prerogative as home team to wear white jerseys. That forced Dallas to wear its blue jerseys, and it was well known that the Cowboys considered their blue jerseys bad luck.

When team president Tex Schramm was notified about the jersey switch—normally, the Eagles wore green at home—he flew into a rage. The Eagles had scored first in the Gamesmanship Bowl.

"They were very open about which colors they preferred," Vermeil said. "We thought, 'Why let them wear it?' It was just

Wilbert Montgomery's 42-yard touchdown run sparked the Eagles to victory in the NFC Championship game against Dallas. "It looked like someone shot Wilbert out of a cannon," Bill Bergey said.

one more thing for them to think about. I felt we had a lot going for us. The Cowboys had been successful for a long time. There was an air about them, the whole 'America's Team' thing. I thought they might take us for granted, and if they did, I knew we'd whip their ass."

The frigid weather and 25-mile-an-hour winds made it almost impossible to throw the ball, so the game would be decided on the ground. Normally, Vermeil would have welcomed such a battle because he felt his team was physically tougher than the Cowboys. But there was the question of Montgomery's health. He had hobbled through a week of practice in Tampa, where the Eagles trained to escape the cold in Philadelphia. His knee gave out in Thursday's practice, and he was limping when the team flew home the following day.

But on Sunday, on the Eagles' second play from scrimmage, Montgomery took a handoff from quarterback Ron Jaworski, started off left tackle, cut back, and found an open lane through the Dallas defense. He sprinted untouched 42 yards for a touchdown that ignited the crowd and gave the Eagles the confidence they needed to win the game.

"It wasn't just that we scored early, but we scored early on a running play," Jaworski said. "Nobody thought we could run like that on the Cowboys. It sent a message that we could take the ball and shove it down their throats. Weather conditions being what they were, the more physical team was going to win, and we established right away that we had the edge."

"We could run that play a hundred times and never hit it as perfectly as we did there," Vermeil said. "We went with our shotgun personnel, but we shifted to the I formation with three wide receivers. We'd never done that before, and it took Dallas by surprise. They had their 'nickel' on the field with six defensive backs.

"They were in 'man' coverage, so they were running with our receivers and had their backs to the ball. We knew if we got Wilbert through the line, he could run right up their backs and they wouldn't even know it."

Left tackle Stan Walters straightened up Harvey Martin. Left guard Petey Perot blocked future Hall of Famer Randy White. Center Guy Morriss took out linebacker Bob Breunig, and right guard Woody Peoples trapped John Dutton. Right tackle Jerry Sisemore sealed off Ed (Too Tall) Jones, giving Montgomery his cutback lane. Only the safeties, Dennis Thurman and Charlie Waters, saw the play develop, but they could not react in time. Once Montgomery broke to the outside, no one could catch him.

"It looked like someone shot Wilbert out of a cannon," Bergey said. "He exploded through there. I knew right then we couldn't lose."

Dallas did tie the game, 7–7, but the Eagles owned the second half, as fullback Leroy Harris (10 carries, 60 yards) punched over the second touchdown and Tony Franklin barefooted two field goals through the bitter cold. The final score made the game appear more competitive than it really was.

Wrote Bill Conlin in the *Philadelphia Daily News*: "It was the Eagles' primordial defense against the Cowboys' trick, slick offense. Fred Flintstone vs. Luke Skywalker. Give one game ball to Wilbert Montgomery and 11 more to the dock-wallopers who punched holes in Tom Landry's offensive game plan, a wrecking ball loose in the Louvre."

"Dallas didn't give up the game," tight end Keith Krepfle said. "If they got a breath of air, they would've been right back in it. But we didn't give them a breath of air, and I think it's

time somebody gave us the credit we deserve. We kicked the hell out of them."

As the final seconds ticked down, hundreds of fans stormed the field. Said tight end John Spagnola: "I just remember being engulfed by all these people and their breath smelled like a distillery." Owner Leonard Tose hugged Vermeil as the Veterans Stadium scoreboard flashed the message "We're Going to the Super Bowl."

Walters recalls seeing some concession workers on the field, celebrating with everyone else. Said Walters: "I thought that was neat, even the hot dog vendors were losing their minds. It put a Philly kind of stamp on the whole thing."

General manager Jim Murray drifted through the locker room, moving from one embrace to another like a man in a dream. His hat had been smashed down on his head by too many playful hands. There were tears trickling down his cheeks and dropping into this great rain barrel of an Irish smile. Every so often, he would roll his eyes and say the magic word: "Champions."

"No way the Cowboys were going to beat us," Murray said. "Not here, not today. We threw the Polish-American string band at them. We threw Andrea McArdle [singing "God Bless America"] at them. I looked around before the game, and there were 70,000 people holding hands and crying. The Cowboys weren't just playing the Eagles today; they were playing the city of Philadelphia, a city united. They weren't prepared for that."

Tose threw a gala victory party that night at Bookbinder's, but Bergey missed it. He was home on the couch, his swollen knee packed in ice.

"There was so much fluid in the knee that when the doctor put the needle in, the plunger backed up by itself," Bergey said. "But as bad as it was, it was worth it just to be on the field that day."

SUPER BOWL XV
January 25, 1981
Louisiana Superdome, New Orleans, Louisiana
Oakland 27, Eagles 10

On a weekend when America celebrated the release of the hostages from Iran, the Eagles and Oakland Raiders met in Super Bowl XV. It was a festive occasion with a giant yellow ribbon adorning the Superdome in New Orleans, but once the game began, the only ones celebrating were the Raiders and their fans as they won easily, 27–10.

It was a bitter disappointment for the Eagles, who went into the game favored by three points. They won 12 games during the regular season, tied for the best record in the league, and had the No. 1 ranked defense. The Raiders did not even win their own division, the AFC West. They made it into the playoffs as a wild-card team, and wild-card teams aren't supposed to win Super Bowls.

The Eagles defeated the Raiders, 10–7, during the regular season, sacking Oakland quarterback Jim Plunkett eight times. They were confident they could do it again in the Super Bowl, but they fell behind early, 14–0, and never recovered. Plunkett burned the Eagles with three touchdown passes and was voted the game's Most Valuable Player.

The intensity that characterized the Eagles all season was strangely lacking in the Super Bowl. Were they worn out by

Oakland's John Matuszak (72) puts the pressure on Eagles quarterback Ron Jaworski in Super Bowl XV. Jaworski threw three interceptions in the 27–10 loss. The Raiders, coach Dick Vermeil said, "beat our butts."

their workaholic coach, Dick Vermeil? Were they unnerved by their first trip to the Big Game? The Eagles went straight from the New Orleans airport to practice, while the Raiders headed for Bourbon Street and stayed there all week. Did the contrasting approaches account for the Raiders appearing looser on game day?

"I don't think we were physically tired, but we may have been emotionally drained," linebacker Frank LeMaster said. "The week leading up to the game, all the hype and pressure kind of sapped us. I think the Raiders' experience [they had 11 veterans who played in other Super Bowls] helped them. They knew how to handle it. We didn't."

"I just remember it felt different," tackle Stan Walters said. "Normally, there was a buzz in our locker room before a game. Guys talking and going through their different rituals. There was a rhythm to it. At the Super Bowl, it wasn't like that. For one thing we got there early, so we had more time to kill. They had a TV in the dressing room showing the pregame show, and we never had a TV in the locker room before. Guys were saying, 'Turn it off.' I could see guys getting edgy. I thought, 'Uh oh.'"

Leonard Tose may have felt the tension building because he brought his pal Don Rickles into the locker room to crack a few jokes. If the owner thought it would help the players get ready for the game, he was wrong. It was just one more depar-

ture from the norm. Besides, as Ron Jaworski pointed out, "[Rickles'] whole routine is insult jokes. Do you really want to be insulted before you play the biggest game of your life?"

On the third play from scrimmage, Jaworski tried to force a pass to tight end John Spagnola. Oakland linebacker Rod Martin intercepted and returned it to the 30-yard line, setting up a Plunkett to Cliff Branch touchdown pass. The Eagles were down 7–0 just 4:16 into the game.

"That was an example of what happens in a Super Bowl," Jaworski said. "We ran that play a dozen times during the season. I knew exactly what to do. If the tight end is open, I throw it. If not, I lay it off to Wilbert [Montgomery] in the flat. It's an easy read. But you get in the Super Bowl and you're all pumped up and you think, 'I'm gonna stick it in there,' and it costs you."

The Eagles had a chance to get back into the game later in the quarter when they drove to the Oakland 40 and, on third down, Jaworski threw an apparent touchdown pass to wide receiver Rodney Parker. However, the play was wiped out by an illegal motion penalty called on Harold Carmichael. The Eagles were forced to punt, and three plays later Plunkett threw his second touchdown pass, an 80-yard bomb to fullback Kenny King.

On the play, defensive end Carl Hairston was two steps away from sacking Plunkett, but tackle Art Shell pulled Hairston down by his face mask. It was an obvious penalty, but the officials never saw it, and the Raiders had a two-touchdown lead.

The Eagles never recovered. Their only touchdown—a pass from Jaworski to tight end Keith Krepfle—came in the fourth quarter, and by then Oakland was comfortably ahead.

"I think if we could have made a couple of big plays early, we would have been okay," Vermeil said. "But we fell behind, and we seemed to sag emotionally. That happens in football. I think you have to give all the credit to the Raiders. They were a much better team that day. We didn't play at the level we played most of the season, but that's because the Raiders didn't let us. They beat our butts."

The loss was a crushing blow to Tose, who spent a small fortune entertaining in New Orleans. He paid to fly hundreds of people to the game, from the Liberty Belles cheerleader squad to the janitors who cleaned the team's offices. Tose also brought John Cardinal Krol, the archbishop of Philadelphia, to New Orleans as his guest.

Before the game, the cardinal told Tose he prayed for an Eagles victory. Tose was not a religious man—although he attended Notre Dame, he was Jewish, not Catholic—but he was heartened by the thought of such a holy man praying for a win.

When the game ended, a dejected Tose turned to the cardinal, who was seated behind him in his Superdome suite.

"I thought God was supposed to answer our prayers," Tose said.

"God does answer our prayers," the cardinal replied. "But sometimes the answer is 'No.'"

NFC WILD CARD GAME
December 27, 1981
Veterans Stadium, Philadelphia
New York Giants 27, Eagles 21

The Eagles were eliminated from the 1981 playoffs in the Wild Card round, falling to the New York Giants, 27–21. It was a disappointing fate, but one to which the defending NFC champions had been inexorably sliding for weeks.

The Eagles opened the season with six consecutive wins and appeared on course for a return to the Super Bowl. But things began breaking down, and the Eagles lost four of their last five regular-season games to finish 10–6.

They qualified for the playoffs as a wild-card team, but they limped in with little confidence and no momentum. Kick returner Wally Henry fumbled twice in the first quarter to help the Giants build a 20–0 lead, and the Eagles were on their way to their first ever postseason loss at Veterans Stadium.

"We seemed to lose our poise and our confidence," coach Dick Vermeil said. "We played for five years without those kinds of things happening."

"When you fall behind 20–0 in a playoff game, it will rattle anybody," quarterback Ron Jaworski said. "To say you can be a cool, calm professional in that situation would be a downright lie."

Jaworski did his best to bring the Eagles back, throwing a touchdown pass to Harold Carmichael and directing two long drives that ended in Wilbert Montgomery touchdown runs, but they never got closer than six points. For the Giants, it was their first postseason appearance in 18 years and their first playoff win since 1958.

The dispiriting loss effectively ended the Vermeil era in Philadelphia. In 1982, the Eagles would fall to 3–6 in a strike-shortened season, and the coach would resign due to physical and emotional exhaustion.

"Losses all chip a little bit off you," Vermeil said after the Giants game. "It especially hurts when you know you're better than you've shown."

"Somebody has to take the blame for this, I guess it will be me," said Henry, who set an Eagles record by returning 54 punts in 1981. "The fans are no more disappointed than I am. When I fumbled against Atlanta [earlier in the season], I said I felt lower than an ant's ass. Right now, I feel double that."

NFC DIVISIONAL PLAYOFF
December 31, 1988
Soldier Field, Chicago, Illinois
Chicago 20, Eagles 12

Reggie White thought it was smoke from a nearby fire. David Alexander thought someone in the crowd had set off fireworks or tipped over a barbecue grill. Gradually, it thickened and rolled across the playing surface at Soldier Field, enveloping the 1988 NFC Divisional playoff between the Eagles and Chicago Bears. It was the fog blowing off Lake Michigan, a fog that made for an unforgettable scene.

"I was on the sidelines and I couldn't see anything," former Chicago coach Mike Ditka said. "It was crazy. All we needed was Count Dracula at quarterback."

"I still wonder why we played," said Randall Cunningham, who passed for 407 yards, an Eagles postseason record, despite the poor visibility. "The people in the stands couldn't see, the people watching on TV couldn't see, and we couldn't see each other."

"I worked three Super Bowls, but I get more questions about the Fog Bowl than any of the Super Bowls," said Jim Tunney, who refereed the game and made the decision to play on despite the conditions. "I still think we did the right thing."

The Bears won, 20–12, but it is hard to say if the fog had any impact on the outcome. The winners, of course, say no. "Half of the game was played in sunshine, and [the Eagles] couldn't get the ball in the end zone," Ditka said. "If they can't score in the sunlight, that's not our fault."

Keith Byars, who led all receivers with nine catches for 103 yards, offers the counterpoint.

"We were behind at halftime, but not by much [17–9]," Byars said. "We were a comeback team all year, and I think if it wasn't for the fog, we would've come back and won that game, too.

"Of all the years under Buddy [Ryan], that probably was our best chance to win it all. We were young and healthy. It was our first time in the playoffs, and we didn't know how to be nervous. We outplayed the Bears in the first half, but we had two touchdowns called back [on penalties]. We were making plays, and we would've continued to make plays, but the fog took away our deep passing game."

At kickoff, the weather was beautiful. Skies were clear, and the temperature was 34 degrees, unseasonably mild for Chicago on New Year's Eve. Those conditions seemed to favor the Eagles and Cunningham, who passed for a career-high 3,808 yards that season. The fog did not roll in until just before halftime.

The Eagles moved the ball effectively, outgaining the Bears 430 yards to 341, but they could not convert on their scoring opportunities. They were in the Chicago red zone nine times, but settled for four Luis Zendejas field goals. Cris Carter and Mike Quick each caught an apparent touchdown pass, but they were wiped out by penalties. Another huge blow was tight end Keith Jackson letting a sure touchdown pass bounce off his hands.

The Eagles took themselves out of the game in the first half, and the fog took them out of it in the second half. While the Bears were content to sit on the lead, Cunningham had to make plays through the air even though throwing the ball beyond 10 yards was almost impossible.

"[The Bears] knew I couldn't throw long, so they flooded the short zones with extra defensive backs," Cunningham said. "That was how they got their [three] interceptions."

"A lot of what we did, we did by memorization," Byars said. "Randall and I worked so much together that we were in sync. If I told him I was running an 'out,' he knew where to throw the ball and I knew when to look for it. Still, it was hard because I couldn't see the ball until it was right on top of me. This brown thing would come shooting out of the fog."

The central figure, really, was Tunney, the referee. Since the fog did not become a factor until the game was under way, it was his call whether to stop it, to call for a postponement, or to continue. If the fog had rolled in before kickoff, the deci-sion would have been made by the league official in atten-dance, executive director Don Weiss. But once the game began, it was in the hands of the referee.

"Don was in the press box, and we talked by phone during each time-out," Tunney said. "He'd say, 'What do you think?' I asked the coaches and players, and they wanted to keep going. If anyone should have objected, it was Buddy because his team was behind, but he was adamant. He said, 'Hell, it's foggy on both sides of the ball. Let's keep playing.' Even most of the players said it wasn't that bad.

"It looked worse from the stands because they had the lights on and they reflected off the fog," Tunney said. "On the field, the fog was patchy. There were pockets that were clear, others that were thick. But we could see 40 or 50 yards."

Most of the players dispute Tunney's account.

"You couldn't see half the field," said Alexander, the Eagles center. "I had no idea where the sidelines were. The fog rolled over the top of the stadium and across the field like smoke rolling off a concert stage. I vividly remember Tunney coming in our huddle and asking Randall, 'Can you see the goal posts at the other end?' Randall said no. Then he asked, 'Can you see the 30-second clock?' Randall said no. [Tunney] said, 'Don't worry, we won't call it,' meaning a delay-of-game penalty. The heck with the penalty. The point is, we couldn't see."

The ghostly images of the Fog Bowl between the Eagles and Chicago Bears at Soldier Field on New Year's Eve, 1988. "Those officials wouldn't have known if there were 22 players on the field or 16," said Eagles owner Norman Braman.

"I had to weigh the options," Tunney said. "What do I do? Stop the game and hope the fog lifts? How long do we wait? If we wait 45 minutes, the players will get stiff and maybe get hurt [when play resumes]. Do we call the game and pick it up another time? If so, when? The next day? There were other playoff games scheduled that day. If you wait two days, then you're penalizing the team that wins by leaving them less time to prepare for the championship game.

"I felt the conditions, while not great, still were playable," Tunney said. "I could see all 22 players from my position [behind the quarterback]. I occasionally lost sight of the safety, but only for a second or two."

CBS broadcaster Verne Lundquist was shocked that the game was allowed to continue. He said so at the time. The network's press-box-level cameras were useless, so they tried to cover the action with their sideline cameras, but even there, the visibility was extremely limited, 10 to 15 yards at the most. Lundquist gamely tried to call the play by play, but wound up saying things like "[Thomas] Sanders goes right … and … and … he disappears."

Eagles owner Norman Braman abandoned his luxury box and watched the second half from the field. Braman was upset with the decision to keep playing. "I was right there," he said, "and, believe me, those officials wouldn't have known if there were 22 players on the field or 16."

NFC WILD CARD GAME
December 31, 1989
Veterans Stadium, Philadelphia
Los Angeles 21, Eagles 7

In the first NFL playoff game held at the Vet in almost a decade, Los Angeles quarterback Jim Everett threw a pair of touchdown passes on his first two possessions to lead the Rams to a 21–7 win over the Eagles.

It was a disappointing loss for the Eagles and quarterback Randall Cunningham, who had one of his poorest performances of the season. Defensively, the Eagles allowed Everett to throw for 167 yards in the first quarter. Offensively, they failed to capitalize on good field position all day. Cunningham was ineffective in the first half, when he threw for just 78 yards.

"They prepared for what our offense does," Cunningham said. "They took [tight end] Keith Jackson away early. They took our wideouts away and our short passing game."

Running back Keith Byars caught nine passes despite playing with sore ribs. He said the team started pressing after falling behind.

"It took us till about the second quarter to get a first down," Byars said. "We were pressing too hard. We got to looking at the scoreboard and thinking, 'We've got to score before the end of the first quarter; we've got to score before halftime.'"

The Eagles did not score until the fourth quarter when Anthony Toney burst over from the one-yard line to climax an 80-yard drive and cut the deficit to 14–7. The Eagles had good field position on two possessions after that but managed only one first down after starting on their own 31- and 40-yard lines.

The Rams put the game away with 2:46 left, when Greg Bell raced 54 yards down the left sideline and scored a few plays

In three playoff losses under coach Buddy Ryan, the Eagles offense, led by quarterback Randall Cunningham, managed just one touchdown. Cunningham threw five interceptions and was sacked 11 times.

later. Bell finished with 124 yards on 27 carries. Everett completed 18 of 33 passes for 281 yards.

"I wanted us to take that one step forward, but today wasn't the day to do it," Eagles coach Buddy Ryan said. "We didn't make it happen, but we need to do that."

NFC WILD CARD GAME
January 5, 1991
Veterans Stadium, Philadelphia
Washington 20, Eagles 6

The Buddy Ryan era in Philadelphia came to an end after the Eagles were eliminated for the third straight year in postseason play. This time it was the Washington Redskins, who won 20–6, in a game that included an impulsive decision by the head coach.

After the Redskins increased their lead to 13–6 on a 19-yard Chip Lohmiller field goal, Ryan yanked Cunningham—who accounted for 77 percent of the Eagles offense during the regular season—and inserted a rusty Jim McMahon in an effort to spark the team.

McMahon, who hardly played at all during the regular season, threw three straight incompletions, and Ryan went back to Cunningham on the Eagles' next possession. But the emotional damage was done.

"I didn't know what [Ryan] was doing, if he thought maybe I was hurt," Cunningham said. "It was insulting. He didn't tell me I was going to be pulled. I didn't find out until Jim was on the field."

Eagles owner Norman Braman was stunned by Ryan's move. He had an aide call the bench to find out if Cunningham was injured. Later, Braman criticized his coach for "embarrassing" his star quarterback.

"You never know, you got to do something to win," Ryan said. "You can't make changes next week."

Cunningham got the Eagles off to a hopeful start on their first possession when he connected with tight end Keith Jackson on a 66-yard pass play to the Redskins 11. But the drive sputtered, and the Eagles had to settle for a 37-yard Roger Ruzek field goal.

They missed another opportunity in the second quarter after recovering a fumble by Washington's Gerald Riggs and driving to a first and goal on the two-yard line. Again they stalled, and Ruzek connected from 28 yards out for a 6–0 lead.

After that, Washington dominated as quarterback Mark Rypien threw two touchdown passes while completing 15 of 31 attempts for 206 yards. Meanwhile, the Washington defense was sacking Cunningham five times.

The Redskins also got a boost from the replay official to increase their lead just before halftime. After tackling Washington's Ernest Byner and causing an apparent fumble, Eagles cornerback Ben Smith picked up the ball and returned it 94 yards for an apparent touchdown. But the replay official ruled that contact with the ground caused Byner to lose the ball, and the Redskins maintained possession.

"I never thought they'd call it back," Smith said. "Unbelievable, the man fumbled the ball."

Lohmiller kicked a 20-yard field goal four plays later to put Washington ahead 10–6.

After the Cunningham benching, Washington scored again to put the game away, this time driving 55 yards in five plays with Rypien finding Gary Clark with a three-yard touchdown pass. Three days later, Ryan was fired as Eagles head coach.

NFC WILD CARD GAME
January 3, 1993
Louisiana Superdome, New Orleans, Louisiana
Eagles 36, New Orleans 20

Randall Cunningham and Fred Barnett connected on two long touchdown plays, and the Eagles exploded for 26 points in the fourth quarter for a 36–20 come-from-behind triumph over New Orleans.

For the Eagles, it was their first road playoff win in 44 years and their first playoff win *anywhere* in 12 years. The Eagles were inspired by a pregame talk by Willie Brown, the father of Jerome Brown, their former teammate and All-Pro defensive tackle who was killed in an automobile accident six months earlier.

Brown's locker with all his belongings, which was preserved in the team's dressing room at Veterans Stadium, was shipped to New Orleans and placed next to Reggie White's stall before the game. White said he was encouraged to see the memorial to his fallen teammate. After the game, he just felt relieved.

"It just feels so good to finally—finally—break through to the next level," said White, who had never won a championship in his football career going all the way back to the Pop Warner League.

The Eagles trailed 20–7 with 6:22 left in the third quarter, but Cunningham rallied the offense, the defense came to life, and the Eagles scored 29 unanswered points to pick up their first playoff victory under coach Rich Kotite.

Eric Allen began the rally late in the third quarter with the first of his two interceptions off Saints quarterback Bobby Hebert, setting up a 40-yard field goal by Roger Ruzek. Early in the fourth period Cunningham hit Barnett, who made a spectacular leaping catch of a 35-yard touchdown pass to cut the deficit to three points. Barnett had scored earlier on a 57-yard pass.

"Randall put the ball inside, perfectly, where I could catch it," said Barnett, who had four catches for 102 yards. "I turned around, saw it, and jumped. It was a great pass."

The Eagles took their first lead with 6:18 left in the fourth quarter on a six-yard run by Heath Sherman. Less than two minutes later, with the Saints backed up to their own seven-yard line and facing a third and 23, White sacked Hebert for a safety.

"We finally got a bead on what they were doing," said linebacker Seth Joyner, who had the other interception in the second-half comeback. "We just picked up the intensity when we had to. It took us some time to get it done, but, thank God, we put it together when we had to."

The Eagles took the ensuing free kick and methodically drove to the Saints' 22 before Ruzek kicked his second field goal of the game. Allen iced it with an 18-yard interception return for a touchdown.

NFC DIVISIONAL PLAYOFF
January 10, 1993
Texas Stadium, Irving, Texas
Dallas 34, Eagles 10

Troy Aikman threw two touchdown passes and Emmitt Smith rushed for 114 yards as the Dallas Cowboys, the eventual Super Bowl champions, built up a 31-point lead and coasted to a 34–10 triumph.

"I wish I knew," said coach Rich Kotite when asked to explain the team's collapse. "That's just the way the game is. We fought out of the hole so often this season, but all people remember about you is the last game you've played."

Even the return of strong safety Andre Waters, who made his first appearance since suffering a broken leg three months earlier, didn't help. Waters' mission was to slow down Smith, but the Cowboys' star gained 74 of his yards after halftime.

The Eagles did not score a touchdown until the closing minutes when Randall Cunningham scrambled and found Calvin Williams open for an 18-yard scoring play. Cunningham completed only 17 of 30 passes for 160 yards.

Philadelphia's other points came on a 32-yard field goal by Roger Ruzek that gave the Eagles a short-lived three-point lead on their first possession.

"Dallas has a great team, and today they whipped our butts," said Cunningham, who was sacked five times. "We recognize it, and we have to compliment them because of it. They are well coached, and their defense showed today why they are No. 1. They make plays, rock you back on your heels, and keep on coming."

The Dallas defense held the Eagles to one third-down conversion in 14 attempts. The Eagles managed only 63 yards on the ground with Cunningham accounting for 22 of them.

NFC WILD CARD GAME
December 30, 1995
Veterans Stadium, Philadelphia
Eagles 58, Detroit Lions 37

Eagles coach Ray Rhodes used the old bulletin board technique to inspire his team to a record-setting playoff performance. After Detroit tackle Lomas Brown guaranteed the Lions would beat the Eagles in the playoffs, Rhodes posted the quote in the Veterans Stadium locker room.

Quarterback Rodney Peete made his first playoff start a memorable one as he led the Eagles to a 58–37 win in the highest-scoring playoff game in NFL history. It was also sweet revenge for Peete, who once played for the Lions and was criticized by Philadelphia fans who wanted him demoted and replaced by Randall Cunningham.

"The last several weeks I struggled, and the offense struggled," Peete explained. "This week in practice you could see that everyone was really bearing down and focusing. It just carried over."

Peete threw three touchdown passes to tie a club playoff record, and running back Ricky Watters scored twice as the Eagles picked up their first postseason win at the Vet since 1981.

Peete said he detected a lack of respect from his former teammates during the game. "They didn't really respect our passing game," he said. "They thought, 'if you stop the run, you stop the Eagles.' So they were playing guys like Fred Barnett with single coverage."

Philadelphia's Gary Anderson kicked field goals of 39, 31, and 21 yards to extend his consecutive FG streak in the postseason to 16 and break the record of 15 set by Rafael Septien of Dallas.

The total of 58 points scored by the Eagles was not only a franchise postseason record, but also the third-highest total by one team in NFL playoff history. Their 31-point outburst in the second quarter was the second most ever scored by one team in the playoffs. Their total of seven touchdowns was a club record for the postseason, and their 21-point margin of victory tied another team milestone. The Eagles held a 51–7 lead at one point.

"If Brown had been a two-or-three-time Super Bowl champion, I could understand it," Rhodes said. "If you haven't been there, keep your mouth shut. He's talking about walking into your house, slapping your family around, and robbing you. We're not going to let anybody do that."

Ray Rhodes used the words of Detroit's Lomas Brown to inspire the Eagles in their NFC Wild Card game against the Lions. Brown made headlines when he guaranteed a Detroit victory. "We're not going to let anybody do that," Rhodes said.

Defensively, the Eagles held the NFL's No. 1 ranked offense to seven points in the first 40 minutes. Detroit's All-Pro running back Barry Sanders was held to 40 yards on ten carries. Philadelphia had six interceptions and two sacks.

Peete connected on 17 of 25 passes for 270 yards and threw touchdown passes of 45 yards to Watters, 43 yards to Rob Carpenter, and 22 yards to Fred Barnett. Watters also scored on a one-yard run.

Barnett, who caught eight passes for 109 yards, said that it was difficult to concentrate on the game because the Eagles had such a big lead. "At the beginning of the third quarter, I just wanted the clock to keep running," he said.

The Eagles also scored on a 15-yard run by Charlie Garner, and pass interceptions of 30 and 24 yards, respectively, by William Thomas and Barry Wilburn. Garner was the game's top rusher with 78 yards on 12 carries.

NFC DIVISIONAL PLAYOFF
January 7, 1996
Texas Stadium, Irving, Texas
Dallas 30, Eagles 11

The Cowboys used a powerful running game and strong defense to roll up a 30–3 lead and crush the Eagles, 30–11.

"It came down to muscle against muscle, and too many times they had the advantage," Eagles coach Ray Rhodes said.

Philadelphia's only points came on a 26-yard field goal by Gary Anderson on the first play of the second quarter and a four-yard run by quarterback Randall Cunningham in the fourth period.

Bobby Taylor deflected a pass by Troy Aikman into the hands of Mark McMillian to set up the Anderson field goal that tied the game, 3–3. Quarterback Rodney Peete was forced out of the game with a concussion after being hit by Dallas safety Darren Woodson right before Anderson's field goal.

"Based on what people tell me, I think I was scrambling to the right trying to get a first down," Peete said. "It's the worst feeling in the world that I didn't get to play the whole game."

Cunningham, who missed most of the week's practices so he could be with his wife for the birth of their first child, took over for Peete but was ineffective (11 completions in 26 attempts for 161 yards). It was Cunningham's last game as an Eagle. The club made no attempt to re-sign him when he became a free agent after that season.

NFC WILD CARD GAME
December 29, 1996
3Com Park, San Francisco, California
San Francisco 14, Eagles 0

For the second straight season, the Eagles had their starting quarterback knocked out of a playoff game. The previous year, it was Rodney Peete, who suffered a concussion against Dallas. This time, Ty Detmer pulled his right hamstring while trying to avoid a sack by San Francisco's Bryant Young.

The Eagles lost to the 49ers 14–0, the first playoff shutout loss in the club's history.

"Quite naturally, it hurts," said Eagles coach Ray Rhodes. "Any time you lose in the playoffs it's disappointing. You wake up tomorrow, and you're not playing anymore. It's more frustrating because we had the opportunities and didn't score any points."

On their first possession, the Eagles drove 59 yards before stalling at the San Francisco 23. Gary Anderson's 40-yard field goal never had a chance in the blustery weather conditions, which included heavy rain and wind gusts up to 60 miles per hour.

In the second quarter, two Eagles scoring drives ended on Detmer interceptions. The first was picked off in the end zone by Marquez Pope, and the other by Roy Barker on the five-yard line just before halftime.

"Today will stick with me for a while," Detmer said. "It's disappointing for me to not be able to finish. All the mistakes in the red zone will stick with me more than the good stuff. If you told me before the game that we were going to be shut out, I would have been shocked."

The game was a homecoming for running back Ricky Watters, who previously played for the 49ers. Watters ended his second season with the Eagles by rushing for 57 yards, with only nine of them coming in the second half.

"The worst thing is we outplayed these guys," Watters said. "It's not like we laid down for this team. We were moving the ball up and down the field. We should have been on the top side of that score."

NFC WILD CARD GAME
December 31, 2000
Veterans Stadium, Philadelphia
Eagles 21, Tampa Bay 3

Donovan McNabb played well in his first NFL playoff start by accounting for all three Eagles touchdowns in a 21–3 win over the Buccaneers. McNabb completed 24 passes to ten different receivers for 161 yards and two touchdowns. He ran for 32 more yards and scored the other touchdown as the Eagles won their first playoff game under coach Andy Reid.

"I was enjoying myself," McNabb said. "Early in the game, I was just making sure that the whole offense was ready and their spirits were uplifted. In the guys' eyes, you could tell that they were hungry and ready to go."

The Eagles defense held Tampa Bay's Warrick Dunn to one yard rushing. The Buccaneers got their only points when Martin Gramatica booted a 29-yard field goal in the second quarter. On Tampa Bay's next possession, Hugh Douglas sacked quarterback Shaun King and knocked the ball loose. Mike Mamula recovered the fumble on the Buccaneers' 15, and five plays later, McNabb ran it in from the five-yard line. Douglas had two of the Eagles' four sacks.

With less than two minutes to go before halftime, the Eagles drove 69 yards in eight plays with McNabb hitting Na Brown with a five-yard touchdown pass. McNabb later threw a two-yard touchdown pass to tight end Jeff Thomason.

"The nice thing about Donovan is that he will continue to get better here for the next couple of years," Reid said. "We surely haven't seen a finished product yet."

It was the Buccaneers' 20th straight loss in games when the temperature was 40 degrees or colder. The game-time temperature was 34 degrees with winds gusting up to 31 miles per hour for a wind chill of 11 degrees.

NFC DIVISIONAL PLAYOFF
January 7, 2001
Giants Stadium, East Rutherford, New Jersey
New York Giants 20, Eagles 10

Ron Dixon returned the opening kickoff 97 yards for a touchdown, and the New York Giants defeated the Eagles, 20–10, in the NFC Divisional playoff.

Blitzing on virtually every play, the Giants sacked Donovan McNabb six times, forcing him to fumble and throw a costly interception.

"They blitzed on first, second, and third down," McNabb said. "They put us in a lot of holes on third down, and when a defense gets in that position, it can do anything it wants."

McNabb completed only 20 of 41 passes for 181 yards, and he was held to 17 yards on five carries.

"When Donovan tried to run, the big guys were popping him all over the place," said tight end Chad Lewis.

Cornerback Jason Sehorn made the game's most spectacular play, a juggling interception of a McNabb pass that he returned 32 yards for a touchdown. The Eagles' only touchdown came on a 10-yard McNabb pass to Torrance Small. It was set up by a blocked punt by Jason Bostic.

NFC WILD CARD GAME
January 12, 2002
Veterans Stadium, Philadelphia
Eagles 31, Tampa Bay 9

With Donovan McNabb throwing two touchdown passes and the defense playing superbly, the Eagles turned in their finest all-around performance of the season in defeating Tampa Bay, 31–9.

McNabb threw scoring strikes of 16 and 23 yards to Chad Lewis and Duce Staley.

"I thought Donovan McNabb showed a lot of poise and patience in the pocket," coach Andy Reid said. "Remember that you're looking at a third-year quarterback, a second-year starter. His maturity continues to improve every game. It's a special thing to watch."

McNabb constantly shook off defenders to gain an extra step and throw the ball. He was forced to flee the pocket several times, but he usually was able to complete the pass as he did on the Lewis touchdown.

"That breaks your back defensively," Eagles cornerback Troy Vincent said. "It kills your will. It kills your desire to keep going."

McNabb set up the Lewis touchdown by completing all four passes in the 73-yard drive, including a 41-yard strike to Todd Pinkston. For the day, McNabb passed for 194 yards and ran for 57 more.

"I don't think anybody knows how to keep a play alive like Donovan," Lewis said. "We know that he causes so much confusion and indecision."

David Akers kicked a 26-yard field goal in the first quarter to help the Eagles take a 17–9 halftime lead.

Midway through the third quarter, Correll Buckhalter broke four tackles and went 25 yards to score.

Damon Moore had two of the Eagles' four interceptions off Tampa Bay's Brad Johnson, including a 59-yard return for a touchdown, the longest playoff interception in club history.

The 22-point margin of victory was also a playoff record for the Eagles, who rushed for 148 yards while limiting the Buccaneers to 63 yards on the ground.

Martin Gramatica accounted for all of the Buccaneers scoring with field goals of 36, 32, and 27 yards. Tampa Bay's only other scoring opportunity was thwarted when Vincent made a spectacular over-the-shoulder interception in the end zone in the third period.

"To throw a shutout like that in the second half again, I think that speaks for itself," Reid said. "Our defense has taken a lot of pride in stepping up and stopping the run. I think they did a nice job with that."

NFC DIVISIONAL PLAYOFF
January 19, 2002
Soldier Field, Chicago, Illinois
Eagles 33, Chicago 19

With Donovan McNabb enjoying a triumphant homecoming, the Eagles routed the Chicago Bears, 33–19, and advanced to the NFC Championship game for the first time in 21 years.

McNabb, who attended Chicago's Mount Carmel High School, threw for 262 yards and two touchdowns and ran for another score as the Eagles rolled up 336 yards on one of the NFL's top defenses.

"Coming back home and seeing family and friends yesterday, I knew today I just had to be focused on my job, and that was going out, playing well, and leading this team," McNabb said. "We've taken it one step farther than we did last year."

David Akers kicked four field goals to tie an Eagles playoff record. His 46-yarder in the fourth quarter was the longest in the club's playoff history.

With the Eagles trailing, 7–6, McNabb directed an 11-play, 69-yard drive, climaxed by a 13-yard touchdown pass to Cecil Martin just 25 seconds before halftime.

After a Chicago touchdown, McNabb responded by throwing a six-yard scoring pass to Duce Staley. Jeff Thomason set up the touchdown by catching a short pass from McNabb, hurdling a would-be tackler, and running 30 yards to convert a third and 14 into a first down at the Bears' 10.

"I think Donovan showed that in the biggest games that's what he's all about," said Eagles coach Andy Reid. "That's all part of his journey."

A 38-yard field goal by Paul Edinger cut the Eagles' lead to 20–17 early in the fourth quarter. After Akers drilled a 40-yard field goal, teammate Tim Hauck forced a fumble on the ensuing kickoff that was recovered by Quinton Caver. Akers then kicked a 46-yard three-pointer.

An interception by Philadelphia's Rashard Cook, a former Chicago draft choice, set up McNabb's five-yard TD run later in the quarter.

"McNabb just killed us," said Bears tackle Blake Brockermeyer. "We had him wrapped up many different times, and the guy just made plays."

The Eagles' defense held Chicago running back Anthony Thomas, the NFL's Offensive Rookie of the Year, to 36 yards on 15 carries. Hugh Douglas knocked Bears quarterback Jim Miller out of the game with a crushing block after an interception by Damon Moore.

NFC CHAMPIONSHIP GAME
January 27, 2002
Edward Jones Dome, St. Louis, Missouri
St. Louis 29, Eagles 24

The Eagles came within inches—and one good offensive drive—of pulling off the upset, but in the end they were unable to stop All-Pro running back Marshall Faulk as the St. Louis Rams dominated the second half for a 29–24 victory.

"We were one drive, one play away from being in the Super Bowl," owner Jeffrey Lurie said.

The Eagles took a 17–13 halftime lead before the heavily favored Rams took charge in the third quarter and held on to clinch their second Super Bowl appearance in three years.

"They ran the ball a lot more than they usually do," defensive end Hugh Douglas said after Faulk rushed for 159 yards and two touchdowns. "They ran with a lot of determination. No excuses. We couldn't get off the field."

The Eagles lost Correll Buckhalter with a sprained ankle after he gained 50 yards on six carries in the first half. Then two of their starters in the defensive secondary went down in the second half.

Troy Vincent, who suffered a pulled groin in the win over Chicago, was forced to leave the game in the third quarter with the Eagles clinging to a 17–16 lead. Safety Damon Moore was sidelined in the fourth quarter with a sprained left knee.

"My body was just getting worn out," Vincent said. "I was dragging my leg around, but it was getting heavier and heavier. I finally had to shut it down."

The Eagles fell behind three minutes into the game after McNabb fumbled on the second play from scrimmage. Five plays later, Kurt Warner found Isaac Bruce with a five-yard scoring pass. It was the only touchdown pass of the day for Warner, who completed 22 of 33 attempts for 212 yards.

The teams traded field goals, with David Akers connecting from 46 yards and Jeff Wilkins, of the Rams, answering from 27 yards out.

The Eagles dominated the second quarter. Buckhalter broke loose for 31 yards to set up a one-yard scoring plunge by Duce Staley. Then, after Wilkins hit a 39-yard field goal, McNabb clicked with the two-minute offense and found Todd Pinkston with a 12-yard scoring pass with 46 seconds left before halftime.

After that, the Rams took over.

St. Louis controlled the ball for 18 of the first 23 minutes of the second half as the Eagles ran five plays in the third quarter. As the Eagles gained only 17 yards on three possessions, the Rams mounted two time-consuming drives and scored nine points to take a 22–17 lead.

Faulk rushed for 27 yards on the Rams' first seven plays from scrimmage to set up a 41-yard field goal by Wilkins. Then after the Eagles went three and out, Warner drove the Rams to a pair of touchdowns, both scored by Faulk on one-yard plunges.

"We prided ourselves all year long on keeping teams out of the end zone," linebacker Jeremiah Trotter said. "We prided ourselves on not giving up the big plays and coming up with turnovers. We prided ourselves on getting to the quarterback. We didn't do any of those things today."

Although a two-point conversion failed after Faulk's first TD, the Rams led, 29–17 before the Eagles mounted a comeback with less than seven minutes left in the game.

Brian Mitchell started the rally with a 41-yard kickoff return to the Rams' 48. Facing a fourth and seven, McNabb hit Chad Lewis for 11 yards and a first down. A few plays later, McNabb barreled into the end zone to cut the Rams' lead to 29–24 with 2:56 left.

The Eagles forced St. Louis's John Baker to punt. Defensive end N. D. Kalu broke through and just missed getting his hands on the ball. "I don't know how I could have missed it," Kalu said.

The Eagles had one last chance to win the game. They got the ball on their own 45-yard line with 2:20 left. On third and seven, Freddie Mitchell couldn't hold on to a high pass from McNabb. On fourth down, Rams cornerback Aeneas Williams jumped in front of Mitchell and picked off McNabb's pass to end the Eagles' Super Bowl hopes.

"We lost an opportunity," coach Andy Reid said. "At the same time, this was a step forward. You can look at it optimistically or pessimistically. I see it very positively from where I'm sitting."

After the game, McNabb stood near the tunnel to the Eagles' locker room and watched the Rams celebrate their NFC championship. "I wanted to feel the excitement," he said. "I wanted to see what it was like. We were so close. A couple of plays and it could have been us out there."

NFC DIVISIONAL PLAYOFF
January 11, 2003
Veterans Stadium, Philadelphia
Eagles 20, Atlanta 6

With Donovan McNabb returning to action for the first time since breaking his ankle against Arizona on November 17 and the defense playing another strong game, the Eagles defeated Atlanta, 20–6, to advance to the NFC Championship Game for the second straight year.

McNabb completed 20 of 30 passes for 247 yards and one touchdown. He dispelled any concerns about his mobility when he raced out of the pocket for a 19-yard gain on the second play from scrimmage.

"I always said I could move," McNabb said. "Everybody else said I couldn't."

Cornerback Bobby Taylor provided all the scoring the Eagles needed midway through the first quarter when he inter-

Cornerback Bobby Taylor played in a club-record 12 postseason games. His 39-yard interception return for a touchdown helped the Eagles to an NFC Divisional playoff win over Atlanta in January 2003.

cepted a Michael Vick pass and returned it for a 39-yard touchdown. It was the longest interception return of his career.

David Akers kicked field goals of 39 and 34 yards to help the Eagles take a 13–6 halftime lead. He later missed a 51-yard attempt when the ball hit the upright, but he still finished the game as the club's all-time postseason leader in points scored, field goals, and extra points.

The Eagles' lone offensive touchdown came when coach Andy Reid went for a first down on a fourth and one at the Falcon 35 with 6:34 left in the game. McNabb hit James Thrash for what appeared to be a 10-yard completion, but Thrash eluded Atlanta cornerback Ray Buchanan and raced the final 25 yards into the end zone.

The Eagles did not commit a turnover in a playoff game for the first time in the club's history.

"I got rid of a little bit of rust," McNabb said. "There were some plays in the game that I felt I could have made better plays with. That's something I can learn from."

The defense did an excellent job containing Vick, sacking the Atlanta quarterback three times, intercepting him twice, and holding him to 30 yards rushing. Brian Dawkins had the other interception in the fourth quarter.

NFC CHAMPIONSHIP GAME
January 19, 2003
Veterans Stadium, Philadelphia
Tampa Bay 27, Eagles 10

For the second straight year, the Eagles missed a chance to go to the Super Bowl. Only this time the loss hurt considerably more because the Eagles were heavily favored and had home-field advantage in the final game at Veterans Stadium.

Tampa Bay played its best game of the year and took advantage of the Eagles' mistakes. The Buccaneers turned two big plays into a 27–10 win that avenged an earlier 20–10 loss to the Eagles.

"For us to play this bad for a Super Bowl appearance, I'm in disbelief," said defensive end N. D. Kalu. "I'm more in shock than upset. I said last week if we did not win this game, the season was a failure. We did this last year. We did not improve. We failed."

The game started auspiciously for the Eagles when Brian Mitchell returned the opening kickoff 70 yards to the Tampa Bay 26. Two plays later, Duce Staley scored from the 20, and the Eagles led 7–0 just 52 seconds into the game.

After that, the Buccaneers, coached by former Eagles assistant Jon Gruden, shut down the Philadelphia offense. Tampa Bay got three points back on the ensuing drive when Martin Gramatica hit a 48-yard field goal.

Later in the quarter Bobby Taylor intercepted a Brad Johnson pass, but the Eagles were unable to move the ball. Instead, punter Lee Johnson put a pooch punt against the wind inside the Tampa Bay five-yard line.

The Buccaneers got some breathing room and faced a third and two at their own 24. Brad Johnson and Joe Jurevicius teamed up on a pass play designed for a quick first down over the middle. Instead, it turned into a 71-yard gain as Jurevicius raced down the sideline to the Eagles' five. Two plays later, Mike Alstott plunged over from the one.

The Eagles were unable to get pressure on Johnson, who completed 20 of 33 passes for 259 yards. He kept the defense off balance by spreading the ball around with a quick release and short, crisp passes to eight different receivers.

"We didn't get enough pressure, and they did a good job protecting him," Reid said. "That's something you have to do with him. He's a good quarterback."

The Buccaneers frequently ran a no-huddle offense to confuse the Eagles. "They caught us off guard with the hurry-up," defensive end Brandon Whiting said. "That's the kind of thing you can't really prepare for. You either adjust to it or you don't."

The Eagles tied the game at 10 on David Akers' 30-yard field goal in the second quarter. The Buccaneers went ahead for good on a nine-yard scoring pass from Johnson to Keyshawn Johnson to climax a 12-play, 80-yard drive.

The Eagles moved into field-goal range just before halftime. But Simeon Rice sacked Donovan McNabb, his former high school teammate, and forced a fumble that Rice recovered.

The Eagles had excellent field position throughout the first half—with drives starting on their own 40, their own 44, the Tampa Bay 46, and the Tampa Bay 38—but could do no better than three points.

"It's my responsibility for us to perform better in this game, and I didn't get that part done," Reid said. "I could have done a better job, and that's where it has to start."

Late in the third quarter the Eagles were called for a 15-yard penalty for interfering with the opportunity to make a fair catch on a punt. After the Buccaneers got the ball back at midfield, Gramatica kicked a 27-yard field goal to extend the lead to 20–10.

The Eagles drove to the Tampa Bay 10 and had a first and goal with less than 4:00 to play. But Ronde Barber stepped in front of Eagles wide receiver Antonio Freeman, picked off McNabb's pass, and raced 92 yards for the clinching touchdown.

McNabb, who lost two fumbles, was unable to escape the pocket all day. He completed 26 of 49 passes for 243 yards and afterward took the blame for one of the most devastating losses in Eagles history.

"I just played poorly," McNabb said. "There were opportunities to make plays. Me, being the quarterback and the leader of the team, I have to make them. This being the last game here at the Vet, we wanted to make it special. Obviously, it didn't happen that way."

"You couldn't have a better stage set," Troy Vincent said. "The fans were ready. The city was ready. The atmosphere was right. For us to lose this football game—this is a tough one to swallow."

NFC DIVISIONAL PLAYOFF
January 11, 2004
Lincoln Financial Field, Philadelphia
Eagles 20, Green Bay 17 (OT)

The Eagles turned the first playoff game at Lincoln Financial Field into an all-time classic. They were down 14 points in the first quarter and they were down three points in the closing seconds, yet they squeezed out a 20–17 overtime win over Green Bay to move into the NFC Championship Game for the third straight year.

Freddie Mitchell's spectacular 28-yard reception on fourth and 26 kept the Eagles alive in their NFC Divisional playoff against Green Bay. With typical modesty, Mitchell suggested the city erect a statue of him and place it next to the Rocky statue on Pattison Avenue.

The Eagles played without Brian Westbrook, their explosive running back and kick returner, who suffered a torn tendon in his left arm in the final regular-season game.

David Akers kicked a 31-yard field goal for the game winner after Brian Dawkins intercepted a pass from Brett Farve on the Packers' first play in overtime.

The Eagles pulled off one of the most remarkable plays in the franchise's history—a season-saving 28-yard completion from Donovan McNabb to Freddie Mitchell on a fourth-and-26 situation—which allowed Akers to kick a 37-yard field goal to send the game into overtime.

"Fourth and 26 and Freddie comes up with a humongous play," said tight end Chad Lewis. "We've got a team full of warriors who just want to battle."

Despite being sacked eight times, McNabb set a NFL playoff record for quarterbacks by gaining 107 yards on 11 rushing attempts. He also threw for 248 yards and two touchdowns.

The Eagles fell behind early when Favre threw touchdown passes of 40 and 17 yards to Robert Ferguson, the first one set up by a McNabb fumble. Meanwhile, the Eagles were going three and out on their first two possessions and committing a turnover on their third.

McNabb pulled the Eagles closer with a 77-yard, six-play drive that ended with a seven-yard touchdown to Duce Staley.

Green Bay responded by driving to a first and goal at the four. But the Eagles came up with one of their biggest defensive plays of the season after they forced the Packers into a fourth and goal from the one. Mark Simoneau and Jerome McDougle stopped Ahman Green short of the goal line.

The Eagles tied it in the fourth quarter when McNabb made a brilliant scramble and 12-yard pass to Todd Pinkston in the corner of the end zone. Ryan Longwell kicked a 21-yard field goal to put Green Bay back in the lead after the Eagles defense stopped a Packers drive on the five. That set the stage for the closing heroics by McNabb and Mitchell with 1:12 left in regulation.

"It was just a great play by Freddie," McNabb said.

"I just tried to beat my man and go deep," Mitchell explained. "Donovan read the play perfectly."

"I don't know how to explain it," Reid said. "I've said it before that this is a unique group, and they all thought that it was going to get done there. The odds were pretty high, but it shows how confident this bunch is and how they keep battling."

NFC CHAMPIONSHIP GAME
January 18, 2004
Lincoln Financial Field, Philadelphia
Carolina 14, Eagles 3

For the third straight year, the Eagles were eliminated in the NFC Championship game.

This time it was the Carolina Panthers who took advantage of four pass interceptions—three by rookie cornerback Ricky Manning, Jr.—and an injury to Donovan McNabb to defeat the Eagles, 14–3, and earn their first Super Bowl berth.

McNabb, who was sacked four times, suffered a torn rib cartilage on a late hit by linebacker Greg Favors in the second quarter. McNabb missed one play and returned but struggled until he was replaced by Koy Detmer in the fourth quarter.

"It hurt to breathe," McNabb said. "I was still willing to go in there. You want to be out there with your teammates."

"I felt we needed to take him out," coach Andy Reid said. "Donovan would have continued to play until he passed out."

When McNabb was injured, the Eagles were trailing 7–0 on a 24-yard touchdown pass from Jake Delhomme to Muhsin Muhammad. They eventually got a 41-yard field goal from David Akers on the series in which McNabb was injured.

That was the end of Philadelphia's scoring. Later in the second quarter, McNabb threw the first of three interceptions. He was picked off again after the Eagles took the second-half kickoff and drove to Carolina's 18.

Later in the period, James Thrash was hit hard by Carolina's Mike Minter after apparently catching a McNabb pass. The ball popped into the hands of Manning, who returned it to the Eagles' 37. Five plays later, DeShaun Foster broke three tackles to score on a one-yard run and increase Carolina's lead to 14–3.

"You get into a championship game, and you've got to make plays when you have the opportunity," Reid said. "I'm sure there are a handful of plays we'd like to have back."

McNabb played two more series before being replaced by Detmer, who drove the Eagles to the 11-yard line with 5:22 left. But Carolina linebacker Dan Morgan intercepted Detmer's pass to end the Eagles' season and make them the first team ever to lose back-to-back conference championship games at home.

"We emptied our tank to get here," linebacker Ike Reese said. "I thought we played defensively a little better than last week. It's tough to say they're the better team. But they're going to the Super Bowl and we're not."

NFC DIVISIONAL PLAYOFF
January 16, 2005
Lincoln Financial Field, Philadelphia
Eagles 27, Minnesota 14

Even though most of their starters hadn't played for nearly a month, the Eagles had no trouble with the Minnesota Vikings, building a 14-point lead less than a minute into the second quarter and coasting to a 27–14 victory.

"I guess we weren't too rusty," said quarterback Donovan McNabb, after completing 21 of 33 passes for 286 yards and two touchdowns. McNabb threw another scoring pass, but L. J. Smith bobbled the ball after making a catch and Freddie Mitchell recovered the fumble in the end zone.

McNabb and running back Brian Westbrook were among a group of starters who sat out most of the final two regular-season games against St. Louis and Cincinnati. After Terrell

Linebacker Ike Reese intercepted a Daunte Culpepper pass in the NFC Divisional playoff win over Minnesota.

Owens was injured against Dallas on December 19, coach Andy Reid took no chances and rested a number of key players for the balance of the regular season.

Westbrook rolled up 117 total yards against the Vikings, 70 of them on the ground. He caught a seven-yard touchdown pass from McNabb early in the second quarter to climax a 92-yard, seven-play drive.

Mitchell enjoyed the best postseason game of his four-year NFL career: five catches for 65 yards and two touchdowns. His two-yard TD reception at 6:18 of the first quarter capped a 53-yard drive and put the Eagles ahead to stay.

"I want to say 'Hi' to all my new friends out there, those people who doubted me and the receivers," Mitchell said.

Freddie was one of the receivers counted on to fill the void left by the loss of Owens. They performed well against the Vikings. In addition to Mitchell and Westbrook, L. J. Smith caught four passes for 52 yards, Todd Pinkston had three catches for 46 yards, and Greg Lewis had two receptions for 64 yards, with 52 of them coming on a brilliant stop-and-go pattern that set up Westbrook's touchdown.

"We stayed together as a group," Pinkston said. "I don't think it was a matter of stepping up, but just continuing to do what we can do."

David Akers added some insurance with field goals of 23 and 21 yards in the fourth quarter.

The Eagles took advantage of numerous Viking mistakes. Minnesota committed several costly defensive penalties, including three pass-interference calls totaling 70 yards.

Quarterback Daunte Culpepper, who threw only 11 interceptions during the regular season, had two passes picked off in the third quarter. Ike Reese intercepted one, Jeremiah Trotter the other.

NFC CHAMPIONSHIP GAME
January 23, 2005
Lincoln Financial Field, Philadelphia
Eagles 27, Atlanta 10

Four years of frustration finally ended for the Eagles, who defeated the Atlanta Falcons, 27–10, to earn their first Super Bowl trip in 24 years.

Leading only 14–10 at the half, the Eagles erased the memory of three straight losses in the NFC Championship game by dominating play after intermission on a bitterly cold day with a wind chill hovering around zero.

A foot of snow fell in Philadelphia the day before, but the playing field was in excellent shape as Donovan McNabb ignored the 35-mile-per-hour wind gusts to pass for 180 yards and two touchdowns.

"It's just a great feeling for the city of Philadelphia," McNabb said as fireworks erupted over Lincoln Financial Field. "Obviously we know what happened in the last three years—being this close and never being able to pull it out."

With injured wide receiver Terrell Owens leading cheers from the sidelines, Brian Westbrook gained 96 yards on 16 carries and caught five passes for another 39 yards as the Eagles rolled up 156 yards on the ground.

Greg Lewis caught two passes for 65 yards, including a brilliant 45-yard reception on which he fought off a defender and carried the ball to the four-yard line in the second quarter. His

Having a healthy Brian Westbrook (36) was a key to the Eagles finally winning the NFC title. He had 117 total yards and one touchdown in the Divisional playoff win over Minnesota. He had 135 yards, including a game-high 96 rushing, in the conference championship game against Atlanta.

effort set up the first of two touchdown catches by Chad Lewis, who managed to keep both feet inbounds in the corner of the end zone after reaching high to grab a three-yard pass from McNabb.

It was a bittersweet day for Lewis, who suffered a season-ending Lisfranc sprain to his left foot while making his second touchdown catch with 3:21 left in the game.

The timing couldn't have been worse for Lewis, a seven-year veteran who survived two trips to the waiver wire and developed into a three-time Pro Bowl player with the Eagles. He was replaced on the Super Bowl roster by Jeff Thomason, who spent the final three years of his ten-year NFL career with the Eagles before being released in 2002.

Thomason caught ten passes for 128 yards and two touchdowns with the Eagles in 2002, but was released the next year when L. J. Smith was drafted. He took a job with a construction company, but had to ask for time off to rejoin the Eagles for the two weeks leading up to Super Bowl XXXIX.

Lewis's touchdown set off a wild celebration among Eagles fans, who had waited ever since the classic win over Dallas in the 1980 NFC Championship game that sent the team to its first Super Bowl.

Chanting "Super Bowl! Super Bowl!" the fans cheered as linebacker Ike Reese and defensive tackle Corey Simon showered coach Andy Reid with Gatorade.

"You know it was great," Reid said. "I think it makes it even more worthwhile that we had to do it four times to get over the hump. This team has great personality. Everybody here in Philadelphia loves them."

The defense, led by Derrick Burgess, Hollis Thomas, and Jevon Kearse, sacked elusive Atlanta quarterback Michael Vick four times. It held him to 136 passing yards and only 26 rushing yards, his lowest offensive output of the season.

The Falcons were the NFL's top rushing team in the regular season, but they managed only 99 yards on the ground and 202 total yards. Burgess, playing the best game of his career, had two sacks and six tackles. Thomas and Kearse each had one sack, and Jeremiah Trotter added a team-high eight tackles.

"I'm gratified we won," said Burgess, who missed all but one game of the 2002 and 2003 seasons with injuries. He was sidelined again for the final month of the 2004 regular season after separating his sternum against Green Bay.

Brian Dawkins intercepted a pass by Vick in the third quarter to set up a 34-yard field goal by David Akers that put the Eagles ahead, 20–10. Akers had converted a 31-yarder in the opening drive of the second half, a score set up by Westbrook's running and receiving.

"Nobody thought we were able to run the ball," Westbrook said. "Nobody thought we had a running attack at all. We were able to run the ball efficiently as well as throw it downfield."

The Eagles established the running game midway through the first quarter when they drove 70 yards to score after they appeared to be stopped on downs. An illegal-use-of-the-hands penalty against Atlanta's DeAngelo Hall gave the Eagles a first down on their own 35-yard line.

Two plays later, Westbrook took advantage of great blocks by Jon Runyan and Artis Hicks and burst up the middle for 36 yards to the Atlanta 25. McNabb then hit L. J. Smith with a 21-yard pass, and Dorsey Levens scored on a four-yard run. Levens appeared stopped at the two, but he bounced off a defender to score.

SUPER BOWL XXXIX
February 6, 2005
Alltel Stadium, Jacksonville, Florida
New England 24, Eagles 21

Tom Brady, Deion Branch, and Terrell Owens turned in spectacular performances in Super Bowl XXXIX, but in the end, four turnovers were the difference as the Eagles failed in their bid to win the NFL's ultimate prize.

The Eagles were seven-point underdogs, but they pushed the New England Patriots to the limit before the defending champions held on for a 24–21 win. It was New England's third Super Bowl victory in four years. Working against an Eagles secondary that sent three starters to the Pro Bowl, Brady passed for two touchdowns, and Branch, who was voted the game's Most Valuable Player, caught 11 passes for 133 yards.

"We did a pretty good job against [Brady] in the first half," cornerback Lito Sheppard said. "In the second half, they spread us out more, ran some screens, and made some plays in the middle of the field. You can't let a team like this do that against you. We just didn't play to the best of our ability."

The same could be said for the Eagles offense, which was unable to run the ball against the Patriots, who shifted from a 3–4 defense to a 4–3 and even an occasional 2–5 look with extra linebackers filling the cutback lanes and limiting Brian Westbrook to 44 yards rushing. Half of those yards came on a meaningless carry at the end of the first half.

The Patriots also did a good job pressuring quarterback Donovan McNabb. They played man-to-man coverage on the outside, which allowed their linebackers to blitz on almost every passing situation. The result was McNabb taking four sacks and throwing a season-high three interceptions. Those mistakes outweighed his 30 completions (on 51 attempts) for 357 yards and three touchdown passes.

"I don't look at any of that," McNabb said, referring to his statistics. "I look at the three interceptions. This game could

have been a blowout [for the Eagles]. You take away those three interceptions and we're probably up two or three touchdowns. As the quarterback, you want to make sure you take care of the ball."

After the game, much of the focus was on the Eagles' failure to run a hurry-up offense in the final minutes when they were trying to make a comeback from a 10-point deficit. But the truth is, the Eagles really lost the game much earlier than that. As McNabb pointed out, they had opportunities to score in the first half and force the Patriots into the unfamiliar position of playing catch-up, but they failed to capitalize.

The first opportunity came when McNabb completed a 30-yard pass to Owens, who showed no ill effects of the fractured fibula and severe ankle sprain that he suffered six weeks earlier. Owens played against the advice of his surgeon, and he played brilliantly, finishing with nine receptions for 122 yards. His first big play gave the Eagles a first down on the New England eight-yard line. McNabb was sacked for a 16-yard loss

Donovan McNabb passed for 357 yards and three touchdowns, but he also threw three interceptions in the Super Bowl XXXIX loss to New England.

on the next play, then he threw an interception to Rodney Harrison that killed the threat.

On their next possession, the Eagles had excellent field position, but tight end L. J. Smith fumbled after catching a McNabb pass at the New England 38.

"Everybody knows the statistics," Owens said. "You can't win when you turn the ball over. We just made too many mistakes."

The Eagles did manage to score first on a nine-play, 81-yard drive, kept alive by a leaping 40-yard reception by Todd Pinkston. The touchdown came on a six-yard pass from McNabb to Smith.

The Patriots responded by driving 83 yards to the Eagles' four-yard line. On second and goal, Brady went back to pass, but dropped the football. Jevon Kearse pushed Brady aside and allowed defensive tackle Darwin Walker to recover for the Eagles.

Later in the second quarter, a 29-yard punt by Dirk Johnson gave New England the ball on the Eagles' 37. Brady finally settled into his big-game groove, completing five of six passes, the last one to David Givens in the end zone, tying the score 7–7 at halftime.

New England took the lead in the third quarter as Brady threw a touchdown pass to Mike Vrabel, the versatile linebacker who sometimes lines up as a second tight end on offense.

"They drove the ball right down the field," linebacker Jeremiah Trotter said. "They got us back on our heels. That's what happens when you're playing against a great team."

The Eagles tied the score, driving 74 yards on 10 plays with McNabb threading a 10-yard touchdown pass to Westbrook, slanting between two defenders in the end zone.

For the first time in Super Bowl history, the score was tied going into the fourth quarter, but the Patriots broke the deadlock on the third play of the period as Corey Dillon scored on a two-yard run. New England was moving the ball using a mixture of running plays and screens to burn the Eagles' blitz.

The Philadelphia offense did nothing on its next possession, so Johnson was forced to punt from his own 16. Brady took over at midfield and completed a 19-yard pass to Branch. A roughing the passer penalty on Corey Simon put the ball on the Eagles' 16. Six plays later, Adam Vinatieri kicked a 22-yard field goal to extend the New England lead to ten points.

When McNabb threw an interception to linebacker Tedy Bruschi on the next series, it appeared the game was over. But the Eagles defense forced a quick three-and-out, so McNabb and the offense got the ball back at their own 21 with 5:40 left on the clock.

To the surprise—and dismay—of Eagles fans in Alltel Stadium, coach Andy Reid did not go to a hurry-up offense. The Eagles huddled after every play and walked to the line of scrimmage. McNabb completed several short passes that ate up valuable time. They used 12 plays to gain just 49 yards. They ran only four plays from the 3:28 mark to the two-minute warning.

Fox broadcaster Troy Aikman said what most viewers were thinking: "The Eagles need to show a greater sense of urgency. They have to score twice."

The Eagles finally did score as McNabb hit Greg Lewis with a 30-yard touchdown pass, but by that time only 1:48 remained. Trailing by three points, Reid called for an onsides kick, which the Patriots recovered. They ran off three plays and forced the Eagles to use their remaining timeouts, so when McNabb got the ball back, there were only 46 seconds left and he was starting at his own four-yard line. Three plays later, McNabb threw his final interception, this one to Harrison, his second of the game.

Asked to explain his clock management, Reid offered a cryptic nonanswer. "Well, we were trying to hurry up," he said. "It was the way things worked out."

Tackle Jon Runyan said the Eagles were aware of the clock, but they wanted to avoid rushing and making another costly error. "If you get too hurry-up, you end up making mistakes," he said. "We had plenty of time."

In the days following the game, several Eagles said McNabb was sick almost to the point of vomiting on the final touchdown drive. On Comcast SportsNet, center Hank Fraley said McNabb "could hardly call the plays, that's how exhausted he was. One play had to be called by Freddie Mitchell because Donovan was mumbling because he was almost puking."

McNabb denied the story. Reid, likewise, said it was not an issue, although the coach did acknowledge that McNabb took a big hit from Bruschi on that scoring drive and could have been feeling the effects. Still, Reid said, it had no bearing on how the drive was conducted or how McNabb played in the final minutes.

Things quieted down until April, when Owens began squabbling with the Eagles in an effort to have his contract renegotiated. At that time, Owens told an ESPN interviewer, "I wasn't the one who got tired at the end of the Super Bowl." It was an obvious reference to McNabb.

When the Eagles reported to their spring minicamp, McNabb was emphatic in his response: "I wasn't tired. Just to set the record straight on any comments that were made, I was not tired."

Clearly annoyed by the lingering controversy, McNabb said, "If you make mistakes in the game, then come out and say it and be a man. But don't try to throw names or guys under the bus to better yourself. You've never heard me say any names in any situation. I'm the guy to be professional and a man about things."

9

The Hall of Fame

THERE ARE 17 busts in the Pro Football Hall of Fame in Canton, Ohio, representing men who have at least some connection to the Philadelphia Eagles.

Six earned their place in Canton due primarily to their service with the Eagles: center-linebacker Chuck Bednarik, offensive tackle Bob Brown, flanker Tommy McDonald, coach Earle (Greasy) Neale, end Pete Pihos, and halfback Steve Van Buren.

Other enshrinees, such as quarterbacks Norm Van Brocklin and Sonny Jurgensen, halfback Ollie Matson, center Jim Ringo, and linebacker Alex Wojciechowicz, played well for the Eagles but were voted into the Hall of Fame mainly for what they did with other NFL teams.

There is a third group that consists of players who were great earlier in their careers but played minor roles with the Eagles. They are tight end Mike Ditka, end Bill Hewitt, and wide receiver James Lofton.

Sid Gillman was a valuable offensive assistant on Dick Vermeil's Super Bowl coaching staff, but he earned his spot in the Hall for his work as a head coach with the Los Angeles Rams and San Diego Chargers. Bert Bell was honored primarily for his visionary leadership as NFL Commissioner from 1946 until his death in 1959. Marv Levy spent one year as the Eagles special teams coach but he won his place in Canton for his success as head coach of the Buffalo Bills.

CHUCK BEDNARIK
Center-Linebacker

College: Pennsylvania • **Years with the Eagles:** 1949–62 • **Birthplace:** Bethlehem, Pennsylvania • **Born:** May 1, 1925 • **Elected:** 1967

In Philadelphia, the name Chuck Bednarik is synonymous with football. A native of Bethlehem, Bednarik earned All-America honors at the University of Pennsylvania and played a record 14 seasons with the Eagles. For much of his career, Bednarik played both ways, center on offense, linebacker on defense. He also was one of the game's surest long snappers, so he handled those duties as well. He is best remembered for playing both ways for much of the 1960 championship season. At 35, Bednarik was the oldest player on the roster, and he began the season as the starting center. However, when Bob Pellegrini was injured in Week 5, coach Buck Shaw asked Bednarik to fill in at outside linebacker. The man known as "Concrete Charlie"

averaged more than 50 minutes a game for the rest of the season. His jarring tackle on Frank Gifford saved a crucial 17–10 win over New York and was selected as "The Greatest Hit of All Time" by NFL Films. Bednarik played all but two minutes of the championship game against Green Bay, and he preserved the Eagles 17–13 victory by tackling Jim Taylor at the eight-yard line on the final play. Bednarik was a true iron man, missing only three games in his pro career. He was chosen "Lineman of the Decade" in the 1950s. He was voted into eight Pro Bowls, more than any other Eagle, and he won Most Valuable Player honors in the 1954 game. He was inducted into the Pro Football Hall of Fame on August 5, 1967. His presenter was Earle (Greasy) Neale, his first coach with the Eagles.

BERT BELL
Owner–Head Coach

College: Pennsylvania • **Years with the Eagles:** 1933–40 • **Years in the NFL:** 1933–59 • **Birthplace:** Philadelphia, Pennsylvania • **Born:** February 25, 1895 • **Died:** October 11, 1959 • **Elected:** 1963

Bert Bell founded the Eagles franchise in 1933, buying the rights to the financially strapped Frankford Yellow Jackets for

Chuck Bednarik

Bert Bell

Bob Brown   Mike Ditka

much as five hours a day in the off-season. He could lift more than 400 pounds, but he was also nimble enough to skip rope like a bantamweight boxer. Hugh Brown of the *Philadelphia Bulletin* described Brown as "a splendid specimen of young manhood. His shoulders, without any pads, mind you, are wider than a water buffalo's." Brown was a proud man who set high standards. In a 1967 interview, Brown said, "I don't ever want to be considered just another tackle in this league. You know the way intelligent football people talk. Somebody mentions blockers, and Jim Parker [Baltimore Hall of Famer] is sure to be talked about. I want them to say, 'What about Bob Brown?' I want to become a household word." He achieved that level of recognition, despite suffering a severe knee injury in 1967. He was traded to the Los Angeles Rams in 1969 and finished his career with the Oakland Raiders in 1973. He was named to the NFL's All-Decade team for the 1960s. He was inducted into the Pro Football Hall of Fame on August 8, 2004. His presenter was his son, Robert, Jr.

MIKE DITKA
Tight End

College: Pittsburgh • **Years with the Eagles:** 1967–68 • **Years in the NFL:** 1961–72 • **Birthplace:** Carnegie, Pennsylvania • **Born:** October 18, 1939 • **Elected:** 1988

Mike Ditka was the first tight end voted into the Pro Football Hall of Fame, a fitting tribute to a great career. But when Ditka looks back on his 12 seasons in the NFL, he would just as soon forget the two years he spent in Philadelphia. Injuries and a falling out with coach Joe Kuharich resulted in a brief, unhappy

Chuck Bednarik (60) tries to break up a pass in the 1960 NFL championship game against Green Bay. Bednarik holds the Eagles record for interceptions by a linebacker with 20.

$4,500. He renamed the team the Eagles in honor of Franklin Roosevelt's National Recovery Act, which had the eagle as its symbol. Bell kept the team afloat through difficult times. The franchise lost $90,000 in its first four years, but Bell never wavered in his commitment to the Eagles and the National Football League. A former quarterback at the University of Pennsylvania, Bell coached the Eagles for five seasons (1936–40), but the team's 10–44–2 record indicated that his future was in the front office, not on the sidelines. His boundless energy and love for the game convinced the other club owners to appoint him commissioner of the league, succeeding Elmer Layden, in 1946. For 14 years, Bell ran the NFL from a small office in Bala Cynwyd. He spent so much time on the telephone that he was known as "The Walkie-Talkie Commissioner." A true visionary, Bell created the modern draft, which allows teams to select players in reverse order of the standings, thereby giving weaker teams first shot at the top college talent. He also is credited with selling the NFL to network television and creating the "sudden-death" overtime rule, which was first used to decide the 1958 championship game. On October 11, 1959, he suffered a fatal heart attack while attending an Eagles-Steelers game at Franklin Field. Bell was in the Pro Football Hall of Fame's first induction class in 1963. He was represented by Art Rooney, president of the Pittsburgh Steelers. His presenter was David McDonald, president of the United Steelworkers of America.

BOB BROWN
Offensive Tackle

College: Nebraska • **Years with the Eagles:** 1964–68 • **Years in the NFL:** 1964–73 • **Birthplace:** Cleveland, Ohio • **Born:** December 8, 1941 • **Elected:** 2004

Bob Brown was a dominating drive blocker who combined world-class strength with speed and agility. He was the Eagles' first-round draft pick in 1964, and in five years with Philadelphia he was voted into three Pro Bowls. Brown was one of the first NFL players to work extensively with weights, training as

Sid Gillman

Bill Hewitt

stay. Ditka was a three-time All-Pro with the Chicago Bears, but when he threatened to play out his option and sign with Houston of the American Football League, George Halas traded him to the Eagles for quarterback Jack Concannon. The Eagles expected Ditka to fill the void created by the retirement of Pete Retzlaff, but he was slowed by injuries. Foot surgery and a hamstring tear limited him to 26 catches in nine games in 1967. He was sidelined by knee surgery for part of the 1968 season and finished with 13 catches for 111 yards. During the 1968 season, Ditka was suspended by Kuharich for making critical comments about the team's management. Ditka was quoted as saying, "I was asked if I would come back to play for the Eagles under Kuharich next season. I replied, 'No, I wouldn't.'" After the season, Ditka was traded to Dallas for wide receiver David McDaniel, who did not even make the Eagles roster in 1969. Ditka enjoyed a resurgence in Dallas, playing four more seasons and catching a touchdown pass in Super Bowl VI. He later won another Super Bowl as head coach of the Bears in January 1986. He was inducted into the Pro Football Hall of Fame on July 30, 1988. His presenter was Ed O'Bradovich, his former Chicago teammate.

SID GILLMAN
Coach

College: Ohio State • **Years with the Eagles:** 1979–80, 1982, 1985 • **Years in the NFL (Head Coach):** 1955–69, 1971, 1973–74 • **Birthplace:** Minneapolis, Minnesota • **Born:** October 26, 1911 • **Died:** January 3, 2003 • **Elected:** 1983

Sid Gillman was one of pro football's keenest offensive minds. He was a head coach for 18 seasons, and, in that time, he won a conference championship with the Los Angeles Rams (1955), and four AFL Western Division titles and one AFL championship (1963) with the San Diego Chargers. Gillman's teams all had one thing in common: a prolific offense built around the forward pass. Gillman was 68 and retired in Palm Springs in 1979 when Dick Vermeil asked if he would join his staff

as quarterback coach. Gillman accepted, and his influence brought dramatic change to the Eagles' offense. Vermeil's approach was conservative and leaned heavily on the running game. Gillman put in more motion and spread formations. In 1980 the Eagles set six team records, including most points (384), most yards (5,519), and most passes completed (275) as they won the NFC championship and advanced to Super Bowl XV. "Sid was an innovator," Vermeil said. "He wasn't afraid to be different." Gillman went back to Palm Springs after the 1980 season, worn out by the 18-hour workdays demanded of the Vermeil staff. He returned twice more, in 1982 and again in 1985, to assist with the Eagles offense. "Meeting with Sid was like going to a football library," said quarterback Ron Jaworski. "Every day you learned something new." He was enshrined in the Pro Football Hall of Fame on July 30, 1983. His presenter was Joe Madro, a long-time coaching associate.

BILL HEWITT
End

College: Michigan • **Years with the Eagles:** 1937–39, 1943 • **Years in the NFL:** 1932–39, 1943 • **Birthplace:** Bay City, Michigan • **Born:** October 8, 1909 • **Died:** January 14, 1947 • **Elected:** 1971

Bill Hewitt is best remembered for his refusal to wear a helmet on the football field. He only began wearing one in 1939 when the NFL made it mandatory for all players. By then, Hewitt had played seven seasons and earned All-NFL honors four times. He played five seasons with the Chicago Bears as a two-way end. He was so quick off the ball that he was nicknamed "The Offside Kid" because opponents could not believe anyone could get across the line that quickly without jumping the count. But Hewitt did it, fairly, time and again. He was traded to the Eagles in 1937 and earned All-NFL honors again, becoming the first player to earn that distinction with two different teams. He led the team with 16 receptions for 197 yards and five touchdowns. He played two more years with the Eagles and retired in 1939. He came back in 1943 when the Eagles and Pittsburgh Steelers, their rosters depleted by the war, merged for one season as the Phil-Pitt Steagles. Following that season, Hewitt retired for good. Four years later, he died in a car crash. He was inducted into the Pro Football Hall of Fame on July 31, 1971. He was represented by his daughter, Mary Ellen Cocozza. His presenter was Upton Bell, son of former NFL Commissioner Bert Bell.

SONNY JURGENSEN
Quarterback

College: Duke • **Years with the Eagles:** 1957–63 • **Years in the NFL:** 1957–74 • **Birthplace:** Wilmington, North Carolina • **Born:** August 23, 1934 • **Elected:** 1983

Sonny Jurgensen was voted into the Pro Football Hall of Fame primarily for his 11 seasons with the Washington Redskins, but he had some shining moments in an Eagles uniform as well. He was a fourth-round draft pick in 1957, and as a rookie, he accounted for three of the team's victories in a 4–8 season. In

Sonny Jurgensen

Marv Levy

James Lofton

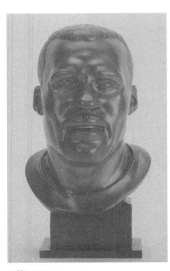

Ollie Matson

1958 the Eagles traded for Norm Van Brocklin, so Jurgensen rode the bench for the next three years. When Van Brocklin retired following the 1960 championship season, Jurgensen took over as the starting quarterback. Many experts predicted the Eagles would collapse without Van Brocklin, but Jurgensen performed brilliantly, leading the league in pass completions (235), yardage (3,723), and touchdown passes (32). Under his direction, the Eagles finished 10–4, one-half game behind New York in the Eastern Conference. However, Jurgensen suffered a shoulder injury in the Playoff Bowl following the 1961 season, and when the team slumped the next two years, he took an undue amount of blame. He was traded to the Redskins in 1964 in exchange for Norm Snead. He resurrected his career in Washington, leading the NFL in passing three times from 1966 through 1969. He was enshrined in the Pro Football Hall of Fame on July 30, 1983. His presenter was Redskins owner Edward Bennett Williams.

MARV LEVY
Coach

College: Coe College • **Years with the Eagles:** 1969 • **Years in the NFL (Head Coach):** 1978–82, 1986–97 • **Birthplace:** Chicago, Illinois • **Born:** August 3, 1925 • **Elected:** 2001

Most Eagles fans probably don't even remember Marv Levy's brief stay in Philadelphia. He was with the Eagles for one year, 1969, as special-teams coach under Jerry Williams. It was his first NFL coaching job. Prior to that, Levy was a college coach with stops at William and Mary, New Mexico, and California. He is a Phi Beta Kappa graduate of Coe College and earned a master's degree in English literature at Harvard. He left the Eagles to join George Allen's staff with the Los Angeles Rams, and when Allen went to Washington in 1971, Levy went with him. He became an NFL head coach in Kansas City in 1978, but he enjoyed his greatest success as head coach in Buffalo, where he won AFC Coach of the Year honors three times and led the Bills to four consecutive Super Bowls. When Levy retired in 1997, he was the 10th-winningest coach in NFL history. His presenter was former Buffalo general manager Bill Polian.

JAMES LOFTON
Wide Receiver

College: Stanford • **Years with the Eagles:** 1993 • **Years in the NFL:** 1978–93 • **Birthplace:** Ford Ord, California • **Born:** July 5, 1956 • **Elected:** 2003

When James Lofton retired following the 1993 season in Philadelphia, he held the NFL record with 14,004 receiving yards. He was the first player to score a touchdown in the 1970s, 1980s, and 1990s. He was a four-time All-Pro, who enjoyed his best seasons in Green Bay from 1978 through 1986. He also played four years with Buffalo and appeared in two Super Bowls. The Eagles acquired him early in the 1993 season when Fred Barnett was injured. Lofton was well past his peak at age 37. He appeared in nine games with the Eagles and caught 13 passes for 167 yards. He was enshrined in the Pro Football Hall of Fame on August 4, 2003. His presenter was his son, David.

OLLIE MATSON
Halfback

College: San Francisco • **Years with the Eagles:** 1964–66 • **Years in the NFL:** 1952–66 • **Birthplace:** Trinity, Texas • **Born:** May 1, 1930 • **Elected:** 1972

In 1959 the Los Angeles Rams traded nine players to the Chicago Cardinals to acquire Ollie Matson, a 6–2, 220-pound halfback with world-class speed. Matson won a bronze medal in the 400 meters at the 1952 Olympic Games in Helsinki, Finland. He was the Cardinals' first-round draft pick that year, and he shared rookie of the year honors with Hugh McElhenny of the San Francisco 49ers. He played six seasons with the Cardinals, four with the Rams, and one with Detroit before the Eagles acquired him in a 1964 trade. Matson was 34 and coming off his poorest season (13 rushing attempts for 20 yards), but Joe Kuharich coached Matson during his All-America career at the University of San Francisco, and he believed the old pro had something left. Matson proved him right, rushing for 404 yards and scoring five touchdowns in 1964. In his final season, 1966, he came off the bench to score the winning touchdown in a driving rainstorm as the Eagles defeated the 49ers, 35–34, at Kezar Stadium. "Ollie Matson is the finest football player I've ever seen or coached," Kuharich said. Matson was enshrined in the Pro Football Hall of Fame on July 29, 1972. Kuharich was his presenter.

TOMMY McDONALD
Flanker

College: Oklahoma • **Years with the Eagles:** 1957–63 • **Years in the NFL:** 1957–68 • **Birthplace:** Roy, New Mexico • **Born:** July 26, 1934 • **Elected:** 1998

Tommy McDonald was a spectacular playmaker who overcame his lack of size with determination and acrobatic daring. An All-America halfback at Oklahoma, who helped the Sooners compile a 47-game winning streak, McDonald was a third-round selection in the 1957 draft. He found a home at the flanker position, and with his blazing speed and sure hands, he became one of the most lethal receivers of the 1960s. He scored 56 touchdowns in 63 games from 1958 through 1962. In 1960, McDonald scored 13 touchdowns on just 39 receptions. He climaxed that season by pulling in a touchdown pass from Norm Van Brocklin as the Eagles defeated Green Bay, 17–13, in the NFL championship game. In 1961, McDonald teamed with Sonny Jurgensen for 64 completions, 1,144 yards, and 13 touchdowns. Both the yardage and touchdown totals led the league. The following year, McDonald caught 58 passes for 1,146 yards, a 19.8-yard average, and 10 touchdowns. "Pound for pound, Tommy is the toughest player I ever faced," said Jimmy Johnson, the Hall of Fame cornerback who played 16 seasons for San Francisco. "I covered all the top receivers, but he was the one who gave me the most trouble." His 1964 trade to Dallas was one of the most unpopular deals in Eagles history. When he retired following the 1968 season, McDonald

Tommy McDonald   Earle (Greasy) Neale

ranked sixth all-time in receptions (495), fourth in receiving yards (8,410), and second only to Don Hutson in touchdown catches (84). He was enshrined in the Pro Football Hall of Fame on August 1, 1998. His presenter was Ray Didinger, a senior producer for NFL Films.

EARLE (GREASY) NEALE
Coach

College: West Virginia Wesleyan • **Years with the Eagles:** 1941–50 • **Birthplace:** Parkersburg, West Virginia • **Born:** November 5, 1891 • **Died:** November 2, 1973 • **Elected:** 1969

The Eagles were a losing organization until owner Lex Thomson hired Earle (Greasy) Neale as coach in 1941. By his th

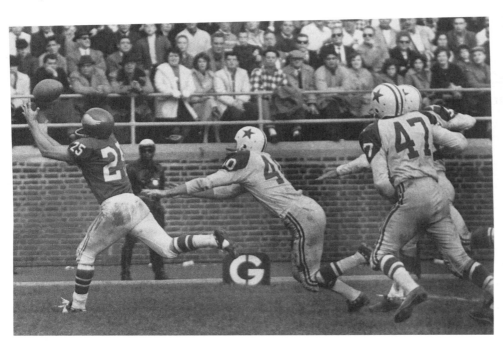

Tommy McDonald, scoring her against Dallas, was the NFL lea in receiving yards (4,540) and touchdown catches (55) in th five-year period from 1958 through 1962.

season, Neale had molded the Eagles into a winner, and by the end of the decade, he had built them into a powerhouse. Under Neale, the Eagles won three consecutive Eastern Division titles and back-to-back NFL championships in 1948–49. In the two championship seasons, the Eagles won 22 games, lost only three, and tied one. Neale was an innovator who put in the T-formation offense and pioneered a 5–2 defensive front that became known as "the Eagle defense." In his youth, Neale played for Jim Thorpe's Canton Bulldogs and coached Washington and Jefferson College to the 1922 Rose Bowl. He also played professional baseball for the Cincinnati Reds and batted .357 in the 1919 World Series against the Chicago White Sox. He played 22 games as an outfielder for the Phillies in 1921. He was inducted into the Pro Football Hall of Fame on September 13, 1969. His presenter was Chuck Bednarik, who began his pro career under Neale as a rookie on the 1949 Eagles.

PETE PIHOS
End

College: Indiana • **Years with the Eagles:** 1947–55 • **Birthplace:** Orlando, Florida • **Born:** October 22, 1923 • **Elected:** 1970

It was no coincidence the Eagles became a championship team when Pete Pihos joined them in 1947. At 6–1 and 210 pounds, Pihos was a rugged competitor capable of winning games on both sides of the ball. He was a six-time All-Pro choice as an offensive end. He also made All-Pro on defense in 1952. Known as "The Golden Greek," Pihos earned a battlefield commission with the U.S. Army in World War II. He was 24 when he joined the Eagles after completing his military service. In 1948, Pihos had 11 touchdown catches in a 12-game season. In 1953 he became the first Eagles receiver to reach the 1,000-yard plateau when he caught 63 passes for 1,049 yards and ten touchdowns. Pihos led the league in receiving each of

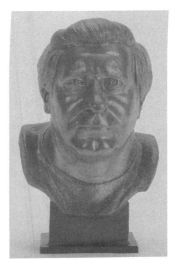

Pete Pihos   Jim Ringo

his last three seasons (1953–55). He blocked a punt to set up the first touchdown in the Eagles' 21–0 Eastern Division playoff win over Pittsburgh in 1947. He scored the first touchdown in the Eagles' 14–0 win over Los Angeles in the 1949 championship game. "Pihos is like a bull," coach Greasy Neale said. "When he gets his hands on the ball, there isn't much a defense can do. He just runs over people." Pihos missed only one game in nine seasons with the Eagles. He was enshrined in the Pro Football Hall of Fame on August 8, 1970. His presenter was Howard Brown, a former teammate at the University of Indiana.

JIM RINGO
Center

College: Syracuse • **Years with the Eagles:** 1964–67 • **Years in the NFL:** 1953–67 • **Birthplace:** Orange, New Jersey • **Born:** November 21, 1931 • **Elected:** 1981

Jim Ringo was 32 when Vince Lombardi traded him from Green Bay to Philadelphia along with fullback Earl Gros for a young linebacker named Lee Roy Caffey. At 6–1 and 235 pounds, Ringo was small for a center, and while he had a great career with the Packers, appearing in seven Pro Bowls in 11 seasons, he was thought to be too old and too battered to help the Eagles. Instead, Ringo started every game for four seasons with the Eagles, and he was voted into three more Pro Bowls. In 1964 he played through bronchial pneumonia, and in 1966 he played despite a painful knee injury. He set an NFL record by starting 182 consecutive games, a streak that ended with his retirement following the 1967 season. "I really wanted that record," Ringo said. "After all, that's the only way a center can be remembered." Ringo was a superb technician with good agility who could block effectively inside and also get downfield to block on sweeps and screens. After he retired, Ringo went into coaching. He was head coach of the Buffalo Bills in 1976–77. He was inducted into the Pro Football Hall of Fame on August 1, 1981. His presenter was Willard "Whiz" Rinehart, his coach at Phillipsburg (New Jersey) High School.

Pete Pihos signs an autograph for a young fan during an Eagles Alumni gathering at Veterans Stadium.

Norm Van Brocklin   Steve Van Buren   Alex Wojciechowicz

NORM VAN BROCKLIN
Quarterback

College: Oregon • **Years with the Eagles:** 1958–60 • **Years in the NFL:** 1949–60 • **Birthplace:** Eagle Butte, South Dakota • **Born:** March 15, 1926 • **Died:** May 2, 1983 • **Elected:** 1971

Norm Van Brocklin led the Los Angeles Rams to the 1951 NFL championship and set a league record by passing for 554 yards in a single game against the New York Yanks, but he considered his 1960 season in Philadelphia his ultimate achievement. That was the year Van Brocklin led the Eagles to a 10–2 regular season mark and a 17–13 win over the Green

Steve Van Buren led the NFL in rushing yardage and rushing touchdowns each season from 1947 through 1949.

Bay Packers in the championship game. The Eagles acquired Van Brocklin in a 1958 trade with the Rams, and the team won only two games that season. But with the fiery Dutchman—or "Dutch" as he was called—providing the leadership, the Eagles won seven games the following year and won it all the year after that. Van Brocklin was voted the NFL's Most Valuable Player for the 1960 season as he passed for 2,471 yards and 24 touchdowns. He also was named MVP of the championship game. "We could have replaced anyone else on the team, but not Van Brocklin," said Tommy McDonald, who caught a touchdown pass from Van Brocklin in the title game against Green Bay. "You could take me away, you could take [Chuck] Bednarik away, but you couldn't take Dutch away. The whole thing would've fallen apart." Van Brocklin retired after the championship win over Green Bay. He went on to serve as head coach in Minnesota (1961–66) and Atlanta (1968–74). He was enshrined in the Pro Football Hall of Fame on July 31, 1971. His presenter was Rankin Smith, president of the Atlanta Falcons.

STEVE VAN BUREN
Halfback

College: LSU • **Years with the Eagles:** 1944–51 • **Birthplace:** La Ceiba, Spanish Honduras • **Born:** December 28, 1920 • **Elected:** 1965

It was only fitting that Steve Van Buren was the first Eagle player enshrined in the Pro Football Hall of Fame. He was the centerpiece of the Eagles' first championship team, and more than a half century after his retirement, he still holds nine club records. He won four NFL rushing titles and earned All-Pro honors five times. The Eagles selected him in the first round of the 1944 draft and signed him to a $4,000 contract. The Eagles had not finished higher than third place in any season prior to Van Buren's arrival, but when he stepped on the field, they became a different team. Over the next six seasons, the Eagles won 51 games, lost 17, and tied three. They finished first in the Eastern Division three times and won the NFL championship in 1948 and '49. With his rare combination of speed and power, Van Buren was the dominant running back of his era. He led the league with 18 touchdowns in a 12-game season in 1945. He went over the 1,000-yard mark twice (1947 and '49). He scored the only touchdown as the Eagles defeated the Chicago Cardinals, 7–0, to win the 1948 NFL championship, a game played in a blizzard at Shibe Park. The next year, he ran for 196 yards as the Eagles defeated the Los Angeles Rams, 14–0, to win their second title, this time in a torrential rain. Injuries forced Van Buren to retire in 1952, but when he left the game, he held the league rushing record with 5,860 yards. He was enshrined in the Pro Football Hall of Fame on September 12, 1965. His presenter was Clarke Hinkle, a Hall of Fame fullback for the Green Bay Packers.

ALEX WOJCIECHOWICZ
Linebacker

College: Fordham • **Years with the Eagles:** 1946–50 • **Years in the NFL:** 1938–50 • **Birthplace:** South River, New Jersey • **Born:** August 12, 1915 • **Died:** July 13, 1992 • **Elected:** 1968

When Alex Wojciechowicz gained fame as one of Fordham's "Seven Blocks of Granite," he considered shortening his name to "Wojack" to make it easier for newspaper reporters and broadcasters. His coach, Jim Crowley, the former Notre Dame star, talked him out of it. "With a name like Wojack, you might get lost in the crowd," Crowley said. "But no one could ever overlook a name like Wojciechowicz or the man who wears it." Crowley was right, although Wojciechowicz earned his lasting fame with his play, not his name. He was a first-round draft pick of Detroit in 1938 and played nine seasons with the Lions as a center and linebacker. In 1946, Wojciechowicz was 31 and appeared to be slowing down. The Lions traded him to the Eagles, where coach Greasy Neale made him a defensive specialist, playing him at outside linebacker in his 5–2 defense. Wojciechowicz thrived in the new role and was a key contributor to the unit that posted eight shutouts in the 1948 and '49 seasons, including back-to-back shutouts in the championship games against the Chicago Cardinals and Los Angeles Rams. "Wojie looked like he was falling asleep half the time, but he flipped the switch on game day," said halfback Bosh Pritchard. "He was one of the best tacklers I ever saw. He didn't just stop [ball carriers], he knocked them backwards." Wojciechowicz was enshrined in the Pro Football Hall of Fame on August 3, 1968. Neale was his presenter.

MEDIA MEMBERS IN THE HALL OF FAME

Four other members of the Hall of Fame are connected with the Eagles and Philadelphia. They all worked in the media. Three of the honorees are newspaper reporters who received the Dick McCann Award, which is presented annually to a journalist for "long and distinguished reporting in the field of professional football." The award is voted on by the Pro Football Writers of America.

Hugh Brown won the McCann Award in 1983. A native of Edinburgh, Scotland, Brown came to the United States when he was five years old. He attended New York University and landed his first newspaper job at the *Waterbury* (Connecticut) *Republican*. He was hired by the *Philadelphia Bulletin* in 1945 and spent 20 years covering the Eagles.

Gordon Forbes was honored in 1988 after covering the Eagles for the *Philadelphia Inquirer* from 1967 until 1982 when he moved to *USA Today*. A native of Patchogue, New York, Forbes began writing sports as a high school stringer for the local paper, earning a nickel for every inch of copy. He authored the book *Tales from the Eagles Sidelines* in 2002.

Ray Didinger won the McCann Award in 1995. He covered the Eagles for 26 years, starting as the beat man with the *Philadelphia Bulletin* in 1970 and continuing as a columnist with the *Philadelphia Daily News* from 1980 through 1995. He joined NFL Films as a writer and producer in 1996. A native of Philadelphia, Didinger was named Pennsylvania Sportswriter of the Year five times.

Ed Sabol, the founder of NFL Films, won the Pete Rozelle Radio and Television Award in 1991. The award is presented annually for "long and exceptional contributions to radio and television in professional football."

Sabol began his filmmaking career by taking home movies of his son Steve playing football with the Little Quakers. In 1962, Sabol convinced Rozelle, the NFL commissioner, to allow him to film the NFL Championship game between Green Bay and the New York Giants. With a crew of six, Sabol shot the game and produced a one-hour film complete with music and narration.

Rozelle was so impressed that he convinced the NFL owners to kick in $10,000 apiece to launch the company now known as NFL Films. More than 40 years later, the company has 260 full-time employees working in a $60 million state-of-the-art facility in Mount Laurel, New Jersey. Ed Sabol is retired, but Steve now serves as president, overseeing the operation, which has won 91 Emmy Awards.

10

The Stadiums

THE EAGLES have hosted their NFL opponents in eight separate venues stretching from one end of Pennsylvania to the other. Two of their "home" games were played at Forbes Field, in Pittsburgh. All the other games were held in Philadelphia, where the club has appeared in two stadiums considered to be among the best in football and one that was rated the worst. Seating capacity at the Eagles' home stadiums ranged from 20,000 at Temple Stadium, at the northern tip of the city, to more than 100,000 at Municipal Stadium, later known as John F. Kennedy Stadium, at the southern edge of Philadelphia.

BAKER BOWL (1933–35)

The Baker Bowl, the baseball stadium owned by the Philadelphia Phillies, was the Eagles' home field when they joined the National Football League in 1933. They went 3–11–1 in three seasons at that stadium, which was known as "The Hump" because it was located at the top of a hill on Broad Street at Lehigh Avenue, in North Philadelphia.

Originally called the *Philadelphia Base Ball Park*, the stadium's name was changed to the *Baker Bowl* shortly after William F. Baker became the Phillies president in 1913. By the time the Eagles played there, the stadium was commonly known as the *Phillies Ball Park*.

Constructed at a cost of $101,000 by Phillies owner Al Reach in 1887, the Baker Bowl served as the home of Philadelphia's National League baseball team until July 1938.

The stadium's capacity was only 12,500 at the start, but more than 20,000 fans jammed the place to witness the first game, a 19–10 Phillies triumph over the New York Giants on April 30, 1887.

Over the next 40 years, the stadium was the site of two tragic mishaps.

On August 8, 1903, a section of the left-field balcony collapsed onto 15th Street killing 12 people and injuring another 232. The accident happened during the second game of a doubleheader with the Boston Braves when a large group of fans rushed to the overhang to watch a disturbance caused by a pair of drunks, who were accosting some young girls outside the stadium.

On May 14, 1927, a 30-foot section of the right-field grandstand collapsed. One man died of a heart attack, and 50 others were injured. The accident was caused by fans rocking the

stands in the seventh inning during a Phillies eight-run rally against the St. Louis Cardinals.

When Bert Bell purchased the Eagles franchise, he hoped to use Shibe Park, the Philadelphia Athletics' baseball park, which had a much larger seating capacity (33,000) than the Baker Bowl. But when those talks became bogged down in political red tape, Bell struck a deal with Phillies owner Gerry Nugent to use Baker Bowl, a stadium located just seven blocks from Shibe Park.

As part of the deal, 5,000 temporary bleacher seats were erected along the right-field wall. There was no written agreement, just an understanding that the Eagles would pay a percentage of the gate and have use of the park for football as needed.

The Eagles beat a U.S. Marine team, 40–0, in their first game at the Baker Bowl, a preseason contest played on October 4, 1933, under rented floodlights. The lights were powered by a generator and mounted on poles. Players had no trouble seeing

Fans taking in the action at Baker Bowl, where the Eagles won only three games in three seasons.

The 1935 Eagles squad at the Baker Bowl.

the ball at ground level, but punts and forward passes went above the lights and into the darkness. Receivers had to guess where the ball would come down.

The first regular-season home game was played at the Baker Bowl on October 18, 1933. Only 1,750 people turned out to watch the Portsmouth Spartans walk away with a 25–0 victory.

The Eagles were a tough sell because they won only three of the 15 games they played in the Baker Bowl. As an inducement in 1933, fans were given a free car wash if they purchased tickets to an Eagles home game.

Art Rooney, the owner of the Pittsburgh Steelers, loved to tell the story about the day the Eagles were playing at the Baker Bowl at the same time the Athletics were playing baseball just down the street.

"It was a cloudy day, but everybody was going to the baseball game," Rooney said. "Bert gave some guy $5, handed him a megaphone, and sent him over to the baseball park to yell, 'No game today. Rain!'"

One of Bell's proudest possessions was the first license ever issued in the Commonwealth of Pennsylvania granting permission to play a game on Sunday, something that was prohibited for years by the state's strict blue laws.

It happened on November 12, 1933. The Eagles, who dropped three of their first four games by a combined 116–9 margin, held the mighty Chicago Bears, the defending NFL champions, to a 3–3 tie before 17,850 fans.

The Bears, led by Red Grange and Bronko Nagurski, took a 3–0 lead in the second quarter when Jack Manders kicked a 20-yard field goal "from an oblique angle with a host of Eagles charging in on him like angry bees," according to Stan Baumgartner, of the *Philadelphia Inquirer.*

Philadelphia's Guy Turnbow connected from the 18-yard-line to tie the game in the final quarter, setting off a wild celebration led by Philadelphia A's catcher Mickey Cochrane, the future Baseball Hall of Famer.

"Mickey forgot all his dignity as he tossed his hat in the air, jumped from seat to seat, and cheered," Baumgartner reported.

The Eagles defeated the Pittsburgh Pirates, 25–6, the following Sunday for their first victory ever at the Baker Bowl, before an estimated crowd of 6,000. Philadelphia's Joe Carter caught two touchdown passes from Roger Kirkman, including a spectacular 63-yard play. The *Inquirer* story describes Carter snatching a long pass "out of the waiting arms of two Pittsburgh interceptors and cutting loose with a thrilling bit of

open field running that would have been a credit to Red Grange as he zigzagged his way across the visitors' goal."

The Eagles won again at home on November 26, this time over the Cincinnati Reds, 20–3. Swede Hanson, whom Baumgartner described as "the lantern-jawed, lank-limbed will o' the wisp of the professional gridiron," set up two Eagles touchdowns with his brilliant running.

Philadelphia's last win at the Baker Bowl occurred on December 3, 1934, when they blanked the New York Giants, 6–0. Jim Leonard, a local star from St. Joseph's Prep and Notre Dame, scored the only touchdown.

After going winless at the Baker Bowl in 1935, the Eagles moved their home games to Municipal Stadium the following season. Three years later, the Phillies moved out, and the stadium was damaged by fire three times before it was finally demolished in 1950. The site is now home to a Philadelphia School District bus maintenance facility.

TEMPLE STADIUM (1934–35)

Temple Stadium, located in Northwest Philadelphia, served as the Eagles' home for only two games, but it was the site of the most explosive performance in their history.

On November 6, 1934, the Eagles demolished the winless Cincinnati Reds, 64–0. That is the most lopsided regular-season game in the league's history and the highest single-game point total for the Eagles.

Only 2,000 fans were on hand to see Swede Hanson rush for 170 yards and three touchdowns as the Eagles opened a 28–0 lead in the first quarter. If the Reds were uninspired, it may have been because they knew the team was being disbanded after the game in Philadelphia.

The Eagles drew 20,000 to their 1935 opener at Temple Stadium, the largest crowd to see Bell's team up to that point. Many came to see Alabama Pitts, the halfback the Eagles had just signed from Sing Sing Prison. Philadelphia took the lead on a touchdown plunge by Jim Leonard less than two minutes into the game, but the Pittsburgh Pirates rallied for all of their points in the next five minutes for a 17–7 win.

In 1952, when the Eagles were unhappy with their lease at Shibe Park, they considered purchasing Temple Stadium, but the club backed off when university officials announced the property was appraised for $1 million and they had no intention of selling.

The 20,443-seat stadium served as home to Temple University's football team from 1928 until 1974 when the Owls moved their home games to Veterans Stadium.

Constructed with brick facing and wooden seats set in concrete, Temple Stadium cost about $400,000 to build. Its funding came from the late Charles G. Erny, the former chairman of the university's board of trustees. The stadium was torn down in 1997.

MUNICIPAL STADIUM/JFK STADIUM (1936–39, 1941, 1947, 1950, 1954)

In announcing plans for the construction of Municipal Stadium on February 1, 1925, Mayor W. Freeland Kendrick touted it as the "world's largest stadium" with "absolutely unlimited parking facilities." He said that it would have a total seating and standing capacity of 250,000, and that its design would be patterned after Wembley Stadium in London.

"At the south end of the arena and enclosing it will be a stadium seating 100,000," Kendrick said. "The northern end of the arena will be enclosed by terraces affording standing room for 150,000." Outside, he promised "a large parking space accommodating approximately 30,000 automobiles."

In the November 1924 election, voters had approved a $2 million loan for construction of the stadium. Years earlier, there was a proposal to build a similar stadium on the east bank of the Schuylkill River, the present site of the Philadelphia Art Museum, but that idea never got off the drawing board.

"Within the arena," said Kendrick, "there will be an ample space for a football gridiron, a baseball diamond, a quarter-mile track, and two 220-yard straightaways for the short distance runners. The track will extend to the north end of the playing field, providing the only half-mile track in the country."

Kendrick added that the stadium could be flooded with water during the winter to provide ice skating facilities.

Ground was broken for the stadium on May 18, 1925. The contract was awarded to the Turner Construction Company, the same firm that built Franklin Field in 1922. The stadium's superstructure was comprised of almost 2 million bricks with limestone trimmings as the exterior enclosing wall. Its entrances were designed with the capacity to pass 50,000 people through within 15 minutes. Wood seats were built on 71 rows.

Municipal Stadium officially opened on May 1, 1926, in time for the city's Sesquicentennial Exposition. But it never achieved Mayor Kendrick's projection as the world's largest stadium.

Its top seating capacity was 102,000 when temporary field seats were installed. Its official capacity of 98,593 was eventually reduced to 86,443. Provisions were never made for 150,000 standees, and major league baseball was never played in the facility.

By the time it was dedicated, the original $2 million price tag had ballooned to $4,227,000.

The stadium attracted its largest crowd in its first year, 1926, when more than 175,000 people attended a mass celebrated by Philadelphia's Dennis Cardinal Dougherty.

In the same year, 120,757 fans watched the Jack Dempsey–Gene Tunney world heavyweight championship fight. In 1941, 116,000 people attended the Thrill Show staged by the city's police and fire departments. The annual Army-Navy football classic was played there between 1936 and 1979 and often attracted crowds of 102,000.

Originally known as Municipal Stadium, its name was changed to Philadelphia Stadium in 1959 and then to John F. Kennedy Stadium in 1963.

For many years, the stadium was a seldom-used white elephant and a cash drain on the city. In 1932, only six years after it opened, Philadelphia Mayor J. Hampton Moore recommended that it be demolished. In 1938 it cost $133,576 to maintain the facility when total income for that year was only $16,556. In 1947 the stadium hosted only eight events—six of them Eagles games—and suffered an operating loss of $3,579.

Steve Van Buren running against a backdrop of empty seats at Municipal Stadium. The seating capacity for football was 102,000, so even though 35,406 fans attended this 1947 game against Washington, the stadium looked—and felt—deserted.

The Eagles had only two winning seasons in the eight years they played at Municipal Stadium. One of those was 1947, when they won five consecutive home games, three by shutout, en route to their first Eastern Division championship. The other year was 1954, their last season at Municipal Stadium, when they finished 7–4–1. In the 1970s, the Eagles sometimes used the grass field at Kennedy Stadium for practice because it was easier on the players' legs than the artificial turf at Veterans Stadium.

The Eagles played their first full season of home games in Municipal Stadium in 1936. Their only victory of the season came there in Game 2 when Hank Reese booted a field goal from the 10-yard line to give them a 10–7 win over the New York Giants.

In 1939, Eagles owner Bert Bell came under heavy criticism when he postponed the regular-season opener at Municipal Stadium against Pittsburgh because of "threatening weather." Meanwhile, the Athletics were playing a doubleheader against Boston a few miles away at Shibe Park under clear skies before a crowd of 23,235.

The following week, 33,258 fans—the largest crowd to witness professional football in Philadelphia—watched the much-heralded debut of the Eagles' No. 1 draft pick, former TCU All-America quarterback Davey O'Brien. The Washington Redskins won, 7–0, as Sammy Baugh threw a 29-yard touchdown pass to Charlie Malone in the fourth quarter.

The game against Pittsburgh was rescheduled for Thanksgiving Day, and the Eagles defeated the Pirates, 17–14, despite being forced to play three games in seven days.

The Eagles enjoyed one of the NFL's highest gate increases with a total Municipal Stadium attendance of 80,000 that year. The total included 10,000 children who were admitted for 10 cents each. The team won only one game, but people came to see O'Brien.

The city of Philadelphia increased the Eagles' rent from $600 to $1,000 a game for the 1940 season. Bell immediately threatened to move the franchise.

"I don't know where we'll play next year, but it won't be at Municipal Stadium unless the city changes its attitude," Bell said. "Perhaps we'll try to make arrangements at Shibe Park, or maybe we'll go out of the city altogether. I already have started to look into possible sites at Hershey and Camden.

"It just doesn't make sense to me. Here they are yelling about business conditions in the city, and then they try to drive people out by unfair practices such as this. I guess it was that 30,000 crowd which saw Davey O'Brien that put this idea into the city fathers' bonnets. Somebody should tell them about the Brooklyn game. We played it here in the rain, and it cost us $11,600."

The Eagles played that game in a torrential downpour before a grand total 50 fans and 102,000 empty seats. Conditions were so awful that Bell invited all the fans into the press box to watch the game.

Bell wanted to postpone the game, but Dodgers owner Dan Topping had made the trip from New York with some influential friends. "It's silly to play, Dan," Bell said. "We'll take a beating [at the gate]."

"But I can't disappoint my friends," Topping replied.

Responding to the city's rental hike, Bell admitted that the Eagles "made a little money" the previous two seasons after operating at a "large deficit" for several years before that.

"It will be a long, long while before we're out of the red," he said. "Philadelphia needs education as far as professional football is concerned. We can't afford to take chances that

might bankrupt us. You can lose your shirt on a rainy day in this business. Still and all, perhaps we'll be willing to pay the rent—if the city is willing to guarantee the crowds and the weather conditions."

The city *wasn't* willing, nor was Bell willing to pay the higher rent. For the 1940 season he moved the Eagles home games to Shibe Park—only to return to Municipal Stadium in 1941.

The 1947 season opener, a 45–42 Eagles victory over Washington on September 28, was one of the wildest games in NFL history. Both teams set league records for combined points, total touchdowns, and touchdown passes.

Municipal Stadium also was the site of one of the most memorable games in league history. On September 16, 1950, coach Paul Brown brought his Cleveland Browns to town, and 71,237 fans, the largest regular-season home crowd in the Eagles' history to that point, watched the defending All-America Football Conference champions crush the Eagles, 35–10, in the Browns' debut as a member of the NFL.

The Eagles were coming off back-to-back NFL championships. The Browns had won all four AAFC titles, but few in the NFL took the "other" league seriously. George Preston Marshall, the owner of the Washington Redskins, spoke for most NFL people when he said, "The worst team in our league could beat the best team in theirs."

Bell, who was then the NFL Commissioner, scheduled the game as the opener of the 1950 season. He fully expected the Eagles to thrash the upstarts from the AAFC. The demand for tickets was so great that Bell moved the contest from the smaller Shibe Park to Municipal Stadium and changed the kickoff from Sunday afternoon to Saturday night. But the Browns' dominant performance stunned the huge Philadelphia crowd into silence.

How many fans actually paid their way in that night is anyone's guess because the stadium was known for many years as a safe haven for gate-crashers.

"When the lights go down, the gates have a way of opening up," concessionaire Robert Nilon told a U.S. Senate antitrust and monopoly subcommittee in Washington, D.C., in 1964.

Nilon testified that Kennedy Stadium had 45 entrance gates. He said that he often saw crowds gather at gates that would suddenly open up after events had begun. People would then pay unauthorized ticket collectors $2 or $3 apiece—"whatever the traffic will bear"—to get in illegally.

The stadium, which housed everything from the Rolling Stones to the Beatles, from rodeos to bicycle racing, was finally torn down in 1992 after city officials declared that the structure was unsafe. The Wachovia Center, home of the NBA Seventy-Sixers and NHL Flyers, was built on the site.

SHIBE PARK/CONNIE MACK STADIUM (1940–57)

The Eagles first played at Shibe Park, a stadium with a capacity of 33,000 for baseball and 39,000 for football, in 1940.

Philadelphia city officials triggered the move by raising the rent at Municipal Stadium from $600 to $1,000 after the 1939 season. Eagles owner Bert Bell responded by moving his home games to Shibe Park.

"I'm delighted to have Bert Bell as a tenant and also think his Eagles will make Shibe Park more popular," said Connie Mack, the A's president. "If our lights are good enough for

The most famous football game played at Shibe Park was the Blizzard Bowl, the 1948 NFL championship game between the Eagles and the Chicago Cardinals. So much snow fell that day that the officials had to use ropes to mark the sidelines.

American League teams to play baseball at its best, they certainly are going to be more than satisfactory for football."

The ballpark was named for Benjamin Shibe, the owner of the Philadelphia Athletics. It was built on a city block that was once a farm at 21st Street and Lehigh Avenue in North Philadelphia. Its cost of $377,000 included substantial renovations that were made four years after it opened. Considered state of the art at the time, it was the first ballpark constructed with concrete and steel.

Shibe Park opened on April 12, 1909, as a crowd estimated at 35,000 watched the A's beat the Boston Red Sox 8–1. Philadelphia Mayor John Reyburn threw out the first ball and declared afterward that the ballpark was a "pride to the city."

In its 62 years of existence, the stadium attracted almost 47 million baseball fans. The Athletics played there for 46 seasons until they moved to Kansas City in 1954. The Phillies came in 1938 after the Baker Bowl fell into disrepair, and they stayed for 33 years until Veterans Stadium opened in 1971.

The stadium hosted eight World Series, seven of them featuring the American League champion Athletics, and two baseball All-Star games—in addition to numerous other events.

It never was intended to be a football field, but Shibe Park—later known as Connie Mack Stadium—was the site of the Eagles' first two world championship teams and three Eastern Division winners, as well as some outstanding offensive and defensive performances.

In 1949 the great Steve Van Buren rushed for 205 yards against the Pittsburgh Steelers, establishing a club record that still stands.

The 1943 opener against Brooklyn produced one of the greatest defensive efforts in franchise history when the Steagles held the Brooklyn Dodgers to *minus 44 yards* rushing.

Once considered among the nation's finest ballparks, Shibe Park eventually went the way of many inner-city athletic facilities and became a crumbling eyesore. But it never was a particularly good football facility.

"What a place," recalled Marion Campbell, who played there for the Eagles in 1956 and '57. "I don't think the groundskeepers ever showed up except to collect their pay. The field was so bad, you could've played hockey and basketball on it and not hurt it. Late in the season, you couldn't put a hole in that field with a jackhammer. Our locker room? I don't think we had one."

The field was in such bad shape that coach Greasy Neale frequently took the team across the street to practice at Funfield Recreation Center. Still, the Eagles had a 57–35–6 overall record in Shibe Park and won their first NFL title while playing there.

The only NFL championship game played there took place in a blizzard on December 19, 1948. After players from both teams helped drag the tarp off the field, Van Buren scored from the five-yard line to give the Eagles a 7–0 win over the Chicago Cardinals before 28,864 frozen fans.

The Eagles finished unbeaten in six games at Shibe Park that year as they won the Eastern Division championship with a 9–2–1 record. They also went unbeaten in all six games at Shibe Park the following season when they repeated as NFL champions and finished with an 11–1 mark.

Tackle Frank (Bucko) Kilroy had a number of relatives living in the neighborhood surrounding Shibe Park. His great uncle, Matt, ran a bar across the street from the stadium.

The name of the ballpark was officially changed from Shibe Park to Connie Mack Stadium before the start of the 1953 baseball season.

In 1954, after the Athletics moved to Kansas City, the Phillies purchased Connie Mack Stadium from new A's owner Arnold Johnson for a reported $1,650,000. Even though the Eagles drew a total of 158,175 fans to Connie Mack Stadium in 1954—an increase of more than 10,000 over the previous season—there were complaints about poor parking and congestion around the stadium.

"There is no ballpark in the entire circuit that presents the problems of congestion and parking that are provided by that hemmed-in eggcrate known as Connie Mack Stadium," wrote *Philadelphia Bulletin* columnist Hugh Brown.

"There is no doubt that parking is the big problem here, and in Washington and Pittsburgh," Eagles president Frank McNamee said in 1956. "We are in the auto age, and parks erected 50 years ago in built-up sections of a city won't do. People want the maximum of comfort, and if we want them to come out we have to give it to them."

Only 12,555 fans came out to watch the last Eagles game at Connie Mack Stadium, on December 14, 1957. The Chicago Cardinals won, 31–27. The game ended with the Eagles' Bill Stribling fumbling on the one-yard line.

Phillies president Bob Carpenter didn't appear overly upset when the Eagles announced that they were moving their home games to Franklin Field in 1958.

"We're sorry to see them go, but wish them the best of luck in the college stadium," he said. "When the smoke clears away, I think we'll find that the loss of revenue to us won't amount to much."

The Eagles paid 15 percent of their gate receipts annually for rent, usually in the $60,000 range.

Carpenter explained that the Phillies had to resod the field every baseball season. That cost, plus the expense of keeping the ballpark open for Eagles games, cut substantially into the revenue they collected from the football team.

The park had to be reconfigured every season for football. Temporary stands were installed in right field, and goalposts were built along the first base line and in left field.

The Phillies played their final season there in 1970. The stadium was heavily damaged by fire in 1971 and demolished in 1976. Today the Deliverance Evangelistic Church stands on the site.

FORBES FIELD (1943)

Because of restrictions imposed by World War II, the Eagles and Pittsburgh Steelers merged into one team, the Phil-Pit Eagles-Steelers, in 1943. Two of the *Steagles'* home games were played at Forbes Field, in Pittsburgh, 300 miles west of Philadelphia, with both contests won by the "home" team.

The Steagles scored three touchdowns in less than four minutes to defeat the Chicago Cardinals, 34–13, in their Pittsburgh debut, on October 31, before 16,351 fans.

Roy Zimmerman threw a pair of touchdown passes of 31 and 26 yards to Tony Bova, a rookie from St. Francis College. Ben Kish returned an interception 86 yards for another touchdown.

Later, the Steagles pulled out a 35–34 win over the Detroit Lions, on November 21, as a crowd of 23,338 watched Jack Hinkle rush for a season-high 132 yards. Zimmerman threw a touchdown pass to Larry Cabrelli and scored on a quarterback keeper.

Forbes Field was named for General John Forbes, a British general who captured Fort Duquesne and renamed it Fort Pitt during the French and Indian War in 1758.

The park was located in the Oakland district of Pittsburgh, a new cultural area that appealed to Pirates owner Barney Dreyfuss. But many people felt that the ballpark was too far from downtown and referred to it as "Dreyfuss's Folly." Like Shibe Park, it was primarily a baseball stadium. It served as the home of the Pirates until 1970, and it was demolished one year later. Today the University of Pittsburgh library stands on the site.

FRANKLIN FIELD (1958–70)

For 13 years, the Eagles played their home games at Franklin Field, still considered one of America's best venues for watching football. The move in 1958 put the Eagles in an attractive setting for the first time.

"Franklin Field moved us uptown," cornerback Tom Brookshier said. "We became socially acceptable. We began to feel like we really belonged. It was an incredible amphitheater. There wasn't a bad seat in the house."

Before moving to Franklin Field in 1958, the Eagles struggled at the gate. "People look at me like I'm crazy when I make that statement," said Bill Campbell, who broadcast the Eagles games on radio from 1956 to 1964. "Penn football used to average 70,000 fans. They were playing a schedule with teams like Notre Dame, Ohio State, Southern Cal, and Michigan. The Eagles were an afterthought. They were playing in Connie Mack Stadium, and they were lucky to get 15,000. After they won the NFL championship in 1960, pro football shot right to the top of the heap."

The original Franklin Field was built by the University of Pennsylvania's alumni association in 1895 at a cost of $100,000. Seating 24,000, it was completed in time for the first running of the Penn Relays. After the old stadium was demolished in 1922, the current facility began taking shape when the lower stands were constructed. President Warren G. Harding presided at dedication ceremonies between halves of the Penn-Navy game on October 28, 1922. The upper stands were completed three years later. An artificial-turf surface was installed in 1969.

Until the 102,000-capacity Philadelphia Municipal Stadium opened in 1926, Franklin Field, located at 33rd and Spruce streets, was the largest sports stadium in the city.

During the 1930s and 1940s, when temporary stands were constructed in the end zone, Penn often led the nation's college football teams in attendance. Crowds exceeded 80,000. The stadium's capacity was 60,658 when the Eagles played there, although temporary seating allowed 67,325 fans to watch the 1960 NFL championship game.

Franklin Field can claim many historic milestones. The nation's first scoreboard was installed there in 1895. The first football radio broadcast was conducted by Philadelphia's WIP in 1922. The first commercial football telecast took place in 1939. A year later, Philadelphia's new Philco station carried all of Penn's home games on television.

Franklin Field hosted the Army-Navy football classic 18 times between 1899 and 1935. On June 27, 1936, more than 100,000 people crowded into the stadium to watch Franklin D. Roosevelt accept the Democratic Party's nomination for president.

The announcement that the Eagles were moving to Franklin Field was made on January 20, 1958, by Eagles president Frank L. McNamee and University of Pennsylvania vice president John L. Moore. The two were good friends who worked together on the War Assets Administration during World War II.

To many observers, the fact that the Eagles were even playing on Penn's campus was a major surprise, even though they had played three exhibition games there.

"It was an awful shock when I first heard about it," said Crawford C. Madeira, a Penn graduate and major fund-raiser for the university. "But after thinking it over, I don't feel so bad about it. By letting the Eagles use it, it won't become the white elephant it has been during the past two or three years. Since it's a case of letting the stadium either crumble or letting the Eagles play there on Sundays, I'd say let the Eagles use it."

Even Bert Bell, a University of Pennsylvania alumnus, was taken aback when McNamee informed him of the move. After the deal was ironed out, McNamee went to see Bell at Philadelphia's Racquet Club. "When I told him the Eagles were going to get Franklin Field, he said, 'Aw, you're crazy,'" McNamee recalled. "So I took him to see Moore to prove it."

Bell said the move to Franklin Field "saved pro football for Philadelphia."

Under the terms of the unwritten agreement—"We have nothing in writing at all," said McNamee—the Eagles did not pay rent for use of the stadium because of the nonprofit status of the university. Instead the NFL club agreed to pay for maintenance and other expenses, reportedly donating between $75,000 and $100,000 annually. All concessions and parking revenue went to the university.

"Next to the Coliseum in Los Angeles, where the Rams play their home games, we now have the largest stadium where a professional football team will play," said McNamee, noting that the Eagles were moving from Connie Mack Stadium with a football capacity of 39,000 to Franklin Field, with a capacity of 60,237.

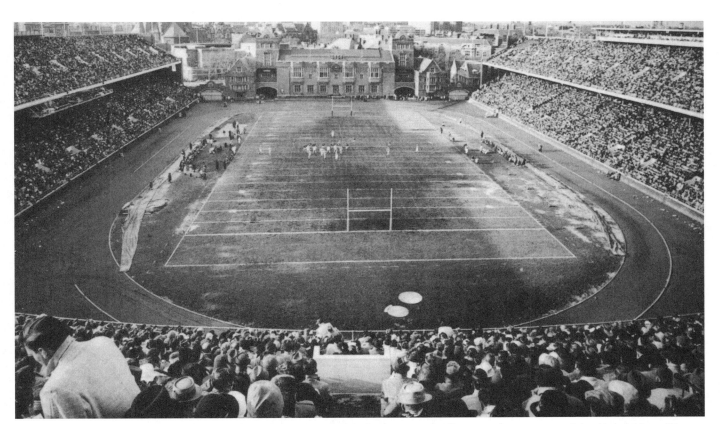

Attendance jumped when the Eagles moved to Franklin Field, the historic stadium on the campus of the University of Pennsylvania. "It was an incredible amphitheater," Tom Brookshier said. "There wasn't a bad seat in the house."

Moore said that the Eagles were moving into one of the "finest" stadiums in the country. "It is situated in an urban area in close proximity to mass public transportation," he said. "Its location—bounded on the east by the Schuylkill River and on the north, west, and south by university buildings—is such that athletic events held inside its walls are of minimum inconvenience to neighbors of the university."

It proved to be a brilliant move for the Eagles—so brilliant that in 1962, when Philadelphia city officials started talking about constructing a multipurpose stadium, McNamee said that his team wasn't interested. He cited a poll indicating that 80 percent of the Eagles season ticket holders preferred Franklin Field.

The Eagles were only the second NFL franchise in history to play a full season in a college stadium. The Detroit Lions once spent a year at the University of Detroit field.

In their regular-season debut in Franklin Field, on September 28, 1958, the Eagles lost to the Washington Redskins, 24–14. Only 36,850 fans showed up to watch the first football game ever played on a Sunday in that historic stadium.

The Eagles picked up their first Franklin Field victory the following week, upsetting the New York Giants, 27–24, before another small gathering of 23,178. Norm Van Brocklin and Tommy McDonald teamed up on a sensational 91-yard scoring play. Standing on his own one-yard line, Van Brocklin almost brushed the goalpost launching a long pass to McDonald, who flew the remaining 45 yards down the sideline.

When the Eagles won the championship in 1960, they drew 254,017—almost doubling the home attendance for their previous NFL championship in 1949 when they drew fewer than 130,000 fans to Shibe Park. Following the championship win over Green Bay, the Eagles sold a record 32,845 season tickets for the 1961 campaign. The total attendance for that year was 395,246. Single-game tickets cost $3 and $5.

"Franklin Field was a good field," said fullback Clarence Peaks. "The only bad thing for passing attacks was that, since it was a horseshoe shape, if the wind was blowing a certain direction, your passing game might change. Other teams weren't always ready for that, so they'd catch hell."

"It was like a dungeon," Green Bay guard Fuzzy Thurston said. "It wasn't much of a place to play. It was kind of scary and ugly. It wasn't anything like Lambeau Field, our home stadium."

"If you're looking for nostalgia, don't contact me about that dump," Eagles defensive tackle Gary Pettigrew said.

"I always thought Franklin Field was a very good place to play," said Eagles middle linebacker Dave Lloyd, who first played there as a member of the Cleveland Browns in 1958. "The locker rooms, things like that are horrible, especially the visiting locker room. Of course, a team coming in, you don't really care how well you put them up."

Franklin Field was both a joyous and sorrowful place for the Eagles, who compiled a 41–45–2 regular-season record at the stadium. The joy was provided by the 1960 team that won the NFL title in the only playoff game ever held in the nation's oldest two-tiered stadium. On December 26, 1960, the Eagles beat the Green Bay Packers, 17–13, and handed Vince Lombardi his only postseason loss as a head coach.

The sorrow was felt one year earlier, on October 11, 1959, when NFL commissioner Bert Bell, the Eagles' founder, collapsed and died in the stands while watching his former team defeat the Pittsburgh Steelers, 28–24.

One of Tom Brookshier's favorite memories of Franklin Field came after the 1960 championship game. Fans were warned by Philadelphia Mayor Richardson Dilworth not to tear down the goalposts. Mounted police were on hand to enforce the mayor's ruling, but the jubilant fans stormed the field anyway.

"We watched the fight for the goalposts; that was better than the game," Brookshier said. "The fans battled for them but there was not a serious injury, even though guys were under the horses and the fans were rolling around."

Afterward, Joseph A. Donoghue, the team's executive vice president, came up with an innovative idea. "After each game we're going to cut up the goalposts," he said. "And any spectator who wants a piece of goalpost can write and ask for it, and we'll send it to him as a souvenir."

The Eagles played their last game at Franklin Field on December 20, 1970, defeating the Steelers, 30–20, for only their third victory of the season. The game ended with a free-for-all between the two last-place teams.

VETERANS STADIUM (1971–2002)

When Veterans Stadium opened in 1971, its design was similar to other cookie-cutter venues of the day, including Riverfront in Cincinnati, Three Rivers in Pittsburgh, and Busch Stadium in St. Louis. The multipurpose stadium, designed to serve both football and baseball on artificial turf, was considered the wave of the future. It seemed more cost-efficient, but these stadiums did not age well.

"At one time this *was* a state-of-the art stadium," said Harold Carmichael, who appeared in more games at Veterans Stadium than any other NFL player. "I really hated people when they talked about the Vet because I had been away from it for six or seven years. When I came back here to work for the Eagles [in 1998], it had really gone down. But this was my first home. A lot of my blood, sweat, and tears went into this place."

Although polls conducted by Philadelphia newspapers indicated various other preferences, the name *Philadelphia Veterans Stadium* was selected by city council in honor of the city's war veterans. Ground was broken at Broad Street and Pattison Avenue on October 2, 1967, with Mayor James H. J. Tate presiding.

The stadium sat on a 74-acre site that was once marshland. Its appointments included a 126,000-square-foot AstroTurf playing surface that was replaced numerous times over the years.

When the stadium opened, its high-tech scoreboard system was called "the largest, most expensive, and most sophisticated in all of sports." But not by Eagles officials, who were irritated because they were forced to use two 90-by-13 foot auxiliary scoreboards. The three firms supporting the high-tech scoreboard—Schmidt's, Western Savings, and Sunoco—elected not to show their messages during Eagles games.

The large scoreboards were eventually replaced by a new giant screen, *Phanavision*, an animated scoreboard. The original orange, yellow, and brown seats were replaced by blue seats in 1996, just before the Phillies hosted the All-Star Game.

In May 1953, Philadelphia recreation commissioner Frederick R. Mann first initiated a public discussion of a new baseball and football stadium in Philadelphia. Mann, one of Philadelphia Mayor Joseph S. Clark's top advisers, suggested putting the stadium in Fairmount Park. He also argued that

Veterans Stadium was known for its treacherous turf and the throaty fans in the 700 level. Defensive end Hugh Douglas called it "The Nest of Death."

unless the city acted quickly, there was a real danger of losing one of its two major league baseball teams.

That's exactly what happened. After the 1954 season, Connie Mack sold the Philadelphia Athletics to Arnold Johnson, who moved the team to Kansas City—leaving the Phillies and Eagles to play their home games in Shibe Park, an antiquated stadium with limited seating and inadequate parking.

Dozens of sites were considered for the new stadium. One idea was to build it on stilts over the railroad station at 30th and Market streets. Penn's Landing also was suggested, and so was a site along the Delaware in Northeast Philadelphia. Locations at 11th and Vine streets and Eighth and Race streets were considered. The Phillies hinted they might move across the Delaware River to Cherry Hill, New Jersey.

But by April 1962 all the proposals were dead except for one: a South Philadelphia location on land just north of Kennedy Stadium. The estimated cost was $22.7 million.

The Eagles, however, were reluctant to commit to the new stadium, prompting Mayor Tate to describe Eagles president Frank McNamee as a man who is "pretty slow with a buck."

In July, McNamee announced that the Eagles would play in the city's new stadium only if they were forced to leave Franklin Field, an unlikely scenario, since Penn had no intention of razing the historic structure.

McNamee cited a poll indicating that 80 percent of the Eagles season-ticket holders wanted the team to remain in Franklin Field. Tate warned the Eagles they would have no

chance to come in later because the city was prepared to build a baseball-only stadium scheduled to open by 1966.

The Eagles were given a deadline of August 15 to sign a lease for the new stadium. That was the deadline for submitting loan questions to printers for the November 6 election ballot when voters would decide whether to support a $23 million bond issue to finance construction of the new facility.

On July 10, McNamee agreed to leave Franklin Field and play in the proposed new facility. Asked what caused him to change his position, McNamee replied, "Civic responsibility."

By the time voters approved the bond issue to construct the new stadium, its cost had risen to $25 million. The Eagles also had a new owner. Jerry Wolman had purchased the club for $5,505,000 from the partnership group known as the 100 Brothers.

In May 1965 the Eagles' future in the new stadium appeared in jeopardy when Wolman accused Mayor Tate of trying to force the team out of the city. The Eagles owner charged the mayor had reneged on an agreement made the previous October to give the Eagles the exclusive right to use the proposed stadium. Wolman said the mayor was "committed to friends who want to bring an American League football club into this city."

Opening a news conference by saying, "We'd like to combat the lies by Mayor Tate," Wolman announced he was suing the city.

"I gave my word that we would lease the stadium for 30 years with a guarantee of $100,000 a year minimum against

10 percent of gross income," Wolman said. "I consider myself as bound by that promise today as I was when I made it on October 22, and I have every intention of carrying it out."

Wolman said he had read a quote attributed to Mayor Tate that the Phillies could have an exclusive lease, but not the Eagles. "He was quoted as saying that the Eagles play only seven games a year and the city couldn't bar an American Football League team from playing in a municipal stadium."

Wolman also contended the architects were instructed to cut the seating capacity from 72,000 to 65,000 "without consulting us—certainly an act of breaking one's word."

Claiming the Eagles rejected "fabulous, unbelievable offers and guarantees to move to other cities," Wolman said, "So long as I am the owner, I will never move the team from Philadelphia."

Wolman said the Eagles would build their own stadium if Tate forced them out of the new facility and brought political pressure on Penn to oust the team from Franklin Field.

"If necessary, we will play out on Market Street, or in the subway, but we will not be driven from this city," Wolman said.

Disavowing any promise to the Eagles, Tate insisted there was "no doubt" there would be "no exclusive clause" for the new stadium. "It is a public stadium to be put up by public money," the mayor said, "There is no reason why the entire stadium should be tied up during the fall and winter when the Eagles play only seven games."

On June 28 the Eagles and the mayor reached a compromise: the Eagles would have exclusive rights to the new stadium for ten years while any American Football League team would play in Franklin Field. In return for exclusive use, the Eagles agreed to guarantee the city an annual rental of $150,000.

For the rest of the year, the city, Eagles, and Phillies squabbled over the stadium's design, seating capacity, and configuration. The Phillies threatened to pull out of the lease agreement unless their demands were met. The Eagles balked when architects proposed putting a roof over the facility.

Finally on February 2, 1966, after 15 months of bickering, the Eagles and Phillies agreed on the design and signed leases to play in the stadium. It would be constructed in the shape of an *octorad*, an architect's term taken from the Latin words for "eight" and "radius," or eight *points* on eight *radii*. The lease included a provision for a retractable dome if the city council asked the taxpayers for more money, a request that never was made.

Wolman called the design for the South Philadelphia venue "without question, the finest that we have ever seen."

The stadium was scheduled to be completed in 1967. But because of construction delays, a labor strike, and a grand jury probe, the opening was pushed back to 1968, then 1969, and finally 1970 when the Eagles sold 50,000 season tickets and planned to open with a preseason game against Oakland. Three months before the first game, the superstructure of the stadium was incomplete. The team had no choice but to return to Franklin Field for the 1970 season. They lost $560,000 because they sold tickets to a 65,000-seat capacity stadium and Franklin Field could hold only 60,658.

At a final cost of $52 million, Veterans Stadium officially opened on April 10, 1971, when the Phillies defeated the Montreal Expos, 4–1, before 55,352 fans. It was the largest crowd ever to attend a baseball game in the Commonwealth of Pennsylvania.

The first football game at the Vet was played on August 16, 1971, when the Eagles defeated the Buffalo Bills, 34–28 in a preseason game. But behind the scenes, things did not go smoothly.

On the night before the game, Eagles general manager Pete Retzlaff examined the playing field while it was being converted from baseball to football. He was infuriated when he stepped on the freshly painted 15-yard line and his brown loafer dropped out of sight.

"It's like stepping in a gopher hole," Retzlaff said. "It isn't safe to play on a field like this. It makes me sick just to look at it."

The players, who went through a light workout that evening, were shocked to learn the locker rooms were not air-conditioned. The heat was so oppressive that many players dressed in the corridor. The air conditioning was repaired. The field, however, remained a problem forever.

The Eagles dropped their first regular-season contest at the Vet to Dallas, 42–7, on September 26 as a capacity crowd of 65,358 saw quarterback Pete Liske tie a club record by throwing six interceptions in his Philadelphia debut.

The Eagles recorded their first win at the Vet on October 24 with a 24–7 decision over the New York Giants.

It took eight years before the Eagles hosted a postseason playoff game at the Vet. It finally happened on December 23, 1979, when they defeated the Chicago Bears, 27–17, in an NFC Wild Card game before 69,397 fans, the largest crowd to see a playoff game in Philadelphia. Ron Jaworski threw three touchdown passes, including a 63-yarder to Billy Campfield for the winning score.

Over the years, the Vet became famous for "the 700 Level," the uppermost reaches of the stadium where the rowdiest fans gathered. It also was known for its playing surface, which everyone—Eagles players and visitors alike—agreed was the worst in the NFL.

Bears wide receiver Wendell Davis ruptured the patellar tendons in both knees attempting to change direction while reaching for a pass against the Eagles on October 10, 1993. Later that season, Chris Mortensen of ESPN was assigned to do a story on the Vet. Eagles safety Mike Zordich walked him around the playing surface.

"He took me around to all the crevices and the seams and the soft spots," Mortensen said. "Even kicking up the base coverage areas where there was soft wood underneath. I'm saying, *It's unbelievable that a professional team in this era would be subject to playing on such a horrible surface.*"

Michael Irvin, the All-Pro wide receiver of the Dallas Cowboys, suffered a career-ending spinal injury when he hit his head on the turf after making his 750th career catch on October 10, 1999.

Bears quarterback Cade McNown separated his throwing shoulder after being driven into the turf by Eagles linebacker Mike Caldwell on October 22, 2000.

"The whole league knows about the Vet turf," said Eagles quarterback Donovan McNabb. "There [are] two things you can get hit by—our defenders or our stadium. They're both hard hits."

The players were not the only ones injured at the Vet. Nine fans were hurt when a railing collapsed during the Army-Navy game on December 5, 1998.

Even coaches were at risk. Juan Castillo, the Eagles offensive line coach, suffered a broken leg in 1998 when he was struck by a golf cart driven by a stadium employee.

The most celebrated incident occurred on August 14, 2001, when the preseason opener between the Eagles and the Super Bowl champion Baltimore Ravens was canceled because of the field conditions.

"We're disappointed," Eagles president Joe Banner said after the teams agreed that the field was unsuitable for playing. "We've been going through this for years. The conditions this team is forced to play in [are] absolutely unacceptable and an embarrassment to the city of Philadelphia."

When Eagles and Ravens players came out for pregame warm-ups, they noticed that the surface, which had just been converted from baseball, was dangerously uneven. Eagles cornerback Troy Vincent said the players actually sank into the turf near the infield cutouts. Ground crews attempted to remedy the problem by adding layers of dirt under the affected areas, but it was no use.

"The surface underneath the turf was not smoothed properly, so that when you lay the turf on it you've got, not a ripple, but ruts to the point where it was unsafe," Banner said.

In addition to the problems on the field, 18 people were trapped in the press elevator when it was stuck between the first and second levels for 41 minutes.

Despite its obvious shortcomings, many fans and players still had a warm spot in their hearts for the Vet.

"It's all gritty, grimy, dirty and filthy," said defensive end Hugh Douglas. "I'm sure a lot of other guys are going to say they won't miss the Vet. But that's what Philadelphia is known for. When a lot of people think about Philadelphia, they think about football and they think about the Vet."

As Vincent told Dave Spadaro, editor of *Eagles Digest*, before the 2003 playoffs, "It's our Taj Mahal for the next two weeks. I don't care how ugly it is, how bad the turf is, how nasty the fans are. Right now, I love the Vet."

Philadelphia fans hoped the Eagles would close the Vet in glorious fashion by winning the NFC championship in the final game. However, Tampa Bay spoiled the party by shocking the favored Eagles, 27–10.

Veterans Stadium was imploded in the early morning hours of March 21,2004, as a subdued gathering of 2,000 fans, officials, and other dignitaries watched. The Eagles had a 144–111–2 regular-season record in the stadium and a 7–4 mark in the postseason.

LINCOLN FINANCIAL FIELD (2003–)

In 1995, after their first season with the Eagles, chairman and CEO Jeffrey Lurie and club president Joe Banner identified their top priorities. A state-of-the-art stadium was at the top of the list.

Since 1971, the Eagles had played in Veterans Stadium, and it was literally falling apart. Its AstroTurf field was installed

The Eagles never had a stadium of their own until Lincoln Financial Field was built in 2003. The Linc, as it is known, cost an estimated $512 million and is the only NFL stadium to host a conference championship game in each of its first two seasons.

Comparing the Old and the New

Veterans Stadium	Stadium Facts	Lincoln Financial Field
$63 million	Cost	$512 million
65,352	Seating capacity	68,532
120 feet	Front row from sidelines	60 feet
33	% of seats along sideline	66
256	Wheelchair-accessible seats	685
89	Luxury suites	172
1,210	Luxury suite seats	3,040
0	Club seats	10,828
0	Club lounges	2 (40,000 sq. ft. each)
16,000	Parking spaces at complex	22,000
84	Concession points of sale	308
2	Number of concourses	2
45 feet	Width of concourses	60 to 90 feet
10	Total novelty locations	22
0	Eagles pro shop	1
Standard Phanavision	Video screens	Daktronics-HDTV
1 (31 × 42 feet)	Size of video screens	2 (27 × 96 feet)
		1 (14 × 25 feet)
14.5 acres	Stadium footprint	15 acres
1 for every 319	Men's restroom facilities	1 for every 58

over concrete, resulting in a high rate of injuries. It was the object of ridicule across the country.

Lurie and Banner went to work. It was a difficult process. Some city officials didn't see the need for separate stadiums for football and baseball. The Eagles executives made it clear that anything less than a stadium built exclusively for football was unacceptable.

There was considerable opposition for publicly financed new stadiums. A report prepared in 1996 by Philadelphia's city council emphasized that professional sports teams like the Phillies and Eagles should find private financing to build new stadiums because the city was in no position to foot the bill.

A copy of the report, which was prepared at the request of city council president (and future Philadelphia mayor) John Street, was obtained by the Philadelphia *City Paper*.

"Despite government rhetoric to the contrary, the trend in stadium and arena development is slowly becoming more and more private," as it was in the early days of professional sports, the report said. "If there is to be a new stadium in Philadelphia for either baseball or football, it should be truly traditional. That is, it should be privately financed, owned, and operated."

The report pointed out that taxpayers in other states have refused to pay for new stadiums: "On five separate occasions in the late '80s and early '90s, Northern California voters rejected proposals for a new ballpark for the San Francisco Giants. If the taxpayers say 'NO' loudly enough, owners can and do find ways to finance ballparks."

It was Banner's responsibility to structure the financing for the new stadium. By the time he was finished—after countless hours, days, and weeks of negotiating—the Eagles were assured of owning their own stadium for the first time in their 70-year history.

The Eagles contributed an unprecedented $330 million to the project. Part of this came from $130 million in loans and grants from the new NFL Stadium Loans Program. Another $180 million came from what is believed to be the largest private sports facility construction loan ever issued, an arrangement negotiated by Banner with FleetBoston Financial Corporation.

As a result, the Eagles assumed more than $30 million in annual debt service for more than 20 years to finance their share of the stadium costs. They also agreed to donate $1 million to a Philadelphia charity. No other NFL team ever made as large a contribution for construction of a stadium or incurred as much debt service as the Eagles did for their new stadium.

The City of Philadelphia contributed $95 million for land acquisition and the warehouse demolition and site clearance. The Commonwealth of Pennsylvania added another $85 million for construction. The Delaware River Port Authority, which operates the region's major toll bridges, gave a $2 million grant and a $5 million loan to close a funding gap.

The Eagles generated an estimated $50 to $60 million in additional revenue by selling "Stadium Builder Licenses," ranging in price from $1,530 to $3,145, for the right to purchase the best 29,000 seats.

Naming rights to the new stadium were awarded to Lincoln Financial Group, a finance company that is paying the Eagles more than $6.6 million annually over 21 years.

With the Philadelphia-based construction management consortium of Turner-Keating-McKissack overseeing the project, construction began on May 7, 2001, when an old warehouse on the south side of Pattison Avenue was demolished.

Less than 27 months later, on August 3, 2003, the new stadium hosted its first ticketed event, a soccer game between Manchester United and FC Barcelona.

Eagles fans got their first look at the Linc, as it became known, during a two-day open house late in July 2003. The only complaint was the lack of drinking water fountains in the main concourses, upper and lower levels. The problem, termed an oversight by the city and the team, was corrected in time for the first game.

Otherwise, the stadium, which was designed by architects NBBJ Sport, offered plenty of new features:

- Fans are closer to the field, with improved sightlines due to the horseshoe-shaped design. The closest seats are only 60 feet from the field, with nearly two-thirds of them along the sidelines. No seats have an obstructed view.
- The exterior of the stadium has a pair of Eagle winglike coverings over the upper deck. These provide some protection from the elements and redirect crowd noise back toward the field.
- The stadium features two liquid-crystal-display HDTV video boards, each measuring 27 by 96 feet. Each screen spans nearly the entire width of the field, with one located behind each end zone. Each screen is the equivalent of four Phanavision screens.
- The sound reinforcement system, designed by Acoustic Dimensions, covers the seating bowl, reduces echoing, and allows for section-specific messaging.
- Some 150 luxury suites are located above and below the club seating sections. All of the suites feature retractable glass windows, allowing fans to watch games in climate-controlled comfort or with an open-air experience.

"In terms of technological enhancements, the stadium represents a world of difference from what fans have experienced at Veterans Stadium, and even from what is available in some of the newest facilities around the country," Banner said. "A dramatic new venue such as this can play a major role in enhancing the city's profile while at the same time having a positive economic impact. In all, we're conceivably talking about 30–50 major events a year."

The annual Army-Navy game, which has been played in Philadelphia for most of its 100-plus years, was scheduled for the Linc from 2003 to 2006 and again in 2008.

The new stadium served as a site for the 2003 FIFA Women's World Cup, the largest women's soccer tournament in the world. It also was booked as the host field of the 2005 and 2006 NCAA men's lacrosse championships.

"We used to come in and practice at the Vet, and you never felt like you were practicing on a football field," Lurie said. "Here we've got a true state-of-the-art football stadium."

"Finally. Finally it's happened," quarterback Donovan McNabb said, after the Eagles went through their first practice at the Linc in June 2003. "We're excited."

Referring to the construction crews that were on hand—still working on the new facility and chanting, "E-A-G-L-E-S … E-A-G-L-E-S," from the upper deck—McNabb added, "It was good that they got a chance to come out and watch us practice because they've worked extremely hard to get us here right now."

The Eagles played their first game at the Linc on August 22, 2003, when they dropped a preseason contest to the New England Patriots, 24–12. But the grand opening came on September 8, 2003.

With a national TV audience watching on "Monday Night Football" and a sellout crowd of 67,772 fans cheering, the lights dimmed and the Linc exploded with a spectacular 30-minute pregame show with fireworks and a laser light display.

Philadelphia native Teddy Pendergrass, confined to a wheelchair since a 1982 automobile accident, delivered an emotional rendition of "The Star-Spangled Banner." Then, just before kickoff, Sylvester Stallone appeared atop a staircase in the north end zone. Dressed in a number 22 Eagles jersey, Stallone struck his classic *Rocky* pose to the delight of the cheering crowd.

"This was a bizarre scene for me," said Tampa Bay coach Jon Gruden, who served as an Eagles assistant under Ray Rhodes. "I've never seen a pregame warm-up like that. This place was juiced, man. And it was loud."

The Buccaneers doused all that emotion by defeating the Eagles, 17–0. It was Philadelphia's first shutout since a 26–0 loss to Buffalo on September 26, 1999. It came against the same team that denied them a trip to the Super Bowl at the end of the 2002 season when the Bucs battered the Eagles 27–10 in the NFC Championship game.

"It was like the whole Rocky Balboa and Apollo Creed fight," said Bucs safety John Lynch. "They had us down at one point, and then we knocked them down. But I thought we set the tone pretty early and then just kept coming at them."

The Eagles also lost their next home game to New England, 31–10, on September 14. Duce Staley scored the first Eagles touchdown in the new stadium. David Akers kicked the first field goal, a 57-yarder that was the longest ever kicked anywhere in Philadelphia and the second longest in team history.

The Eagles finally recorded their first victory at the Linc on October 5, defeating Washington, 27–25.

Their regular-season home-field record in the first two years was 12–4. At home in the NFL playoffs over those two years, the Eagles were 3–1, with the most memorable triumph being the 27–10 win over Atlanta, the win that put them into their first Super Bowl in 24 years.

That game also gave the Linc the distinction of being the first stadium ever to host National Football Conference championship games in each of its first two years of existence.

In 2003 the Eagles defeated the Green Bay Packers, 20–17, in the NFL Divisional playoff, then lost to the Carolina Panthers, 14–3, in the NFC Championship game. In 2004 the Eagles beat the Minnesota Vikings, 27–14, in the Divisional playoff before winning the NFC title against the Falcons.

Milestone Moments

THE EAGLES' HISTORY is full of milestone moments: dramatic wins, record-setting performances, unforgettable games that became part of the lore surrounding the team.

Certainly, some of the most memorable games were the championship contests in 1948 and '49 as well as 1960. Also, the 1980 NFC Championship game, the Fog Bowl in Chicago, and Super Bowl XXXIX in Jacksonville. Those games are duly chronicled in Chapter 8.

This chapter focuses on landmark events from the regular season, which include the Eagles participation in the first televised professional football game in 1939, the 1965 game in which the Eagles set an NFL record by intercepting nine passes against Pittsburgh, and the 1979 game in which Tony Franklin set a team mark by kicking a 59-yard field goal to defeat Dallas.

The milestone moments include legendary players such as Chuck Bednarik, who delivered one of the most famous hits in NFL history on Frank Gifford in 1960. But there are also players who are almost forgotten—Adrian Burk, Norm Willey, Joe Scarpati, and James Willis—but who wrote their names into Eagles history once upon a time.

From the Miracle of the Meadowlands to the Pickle Juice game in Dallas, the milestone moments will be talked about for as long as people follow the Eagles.

FIRST TELEVISED GAME— OCTOBER 22, 1939

History was made on October 22, 1939, although hardly anyone bothered to notice. The Eagles and Brooklyn Dodgers played in the first televised professional football game. The telecast, with its fuzzy black-and-white images, reached approximately 500 TV sets in New York City.

The broadcast was an experiment more than anything else. There was very little interest in the game. The Eagles and Dodgers both were losing teams. Only 13,057 fans bothered to show up at Ebbets Field in Brooklyn. But NBC had telecast the first college game—Fordham versus Waynesburg (Pennsylvania)—three weeks earlier and wanted to add a pro game to its credits. The fact that the teams were lousy was irrelevant.

The Dodgers won 23–14 as Ralph Kercheval kicked three field goals (40, 44, and 45 yards) to provide the margin of victory. Most of the players had no idea the game was being televised. Only one player, Brooklyn fullback Harrison Francis, admitted to seeing a "big trailer thing" parked outside Ebbets Field. The *New York Times* account of the game did not even mention the telecast.

There was only one announcer, Allen "Skip" Walz, who was paid $25 for calling the action. Said Walz: "I was doing the game with no monitors, no spotters, and no visual aids of any kind. This was flying blind at best. It was up to the cameramen to somehow follow my commentary, and that got sticky, particularly late in the game when the light got bad."

Walz's crew consisted of eight people, including the guy who drove the truck. Today, the crew assigned to a typical NFL telecast numbers around 200. There were two cameras at the 1939 game, one in the 40-yard-line box seats, the other in the upper deck. Now there are 14 cameras, sometimes more, covering every angle of every game.

"It was a cloudy day," Walz told Greg Greenday of *Eagles Digest*. "And when the sun crept behind the stadium, there wasn't enough light for the cameras. The picture would get darker and darker, and eventually it would go completely blank and we'd revert to a radio broadcast."

STEVE VAN BUREN'S BIG DAY

Steve Van Buren was not expected to play on November 27, 1949, when the Eagles met the Pittsburgh Steelers. He was sick all week and unable to practice. An hour before kickoff, he was shivering with a fever.

Coach Greasy Neale planned to rest Van Buren. The Eagles were 8–1 and rolling toward their third consecutive NFL championship game. There was no reason for Neale to put his great running back at risk. The coach started Russ Craft in Van Buren's place, but the Steelers roughed up the 5–9 Craft so badly that Van Buren insisted on playing.

"They made me mad," Van Buren said. "They gave Russ a terrible time. They twisted his helmet around, hit him late, kneed him. It was dirty football and I couldn't stand for it.

"I told Greasy, 'I feel better, put me in.' I didn't feel better at all, but I wanted to pay the Pittsburgh guys back. I kept telling [quarterback Tommy] Thompson to give me the ball. I didn't realize how many yards I had until someone told me after the game. I just knew I ran over a lot of guys."

Van Buren had 205 yards, an Eagles record, on 27 carries. He finished the 1949 season with 1,146 yards rushing, a league record at that time. He also led the NFL in rushing attempts (263) and touchdowns (11). He capped the season with his 196-yard rushing performance in the championship game win over the Rams.

The game against Pittsburgh, which the Eagles won handily 34–17, epitomized Van Buren's stoic toughness.

"Great competitor, great teammate," said end Pete Pihos. "If somebody did something dirty, Steve would go after him. He wouldn't try to fight him because he didn't want to get thrown out of the game. But he'd run the guy into the ground."

"That day one guy, I can't remember his name, but he was pulling some stuff, roughing guys up under the pile," said Chuck Bednarik. "Steve said, 'Nobody block him. Give me the ball and get out of the way.' Steve lowered his shoulder and went right into him, knocked him flat. We didn't see the guy for the rest of the day."

WILDMAN WILLEY: 17 SACKS IN ONE GAME

In 1952, the NFL was not keeping track of quarterback sacks. In fact, the term "sack" did not exist until the 1970s when Deacon Jones, the All-Pro defensive end of the Los Angeles Rams, introduced it. And it did not become an official statistic until 1982.

"I guess I came along too soon," said Norm Willey, better known as Wildman Willey, the ferocious pass rusher who played for the Eagles from 1950 through 1957. "I'd get two or three sacks a game, but no one kept count. If I played today, I'd be setting records and getting rich. Back then, no one paid attention to defense."

But on October 26, 1952, Willey made people take notice when he tackled New York Giants quarterback Charlie Conerly 17 times while he was attempting to pass. Today, those would be counted as sacks and Willey would have the league record. As it is, Derrick Thomas of Kansas City has the official record: seven sacks in one game against Seattle (1990). Willey more than doubled that in a 14–10 win over the Giants.

How do we know it happened? Hugh Brown covered the game for the *Philadelphia Bulletin* and wrote, "Willey awed inhabitants of the Polo Grounds by dumping Charlie Conerly 17 times while he was attempting to pass. Eleven of the dumpings came in sequence, causing New York scribes to remark, 'He's the greatest defensive end we've ever seen and probably the greatest we'll ever see.'"

Frank Gifford, the Giants' All-Pro halfback, wrote about the game in his book *The Whole Ten Yards*. In a 1996 interview, Gifford explained it simply enough. "Norm Willey was very fast," he said, "and we were very slow."

"I almost felt sorry for Charlie," said Eagles coach Jim Trimble. "I remember vividly Charlie having a heckuva time just getting up. He was mauled by Norm. I had a fight with the Giants chaplain, Father Dudley, after the game because he felt we were abusing Charlie Conerly. We had an argument going off the field."

"The Giants complained I was hitting Conerly late, but that was sour grapes," Willey said. "I mean, he was going down with the ball, so how could it be late? He was bleeding and limped off the field, he said he'd had enough. You hate to blow your own horn, but I had a good day. I was named [NFL] Player of the Week.

Norm (Wildman) Willey was a one-man wrecking crew in a 1952 win over the New York Giants.

"To me, the real highlight was when I got my bonus. We had an incentive clause: $10 for each hit on the quarterback. It was illegal, but the coaches did it anyway. They would look at the films and decide who got what. That week I got an envelope with $170 in it. Seventeen [sacks] times $10.

"That was big money in those days," said Willey, who never made more than $9,000 a season despite earning All-Pro honors three times. "There really was an incentive [to the cash bonus]. An extra $10 or $20 was important. You'd get that envelope and think you were rich."

Willey was 6–2 and 225 pounds during his playing career, a big man for that era, and he combined that size with surprising quickness—he was a basketball standout at Marshall College—to defeat even the best pass blockers. The day he recorded the 17 sacks, he was matched against a future Hall of Fame tackle, Roosevelt Brown.

"I wish they kept [defensive] records when I played, I'd like to see those 17 sacks in the books," Willey said. "Anytime you hold a record, people remember you. Look at Joe DiMaggio. Kids today know about his hitting streak. We can all relate to numbers.

"But I think they're getting ridiculous now. I look at the [defensive] stats after a game and they've got 'hurries' and 'pressures' and 'forced fumbles.' They probably keep track of how many times these guys burp during a game. But that's how the game has grown."

ADRIAN BURK'S SEVEN TOUCHDOWN DAY

On October 17, 1954, Eagles quarterback Adrian Burk wrote his name in the NFL record book by tossing seven touchdown passes in a 49–21 rout of Washington at Griffith Stadium. He tied the league record set by Chicago's Sid Luckman in 1943. The mark was later equaled by George Blanda of the Houston Oilers (1961), Y. A. Tittle of the New York Giants (1962), and Joe Kapp of Minnesota (1969).

"No one could have foreseen what would happen that day, least of all me," Burk said in a 1988 interview. "Our game plan was to run the ball. We spent the whole week practicing plays for [halfbacks] Jerry Williams and Jim Parmer. We felt we could control the ball on the ground."

But when the Eagles were near the goal line, Burk would fake a handoff and flip a pass to a receiver who usually was wide open in the end zone. None of his scoring passes was longer than 26 yards. Four of the touchdowns covered nine yards or less. He threw three apiece to ends Pete Pihos and Bobby Walston and one to halfback Toy Ledbetter.

Burk finished with 19 completions in 27 attempts for 229 yards. Those are almost paltry numbers compared to the totals amassed by Luckman (433 yards), Blanda (418), Tittle (505), and Kapp (449) in their record-setting games.

"It seemed like every time I threw a pass, it was six points," Burk said. "It was one of those days."

Because so many of the touchdown passes were short ones, it did not occur to Burk or his teammates that he was on the verge of history. Coach Jim Trimble lifted Burk in the fourth quarter after his sixth touchdown pass. Ed Hogan, the team's publicity director, checked the record book and discovered Burk needed one touchdown pass to tie Luckman. Hogan sent word to the bench, and Trimble sent Burk back into the game with instructions to go for the record.

"We didn't know what was going on," said Pihos, who led the league in receiving that season. "I couldn't figure out why they were lifting Bobby [Thomason, the other quarterback]. We were in the middle of a drive, we had the ball inside the 20. We didn't know anything about the record. I'm glad I didn't know or I might have dropped the damn ball when Adrian threw it to me [for the seventh touchdown]."

"After the game, there was no big to-do," Trimble said. "If someone threw seven touchdown passes in a game today, it would be all over the TV. As it was, we took a bus back to Philadelphia and there was no great elation. Part of that was Adrian himself. He was such a modest person. As I recall, he gave all the credit to his receivers."

THE HIT HEARD 'ROUND THE WORLD

Steve Sabol, president of NFL Films, calls it "the greatest tackle in pro football history": Chuck Bednarik's knockout shot on Frank Gifford. The hit took place on November 20, 1960, yet it still echoes from New York, where it occurred, to Philadelphia, where it is legend, to Canton, Ohio, where both players are enshrined in the Pro Football Hall of Fame.

"I'm still asked about it at least once a week," Bednarik said. "If I play in a golf tournament or go to a banquet, somebody asks about the time I got Gifford. It's amazing how many people know about that play."

Not so amazing, really, when you consider who was involved in the play and what it meant. It was one future Hall of Famer hitting another future Hall of Famer, knocking him cold and forcing a fumble that changed the destiny of two teams, the Eagles and the New York Giants.

The fumble, which Bednarik forced and the Eagles recovered, killed a New York drive and preserved a 17–10 victory for the Eagles at Yankee Stadium. The win put the 7–1 Eagles one and a half games ahead of the second-place Giants and keyed their improbable drive to the NFL Championship.

The Giants, meanwhile, lost the services of Gifford, their star halfback, for the rest of the 1960 season and all of the following season due to a severe concussion. Gifford came back in 1962 and moved to flanker, where he played three more years before retiring after the 1964 season.

What helped to immortalize the play was a series of photographs taken by *Sports Illustrated*'s John Zimmerman that showed Bednarik hitting Gifford and then dancing gleefully over the unconscious halfback. It appears Bednarik is gloating over Gifford's injury, but Bednarik has said a million times that was not the case. He was celebrating the fumble recovery that iced the win for the Eagles.

Adrian Burk tied an NFL record by throwing seven touchdown passes in one game against the Washington Redskins on October 17, 1954.

Chuck Bednarik's devastating hit on Frank Gifford sealed a huge win over the New York Giants on November 20, 1960. Gifford was knocked unconscious and suffered a severe concussion that sidelined him until the 1962 season.

"I didn't even see Gifford there," Bednarik said. "All I saw was the ball and Chuck Weber [Eagles linebacker] fell on it. I jumped up and pumped my fist and said, 'This f——ing game is over.' That's when [Zimmerman] took the picture.

"I did an appearance last year and was given a stack of photos to autograph. Don't you know that was the photo? One guy asked me about the play and I told him exactly what happened. He said, 'Would you write that on the picture for me?' So I did. I signed it, 'Best Wishes, Chuck Bednarik. This F——ing Game Is Over.'"

On the play, Gifford was running a crossing pattern through the Eagles defense. He caught the ball, but he was hit almost immediately by Bednarik, who was coming full speed in the opposite direction. "It was like a truck hitting a Volkswagen," Bednarik said. Gifford went down and never moved.

When you see the hit on film, it doesn't look that bad. Sabol had the same reaction when he saw it for the first time, saying, "I see four or five hits a week that look worse." But Sabol has talked to enough players who were on the field to know it was truly frightening. Hardened veterans, such as defensive end Marion Campbell, insist they never heard anything like it.

"It was like a bomb went off, I still remember seeing the turf fly," Campbell said. "There was nothing dirty about it. Chuck just hit Frank a good lick and put him out. But it gave us all a chill to see them put Frank on the stretcher. His eyes were rolled up in his head. His whole body was limp. I thought Chuck killed him."

The camera work of the time did not adequately convey the force of the blow delivered by the 6–3, 235-pound Bednarik on the 6-foot, 185-pound Gifford.

"The fact that the film is black-and-white and the camera is so far away really diffuses the impact," Sabol said. "If the same play happened now, with all our field-level cameras and the field microphones to pick up the live sound, it would be incredible."

What made the hit even more remarkable was that Bednarik was playing both ways—center on offense, linebacker on defense—as he did for much of the 1960 season. He was 35 years old, playing every down, and he still had the strength to KO Gifford in the final two minutes of the game.

Bednarik forced another key fumble on the previous series, hitting Giants fullback Mel Triplett and popping the ball straight up in the air. Cornerback Jimmy Carr caught it on the dead run and raced 36 yards for the winning touchdown. Many defensive players go an entire season and don't force two fumbles. Bednarik forced two in less than two minutes: one gave the Eagles the lead, the other sealed the victory that springboarded them to the NFL Championship.

There was an irresistible symbolism to the final play. Here was Bednarik with his flattened nose and mangled fingers, the working stiff from the steel mills, taking out Gifford, the golden boy from Southern Cal who was modeling clothes and making movies when he was not playing football. The contrast between the grit and the glamour is another reason why the play is so memorable. Concrete Charlie hung it on the handsome prince, right there in his own palace.

"It was like the New York press wanted me to apologize for hitting Gifford," Bednarik said. "They came to me after the game and said, 'Did you know Frank is hurt?' I said I didn't know, but it was a clean shot and that's part of the game. They carried Frank off on a stretcher, but I was in another world. I was busy celebrating the win. I played to win and so did Frank, that's why we're in the Hall of Fame. You don't hear him whining about it. He says I hit him a clean shot, and that's the truth."

The play has been talked about so much that it has become a love-hate thing with Bednarik. Sometimes he growls when he is asked about it. Other times he revels in the retelling. At a Maxwell Club football banquet, someone asked about the play and, flashing a wicked grin, Bednarik asked the man to lean forward.

"Here," Bednarik said, rubbing his shoulder. "You can still smell Gifford right here."

"If that was Kyle Rote or Alex Webster or any other Giant, it would have been forgotten long ago," Bednarik said. "But Frank's [TV] visibility kept it alive. [Howard] Cosell talked about it for 10 years on "Monday Night Football." Every time there was a hard hit, Cosell would say, 'Just like when Chuck Bednarik blindsided you, Giff, at Yankee Stadium.' I'd sit there on my couch and say, 'Blindside, my ass.' It was a good shot, head-on."

The play occurred near the New York bench, and several players, including quarterback Charlie Conerly, shouted at Bednarik, accusing him of a cheap shot. Enraged, Bednarik pointed at Conerly and said, "I'll get you next week."

A scheduling quirk had the Eagles and Giants rematched the next Sunday at Franklin Field. The buildup to the game was intense. The Giants talked about avenging Gifford, who remained hospitalized. First place in the Eastern Conference was at stake with the Giants needing a win to stay alive. One Giants fan, a woman, got Bednarik's phone number and called his house all hours of the day and night. She called several times the night before the game, jolting Bednarik and his wife Emma awake. It didn't matter. The Eagles defeated the Giants again, 31–23, and Bednarik played another brilliant 60-minute game.

"I sent a basket of flowers and a letter to Frank in the hospital," Bednarik said. "I told him I'd pray for him. I'm a good Catholic, but I'm also a football player. When I was on the field, I knocked the hell out of people, but that's the name of the game.

"Frank and I see each other at the Hall of Fame. We've played in golf tournaments together. There are no hard feelings. The only thing that ticked me off was the book he wrote. In the book, he tells his wife [Kathie Lee] that she is going to hear the name 'Bednarik' a lot. And she says, 'Bednarik? What's that, a pasta?' I read that and said, 'Pasta, my ass.'"

A RECORD DAY IN PICKS-BURG

On December 12, 1965, the Pittsburgh Steelers thanked the 22,002 fans who came out to Pitt Stadium by having a club employee dressed as Santa Claus toss footballs into the stands. On the field, the Steelers quarterbacks did their own version of a Christmas giveaway, throwing nine interceptions to the Eagles, tying an NFL single-game record.

"What are you going to with young quarterbacks like that?" Steeler coach Mike Nixon said, referring to Bill Nelsen, who threw two interceptions, and Tommy Wade, who threw the last seven, as the Eagles routed Pittsburgh, 47–13.

Rookie Jim Nettles, who replaced an injured Nate Ramsey at safety, intercepted three passes. Free safety Joe Scarpati intercepted two. Linebacker Maxie Baughan, cornerback Irv Cross, defensive end George Tarasovic, and Ramsey had one apiece. Baughan, Nettles, and Tarasovic each returned an interception for a score, tying the league record for most touchdowns on interception returns in a single game.

"This day was just one of those things," Nettles said. "It might not have been as good as it looked."

The truth is, it didn't look all that good. The Steelers had more first downs than the Eagles (19–17) and outgained them, 324 yards to 302, but they turned the ball over so often that they allowed the Eagles to build a 27–0 lead in the first quarter.

"It was a weird, sloppy game, almost a travesty on the sport," wrote Herb Good in the Philadelphia Inquirer. "Brief flurries of fisticuffs broke out three times as frustrations ignited tempers."

Bill Shefski of the Philadelphia Daily News described the scene in the Pittsburgh locker room, where Nelsen and Wade "were seated despondently next to each other like two old ladies whose purses had just been snatched."

For the Steelers, the loss was their sixth in a row and their 11th in 13 games. The Eagles were not much better at 5–8, having lost six of their previous eight games.

Nettles was signed by the Eagles as an undrafted free agent after his graduation from the University of Wisconsin. Nettles was listed at 5–10 and 175 pounds, but he was actually smaller than that. The pro scouts rejected him because of his size, but he earned an invitation to training camp by writing a letter to coach Joe Kuharich.

Nettles played a total of eight seasons in the NFL, four with the Eagles, four with the Los Angeles Rams, but he never had another day like the one in Pittsburgh. There must have been something in the air because on the same day Gale Sayers scored a record six touchdowns for Chicago against San Francisco, and Paul Hornung scored five touchdowns for Green Bay against Baltimore.

SCARPATI STEALS THE BALL

The Eagles have been around since 1933, they have played almost 1,000 regular-season games, but they never played a wackier one than the 24–23 win over Dallas on November 6, 1966. That was the day Joe Scarpati stole the ball. In Eagles history, it will go down as the Grand Larceny.

"[That play] still comes up when I'm introduced to people," said Scarpati, who played free safety for the Eagles for seven seasons. "Very often they will say, 'I was there the day you stole the ball from [Dan] Reeves.'

"A couple guys I work with saw Reeves recently. They introduced themselves and said, 'We're friends of Joe Scarpati.' They said Dan talked for 10 minutes about that play. The guy's been to, like, 20 Super Bowls since then and he still remembers that play. It must've been pretty good."

Scarpati snatched the ball from Reeves after the Dallas halfback carried a Don Meredith pass down to the Eagles' 13-yard line with 90 seconds left in the game. The pass play gained 23 yards, and the Cowboys were in position to milk the clock and kick a chip-shot field goal in the closing seconds to win.

But Scarpati's theft, witnessed by 60,658 slack-jawed fans at Franklin Field, saved the day and so enraged Reeves he chased after one official to protest and accidentally knocked him down. For that, Reeves was ejected from the game, the first and only time in his 30-year career as an NFL player and coach.

"I didn't know I was ejected until Tex [Schramm, the team president] told me on the flight back to Dallas," Reeves said. "Our offense never got back on the field [after the turnover] so no one ever bothered to tell me I was out. That game cost me a lot of money. I was supposed to stay in Philly and speak at a banquet, but I had to fly back to Dallas to get treatment for an injury. So I canceled the appearance, which was for $200, and I got fined another $200 for the ejection on top of that.

"Four hundred dollars was a heckuva lot of money back then," Reeves said. "I give Joe credit for making a heads-up play, but to this day, I still think it was a bad call. The whistle should have blown."

"Tell Dan it's too late. The statute of limitations ran out," Scarpati said.

The irony of the play: Scarpati was given a poor grade in film review by assistant coach Fred Bruney, who pointed out that (1) Scarpati was beaten by Reeves on the pass completion and (2) he missed a tackle on Reeves before catching him from behind and swiping the ball.

It was a fitting epilogue to a crazy day, during which

- the Eagles scored three touchdowns, all on kick returns. Two were kickoff returns by Timmy Brown (93 and 90 yards); the other was a punt return by Aaron Martin (87 yards).
- the Eagles upset a very good Dallas team despite an anemic offense that managed only five first downs and completed just five passes in 17 attempts.
- the home team avenged a 56–7 whipping at the hands of the Cowboys just four weeks earlier.

In the week leading up to the rematch, Eagles coach Joe Kuharich made the players watch the film of that game every day to remind them how thoroughly they were humiliated in Dallas. "We all squirmed in our seats watching that film," defensive tackle Don Hultz said.

The Eagles could have been routed again at Franklin Field if it hadn't been for the defense, which forced the Cowboys to punt nine times, and the special teams, which scored three touchdowns. Brown's two kickoff return touchdowns set an NFL record. Martin's touchdown return was the first and last of his pro career.

"I was happy for Aaron because he was going through a rough time," Scarpati said of the cornerback who was dropped from the starting lineup that week. "He wasn't a great corner, but he had better than average skills. The mental part was what killed him. The fans got on him and broke his confidence. The punt return got the fans off his back for a day at least."

In the end, the game came down to the final drive. The Eagles were clinging to a one-point lead, but Dallas marched down the field with Meredith completing four consecutive passes, three to Reeves, one to flanker Buddy Dial. With a first down at the Eagles 36-yard line, Meredith hit Reeves in the flat, and he spun away from a diving Scarpati and headed upfield. He had a chance to step out of bounds, but cut back and tried for the end zone.

Cornerback Jim Nettles, starting in place of Martin, grabbed Reeves at the 13-yard line and was struggling to bring him down when Scarpati came up from behind.

"I was coming in to help with the tackle, and as I got there, Dan kind of turned," Scarpati said. "He was still on his feet and had his arm extended. The ball was right there. I just reached in and grabbed it. The official was coming in, and he had his whistle raised. He was ready to blow the play dead, but I got the ball first. A split second later would have been too late."

Joe Scarpati accepts congratulations on the bench after stealing the ball from Dan Reeves to clinch the 24–23 win over Dallas on November 6, 1966. "[That play] still comes up when I'm introduced to people," Scarpati said.

"I started back up the field," said Scarpati, who returned the ball 13 yards before the Cowboys realized what happened and knocked him out of bounds. "I still wasn't sure it was legal until one official took the ball and spotted it there. I thought they might overturn it. It seemed like the Cowboys always got those calls. We suspected Schramm had some extra influence on the officials. He was on all those committees."

Reeves has two postscripts to the story. One, a few days after the game, Dallas owner Clint Murchison sent a gift-wrapped box to Reeves' locker. Inside, Reeves found an old football with half the cover ripped off. Said Reeves: "There was no note, but I think the idea was, 'See if you can hang onto this.'"

Postscript No. 2: The Cowboys were preparing for the Eagles the following year, and coach Tom Landry was going over the scouting report. When Landry got to Scarpati, he stumbled over his name.

"Tom always slaughtered people's names," Reeves said. "He was saying, 'Here's No. 21. Scar-peter, Scar-pappy. Aw, what's his name? Then he said, 'Reeves, you must know his name. What is it?'"

FIRST MONDAY NIGHT WIN AT THE VET

Like most players, Bill Bergey enjoyed the adrenaline rush of "Monday Night Football." What he did not enjoy was Monday afternoon, trapped in a hotel room, waiting.

"It can drive you crazy; the minutes pass like hours," the former All-Pro middle linebacker said. "All you can think about is the game, and it seems like it will never get there."

That was especially true on September 23, 1974, when the Eagles played their home opener on a Monday night against Dallas. It was Bergey's first regular-season appearance at Veterans Stadium. He knew how tough the Philadelphia fans could be, so he wanted to impress them right away. The Eagles paid a steep price to acquire him—two first-round draft picks and a second-round pick—so he knew he was under a microscope.

Also, with the game on national TV, Bergey wanted to make a point to his previous employers in Cincinnati. Bergey played five seasons with the Bengals and was one of the top linebackers in the game, but the team dealt him to Philadelphia when he threatened to sign with the rival World Football League.

"I wanted to show the Bengals what a horrible mistake they made," Bergey said. "The Bengals as much as said, 'You're our meat; we will decide what happens to you.' I wanted to stick it to them. Playing well on Monday night was one way to do it."

Bergey stuck it to the Cowboys as he made 18 tackles in a 13–10 Eagles win. "It seemed like there were six of him out there," said Dallas coach Tom Landry.

Bergey made the biggest play of the game, hitting rookie Doug Dennison and forcing a fumble that cornerback Joe Lavender returned 96 yards for a touchdown. It was the longest fumble return in Eagles history, and it gave the team the lift it needed on a night when the offense did next to nothing.

Bergey's hit turned the game around. The Cowboys led 7–0 and Dennison was one step away from making it 14–0 when Bergey drilled him at the goal line. The ball popped loose, Lavender scooped it up and raced away untouched to tie the score.

"Once I saw Joe in the clear, I knew he was gone," Bergey said. "Roger [Staubach] chased him, but there was no way Roger was going to catch him. I got a big smile on my face. As a linebacker, you don't get those moments too often, where you make a play that actually puts points on the board. To do it in a big game like that, especially against the Cowboys, was a tremendous thrill."

Dennison was playing in place of the injured Calvin Hill. The fumble was a bitter blow for Dennison, who played at Kutztown State and had a dozen relatives at the game.

"That [touchdown] gave the Eagles life," Landry said. "If we had gone ahead 14–0, it would have been hard for them to catch up. But give Bergey credit, he made a great play."

That play launched the Bergey legend in Philadelphia. It started a chant at the Vet that echoed for the next six seasons. Ber-gey … Ber-gey …

"That game got me over the hump," Bergey said. "There were all those banners in the stands with my name on them. One said, 'Thanks for coming to Philly.' Another said 'Dallas sinks after hitting an Ice-Bergey.' It was great, knowing the fans were behind me."

For the Eagles, it was the first "Monday Night Football" win at Veterans Stadium. Kicker Tom Dempsey provided the winning points, kicking a 45-yard field goal with 25 seconds left in regulation time. It was only the second win for the Eagles in 14 meetings with the Cowboys dating back to 1967. Bergey's hit was the key blow.

"I don't know if it was my best hit," Bergey said, "but it surely came at the best time."

THE MIRACLE OF THE MEADOWLANDS

As head coach of the New York Jets, Herman Edwards preaches one message above all others: "Finish the play." Every day at practice and right before each game, he calls his players together and reminds them. No matter what happens, no matter what the score is, finish every play.

"Like I tell them, 'You never know. Funny things happen in this game,'" Edwards said.

Coming from some coaches, it would sound like a cliché. But when Edwards says it, it rings true because finishing the play—one play in particular—is what earned him a place in football history.

Edwards was the Eagles cornerback who scooped up a fumble and ran it in for a touchdown in the closing seconds, turning an apparent loss into a storybook 19–17 victory over the New York Giants. The play will forever be known as "The Miracle of the Meadowlands." It took place on November 19, 1978, but it still pops up on NFL highlight shows and in Joe Pisarcik's nightmares.

Pisarcik was the quarterback who fumbled the handoff to fullback Larry Csonka as the Giants were running out the clock with a 17–12 lead. The Eagles were out of timeouts and seemingly out of hope. But Pisarcik's last handoff hit Csonka on the hip and fell to the ground. The ball bounced off the artificial turf, and few people even realized it. Most of the players were piled up at the line, and most of the fans were headed for the exits, figuring the game was over.

Eagles quarterback Ron Jaworski was sitting on the bench with his head down. He had just thrown his third interception and thought he cost the Eagles the game. He could not bear to watch as the Giants ran out the final seconds. "That was

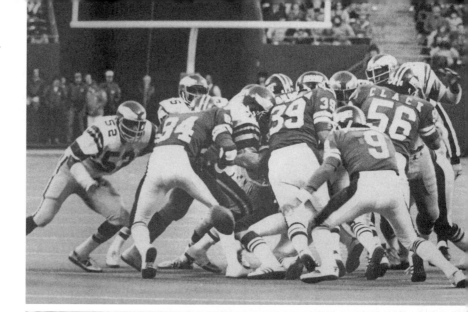

about as low as I've ever felt," Jaworski said, "until I heard someone shout, 'Hey, Herman's got the ball.' Then it was about as happy as I've ever felt."

Edwards should not have been in the game at that time. He normally came out when the other team went into a formation with no split receivers, and that was what the Giants were using to run out the clock. So why was Edwards on the field? He has no idea.

"We stayed with our base [defense]," Edwards said. "I don't know why. Maybe Marion [Campbell, defensive coordinator] thought it was the end of the game so it didn't matter who was out there. Looking back, that was one of the ironies. It was like fate. I know that sounds weird, but how else can you explain it? The NFL has been around for more than 80 years, and there never has been another play like that one. There had to be something crazy going on that day."

Fate …

The Giants run a play that never should have been called—why hand off when the quarterback can simply kneel down?—and the ball hops into the lap of a player who shouldn't even be on the field, and he takes it into the end zone to win the game. Toss in the fact that Eagles owner Leonard Tose was in a Houston hospital recovering from open-heart surgery and listening to the game on a special radio hookup. It was a day with so many story lines and mood swings, it seemed lifted from a pulp novel.

But it was all real: crazily, wonderfully, memorably real.

"I still believe [linebacker] Frank LeMaster made that play happen," said Bill Bergey, the All-Pro linebacker.

On the previous play, he shot through the line and hit Pisarcik when Joe went down to one knee to run out the clock. It was a frustration play on Frank's part, and it really ticked the Giants off. A fight started, and guys were rolling around. I said to Frank, "What the hell are you doing? Let's get this over with and get outta here."

When the Giants lined up for the next play, I heard them arguing. Guys were saying, "Joe, just fall on the damn ball." I thought, "What the heck is this all about?" Then I saw

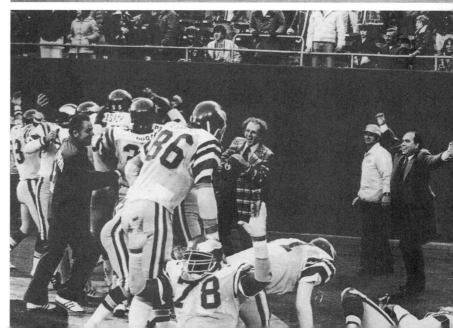

A botched handoff from Joe Pisarcik (9) to Larry Csonka (39) resulted in one of the most memorable plays in Eagles history: The Miracle of the Meadowlands. Herman Edwards (46) picked up the loose ball and raced 26 yards for the touchdown that turned certain defeat into a 19–17 win over the New York Giants on November 19, 1978. Assistant director of public relations Chick McElrone (plaid jacket) and general manager Jim Murray (far right) join in the celebration.

Joe turn and hand off to Csonka. I really think they were running Csonka at Frank as a payback for him hitting the quarterback.

Joe never got the ball to Csonka. He dropped it; it hit the ground and bounced right to Herman. He took it in stride and headed for the end zone. I was so excited, I almost jumped out of my shoes.

Edwards remembers the scuffle following LeMaster's hit on Pisarcik. He stood off to one side with Doug Kotar, the Giants halfback. "There were only a few seconds left, and I said to Kotar, 'Okay, man, we'll see you in a couple weeks back in Philly,'" Edwards said. "He said, 'Okay, see you then.' Next play was the fumble. Unbelievable."

"It seemed like everything about that play happened in slow motion," Edwards said. "The ball fell right in front of me and took a perfect hop. I picked it up, and I don't remember anything else until I was in the end zone and the guys were mobbing me. All I could think was 'Did this really happen?' I remember how quiet the stadium was. A lot of fans were gone by then, and the ones who stayed were sitting there in shock."

The improbable victory lifted the Eagles record to 7–5 and gave them the impetus to finish 9–7, their first winning season since 1966. That also was the first of four consecutive playoff seasons for the Eagles under coach Dick Vermeil.

"That was a turning point for our team," tackle Stan Walters said. "Prior to that, we were losing games we should've won. That day, we won a game we should've lost, and all of a sudden we became a team that expected to win. Even if we were losing, we felt we'd find a way to win. We didn't have that feeling before."

"I remember standing on the field, thinking, 'How am I going to explain this [loss] to Leonard?'" said general manager Jim Murray. "Then all of a sudden, here's Herman Edwards running toward me with the football and I'm thinking, 'Is this a dream?' This was the miracle, no doubt about it.

"It was funny, we got Pisarcik [in 1980] as the backup to Jaworski. We talked about that play. I told him, 'Joe, you're Catholic. All you had to do was genuflect and the game would've been over.'"

That night, the team celebrated at the South Jersey home of Vince Papale. The party went into the wee hours of Monday, and Papale's neighbors finally called the police. "[The police] came to the door," Papale said, "and saw it was an Eagles party. One guy said, 'Hey, great game.' I invited them in and they partied with us. We went all night."

Edwards may be the only defensive player ever to inspire an offensive formation. Today, when you see most teams run out the clock, they position one man 10 yards deep so he can make the tackle in case there is a fumble.

"My players kid me about that," said Edwards, who as head coach of the New York Jets plays his home games on the site of his famous play. "They say, 'Look, coach, it's your formation.' Then they say, 'Man, you must've been good. You revolutionized the game.'"

CARMICHAEL'S RECORD STREAK

It began humbly enough with one catch against Washington in the fourth week of the 1972 season. But week by week, season by season, it grew into The Streak: 106 consecutive games

Harold Carmichael made history by catching at least one pass in 106 consecutive games, a streak that spanned eight seasons.

with at least one pass reception for Harold Carmichael. At the time, it was an NFL record, breaking the mark set by Danny Abramowicz of the New Orleans Saints.

Carmichael did not even realize he had a streak until 1977 when a local TV sports producer, Bill Werndl, started counting up the games. "I never kept track of statistics," Carmichael said. "But Bill said, 'You have a chance to make history.'"

When The Streak began, the Eagles were a lousy team (2–11–1), and Carmichael was still something of a curiosity. He was a gangly 6–8 receiver who was trying to prove he belonged in the NFL. But as The Streak continued over the next seven years, the Eagles developed into a Super Bowl contender, and Carmichael matured into one of the league's top receivers.

Carmichael set the record on November 4, 1979, at Veterans Stadium. The Eagles were playing Cleveland, and The Streak was on everyone's mind. For that very reason, Ron Jaworski threw Carmichael a five-yard hitch pass on the game's first series so he could get the record safely tucked away. "There was a sigh of relief," Carmichael said.

Carmichael still was untangling himself from the pileup when a golf cart whizzed onto the artificial turf carrying Eagles owner Leonard Tose, Carmichael's wife Bea, and his infant son, Lee Harold II. They brought with them a trophy to commemorate his record: the world's tallest trophy (23 feet, 9 inches) for the world's tallest wide receiver.

The game was stopped for a brief ceremony, which embarrassed Carmichael, and the crowd responded with a standing ovation. Carmichael kissed his wife and son, buckled his chin strap, and went back to work. It was a wonderful day, except for one thing: the Eagles lost the game, 24–19, blowing a nine-point lead in the fourth quarter.

"I'm happy to have the record," Carmichael said, "but I have feelings for the other 44 guys, too, and they have no record to celebrate. Everything went so beautifully today, until we lost. There is nothing that can happen to you in this game that is as much fun as winning."

Regarding the trophy: It was created by the Action Trophy Manufacturing Company in Philadelphia to earn a place in the Guinness Book of World Records. The previous tallest trophy was 15 feet. They wanted to top that, and they did. But once they had the record, they did not know what to do with the trophy.

They called the Eagles to ask if they had a use for it. General manager Jim Murray immediately thought of Carmichael, who was closing in on the record. Wrote Tom Cushman in the *Philadelphia Daily News*: "Like the man it honors, [the trophy] is tall, unique, a world record holder, and we can be reasonably certain that Harold did not already have one."

The trophy, obviously, was too big to display in Carmichael's house, so it was sent to the Pro Football Hall of Fame in Canton, Ohio, where it was placed in the lobby. Carmichael extended his streak to 127 games until December 21, 1980, when he was knocked out of a game in Dallas and finished without a catch. His record stood until Seattle's Steve Largent passed him in 1986.

TONY FRANKLIN BOOTS THE COWBOYS

The Eagles had lost three consecutive games to see their record fall to 6–4. Their confidence was shaken, their early season optimism fading fast as they traveled to Dallas for a Monday night game on November 12, 1979.

The night before the game, there was the usual team meeting at the hotel with Dick Vermeil addressing the squad. In his four years as coach, Vermeil had talked endlessly about beating Dallas. The Eagles could not go anywhere, he reasoned, until they got past the Cowboys.

Vermeil hammered away at that theme, reading off a checklist that began, "What will it take to beat the Dallas Cowboys?" He would enumerate dozens of things from improving the pass rush to adding X-number of yards to the net punting average. He had improved the team, yet he had not found a way to beat the Cowboys in six tries. This hardly seemed like the time for a breakthrough with his team reeling and the Cowboys riding high at 8–2.

The night before the game, Vermeil began the meeting by asking, "What will it take to beat the Dallas Cowboys?" Some players rolled their eyes, thinking, "Here we go again." This time, however, there was no long checklist. This time, Vermeil said, "Just another 24 hours." With that, he left the room.

"Guys were saying, 'Did he say what I think he said?'" tackle Stan Walters said. "Talk about impact. He was saying, 'We've arrived. We're ready to beat those guys.' We walked out of that room really believing."

The next night, while the Cowboys awaited their pregame introductions, Eagles rookie Tony Franklin practiced his kick-offs by knocking the ball into the end zone where the Dallas players were standing. One after another, the balls rained down on the Cowboys, who were none too happy about it. They shouted some unkind remarks at the cocky barefoot kicker from Texas A&M.

"I was standing next to [tackle Jerry] Sisemore," Walters recalled, "and he was saying, 'Franklin is doing this on purpose, f——ing rookie.' We thought he was gonna tick the Cowboys off, and he did."

It didn't matter as the Eagles won the game, 31–21. Wilbert Montgomery rushed for 127 yards, and Harold Carmichael scored two touchdowns, including one on a fourth-and-inches play that took the Dallas defense by surprise. There was even a cameo appearance by backup quarterback John Walton, who came into the game for two series when Ron Jaworski was shaken up and threw a clutch 29-yard touchdown pass to Charlie Smith.

But the play that stands out is the 59-yard field goal that Franklin booted right before halftime. It was the longest field goal in Eagles history, topping the 54-yarder kicked by Tom Dempsey in 1971. It also tied for the fourth-longest in league history. Wrote Gary Smith in the *Philadelphia Daily News*: "It left his naked right foot with a satisfying thump, climbed majestically, and dipped several yards behind the crossbar … sending Franklin into jackrabbit ecstasy."

The Eagles had gone through four different kickers the previous two seasons, so they invested a third-round draft pick in Franklin. He immediately improved their kicking game, hitting on 13 of his first 17 field goal attempts. He had kicked a 65-yard field goal in college, but when he was lining up for his 59-yarder that night at Texas Stadium, no one outside the Eagles bench thought he could make it.

"We thought he couldn't hit from that distance," said Dallas coach Tom Landry, who declined a five-yard penalty on the Eagles immediately prior to the kick. "But he did hit it, and that really took the juice out right before half."

"So help me God, Tony said, 'Coach, I can hit that,'" Vermeil said. "So I said, 'Go ahead.'"

Franklin was not celebrating after the game, however. He missed on three other field goal attempts, two from 45 yards, one from 52. They were hardly chip shots, but it upset Franklin who said, "I kicked like a damn first-grader. I hate to kick so damn bad in front of all these Texas people. I guess Howard [Cosell, the ABC broadcaster] had a field day."

JAWORSKI TO QUICK: 99 YARDS

The Eagles had the ball at their own one-yard line. Actually, the ball was inside the one-yard line. "It was this far from the goal line," Ron Jaworski said, holding his thumb and forefinger an inch apart. "It was that close."

The Eagles had squandered a 17–0 lead against the Atlanta Falcons and found themselves tied 17–17 in sudden-death overtime. Surely, they would not take any chances with the ball so close to their own goal line.

"We figured they'd play it safe and keep it on the ground," Falcon coach Dan Henning said. "We didn't expect them to throw the ball, and we didn't expect them to throw to the inside."

Wrote Paul Domowitch in the *Philadelphia Daily News*: "A word of advice: Don't take any stock tips from Dan Henning."

On second down, Jaworski stepped back into the end zone and threw a strike to wide receiver Mike Quick, who split two Atlanta defenders, cornerback Bobby Butler and safety Scott Case. It was a perfectly executed slant route, which Quick took the distance, officially 99 yards to win the game and tie the NFL record for longest touchdown pass.

"The safety went for the interception," Jaworski said. "I guess he underestimated my ability. But my arm still has a little zip on it."

"That play was there for the better portion of the day," Quick said. "I knew I could get the slant on them. And I knew if the outside guy [Butler] didn't get me that I had a chance to go all the way. When the safety didn't slow me up, I knew there was no stopping me unless I tripped and fell."

"We got beat on a great play by a great athlete," Henning said. "If we have to get beat, that's the way I'd like to see us get beat."

A tragic footnote to that day: November 10, 1985. That morning, Flyers goaltender Pelle Lindbergh was involved in a fatal car wreck in South Jersey. Eagles cornerback Herman Edwards reflected on that after the game. "It makes the winning and losing of a game mean nothing," Edwards said. "You realize the important thing is being here. Living."

RANDALL STRIKES IT RICH

Keith Byars recalls noticing something in pregame warm-ups that day in Washington, D.C. Something different, something good, and, as it turned out, something prophetic.

"Randall was really sharp … I mean, sharper than sharp," Byars said, flashing back to September 17, 1989. "He was zipping the ball, hitting us right in the hands. I remember saying to Mike Quick, 'Man, Randall looks goooood.' Mike said, 'Yeah, he does. He's in the zone today.'"

No one else on the team knew it, but that morning Randall Cunningham signed a five-year, $14 million contract extension that made him the NFL's highest paid player. The deal was negotiated by Eagles president Harry Gamble and Cunningham's agent Jim Steiner, and it was settled early Sunday morning in Gamble's hotel suite in suburban Washington.

Cunningham signed the papers, then boarded the team bus. He did not tell anyone about the deal because he did not want to distract them from the job at hand: finding a way to win at RFK Stadium, where the Eagles were 1–7 since 1981.

Once Cunningham was on the field, the good vibes took over, and he had the greatest game of his Eagles career. He completed 34 passes for 447 yards (both club records at the time) and five touchdowns (a personal best) as the Eagles stunned the Redskins, 42–37.

The game had everything: 966 yards in combined total offense, nine turnovers between the two teams, the Redskins scoring on their first two plays from scrimmage (an 80-yard pass from Mark Rypien to Gary Clark and a 41-yard run by Gerald Riggs), and the Eagles stealing a win in the final minute on a Wes Hopkins fumble recovery followed by a four-yard touchdown pass from Cunningham to tight end Keith Jackson.

"A miracle from the sky," Eagles defensive end Reggie White called it.

For the Redskins, it was such a shattering loss that Rypien canceled a postgame dinner with Vice President Dan Quayle. Said Rypien, "I don't think I'd be very good company."

Randall Cunningham set an Eagles team record by passing for 447 yards in a 42–37 win over Washington in 1989. Later that season, he set another team mark when he boomed a 91-yard punt against the New York Giants.

The Eagles played most of the game in a spread formation with Jackson and Byars working against either a linebacker or a safety. Either way, it was a mismatch. Jackson finished with 12 catches for 126 yards and a career-high three touchdowns. Byars had eight receptions for a career-high 130 yards. Quick and Cris Carter also caught touchdown passes from Cunningham.

"We were losing pretty bad at halftime, but we were in a good rhythm offensively," Byars said. "I remember Randall saying, 'We can win this game. They can't stop us.' I could see in his eyes, he was really into it. After the game, I heard about the new contract and I laughed. I said, 'Oh, now I know why you played so good.'"

"I was up all morning [with Steiner] going over the details," Cunningham said, "so my body was nice and warm. Plus, there was the satisfaction of knowing I had a contract like that. Going into the game, I felt relaxed, knowing everything was taken care of. It was like, 'Hey, we took care of business, now let's have some fun.'"

RANDALL CUNNINGHAM'S 91-YARD PUNT

On a brutally cold December 3, 1989, with the temperature in the teens and the winds gusting at 35 miles per hour, Randall Cunningham stood eight yards deep in the end zone awaiting the snap. There were many quizzical looks in the Giants Stadium press box. Why wasn't Max Runager, the Eagles regular punter, in the game?

With one mighty swing of his leg, Cunningham answered that question. The Eagles starting quarterback and part-time punter boomed a 91-yard kick through the biting wind. It was the longest punt in Eagles history, topping Joe Muha's 82-yard effort against the Giants in 1948, and it was the third-longest punt in NFL history behind the Jets' Steve O'Neal (98 yards) against Denver in 1969 and Green Bay's Joe Lintzenich (94) against the Giants in 1931.

Jay Searcy of the *Philadelphia Inquirer* described Cunningham's punt as "so high and so long and so beautiful, it must have passed through heaven." He kicked it from eight yards deep in his end zone and it traveled 70 yards in the air. It landed at the Giants 38-yard line and skipped past return man Dave Meggett, who finally chased the ball down at the seven. He returned it only as far as the 16.

The score was tied 17–17 in the fourth quarter, and Cunningham's punt changed the field position. Two plays later, defensive tackle Mike Golic sacked Giants quarterback Phil Simms and forced a fumble, which Mike Pitts recovered at the 7. Three plays later, Keith Byars powered into the end zone with the winning touchdown.

"That [punt] was the ball game," said Al Roberts, the Eagles special-teams coach. "We knew we were going to win then. After that, we felt with any kind of accident that might happen—a blocked punt, an interception, or a fumble—we'd be in position to take advantage."

"I never played in a game where the [weather] conditions were so bad," Runager said. "Randall has a tremendous leg. You've got a weapon like that, you use it. I'm more of a directional kicker. I don't have the power Randall has. That was the right spot to use him."

Cunningham averaged 45.2 yards per punt during his college career at UNLV. He rarely punted in the pros, but he worked on it at least one day a week at practice, just in case. Cunningham's punting was inconsistent, which is why he was called on infrequently. He would hit three booming kicks, then shank one for 15 yards. A punter like Runager was more reliable. But in certain situations, when the Eagles needed a big kick, they called on Randall and hoped for the best.

"Randall has no form," Roberts said. "You can talk mechanically and structurally about how to place the ball on the foot and the power zone, but Randall has such outstanding athletic ability, he just gets his foot on the football and God does the rest. You don't coach that. You just let it go. You just say, 'Randall, kick.'"

"That was the longest punt I've ever had in my life, even without the bounce," Cunningham said.

THE SACKING OF TROY

Bud Carson was overwhelmed by the Eagles pass rush. Not as overwhelmed as Dallas quarterback Troy Aikman perhaps, but overwhelmed nonetheless. The Eagles' defensive coordinator could not remember another game in which his unit dominated the opposition as thoroughly as the Eagles dominated the Cowboys on September 15, 1991.

That's a huge statement considering Carson coached the fearsome Pittsburgh defense in the 1970s, the Steel Curtain that has sent four players to the Pro Football Hall of Fame.

"We had some great games," Carson said, reflecting on those Super Bowl seasons in Pittsburgh, "but nothing like this."

The Eagles had a club-record 11 sacks against Aikman as they blanked the Cowboys 24–0 at Texas Stadium. What was remarkable about the Eagles rush was that it was achieved with very little blitzing. Carson occasionally rushed linebacker Seth Joyner, but most of the time it was the front four and only the front four storming the gates.

"There hasn't been this one-sided a struggle on Texas soil since Davy Crockett got trapped in the Alamo," wrote Stan Hochman in the *Philadelphia Daily News*.

Jerome Brown had two and a half of the 11 sacks on Dallas quarterback Troy Aikman. "We had Troy running for his life," Clyde Simmons said.

"[The Eagles] had guys all over the place," Aikman said. "It felt like there was 20 guys out there, all chasing me. We couldn't do anything."

Clyde Simmons set a team record with four and a half sacks, Jerome Brown had two and a half, Mike Golic had two, and Reggie White and Mike Pitts had one each. The most surprising aspect of the rout was that White, the league's premier pass rusher, had only one of the 11 sacks.

"How Golic got more than me, I still don't know," White said in mock disgust. "That's ridiculous."

The victory extended the Eagles winning streak over Dallas to eight games, the longest winning streak for any opponent ever against the Cowboys. They came into the game with the NFL's top-ranked offense, and the Eagles limited them to 90 total yards, the lowest single-game output in Cowboys history.

"After that game, people said we couldn't win with our line," said Norv Turner, the former offensive coordinator in Dallas. "They said Nate [Newton] was too fat, [Kevin] Gogan was too slow, and [Mark] Stepnoski was too small. But with the exception of Erik Williams, who broke in [right tackle] the next year, it was the same line that took us to two Super Bowls and helped Emmitt [Smith] win three rushing titles. It was a good line; it just happened to have a real bad day against the Eagles."

The Eagles defense was at its peak in 1991, ranking first in the NFL against both the run and the pass. In its first season under Carson, the defense led the league with 55 sacks and tied for the lead with 48 takeaways.

"It was a great day for the whole line," said Simmons, who was named NFC Defensive Player of the Week. "I don't know if it was my best game. I don't look at things that way. But it was the best from a team standpoint. We had everything going our way. We stopped the run early, got the lead, and we had them in long-yardage situations all day. We had Troy running for his life."

FOURTH AND ONE, TIMES TWO

It was a typically cold winter's day—December 10, 1995—when the Eagles and Dallas Cowboys met at Veterans Stadium. The wind chill was minus seven degrees, but the Eagles still were feeling the heat from coach Ray Rhodes' speech the night before. It was a profane rant about fighting for respect and protecting your home and manhood.

"It was more like street talk than a pep talk," guard Guy McIntyre said. "What Ray said, basically, was the Cowboys didn't respect us and they were coming into our house to slap us around. Ray put it to each guy on the team: 'What are you gonna do about it?'"

The Eagles were a surprising 8–5 in their first season under Rhodes, and they were two games behind Dallas (10–3) in the NFC East. Early in the game, the Cowboys were in control, opening a 17–6 lead as Emmitt Smith ran for 98 yards in the first half. But Rhodes adjusted, bringing an extra defender into the box to slow the run, hoping the cold, windy conditions would discourage quarterback Troy Aikman from passing.

Rhodes strategy worked, and the Eagles, led by the relentless pounding of Ricky Watters (33 carries, 112 yards), clawed their way back to tie the game, 17–17. With just over two minutes remaining, the Cowboys had fourth down and less than a foot to go for a first down at their own 29-yard line.

Barry Switzer, in his second season as head coach after succeeding Jimmy Johnson, decided to go for the first down rather than punt. It was a strange call, risking the loss of possession deep in your own territory late in the game. John Madden, calling the game on the Fox TV network, said, "I wouldn't do this."

The Cowboys went with their best short yardage play—Load Left—a straight handoff to Smith running behind fullback Daryl Johnston, left tackle Mark Tuinei, and guard Nate Newton. But tackle Andy Harmon and linebackers Kurt Gouveia and Bill Romanowski penetrated and stopped Smith for no gain.

Over the roar of the crowd, Eagles radio analyst Stan Walters could be heard saying, "Uh oh, the officials are talking. We might have a problem."

Referee Ed Hochuli ruled the clock had ticked down to the two-minute warning before the ball was snapped. Therefore, it was a dead ball, no play. Switzer was handed a reprieve. He had seen his gamble blow up in his face. Surely, he wouldn't try it again. But he did. Not only did Switzer go for it again, he went with the same play.

"One yard to go and they run the same exact play? You don't see that very often," defensive end William Fuller said. "You would've thought we'd have an emotional letdown after stopping them and having the play waved off. But we were fired up. We were saying, 'Come on, bring it on.'"

"We got a lot of energy from the fans," Romanowski said. "I don't know if I ever heard a crowd that loud. The whole stadium was shaking."

Aikman handed off to Smith, and Harmon, Romanowski, and end Mike Mamula stopped him cold. The Eagles took possession and won the game on a 42-yard field goal by Gary Anderson, his fourth of the day. Final score: Eagles 20, Cowboys 17.

"Hell, yes, it was my decision," Switzer said. "I wanted to control the ball. Move it down there so we could do something with the time that was left. That [decision] wasn't the difference. The way we played the final 30 minutes, that was the difference."

At the time, it seemed like a monumental win for the Eagles. Bill Lyon of the *Philadelphia Inquirer* wrote, "This has the feel of a game that will be pointed to two or three years from now, when Ray Rhodes has everything in place and the Eagles have become members of the elite class. This will be recalled as the game that was the springboard."

The victory helped the Eagles finish the 1995 season with a 10–6 record and make the NFC playoffs as a wild card, but it did not have long-term resonance. One month later, the Cowboys crushed the Eagles in the divisional playoff, 30–11, and went on to win the Super Bowl. Rhodes' career in Philadelphia collapsed in ruins, but that one moment—with Merrill Reese shouting, "They stopped them *again*"—remains a lasting memory.

THE 104-YARD INTERCEPTION RETURN

On November 3, 1996, James Willis accomplished a rare trifecta. On one play, Willis (1) made the interception that preserved an Eagles victory, (2) helped to set an NFL record for the longest interception return, and (3) incurred the wrath of head coach Ray Rhodes. How, you wonder, is it possible to do all three?

Here's how: Willis made a clutch interception of a Troy Aikman pass in the end zone with the Eagles clinging to a 24–21 lead with just 15 seconds left in regulation time. So far so good. But instead of taking a knee in the end zone, which would have been the safe thing to do, Willis decided to run the ball out. That was his first mistake.

Then around the 10-yard line, Willis lateraled the ball to cornerback Troy Vincent, who returned it for a touchdown. Since Willis intercepted the ball four yards deep in the end zone, the play was officially recorded as a 104-yard interception return, the longest in NFL history. That's all well and good, but what was Willis doing lateraling the ball?

What if he botched the exchange? What if Vincent dropped the ball? The Cowboys could have recovered the loose ball with enough time to run three more plays and salvage the victory. That's why Rhodes was upset.

"I saw [Willis] with the ball and I thought, 'Great play,'" Rhodes said. "Then I saw him looking around [to lateral] and I couldn't believe it. You have to be smarter than that."

"It was the biggest play of my life," Willis said after the 31–21 victory. "But I know when we watch the tapes, I'm gonna take some heat from Ray. I'd take [the lateral] back right now if I could. I could have blown the whole game. I'll never do it again."

It ended an Eagles six-game losing streak in Dallas, and it came at a time when the Cowboys were the defending Super Bowl champions. The Eagles were beaten badly twice in Texas Stadium the previous year under Rhodes, losing 34–12 in the regular season and 30–11 in the playoff. After the latter game, coach Barry Switzer boasted, "We kicked their ass." That remark burned in Rhodes' memory the entire off-season.

As the Eagles prepared for the Cowboys this time, Rhodes talked to the team about "kicking open the closet door and facing the monster." As defensive end William Fuller put it, "He said it was time. It's time to stand up to these guys. We know them, we've played against them, we've been close. It's time to beat them in a meaningful game."

Willis was a free-agent pickup from Green Bay who took over as the starting middle linebacker in 1996 after Kurt Gouveia signed with San Diego. He would play four seasons with the Eagles, three as a starter, a decent player but hardly a star. This one play, however, earned him a lasting place in Eagles history. Who could forget Merrill Reese's euphoric radio call "The Eagles win, the Eagles win, the Eagles win …"

It was an improbable victory, considering the Cowboys had a first down at the three-yard line with a minute left. Down three points, the Cowboys seemed assured of at least a field goal that would have forced overtime. More likely, they would score a touchdown and deal the Eagles another Texas Stadium heartbreak.

Two running plays to Emmitt Smith gained nothing, so on third and goal, Aikman faded to pass. Fuller beat tackle Erik Williams to the inside and hit Aikman just as he released the ball. His throw was intended for tight end Tyji Armstrong, but Willis came off his man, fullback Daryl Johnston, and made the interception, setting off the mad dash to the other end zone.

Wrote Bill Lyon in the *Philadelphia Inquirer*: "It was a play that will live on in Philadelphia sporting lore, to be replayed lovingly on cold winter nights by Iggles zealots. It will rank right up there with the Miracle of the Meadowlands."

PICKLE POWER

On September 3, 2000, the Eagles and Dallas Cowboys played the hottest game in NFL history. The temperature at kickoff was 109 degrees, but the thermometer on the artificial turf at Texas Stadium was reading 150 degrees. That's not a football field, it's a frying pan.

Yet the Eagles overcame the oppressive heat. They trounced the Cowboys 41–14, and Duce Staley carried the ball 26 times for 201 yards, the biggest game for an Eagles running back since Steve Van Buren set the franchise record with 205 yards against Pittsburgh in 1949.

So how did they do it? Would you believe, pickle juice?

Trainer Rick Burkholder started the players drinking pickle juice during training camp to prevent dehydration. The high sodium content in the briny liquid helps the body retain water and also makes the players thirsty, so they drink even more water. The combination keeps the players hydrated and less likely to suffer heat cramps.

"I know it helped me," safety Brian Dawkins said. "I'm a crampee. I cramp up all the time. I didn't have a single cramp today."

The players drank the pickle juice in two-ounce shots. Some players, such as quarterback Donovan McNabb, declined. He thought it looked and smelled "nasty."

Pickle juice helped the Eagles win the war of attrition with the Cowboys, but there were other factors as well. Burkholder wisely suggested coach Andy Reid cut short the pregame warm-up. The Eagles were back in the locker room cooling down for a full eight minutes while the Cowboys were still running drills in the scorching heat. No doubt that helped.

Also, the Eagles jumped to an early lead, thanks to a daring call by Reid executing a successful onsides kick on the opening kickoff. The Eagles scored on that possession, scored again on a Staley run and again on a Jeremiah Trotter interception return, and took a 24–6 lead into halftime. It's far easier to play with a lead than it is to play catch-up. As defensive tackle Hollis Thomas told Phil Sheridan of the *Philadelphia Inquirer*, "I think it feels hotter when you're behind than when you're winning."

The game signaled a shift in power in the NFC East. The Eagles established themselves as a team on the rise. Coming off a 5–11 season in their first year under Reid, the Eagles were projected by most NFL experts to win seven, maybe eight games, in 2000. Their dominating performance in the opener was a clear indication Reid's team was improving ahead of schedule. Indeed, the Eagles went on to win 11 games and qualify for the NFC playoffs.

The Cowboys, meanwhile, were exposed as an aging dynasty at the end of its run. They finished the season at 5–11, the first of three straight losing years under coach Dave Campo.

Several new acquisitions made their presence felt. Tackle Jon Runyan, signed as a free agent from Tennessee, was a force, blasting open holes for Staley. Linebacker Carlos Emmons, signed from Pittsburgh, started on the strong side and intercepted a pass. Corey Simon, the No. 1 draft pick from Florida State, sacked Troy Aikman on the Cowboys' first offensive play.

Asked what the victory meant, owner Jeffrey Lurie said, "We beat a team Philadelphia loves to beat, and we beat them convincingly. Hopefully, it means we'll be a lot of fun to watch for a lot of years."

McNABB PASSES FOR FOUR TDS ON BROKEN ANKLE

On November 17, 2002, the Eagles were 6–3 and rolling methodically toward their second consecutive NFC East Division title. A home game against the Arizona Cardinals looked like an easy day's work. But on the third play from scrimmage, the Eagles' season took a frightening turn.

Quarterback Donovan McNabb was sacked by Adrian Wilson and LeVar Woods. As he fell, McNabb's right leg twisted beneath him. McNabb fumbled the ball, but the real concern was the way he clutched his leg and limped off the field. He told the trainers he felt the ankle was sprained, so he had it retaped and returned to the game.

McNabb hobbled through the next three quarters, and when he left the game with 4:49 to play, the Eagles led 38–14 and he had completed 20 of 25 pass attempts for 255 yards and four touchdowns, equaling his career high. His quarterback efficiency rating was a glittering 132.1, his best since 2000.

The shock came an hour after the game when coach Andy Reid announced that X rays revealed McNabb had suffered a fractured right fibula, one of two bones in the lower leg near the ankle. He would be sidelined for the remainder of the regular season. He did not play again until the NFC Divisional playoff round against Atlanta, January 11.

Two questions arose: (1) Why did the team wait until after the game to X-ray McNabb? (2) How did he play so well on a broken ankle?

Donovan McNabb passed for a club record 464 yards in a 47–17 win over Green Bay on December 5, 2004. Two years earlier, McNabb threw four touchdown passes in a game against Arizona while playing on a broken ankle.

The answer to (1) was simple: McNabb insisted he was all right. It was a sprain, he said, nothing more. When the doctor suggested X-raying the ankle at halftime, McNabb said no. He told the trainers to simply apply more tape.

"I didn't want anybody to touch it," McNabb said. "When the game was going on, I just tried to do whatever it took to win the game."

"We obviously didn't know this," Reid said, referring to the extent of the injury. "We thought he sprained his ankle, and I wanted to make sure he could push off it and he was able to do that. He wasn't going to come out. He showed a lot of guts."

But how was he able to play through the pain and throw four touchdown passes?

"I tried not to think about it," McNabb said. "I just blocked it out. You've got to keep fighting. On the sidelines, [the pain] hit me a couple times. But I just focused on what we needed to do in order to put points on the board. That's all that was on my mind."

"Donovan is a strong player, he's a warrior," said running back Duce Staley.

For McNabb, it was the first serious injury of his career. He did not miss a game in his four seasons at Syracuse. He had started 43 consecutive games for the Eagles, the fifth-longest streak among NFL quarterbacks at the time, trailing only Brett Favre (168), Peyton Manning (73), Rich Gannon (57), and Kerry Collins (48).

"It definitely is a shock," McNabb said. "But if Koy [Detmer] is going to be in there, then we won't miss a beat. St. Louis lost a Pro Bowl quarterback [Kurt Warner], and they've won four in a row with their backup [Marc Bulger]. We'll be fine."

At the time, most people felt McNabb was simply putting on a brave face for the organization. But the Eagles did keep things together in his absence as Detmer (who was injured in the next game) and A. J. Feeley led the team to five consecutive wins and a 12–4 regular season finish.

A RECORD-BREAKING DAY

For the Eagles, December 5, 2004, was a landmark day. They routed the Green Bay Packers 47–17 to extend their record to 11–1, and coach Andy Reid, quarterback Donovan McNabb, and wide receiver Terrell Owens all set franchise marks.

- For Reid, it was his 67th regular-season victory, making him the winningest coach in Eagles history, passing Hall of Famer Greasy Neale.
- Owens caught his 14th touchdown pass of the season, breaking the club record shared by Hall of Famer Tommy McDonald (who did it twice, 1960–61) and Mike Quick (1983).
- McNabb set a team record with 464 passing yards, topping the 447 yards that Randall Cunningham rolled up against Washington in 1989. McNabb also set an NFL record by completing 24 consecutive passes: his first 14 passes in this game and his last 10 passes the previous week against the New York Giants. He broke the record of 22 set by Joe Montana in 1987.

It must have been particularly satisfying for McNabb because the consecutive completion record is all about accuracy, and Montana is considered the most efficient passer in

Andy Reid became the winningest coach in Eagles history with a rout of his former team, the Green Bay Packers.

pro football history. For years, McNabb was characterized as a quarterback who won games and made big plays, but was not a pure passer. The label should have been put to rest earlier—in his previous 22 games, he completed better than 60 percent of his passes 16 times—but eclipsing Montana in the record book should finish it once and for all.

"I don't listen to what people say about my accuracy," McNabb said after throwing for a career-high five touchdowns against the Packers. "People who have a problem with my accu-racy can take a look at my winning percentage. If they have a problem with that, then tough luck."

McNabb's winning percentage in that 22-game stretch was .909. He won 20 games, lost only two.

His performance against the Packers was nothing short of stunning. He completed 32 of 43 attempts with no intercep-tions, a passer rating of 147.8. He threw five touchdown passes on the first seven possessions as the Eagles built a 35–3 halftime lead on a Green Bay team that came into Lincoln Financial Field riding a six-game winning streak.

At intermission, Ron Jaworski, the Eagles' all-time leading career passer, stood in the press box, shaking his head. "That's the best half of offensive football I've ever seen the Eagles play," he said, including his own years playing under Dick Vermeil.

The 35 points the Eagles scored in the first half tied a club record, as did the 28 points they scored in the second quarter.

"I just think we played the game at another level," said half-back Brian Westbrook, who caught 11 passes for 156 yards and three touchdowns. "It's hard to say why, but we were so focused, it was sort of scary. I mean, when you look at the scoreboard and it's 35–0 against a team as good as the Packers, you're a lit-tle bit in shock."

If the Eagles were in shock, imagine how the Packers felt. They spent the week leading up to the game vowing to avenge their 20–17 loss to the Eagles in the Wild Card playoff round the previous season. That was the game the Eagles won in overtime, but only after McNabb's miracle 4th-and-26 com-pletion to Freddie Mitchell kept them breathing in regulation.

"There were a couple quotes we read and heard," McNabb said. "They were fired up about coming in here and beating us on our home field. That added a little more fire to us."

As it turned out, the game was a mismatch. The Eagles took full advantage of Green Bay's pass defense, which ranked 29th among the 32 teams. Reid spread the field with multiple receiver sets, often using Westbrook split wide, and allowed McNabb to find open receivers all over the field. Westbrook and Owens (eight catches, 161 yards) became the first pair of Eagles to crack the 150-yard receiving mark in the same game since McDonald and Timmy Brown did it in 1962.

"Sometimes you go through a game where you are in a groove," McNabb said. "You hope the next play call will be a pass. We were clicking on all cylinders. It was one of those games where you want to send out a message. I think we sent that message. Week in and week out, we come ready to play."

"They brought out all the guns," said Green Bay corner-back Al Harris, a former Eagle. "And when they do that, they're hard to beat."

12

Eagles Fans: Portrait in Passion

OTHER NFL CITIES might do the same thing, but only in Philadelphia is it considered part of the culture. You know what we're talking about …

"Booooooooooo!"

"Sometimes I can still hear it, and I've been retired for 30 years," said Adrian Burk, who quarterbacked the Eagles for six seasons (1951–56).

"Philly is a tough town," said Sonny Jurgensen, the Hall of Fame quarterback who began his career with the Eagles in 1957.

My rookie year, I won three of my four starts, and they still threw beer cans at me when I came through the tunnel. I said, "My God, what's going to happen if I do bad?"

One game against Dallas in 1961, I was booed when I was introduced. I mean, I was booed by everybody. The first pass I threw was intercepted. The booing got worse. The second pass I threw was intercepted, and fans started coming out of the stands. Our trainer got into a fight with a couple of them behind the bench. I thought we were going to have a riot.

I wound up throwing five touchdown passes, and we won going away. The fans were cheering me by the end, but they weren't loud cheers. It was polite applause, like you'd hear at a tennis match. I couldn't please them. A friend of mine went to the game. He told me, "Man, I never heard anything like that. Everybody around me was booing you." I asked him what he did. He said, "I booed you, too." It was the thing to do.

The Philadelphia fans were rough on Jurgensen. Part of the reason was that he followed Norm Van Brocklin after the Dutchman quarterbacked the Eagles to the NFL championship in 1960. Jurgensen had a great season in 1961—he set the club record with 32 touchdown passes—but he wasn't Van Brocklin. He did not take the Eagles back to the championship—although a 10–4 season was no small achievement—and there was just something about Jurgensen that irritated the fans. With his easy grin and playboy reputation, he seemed too cavalier. To the fans, he was the opposite of the fiercely competitive, driven-to-win Dutchman.

Jurgensen recalls one fan shouting, "Go back to the taproom, you bum." To which he replied, "It's Sunday, they're closed." In 1983, when Jurgensen was inducted into the Hall of Fame, he reflected on his seven seasons in Philadelphia and admitted the booing bothered him more than he let on. "The

thing is, you don't understand it," he said. "You're out there trying to win, trying to do good, and they boo. Why?"

Generations of players—and not just quarterbacks—have asked the same question. There is no simple answer. Indeed, it is one of the most complex issues surrounding the team. Eagles fans: Are they the NFL's best—or worst?

In truth, they can be both depending on the day, the season, and the score. If the team is winning, they are the loudest, most supportive fans in the league. If the team is losing, all that emotion swings the other way.

But even that formula—win = cheers, lose = boos—is not absolute. The fans booed Jurgensen when he won *and* lost, then they booed when Joe Kuharich traded him to Washington for Norm Snead. Philadelphia fans like to say they never boo anyone who gives an all-out effort, yet they booed Ron Jaworski and no one could have left more of himself on the field than Jaworski did in his 10 seasons at the Vet. So the Philly fans are an unpredictable lot. Knowledgeable, yes, but also more fickle than they like to admit.

One thing is constant: They show up. Eagles fans have filled the seats from Shibe Park to Franklin Field to Veterans Stadium to Lincoln Financial Field, year after year, for almost half a century. Club president Joe Banner recalls the team winning just three games in 1998 and having an increase in season-ticket requests the following year.

"This is the most passionate fan base in the NFL," Banner said. "We had 25,000 people come to training camp one day to watch practice. There were probably another 5,000 who tried to get there but couldn't because the roads were so jammed. Andy [Reid] needed a police escort to get from the dorm to the practice field."

"This is a football town," said quarterback Donovan McNabb. "If the other sports don't win, they say, 'Well, football is getting ready to start.' And when football season starts, they don't care about anything but winning. And when you're winning, they love you. And when you lose, they're trying to find answers as to what's going on."

"When I first got here, I thought these fans were crazy," linebacker Ike Reese told Bob Brookover of the *Philadelphia Inquirer*. "Looking back, we only won three games that year, so I can understand it now. But I never experienced the verbal abuse or some of the booing that went on during 1998. Now I understand how passionate these people are."

"The fans are tough, I know from experience," Jaworski said. "I didn't like being booed. No one does. We all want to be liked.

But I knew where [the fans] were coming from. The team had been losing for years, and the fans were sick of it. It was honest and I understood it. It was better than what we had in LA [with the Rams] where you had a Hollywood crowd, 93,000 people, and you could hardly hear them.

"I look back on those [Eagles] years, and I wouldn't trade them for the world because I really believe they made me stronger. They made me tougher and taught me how to deal with adversity. Although [the boos] hurt at the time, they built my character."

"I've heard Ron say that," said tight end John Spagnola, who played with Jaworski for eight seasons. "He says the fans were like a parent scolding him to make him better. That's one way of looking at it, I guess. I think Ron's being very gracious. It's not everyone who could handle it that way. Some guys would collapse under that [booing]."

Philadelphia fans were known as pretty tough lot as far back as the 1950s when they booed Del Ennis, who was a hometown boy and All-Star outfielder with the Phillies. They booed the Eagles, too, except for the magical 1960 season when Van Brocklin led the entire city, Pied Piper–like, to the NFL championship. The booing resumed shortly after that.

But an interesting thing happened in the late '60s: The fans organized. They focused their dissatisfaction. Instead of 60,000 separate boobirds, they formed one angry flock. The man responsible was Joe Kuharich, who presided over perhaps the darkest era in Eagles history. In 1968, Kuharich's fifth season as head coach and general manager, the Eagles lost their first 11 games, and the fans formed a "Joe Must Go" campaign with buttons and banners. They even paid to have a plane fly over Franklin Field trailing a "Joe Must Go" sign.

"[Kuharich] has pulled the city together as though he had tightened a noose around its neck," wrote Milton Gross in the *New York Post*. "He has rallied it as one around a funeral pyre. He has made the City of Brotherly Love forget about water pollution, the departure of Wilt Chamberlain, and the roof blowing off the Spectrum. He has been responsible for a kind of cultural explosion which may be without precedent in the history of professional sports."

Wrote Sandy Grady in the *Philadelphia Bulletin*: "Any machine politician would marvel at the way Kuharich has united 3,000,000 people. Richard Nixon has promised to pull the country together, but Kuharich has already done it."

One fan, Frank Sheppard of Cherry Hill, was not content to just wear a "Joe Must Go" button. He created the Committee to Rejuvenate the Philadelphia Eagles (CRPE) and bought advertising in the local papers, urging a fan boycott. He wanted the Eagles to play the New Orleans Saints in an empty Franklin Field. Sheppard felt that would send a more powerful message to Eagles owner Jerry Wolman than a lot of buttons and boos.

Several days before the game, Sheppard told Grady his movement was taking hold. "Amazing the way it's mushrooming," he said. "It shows that all you need is the right idea at the right time."

Sheppard must have been disappointed on Sunday. For one thing, 57,128 fans came to Franklin Field to see the pitiful 1–11 Eagles play the 3–8–1 Saints. And to make matters worse, the Eagles actually won, 29–17, a victory that cost them the first overall pick in the college draft. The fans had consoled themselves throughout the miserable 1968 season with the knowledge that, as the worst team in football, the Eagles would be able to draft O. J. Simpson, the Heisman Trophy winner from

Ron Jaworski did not allow the boos at Veterans Stadium to spoil his relationship with the Philadelphia fans.

USC. But by beating the Saints, the Eagles fell to third in the draft, behind Buffalo and Atlanta, so instead of O. J. Simpson, the Eagles wound up with Leroy Keyes, whose NFL career was brief and forgettable.

The national press celebrated. "The bush league fans in that city don't deserve an O. J. Simpson," wrote Brent Musburger, who was then a columnist for the *Chicago Daily News*. Jimmy Cannon, the syndicated columnist, called Philadelphia "a bog of nastiness" and concluded, "O. J. Simpson doesn't belong there … the Devil's Island of football."

For the fans, the frustration boiled over when the Eagles finished the season at home against Minnesota. A crowd of 54,530 trudged through the snowy streets and sat in the biting cold, watching the Eagles lose to the Vikings, 24–17. At halftime, Frank Olivo, a 20-year-old South Philadelphian dressed as Santa Claus, came onto the Franklin Field track and waved to the crowd as the public address announcer said, much too cheerfully, "The Eagles wish you a Merry Christmas."

At first, there were boos. Then someone threw a snowball. Quickly, the idea spread. Soon, hundreds of fans were venting their anger by throwing snowballs. Olivo tried to make the best of it, smiling and waving, but finally the barrage became too intense. He began ducking, then holding his hands over his face to protect himself. He was fortunate not to be injured.

Matt Millen, who won three Super Bowl rings as an NFL linebacker, was at the game with his father. Millen was 11 at the time and rode to Philadelphia on a bus from his home in upstate Pennsylvania. "It was a miserable day and a miserable team," Millen was quoted as saying in *The Great Philadelphia Fan Book*. "[Throwing snowballs] was the only fun part of the game. Everybody joined in—fathers, sons, even the old ladies."

When the Eagles returned to the field, the fans began throwing snowballs at Kuharich. Fullback Tom Woodeshick tried to stay as far away from the coach as he could, lest he catch a stray one.

"It wasn't easy because Joe paced the whole game," Woodeshick said. "I'd go to the end of the bench where I thought I was safe, and pretty soon snowballs were flying over my head. I'd look up and there was Joe."

After the game, Kuharich hardly mentioned the fans, saying only, "They boo the president. They probably boo their wives. That's the nature of America today." But Bob Brown, the All-Pro tackle, was furious. He called the fans "creeps" and said he wanted out of Philadelphia. (Brown forced the team to trade him to the Los Angeles Rams in the off-season.)

"The fans in Baltimore are not like that," said kick returner Alvin Haymond, who was in his first season with the Eagles after four years with the Colts. "I don't know what you'd call the fans here. Animals, I guess."

That is how the legend began: Philadelphia fans are so mean, they threw snowballs at Santa Claus. It has been repeated so often, some people think it is a banquet joke. Jeffrey Lurie did

Eagles fans have a long and colorful history with Santa Claus. In 1973, they made this Christmas wish on behalf of quarterback Roman Gabriel.

not believe it until shortly after he purchased the team when he was having lunch with a Philadelphia writer and asked, "Did they really throw snowballs at Santa Claus?"

When Lurie was told yes, his eyes widened. "Really?" he said.

Lurie was told about a similar incident in December 1989, when the fans at Veterans Stadium threw snowballs at Dallas coach Jimmy Johnson. They hit Al Jury, the back judge, in the head and knocked him to the ground. They even threw snowballs into the CBS broadcast booth, where play-by-play man Verne Lundquist likened Philadelphia to Beirut.

Some of the snowballs were taken to the washroom and run under water to turn them into ice. Others were loaded with rocks, batteries, or crushed beer cans. It was so perilous on the field that the Eagles mascot and cheerleaders headed for cover early in the fourth quarter. Wrote Bill Conlin in the *Philadelphia Daily News*: "Tough as it was to do, we thrust our richly earned reputation for mean-spirited crowd violence to a new low."

Owner Norman Braman called the fans' behavior "a disgrace." He ordered a ban on beer sales at the stadium for the remainder of the season, which was only two games.

In 11 years as owner, Lurie has seen both faces of the Eagles fan: the good and the ugly. In 1997 the team played a Monday night game against San Francisco, and the national TV audience saw a record number of brawls—police reported 60 fistfights in the stands—and one fan was arrested after firing a flare into the upper deck. There were no injuries, but the game was such an embarrassment that the team and the city decided to take action.

A court was created in the basement of the Vet with Judge Seamus McCaffery dispensing justice on the spot. Where in the past, a drunken or abusive fan would simply be ejected from the stadium, now he was handcuffed and taken to the courtroom—actually, it was a storage area for the Phillies grounds crew—where Judge McCaffery, a no-nonsense former homicide detective, would issue a stiff fine, and if the offender couldn't pay, he was sent to jail.

City Councilman James Kenney supported the court. "I'm a lifelong Philadelphian, I'm a lifelong Eagles fan, I like my Coors Light," he said. "But there is no excuse to start drinking at 10 o'clock on a Sunday morning with the intention of going to the Eagles game and rolling around in the aisles. You start acting like a creep, it's going to cost you $250 or $300, which puts a big hole in your beer money."

On the first day of the court—while the Eagles were defeating Pittsburgh 23–20—20 fans were brought before McCaffery. Eighteen were found guilty of disorderly conduct and fined. They also were forced to give up their season tickets.

The Eagles court cut down on rowdy behavior, but it did not eliminate it. In 1999, Michael Irvin of the Cowboys was injured when he fell headfirst onto the hard turf at the Vet. As he lay motionless, many in the crowd of 66,669 cheered. When paramedics wheeled a stretcher onto the field, there was another cheer. Irvin had suffered a spinal cord injury that would end his career, yet a large number of Eagles fans reveled in the sight of the All-Pro receiver being loaded into an ambulance.

"This cannot pass by as just another incidence of our peculiar civic charm," wrote Rich Hofmann in the *Daily News*. "You can't put it in there with the snowballs or the night the guy launched the flare at the seats across the field. This isn't booing or badgering or anything like that. This is twisted. This is sick."

The 700 level at Veterans Stadium. "They call this the City of Brotherly Love, but it's really a banana republic," Bill Parcells said. "[The fans] let you know what they thought of you and it was almost always in very negative terms."

Dallas running back Emmitt Smith said he was "disgusted to death." Even the Eagles were appalled. Said wide receiver Charles Johnson, "Our fans pride themselves on being tough, but that wasn't tough. That was plain ignorant."

"The fans who booed are idiots, there's no question about it," said Ed Rendell, a season-ticket holder who was then mayor of Philadelphia. "It's one thing to root hard, but it's a game. How important is a game that we would cheer somebody that may be paralyzed? It's inconceivable to me."

Rendell went on to say, "I've heard comments from fans who said, 'Anyone who goes to an Eagles game should know they can't bring their kids with them.' That is unacceptable to us as a city, and it's certainly unacceptable to the Eagles organization. Taking your kids to a sporting event is one of the best experiences you can have."

That became the image of Philadelphia fans. In January 2003 a Florida travel agent refused to book packages for Tampa Bay fans who wanted to see the Buccaneers play the Eagles in the NFC Championship game. The agent, Dennis Pfeiffe, was quoted as saying, "The potential for client injury [in Philadelphia] has our insurance agent lying awake at night. There is a portion of [Eagles] fans who are terrible; they're rude and obnoxious. That's a known fact."

Even when the Eagles moved across the street to the swankier Lincoln Financial Field—with a decidedly more upscale crowd—the image of the beer-swilling, itching-to-start-trouble Philly fan lived on. When Minnesota earned a trip to Philadelphia in the 2005 Divisional playoff, a Twin Cities travel agent warned Viking fans that if they attended the game they would be doing so at their own risk.

"Don't look like a Vikings fan if you value your safety and possessions," said Steve Erban, president of Creative Charters. "The stadium is beyond civilization." Erban told the *St. Paul Pioneer-Press* he brought some Green Bay fans to the Linc for the 2004 wild-card game, and he claimed some Eagles fans doused them with beer and then tried to shove them down the steps.

Obviously, it is impossible to condone or excuse such behavior. But it should not be exaggerated or offered as representative of all Eagles fans. The louts and bullies are a minority. Most of the people who attend Eagles games are good fans: fiercely loyal, loud, and, yes, tough on the visiting team, but not in a threatening way. In fact, crowd behavior has improved so much since the move to the Linc that the Eagles court was discontinued in December 2003.

Most visiting coaches and players understand it. When Atlanta was preparing to come to Philadelphia for the NFC championship game in January 2005, running back Warrick Dunn said, "I would say [Philadelphia is] one of the most hostile environments a player can play in because the fans are rude, the crowd is definitely behind the Eagles, and it's a situation of you against them."

Eagles fans gather on "The Roost" at Lincoln Financial Field. "This is the most passionate fan base in the NFL," team president Joe Banner said.

Dunn went on to say he preferred that atmosphere to what the Falcons typically experience at home. He said that when the Falcons defeated St. Louis in the NFC wild-card game, it was "the first time you could really feel the electricity of football [in the Georgia Dome], and that's how games are supposed to be. I know in Philadelphia it's like that week in and week out."

NFL Films once caught Giants coach Bill Parcells talking to Lawrence Taylor prior to a game at Veterans Stadium. "They call this the City of Brotherly Love," Parcells said, "but it's really a banana republic." In a 2002 interview, Parcells was reminded of the sound bite and asked for his final thoughts on the Vet, which was coming down after the season.

"It's a place I grew to really like in a kind of distorted, perverted way," Parcells said. "It's a place where they let you know what they thought of you, and it was almost always in very neg-

ative terms. But the more they [abused] you, the more you began to understand that it was part of a respect they had for you. It was kind of a vile way of doing it, but at the end of the day, you knew they really did have respect for you."

Jim Fassel, who also coached the Giants, had similar feelings. "The Vet was the one place we wouldn't let our families come because of the fans," Fassel said. "It's a rough environment. Those fans are on you. As a coach, if you were walking to the press box, they'd be throwing beer on you. But if you beat them, it all stopped. The same fans would say, 'Congratulations. Nice job.' I respect that."

"I've traveled to other countries, and when I told people I was from Philadelphia, they knew about the booing, that's how widespread the reputation is," said Dr. Joel Fish, a sports psychologist.

It's this whole negative thing which is unfortunate because it's only half the picture. That's because when something happens in Philadelphia, it makes the network news. It's like, "Look, they're throwing things. They're booing." It reinforces the notion that this is a horrible place.

But that passion and energy is part of a genuine caring the people of the city have for their teams. That isn't appreciated enough. I remember when the Eagles were winning two games a season and still selling out. Where else do you find that? Philadelphia fans identify with their teams, especially the Eagles, in a unique way. Listen to talk radio. If the Eagles win, the fans say, "We won." If they lose, it's "We lost." Our identity is wrapped up in our sports teams more than other cities.

This is a blue-collar town that likes to think of itself as a tough, hard-nosed place, and football is a perfect fit. Philadelphians love Rocky because they identify with the guy from the neighborhood who fought his way to the top. And in the movie, when Rocky gets a dog, what does he buy him? An Eagles jersey.

Vai Sikahema has seen this issue from both sides. He was a kick returner with the St. Louis Cardinals coming to Philadelphia as a visiting player. He recalls the team bus pulling into the Vet on Sunday morning and immediately being surrounded by Eagles fans "who looked like they wanted to kill us." Sikahema thought Philadelphia was an awful place filled with nasty people. When he became a free agent, he told his wife, "I can tell you one place we aren't going, and that's Philadelphia."

But Jim McMahon, a former Brigham Young teammate, convinced Sikahema that Philadelphia wasn't a bad place. Largely on McMahon's recommendation, Sikahema signed with the Eagles in 1992 and settled so comfortably into the community that he became a fixture as sports director of WCAU television.

"Jim tells a story that describes Philadelphia fans perfectly," Sikahema said.

He was leaving the Vet, and there were two guys standing over the tunnel, shouting at the players, "You stink, you suck." Most of the players kept walking, but when the two guys shouted at Jim, he turned and gave them the finger. They looked at each other and as Jim walked away, they started shouting, "McMahon, you are the man."

That's the Philly fans. They're tough, they're confrontational, and they respect you if you give it back. They want their athletes to be like the guys they hang with. They poke you in the chest and tell you off, and they like it when you poke back. They say, "That's a man's man." Look at the guys who are popular here. Charles Barkley, Larry Bowa, Buddy Ryan. They're guys who didn't take any crap, and this is a no-crap town.

If Philadelphia fans seem quick to anger, it is easy to understand. The end of the 2004 season marked 21 years since any Philadelphia team in one of the major sports has won a championship. It is the longest drought of any American city with franchises in the four major sports. And of all the Philadelphia teams, the Eagles have gone the longest—45 years—without a title. Still, from Fishtown to Bryn Mawr, the fans keep the vigil.

"Their loyalty is without limit, their tolerance for suffering bordering on masochism," wrote Bill Lyon in the *Philadelphia Inquirer*. "Each year they tell themselves this will be the year of 76 trombones leading the big parade. And then follows another crushing emotional bender, and you are sure that this time they will be scared away for good, fed up and sworn off. But then another season rolls around, and there they are back for more, hopeful beyond reason, expectant beyond logic."

In the 2004 season, the Eagles rewarded their fans by finally winning the NFC Championship game after stumbling each of the three previous years. After the 27–10 win over Atlanta, the fans celebrated in the Linc and on the streets of Philadelphia, braving subzero wind chill to revel in the moment.

"I'm a grown man, and I was crying walking away from those other championship games; it was like death," said Sandy Stern, a fan from Fort Washington who was interviewed by the *Inquirer* on his way out of the stadium. "But this just feels so unbelievable. My wife is pregnant with twin boys. Nothing except for their birth could match this. Twin Eagle fans."

Paul Campise watched the game from his Moorestown, New Jersey, home. A retired court stenographer, the 74-year-old Campise stopped going to the games after his second triple bypass. Before the last surgery, he told his doctor he wanted

An Eagles fan cannot bear to watch as the team loses its third consecutive NFC title game, this one to Carolina in January 2004.

to live long enough for three things: one, to celebrate his 50th wedding anniversary (he did); two, to make a hole in one (not yet); and three, to see the Eagles win a Super Bowl. He thought the 2004 season would be it, but the Eagles lost Super Bowl XXXIX to New England, 24–21.

"It will hurt for a while, but I'll be back," said Campise, who spent six months building a train platform and scale-model Eagles stadium (complete with a miniature Andy Reid) in his basement. "I've been following the team since the Steve Van Buren days, so I'm going to stick with them. That's what true fans do."

The Eagles fans made an impressive showing at the Super Bowl. An estimated 40,000 of them poured into Jacksonville, many without tickets to the game or places to stay, but they wanted to be there to show their support. They took over the city—people began calling it Philly-ville—wearing their Eagles colors and singing the fight song from morning until night.

But when the game ended and they were left with yet another heartache, most of the fans handled it with grace.

In a letter to the *Philadelphia Daily News*, Mike Marquis, a Patriots fan, wrote:

> Your fans were in full force Sunday, booing the Patriot players, coaches, and even the cheerleaders. They turned the Super Bowl into a home game atmosphere. The E-A-G-L-E-S chants were nonstop. The "Fly Eagles Fly" song loud and clear. They did the rabid fan base in Philly proud.
>
> But an untold story is that when the game was over, these same fanatics walked past those of us wearing blue and silver and congratulated us, offering a hand or even a hug. Those fans not only represented Philly well, but the atmosphere that is championship football. Your city should be proud of those fans who laid out the money to make the trek. They did it with passion and class.

Eagles fans tailgating before the long drive to Super Bowl XXXIX. The *Florida Times-Union* estimated that Eagles fans outnumbered New England fans 10 to 1 on the streets of Jacksonville.

13

Sidelines

WHEN YOU ATTEMPT to chronicle something as sprawling as the history of a professional football team, it is inevitable that some statistics, quotes, and anecdotes will fall outside the conventional encyclopedia framework.

For example, where do you put the story of Alabama Pitts, the only Eagle signed from Sing Sing Prison? Where do you list the preferred brand of glassware eaten by Tim Rossovich? Where do you tell the tales of the Praying Tailback and Bow Wow? And we can't very well forget Terrell Owens and Nicollette Sheridan.

So we created this chapter to collect those, and other, loose ends.

TOP FIVES: THE BEST AND WORST

A wholly subjective look back at the best and worst personnel decisions in Eagles history:

Best Trades

1. Mark Nordquist to Chicago for a ninth-round draft choice in 1976 and a sixth-round draft choice in 1977. The Eagles traded a journeyman guard to the Bears for two draft picks. The Eagles used the first to select Mike Hogan, who led the team in rushing in 1976 and '77. They used the second to select Wilbert Montgomery, who became the top rusher in franchise history.
2. Tackle Buck Lansford, defensive back Jimmy Harris, and a first-round pick in the 1959 draft to Los Angeles for quarterback Norm Van Brocklin. It seemed like a hefty package at the time, but Van Brocklin was the key to the 1960 championship season.
3. In a three-team deal, the Eagles traded a fifth-round draft choice in 2004 to Baltimore and defensive end Brandon Whiting to San Francisco for the rights to wide receiver Terrell Owens. Owens had perhaps the most dynamic first season of any player in team history, setting a club record with 14 touchdown receptions and coming back from a severe leg injury to catch nine passes for 122 yards in the Super Bowl.
4. A second-round pick and a fifth-round pick in the 1998 draft to the New York Jets for defensive end Hugh Douglas. Douglas is third on the Eagles' all-time list with 54 and a half career sacks.

5. Quarterback John Reaves and a second-round draft pick in 1976 to Cincinnati for tackle Stan Walters and quarterback Wayne Clark. The Eagles gave up a failed first-round pick in Reaves (winless in seven starts) for Walters who was a solid left tackle for nine seasons. He started 122 consecutive games for the Eagles and was voted into two Pro Bowls.

Worst Trades

1. Quarterback Sonny Jurgensen and defensive back Jimmy Carr to Washington for quarterback Norm Snead and defensive back Claude Crabb. Jurgensen had a Hall of Fame career with the Redskins, while Snead had only one winning season in seven with the Eagles.
2. Traded a first-round draft choice in 1989 and a fourth-round pick in 1990 to Indianapolis for guard Ron Solt. Solt was an injury-plagued bust with the Eagles, while the Colts used the first-round pick (22nd overall) to select wide receiver Andre Rison.
3. Traded a sixth-round pick in 1975 and a first-round pick in 1976 to Cincinnati for the rights to quarterback Mike Boryla. Why the Eagles paid so dearly for Boryla, who was just a fourth-round pick by Cincinnati, remains a mystery. He lasted just three seasons in Philadelphia.
4. Traded their own first-round pick in 1991 and their first-round pick in 1992 to Green Bay to move up in the draft and select offensive tackle Antone Davis, who played five lackluster seasons with the Eagles. Davis was the eighth overall pick. A footnote: The Eagles could have stayed in their original spot (19) and taken Brett Favre, who went number 33.
5. Traded Tommy McDonald to Dallas for kicker Sam Baker, offensive lineman Lynn Hoyem, and defensive tackle John Meyers. McDonald was a Hall of Famer and one of the most popular players in team history. Joe Kuharich traded him for a kicker and two mediocre linemen.

Best Draft Picks

1. Harold Carmichael. A seventh-round pick out of Southern University in 1971, the 6–8 wide receiver played more games (180), caught more passes (589), and scored more touchdowns (79) than any other player in franchise history.

2. Bobby Walston. A 14th-round pick out of Georgia in 1951. A fine receiver and placekicker, he is the leading scorer in team history (881 points). He played 12 seasons and appeared in 148 consecutive games, the third-longest streak in club history. He set the team mark for most points in a game with 25 against Washington in 1954.

3. Seth Joyner and Clyde Simmons. We will make them an entry since they came in back-to-back picks in the 1986 draft. Joyner, an eighth-round pick from Texas–El Paso, was a Pro Bowl linebacker. Simmons, the ninth-round pick from Western Carolina, had 76 and a half sacks, second only to Reggie White, in team history.

4. Tom Brookshier. A 10th-round pick out of Colorado in 1953, Brookshier had eight interceptions as a rookie and was a starter for seven seasons with the Eagles. A key performer on the 1960 championship team.

5. Russ Craft. A 15th-round pick out of Alabama in 1943, Craft excelled as an all-around player with the championship teams of the late '40s. An All-Pro defensive back, he also played running back and returned kicks.

Worst Draft Picks

1. Kevin Allen. The Eagles were desperate for a left tackle, so they used the ninth pick in the 1985 draft for Allen, who was projected as a third- or fourth-round pick by most NFL teams. Allen, from Indiana, played one dismal season, then was convicted of rape and spent the next three years in prison. (A footnote: Jerry Rice was the 15th pick in that draft.)

2. Jon Harris. Ray Rhodes wanted a defensive end to replace William Fuller, so in the first round of the 1997 draft, he reached for this 6–7, 280-pounder from Virginia. Harris had two sacks in two seasons before he was traded to Green Bay.

3. Leroy Keyes. Okay, so the Eagles missed out on O. J. Simpson in the 1969 draft, but they still had the third overall pick. They could have taken Mean Joe Greene (he went fourth), Ted Kwalick (seventh), or Calvin Hill (24th). Instead, they selected Keyes, a halfback from Purdue, who played just 48 games in five NFL seasons.

4. Walt Kowalczyk. In 1958 the Eagles had the fifth pick and selected the "Sprinting Blacksmith" from Michigan State. In two seasons with the Eagles, Kowalczyk had 43 rushing attempts for 80 yards, a 1.86-yard average. (A footnote: In the same draft, Vince Lombardi acquired fullback Jim Taylor, 14th overall, linebacker Ray Nitschke, 35th, and guard Jerry Kramer, 38th.)

5. The entire 1993 draft. The Eagles had eight picks, including two in the first round and five choices in the first 77 overall, and came away with nothing. Guard Lester Holmes was their first pick, and he was gone after 46 games. They used their second number 1 (24th overall) for defensive tackle Leonard Renfro, passing up Dana Stubblefield, who went to San Francisco at 26, two picks later.

Best Free-Agent Signings

1. Troy Vincent. Signed in 1996 from Miami. Started at cornerback for eight seasons, voted into the Pro Bowl five times.

2. Ricky Watters. Signed in 1995 from San Francisco. Played three seasons with the Eagles and left as the fourth-leading rusher in team history. His 353 rushing attempts in 1996 was a franchise record.

3. Jon Runyan. Signed in 2000 from Tennessee. Solid anchor at right tackle. At the end of the 2004 regular season, he had started 128 consecutive games, the fifth-longest streak in the NFL.

4. William Fuller. Signed in 1994 from Houston. Led the team in sacks all three seasons (1994–96). Went to the Pro Bowl each year. Set a team record in 1994 recording at least one full sack in seven consecutive games.

5. Irving Fryar. Signed in 1996 from Miami. In his first season as an Eagle, he set a team record with 88 receptions. He tied the club mark with four touchdown catches in one game against Miami the same year.

Worst Free-Agent Signings

1. Tim Harris. Signed in 1993 from San Francisco. Was billed as the replacement for the departed Reggie White. He played four games before going on injured reserve with an infected elbow. He was released after the season and re-signed with the 49ers.

2. Steve Everitt. Signed in 1997 from Cleveland. A former first-round pick and All-Pro center with the Browns, he had lost interest in football by the time he signed with the Eagles. Played three seasons and was released in 2000.

3. Chris Boniol. Signed in 1997 from Dallas. One of the NFL's most accurate kickers in Dallas—he was successful on 27 of 28 field goal attempts in 1995—Boniol unraveled in his two seasons with the Eagles.

4. Steve Wallace. An offensive tackle who earned a reputation as a bruising—some would say dirty—blocker in ten seasons with the San Francisco 49ers. In 1996 the Eagles signed Wallace as a free agent, but he performed so poorly during the preseason that the team released him. He re-signed with the 49ers and actually played *against* the Eagles in the NFC Wild Card game later that year.

5. Nate Wayne. Signed in 2003 from Green Bay. The Eagles overpaid for Wayne (a four-year contract for a reported $13 million with a $4 million signing bonus), an inconsistent linebacker who was replaced midway through his second season.

THE FIRST DRAFT PICK: JAY BERWANGER

One of Bert Bell's greatest achievements was selling the other NFL owners on the idea of a draft. Bell believed a draft would provide an orderly distribution of college talent each year. Rather than teams bidding against each other for the top players—and driving up the price—a draft would put all the players in a pool, and the teams would select them, one by one.

It was a brilliant idea, and it was instrumental in creating the competitive balance that is the foundation of the NFL's success, but it was not entirely selfless on Bell's part. He was tired of seeing the top teams—Chicago, Washington, Green Bay, and the New York Giants—attract the best players. As the owner of the Eagles, the worst team in the league, he knew the free-enterprise system was not helping him at all.

So Bell created the draft and set it up in the reverse order of the league standings, an arrangement under which the poorer teams had the higher picks, and the worst team—it just happened to be Bell's Eagles—went first. He even arranged for the first draft to be held in Philadelphia at the Bellevue-Stratford Hotel on February 8, 1936.

Everything was set up for Bell to make a big splash with the first selection in the first draft, and he did not disappoint, selecting Jay Berwanger, the Heisman Trophy winner from the University of Chicago. There was only one problem: Berwanger did not want to play pro football. He had a business degree, and he felt he could make more money in the corporate world.

Bell tried to change Berwanger's mind without success. Bears owner George Halas paid Bell $16,000 for the rights to Berwanger, figuring he could talk the talented 6–0, 190-pound tailback into playing for the hometown team. However, when Berwanger told Papa Bear his price—a two-year, no-cut contract for $25,000—it was the end of the courtship.

Berwanger never did play pro football. Instead, he started his own company, which manufactured rubber and plastic parts for industry. He became a wealthy man and claimed he never regretted his decision. But in a 1972 interview, Berwanger said, "If I was coming out of college today, with the money these teams are paying, I couldn't afford not to play."

EAGLES AND THE HEISMAN

Winning college football's most prestigious award is no guarantee of success in the NFL. The Eagles' track record with Heisman Trophy winners is proof of that. We won't even count Jay Berwanger, who chose not to play pro football. The Heisman winners who actually did show up did not exactly carry the Eagles to great heights.

- Davey O'Brien, quarterback from TCU, was their first pick in 1939. The 5–7, 150-pound O'Brien played valiantly, but he only won two games in two seasons because his supporting cast was so woeful. He quit following the 1940 season to join the FBI.
- Howard (Hopalong) Cassady, receiver from Ohio State, was acquired from Cleveland in 1962. Cassady was a great college runner, but he had a mediocre pro career. The Eagles were his third NFL team, and he played just five games before breaking his leg.
- John Huarte, quarterback from Notre Dame, was signed in 1968. The Eagles were his third stop after failing with the New York Jets and Boston Patriots. He was the third quarterback, behind Norm Snead and King Hill, in the 2–12 season that culminated with the snowball attack on Santa Claus. He played in only two games and was released.
- Herschel Walker, running back from Georgia, had the most impact. Signed as a free agent in 1992, Walker gave the Eagles three solid years. In his first season, he rushed for 1,070 yards and scored 10 touchdowns. In 1994 he became the first player in NFL history to record a 90-yard, or longer, running play, pass reception, and kickoff return, all in the same season. But the team had only one winning season in his three years.
- Ty Detmer, quarterback from BYU, signed as a free agent in 1996. Replaced the injured Rodney Peete and led the

Eagles to seven wins in their last 11 regular-season games that year. Lost the starting job to Bobby Hoying the following season.

Bottom line for the Eagles: Nine seasons with a Heisman Trophy winner on their roster. Only two of those seasons produced a winning record.

FROM SING SING TO THE NFL

In the 2000 media guide, the Eagles made a change in their all-time roster. It probably went undetected by most people, but it was interesting nonetheless. Next to the name Alabama Pitts, it now reads, "No College," which is technically correct. But there was a time when it read, "Sing Sing," as in the prison.

The Eagles probably did not like advertising the fact they once had a convicted felon on their roster, even if it was only

Edwin (Alabama) Pitts was an outstanding athlete at Sing Sing, playing football and baseball for the prison team, which was known as "The Black Sheep." When he was released, Pitts signed with the Eagles and appeared in three games during the 1935 season.

for three games in 1935. But Edwin (Alabama) Pitts was a fascinating character who lived a short but eventful life.

Pitts was born in Opelika, Alabama, and lost both his father and stepfather at an early age. He joined the Navy at 15, served three years, and was discharged with no real skills. At 19, Pitts and three accomplices robbed a grocery store in New York. The robbery netted $78.25, and when the four men were arrested, they were sentenced to 8-to-15 year stretches at Sing Sing Prison in Ossining, New York.

The prison had an athletic program under the direction of warden Lewis Lawes, and the 5–10, 185-pound Pitts joined the baseball and football teams, which competed under the name "The Black Sheep." Soon, Pitts was dominating the prison competition, and he became something of a legend in upstate New York.

Pitts was eligible for parole after five years, and Johnny Evers—the former Cubs star, best known as the middle man in Tinkers-to-Evers-to-Chance—was managing a minor league team in Albany. He offered Pitts $200 a month to play for his team. League officials tried to block it, claiming it would be a black mark for the sport to have a man with a criminal record playing in the league.

Other people—including John Costello, the robbery victim—took up Pitts' cause and campaigned for his right to make a living. The case was appealed all the way up to the office of Commissioner Kenesaw Mountain Landis, who ruled in favor of Pitts. It proved to be much ado about nothing, however, as Pitts hit .233 and committed eight errors in 43 games with the Albany team.

Still, Pitts was capable of generating headlines, so the Eagles signed him to a $1,500 contract as a running back. His signing in September 1935 was big news in Philadelphia, and the photograph of Pitts in his number 50 jersey was splashed across every newspaper in the country. Bert Bell and Lud Wray, the owner and coach, knew Pitts would draw fans, and if he could play a little bit, well, that was a bonus.

Published reports indicate 20,000 people attended the Eagles regular-season opener against Pittsburgh. That was four times the normal attendance. The fans spent the second half calling for Wray to put Pitts in the game, which he never did. Pitts did play briefly in the next two games, and he finally got to handle the ball—two receptions for 21 yards—in the fourth game, a 39–0 loss to the Chicago Bears.

His original contract with the Eagles was for four games, so after the Chicago loss, Bell and Wray had to make a decision. They offered Pitts a new deal, but for considerably less money: $50 a game. He rejected the offer and went back to baseball.

Why did the Eagles give up on Pitts? Two reasons: One, Pitts did not play organized sports before going to prison, so he had trouble keeping up with the other NFL players, most of whom had college experience. Said Bell: "He needs a lot of work." Two, the other players may have resented the fact that Pitts made more money, at least initially, and that caused some grumbling in the ranks.

Pitts knocked around baseball's bush leagues for the next five years, and he also landed a job at a knitting mill in Valdese, North Carolina. On June 7, 1941, Pitts went to the local dance hall, where he made a pass at a pretty girl and was fatally stabbed by her jealous boyfriend. He was just 33 years old.

THE YEAR OF THE STEAGLES

The Eagles were playing in Washington on December 7, 1941, the day the Japanese attacked Pearl Harbor. The game was already under way when the news swept through Griffith Stadium.

"There was a buzz through the crowd, we could tell something was up," Eagles halfback Jack Hinkle said. "Being in Washington, there were lots of government officials in the stands, so every few minutes there was an announcement,

During the war years, NFL teams sometimes used military transport planes for travel. Obviously, these were no-frills flights. On this 1945 trip to Detroit, the cabin was so hot one Eagles player stripped down to his trousers. Is it any wonder that coach Greasy Neale preferred to travel by train?

Tommy Thompson looks understandably embarrassed in this 1948 publicity photo. It was a cheap play on words—Tommy is armed with a Tommy-hawk—and an attempt by the Eagles to make Thompson as well known as other quarterbacks of the day, such as Otto Graham, Sid Luckman, and Sammy Baugh. But Thompson did not need any gimmicks. He led the Eagles to back-to-back world championships, and he threw 25 touchdown passes in a 12-game regular season in 1948.

'Senator so-and-so, General so-and-so, report to your office.' By the fourth quarter, the stadium was almost empty."

The teams finished the game with the Eagles losing to the Redskins, 20–14. But for the next five years, nothing was the same. America was at war and, like the rest of the country, the NFL had to make sacrifices. More than 600 NFL people (players, coaches, and staff) went into the service, but the league kept going. Teams filled out their rosters as best they could, signing players with medical deferments or calling former players, such as Bronko Nagurski, out of retirement.

In 1943 the Eagles and Pittsburgh Steelers were short on both players and money. The only way they could survive was to pool their resources, so for one season, the teams merged. Officially, their name was the Phil-Pitt Eagles-Steelers, but they were best known as the Steagles. The two head coaches, Greasy Neale of the Eagles and Walt Kiesling of the Steelers, were named co-coaches, which, given the personalities of the two men, was a recipe for disaster.

"It sounds like we had a big advantage, putting two teams together as one," said tackle Al Wistert. "But all it meant was we had twice as many lousy players. Look at the teams. The Eagles had never had a winning season, and the Steelers were almost as bad."

The Steelers actually had their first winning season (7–4) the previous year, but the Eagles still had not reached the .500 mark in ten seasons. The "Steagles" were a motley bunch, splitting their home games between Philadelphia and Pittsburgh, but somehow they managed to finish 5–4–1.

"I think we surprised ourselves," Wistert said. "We had a couple good players. They brought Bill Hewitt out of retirement [he last played in 1939]. He was a great player, a Hall of Famer, who didn't wear a helmet. When he came back in '43 they had a rule that said everyone had to wear a helmet, so he did. He didn't like it, though."

Hinkle had a career year, carrying the ball 116 times for 571 yards, a 4.9-yard average. He finished one yard behind NFL rushing leader Bill Paschal of the New York Giants, but it was later discovered that one of Hinkle's runs, a 45-yarder, was erroneously credited to a teammate. The mistake never was corrected, and Hinkle lost his chance for the rushing title.

"That was a strange year; a lot of things went on," Hinkle said. "The fun was watching Greasy and Kiesling go after each other. They were stubborn and wouldn't give an inch. Kiesling accused Greasy of picking on his guys [Steelers]. We said, 'Nah, Greasy talks that way to everybody.'"

THEIR 15 MINUTES

Don Looney played only one season with the Eagles, but he left his mark. A lanky 6–2 split end from TCU, Looney set an NFL record with 58 catches in 1940. He finished well ahead of Green Bay's Don Hutson, the dominant receiver of that era, who had 45 catches.

Looney had the advantage of playing with his college quarterback, Davey O'Brien, for that one season in Philadelphia. The two put on quite a show, especially in the final game of the season when O'Brien threw 60 passes and completed

Don Looney (left) and Davey O'Brien were one of the first great passing combinations. Teammates at TCU where O'Brien won the Heisman Trophy, they played one season together with the Eagles, 1940. O'Brien (shown here with his wife) led the NFL in passing and Looney led the league in receptions.

In the 1950s, most pro football teams had to work to create fan interest. The Eagles were no exception. The team's publicity director, Ed Hogan, came up with this idea: He gave the defense a colorful nickname, The Suicide Seven, and dressed the players as pirates, complete with eyepatches and pistols. The Seven are (front row, left to right) end Norm (Wildman) Willey, tackle Mike Jarmoluk, tackle Frank (Bucko) Kilroy, tackle Jess Richardson, and end Tom Scott; (second row) linebackers Chuck Bednarik and Wayne Robinson. Dealing the cards is tight end Bobby Walston. As hokey as it was, the nickname had some merit. The Eagles defense during that period was accused of dirty play by *Life* magazine.

33 (both NFL single-game records) and Looney caught 14 (an Eagles record) for 180 yards. Still, the Eagles lost the game, 13–6, to Washington.

Looney went to Pittsburgh after that season as the Eagles and Steelers owners swapped franchises. He played just 12 games in Pittsburgh and retired. He came back to the NFL ten years later as a referee. His son, Joe Don, played five seasons in the league as a running back.

Leo Skladany had an even shorter career with the Eagles—just four games in 1949—but he made one of the biggest plays in team history. He blocked a Bob Waterfield punt and scooped up the ball for a touchdown in the Eagles' 14–0 win over the Los Angeles Rams in the 1949 championship game.

Skladany was a 17th-round draft pick from Pitt who was released during training camp, but coach Greasy Neale felt he had potential, so he sent Skladany to a semipro team in Paterson, New Jersey, so he would be close by in case the Eagles needed him. When defensive end Johnny Green was injured late in the season, Neale called Skladany.

"I couldn't believe my good fortune," Skladany said. "I spent that season making $200 a game in Paterson. I had a day job working in a factory, making storm windows. All of a sudden, I was with the Eagles, playing with guys like [Steve] Van Buren, [Chuck] Bednarik, and [Pete] Pihos."

In the championship game, the Eagles were leading 7–0 in the third quarter. The game was played in a driving rain, and the field was ankle-deep in mud. Skladany used his speed to block the Waterfield punt, then fell on the ball for the touchdown that locked up the Eagles' second consecutive NFL championship.

"I just took a straight line to Waterfield," Skladany said. "I threw myself through the air, and I was lucky enough to get the ball just as it was coming off his foot. The ball stuck in the mud, that's how deep it was. I just grabbed it and skidded across the goal line. The other players all mobbed me. What a feeling."

At the victory party, while the champagne was flowing, one of the team owners promised Skladany he would be rewarded by having his half share of the winner's check boosted to a full share.

"The next day everybody sobered up, and I never heard about my bonus again," Skladany said. He never complained, however. "I figured I had an experience I'd never forget," he said. "I would've played for nothing that day. Today, it's all about the money. Back in those days, football was football."

The Eagles traded Skladany to the New York Giants the following season. He played just four games in New York before ending his career.

BUD GRANT—AND OTHER SUPER COACHES

Long before Harold (Bud) Grant became a Hall of Fame coach, he was an outstanding two-way player for the Eagles. The fact that he played only two years in Philadelphia is a reflection of Grant's iconoclastic nature. He was not one to compromise, even then.

Grant was the Eagles' first-round draft pick in 1950, but when they offered him only $7,000 to sign, he chose to play pro basketball with the Minneapolis Lakers. He spent two seasons with the Lakers as a 6–3 forward, playing in the same frontcourt as the great George Mikan and helping the Lakers win back-to-back NBA championships.

"At that point, I felt I had gone as far as I could go in basketball," Grant said.

So he signed with the Eagles in 1951. He played his first season at defensive end and led the team in tackles. In 1952 coach Jim Trimble switched Grant to offense to take advantage of his height. The former Minnesota All-America caught 56 passes for 997 yards and seven touchdowns. He was the league's second-leading receiver, trailing only Mac Speedie of Cleveland, who had 62 catches, but less yardage (911) and fewer touchdowns (five) than Grant.

Grant was so good that Trimble played Pete Pihos, a future Hall of Fame receiver, on defense most of the season. Said quarterback Adrian Burk, "From playing basketball, Bud had great hands, and with his height, he had a deceptive stride. He always seemed to be open."

Grant played the 1952 season without a contract. He refused to sign because he felt the $7,000 offer was less than fair. By not signing, he played out his option and was a free agent at the end of the season. He claims he would have stayed if the Eagles had made a good offer, but instead they offered a token raise of $1,000.

In his book *Bud: The Other Side of the Glacier*, Grant said, "I thought I was worth more than that. They said I couldn't make more than the veterans. I asked why. The answer was 'You just can't.' I told them I couldn't sign. They told me if I didn't sign, I couldn't play in the Pro Bowl. I told them what they could do with the Pro Bowl invitation and their contract offer."

Grant signed with Winnipeg of the Canadian Football League, where he played for four seasons and led the league in receiving three times. In 1957, at age 30, Grant was named

Bud Grant is best known for coaching the Minnesota Vikings to four Super Bowls, but in 1952, he starred as an end with the Eagles, catching 56 passes and scoring seven touchdowns.

head coach in Winnipeg. In ten seasons, he won four Grey Cup championships. In 1967, he was hired to coach the Minnesota Vikings. In 18 years with the Vikings, he won 11 division championships and led the team to four Super Bowls. He was inducted into the Pro Football Hall of Fame in 1994.

Three other men who wore the Eagles uniform—like Grant, briefly—coached teams to the Super Bowl:

- Bill Cowher was cut by Dick Vermeil in the 1980 preseason, but returned and made the team as a reserve linebacker and special-teams player in 1983–84. He coached Pittsburgh to Super Bowl XXX.
- Mike Ditka made the Hall of Fame on the strength of six great years in Chicago, but he caught only 39 passes in two injury-plagued years with the Eagles (1967–68). He coached the Bears to victory in Super Bowl XX.
- John Madden was a 21st-round draft pick of the Eagles in 1958. A tackle from Cal-Poly, Madden came to training camp, but suffered a knee injury that ended his playing career. He went into coaching and led Oakland to victory in Super Bowl XI. Today, he is an Emmy-winning football analyst on ABC-TV.

EAGLES BREAK THE COLOR BARRIER

Ralph Goldston had no idea he was a pioneer. When he reported to the Eagles training camp in 1952, he was only concerned with one thing, and that was making the team. He did not realize he made history just by walking through the door.

Goldston and fellow rookie Don Stevens were the first African Americans to wear an Eagles uniform. Goldston was an 11th-round draft pick from Youngstown State; Stevens was a 30th-round pick from Illinois. Both were running backs.

"I didn't know about any color line," Goldston said in a 2005 interview from his home in Columbus. "I didn't find out I was the first [black player] until I was there a while. It wasn't a big deal. Don and I were treated the same as the other rookies."

Jim Gallagher, an Eagles executive from 1949 until his retirement in 1995, agreed. "It wasn't an issue," he said. "The papers didn't make a point of it. None of us talked about it. We were just looking for good players."

The number of black players in the NFL was slowly increasing by 1952. There were none in the league from 1934 through 1945. The reintegration of pro football took place in 1946—the year before Jackie Robinson broke the color line in major league baseball—with Kenny Washington and Woody Strode signing with the Los Angeles Rams and Bill Willis and Marion Motley joining the Cleveland Browns.

In 1949, Detroit signed three black players, including Bob Mann, who became a star receiver, and Wally Triplett, who led the league in kickoff returns. The Browns signed Horace Gillom, who led the league in punting. The teams that played for the championship in 1950 and '51, the Browns and Rams, were the teams with the most black players. It was no coincidence that other clubs, such as the Eagles, began drafting black players right about that time.

In 1952, the Eagles were coming off two poor seasons, and Steve Van Buren, their great halfback, was at the end of his career. They needed to add speed to their backfield, so they drafted Goldston and Stevens. They used their first pick on

Johnny Bright, a tailback from Drake, but he signed with Calgary of the Canadian Football League. Bright later said he went to the CFL because he did not want to be the first black player on the Eagles.

"There was a tremendous influx of southern players into the NFL, and I didn't know what kind of treatment I could expect," Bright told an interviewer in 1963.

Goldston had no such fears. "I didn't know the history," he said. "I felt if the Eagles drafted me, there wasn't a problem. Other [black] players were doing well in pro football. What [Bright] was thinking, I can't say. I was just grateful for the opportunity. It worked out well for me."

The Eagles did have issues when they traveled. Goldston and Stevens usually were forced to stay in a different hotel. Said Goldston: "All it meant was Don and I didn't have a curfew. The other players had bed check at 9, but we were on our own."

While Goldston was in Philadelphia, he lived with a minister and his wife at 24th and Montgomery. He walked to and from practice at Shibe Park, 21st and Lehigh. As a rookie, Goldston cracked the starting lineup and led the Eagles with three rushing touchdowns. He finished the season with 210 yards on 65 carries, a 3.2-yard average. Stevens was a part-time running back and kick returner.

Hugh Brown of the *Philadelphia Bulletin* described the 5–11, 195-pound Goldston as "a powerful and shifty runner [who is] in the opinion of many, the best all-around back in camp." Reporters made occasional references to race, such as an *Inquirer* story on Goldston that predicted "a great year for the hard-hitting Negro," but the fact that he and Stevens were

Halfbacks Ralph Goldston (above) and Don Stevens were the first African Americans to play for the Eagles. They joined the team in 1952.

the first black players in the team's 20-year history was never addressed.

"The way we fit in, I guess no one thought twice about it," Goldston said.

Coach Jim Trimble had high hopes for Goldston, but a broken leg suffered in a 1953 exhibition game sidelined him for the entire season. When he came back the next year, Goldston was switched to defense, where he played two more seasons before the Eagles released him. In 1956, Trimble was hired as head coach of Hamilton in the CFL, and he brought Goldston with him. He played ten seasons in the CFL before beginning a 30-year career as a college coach (Harvard, Colorado) and NFL scout (Seattle).

Stevens was with the Eagles in 1952 and briefly in '54, but his NFL career lasted only 15 games.

SAVAGERY ON SUNDAY

In October 1955, *Life* magazine published a cover story entitled "Savagery on Sunday." The article claimed there was an epidemic of dirty play in the National Football League, and it identified the Eagles—middle guard Bucko Kilroy and linebacker Wayne Robinson, in particular—as the worst offenders.

The article called Kilroy the toughest of the league's "bad men" and claimed he deliberately injured Giants quarterback Arnold Galiffa. One of the photos showed Robinson kneeing Cleveland's Pete Brewster in the groin. The story indicated that Robinson's action was deliberate.

When the story appeared, Commissioner Bert Bell was furious. He was trying to polish the image of pro football and sell it to the TV networks. Getting smeared on the cover of *Life* magazine was a serious blow. Bell had no choice but to defend the honor of his league.

"Bert called and said, 'We're suing,'" Kilroy said. "I said, 'What are you talking about?' He said, 'We're suing *Life* magazine over this story.' I said okay. My name was on the suit [along with Robinson's], but Bert was the one behind it."

The case did not come to trial for two years. By then, Kilroy and Robinson were retired, but the case was heard in U.S. District Court in Philadelphia. It was a home-field advantage for the two ex-Eagles, who sued Time, Inc., the publisher of *Life*, for $250,000 apiece, claiming the article subjected them to "scorn, contempt, and ridicule."

The trial lasted eight days, and the testimony was often hilarious. Asked to explain the photograph where he appears to be kneeing Brewster, Robinson said he was blocked into him by another player. "If my knee went in his groin," Robinson said, "it was with help."

Robinson was asked about an incident that caused him to be ejected from a 1952 exhibition game. "Didn't you chase a fellow 30 yards down the field and throw a punch at him?" asked attorney Phil Strubing. Robinson replied, "Yes, but I didn't hit him."

Detroit end Cloyce Box called the Eagles a bunch of "ornery critters." Asked to define the term, Box said, "A domesticated animal which at periods of time acts without the scope of that domestication."

Kilroy agreed he was a tough player, but insisted he played within the rules. As proof of his good character, Kilroy told the court he once was a choirboy at St. Anne's Roman Catholic Church in Port Richmond.

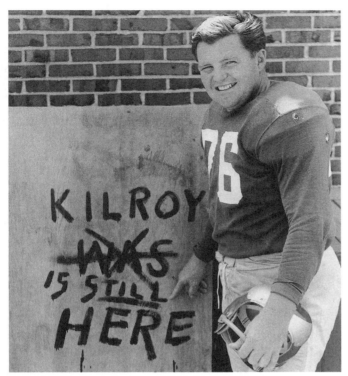

Life magazine described Eagles tackle Frank (Bucko) Kilroy as "the orneriest of ornery [NFL] critters." At the urging of Commissioner Bert Bell, Kilroy sued the magazine for slander.

The jury—11 men, one woman—found in favor of Kilroy and Robinson, although they reduced the award to $11,600 apiece. It was considerably less than the quarter of a million the players sought, but as Robinson pointed out, it still was more than he made in his best season as a player.

The real winner was Bert Bell because after the verdict was rendered, no other publication ever tried to establish a similar pattern of dirty play in the NFL, and that result was exactly what the commissioner hoped to accomplish.

TOMMY McDONALD: THE KISSING BANDIT

Tommy McDonald will never forget his first visit to Philadelphia. It was January 1957, and he was in town to receive the Maxwell Award as college football player of the year. The Eagles had selected him in the third round of the draft, so McDonald was walking through Center City, getting acquainted with his new home.

He did not know there had been a series of robberies in the downtown area committed by a man the police called "the Kissing Bandit." He targeted offices with female staff, and after he grabbed the money, he also stole a kiss from the woman behind the counter. The police circulated a sketch of the suspect, and he looked just like Tommy McDonald.

So when the Oklahoma All-America walked into an airline ticket office, the female ticket agent screamed, "It's him." Two plainclothes detectives rushed in, shoved McDonald against the wall, and stuck a gun in his ribs.

"I had no idea what was going on," McDonald said. "I kept saying, 'You're making a big mistake. I'm Tommy McDonald. Call Vince McNally with the Eagles. He'll tell you.'"

The police did call McNally, the Eagles general manager, who rushed over from the team's offices at 15th and Locust and straightened everything out. As McDonald was leaving, he told one detective, "You know, I was ready to belt you." The detective said, "It's a good thing you didn't." A third cop stepped out of the back room and said, "I had a gun trained on you the whole time. I would've had to shoot you."

A week later, McDonald received an official apology from the mayor's office.

REACHES AND LONG SHOTS

In the never-ending search for talent, NFL teams have been known to sign track athletes, basketball players, wrestlers, anyone they think has raw skill worth developing. The Eagles have tried it a few times, without much success.

In 1962 they selected Villanova sprinter Frank Budd in the seventh round of the draft. On the day he signed, he posed for photographers in a green jersey with the number 09.2, which was his world-record time in the 100-yard dash. He actually was given number 20.

"I expect to work, and I expect to make it," said Budd, who was signed as a wide receiver even though he had not played

Villanova's Frank Budd set world records in track, but he went nowhere fast as a wide receiver with the Eagles in 1962.

football since his days at Asbury Park (New Jersey) High School. General manager Vince McNally raved about Budd's first workout. "He showed us he has a beautiful pair of hands," McNally said.

Budd made the team, but lasted only one season. He caught five passes for 130 yards, an impressive 26-yard average, but his hands turned out to be not so beautiful, after all. He dropped too many passes, and the quarterbacks lost confidence in him. The Eagles released him and Washington claimed him, but he was dropped after one season there. He played briefly with Calgary in the Canadian Football League, then retired.

In 1970 the Eagles selected John Carlos in the 15th round of the draft. He was even more of a reach than Budd because he never had played organized football and he still was carrying the baggage of the 1968 Mexico City Olympics where he drew worldwide attention for giving the black power salute on the medal platform after finishing third in the 220-yard run.

Carlos had two things going for him: world-class speed and impressive size (6–3, 210 pounds). But he was hopelessly far behind in football fundamentals. In fact, he did not even know how to put on the equipment for his first training camp practice. Two sportswriters took pity on him and helped him get dressed.

Like Budd, Carlos worked hard, but running pass patterns, with the cutting and pivoting, was nothing like running on a track. The long stride that served him so well in the 220 worked against him on a football field with its short, violent bursts of action.

Pete Retzlaff with his number 44 jersey, which was retired after his final game in 1966. The Eagles have retired seven numbers: 15, Steve Van Buren; 40, Tom Brookshier; 44, Retzlaff; 60, Chuck Bednarik; 70, Al Wistert; 92, Reggie White; 99, Jerome Brown.

Carlos blew out his knee trying to catch a pass one day and spent the entire 1970 season on the injured reserve list. The Eagles coaches hoped being around the game for a full year would increase Carlos's football knowledge and improve his chances of making the team the following summer. But in the 1971 camp, the coaches had a choice: They could keep Carlos or a 6–8 rookie named Harold Carmichael. They kept Carmichael. Clearly, it was the right decision, but it meant the end of Carlos's football career.

"There was no doubt about his courage, no doubt about his effort," head coach Jerry Williams said in releasing Carlos. "He was a good team man. He was good to have on the squad. The determining factor was a lack of consistency in catching the ball."

In 1973 the Eagles went even farther afield, signing Australian rugby star Mark Harris as a running back and kicker. Harris was 24 with a chiseled 6–2, 225-pound body and 4.5 speed in the 40-yard dash. He knew nothing about American football, starting with the name. He called it "gridiron."

But Harris was such a natural talent that he fascinated the Eagles coaches. He once punted a ball from the warning track in right field at Veterans Stadium into the box seats behind third base on one hop. "The ball went 75 yards in the air," coach Mike McCormack said. "The man is a great, great athlete."

Harris was baffled by NFL football and its terminology. A superstar in his homeland, Harris grew frustrated standing on the sidelines at Eagles camp. He asked for and was given his release before the first preseason game. However, he did leave behind a wonderful entry in his player questionnaire.

Q: Do you recall any humorous incidents in your career?
A: Yes, in a World Cup game in England. It was raining and foggy. No one could see. One player decided to relieve himself at center field knowing the spectators could not see further than 20 feet.

KUHARICH'S THREE-HEADED QUARTERBACK

Joe Kuharich had one winning season in Philadelphia—a 9–5 finish in 1966—but even that year had people shaking their heads. That's because the Eagles coach used three different quarterbacks and shuffled them around in a way that confused everyone, most of all the three quarterbacks.

Kuharich practiced all three—Norm Snead, King Hill, and Jack Concannon—with the first unit during the week, then decided on his starter just before game time. You could almost see the coach standing in the locker room, saying, "Eenie, meenie, miney, moe."

"It became a joke around the league," Hill said, "but the three of us weren't laughing. I thought Joe was a nice fellow, but I can't say I understood him too well."

Snead said:

The thing was, we were different styles. I was a drop-back passer. King used play action. Jack was a scrambler. The other players had to adjust to whichever quarterback was in the game. It was hard all the way around. We [the quarterbacks] didn't know what Joe was thinking half the time. We'd be asking each other before the game, "Did he tell you anything? He didn't tell me anything either."

Eagles quarterbacks (from left) Jack Concannon, Norm Snead, and King Hill study the game plan on a team flight in 1966. They knew the plays; they just didn't know who was playing.

One day Joe came up to me during warm-ups. He said, "Are you ready?" I said, "You bet." He said, "Good. You're going today." I was all charged up. Then he went to King and said, "Be ready. If we get the ball inside our 40, you're starting." King said to me, "Didn't he say you were starting?" At that point, we were both confused.

As we were heading to the locker room, Joe said to Concannon, "If we get the ball inside their 20, you're starting," We looked at each other. The other team got the ball first and we held them on downs. They punted and the ball was bouncing around midfield. King and I were watching. We figured if it bounced one way, he was starting. If it bounced the other way, I was starting. We both had our helmets on, ready to go.

The ball stopped rolling right around the 50, and Joe said, "Concannon, get in there." King and I just looked at each other. There didn't seem to be a whole lot of logic to what was going on.

No one thought the juggling act made much sense, but somehow it worked. The Eagles recovered from embarrassing losses to St. Louis (41–10) and Dallas (56–7) to win seven of their final nine games. They finished in a tie for second place in the Eastern Conference and went to the Playoff Bowl, where they lost to Baltimore, 20–14. Kuharich used all three quarterbacks against the Colts with Hill starting, Concannon playing the second half, and Snead coming in for one play: a Hail Mary pass that fell incomplete.

"Norm was steamed," Hill said. "He didn't play the whole game, then with five seconds left, Joe tells him, 'Get in there and throw it as far as you can.' Norm said to me, 'I'd like to throw it in the stands.'"

For the season, Snead completed 45 percent of his passes, eight for touchdowns with 11 interceptions. Hill completed 54 percent of his attempts, but his long gain was 30 yards, and he, too, had more interceptions (7) than touchdowns (5). Concannon made some plays with his legs (195 yards rushing), but he completed just 21 of 51 passes (41 percent) with one touchdown and four interceptions. Their combined efficiency rating was 53.4, one of the lowest in team history.

Those numbers beg the question: Did Kuharich's constant shuffling of the deck cause the lousy quarterback play? Or did their lousy play leave Kuharich no choice but to keep changing quarterbacks? Whatever, it remains some kind of miracle that team actually won nine games.

THE O. J. BOWL

It was called "The O. J. Bowl," a 1968 matchup of the 0–6 Eagles and 0–6 Pittsburgh Steelers. They appeared to be the two worst teams in the NFL that season, so whichever team lost this game figured to lose every game on the schedule.

Ordinarily, that would be a very bad thing, but in 1968 there was a nice consolation prize to being at the bottom of the standings. It meant having the top pick in the next draft, so that team could select O. J. Simpson, the Heisman Trophy winner from Southern California.

In the days leading up to the game, the newspapers in Philadelphia and Pittsburgh focused on the "O. J." angle and ran stories about how long-time fans were openly rooting for their teams to lose. Their feeling was that one win was not going to reverse the fortunes of their team, but the addition of a great running back like Simpson could. So the idea was to lose and keep losing until the No. 1 draft pick was safely in hand.

A sparse crowd of 26,908 at Pitt Stadium saw one of the worst games in modern NFL history. The two teams combined for 303 yards in penalties. The Steelers replaced an ineffective quarterback (Dick Shiner, who completed six of 12 passes) with one who was worse (Kent Nix, who completed three of 15). The score was tied 3–3 in the final minute, but a bizarre decision by Eagles coach Joe Kuharich allowed the Steelers to pull out a 6–3 victory.

The Eagles had fourth down at their own 10-yard line with 50 seconds left. They had inches to go for the first down, and Kuharich decided to gamble. He sent in his best short yardage play—Tom Woodeshick running behind All-Pro tackle Bob Brown—but the Pittsburgh defense knew what was coming and stopped Woodeshick cold.

Three plays later, Booth Lusteg—who earlier missed field-goal attempts from 22 and 34 yards—kicked one through from the 15, giving the Steelers the victory.

Wrote Gordon Forbes in the *Philadelphia Inquirer*: "Joe Kuharich's career as a pro football coach and maker of wrong decisions sank to its lowest depth Sunday and the Eagles were forced to crawl into the same dungeon." Bill Conlin of the *Philadelphia Daily News* wrote, "[The game] was like a Soviet beauty contest. Nobody won. The NFL lost."

Kuharich tried to justify his decision by saying he wanted to control the ball and drive down the field to either a game-winning field goal or touchdown. What made him think the Eagles were capable of mounting that kind of drive—when they could only manage one field goal in the previous 59 minutes—was anyone's guess.

"It was one of those games that teeter-tottered until somebody got the last break," Kuharich said.

As it turned out, neither the Steelers nor the Eagles landed O. J. Each team finished the 1968 season with two wins, so the 1–13 Buffalo Bills got the first pick in the draft, and they took Simpson.

THE ROSSOVICH FILE

Tim Rossovich was a defensive end and linebacker who played with the Eagles from 1968 through 1971. It was just four years—and they were four awful years at that as the team won exactly 15 games—but Rossovich made a lasting impression, mostly for his antics off the field. They included

- Dousing his long hair with lighter fluid and setting himself on fire. He did this to amuse his friends at parties, and he also did it for a *Sports Illustrated* photographer for a 1971 feature story.
- Biting the caps off beer bottles and eating glass. He preferred leaded Belgian crystal.
- Diving headfirst into the whirlpool.
- Wearing tie-dyed capes and leotards and listening to Gregorian chants on the stereo.
- Grabbing a spider off a table and eating it.
- Crawling into a shoe store and biting the toes of lady customers.
- Hiding in the bushes at training camp and leaping out to startle unsuspecting journalists.

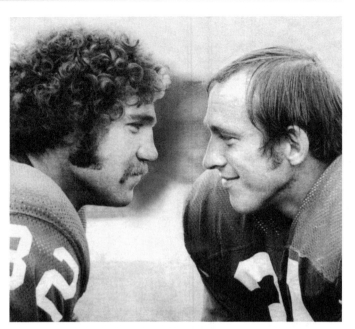

Tim Rossovich (left), here in a playful staredown with teammate Tom Woodeshick, was famous for his antics off the field. "The team wasn't winning," he said, "so I had to find other ways to have fun."

When the 6–4, 240-pound Rossovich quit football, he found work in Hollywood as an actor and stunt man. On screen, he boxed Ryan O'Neal (*The Main Event*), he was tossed off a hotel balcony by Kate Jackson (*Charlie's Angels*), and he was gunned down in a bank robbery (*The Long Riders*).

You were expecting Shakespeare?

EAGLES ON "MONDAY NIGHT FOOTBALL"

"Monday Night Football" debuted to great fanfare in 1970. There was a carnival atmosphere to the games, and when the crew of Keith Jackson, Don Meredith, and Howard Cosell came to town, it was a major event.

The Eagles got their first taste of the Monday night spotlight when they hosted the New York Giants at Franklin Field on November 23. The ABC network executives were less than thrilled with the way it turned out. For one thing, the Eagles were a dismal 1–7–1, so they were hardly a prime-time attraction. The other problem was Cosell: He was unable to finish the game.

Cosell downed a few vodka martinis at a pregame party thrown by Eagles owner Leonard Tose. He continued drinking during the game in an effort to stay warm. It was an unusually cold night for November. Wind chill was below zero, and the players put Saran Wrap around their feet to ward off frostbite. The ABC broadcast location was an open, unheated platform on the facing of the upper deck. Cosell had complained earlier in the day of flulike symptoms, so whether it was the flu, the wind chill, the vodka, or a combination of the three, Cosell became violently ill late in the second quarter.

As authors Marc Gunther and Bill Carter wrote in the book *Monday Night Mayhem*, "Suddenly, with a few minutes to go [before halftime], Cosell went white. He pitched forward and threw up all over Meredith's cowboy boots."

Executive producer Roone Arledge met with Cosell at halftime and decided he was in no shape to continue. Cosell climbed into a cab outside Franklin Field and went straight to his home in Manhattan. He missed an exciting finish as the Eagles upset the Giants, 23–20, and the jubilant fans tore down the goalposts and carried them into the night.

Overall, the Eagles have fared well on "Monday Night Football." Through the 2004 season, the Eagles are 22–17 on ABC's prime-time showcase. They are 13–8 at home, 9–9 on the road. They were 0–6 on Monday night from 1995 through 1998, and ABC dropped them from the schedule. But when the team rebounded under Andy Reid, the network was back, putting the Eagles on Monday night three times in each season from 2002 to 2004. The Eagles were 7–2 in those nine games.

WHAT'S IN A NAME?

Eagles general manager Jim Murray knew he wanted to draft Will Wynn. He did not study film on Wynn. He did not even know what position Wynn played. But Murray knew one thing: He liked the name.

"With the record we've had," Murray said, "how could we not draft a guy named Will Wynn? I feel better just saying it, Will Wynn."

So the Eagles selected Wynn, a defensive end from Tennessee State, in the seventh round of the 1973 draft. He made the team and cracked the starting lineup as a rookie. He had three sacks of Roger Staubach in a 30–16 win over Dallas, helping the Eagles snap an 11-game losing streak against the Cowboys.

Here are other entries in an Eagles' All-Name Team:

Best Names

Ephesians Bartley, LB, 1992
Claude Crabb, DB, 1964–65
Smiley Creswell, DE, 1985
Happy Feller, K, 1971
Clark Hoss, TE, 1972
Proverb Jacobs, T, 1958
Israel Lang, RB, 1964–68
Toy Ledbetter, RB, 1953–55
Baptiste Manzini, C, 1944–48
John Outlaw, DB, 1973–78
Junior Tautalatasi, RB, 1986–88
Tuufuli Uperesa, OG, 1971
Dean Wink, DT, 1967–68

Best Nicknames

Walter (Piggy) Barnes, OG, 1948–51
Ed (Bibbles) Bawel, RB, 1952–56
Chuck (Concrete Charlie) Bednarik, C-LB, 1949–62
Jim (Gummy) Carr, DB, 1959–63
Bill (Popeye) Dunstan, 1973–76
Eric (Pink) Floyd, OG, 1992–93
Hank (Honey Buns) Fraley, C, 2000–
William (Lefty) Frizzell, DB, 1986–90, 1992–93
Hal (Skippy) Giancanelli, RB, 1953–56

Ron (The Polish Rifle) Jaworski, QB, 1977–86
Frank (Bucko) Kilroy, DT, 1943–55
Joe (Big Bird) Lavender, CB, 1973–75
Earle (Greasy) Neale, Coach, 1941–50
Pete (The Golden Greek) Pihos, E, 1947–55
Pete (The Baron) Retzlaff, E, 1956–66
Clyde (Smackover) Scott, RB, 1949–52
Ralph (Catfish) Smith, TE, 1962–64
Norm (The Dutchman) Van Brocklin, QB, 1958–60
Reggie (Minister of Defense) White, DE, 1985–92
Norm (Wildman) Willey, DE, 1950–57

Best Same Names

Neill Armstrong, E, 1947–51
Glenn Campbell, E, 1935
Hopalong Cassady, WR, 1962
Rocky Colavito, LB, 1975
Jack Dempsey, T, 1934–37
Glenn Frey, RB, 1936–37
Richard Harris, DE, 1971–73
Don Johnson, RB, 1953–55
Spike Jones, P, 1975–77
Don King, T, 1956
Ted Williams, RB, 1942

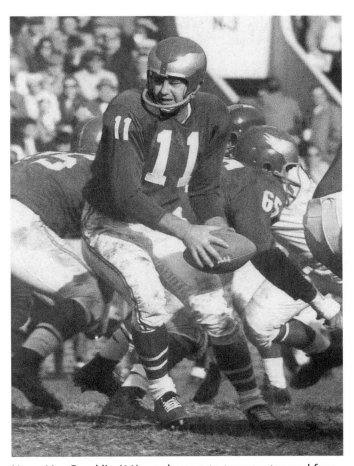

Norm Van Brocklin (11) was known to teammates and fans alike as "The Dutchman."

THE DEATH OF BLENDA GAY

The Eagles had just concluded the 1976 season, their first under coach Dick Vermeil. They finished with a 4–10 record, but they closed it out with a 27–10 win over Seattle, which sent the players into the off-season with a good feeling.

But on Monday, December 20, they were shaken by the news that a teammate, defensive end Blenda Gay, was found dead in his South Jersey apartment. His throat was slashed, and his wife, Roxanne, was charged with the murder.

"It's a tragic thing," Vermeil said. "Here's a young guy with everything going for him, and now he's gone. He didn't have great talent, but he had great character. He worked hard to make himself into an NFL player. We felt he would keep improving because he was so dedicated."

Gay came up the hard way, playing at tiny Fayetteville (Arkansas) State, then playing for the Model City (New York) Diplomats, a semipro team that paid him $75 a game. He signed with Oakland as a free agent, was cut and re-signed four times, before finally catching on with the Eagles in 1975. Gay worked his way into the starting lineup, and in 1976 he had 36 tackles, 43 assists, and two sacks.

After Gay's death, people within the Eagles organization wondered if they should have recognized the signs of potential trouble. Roxanne, a petite woman of 25, had called people in the front office at odd hours, complaining about petty things, like the length of practice, or her suspicions that her husband was involved with other women. She would just appear at the team's Veterans Stadium office and sit in the lobby for hours.

When the Eagles were on the road, she made so many phone calls to her husband's room that no one on the team

Defensive end Blenda Gay was stabbed to death by his wife in December 1976.

would share a room with him. She claimed the 6–5, 255-pound Gay assaulted her, but no formal charges were filed and no one could recall seeing visible evidence of abuse. Finally, she picked up an eight-inch kitchen knife and stabbed her husband while he slept.

Gay was able to call the Camden County emergency operator. He said, "My wife stabbed me. I'm bleeding. Please send help." The 27-year-old Gay died en route to John F. Kennedy Memorial Hospital in Stratford, New Jersey.

Roxanne Gay was tried for the murder, but found not guilty by reason of insanity. Judge I. V. DeMartino ordered her confined to the Trenton State Psychiatric Hospital. He said, "If not committed and treated extensively, she presents a risk … to herself and others for the foreseeable future."

THE PRAYING TAILBACK

The prayer of thanksgiving—an end-zone celebration that is almost commonplace in today's NFL—began with Eagles running back Herb Lusk. Now senior pastor of Greater Exodus Baptist Church in North Philadelphia, Lusk started dropping to his knees after scoring touchdowns for Long Beach State University in 1975, and he continued to do it with the Eagles.

"I was the first one," said Lusk, who was known as "the Praying Tailback." "It was my way of saying thanks. I hurt my knee in junior college, and the doctors said I'd never play football again. But I put my fate in God's hands. I prayed every day, and I knew if my knee healed, it was His will for me to continue playing."

Lusk recovered well enough to rush for 1,596 yards and 13 touchdowns as a senior at Long Beach. The Eagles selected the 6–0, 190-pound Lusk in the tenth round of the 1976 draft. He made it clear from the start that even if he made the team, he would be gone after three seasons. At that point, Lusk planned to follow in his father's footsteps and become a minister.

Lusk was true to his word. He played three seasons with the Eagles and walked away. He finished his pro career with 113 rushing attempts for 483 yards, a 4.3-yard average, and 18 pass receptions for 221 yards. He scored three touchdowns and said a prayer of thanksgiving after each one.

His career highlight was an October 9, 1977, game against the New York Giants at the Meadowlands. Tom Sullivan, the starting halfback, bruised his knee, and Lusk came off the bench to carry the ball 17 times for 117 yards and two touchdowns. One of his scoring runs was a 70-yard dash around end, the longest run by an Eagle in 19 years. Tackle Stan Walters threw the key block, wiping out cornerback Ray Rhodes, who later would become the Eagles head coach.

When Lusk informed the Eagles he was retiring at age 26, he said, "I'm leaving the game very happy and very proud. I don't feel like I'm going to miss the game. I'm moving up to better things."

Lusk began his seminary studies and preached his first sermon on April 13, 1980, at the First African Baptist Church in Sharon Hill. Two years later, he became pastor of a troubled Greater Exodus Baptist Church on North Broad Street. The church had only 17 active members and was more than $1 million in debt. Working tirelessly, Lusk put the church back on its feet. Today, the church has more than 2,000 members, and in addition to its religious activities, it has a job training and placement program that serves the North Philadelphia

Herb Lusk, "The Praying Tailback," quit pro football after three seasons to study for the ministry. He is now the pastor of the Greater Exodus Baptist Church in North Philadelphia.

community. In June 2004, President George W. Bush visited the church and praised Lusk as a model for leadership in America's inner cities.

THE MAN KNOWN ONLY AS BOW WOW

All professional sports teams attract characters, but Dick Vermeil's Eagles had a true original in Wojtkiewicz Stanley Wojciechowicz, better known as "Bow Wow." How he got the nickname was something of a mystery, like most things about Bow Wow, but he was a fixture around Veterans Stadium during the Vermeil years.

He was not listed in the media guide, and he was not in the official team directory, but he was everywhere else—on the practice field, in the locker room, in the executive offices. Mostly, he was attached at the hip to Vermeil, the coach he befriended at UCLA.

Bow Wow was born in Pittsburgh, but he bounced around the country, attending 13 different colleges ("I was one of those tramp athletes," he said) before settling on the West Coast where he met and married Sheila Graham, the columnist for *Variety*. It was through his marriage to Graham (which lasted three years) that Bow Wow claimed to have become something of a player in Hollywood, producing various TV and radio shows.

Bow Wow (who was not related to former Eagles great Alex Wojciechowicz) claimed to know Frank Sinatra, Jackie Onassis, Cary Grant, and on and on. He claimed to have won six Emmys. He claimed to have his own TV production company. He claimed a lot of stuff. Maybe it was true, maybe half of it was true, maybe none of it was true. No one knew for sure, just as no one knew his age or where he actually lived, but that was part of Bow Wow's charm.

This much was known: While living in Los Angeles, he became friendly with Tommy Prothro, who coached UCLA and the Rams. He started hanging out at UCLA football practices, and that was where he met Vermeil. They were an odd couple—the laser-focused Vermeil and the winking rogue known as Bow Wow—but they hit it off.

When Vermeil came to Philadelphia in 1976, Bow Wow was part of the package. Stan Hochman of the *Philadelphia Daily News* described their relationship as "Bow Wow playing Sancho Panza to Vermeil's Don Quixote."

Mostly, Bow Wow ran errands. With Vermeil rarely leaving his office, Bow Wow functioned as a valet. He picked up pizzas, aspirin, birthday cards, all the things the coach was too busy to get for himself. Bow Wow also knew how to make Vermeil laugh, which was perhaps his most important role, using his sly needle to ease the pressure.

"When things get grim, he can make me smile," Vermeil said. "I like to have him around. The players like having him around. You've got to have some laughs."

When the football season ended, Bow Wow would disappear and not reappear until the next training camp. No one knew where he went, but it was assumed he went to Los Angeles. When Vermeil resigned after the 1982 season, Bow Wow also departed the Philadelphia scene.

1980 EAGLES: THE VATICAN'S TEAM

The Eagles went into the 1980 postseason as the first NFL team with a papal blessing. Whether it had anything to do with the Eagles winning the NFC championship and earning a trip to the Super Bowl, you can draw your own conclusions, but it surely is a unique chapter in the team's history.

The story actually began one year earlier when Pope John Paul II visited Philadelphia. Jim Murray, the Eagles general manager, stationed his infant son, named John Paul, in a prominent place along the pope's parade route. Murray had his son dressed in a John Paul T-shirt, holding a sign that read, "I, too, am called John Paul, named in your honor for His glory."

The pope somehow picked the child out of the huge crowd. He broke from his procession and walked over to bless his namesake. Ed Mahan, the Eagles photographer, was there and captured the moment in a remarkable picture, which received widespread exposure, including a halftime piece on ABC's "Monday Night Football."

Ed Piszek, head of Mrs. Paul's Foods, was a good friend of Eagles owner Leonard Tose and Murray. He also was a longtime friend of the pontiff, having met him when John Paul was still a cardinal in Poland. In December 1980, Piszek went to Rome to visit the pope and brought along a copy of Mahan's picture.

When Piszek and his wife Olga handed the pope the photograph, he smiled and said, "Yes, I remember this." The pope signed the photo and asked the Piszeks to return it to the baby's family as a memento.

"Then I told the pope who Jim Murray was, that he was general manager of a professional football team," Piszek said. "The pope is an avid sportsman, so he was very interested. I told the pope that Murray's team was entering its championship round and it has two Polish quarterbacks [Ron Jaworski and Joe Pisarcik]. He didn't know what a quarterback was, but I said, 'They're the big shots. They throw the ball.'

The Worst of Times

In 112 games during an eight-year period between 1968 and 1975, the Eagles were minus 35 in turnovers. During that span, they allowed 149 yards per game rushing while averaging only 107 yards on the ground.

After the first five games of 1971, the Eagles had won only nine of their previous 47 contests (9–36–2). In 1971, the Eagles won only six games and rushed for only six touchdowns all season. The following year, the won only two games and scored only two touchdowns on the ground all season.

From 1983 to 1985, the Eagles went 18–29–1 and were minus 25 in turnovers, In addition to ranking near the bottom of the league in pass defense, the team could neither run the ball nor stop the run during that 48-game span, when they averaged 91 yards per game on the ground while allowing an average of 146 yards.

"The pope said, 'I wouldn't want them to get hurt,' so he got two papal medals and blessed them. He told me to give them to the two players. He said they were for their protection."

Piszek brought the medals home and presented them to Jaworski and Pisarcik at a team meeting during the bye week before the playoffs. Piszek told the squad about his audience with the pope and the Holy Father's interest in Philadelphia and the Eagles.

"We all just sat back and listened," Murray said. "The more Ed spoke, the faster my head spun. Think about it. The pope comes to town and picks John Paul out of two million people. Then Eddie gets the great picture. Ed Piszek is friends with Leonard, and he's a personal friend of the pope. The pope just happens to be Polish, and we have two Polish quarterbacks. Hey, Jimmy the Greek wouldn't touch odds like that.

"Our two quarterbacks have got to feel pretty good," Murray said. "Now they've got Stan Walters, Jerry Sisemore, and the pope protecting them. That's three Pro Bowlers right there."

THE CONWELLS: THE TACKLE AND THE ROCK STAR

Joe Conwell was a starting offensive tackle for the Eagles, but he was only the second-biggest name in his own family. He was overshadowed by his younger brother, star of the rock band Tommy Conwell and the Young Rumblers.

"I love football," Joe said, "but if there is anything in the world that I would trade what I'm doing for, it would be to be doing what he's doing."

Tommy taught Joe to play the guitar, and Joe would sometimes join his brother on stage, but Joe was more comfortable on the football field. A native of Philadelphia who grew up in Lower Merion, Joe always wanted to play for the Eagles, and he did for two seasons under coach Buddy Ryan.

Conwell played at the University of North Carolina and signed with the Philadelphia Stars of the USFL. When the league collapsed, he joined the Eagles and won a starting position in 1986. In his first game, Conwell held Richard Dent, the Chicago Bears' All-Pro end, without a sack. In the final game of the season, he was named the team's MVP for his performance against Washington.

"I didn't know a whole lot about him when we got him," Ryan said, "but he's a player. He puts people on the ground."

"With myself in sports and Tommy in music, those are two industries that almost always take you far away from your roots," Conwell told Phil Anastasia of the *Courier-Post.* "I don't think there's anyone else in this locker room who isn't away from home. But to be here, playing for the team I grew up watching and to have my family get to share in this with me, it's pretty amazing."

THE BODY BAG GAME

For the record, the number is six. That's how many Washington Redskins were injured in the 28–14 loss to the Eagles on November 12, 1990. The game will forever be remembered as "the Body Bag Game." That's because defensive back William Frizzell turned to the Washington bench at one point and asked, "You need any more body bags?"

Here was the casualty report: Quarterback Jeff Rutledge (broken thumb), quarterback Stan Humphries (sprained knee), running back Gerald Riggs (sprained foot), kick returner Walter Stanley (sprained knee), kick returner Joe Howard (concussion), and linebacker Greg Manusky (sprained knee). All left the game. Howard was taken off on a stretcher.

"This was a big setback for us," Washington coach Joe Gibbs said. "We not only lost the game, but we got a lot of people hurt."

Just three weeks earlier, the Eagles had lost to the Redskins in Washington, 13–7, and their record dropped to 2–4. But this decisive victory on "Monday Night Football" was their third win in a row as they built momentum toward a 10–6 finish and a wild-card playoff berth.

"When we're playing like that, we're scary," defensive tackle Mike Golic said. "We showed the whole package tonight. You could see it in their eyes, the way we were dominating them."

The defense scored two touchdowns—an interception return by Frizzell and a fumble recovery by Clyde Simmons—and Reggie White made his first career interception. On offense, Heath Sherman had 35 rushing attempts, tying Steve Van Buren's club record set in 1949.

"The next morning, our phone lines lit up like you wouldn't believe," said Angelo Cataldi, talk show host on WIP sports radio. "People couldn't wait to talk about the game. They loved that the Eagles kicked the crap out of the Redskins. That's when I realized, there's a different set of rules in

Clyde Simmons (96) scored a touchdown, Reggie White (92) intercepted a pass, and Eric Allen (21), Jerome Brown (99), and Seth Joyner (59) all pitched in as the Eagles' Gang-Green defense pounded Washington, 28–14, in the "Body Bag Game" in 1990.

Philadelphia. It's not just about winning games; it's about proving your manhood."

But the Redskins did not forget that ugly night. "The Body Bag Game" became a rallying cry for Gibbs' team, and when they returned to Veterans Stadium on January 5 in the NFC wild-card game, the Redskins defeated the Eagles, 20–6. Three days later, head coach Buddy Ryan was fired.

VAI SIKAHEMA—A TD AND A TKO

Vai Sikahema set an Eagles record with the longest punt return in team history, 87 yards against the New York Giants on November 22, 1992. But it is what he did *after* he reached the end zone that made the play so memorable.

Sikahema ran to the padded goalpost and began pounding away with both fists. He was throwing lefts and rights like a miniature Joe Frazier working on the heavy bag. We thought we had seen every kind of touchdown celebration, from slam dunks to choreographed dances, but this was something new.

Sikahema explained that it was a tribute to his father, who once thought young Vai would become a boxer. Sikahema did some boxing in his native Tonga, and he displayed excellent form that day in the Meadowlands. He demonstrated a left hook worthy of any fight club in Philadelphia.

Sikahema described what happened:

My father had just visited me. It was my first season in Philadelphia, and we're both big fight fans. I took him to the Blue Horizon to see a fight. We had a ball, so that was still on my mind when I scored the touchdown. I saw the goalpost and it was just a reaction: Go punch it.

People thought I was doing it because of Philly and the Rocky thing. I wasn't thinking that at all. I knew my father would see it on TV, so it was for him. But the fans took it as a Philly thing, and that's fine. This is a fight town. Joe Frazier, Meldrick Taylor, Bennie Briscoe, that's Philly.

To this day, if I stop in South Philly to get a cheese steak at Pat's or Geno's, someone will shout, "Yo, Sikahema." When I look over, they start throwing punches. I always throw a few back.

Sikahema set an Eagles record for most punt-return yardage in a season (503 yards in 1992), and his career punt-return average (10.7) ranks among the best in club history. He scored just one touchdown in two seasons with the Eagles, but his celebration insured no one will ever forget it.

THE BROTHERS DETMER

The 2004 season marked the ninth consecutive year the Eagles had a quarterback named Detmer on their roster. It started with Ty, who signed as a free agent in 1996, then Koy was added the following year as a seventh-round draft pick. Ty left for San Francisco in 1998, but Koy stayed on as the backup to Donovan McNabb and the holder for kicker David Akers.

Ty and Koy are similar players: undersized at 6–0, 190 pounds and underrated. Ty was a ninth-round draft pick despite setting 59 NCAA records at Brigham Young and winning the 1990 Heisman Trophy. Koy also was written off by many pro scouts, even though he was the first quarterback in Colorado history to pass for more than 3,000 yards in a season.

"Everybody is looking for the power pitcher," said Jon Gruden, who worked with both Detmers in 1997 in his role as Eagles offensive coordinator. "Sometimes you forget this game is not a punt, pass, and kick competition. It's about managing a game plan and making the throws. These guys have been doing it all their lives."

Ty played well after taking over for an injured Rodney Peete five weeks into the 1996 season. He won his first four starts against the Giants (19–10), Miami (35–28), Carolina (20–9), and Dallas (31–21). In the Miami game, Detmer threw four touchdown passes, all to Irving Fryar. He finished the season as the fourth-leading passer in the NFC with a 59.4 completion percentage and 15 touchdowns.

"I can't say enough about him," running back Ricky Watters said. "He's just this little skinny guy, but he's always so poised. He's something else."

Koy was given his chance to play in 1998, appearing in eight games and starting five, including an impressive effort (22 for 36, 185 yards, and two touchdowns) in his first start against Green Bay on "Monday Night Football." He settled into a backup role the next year when McNabb joined the team, but in 2002 he took over after McNabb went down with a broken ankle, and he played brilliantly (18 for 26, 227 yards, and two touchdowns) against San Francisco before he was knocked out of the game with a dislocated elbow.

The Detmers are the only pair of brothers to start NFL games at quarterback. They were on opposite sidelines in the NFC Championship game in January 2005. Koy was the backup for McNabb, while Ty was the backup for Atlanta's Michael Vick. Said Koy: "Only thing we know is, one way or another, Mom and Dad are going to the Super Bowl."

THE JACKSONVILLE CONNECTION

When the Eagles traveled to Jacksonville for Super Bowl XXXIX, it was a homecoming for safety Brian Dawkins, cornerback Lito Sheppard, and former wide receiver Harold Carmichael, the team's director of player development. All three grew up in the Florida city and attended William Raines High School.

Raines has produced a number of NFL players over the years, including Ken Burrough, the former All-Pro receiver with Houston, and Rod Gardner, a receiver with Washington, but the richest pipeline is the one to Philadelphia, with three players, all Pro Bowlers, graduating from Raines to the Eagles.

"There is a lot of talent in Jacksonville, which makes for good competition," Dawkins said. "As a player, it definitely pushes you."

Raines has produced top athletes in other sports, including former NBA all-star Truck Robinson and major league all-star Vince Coleman, but the No. 1 sport is football. The high school field is nicknamed "The Graveyard," and there is a fake cemetery behind the end zone where the name of every defeated opponent is written on a stake and planted in the ground.

"Raines is where people want to be," head football coach Ben Simmons told Christian Red of the New York Daily News. "It's the measuring stick of success for football programs around here."

Dawkins donated $100,000 so the school could refurbish its weight room. It is now known as the Brian Dawkins Strength Room. "It was run-down," he said, "and I wanted those kids to take pride in what they have."

T. O.'S GREATEST HITS

Ever since Terrell Owens pulled a Sharpie from his sock and autographed the football after scoring a touchdown in 2002, he has been known as a master of the end-zone celebration. He continued in that role with the Eagles, and, with a club-record 14 touchdown receptions, he had ample opportunity to express himself.

Here is a totally subjective ranking of T. O.'s top five celebrations from 2004:

1. His dead-on imitation of Ray Lewis's "this-is-my-house" pregame dance. He did this after scoring what proved to be the winning touchdown against Lewis's Baltimore Ravens on October 31.
2. Striking a pose on the small star in the Texas Stadium end zone. This was after scoring one of his three touchdowns in a 49–21 win over the Cowboys on November 15. It

played off the 2000 game when he ran to midfield and stomped on the Dallas logo, almost setting off a riot.
3. Flapping his arms to simulate an Eagle in flight. He did this on several occasions, the first time in the regular-season opener at Lincoln Financial Field when he scored three touchdowns against the New York Giants.
4. Placing his right foot on the ball and giving a military salute after scoring a touchdown in Detroit, September 26. He said it was a tribute to the troops, especially Eagles fans, serving in Iraq.
5. His sit-ups in the end zone at Chicago, October 3. Major points for originality.

Mike Vaccaro of the New York Post wrote, "On Sunday, we had Terrell Owens catching another touchdown pass and you know what I heard? I heard laughter. I heard a delightful buzz. I heard people yelling at their friends, saying: 'You gotta see what he did now.' Owens, remarkable as this may be to say, is exactly what we need. Every now and again, it really is OK to remind ourselves of something: Sports is supposed to be fun."

T. O. AND NICOLLETTE

Terrell Owens had the best season of any Eagle receiver in history, and his performance in the Super Bowl, playing on an injured leg and catching nine passes for 122 yards, was inspiring. But nothing Owens did during the 2004 season was as talked about as his costarring role opposite Nicollette Sheridan, the actress from "Desperate Housewives."

ABC produced the Owens-Sheridan skit as the opening for the November 15 Monday night game between the Eagles and Dallas. It was filmed in an empty locker room with Owens ready to take the field and Sheridan, wearing only a towel, trying to convince him to skip the game for her. The skit ended with Sheridan dropping the towel (she was shown from behind) and Owens saying, "Aw, hell, the team's going to have to win without me." With that, the naked (or so it appeared) actress jumped into his arms.

The response was swift and stinging. The Federal Communications Commission reported more than 50,000 complaints. The offices of ABC and the NFL were flooded with similar calls and angry e-mails. "Disgraceful," said Senator John McCain of Arizona.

"It is yet another symptom of television network arrogance, piping sexual content into America's living rooms at a time when millions of children are watching," said Tim Winter, executive director of the Parents Television Council. "And now, apparently, a football game is fair game for their raunch. Families across our nation are sick and tired of this wanton, reckless behavior."

Gene Upshaw, executive director of the NFL Players Association, was with Commissioner Paul Tagliabue when the piece aired. "[Tagliabue] looked at it and, God, he was really upset," Upshaw told USA Today. "He knew nothing about it."

Tagliabue was particularly sensitive to the risqué subject matter because the NFL still was reeling from the baring of Janet Jackson's breast during the Super Bowl XXXVIII halftime show, an act that drew a $550,000 FCC fine for CBS.

NFL spokesman Greg Aiello issued the following statement: "ABC's opening was inappropriate and unsuitable for our 'Monday Night Football' audience. While ABC may have gained attention for one of its shows ['Desperate Housewives'], the NFL and its fans lost."

"You don't have to be a pilgrim or a follower of the far right to understand that what ABC did was outrageous," wrote Jerry Izenberg of the *Newark Star Ledger.* "Just look at the key characters. Ms. Sheridan brought nothing to the moment but a view that flirted with her derriere. Terrell Owens brought nothing but a me-Tarzan-you-Jane act."

Indianapolis coach Tony Dungy claimed the skit played off the stereotype of athletes, especially black athletes, as sexual predators. Said Dungy: "That a guy was more concerned with that [sex] than the game, that's a terrible message to send. It could have been any player and I would've been outraged, but being an African American, it particularly hurt me. I don't think they would've had Bill Parcells or Andy Reid or one of the owners involved in that.

"If that's what we have to do to get ratings, I'd rather not get them," Dungy said. "I realize [TV] pays us in this league, but if that's what we have to do, I'm willing to take a pay cut."

Under the barrage of criticism, ABC's vice president for sports Mark Mandel expressed regret: "We have heard from many viewers about [Monday's] opening segment. We agree that the placement was inappropriate. We apologize."

The Eagles issued their own statement, which read, "We appreciate that ABC has taken responsibility and apologized for the opening to the 'Monday Night Football' broadcast. It is normal for teams to cooperate with ABC in the development of an opening for its broadcast. After seeing the final piece, we wish it hadn't aired."

What was almost forgotten amid all the outrage was what happened *after* the taped opening; that is, Owens had perhaps his best game of the season. He had six catches for 134 yards (a season high) and three touchdowns as the Eagles crushed Dallas, 49–21. Owens was puzzled by the furor.

"The [Eagles] organization felt it was a clean skit," he said. "I think it just got really taken out of context with a lot of people … Personally, I didn't think it would have offended anyone, but if it did, we apologize."

VOICES OF THE GAME

When the Eagles and New England Patriots met in Super Bowl XXXIX, the two longest-tenured radio play-by-play men in the NFL called the action: Merrill Reese for the Eagles and Gil Santos for New England. It was their 28th consecutive season behind the microphone covering their respective teams through good times and bad.

"There is nothing in the world I'd rather do; I love it," said Reese, a Philadelphia native and Temple University graduate who learned his trade broadcasting Owls football on the campus radio station, WRTI. (As an undergrad, Reese cohosted a weekly radio show with an Owls fullback named Bill Cosby.)

Generations of Eagles fans have grown up listening to—and often imitating—Reese's distinctive baritone. He has not missed a game in those 28 seasons, making him radio's ironman equivalent of Chuck Bednarik. He begins every game day the same way—with a hot bath and a plate of pancakes—then he settles in for another three-plus hours of unscripted drama.

Perhaps his most memorable call was the "Miracle of the Meadowlands" when Herman Edwards scored the winning touchdown against the New York Giants. Reese's call has been replayed countless times: "Pisarcik fumbles the football. It's picked up by Herman Edwards. Touchdown, Eagles. I don't believe it. I don't believe it. I do not believe what has just occurred here, ladies and gentlemen."

Reese joined the Eagles broadcast team in 1977 as color analyst working with veteran play-by-play man Charlie Swift. In December of that year, Swift, who was in his ninth season as the voice of the Eagles, committed suicide. The news shocked everyone in the organization. Swift had worked the Eagles-Dallas game three days earlier and seemed fine. Suddenly, he was gone, dead in his kitchen with a gunshot wound to the head.

Reese took over the play-by-play duties for the final two games of the season. Ex–Packer great Herb Adderley filled in as the color analyst. On the Sunday after Swift's death, there was a moment of silence at Veterans Stadium, and the public

Merrill Reese (left), the voice of the Eagles radio network, with broadcast partner and former All-Pro wide receiver Mike Quick.

Tom Brookshier began his broadcasting career at WCAU radio after a broken leg forced him to retire in 1962. Brookshier was the first ex-player to serve as color analyst on the Eagles radio network. From there, he went to CBS Sports, where he joined Pat Summerall to form the network's top NFL broadcast team.

Eagles Radio Broadcasters Through the Years

Year	Station	Play-by-Play	Color Analyst
1939	WCAU	Taylor Grant	Bob Hall, Harry McTique
1940–41	WCAU	Byrum Saam	Bob Hall
1942–44	WCAU	Byrum Saam	Chuck Thompson
1945	WCAU	Byrum Saam	Claude Haring
1946–49	WIBG	Byrum Saam	Claude Haring
1950	WPEN	Franny Murray	Del Parks, Jules Rind
1951	WCAU	Bill Sears	—
1952–54	WCAU	Byrum Saam	Claude Haring
1955	WCAU	Byrum Saam	Claude Haring, Bill Bransome
1956	WCAU	Bill Campbell	Bill Bransome
1957	WCAU	Bill Campbell	Bill Bransome, Ed Romance
1958–59	WCAU	Bill Campbell	Bill Bransome
1960	WCAU	Bill Campbell	Ed Harvey, Russ Hall
1961	WCAU	Bill Campbell	Ed Harvey, Russ Hall, Jack Buck, Tommy Roberts
1962	WCAU	Bill Campbell	Bobby Thomason, Tom Brookshier
1963	WCAU	Bill Campbell	Tom Brookshier
1964	WCAU	Bill Campbell	Byrum Saam, Tom Brookshier
1965	WCAU	Andy Musser	Charlie Gauer, Stan Hochman
1966–67	WCAU	Andy Musser	Charlie Gauer, Ed Harvey
1968	WCAU	Andy Musser	Charlie Gauer
1969	WIP	Charlie Swift	Clarence Peaks, Thatcher Longstreth
1970	WIP	Charlie Swift	Al Pollard, Clarence Peaks, Thatcher Longstreth
1971–76	WIP	Charlie Swift	Al Pollard
1977	WIP	Charlie Swift	Merrill Reese, Herb Adderley
1978–81	WIP	Merrill Reese	Jim Barniak
1982	WIP	Merrill Reese	Jim Barniak, Bill Bergey
1983	WIP	Merrill Reese	Bill Bergey
1984–91	WIP	Merrill Reese	Stan Walters
1992–97	WYSP	Merrill Reese	Stan Walters
1998–2004	WYSP	Merrill Reese	Mike Quick

address announcer asked everyone to turn toward the radio booth as a tribute to the late broadcaster. Reese recalls seeing all those eyes looking up at him and feeling his heart pound.

"I never was so nervous in my life," he said.

Reese did a remarkable job under difficult circumstances, and following the season he was named the permanent play-by-play man. Today, his voice is as identified with Eagles football as the winged helmets.

"It never gets old," said Reese, who has worked with five different color analysts, including current sidekick, former Pro Bowl receiver Mike Quick. "I'll never retire. They'll have to pry me out of the booth."

Older fans will recall Bill Campbell as the voice of the 1960 championship team. Like Reese, Campbell is a Philadelphia native who graduated from St. Joseph's College. Over the past half century, Campbell has broadcast games for the Phillies, the 76ers, and Big Five basketball, but he is best remembered as the man who painted the verbal pictures of the Eagles drive to their last NFL title.

"I broadcast Wilt Chamberlain's 100-point game, I did the '64 Phillies, but that [1960] season was probably what I'll remember most," said Campbell, who called the Eagles games for nine years, beginning in 1956. "Watching [Norm] Van Brocklin bring that team from behind in the fourth quarter, week after week, kept you on the edge of your seat."

Appendix A

Year-by-Year Highlights

1933

Record: 3–5–1, 4th in Eastern
Head Coach: Lud Wray

Date	W/L	Score	Opponent	Att.
10/15	L	0–56	@NY Giants	NA
10/18	L	0–25	Portsmouth Spartans	1,750
10/29	L	9–35	@Green Bay Packers	3,007
11/05	W	6–0	@Cincinnati Reds	NA
11/12	T	3–3	Chicago Bears	17,850
11/19	W	25–6	Pittsburgh Pirates	6,000
11/26	W	20–3	Cincinnati Reds	NA
12/03	L	0–10	Green Bay Packers	9,500
12/10	L	14–20	NY Giants	18,000

Bert Bell and Lud Wray are awarded the Frankford Yellow Jackets for $2,500 and rename the NFL franchise the *Philadelphia Eagles.* Wray is appointed coach. Some 40 candidates attend the team's first training camp for three weeks at Bader Field, in Atlantic City.

After finishing the exhibition season with a perfect 5–0 record, the Eagles lose their league opener to the New York Giants, 56–0. Their first regular-season home game is played under rented portable lights at the Baker Bowl with only 1,750 fans turning out to watch the Portsmouth Spartans win, 25–0. The Eagles drop their next contest to the Green Bay Packers, but go unbeaten in their next four games in what would turn out to be the most successful month in the club's first decade of existence.

Swede Hanson scores the only TD on a nine-yard reverse on a fourth-down play to give the Eagles their first win, 6–0, at Cincinnati. Then in the upset of the year, the Eagles hold the mighty Chicago Bears, the defending NFL champions, to a 3–3 standoff as Guy Turnbow kicks the tying field goal from the 28-yard line in the opening seconds of the fourth quarter. It is the first professional event ever held on a Sunday in Philadelphia.

The Eagles' first two home wins come over the Pittsburgh Pirates, 25–6, and Cincinnati Reds, 20–3. Roger Kirkman triggers the victory over Pittsburgh with a pair of scoring passes to Joe Carter. Red Roberts, Lee Woodruff, and Sylvester Davis score the touchdowns against the Reds.

1934

Record: 4–7, 3rd in Eastern (tie)
Head Coach: Lud Wray

Date	W/L	Score	Opponent	Att.
9/16	L	6–19	@Green Bay	5,000
9/26	W	17–0	@Pittsburgh	NA
10/07	L	7–9	Pittsburgh	NA
10/14	L	0–10	Detroit	9,860
10/21	L	0–6	@Boston Redskins	10,344
10/28	L	0–17	@NY Giants	NA
11/06	W	64–0	Cincinnati Reds	NA
11/11	L	7–10	Brooklyn Dodgers	NA
11/18	L	7–14	Boston Redskins	8,500
11/25	W	13–0	@Brooklyn Dodgers	NA
12/03	W	6–0	NY Giants	12,471

The Eagles register shutouts in all four of their triumphs, but are also a victim of one of the most amazing streaks in NFL history when the Detroit Lions record seven straight shutouts and don't allow an opponent inside the 20-yard line during that span.

The Lions blank the Eagles in Game 4, holding them to only eight first downs and causing them to misfire on 21 of 26 pass attempts.

But the Eagles get themselves into the record books later when they destroy the winless Cincinnati Reds, 64–0, for their only victory ever at Temple Stadium. It is the worst regular-season defeat by any NFL team in the league's history and the highest single-game point total for the Eagles. Swede Hanson rushes for 170 yards and three touchdowns for the Eagles, who lead 28–0 after the first quarter.

Two of the Eagles wins come on the road. They blank Pittsburgh, 17–0, as Swede Hanson scores on lateral plays of 34 and 15 yards, and Brooklyn, 13–0, as Hanson and Ed Storm score touchdowns. Hanson also runs 60 yards with a pass interception against the Dodgers.

At the Baker Bowl, the Eagles blank the New York Giants, 6–0. Jim Leonard, a local star from St. Joseph's Prep, scores the only touchdown. Joe Carter leads the NFL with 16 receptions for 238 yards and four touchdowns.

> *The Eagles' four regular-season shutouts in 1934 set a club record that was equaled only once, and that was in the 1948 world championship season.*

1935

Record: 2–9, 5th in Eastern
Head Coach: Lud Wray

Date	W/L	Score	Opponent	Att.
9/13	L	7–17	Pittsburgh	20,000
9/20	L	0–35	@Detroit	12,000
10/09	W	17–6	@Pittsburgh	6,271
10/13	L	0–39	Chicago Bears	NA
10/27	L	6–17	@Brooklyn Dodgers	NA
11/03	W	7–6	@Boston Redskins	10,000
11/05	L	0–3	Brooklyn Dodgers	NA
11/10	L	3–12	@Chicago Cardinals	6,000
11/24	L	0–10	@NY Giants	NA
12/01	L	14–21	NY Giants	NA
12/08	L	6–13	Green Bay	4,000

Bert Bell proposes an annual draft of college players to equalize the talent among NFL teams. It is adopted on May 19 to begin before the 1936 season.

The Eagles move their home games to Municipal Stadium, but their only two wins come on the road. They defeat Pittsburgh, 17–6, as Ed Matesic scores on a run and connects with Joe Carter on a 68-yard pass. Alabama Pitts, who gained fame as an athlete at Sing Sing Prison, signs with the Eagles upon his release.

A wild free-for-all involving at least a dozen players mars the Eagles' 7–6 win at Boston's Fenway Park. The Redskins go ahead 6–0 in the first quarter when Bill Shepherd races 56 yards to score, but Shepherd misses the extra point. The Eagles come back later in the period when Ed Storm throws a 54-yard pass to Ed Manske and Hank Reese kicks the extra point.

1936

Record: 1–11, 5th in Eastern
Head Coach: Bert Bell

Date	W/L	Score	Opponent	Att.
9/06	L	7–13	Brooklyn Dodgers	NA
9/13	W	10–7	NY Giants	20,000
9/20	L	3–26	Boston Redskins	20,000
9/27	L	0–17	Chicago Bears	25,000
10/04	L	0–18	@Brooklyn Dodgers	NA
10/11	L	0–23	Detroit	15,000
10/14	L	0–17	@Pittsburgh	10,042
10/18	L	7–17	@Boston Redskins	4,000
10/25	L	17–21	@NY Giants	15,000
11/05	L	0–6	Pittsburgh (Johnstown, PA)	NA
11/08	L	0–13	@Chicago Cardinals	1,500
11/22	L	7–28	Chicago Bears	NA

Bell becomes sole owner of the team after making the only bid, $4,000. Bell also assumes the role of head coach, succeeding Lud Wray. The Eagles have the first pick in the draft and select Heisman Trophy winner Jay Berwanger, of the University of Chicago, but he chooses not to play professional football.

The Eagles are shut out six times during the season. Their only win comes over the heavily favored New York Giants, 10–7, at Municipal Stadium.

Ed Manske scores the Eagles' touchdown on a 24-yard pass from Dave Smukler.

"As [the Giants] closed in about him like giant claws, there did not seem an avenue of escape," reported Stan Baumgartner, in the *Philadelphia Inquirer.* "But quick as a flash, [Manske] made a complete pivot, left his foes riveted to the ground, and shot toward the sidelines. By this time, other Giant tacklers thundered in upon him. Again, he seemed at the end of the trail. But with a lightning-like stroke of genius, the blond spiraled a lateral pass to Joe Carter, captain and end, 20 yards away. Carter snuggled the pigskin to his jersey on the dead run and raced over the goal line unmolested."

After the Giants tie it early in the fourth quarter, the Eagles drive 58 yards and Hank Reese kicks the deciding field goal.

The Giants get revenge later in the season with a controversial 21–17 win at home. Field judge George Vergara is given a police escort off the field after making a questionable pass interference call that leads to the winning touchdown. Vergara is surrounded by an angry group of Eagles and comes off the field with "his tie pulled, his shirt torn, and his hair mussed," according to the *New York Times.*

Reese leads the team in scoring with *nine* points for the entire season.

> *The 1936 season stands as the worst in franchise history—1 win and 11 losses, a winning percentage of .083.*

1937

Record: 2–8–1, 5th in Eastern
Head Coach: Bert Bell

Date	W/L	Score	Opponent	Att.
9/05	L	14–27	@Pittsburgh	8,588
9/10	L	7–13	Brooklyn Dodgers	5,221
9/21	L	3–21	Cleveland Rams	3,107
9/28	T	6–6	Chicago Cardinals	3,912
10/03	L	7–16	NY Giants	4,878
10/10	W	14–0	@Washington	7,320
10/17	L	0–21	@NY Giants	20,089
10/24	L	7–10	Washington	6,580
10/31	L	7–16	@Pittsburgh Pirates	2,772
11/07	W	14–10	@Brooklyn Dodgers	8,373
11/14	L	7–37	@Green Bay	13,340

Future Pro Football Hall of Fame end Bill Hewitt, the last NFL player not to wear a helmet, joins the Eagles after starring for the Chicago Bears. Bert Bell doubles his salary to $200 a game and arranges for a $24-a-week, off-season job as a repairman in a service station.

The Eagles win only two games, both upsets on the road. Using only 15 players, they knock Washington out of first place in the East, 14–0. Hewitt sets up the first TD with a sensational one-handed catch of a pass from Emmett Mortell. He laterals to Johnny Kusko for a 47-yard gain, and scores the touchdown on the next play after catching a nine-yard pass from Dave Smukler. Rookie Maurice Harper returns an interception 15 yards for the other score.

Smukler passes nine yards to Hewitt for one touchdown and scores the other on a short plunge to lead the Eagles over the Brooklyn Dodgers, 14–10. The second score erases a 10–7 Dodgers lead in the fourth quarter.

1938

Record: 5–6, 4th in Eastern
Head Coach: Bert Bell

Date	W/L	Score	Opponent	Att.
9/11	L	23–26	Washington	20,000
9/16	W	27–7	Pittsburgh (Buffalo, NY)	19,749
9/25	W	14–10	NY Giants	20,000
10/02	L	6–28	Chicago Bears	NA
10/16	L	7–17	@NY Giants	33,187
10/23	L	14–20	@Washington	3,000
10/26	W	7–0	Chicago Cardinals (Erie, PA)	15,000
11/06	L	7–10	Brooklyn Dodgers	12,000
11/13	L	14–32	@Brooklyn Dodgers	13,052
11/20	W	14–7	Pittsburgh Pirates (Charleston, WV)	6,500
12/04	W	21–7	@Detroit	19,000

The Eagles move their preseason camp to West Chester State Teachers College, the first time the team trains on a college campus.

Jay Arnold scores three touchdowns and plays excellent defense in a 27–7 win over the Pittsburgh Pirates. Bob Pylman and Joe Carter each race 90 yards to score as the Eagles upset the New York Giants, 14–10. Pylman later rips the ball out of the arms of New York's Dale Burnett as the Giants back appears headed for a touchdown.

After three losses, the Eagles force six Chicago Cardinals fumbles in the driving rain and record the only touchdown in a 7–0 win. George Rado sets the score up by recovering a fumble on the Cardinals 6-yard line. Dave Smukler then hits Carter with a four-yard touchdown pass.

The Eagles win their last two games, defeating the Pirates again, 14–7, behind a pair of Smukler-to-Carter touchdown passes, and then knocking the Detroit Lions out of the Western Division title, 21–7, as Smukler throws three scoring passes, two of them to Hewitt.

Smukler is the team's offensive star. He rushes for 313 yards, passes for 524 more, scores eight touchdowns, and goes 6-for-6 on extra points.

> *The 1938 season marked the first time the Eagles had two players selected for All-Pro honors. Ends Joe Carter and Bill Hewitt both were named to the Pro Football Writers of America All-Pro team.*

1939

Record: 1–9–1, 4th in Eastern (tie)
Head Coach: Bert Bell

Date	W/L	Score	Opponent	Att.
9/17	L	0–7	Washington	33,258
9/24	L	3–13	NY Giants	30,600
10/01	T	0–0	Brooklyn Dodgers	1,880
10/15	L	10–27	@NY Giants	34,471
10/22	L	14–23	@Brooklyn Dodgers	13,057
11/05	L	6–7	@Washington	20,444
11/12	L	16–23	Green Bay	23,000
11/19	L	14–27	@Chicago Bears	21,398
11/23	W	17–14	Pittsburgh	20,000
11/26	L	12–24	@Pittsburgh	8,788
12/03	L	13–35	Cleveland Rams (Colorado Springs, CO)	9,189

Texas Christian's All-America quarterback Davey O'Brien signs with the Eagles for a reported $12,000 salary plus a percentage of the gate.

O'Brien is outplayed by Washington's Sammy Baugh in his home debut won by the Redskins, 7–0. But he goes on to set a new single-season NFL passing record with 1,324 yards.

The Eagles' only victory comes at home on Thanksgiving Day over the Pittsburgh Pirates, 17–14, when they snap an eight-game winless streak.

The Eagles, coming off a 27–14 loss to the mighty Chicago Bears, are forced to play three games in eight days.

The Eagles participate in the first televised game in NFL history when they lose to the Brooklyn Dodgers, 23–14, at Ebbets Field. O'Brien completes 11 of 25 passes for 140 yards in a losing cause as Brooklyn's Ralph Kercheval connects on three 40-yard field goals.

1940

Record: 1–10, 5th in Eastern
Head Coach: Bert Bell

Date	W/L	Score	Opponent	Att.
9/15	L	20–27	@Green Bay	11,657
9/22	L	13–21	@Cleveland Rams	15,941
9/28	L	14–20	NY Giants	26,431
10/04	L	17–30	@Brooklyn Dodgers	24,008
10/13	L	7–17	@NY Giants	30,317
10/20	L	17–34	Washington	25,062
10/26	L	7–21	Brooklyn Dodgers	6,500
11/10	L	3–7	@Pittsburgh	9,556
11/17	L	0–21	Detroit	6,327
11/28	W	7–0	Pittsburgh	4,200
12/01	L	6–13	@Washington	25,838

Pittsburgh owner Art Rooney buys a half interest in the Eagles after selling the Pittsburgh Steelers franchise to Alexis Thompson, of New York, a 30-year-old heir to a $6 million steel fortune. The Eagles switch their home games from Municipal Stadium to Shibe Park.

Davey O'Brien and Washington's great Sammy Baugh hook up in a spectacular passing display. Inspired by playing against his TCU predecessor, O'Brien throws a record 60 passes and completes 33, but the Eagles lose, 13–6.

The team wins only once, beating the Steelers, 7–0, to snap a nine-game losing streak on a 17-yard run by Dick Riffle. O'Brien is honored before the game. He has announced that he is retiring from professional football to join the FBI.

Philadelphia's Don Looney leads NFL receivers with 58 catches for 707 yards and four touchdowns.

> *Don Looney's 58 pass receptions in 1940 set a club record that stood for 13 years, until Pete Pihos broke it with a league-high 63 catches in 1953.*

1941

Record: 2–8–1, 4th in Eastern
Head Coach: Greasy Neale

Date	W/L	Score	Opponent	Att.
9/13	L	0–24	NY Giants	25,478
9/21	W	10–7	@Pittsburgh	12,893
9/27	L	13–24	Brooklyn Dodgers	16,341
10/12	L	0–16	@NY Giants	30,842
10/19	L	17–21	Washington	19,071
10/26	W	21–14	Chicago Cardinals	12,683
11/02	L	6–15	@Brooklyn Dodgers	15,899
11/09	T	7–7	Pittsburgh	15,601
11/16	L	17–21	@Detroit	16,306
11/30	L	14–49	Chicago Bears	32,608
12/07	L	14–20	@Washington	27,102

Bert Bell and Art Rooney swap franchises with Alexis Thompson, Rooney returning to Pittsburgh and Thompson taking over the Eagles. Bert Bell joins Rooney as a full-time partner in Pittsburgh. Earle (Greasy) Neale replaces Bell as coach and installs the T formation on offense with Tommy Thompson, who is partially blind in one eye, taking over as quarterback.

The Eagles return to Municipal Stadium for their home games just for the season. They defeat Bert Bell's Pittsburgh Steelers, 10–7, and the Chicago Cardinals, 21–14, for their only wins.

Rookie Danny DeSantis, from Niagara, just back from his dad's funeral in Buffalo, throws a 37-yard pass to Lou Tomasetti for the only touchdown against the Steelers. Len Barnum's 43-yard field goal provides the margin of victory.

The Eagles build a 21-point lead and then hold off the Chicago Cardinals for a 21–14 win. Jimmy Castiglia, a rookie from Georgetown, scores twice, and Thompson throws a 12-yard touchdown pass to Wes McAfee.

1942

Record: 2–9, 5th in Eastern
Head Coach: Greasy Neale

Date	W/L	Score	Opponent	Att.
9/13	W	24–14	@Pittsburgh	13,349
9/20	L	14–24	@Cleveland Rams (Akron, OH)	6,434
9/27	L	14–35	Brooklyn Dodgers (Buffalo, NY)	5,286
10/04	L	10–14	Washington	15,500
10/11	L	17–35	@NY Giants	28,264
10/18	L	0–14	Pittsburgh	12,500
10/25	L	14–45	@Chicago Bears	15,372
11/01	L	27–30	@Washington	32,658
11/08	L	0–14	NY Giants	13,600
11/15	W	14–7	@Brooklyn Dodgers	3,858
11/29	L	0–7	Green Bay	13,700

The Eagles, who return to Shibe Park for their home games, again win only twice, both on the road, behind the passing of Tommy Thompson.

Thompson leads a 24–14 opening-game win over the Pittsburgh Steelers by passing for two touchdowns and running 25 yards to set up the other. Thompson hits Len Supluski and Fred Meyer with tosses of 40 and 13 yards, and Bob Davis scores from three yards out.

The team snaps an eight-game losing streak by defeating the Brooklyn Dodgers, 14–7. William (Loyal) Combs scores on an over-the-shoulder catch of Thompson's 13-yard pass. Meyer sets up the other on a 41-yard reception from Thompson with Richard Erdlitz scoring on a short plunge.

The Eagles are outscored 211–96 during the losing streak.

> *From 1939 until the arrival of Steve Van Buren in 1944,*
> *a different player led the Eagles in rushing each year.*
> *They were, in order, Dave Smukler, Dick Riffle,*
> *Jim Castiglia, Bob Davis, Jack Hinkle, and Van Buren.*

1943 "STEAGLES"

Record: 5–4–1, 3rd in Eastern
Head Coaches: Greasy Neale and Walt Kiesling

Date	W/L	Score	Opponent	Att.
10/02	W	17–0	Brooklyn Dodgers	11,131
10/09	W	28–14	NY Giants	15,340
10/17	L	21–48	@Chicago Bears	21,744
10/24	L	14–42	@NY Giants	42,681
10/31	W	34–13	Chicago (@Pittsburgh)	16,351
11/07	T	14–14	Washington	28,893
11/14	L	7–13	@Brooklyn Dodgers	7,614
11/21	W	35–34	Detroit (@Pittsburgh)	23,338
11/28	W	27–14	@Washington	35,826
12/05	L	28–38	Green Bay	34,294

Because of a manpower shortage and travel restrictions during World War II, the NFL owners consider canceling the season. After a motion is narrowly defeated to suspend operations, Lex Thompson and Pittsburgh owner Art Rooney agree to combine their teams, split their home games, and play one season as the *Steagles*.

All the players are required to work at least 40 hours a week in defense plants. They practice for three hours, Monday through Saturday, at 6:00 P.M. When the team starts its drills, Bert Bell raves to Rooney about how good the new combined Steagles look. But when Rooney sees the team play for the first time, he says to Bert, "They're the same old dogs. The only thing new about them is the uniforms."

Bell convinces Bill Hewitt to come out of his three-year retirement and play for $400 a game. However, Hewitt is forced by a new league rule to wear a helmet.

The Steagles start fast, winning their first two games. In their home opener, they beat the Brooklyn Dodgers, 17–0, on touchdowns by John Butler and Ernie Steele. The Dodgers are held to *minus* 33 yards rushing.

The Steagles also upset the New York Giants, 28–14, despite fumbling an NFL-record ten times. One of the touchdowns is scored by Jack Hinkle on a 91-yard interception return. Hinkle rushes for a season-high 132 yards on 13 carries in a 27–14 win over the Washington Redskins.

The Steagles finish with a 5–4–1 record, the first winning season ever for an Eagles franchise. It is a remarkably successful year considering that the two co-coaches, Pittsburgh's Walt Kiesling and Philadelphia's Greasy Neale, bicker all season.

Hinkle finishes with 571 yards on 116 carries, but he loses the NFL rushing title by a yard to Bill Paschal of the New York Giants because the statisticians credit a 37-yard run to another player.

1944

Record: 7–1–2, 2nd in Eastern
Head Coach: Greasy Neale

Date	W/L	Score	Opponent	Att.
9/26	W	28–7	@Boston Yanks	25,061
10/08	T	31–31	Washington	32,549
10/22	W	38–0	Boston Yanks	24,638
10/29	W	24–17	@NY Giants	42,639
11/05	W	21–7	@Brooklyn Dodgers	15,289
11/12	T	21–21	NY Giants	33,248
11/19	W	37–7	@Washington	35,540
11/26	L	7–28	Chicago Bears	34,035
12/03	W	34–0	Brooklyn Dodgers	13,467
12/10	W	26–13	Cleveland Rams	24,123

Despite losing only one of ten games, the Eagles can do no better than second place. They finish with their best record to date as rookie Steve Van Buren, the No. 1 draft choice, leads the NFL in punt-return yardage and averages 5.6 yards per rushing attempt.

The Eagles grind out a 28–7 win over the Boston Yanks as Roy Zimmerman, Jack Banta, Mel Bleeker, and Ernie Steele each score one touchdown. Then, following a 31–31 tie with the Washington Redskins, the Eagles reel off three straight wins, including an impressive 38–0 shutout of the Yanks.

The franchise scores its first win at the Polo Grounds, erasing a 17–3 deficit and holding on for a 24–17 victory over the New York Giants. Van Buren sets up the winning touchdown with a pass interception.

The Eagles move into first place in the Eastern Division for the first time, beating Washington, 37–7, as Zimmerman throws for two scores and rushes for another against his former team. It is the Redskins' worst defeat since they lost to the Chicago Bears in the 1940 NFL Championship Game, 73–0.

Next, the Eagles hand the Brooklyn Dodgers *their* worst defeat ever, 34–0, as they outgain the Dodgers on the ground, 253–13. Jack Banta scores a spectacular touchdown, taking a lateral from Zimmerman and scooting 60 yards.

Although the Eagles easily defeat the Cleveland Rams, 26–13, in the season finale, they can do no better than second place, one game behind the Giants, because of an earlier 28–7 loss to the Chicago Bears and ties with the Giants and Redskins.

> *Coach Greasy Neale's Eagles set a franchise record by scoring at least one touchdown in 88 consecutive games (1943–50).*

1945

Record: 7–3, 2nd in Eastern
Head Coach: Greasy Neale

Date	W/L	Score	Opponent	Att.
10/07	W	21–6	Chicago Cardinals	25,581
10/14	L	24–28	@Detroit	22,580
10/21	L	14–24	@Washington	35,550
10/28	W	28–14	Cleveland Rams	38,149
11/04	W	45–3	@Pittsburgh	23,018
11/11	W	38–17	NY Giants	30,047
11/18	W	30–6	Pittsburgh	23,838
11/24	W	16–0	Washington	37,306
12/02	L	21–28	@NY Giants	45,372
12/09	W	35–7	Boston Yanks	27,905

The Eagles again finish second in the East with seven wins and lead the NFL in scoring with 272 points. Steve Van Buren leads the league with 832 rushing yards and 110 points.

The Eagles' most impressive triumph comes in midseason, 45–3, at Pittsburgh, as Roy Zimmerman throws for a pair of touchdowns and Jack Ferrante scores twice.

Van Buren has his best single-game performance in the season-ending 35–7 triumph over the Boston Yanks. In addition to rushing for 100 yards and scoring three times, he sets a number of NFL records, including the most touchdowns in a single season (18).

Ferrante, a product of Philadelphia's sandlots who never attended college, is the Eagles' top receiver with 21 catches and seven touchdowns.

1946

Record: 6–5, 2nd in Eastern
Head Coach: Greasy Neale

Date	W/L	Score	Opponent	Att.
9/29	W	25–14	@LA Rams	30,500
10/06	W	49–25	Boston Yanks	33,986
10/13	L	7–19	Green Bay	36,127
10/20	L	14–21	@Chicago Bears	41,221
10/27	W	28–24	@Washington	33,691
11/03	W	24–14	NY Giants	40,059
11/10	L	17–45	@NY Giants	60,874
11/17	L	7–10	@Pittsburgh	38,882
11/24	L	10–27	Washington	36,633
12/01	W	10–7	Pittsburgh	29,943
12/08	W	40–14	@Boston Yanks	29,555

Neale adds some impressive talent, trading for Alex Wojciechowicz, an outstanding center and linebacker, and drafting Joe Muha, a rugged fullback and punter. He also acquires Russ Craft, a versatile halfback from Alabama, with a 15th round draft pick. The speedy Bosh Pritchard rejoins the team after three years of military service.

The Eagles ruin the debut of the Los Angeles Rams, who have just moved from Cleveland, rallying from a 14–6 halftime deficit to win 25–14 in 97-degree heat. Lefty Al Sherman's 38-yard pass to Larry Cabrelli and 29-yard throw to Jack Ferrante provide the scoring. Duke Maronic sets up the second touchdown by dumping Tom Harmon for a 10-yard loss and then stealing the ball from Mike Holovak after throwing him for a four-yard loss.

Agostino (Augie) Lio, a guard from Georgetown, leads the Eagles over the New York Giants, 24–14, before a record Shibe Park crowd of 40,059, by recovering a blocked kick in the end zone for a touchdown and kicking a 28-yard field goal. Steve Van Buren scores two touchdowns.

The Eagles beat the Boston Yankees twice by a combined 89–39 score. Van Buren and Pritchard each score twice in the first game, 49–25, which falls only five points short of the all-time NFL record for single-game scoring. In the season finale at Fenway Park, Roy Zimmerman throws three touchdown passes, and Van Buren returns a punt 50 yards for a score.

Lio finishes as the Eagles' leading scorer with 51 points—27 extra points without a miss, six field goals, and a touchdown—as the Eagles finish second in the East for the third straight year.

> *The Eagles set a club record for the biggest comeback in the October 27, 1946, game at Washington. The Eagles trailed 24–0 at halftime, and outscored the Redskins 28–0 in the second half for the victory.*

1947

Record: 8–4, 1st in Eastern
Head Coach: Greasy Neale

Date	W/L	Score	Opponent	Att.
9/28	W	45–42	Washington	35,406
10/05	W	23–0	NY Giants	29,823
10/12	L	7–40	@Chicago Bears	34,338
10/19	L	24–35	@Pittsburgh	33,538
10/26	W	14–7	LA Rams	36,364
11/02	W	38–14	@Washington	36,591
11/09	W	41–24	@NY Giants	29,016
11/16	W	32–0	Boston Yanks	26,498
11/23	L	14–21	@Boston Yanks	15,628
11/30	W	21–0	Pittsburgh	37,218
12/07	L	21–45	Chicago Cardinals	32,322
12/14	W	28–14	Green Bay	24,216

NFC Divisional Playoff

12/21	W	21–0	@Pittsburgh	35,729

NFL Championship

12/28	L	21–28	@Chicago Cardinals	30,759

The Eagles sign Pete Pihos, a 6–1, 215-pound rookie from Indiana. Since they don't need a fullback, Greasy Neale converts Pihos to an end and devises the "Pihos screen," a short pass behind the line. This forces opposing defenses to spread out, opening holes for Steve Van Buren and Bosh Pritchard.

The Eagles win a franchise-high eight games and finally make it to the NFL Championship Game, but lose to the Chicago Cardinals, 28–21, at Comiskey Park.

The combined total of points in the 45–42 win over the Washington Redskins, as well as the 12 touchdowns scored by both teams in the season opener, are NFL records. Tommy Thompson throws three touchdown passes to players making their NFL debuts—two to Pihos and one to Neill Armstrong. Van Buren runs a kickoff back 95 yards for a touchdown, and Joe Muha wins it with a 40-yard field goal.

The Eagles force a tie for the Eastern Division title by beating Green Bay for the first time in history, 28–14. Van Buren scores three touchdowns and sets an NFL single-season rushing record with 1,008 yards gained.

The Eagles win the division by beating the Pittsburgh Steelers in a playoff game, 21–0.

1948

Record: 9–2–1, 1st in Eastern
Head Coach: Greasy Neale

Date	W/L	Score	Opponent	Att.
9/24	L	14–21	@Chicago Cardinals	24,159
10/03	T	28–28	@LA Rams	24,597
10/10	W	45–0	NY Giants	22,804
10/17	W	45–0	@Washington	35,580
10/24	W	12–7	Chicago Bears	36,227
10/31	W	34–7	@Pittsburgh	32,859
11/07	W	35–14	@NY Giants	24,983
11/14	W	45–0	Boston	22,958
11/21	W	42–21	Washington	36,254
11/28	W	17–0	Pittsburgh	22,001
12/05	L	14–37	@Boston	9,652
12/12	W	45–21	Detroit	15,322

NFL Championship

12/19	W	7–0	Chicago Cardinals	28,864

The Eagles open the season with a loss to the Chicago Cardinals and a tie with the Los Angeles Rams, but then win eight games in a row, including back-to-back 45–0 shutouts over the New York Giants and Washington. Tommy Thompson throws two TD passes against the Giants, then tears a muscle against the Redskins as Van Buren scores three times.

Backup quarterback Bill Mackrides takes over for Thompson and leads the Eagles to their first-ever win over the Chicago Bears, 12–7. Van Buren scores the only touchdown on an eight-yard run, and Cliff Patton kicks a 38-yard field goal.

Thompson passes for 197 yards and throws a career-high four touchdown passes in a 45–0 rout of the Boston Yanks. Van Buren carries 29 times for a season-high 171 yards in a 42–21 win over the Redskins. The Eagles clinch the Eastern Division title by beating Pittsburgh, 17–0, as Bosh Pritchard and Pete Pihos score.

Thompson throws four touchdown passes—three to Jack Ferrante—as the Eagles rout Detroit, 45–21. The team wins its first NFL championship, defeating the Cardinals 7–0 in a blinding snowstorm at Shibe Park before 28,864 fans.

While outscoring their opponents, 376–156, the Eagles produce four individual NFL leaders—Van Buren (945 yards rushing), Thompson (1,965 passing yards), Patton (50-of-50 extra points and 8-of-12 field goals), and Joe Muha (47.2-yard punting average). It is Van Buren's third rushing title in five years. Captain Al Wistert is named an All-Pro tackle.

> *The Eagles set a franchise record with 14 consecutive home victories from December 14, 1947, through December 11, 1949. The streak includes the 1948 NFL championship game, a 7–0 win over the Chicago Cardinals.*

1949

Record: 11–1, 1st in Eastern
Head Coach: Greasy Neale

Date	W/L	Score	Opponent	Att.
9/22	W	7–0	@NY Bulldogs	4,355
10/03	W	22–14	@Detroit	20,163
10/08	W	28–3	Chicago Cardinals	33,716
10/16	L	21–38	@Chicago Bears	47,248
10/23	W	49–14	Washington	28,602
10/30	W	38–7	@Pittsburgh	37,840
11/06	W	38–14	LA Rams	38,230
11/13	W	44–21	@Washington	31,170
11/20	W	42–0	NY Bulldogs	22,165
11/27	W	34–17	Pittsburgh	22,191
12/04	W	24–3	@NY Giants	25,446
12/11	W	17–3	NY Giants	21,022

NFL Championship

Date	W/L	Score	Opponent	Att.
12/18	W	14–0	@LA Rams	22,245

Alexis Thompson sells the Eagles to "100 Brothers," a syndicate of prominent Philadelphia-area business leaders, headed up by James P. Clark, who pay $3,000 for each of 100 shares. Vince McNally is named the club's general manager.

In the first round of the draft, the Eagles select Chuck Bednarik, an All-America center-linebacker from the University of Pennsylvania.

The Eagles win their third straight Eastern Division title by winning 11 of 12 games, a club record. Their only loss comes against the Chicago Bears, 38–21, in Week 4. The Eagles defend their NFL title by defeating the Los Angeles Rams, 14–0.

Cliff Patton shatters the NFL record for consecutive points-after-touchdowns by converting seven PATs in the 49–14 victory over the Washington Redskins to extend his streak to 77.

The Eagles take over first place in the East by beating the Pittsburgh Steelers, 38–7, in Week 6. The game is highlighted by a 70-yard punt return for a touchdown by Clyde (Smackover) Scott. The following week, the Eagles knock off the Rams, the only remaining unbeaten team in the NFL, 38–14, before 38,230, the largest crowd ever to see a football game at Shibe Park. They hold the Rams to 27 yards rushing, prompting coach Greasy Neale to say, "This is a great team. No team ever assembled could have beaten them today."

Van Buren rushes for a career-high 205 yards as the Eagles again beat the Steelers, 34–17. He again breaks his NFL single-season record by gaining 1,146 yards on 263 carries.

The 1949 season was the best in franchise history— 12 wins and 1 loss, a winning percentage of .923.

1950

Record: 6–6, 3rd in American (tie)
Head Coach: Greasy Neale

Date	W/L	Score	Opponent	Att.
9/16	L	10–35	Cleveland	71,237
9/24	W	45–7	@Chicago Cardinals	24,914
10/07	W	56–20	Los Angeles	24,134
10/15	W	24–14	@Baltimore	14,413
10/22	W	17–10	@Pittsburgh	35,662
10/29	W	35–3	Washington	33,707
11/05	L	7–9	Pittsburgh	24,629
11/12	W	33–0	@Washington	29,407
11/19	L	10–14	Chicago Cardinals	28,368
11/26	L	3–7	@NY Giants	24,093
12/03	L	7–13	@Cleveland	37,490
12/10	L	7–9	NY Giants	26,440

With 71,237 fans, the largest regular-season home crowd in Eagles history, sitting in shocked disbelief at Municipal Stadium, the Cleveland Browns, the All-America Football Conference champions, rout the NFL champs, 35–10, in Cleveland's first game as a member of the National Football League.

The Eagles bounce back to win five straight games. They spoil the Chicago Cardinals' home opener, 45–7, forcing Chicago quarterback Jim Hardy to throw an NFL-record eight interceptions. Russ Craft has four of the interceptions, while Joe Sutton adds three.

The Eagles then hand their NFL Championship Game opponent Los Angeles Rams their worst loss in history, 56–20, in a game highlighted by a 103-yard kickoff return by Craft.

Rookie Toy Ledbetter's touchdown sparks the Eagles to a 24–14 win over Baltimore. The team moves into a first-place tie with the New York Giants by defeating Pittsburgh, 17–10. Van Buren scores the go-ahead touchdown following a 74-yard pass from Tommy Thompson to Jack Ferrante.

The Eagles take undisputed possession of first place by routing the Redskins, 35–3, as Joe Muha, Frank Reagan, and Johnny Green all score defensive touchdowns.

With Van Buren hampered by foot and chest injuries, the Eagles drop five of their last six games to fall into a third-place tie. After a 7–3 loss to the New York Giants, Greasy Neale and club president Jim Clark almost come to blows in the locker room. Neale is fired after the season.

1951

Record: 4–8, 5th in American
Head Coach: Bo McMillin (2) and Wayne Millner (10)

Date	W/L	Score	Opponent	Att.
9/30	W	17–14	@Chicago Cardinals	16,129
10/06	W	21–14	San Francisco	23,432
10/14	L	24–37	@Green Bay	18,489
10/21	L	24–26	@NY Giants	28,656
10/28	L	23–27	Washington	20,437
11/04	W	34–13	@Pittsburgh	19,649
11/11	L	17–20	@Cleveland	36,571
11/18	L	10–28	Detroit	25,350
11/25	L	13–17	Pittsburgh	15,537
12/02	W	35–21	@Washington	23,738
12/09	L	7–23	NY Giants	19,322
12/16	L	9–24	Cleveland	16,263

Alvin (Bo) McMillin is named coach but is forced to resign because of illness after directing the Eagles to wins in their first two games. Wayne Millner succeeds him as coach, and the team wins just two of its remaining 10 games.

Van Buren is again slowed by injuries and gains only 327 yards on 112 carries. Adrian Burk succeeds the retired Thompson at quarterback and throws a league-high 23 interceptions.

The Eagles do record one of the top upsets of the season, beating the San Francisco 49ers, 21–14. They switch to a single-wing offense in the second half, and Burk throws touchdown passes of 49 and 28 yards to Clyde Scott.

The Eagles' other victories come on the road at Pittsburgh (34–13) and Washington (35–21). Burk throws touchdown passes to rookie Bobby Walston and Pete Pihos to overcome a 10–0 deficit against the Steelers, then puts the game away with a 30-yard scoring toss to Dan Sandifer. Van Buren and Walston each score a pair of touchdowns as the Eagles tie the NFL record with 32 first downs against the Redskins.

Walston scores 18 points against the Giants at the Polo Grounds and 17 against the Redskins at Griffith Stadium. His longest field goal is a 44-yarder against the Redskins. He is named NFL Rookie of the Year after catching 31 passes, scoring eight touchdowns, and totaling 94 points.

1952

Record: 7–5, 2nd in American (tie)
Head Coach: Jim Trimble

Date	W/L	Score	Opponent	Att.
9/28	W	31–25	@Pittsburgh	22,501
10/04	L	7–31	NY Giants	22,512
10/12	W	26–21	Pittsburgh	18,648
10/19	L	7–49	Cleveland	27,874
10/26	W	14–10	@NY Giants	21,458
11/02	L	10–12	@Green Bay	10,149
11/09	W	38–20	Washington	16,932
11/16	W	10–7	Chicago Cardinals	18,406
11/23	W	28–20	@Cleveland	28,948
11/30	L	22–28	@Chicago Cardinals	13,577
12/07	W	38–21	Dallas	18,376
12/14	L	21–27	@Washington	22,468

Wayne Millner resigns as coach and is replaced by Jim Trimble. Former coach Bo McMillin dies of stomach cancer.

Van Buren suffers a serious knee injury in training camp and retires. Bobby Thomason is acquired from Green Bay and named starting quarterback. Trimble moves the team's top draft choice, Harold (Bud) Grant, ahead of Pete Pihos at offensive end and switches Pihos to defense. Grant catches 56 passes, seven for touchdowns, to rank second among NFL receivers.

The Eagles win seven games, but they miss out on a chance to tie for the American Division title when they lose to the Redskins, 27–21, in Washington in the last game of the season.

The Eagles sign their first African American players, halfbacks Ralph Goldston from Youngstown State and Don Stevens from Illinois. Goldston scores twice in a 28–20 upset of the Browns in Cleveland.

Defensive end Norm (Wildman) Willey earns NFL Defensive Player of the Week honors by tackling New York quarterback Charlie Conerly 17 times (the term "sack" was not yet created) in a 14–10 win over the Giants at the Polo Grounds.

Their final win is a 38–21 rout of the Dallas Texans. In the victory, Grant catches 11 passes for 203 yards and two touchdowns.

Steve Van Buren's Awesome Impact

During a 77-game span between 1943 and 1949, the Eagles had a 53–20–4 record. Steve Van Buren, who joined the team in 1944, ran for at least 100 yards 18 times through 1949 as the Eagles won 15 of those games. He was the first player ever to record four straight 100-yard rushing games in a season. During this 77-game period, the Eagles averaged 172 yards on the ground while allowing an average of only 91 yards. The team was minus 36 on fumbles but plus 61 on pass interceptions, for a turnover ratio of plus 25.

In 1949, when the Eagles lost only one of 12 games, they allowed only 96 points in their 11 wins. They outscored the opposition by 230 points in 12 games.

Contrast that record to the period from 1950 to 1958, after Van Buren retired, when the Eagles went 44–59–5. After opening the 1955 season with a win over the New York Giants, the Eagles slumped to a 12–32–3 record for the final 47 games of this 108-game span. Overall, during these 108 games, the team rushed for only 125 yards a game while allowing 131 yards on the ground. Additionally, the Eagles' turnover ratio dropped to minus 59 in that time.

1953

Record: 7–4–1, 2nd in Eastern
Head Coach: Jim Trimble

Date	W/L	Score	Opponent	Att.
9/27	L	21–31	@San Francisco	27,819
10/02	T	21–21	Washington	19,099
10/10	L	13–37	@Cleveland	45,802
10/17	W	23–7	Pittsburgh	18,681
10/25	W	56–17	@Chicago Cardinals	22,064
11/01	W	35–7	@Pittsburgh	27,547
11/08	W	30–7	NY Giants	24,331
11/15	W	45–14	Baltimore	27,813
11/21	W	38–0	Chicago Cardinals	19,402
11/29	L	28–37	@NY Giants	20,294
12/06	L	0–10	@Washington	21,579
12/13	W	42–27	Cleveland	38,654

The Eagles again win seven games and finish second despite the loss of end Bud Grant, who jumps to the Canadian League. Late-season back-to-back upset losses to the New York Giants and Washington cost the team a shot at the division title.

Trimble switches Pete Pihos back to offense, and he catches a league-high 63 passes for 1,049 yards and ten touchdowns. Thomason and Burk combine to pass for 3,250 yards, with Thomason's best game coming in a 30–7 win over the New York Giants when he completes 22 of 44 passes for a club-record 437 yards and four touchdowns.

Rookie defensive back Tom Brookshier leads the team with eight pass interceptions.

After an 0–2–1 start, the Eagles put together a six-game winning streak, including a 56–17 rout of the Cardinals.

They continue their impressive play against Baltimore, winning 45–14. After allowing the Colts' Buddy Young to return the opening kickoff 104 yards for a touchdown, the Eagles roar back to take a 21–7 halftime lead and add 24 points in the fourth quarter. Rookie Don Johnson scores three touchdowns, and Chuck Bednarik returns an interception 26 yards for his first pro score.

On the final week of the season, the Eagles shock the previously unbeaten Cleveland Browns, dealing them a 42–27 defeat. Thomason outplays the great Otto Graham, passing for 331 yards and three touchdowns. Toy Ledbetter scores twice.

The Eagles' loss to Washington
on December 6, 1953, ended the
longest string of consecutive games
in which the team scored points:
127 games,
beginning more than 10 years before,
on October 2, 1943.

1954

Record: 7–4–1, 2nd in Eastern
Head Coach: Jim Trimble

Date	W/L	Score	Opponent	Att.
9/26	W	28–10	Cleveland	26,546
10/03	W	35–16	@Chicago Cardinals	17,084
10/09	W	24–22	Pittsburgh	37,322
10/17	W	49–21	@Washington	22,051
10/23	L	7–17	@Pittsburgh	39,075
10/30	L	14–37	Green Bay	25,378
11/07	W	30–14	Chicago Cardinals	21,963
11/14	L	14–27	@NY Giants	46,565
11/21	L	0–6	@Cleveland	41,537
11/28	W	41–33	Washington	18,517
12/05	T	13–13	@Detroit	54,939
12/12	W	29–14	NY Giants	28,449

The Eagles win their first four games, then drop four of their next five to finish in second place with seven victories for the third straight year. Burk leads the NFL with 23 touchdown passes and ties a league single-game record with seven scoring passes to trigger a 49–21 win at Washington. Later, he throws for five touchdowns in a 41–33 win over the Redskins at Shibe Park, including the year's longest pass, an 84-yarder to Jerry Williams.

The Eagles shock the defending Eastern Division champion Cleveland Browns, 28–10, in the opener. Burk and Bobby Thomason each throw two touchdown passes, and the defense keeps Otto Graham in check, preventing him from completing a pass for the first 26 minutes.

In the season finale, the Eagles defeat the Giants 29–14. The big plays are a pair of intercepted passes by Wayne Robinson and Jerry Norton and a fumble recovery by Norm (Wildman) Willey. Norton returns his pick 69 yards for a touchdown. Willey recovers his fumble in the end zone after a vicious hit by tackle Mike Jarmoluk on Giants quarterback Bobby Clatterbuck. Jarmoluk is honored prior to the game as he retires after nine seasons with the Eagles.

Bobby Walston sets a club record by scoring 25 points in a single game, the 49–21 romp in Washington. Walston scores three touchdowns and adds seven extra points. He goes on to catch 11 touchdown passes and lead the NFL in scoring with 114 points. Pihos has 60 receptions to share the league lead with the 49ers' Billy Wilson.

1955

Record: 4–7–1, 4th in Eastern (tie)
Head Coach: Jim Trimble

Date	W/L	Score	Opponent	Att.
9/24	W	27–17	NY Giants	29,597
10/01	L	30–31	Washington	31,891
10/09	L	17–21	@Cleveland	43,974
10/15	L	7–13	@Pittsburgh	33,413
10/23	T	24–24	@Chicago Cardinals	24,620
10/30	W	24–0	Pittsburgh	31,164
11/06	L	21–34	@Washington	25,741
11/13	W	33–17	Cleveland	39,303
11/20	L	7–31	@NY Giants	22,075
11/27	L	21–23	Los Angeles	31,648
12/04	W	27–3	Chicago Cardinals	19,478
12/11	L	10–17	@Chicago Bears	34,783

The Eagles overcome a 10-point deficit to beat the New York Giants, 27–17, in the opener. But the victory is costly as All-Pro tackle Bucko Kilroy, starting his 101st consecutive game, suffers a career-ending knee injury. Teddy Wegert, a promising rookie, breaks his foot and misses four games. The Eagles are plagued by an ineffective ground attack the rest of the season and win only three more times.

The highlight of the season is a 33–17 win over Cleveland as the Eagles rally from a 17–0 deficit. The game attracts a season-high crowd of 39,303 to Shibe Park, and another 10,000 fans are turned away.

Trailing 17–16, the Eagles go ahead when Adrian Burk scores from the one-yard line after Bob Hudson recovers a blocked punt. Dick Bielski boots a 40-yard field goal, and Bibbles Bawel dashes 40 yards to score with an interception.

Pete Pihos, playing the final home game of his nine-year pro career, stars in a 27–3 win over the Chicago Cardinals. Pihos catches ten passes for 127 yards and one touchdown. He leads the NFL in receptions for the third straight year with 62 catches for 864 yards and seven touchdowns. He retires with 373 receptions for 5,619 yards and 63 touchdowns.

1956

Record: 3–8–1, 6th in Eastern
Head Coach: Hugh Devore

Date	W/L	Score	Opponent	Att.
9/30	L	7–27	@Los Angeles	54,412
10/06	W	13–9	Washington	26,607
10/14	W	35–21	@Pittsburgh	31,375
10/21	L	6–20	Chicago Cardinals	36,545
10/28	L	3–20	@NY Giants	40,960
11/04	L	17–28	@Chicago Cardinals	27,609
11/11	W	14–7	Pittsburgh	22,652
11/18	L	0–16	Cleveland	25,894
11/25	T	10–10	San Francisco	19,326
12/02	L	14–17	@Cleveland	20,654
12/09	L	17–19	@Washington	22,333
12/15	L	7–21	NY Giants	16,562

Jim Trimble is dismissed as coach and replaced by Hugh Devore. The Eagles lose seven starters to retirement, and 17 other players are lost to injuries during this hard-luck season.

The Eagles win only three games as Ken Keller, a rookie from North Carolina, leads the team in rushing with 433 yards before suffering torn ligaments in the next-to-last game, a 19–17 loss at Washington.

The Eagles earlier defeat the Redskins, 13–9, in their home opener in a drenching rain when Bobby Thomason scores on a one-yard sneak in the last quarter.

The following week, the Eagles squander a 28–0 lead in Pittsburgh but hold off the Steelers with a dramatic goal-line stand to win, 35–21. Jerry Norton tackles Steeler quarterback Ted Marchiborda on a fourth-down run, and Keller puts the game away with a 51-yard touchdown scamper with 25 seconds left.

The Eagles' only other win also comes against the Steelers, 14–7, when Hank Burnine, a rookie from Missouri, catches two touchdown passes from Thomason.

Bobby Thomason's career with the Eagles was marked by extreme highs and lows. He set a club record with 437 passing yards in one game in 1953, but he also set a club record with six interceptions in one game against the Chicago Cardinals on October 21, 1956.

1957

Record: 4–8, 5th in Eastern
Head Coach: Hugh Devore

Date	W/L	Score	Opponent	Att.
9/29	L	13–17	@Los Angeles	62,506
10/05	L	20–24	NY Giants	28,342
10/13	L	7–24	@Cleveland	53,493
10/20	W	17–7	Cleveland	22,443
10/27	L	0–6	@Pittsburgh	27,016
11/03	W	38–21	@Chicago Cardinals	18,718
11/10	L	16–27	Detroit	29,320
11/17	L	0–13	@NY Giants	42,845
11/24	W	21–12	Washington	20,730
12/01	W	7–6	Pittsburgh	16,364
12/08	L	7–42	@Washington	21,304
12/14	L	27–31	Chicago Cardinals	12,555

The Eagles have their best college draft, selecting, in order, Michigan State fullback Clarence Peaks, Wake Forest halfback Billy Ray Barnes, Oklahoma halfback Tommy McDonald, and Duke quarterback Sonny Jurgensen.

Coach Hugh Devore waits until the ninth week to play the 5–9 McDonald at flanker. The rookie catches two touchdown passes from Jurgensen to lead the Eagles to a 21–12 win over Washington. Jurgensen also throws a nine-yard scoring pass to Dick Bielski.

The Eagles win only three other times, but one is a 17–7 upset of the Cleveland Browns, as Jurgensen throws a 31-yard touchdown pass to Rocky Ryan, and later scores on a quarterback sneak.

Jurgensen also triggers a 7–6 win over the Steelers with a seven-yard scoring pass to Bielski. Walston's extra point is the game winner.

Bobby Thomason's best game is the 38–21 win over the Chicago Cardinals. He throws touchdown passes to Bill Stribling and Bobby Walston and scores twice on quarterback sneaks.

Norm (Wildman) Willey, the All-Pro defensive end, retires after an eight-year career.

1958

Record: 2–9–1, 5th in Eastern (tie)
Head Coach: Buck Shaw

Date	W/L	Score	Opponent	Att.
9/28	L	14–24	Washington	36,850
10/05	W	27–24	NY Giants	23,178
10/12	L	3–24	@Pittsburgh	23,153
10/19	L	24–30	San Francisco	33,110
10/26	L	35–38	@Green Bay	31,043
11/02	T	21–21	@Chicago Cardinals	17,486
11/09	L	24–31	Pittsburgh	26,306
11/16	W	49–21	Chicago Cardinals	18,315
11/23	L	14–28	@Cleveland	51,319
11/30	L	10–24	@NY Giants	35,438
12/07	L	14–21	Cleveland	36,773
12/14	L	0–20	@Washington	22,621

Hugh Devore is fired and replaced by Buck Shaw as head coach. The Eagles acquire veteran quarterback Norm Van Brocklin from the Los Angeles Rams and move their home games from Connie Mack Stadium to Franklin Field.

Although the team produces a promising passing attack with Tommy McDonald at flanker and converted fullback Pete Retzlaff at split end, they win only two games.

The Eagles upset the New York Giants, 27–24, in Week 2 as Van Brocklin and McDonald combine on a club-record 91-yard touchdown pass. Standing on his own one-yard line and almost brushing the goal post, Van Brocklin throws a pass that McDonald catches on the other side of midfield and races away to the end zone.

Van Brocklin, who throws another touchdown pass to Clarence Peaks, directs a 66-yard drive in the fourth quarter for the come-from-behind triumph with Billy Barnes plunging six inches for the winning score.

The Eagles later snap a five-game winless streak by beating the Chicago Cardinals 49–21. Peaks scores four touchdowns, and Barnes contributes 244 total yards.

Retzlaff goes on to catch 56 passes and tie Baltimore's Raymond Berry for the NFL receiving title. Nine of McDonald's 29 receptions go for touchdowns.

Tommy McDonald's Place Among the NFL's Leading Receivers, 1958–62

	Rec.	Yds.	Avg. gain	TD
Raymond Berry	303	4,452	14.7	28
Red Phillips	262	3,915	14.9	24
Tommy McDonald	**237**	**4,540**	**19.2**	**55**
Del Shofner	231	4,413	19.1	39
Pete Retzlaff	216	3,540	16.4	19
Lenny Moore	209	3,663	17.5	32
Bobby Mitchell	200	2,846	14.2	27

1959

Record: 7–5, 2nd in Eastern (tie)
Head Coach: Buck Shaw

Date	W/L	Score	Opponent	Att.
9/27	L	14–24	@San Francisco	41,697
10/04	W	49–21	NY Giants	27,023
10/11	W	28–24	Pittsburgh	27,343
10/18	L	7–24	@NY Giants	68,783
10/25	W	28–24	@Chicago Cardinals	20,112
11/01	W	30–23	Washington	39,854
11/08	L	7–28	@Cleveland	58,275
11/15	W	27–17	Chicago Cardinals	28,887
11/22	W	23–20	Los Angeles	47,425
11/29	L	0–31	@Pittsburgh	22,191
12/06	W	34–14	@Washington	24,325
12/13	L	21–28	Cleveland	45,952

After the Eagles drop their opener to the 49ers, 24–14, in San Francisco, Van Brocklin leads them to a stunning 49–21 upset over the New York Giants. Tommy McDonald suffers a fractured jaw but still scores four touchdowns, including one on a sensational 81-yard punt return, the longest in Eagles history.

The team wins six of the next eight games and vaults from last place to a second-place tie in the East, their highest finish in five years.

NFL commissioner Bert Bell collapses and dies while watching the Eagles beat Pittsburgh, 28–24, at Franklin Field in Week 3. McDonald scores the winning touchdown with a leaping catch of an 18-yard Van Brocklin pass in the closing minute. Billy Barnes rushes for 163 yards.

Two weeks later, McDonald again scores the winning touchdown late in the fourth quarter as the Eagles battle back from a 24–0 deficit to beat the Chicago Cardinals, 28–24.

They almost squander a 30–9 halftime lead against Washington but hold on to win, 30–23, with a goal-line stand in the closing seconds. The defense stops fullback Don Bossler three times from the one-yard line as time runs out.

The Eagles defeat the Los Angeles Rams, 23–20, as Paige Cothren, a Rams castoff, kicks the game-winning 14-yard field goal with 16 seconds left.

McDonald finishes the season with 47 receptions for 846 yards and 10 touchdowns. Pete Retzlaff comes back from a broken leg to catch 34 passes for 595 yards in the last eight games.

Tommy McDonald's Place Among the NFL's Touchdown Leaders, 1958–62

	TD
Jim Brown	*71*
Tommy McDonald	**56**
Jim Taylor	*56*
Lenny Moore	*54*
Bobby Mitchell	*50*
John David Crow	*43*
Paul Hornung	*41*

1960

Record: 10–2, 1st in Eastern
Head Coach: Buck Shaw

Date	W/L	Score	Opponent	Att.
9/25	L	24–41	Cleveland	56,303
9/30	W	27–25	@Dallas	18,500
10/09	W	31–27	St. Louis	33,701
10/16	W	28–10	Detroit	38,065
10/23	W	31–29	@Cleveland	64,850
11/06	W	34–7	Pittsburgh	58,324
11/13	W	19–13	Washington	39,361
11/20	W	17–10	@NY Giants	63,571
11/27	W	31–23	NY Giants	60,547
12/04	W	20–6	@St. Louis	21,358
12/11	L	21–27	@Pittsburgh	22,101
12/18	W	38–28	@Washington	20,558

NFL Championship

12/26	W	17–13	Green Bay	67,325

The Eagles are shocked by the Cleveland Browns, 41–24, in their league opener but come back to win their next nine games and clinch their first Eastern Division title in 11 years. Van Brocklin has one of his greatest seasons at quarterback. The 35-year-old Chuck Bednarik begins playing both ways at center and linebacker after a series of injuries deplete the team at midyear.

The key victory of the season comes in the rematch against the Browns in Cleveland, 31–29, when Bobby Walston kicks a 39-yard field goal with two seconds left.

The Eagles take over undisputed possession of first place by beating the Pittsburgh Steelers, 34–7, before 58,324 fans, their largest home crowd in ten years.

The Eagles lock up the division crown with back-to-back wins over the New York Giants, 17–10 and 31–23. Bednarik turns the tide in the first game with two vicious tackles that create fumbles as the Eagles overcome a 10–0 halftime deficit. Bednarik's first tackle jars the ball loose from Mel Triplett. Jimmy Carr catches the ball in midair and races 36 yards for the winning touchdown with 2:37 left. Bednarik's next tackle about a minute later knocks Frank Gifford unconscious after he catches a pass at the Eagles' 30-yard line. Chuck Weber recovers the fumble to lock up the victory.

Ted Dean scores two touchdowns in the second game as the Eagles overcome a 17–0 deficit. Dean, a rookie from Radnor, is now starting in place of Peaks, who broke his leg in the win over Washington. His 49-yard touchdown reception from Van Brocklin gives the home team its first lead, 24–23, in the fourth quarter.

The Eagles clinch the Eastern Conference title by defeating the Cardinals, in St. Louis, 20–6 as Van Brocklin throws touchdown passes to Tommy McDonald and Retzlaff.

McDonald has another spectacular year, scoring 13 touchdowns on just 39 receptions. Van Brocklin passes for a career-high 24 touchdowns.

The Eagles come from behind to beat the Green Bay Packers, 17–13, for the NFL title before a crowd of 67,325 at Franklin Field. After the game, Buck Shaw retires as coach, and Van Brocklin, the overwhelming choice as the league's MVP, retires as a player.

1961

Record: 10–4, 2nd in Eastern
Head Coach: Nick Skorich

Date	W/L	Score	Opponent	Att.
9/17	W	27–20	Cleveland	60,671
9/24	W	14–7	Washington	50,108
10/01	L	27–30	St. Louis	59,399
10/08	W	21–16	Pittsburgh	60,671
10/15	W	20–7	@St. Louis	20,262
10/22	W	43–7	@Dallas	25,000
10/29	W	27–24	@Washington	31,066
11/05	W	16–14	Chicago	60,671
11/12	L	21–38	@NY Giants	62,800
11/19	L	24–45	@Cleveland	68,399
11/26	W	35–13	Dallas	60,127
12/03	W	35–24	@Pittsburgh	21,653
12/10	L	24–28	NY Giants	60,671
12/17	W	27–24	@Detroit	44,231

Playoff Bowl (at Miami)

1/06	L	10–38	Detroit	25,612

Buck Shaw's top assistant Nick Skorich is appointed coach. Sonny Jurgensen takes over as quarterback and guides the Eagles to wins in seven of their first eight games.

Tim Brown returns the opening kickoff of the season 105 yards to help give the Eagles a 27–20 triumph over Cleveland. The biggest offensive explosion comes at Dallas when Clarence Peaks scores twice to spark a 43–7 win. The Eagles rush for 289 yards, score on six of their first seven possessions, and don't have to punt all night.

Jurgensen completes 11 straight passes at one point and hits McDonald with a 41-yard scoring toss with 12 seconds left in the game to give the Eagles a 27–24 win against the Redskins, in Washington. The victory vaults the Eagles into undisputed possession of first place in the division.

But hopes for a repeat championship evaporate in a 16–14 win over Chicago when All-Pro cornerback Tom Brookshier suffers a broken leg. The Eagles are 7–1 when Brookshier goes down, but in the next two weeks, their secondary without Brookshier collapses in losses to the Giants, 38–21, and Cleveland, 45–24.

They still have a chance to win the Eastern Conference, but a 28–24 loss to the Giants in the next-to-last week of the season leaves them in second place.

The Eagles lose to the Detroit Lions, 38–10, in the Playoff Bowl between conference runners-up. The meaningless game proves costly to the Eagles as Jurgensen suffers a shoulder injury that will plague him for the next two seasons. In his first full season as a starter, Jurgensen sets club records for completions (235), passing yards (3,723), and touchdown passes (32).

1962

Record: 3–10–1, 7th in Eastern
Head Coach: Nick Skorich

Date	W/L	Score	Opponent	Att.
9/16	L	21–27	St. Louis	60,671
9/23	L	13–29	NY Giants	60,671
9/30	W	35–7	Cleveland	60,671
10/06	L	7–13	@Pittsburgh	23,164
10/14	L	19–41	@Dallas	18,645
10/21	L	21–27	Washington	60,671
10/28	L	21–31	@Minnesota	30,071
11/04	T	14–14	@Cleveland	63,848
11/11	L	0–49	Green Bay	60,671
11/18	L	14–19	@NY Giants	62,705
11/25	W	28–14	Dallas	58,070
12/02	W	37–14	@Washington	32,229
12/09	L	17–26	Pittsburgh	60,671
12/16	L	35–45	@St. Louis	14,989

The Eagles are plagued with an incredible number of injuries and win only three games. Three receivers—Pete Retzlaff, Bobby Walston, and Dick Lucas—suffer broken arms. Clarence Peaks and Ted Dean break bones in their feet. Fullback Theron Sapp goes down with a separated shoulder. Howard (Hopalong) Cassady suffers a broken leg. Don (The Blade) Burroughs, the team's leading pass defender, is sidelined with cracked ribs.

Only the smallest player on the team, Tommy McDonald, stays healthy, catching 58 passes and scoring 10 touchdowns. He also throws the first touchdown pass of his career, a 10-yard toss to Tim Brown on a broken play, during a 37–14 win at Washington.

The Eagles record their most decisive win ever over Cleveland, beating the Browns, 35–7, while holding Jimmy Brown, the league's leading rusher, to 38 yards.

The Green Bay Packers avenge their 1960 championship game loss by returning to Franklin Field and rolling up 628 yards in total offense to the Eagles' 54 in a 49–0 trouncing. "No professional team should outgun another so badly, offensively and defensively," says coach Nick Skorich after Green Bay amasses an NFL-record 37 first downs to three for the Eagles.

Timmy Brown finishes the year with one of the best all-around individual performances in team history. He compiles 2,306 all-purpose yards (545 rushing, 849 on 52 pass receptions, 831 on kickoffs, and 81 on punt returns), and scores 78 points. Twice Brown runs 99 yards for touchdowns, once with a missed field goal in a 30–27 loss to St. Louis, and later with a kickoff in the 37–14 win over the Redskins.

Chuck Bednarik retires after the season, ending his brilliant 14-year NFL career at age 37. Following the last game, a 45–35 loss in St. Louis, Bednarik's uniform is shipped to the Pro Football Hall of Fame where it remains on display today.

> In 1960, the Eagles won nine consecutive games, a franchise record that would not be equaled until the 2003 season.

1963

Record: 2–10–2, 7th in Eastern
Head Coach: Nick Skorich

Date	W/L	Score	Opponent	Att.
9/15	T	21–21	Pittsburgh	58,205
9/22	L	24–28	St. Louis	60,671
9/29	L	14–37	NY Giants	60,671
10/06	W	24–21	Dallas	60,671
10/13	W	37–24	@Washington	49,219
10/20	L	7–37	@Cleveland	75,174
10/27	L	7–16	@Chicago	48,514
11/03	L	17–23	Cleveland	60,671
11/10	L	14–42	@NY Giants	62,936
11/17	L	20–27	@Dallas	23,694
11/24	L	10–13	Washington	60,671
12/01	T	20–20	@Pittsburgh	16,721
12/08	L	14–38	@St. Louis	15,979
12/15	L	13–34	Minnesota	57,403

With the franchise's 91 outstanding shares now held by 65 stockholders, president Frank L. McNamee puts the club up for sale with an asking price of $4.5 million. Jerry Wolman, a 36-year-old construction magnate from Washington, D.C., purchases the club for $5.5 million.

Problems begin when quarterback Sonny Jurgensen and his backup, King Hill, walk out of training camp to dramatize their salary demands. Management meets their demands, and they return after a one-day absence. The club suffers more injuries as Jurgensen reinjures his arm, Tommy McDonald separates his shoulder, Clarence Peaks dislocates his elbow, linebacker Maxie Baughan breaks his thumb, and tackle Frank Fuller breaks his leg.

The one bright spot is running back Timmy Brown, who sets an NFL record for total offense in a season (2,436 yards: 841 rushing, 487 receiving, 11 passing, 945 on kickoff returns, and 152 on punt returns).

The Eagles win only two games, back to back in early October.

Hill, making only his second start as an Eagle, leads the team past the winless Dallas Cowboys, 24–21. Hill throws touchdown passes of 80 yards to Brown and six yards to Peaks.

Brown has another spectacular day, contributing 211 yards of total offense—91 rushing, 87 on three pass receptions, and 33 on kick runbacks—and scores another touchdown on a two-yard end sweep. Rookie Mike Clark kicks a 12-yard field goal for the winning points in the third period.

Jurgensen's pinpoint passing and Brown's dazzling running help carry the Eagles back from a 17–0 deficit to defeat the Redskins, in Washington, 37–24. Jurgensen throws four touchdown passes—34 and nine yards to McDonald, 36 yards to Brown, and 35 yards to rookie Ron Goodwin, making his NFL debut.

Brown's touchdown is the result of some nifty running as he breaks one tackle and sidesteps another defender. It comes at 5:32 of the third quarter and puts the Eagles ahead 23–17. Brown also scores on a five-yard-run.

After the season, Skorich is fired as coach.

1964

Record: 6–8, 3rd in Eastern (tie)
Head Coach: Joe Kuharich

Date	W/L	Score	Opponent	Att.
9/13	W	38–7	NY Giants	60,671
9/20	L	24–28	San Francisco	57,353
9/27	L	20–28	Cleveland	60,671
10/04	W	21–7	Pittsburgh	59,354
10/11	L	20–35	@Washington	49,219
10/18	W	23–17	@NY Giants	62,978
10/25	W	34–10	@Pittsburgh	38,393
11/01	L	10–21	Washington	60,671
11/08	L	10–20	@LA Rams	53,994
11/15	W	17–14	@Dallas	55,972
11/22	L	13–38	St. Louis	60,671
11/29	L	24–38	@Cleveland	79,289
12/06	W	24–14	Dallas	60,671
12/13	L	34–36	@St. Louis	24,636

Owner Jerry Wolman signs Joe Kuharich as coach, and Kuharich dismantles the team, trading Tommy McDonald to Dallas, Sonny Jurgensen and safety Jim Carr to Washington, Lee Roy Caffey and a first-round draft pick to Green Bay, J. D. Smith to Detroit, Ted Dean to Minnesota, and Clarence Peaks to Pittsburgh.

In return, the Eagles obtain quarterback Norm Snead, running backs Ollie Matson and Earl Gros, center Jim Ringo, defensive tackle Floyd Peters, and kicker Sam Baker, who goes on to set a club record with 16 field goals.

The Eagles go on to win six games—two each over the New York Giants, Pittsburgh Steelers, and Dallas Cowboys—but drop three of their last four contests to finish in a third-place tie in the Eastern Conference.

Snead makes an impressive debut, guiding the Eagles to a surprisingly easy 38–7 win over New York in the opener, snapping a six-game losing streak against the Giants. Snead throws two touchdown passes, and Timmy Brown scores twice, as the Eagles defense, using the safety blitz for the first time, gives Giants quarterback Y. A. Tittle one of the worst days of his 15-year professional career.

Brown has his best day of the year in a 21–7 win over Pittsburgh, rushing for 116 yards on 16 attempts and scoring two touchdowns, one on an 87-yard bomb from Snead.

Matson, subbing for the ailing Brown, provides the spark in the Eagles' second win over the Giants, 23–17. He scores twice, once on a 54-yard run, and the defense forces seven Giants fumbles.

Irv Cross's 94-yard touchdown run with an intercepted pass highlights the Eagles' second triumph over the Steelers, 34–10. Rookie Jack Concannon gets his first extended playing opportunity, and scores on a 15-yard run.

King Hill takes the Eagles on a 96-yard drive in the final minute for a 17–14 win over the Cowboys, in Dallas. The game winner comes on a 38-yard pass to Pete Retzlaff, his second touchdown catch of the day.

Concannon makes his best showing as a starting quarterback in the final home game of the season, a 24–14 victory over the Cowboys. He throws touchdown passes to Retzlaff and Goodwin.

1965

Record: 5–9, 5th in Eastern (tie)
Head Coach: Joe Kuharich

Date	W/L	Score	Opponent	Att.
9/19	W	34–27	St. Louis	54,260
9/26	L	14–16	NY Giants	57,154
10/03	L	17–35	Cleveland	60,759
10/10	W	35–24	@Dallas	56,249
10/17	L	27–35	@NY Giants	62,815
10/24	L	14–20	Pittsburgh	56,515
10/31	L	21–23	@Washington	50,301
11/07	L	34–38	@Cleveland	72,807
11/14	W	21–14	Washington	60,444
11/21	L	24–34	@Baltimore	60,238
11/28	W	28–24	@St. Louis	28,706
12/05	L	19–21	Dallas	54,714
12/12	W	47–13	@Pittsburgh	22,002
12/19	L	28–35	Detroit	56,718

The Eagles win only five games, but they strengthen their offensive line considerably with the addition of rookie Bob Brown, an All-America tackle from Nebraska, and guards Ed Blaine and Jim Skaggs.

Timmy Brown finishes third in the NFL in rushing with 861 yards. Pete Retzlaff switches to tight end at age 34 and catches 66 passes for 1,190 yards and 10 touchdowns.

Two of the Eagles' victories come over St. Louis on late touchdown passes by Norm Snead. They beat the Cardinals in the season opener, 34–27, when Ray Poage makes a sensational sliding catch of a 38-yard Snead throw with Cardinal defender Jimmy Burson draped over his back. Later, Snead pulls out a 28–24 win when he hits Pete Retzlaff with a 10-yard throw with 2:21 remaining.

King Hill is back in the lineup against the Cowboys and scores twice to help cement a 35–24 win in 92-degree heat in Dallas.

Retzlaff has the best game of his 10-year career as the Eagles snap a four-game losing streak and defeat the Washington Redskins, 21–14. Retzlaff catches seven passes for 204 yards and scores on a 78-yard pass play from Snead, who beats his former teammates for the first time.

The Eagles tie an NFL record with nine interceptions in a 47–13 romp over Pittsburgh. Rookie Jim Nettles, who is pressed into service when Nate Ramsey is hurt in the first quarter, has three of the interceptions and returns one 56 yards for a touchdown. Maxie Baughan and George Tarasovic also score with interceptions.

1966

Record: 9–5, 2nd in Eastern (tie)
Head Coach: Joe Kuharich

Date	W/L	Score	Opponent	Att.
9/11	L	13–16	@St. Louis	39,066
9/18	W	23–10	Atlanta	54,049
9/25	W	35–17	NY Giants	60,177
10/02	L	10–41	St. Louis	59,305
10/09	L	7–56	@Dallas	69,372
10/16	W	31–14	@Pittsburgh	28,233
10/23	W	31–3	@NY Giants	63,018
10/30	L	13–27	Washington	60,652
11/06	W	24–23	Dallas	60,658
11/13	L	7–27	@Cleveland	77,968
11/20	W	35–34	@San Francisco	31,993
12/04	W	27–23	Pittsburgh	54,275
12/11	W	33–21	Cleveland	58,074
12/18	W	37–28	@Washington	50,405

Playoff Bowl (at Miami)

Date	W/L	Score	Opponent	Att.
1/08	L	14–20	Baltimore	58,088

Two more popular players are traded away. Maxie Baughan and Irv Cross go to the Los Angeles Rams for tackle Frank Molden, linebacker Fred Brown, cornerback Aaron Martin, and flanker Willie Brown.

Norm Snead, King Hill, and Jack Concannon share the quarterbacking duties as the Eagles enjoy their first winning season in five years and take seven of their last nine games to tie Cleveland for second place.

Sam Baker kicks a 51-yard field goal, the longest in Eagles history, during a 31–14 win over Pittsburgh.

Timmy Brown becomes the first player in NFL history to run two kickoffs back for touchdowns in the same game as the Eagles upset Dallas, 24–23.

Joe Scarpati makes the biggest defensive play of the season in the same game by ripping the ball from the grasp of Dan Reeves on the Eagles' 13 to stop a Dallas drive in the closing minutes.

Al Nelson runs for a 100-yard touchdown on a missed field goal attempt by Lou Groza on the last play of the first half of a 33–21 Eagles triumph over Cleveland.

King Hill starts the Eagles on a four-game winning streak that carries them into the Playoff Bowl by engineering a 35–34 victory over San Francisco. In helping to wipe out a 20–7 halftime deficit, Hill completes 12 of 19 passes for 146 yards and three touchdowns after intermission, with Ollie Matson catching the winning four-yard toss.

The Eagles beat the New York Giants twice. They win 35–17, as Snead throws three touchdown passes and Brown and Earl Gros each score twice. Later, in a 31–3 win, Snead throws a pair of touchdown passes and Gros again scores twice as the Eagles force six Giants turnovers.

The Eagles' other wins come over Atlanta, 23–10, as Snead and Gros score touchdowns on short plunges, and 27–23 over Pittsburgh, with Concannon scrambling for 129 yards, the most rushing yards by a quarterback in franchise history.

The Eagles lead Baltimore, 14–10, at halftime of the Playoff Bowl, but the Colts come back with 10 unanswered points in the second half for a 20–14 win. Hill and Izzy Lang score the Eagles' two touchdowns.

1967

Record: 6–7–1, 2nd in Capitol
Head Coach: Joe Kuharich

Date	W/L	Score	Opponent	Att.
9/17	W	35–24	Washington	60,709
9/24	L	6–38	Baltimore	60,755
10/01	W	34–24	Pittsburgh	60,335
10/08	W	38–7	@Atlanta	53,868
10/15	L	27–28	San Francisco	60,825
10/22	L	14–48	@St. Louis	46,562
10/29	W	21–14	Dallas	60,740
11/05	L	24–31	@New Orleans	59,596
11/12	L	17–33	@LA Rams	57,628
11/19	W	48–21	New Orleans	60,751
11/26	L	7–44	@NY Giants	63,027
12/03	T	35–35	@Washington	50,451
12/10	L	17–38	@Dallas	55,834
12/17	W	28–24	Cleveland	60,658

Jack Concannon is traded to the Chicago Bears for All-Pro tight end Mike Ditka. Earl Gros is sent to the Pittsburgh Steelers for split end Gary Ballman.

Norm Snead passes for 3,399 yards and 29 touchdowns. Ben Hawkins, a second-year flanker from Arizona State, catches 59 passes for a league-leading 1,265 yards and 10 touchdowns.

The Eagles enjoy their highest single-game offensive output in eight years in a 48–21 win over New Orleans. Snead completes 19 of 27 passes for 309 yards and two touchdowns. Hawkins and Tom Woodeshick each score twice.

Snead, Ballman, and Woodeshick play major roles in the Eagles' 35–24 win over Washington. Snead completes 18 of 27 passes for 301 yards and two touchdowns to Ballman. Woodeshick scores the go-ahead touchdown on a 40-yard run.

Woodeshick also triggers a 38–7 triumph over Atlanta by gaining 102 yards on 12 carries, and a 21–14 win over Dallas with 101 yards on 20 attempts as the Eagles hold off the Cowboys after building a 21–0 lead.

Snead and Hawkins lead the Eagles to a 34–24 win over Pittsburgh. Snead throws four touchdown passes, and Hawkins makes eight catches for 187 yards.

Hawkins enjoys his best day during a 48–14 loss to the Cardinals, in St. Louis, by catching six passes for a career-high 197 yards and an 87-yard touchdown, the second longest in club history.

The Eagles win their season finale, 28–24, over Cleveland. Snead throws touchdown passes of 43 and 60 yards to Woodeshick and Hawkins. The team finishes with a losing record due to a porous defense that allows 409 points.

1968

Record: 2–12, 4th in Capitol
Head Coach: Joe Kuharich

Date	W/L	Score	Opponent	Att.
9/15	L	13–30	@Green Bay	50,861
9/22	L	25–34	NY Giants	60,858
9/29	L	13–45	Dallas	60,858
10/06	L	14–17	@Washington	50,816
10/13	L	14–34	@Dallas	72,083
10/20	L	16–29	Chicago	60,858
10/27	L	3–6	@Pittsburgh	26,908
11/03	L	17–45	St. Louis	59,208
11/10	L	10–16	Washington	59,133
11/17	L	6–7	@NY Giants	62,896
11/24	L	13–47	@Cleveland	62,338
11/28	W	12–0	@Detroit	47,909
12/08	W	29–17	New Orleans	57,128
12/15	L	17–24	Minnesota	54,530

After training at Hershey, Pennsylvania, for the past 17 years, the Eagles move their preseason camp to Albright College, in Reading, Pennsylvania. Quarterback Norm Snead suffers a broken leg on the first play of the opening preseason game. Halfback Timmy Brown is traded to Baltimore for kick-return specialist Alvin Haymond.

The Eagles lose their first 11 games, then finish the season by winning two of their last three. In the process, they blow their shot at the top pick in the draft, O. J. Simpson, the Heisman Trophy winner from USC.

The Eagles win at Detroit in Game 12 as Sam Baker kicks field goals of 36, 18, 32, and 35 yards to provide all the scoring in a 12–0 yawner over the Lions. Snead completes only six of 15 pass attempts for 55 yards. He bounces back the following week and throws three touchdown passes to lead the Eagles over New Orleans, 29–17. Ben Hawkins catches two of the scoring throws, and Gary Ballman grabs the other.

Tom Woodeshick rushes for 122 yards on 18 carries and scores on a 30-yard run against the Saints. However, he falls just short of 1,000 yards for the season (947) when he is injured in the final game, a 24–17 loss to Minnesota. At halftime of the game, Eagles fans interrupt their chants of "Joe [Kuharich] must go" by throwing snowballs at Santa Claus.

> The 11-game losing streak at the start
> of the 1968 season is a team record.

1969

Record: 4–9–1, 4th in Capitol
Head Coach: Jerry Williams

Date	W/L	Score	Opponent	Att.
9/21	L	20–27	Cleveland	60,658
9/28	W	41–27	Pittsburgh	60,658
10/05	L	7–38	Dallas	60,658
10/13	L	20–24	@Baltimore	56,864
10/19	L	14–49	@Dallas	71,509
10/26	W	13–10	New Orleans	60,658
11/02	W	23–20	@NY Giants	62,912
11/09	T	28–28	@Washington	50,502
11/16	L	17–23	LA Rams	60,658
11/23	W	34–30	@St. Louis	45,512
11/30	L	17–26	@New Orleans	72,805
12/07	L	29–34	Washington	60,658
12/14	L	3–27	Atlanta	60,658
12/21	L	13–14	@San Francisco	25,391

Due to severe financial setbacks, Jerry Wolman is forced to sell the team to Leonard Tose, a trucking magnate from Norristown, Pennsylvania, for $16.1 million, a record price at the time for a professional sports team. Tose fires Joe Kuharich and replaces him with Pete Retzlaff as general manager. Retzlaff hires former Eagles halfback and assistant coach Jerry Williams as head coach.

Retzlaff trades Bob Brown to the Los Angeles Rams for defensive halfback Irv Cross, guard Don Chuy, and tackle Joe Carollo.

The Eagles select Leroy Keyes with their first draft pick, but the Purdue All-America holds out until September in a contract dispute. Harold Jackson blossoms as a full-time receiver and catches 65 passes for a league-high 1,116 yards. He and Ben Hawkins combine for 17 touchdowns.

Hawkins ties a club record with four touchdown catches in a win over Pittsburgh. Norm Snead completes 22 of 30 attempts for 335 yards and a fifth touchdown pass to Jackson. The 41–27 victory is Snead's finest game as an Eagle.

Snead scores the lone touchdown on a quarterback sneak in a 13–10 win over New Orleans, and he throws a pair of touchdown passes to Hawkins in a 23–20 win over the New York Giants.

The Eagles have a 3–1–1 stretch at midseason that raises their record to 4–5–1, but they lose their final four games to finish 4–9–1.

1970

Record: 3–10–1, 5th in NFC East
Head Coach: Jerry Williams

Date	W/L	Score	Opponent	Att.
9/20	L	7–17	Dallas	59,728
9/27	L	16–20	@Chicago	53,643
10/04	L	21–33	Washington	60,658
10/11	L	23–30	@NY Giants	62,820
10/18	L	20–35	St. Louis	59,002
10/25	L	17–30	@Green Bay (Milwaukee)	48,022
11/01	L	17–21	@Dallas	55,736
11/08	W	24–17	Miami	58,171
11/15	T	13–13	Atlanta	55,425
11/23	W	23–20	NY Giants	59,117
11/29	L	14–23	@St. Louis	46,581
12/06	L	10–29	@Baltimore	60,240
12/13	L	6–24	@Washington	50,415
12/20	W	30–20	Pittsburgh	55,252

Another unbelievable string of injuries plague the Eagles, who drop their first seven games and finish with only three victories.

Coach Jerry Williams' plans to switch Leroy Keyes to defense are dashed when Keyes is sidelined with a torn Achilles tendon. Tom Woodeshick, the team's leading rusher for the past three years, carries the ball only 52 times after injuring his knee. Safety Bill Bradley suffers torn knee ligaments and is out for the year. Tim Rossovich tears ligaments in his ankle in the preseason but refuses surgery. He starts all 14 games at defensive end and leads the team with 174 tackles.

The Eagles win their first game by upsetting the Miami Dolphins, 24–17. Snead throws three touchdown passes—two of them to Harold Jackson and the game winner to Steve Zabel, the first-round draft pick from Oklahoma.

The highlight of the year comes on "Monday Night Football" when Snead rushes for a pair of touchdowns and passes to tight end Fred Hill for another to lead the Eagles to a 23–20 upset over the New York Giants. ABC announcer Howard Cosell becomes ill at halftime and is unable to finish the telecast at Franklin Field, where the wind chill is below zero.

Rookie Lee Bouggess, a third-round draft pick from Louisville, leads all NFL running backs with 50 pass receptions.

Before the first football game was played on Franklin Field's new Astroturf surface in 1969, the grounds crew had to use high-pressure water hoses to clear thousands of dead grasshoppers off the field. "In a fatal miscalculation," wrote Phil Lowry in Total Football, *"the grasshoppers believed that the shiny new green plastic surface would make a great breakfast."*

1971

Record: 6–7–1, 3rd in NFC East
Head Coach: Jerry Williams (3) and Ed Khayat (11)

Date	W/L	Score	Opponent	Att.
9/19	L	14–37	@Cincinnati	55,880
9/26	L	7–42	Dallas	65,358
10/03	L	3–31	San Francisco	65,358
10/10	L	0–13	Minnesota	65,358
10/17	L	10–34	@Oakland	54,615
10/24	W	23–7	NY Giants	65,358
10/31	W	17–16	Denver	65,358
11/07	T	7–7	@Washington	53,041
11/14	L	7–20	@Dallas	60,178
11/21	W	37–20	@St. Louis	48,658
11/28	L	13–20	Washington	65,358
12/05	W	23–20	@Detroit	54,418
12/12	W	19–7	St. Louis	65,358
12/19	W	41–28	@NY Giants	62,774

The Eagles move their home games from Franklin Field to Veterans Stadium. Quarterback Norm Snead is traded to Minnesota.

The team is outscored 110–24 in its first three games. In one of the lopsided losses, 42–7 to the Dallas Cowboys, quarterback Pete Liske throws six interceptions, and his backup Rick Arrington throws another, establishing a record for most interceptions in one game by the Eagles.

At 0–3, owner Leonard Tose fires head coach Jerry Williams and replaces him with defensive line coach Ed Khayat, who orders all the players to cut their hair and shave off their mustaches.

Khayat's first win, which snaps a five-game losing streak, comes over the New York Giants, 23–7. The Eagles hold Fran Tarkenton to 11 completions in 26 attempts, sack the quarterback three times, and force an interception.

The defense carries the Eagles to a 17–16 win over Denver the following week. Bill Bradley intercepts two passes, and linebacker Bill Hobbs scores the winning touchdown on a blocked punt.

Tom Dempsey makes a successful debut with the Eagles by kicking field goals of 41, 27, and 45 yards as the Eagles defeat St. Louis, 37–20.

Liske engineers a 23–20 upset over playoff-bound Detroit, leading a five-play, 79-yard drive in the final 1:49. He passes five yards to Kent Kramer for the winning touchdown.

Dempsey ties a club mark with four field goals, including a record 54-yarder, as the Eagles beat St. Louis for the second time, 19–7. It is the longest field goal in the NFL all season.

The Eagles close out the season with their third consecutive win, 41–28 over the New York Giants. After the game, Tose announces that general manager Pete Retzlaff and Khayat have been rewarded with two-year contracts. Bradley leads the NFL with 11 pass interceptions, a team record.

1972

Record: 2–11–1, 5th in NFC East
Head Coach: Ed Khayat

Date	W/L	Score	Opponent	Att.
9/17	L	6–28	@Dallas	58,850
9/24	L	17–27	Cleveland	65,720
10/02	L	12–27	NY Giants	65,720
10/08	L	0–14	@Washington	53,039
10/15	L	3–34	LA Rams	65,720
10/22	W	21–20	@Kansas City	78,389
10/29	L	3–21	@New Orleans	65,664
11/05	T	6–6	St. Louis	65,720
11/12	W	18–17	@Houston	34,175
11/19	L	7–28	Dallas	65,720
11/26	L	10–62	@NY Giants	62,586
12/03	L	7–23	Washington	65,720
12/10	L	12–21	Chicago	65,720
12/17	L	23–24	@St. Louis	34,827

Leroy Keyes, Lee Bouggess, and Steve Zabel all suffer serious injuries in training camp. Tim Rossovich is traded to San Diego. The Eagles win only two games as Pete Liske is replaced at quarterback by John Reaves, the first-round draft pick from the University of Florida.

After losing their first five games, the Eagles upset the Chiefs, in Kansas City, 21–20. Liske, starting for the first time since Game 2 against Cleveland, throws touchdown passes of 36 and 41 yards to Harold Jackson and 67 yards to Ben Hawkins.

The Eagles and St. Louis play to a 6–6 tie as Tom Dempsey and Jim Bakken, of the Cardinals, each kick two field goals. St. Louis misses a chance to win the game in the last 17 seconds when Bakken's 27-yard field goal attempt sails wide.

Dempsey sets another club record with six field goals, ranging from 12 to 52 yards, and accounts for all the scoring in an 18–17 win over Houston in the Astrodome.

The Eagles drop their last five games, including an embarrassing 62–10 loss to the New York Giants at Yankee Stadium. The morning after the season finale, owner Leonard Tose accepts Retzlaff's resignation and fires the entire coaching staff.

Bill Bradley becomes the first player in NFL history to win the interception title two years in a row. Rookie Ron (Po) James leads the team with 565 yards rushing. Jackson leads the NFL with 62 receptions and 1,048 yards.

In an effort to inspire his last-place team, owner Leonard Tose predicted the Eagles would upset the New York Giants in Week 11 of the 1972 season. His comment made headlines, but the Eagles lost the game, 62–10, their worst defeat in 40 years.
"I'll never do that again," Tose said.

1973

Record: 5–8–1, 3rd in NFC East
Head Coach: Mike McCormack

Date	W/L	Score	Opponent	Att.
9/16	L	23–34	St. Louis	61,103
9/23	T	23–23	@NY Giants	62,289
9/30	L	7–28	Washington	64,147
10/07	L	26–27	@Buffalo	72,364
10/14	W	27–24	@St. Louis	44,400
10/21	L	21–28	@Minnesota	47,478
10/28	W	30–16	Dallas	63,300
11/04	W	24–23	New England	65,070
11/11	L	27–44	Atlanta	63,114
11/18	L	10–31	@Dallas	59,375
11/25	W	20–16	NY Giants	63,086
12/02	L	28–38	@San Francisco	51,155
12/09	W	24–23	NY Jets	34,621
12/16	L	20–38	@Washington	49,484

Mike McCormack, a Hall of Fame lineman with Cleveland, is named head coach. The Eagles have an excellent draft and acquire Texas tackle Jerry Sisemore, USC tight end Charles Young, TCU center Guy Morriss, Michigan safety Randy Logan, and San Diego State cornerback Joe Lavender. Fullback Norm Bulaich is obtained from Baltimore for a draft choice. Harold Jackson and two No. 1 draft choices are dealt to the Los Angeles Rams for Roman Gabriel.

Gabriel becomes the NFL Comeback Player of the Year as he leads the league with 3,219 passing yards and 23 touchdowns. Harold Carmichael is the league's top receiver with 67 catches. Young leads all tight ends with 55, and Tom Sullivan emerges as one of the best halfbacks in the league, rushing for 968 yards.

The Eagles win five games including a 30–16 upset over Dallas, snapping an 11-game losing streak against the Cowboys. Gabriel throws a pair of touchdown passes to Carmichael, and the defense holds the Cowboys to a lone field goal in the second half.

The Eagles trail 17–0 in the third quarter against New England, but win, 24–23, on a 12-yard field goal by Tom Dempsey in the fourth quarter. Steve Zabel saves the victory by blocking Jeff White's 47-yard field-goal attempt on the final play.

Gabriel leads another great comeback in a 27–24 victory over St. Louis. Trailing 24–13 with less than two minutes remaining, Gabriel cuts the deficit to 24–20 with a 27-yard pass to Carmichael. Then, at the final gun, he hits rookie Don Zimmerman with a 23-yard pass, and Zimmerman drags three St. Louis defenders into the end zone.

The Eagles rally from another 17-point deficit to beat the New York Jets, 24–23. John Outlaw scores on a 45-yard interception return, and Dempsey kicks a 40-yard field goal to secure the victory.

Tom Sullivan has the best day of his career, rushing for 156 yards to help beat the New York Giants, 20–16. Dempsey kicks a 51-yard field goal, the fourth straight year that he has nailed a three-pointer of 50 yards or longer.

The Eagles narrowly miss another upset win when Pete Gogolak kicks a 14-yard field goal at the final gun to pull the New York Giants into a 23–23 tie in the last NFL game played at Yankee Stadium.

1974

Record: 7–7, 4th in NFC East
Head Coach: Mike McCormack

Date	W/L	Score	Opponent	Att.
9/15	L	3–7	@St. Louis	40,322
9/23	W	13–10	Dallas	64,088
9/29	W	30–10	Baltimore	64,205
10/06	W	13–7	@San Diego	36,124
10/13	W	35–7	NY Giants	64,801
10/20	L	24–31	@Dallas	43,586
10/27	L	10–14	@New Orleans	64,257
11/03	L	0–27	@Pittsburgh	47,996
11/10	L	20–27	Washington	65,947
11/17	L	3–13	St. Louis	61,982
11/24	L	7–26	@Washington	54,395
12/01	W	36–14	Green Bay	42,030
12/08	W	20–7	@NY Giants	46,889
12/15	W	28–17	Detroit	57,157

All-Pro middle linebacker Bill Bergey is obtained from Cincinnati for two first-round draft picks and one second-round pick. He goes on to have a great year, making 160 tackles and leading the team with five interceptions.

Bergey makes the key play in a 13–10 upset of Dallas in the home opener. His jarring hit on Doug Dennison forces a fumble that Joe Lavender returns 96 yards for a touchdown that ties the game, 7–7. With 25 seconds left in the fourth quarter, Tom Dempsey kicks a 45-yard field goal to give the Eagles their first Veterans Stadium victory on "Monday Night Football."

Tom Sullivan has his best game of the year with two touchdowns and 93 yards rushing in a 30–10 victory over Baltimore. Lavender scores for the second straight week, returning an intercepted pass 37 yards.

The Eagles intercept San Diego quarterback Dan Fouts four times and recover his fumble in a 13–7 win over the Chargers. Randy Logan knocks the ball loose from Fouts, and tackle Bill Dunstan picks it up and runs 46 yards for his first NFL touchdown. Sullivan scores the winning touchdown.

Roman Gabriel passes for two touchdowns, and Sullivan runs for two scores to lead the Eagles over the New York Giants, 35–7.

But a 31–24 loss to Dallas breaks the momentum, and the Eagles lose six straight games. Coach Mike McCormack benches quarterback Roman Gabriel and replaces him with rookie Mike Boryla, who guides the Eagles to victories over Green Bay, the New York Giants, and Detroit to close out the regular season. He is the first Eagle quarterback since Adrian Burk in 1951 to win his first three starts.

Charles Young leads all NFL receivers with 63 receptions. After the season, Jim Murray, the team's administrative assistant, is promoted to general manager.

1975

Record: 4–10, 5th in NFC East
Head Coach: Mike McCormack

Date	W/L	Score	Opponent	Att.
9/21	L	14–23	NY Giants	60,798
9/28	L	13–15	@Chicago	54,392
10/05	W	26–10	Washington	64,397
10/12	L	16–24	@Miami	60,127
10/19	L	20–31	@St. Louis	45,242
10/26	L	17–20	Dallas	64,889
11/03	L	3–42	LA Rams	64,601
11/09	L	23–24	St. Louis	60,277
11/16	W	13–10	@NY Giants	53,434
11/23	L	17–27	@Dallas	57,893
11/30	W	27–17	San Francisco	56,694
12/07	L	0–31	Cincinnati	56,984
12/14	L	10–25	@Denver	37,080
12/21	W	26–3	@Washington	49,385

The Eagles lose their first two games to the woeful New York Giants and Chicago Bears, and they lose seven of their first eight games overall on the way to a 4–10 finish.

The Eagles sweep the Washington Redskins for the first time since 1961, including a 26–3 rout at RFK Stadium highlighted by Frank LeMaster's 89-yard interception return for a touchdown.

Horst Muhlmann kicks a last-minute 30-yard field goal to help the Eagles beat the New York Giants, 13–10, and he boots a 51-yard three-pointer, his longest of the season, to set the stage for a 27–17 win over the San Francisco 49ers.

Mike Boryla completes 23 of 36 passes for 241 yards and three touchdowns against the 49ers, while Bill Bergey plays one of the best games of his career with two interceptions and two fumble recoveries.

Following the season, owner Leonard Tose announces that coach Mike McCormack's contract will not be renewed. He finishes his three seasons in Philadelphia with a 16–25–1 record.

Boryla is added to the NFC Pro Bowl squad when six other quarterbacks decline the invitation. He comes off the bench in the fourth quarter and throws two TD passes to spark a 23–20 NFC victory.

1976

Record: 4–10, 4th in NFC East
Head Coach: Dick Vermeil

Date	W/L	Score	Opponent	Att.
9/12	L	7–27	@Dallas	55,530
9/19	W	20–7	NY Giants	60,643
9/27	L	17–20ot	Washington	60,131
10/03	W	14–13	@Atlanta	45,535
10/10	L	14–33	St. Louis	44,933
10/17	L	13–28	@Green Bay	55,398
10/24	L	12–31	Minnesota	56,233
10/31	W	10–0	@NY Giants	68,690
11/07	L	14–17	@St. Louis	60,760
11/14	L	3–24	@Cleveland	62,120
11/21	L	7–26	Oakland	62,133
11/28	L	0–24	@Washington	54,292
12/05	L	7–26	Dallas	55,072
12/12	W	27–10	Seattle	37,949

Dick Vermeil is hired as the Eagles' fifth head coach in nine years. Quarterback Roman Gabriel is slow recovering from off-season knee surgery and does not rejoin the team until mid-October.

Vermeil wins his home opener, 20–7, over the New York Giants. The Eagles rush for 211 yards as rookie fullback Mike Hogan gains 93 yards on 19 carries. Vince Papale, a 30-year-old rookie from the Delaware County rough touch league, sets up the final Eagles touchdown by recovering a muffed New York punt on the Giants' three-yard line.

The Eagles beat Atlanta, 14–13, as Bill Dunstan blocks a 42-yard field goal attempt on the final play. They lose eight of their next nine games, and the offense scores only two touchdowns in four weeks.

The only win in that span, 10–0 over the New York Giants, is the Eagles' first shutout since 1968. Harold Carmichael catches five passes including the game's only touchdown, a 13-yard pass from Mike Boryla. Bill Bergey leads the defense with 10 unassisted tackles.

The Eagles don't score more than two touchdowns in the same game until the final week when they trounce Seattle, 27–10. Tom Sullivan rushes for 121 yards, and Mike Hogan adds 104, making them the first pair of Eagles runners to rush for more than 100 yards in the same game since 1973.

Eagles in the Pro Bowl

The Pro Bowl originated in 1951 after the merger of the National Football League and the All-America Football Conference. Over the years, four Eagles have earned MVP honors in the Pro Bowl: Chuck Bednarik (1954), Floyd Peters (1967), Reggie White (1987), and Randall Cunningham (1989). The Eagles who have made the most trips to the Pro Bowl are:

8 games	*Chuck Bednarik*
7 games	*Reggie White*
6 games	*Pete Pihos*
5 games	*Eric Allen, Maxie Baughan, Donovan McNabb, Tommy McDonald, Mike Quick, Pete Retzlaff, Troy Vincent*
4 games	*Bill Bergey, Harold Carmichael, Brian Dawkins*

1977

Record: 5–9, 4th in NFC East
Head Coach: Dick Vermeil

Date	W/L	Score	Opponent	Att.
9/18	W	13–3	Tampa Bay	61,549
9/25	L	0–20	@LA Rams	46,031
10/02	L	13–17	@Detroit	57,236
10/09	W	28–10	@NY Giants	48,824
10/16	L	17–21	St. Louis	60,535
10/23	L	10–16	Dallas	65,507
10/30	L	17–23	@Washington	55,031
11/06	W	28–7	New Orleans	53,482
11/13	L	14–17	Washington	60,702
11/20	L	16–21	@St. Louis	48,768
11/27	L	6–14	@New England	57,893
12/04	L	14–24	@Dallas	60,289
12/11	W	17–14	NY Giants	47,731
12/18	W	27–0	NY Jets	19,241

Quarterback Ron Jaworski is obtained from the Los Angeles Rams for the rights to Charles Young. The Eagles win five games, including their first regular-season opener since 1967, 13–3 over Tampa Bay. In his debut, Jaworski throws touchdown passes to Keith Krepfle and Tom Sullivan while the defense limits the Buccaneers to 118 total yards.

Again, the Eagles beat the New York Giants twice. Herb Lusk, the "Praying Tailback," enjoys his best game as a pro with 117 yards on 17 carries and two touchdowns in a 28–10 win at the Meadowlands. Jaworski's one-yard bootleg run around left end with 20 seconds left beats the Giants 17–14 in the rematch.

Jaworski and Harold Carmichael hook up for a pair of touchdown passes in a 28–7 victory over the New Orleans Saints. Free-agent fullback Jim Betterson replaces the injured Mike Hogan and gains 72 yards on 23 carries.

Wilbert Montgomery makes the most of his first NFL start against the New York Jets, as the Eagles record their only shutout of the year, 27–0. Montgomery rushes for 103 yards and scores two touchdowns. Carmichael catches two passes, extending the number of games in which he has caught at least one pass to 80.

Bill Bergey keys defensive coordinator Marion Campbell's 3–4 defense and is selected to play in his third Pro Bowl.

> *Roman Gabriel retired after the 1977 season,*
> *ending a 16-year NFL career.*
> *His last completion was a 15-yard pass to*
> *Vince Papale. It was the 2,366th completion*
> *of Gabriel's career and the first, and only,*
> *reception of Papale's career.*

1978

Record: 9–7, 2nd in NFC East
Head Coach: Dick Vermeil

Date	W/L	Score	Opponent	Att.
9/03	L	14–16	LA Rams	64,721
9/10	L	30–35	@Washington	54,380
9/17	W	24–17	@New Orleans	49,242
9/24	W	17–3	Miami	62,998
10/01	W	17–14	@Baltimore	47,639
10/08	L	14–24	@New England	61,016
10/15	W	17–10	Washington	65,722
10/22	L	7–14	@Dallas	60,525
10/29	L	10–16	St. Louis	62,989
11/05	W	10–3	Green Bay	64,214
11/12	W	17–9	NY Jets	60,249
11/19	W	19–17	@NY Giants	70,318
11/26	W	14–10	@St. Louis	39,693
12/03	L	27–28	@Minnesota	38,722
12/10	L	13–31	Dallas	64,667
12/17	W	20–3	NY Giants	56,396

NFC Wild Card

Date	W/L	Score	Opponent	Att.
12/24	L	13–14	@Atlanta	49,447

Coach Dick Vermeil guides the Eagles to a 9–7 record, their first winning season since 1966. The team qualifies for the postseason, but loses to Atlanta in the NFC Wild Card Game, 14–13.

Wilbert Montgomery makes the most of his first year as a starter by rushing for 1,220 yards to become the first Eagle since Steve Van Buren to pass the 1,000-yard mark in a season.

Cornerback Herman Edwards provides the highlight of the year, the "Miracle of the Meadowlands," as he scoops up a fumbled handoff by Joe Pisarcik and races 26 yards for the winning touchdown in a last-second 19–17 win over the New York Giants.

The Eagles also beat the Giants in their final home game, 20–3, to clinch the playoff spot. Montgomery and Mike Hogan rush for 130 and 100 yards, respectively.

The Eagles snap a nine-game losing streak to St. Louis by defeating the Cardinals 14–10 on a Mike Hogan touchdown.

The Eagles' most dominating performance comes in a 17–3 win over Miami. Montgomery runs for 111 yards, and the defense holds the NFL's best ground attack to just 84 yards.

Montgomery triggers the Eagles' biggest comeback of the season, 17–14 over the Baltimore Colts. The Eagles score all their points in the fourth quarter to erase a 14–0 deficit, with Montgomery scoring the game winner on a 14-yard run with 2:39 left. He ties a club record by scoring four touchdowns in one game against Washington, a 35–30 loss.

The Eagles beat Green Bay, 10–3, on a touchdown by John Sciarra, who was playing as an option quarterback. They defeat New Orleans, 24–17, in their first visit to the Superdome as Ron Jaworski throws a 19-yard pass to Harold Carmichael for the game winner. Carmichael also catches a pair of touchdown passes from Jaworski in a 17–9 win over the New York Jets.

1979

Record: 11–5, 1st in NFC East (tie)
Head Coach: Dick Vermeil

Date	W/L	Score	Opponent	Att.
9/02	W	23–17	NY Giants	67,366
9/10	L	10–14	Atlanta	66,935
9/16	W	26–14	@New Orleans	54,212
9/23	W	17–13	@NY Giants	74,265
9/30	W	17–14	Pittsburgh	70,352
10/07	W	28–17	Washington	69,142
10/14	W	24–20	@St. Louis	48,367
10/21	L	7–17	@Washington	54,442
10/28	L	13–37	@Cincinnati	42,036
11/04	L	19–24	Cleveland	69,019
11/12	W	31–21	@Dallas	62,417
11/18	W	16–13	St. Louis	70,235
11/25	W	21–10	@Green Bay	50,023
12/02	W	44–7	Detroit	66,128
12/08	L	17–24	Dallas	71,434
12/16	W	26–20	@Houston	49,407

NFC Wild Card

Date	W/L	Score	Opponent	Att.
12/23	W	27–17	Chicago	69,397

NFC Divisional Playoff

Date	W/L	Score	Opponent	Att.
12/29	L	17–24	@Tampa Bay	71,402

Dick Vermeil is named Coach of the Year after guiding the Eagles to an 11–5 regular-season record. They tie Dallas for first place in the NFC East and again go to the playoffs as a wild card team. They beat Chicago, 27–17, then are upset by Tampa Bay, 24–17, in a divisional playoff round.

The Eagles start fast, winning six of their first seven games. They suffer a major loss in Week 3, however, when All-Pro linebacker Bill Bergey suffers a season-ending knee injury in a 26–14 win at New Orleans.

Wilbert Montgomery, who goes on to set a club record with 1,512 rushing yards, runs for 126 and scores a touchdown on a 53-yard pass from Jaworski as the Eagles down the New York Giants, 17–13.

The Eagles upset the Pittsburgh Steelers, the defending Super Bowl champions, 17–14. Ken Clarke preserves the win by recovering a Franco Harris fumble on the one-yard line in the fourth quarter.

Montgomery leads the Eagles to a 28–17 win over Washington, rushing for 127 yards and scoring four touchdowns, making him the first player in the club's history to score four times in a game twice in a career.

After dropping three straight games, the Eagles rebound to win four in a row. They defeat Dallas, 31–21, in a Monday night contest for their first win ever at Texas Stadium. Tony Franklin's 59-yard field goal is the second longest in NFL history.

Jaworski's passing plays a major role in wins over St. Louis, Green Bay, and Detroit. His 40-yarder to Keith Krepfle is the difference in the 16–13 triumph over the Cardinals. His three touchdown passes—two to Carmichael and one to Montgomery—defeat the Packers, 21–10.

Two more touchdown passes to Carmichael highlight a 24-point second quarter—the most productive period for the Eagles since 1967—in a 44–7 rout of the Lions. The 37-point margin of victory is the Eagles' largest since they defeated the Chicago Bears, 38–0, in 1953.

1980

Record: 12–4, 1st in NFC East
Head Coach: Dick Vermeil

Date	W/L	Score	Opponent	Att.
9/07	W	27–6	Denver	70,307
9/14	W	42–7	@Minnesota	46,460
9/22	W	35–3	NY Giants	70,767
9/28	L	14–24	@St. Louis	49,079
10/05	W	24–14	Washington	69,044
10/12	W	31–16	@NY Giants	71,051
10/19	W	17–10	Dallas	70,696
10/26	W	17–14	Chicago	68,752
11/02	W	27–20	@Seattle	61,046
11/09	W	34–21	@New Orleans	44,340
11/16	W	24–0	@Washington	51,897
11/23	W	10–7	Oakland	68,585
11/30	L	21–22	@San Diego	51,760
12/07	L	17–20	Atlanta	70,205
12/14	W	17–3	St. Louis	68,969
12/21	L	27–35	@Dallas	62,548

NFC Divisional Playoff

Date	W/L	Score	Opponent	Att.
1/03	W	31–16	Minnesota	68,434

NFC Championship Game

Date	W/L	Score	Opponent	Att.
1/11	W	20–7	Dallas	70,696

Super Bowl XV (at New Orleans)

Date	W/L	Score	Opponent	Att.
1/25	L	10–27	Oakland	75,500

The Eagles reach the Super Bowl for the first time after setting a record with 12 wins in the regular season. They trounce Minnesota, 31–16, in the divisional playoff round, then defeat Dallas, 20–7, to win the NFC title, before losing to Oakland, 27–10, in Super Bowl XV.

Ron Jaworski leads the NFC with a 90.9 passing rating while throwing for 3,529 yards and 27 touchdowns. His three touchdown passes, including the first of tight end John Spagnola's career, highlight a 27–6 win over Denver in the regular-season opener.

That starts a streak in which the Eagles win 11 of their first 12 games, overcoming key injuries along the way. Dick Vermeil's nephew, Louie Giammona, comes off the bench to spell the injured Montgomery and scores two touchdowns to help beat the New York Giants, 31–16.

When Jaworski is forced to leave the Chicago game with a concussion, Joe Pisarcik comes off the bench to direct a 70-yard drive climaxed by Tony Franklin's 18-yard game-winning field goal as the Eagles defeat the Bears, 17–14.

Harold Carmichael enjoys the most productive day of his career with three touchdowns—on passes of 10, 6, and 25 yards from Jaworski—as the Eagles beat New Orleans, 34–21. Charlie Smith also has a career day, catching nine passes for 137 yards.

The Eagles tie a club record by sacking Jim Plunkett eight times in a 10–7 win over Oakland. Montgomery scores the deciding touchdown on a three-yard run after Jaworski keeps the drive alive by barely avoiding a sack and hitting fullback Leroy Harris with a 43-yard pass.

The Eagles lose three of their last four regular-season games but still win the Eastern Division title with a 12–4 record.

Carmichael's streak of 127 consecutive games with a reception is snapped when he fails to catch a pass in the regular-season finale, a 35–27 loss at Dallas. Carmichael leaves the game early with a back injury.

1981

Record: 10–6, 2nd in NFC East
Head Coach: Dick Vermeil

Date	W/L	Score	Opponent	Att.
9/06	W	24–10	@NY Giants	72,459
9/13	W	13–3	New England	71,089
9/17	W	20–14	@Buffalo	78,331
9/27	W	36–13	Washington	70,664
10/05	W	16–13	Atlanta	71,488
10/11	W	31–14	@New Orleans	52,728
10/18	L	23–35	@Minnesota	45,459
10/25	W	20–10	Tampa Bay	70,714
11/01	L	14–17	Dallas	72,111
11/08	W	52–10	@St. Louis	48,421
11/15	W	38–13	Baltimore	68,613
11/22	L	10–20	NY Giants	66,327
11/30	L	10–13	@Miami	67,797
12/06	L	13–15	@Washington	52,206
12/13	L	10–21	@Dallas	64,955
12/20	W	38–0	St. Louis	56,636

NFC Wild Card

Date	W/L	Score	Opponent	Att.
12/27	L	21–27	NY Giants	71,611

After winning their first six games, the Eagles limp to a 10–6 finish before losing to the New York Giants, 27–21, in the NFC Wild Card Game. The defense ranks first in the NFL in fewest yards (4,447) and fewest points allowed (221). Harold Carmichael enjoys his third 1,000-yard receiving year, and Wilbert Montgomery rushes for 1,402 yards.

A 55-yard touchdown pass from Ron Jaworski to Rodney Parker and a one-yard touchdown run by Montgomery highlight a 24–10 opening-game win over the Giants.

Playing a Thursday night game in front of many of his Lackawanna, New York, friends, Jaworski leads the Eagles to a 20–14 win over the Bills, in Buffalo. His 15-yard touchdown pass to Carmichael puts the Eagles ahead, and free safety Brenard Wilson preserves the victory with two second-half interceptions.

With Montgomery sidelined by an injured hamstring, Louie Giammona leads the Eagles over Washington, 36–13, with two touchdowns.

Playing before a national television audience and the largest regular-season crowd to see a game at the Vet (71,488), the Eagles snap a three-game losing streak against Atlanta by jumping out to a 13–0 lead and winning, 16–13. Tony Franklin kicks field goals of 36, 34, and 43 yards.

Booker Russell scores twice on short plunges as the Eagles win their sixth straight game, 31–14, over New Orleans.

After losing two of their next three games, the Eagles roll up their highest point total since 1953, defeating the Cardinals in St. Louis, 52–10. Highlighting a 35-point second half is a 20-yard touchdown pass from Joe Pisarcik to Wally Henry, the first scoring pass as an Eagle for Pisarcik and the first NFL touchdown catch for Henry.

The Eagles crush Baltimore, 38–13, with 574 yards of total offense, then lose four straight before ending the regular season with a 38–0 rout of St. Louis.

1982

Record: 3–6, 13th in NFC
Head Coach: Dick Vermeil

Date	W/L	Score	Opponent	Att.
9/12	L	34–37ot	Washington	68,885
9/19	W	24–21	@Cleveland	78,830
11/21	L	14–18	Cincinnati	65,172
11/28	L	9–13	@Washington	48,313
12/05	L	20–23	St. Louis	63,622
12/11	L	7–23	@NY Giants	66,053
12/19	W	35–14	Houston	44,119
12/26	W	24–20	@Dallas	46,199
1/02	L	24–26	NY Giants	55,797

An NFL players strike after the first two games interrupts the season for eight weeks and reduces the schedule from 16 to nine games. The season, the Eagles' 50th in the NFL, is a disaster as they win only three games and miss the playoffs for the first time since 1977.

The Eagles open the season by dropping a 37–34 overtime thriller to eventual Super Bowl champion Washington despite a career-best 371 passing yards by Ron Jaworski.

Jaworski enjoys his second consecutive 300-yard game and rallies the Eagles to three touchdowns in the fourth quarter for a 24–21 win over the Browns in Cleveland. Leroy Harris scores the deciding touchdown on a two-yard run with 27 seconds left.

After the 57-day work stoppage, the Eagles are not the same team, losing four games in a row. They end the streak with a 35–14 win over Houston as Wilbert Montgomery scores on a 90-yard run, the longest of his career.

A 24–20 Eagles victory at Dallas, decided by a 10-yard touchdown pass from Jaworski to Harold Carmichael, is Dick Vermeil's last win as an Eagles coach. He resigns shortly following the season, citing physical and emotional fatigue.

Rush to Victory

After beginning his career with the Eagles by going 7–19, Dick Vermeil guided the team to a 44–22 record during a period that began with the last two games of 1977 and continued through 1981. For this 92-game span, the Eagles were plus 29 in turnovers. The team averaged 143 yards per game on the ground while allowing 124. The Eagles' record under Vermeil in a game when one of his running backs rushed for 100 or more yards was 25–5.

1983

Record: 5–11, 4th in NFC East
Head Coach: Marion Campbell

Date	W/L	Score	Opponent	Att.
9/03	W	22–17	@San Francisco	55,775
9/11	L	13–23	Washington	69,542
9/18	W	13–10	@Denver	74,202
9/25	L	11–14	St. Louis	64,465
10/02	W	28–24	@Atlanta	50,621
10/09	W	17–13	@NY Giants	73,291
10/16	L	7–37	@Dallas	63,070
10/23	L	6–7	Chicago	45,263
10/30	L	21–22	Baltimore	59,150
11/06	L	20–27	Dallas	71,236
11/13	L	14–17	@Chicago	47,524
11/20	L	0–23	NY Giants	57,977
11/27	L	24–28	@Washington	54,324
12/04	W	13–9	LA Rams	32,867
12/11	L	17–20ot	New Orleans	45,182
12/18	L	7–31	@St. Louis	21,902

After six seasons as the team's defensive coordinator, Marion Campbell succeeds Dick Vermeil as head coach. The Eagles win four of their first six games, then drop seven straight and nine of their last 10 to finish 5–11.

The Eagles are plagued by injuries during an opening day 22–17 win over San Francisco. Wilbert Montgomery is sidelined with a sprained knee, and Ron Jaworski goes out with a concussion. Backup quarterback Joe Pisarcik leads the team to two touchdowns and a pair of field goals on the first four possessions of the second half. Michael Haddix, the team's No. 1 draft choice, leads all rushers with 76 yards and scores his first NFL touchdown.

Spoiling Denver's home opener, the Eagles display their best defensive effort of the year while edging the Broncos, 13–10, on Tony Franklin's 43-yard field goal with 57 seconds remaining.

Jaworski triggers back-to-back wins over Atlanta, 28–24, and the New York Giants, 17–13, with five touchdown throws and 480 passing yards.

The Eagles then begin their nine-game swoon, with the lone victory coming against the Los Angeles Rams, 13–9. Wide receiver Tony Woodruff clinches the Eagles' only win at the Vet by outjumping LeRoy Irvin, of the Rams, in the end zone with 21 seconds left to snatch a 29-yard scoring pass from Jaworski.

All-Pro Mike Quick leads the league with a club-record 1,409 receiving yards on 69 catches.

1984

Record: 6–9–1, 5th in NFC East
Head Coach: Marion Campbell

Date	W/L	Score	Opponent	Att.
9/02	L	27–28	@NY Giants	71,520
9/09	W	19–17	Minnesota	55,942
9/16	L	17–23	@Dallas	64,521
9/23	L	9–21	San Francisco	62,771
9/30	L	0–20	@Washington	53,064
10/07	W	27–17	@Buffalo	37,555
10/14	W	16–7	Indianapolis	50,277
10/21	W	24–10	NY Giants	64,677
10/28	L	14–34	St. Louis	54,310
11/04	T	23–23ot	@Detroit	59,141
11/11	L	23–24	@Miami	70,227
11/18	W	16–10	Washington	63,117
11/25	L	16–17	@St. Louis	39,858
12/02	L	10–26	Dallas	66,322
12/09	W	27–17	New England	41,581
12/16	L	10–26	@Atlanta	15,582

Wilbert Montgomery establishes new Eagles career records for rushing yardage (6,538) and carries (1,465), surpassing marks set by Pro Football Hall of Famer Steve Van Buren. Kicker Paul McFadden is named NFC Rookie of the Year after setting an Eagles single-season scoring record with 116 points, besting the 30-year-old mark of 114 set by Bobby Walston.

The Eagles' first win, 19–17, over Minnesota turns out to be their closest game of the year. John Spagnola catches a one-yard pass from Ron Jaworski for the winning touchdown on fourth down with two seconds left.

The Eagles snap a three-game losing streak, defeating the Bills in Buffalo, 27–17, with Jaworski playing one of his best games in front of friends and family from nearby Lackawanna. He throws two touchdown passes and runs for another on fourth down with 4:01 remaining to clinch the win.

The defense leads the way in wins over Indianapolis (16–7), the New York Giants (24–10), and Washington (16–10). Against the Redskins, the Eagles recover three fumbles, intercept three passes, and hold the defending NFC champions to their lowest point total since 1982. Andre Waters breaks the game open when he returns a kickoff 89 yards for a touchdown.

Jaworski suffers a broken leg during a 17–16 loss to the Cardinals in St. Louis in Week 13, snapping his streak of 116 consecutive starts, a durability record for NFL quarterbacks.

In the final week of the regular season, it is reported that owner Leonard Tose, in dire financial straits due in part to gambling losses, is in negotiations to move the Eagles to Phoenix. Public backlash kills the deal, and Tose keeps the team in Philadelphia.

1985

Record: 7–9, 4th in NFC East
Head Coach: Marion Campbell (15) and Fred Bruney (1)

Date	W/L	Score	Opponent	Att.
9/08	L	0–21	@NY Giants	76,141
9/15	L	6–17	LA Rams	60,920
9/22	W	19–6	@Washington	53,748
9/29	L	10–16ot	NY Giants	66,696
10/06	L	21–23	@New Orleans	56,364
10/13	W	30–7	St. Louis	48,186
10/20	W	16–14	Dallas	70,114
10/27	W	21–17	Buffalo	60,987
11/03	L	13–24	@San Francisco	58,383
11/10	W	23–17ot	Atlanta	63,691
11/17	W	24–14	@St. Louis	39,032
11/24	L	17–34	@Dallas	54,047
12/01	L	23–28	Minnesota	54,688
12/08	L	12–17	Washington	60,737
12/15	L	14–20	@San Diego	45,569
12/22	W	37–35	@Minnesota	49,722

Norman Braman, an automobile dealer from Florida, purchases the Eagles from Leonard Tose for a reported $65 million. Harry Gamble is promoted to vice president–general manager, overseeing the daily operations. Wilbert Montgomery, the team's all-time rushing leader, is traded to Detroit for linebacker Garry Cobb. Defensive end Reggie White signs a free-agent contract in Week 4 and is named NFC Defensive Rookie of the Year.

The Eagles lose four of their first five games and finish 7–9. Head coach Marion Campbell is released, and Fred Bruney serves as interim coach for the final game at Minnesota, a 37–35 victory.

Paul McFadden kicks four field goals for the second time in his career to lead the Eagles to their first win, 19–6, over the Redskins, the defending NFC champions. It is the first time ever that a Washington team coached by Joe Gibbs fails to score a touchdown at RFK Stadium.

Earnest Jackson rushes for a career-high 162 yards in a 24–14 win over St. Louis. His total of 34 rushing attempts is one short of Steve Van Buren's team record, and Jackson's 51-yard touchdown run is a career best.

Ron Jaworski comes back from his broken leg to pass for career highs—with 380 yards in a 16–14 win over Dallas and 394 yards in a 24–13 loss to San Francisco. He helps the Eagles overcome a 17–0 deficit against Buffalo, rallying the team to three touchdowns in the fourth quarter for a 21–17 win. He throws a 32-yard strike to Mike Quick for the game winner.

Jaworski also delivers the first overtime win in team history, 23–17, over Atlanta as he hits Quick with a 99-yard touchdown pass, tying for the longest touchdown pass in NFL history.

1986

Record: 5–10–1, 4th in NFC East
Head Coach: Buddy Ryan

Date	W/L	Score	Opponent	Att.
9/07	L	14–41	@Washington	53,982
9/14	L	10–13ot	@Chicago	65,130
9/21	L	7–33	Denver	63,839
9/28	W	34–20	LA Rams	65,646
10/05	W	16–0	@Atlanta	57,104
10/12	L	3–35	@NY Giants	74,221
10/19	L	14–17	Dallas	68,572
10/26	W	23–7	San Diego	41,469
11/02	L	10–13	@St. Louis	33,051
11/09	L	14–17	NY Giants	60,601
11/16	L	11–13	Detroit	54,568
11/23	L	20–24	@Seattle	55,786
11/30	W	33–27ot	@LA Raiders	53,338
12/07	T	10–10ot	St. Louis	50,148
12/14	W	23–21	@Dallas	46,117
12/21	L	14–21	Washington	61,816

Buddy Ryan, the defensive coordinator of the Chicago Bears' Super Bowl XX Champions, is named the club's 17th head coach. Harry Gamble is promoted to president–chief operating officer. Ryan makes sweeping changes in the roster, but the Eagles win only five games.

Ryan's first win, 34–20, over the previously unbeaten Los Angeles Rams, comes in Week 4. The Eagles blank Atlanta, 16–0, the following week for their first shutout since 1981. Garry Cobb has a career-high four sacks and leads the team with 13 tackles. Mike Quick makes a spectacular diving catch of an eight-yard pass from Ron Jaworski for the game's only touchdown.

Ryan uses an unusual offensive plan with Jaworski playing on first and second downs and Randall Cunningham replacing him on third down. Cunningham's mobility does not save him from being sacked 72 times, and the Eagles' 104 team sacks is a league record.

The team loses six of seven games at midseason, and Jaworski is lost for the season with a torn tendon on the little finger of his passing hand.

Cunningham ends the losing streak by throwing three touchdown passes in a 33–27 overtime win against the Los Angeles Raiders. He scores the game winner on a one-yard sneak in overtime after Andre Waters scoops up a Marcus Allen fumble and races 81 yards to the Raiders' four-yard line.

The Eagles' only win over an Eastern Division opponent comes with a second-half rally at Dallas, 23–21. Matt Cavanaugh starts for an injured Cunningham and passes for 260 yards and two touchdowns to Kenny Jackson, including a 31-yarder in the third period that puts the Eagles ahead. Paul McFadden kicks three field goals including a 50-yarder, his longest of the season.

1987

Record: 7–8, 4th in NFC East
Head Coach: Buddy Ryan

Date	W/L	Score	Opponent	Att.
9/13	L	24–34	@Washington	52,188
9/20	W	27–17	New Orleans	57,485
10/04	L	3–35	Chicago	4,074
10/11	L	22–41	@Dallas	40,622
10/18	L	10–16ot	@Green Bay	35,842
10/25	W	37–20	Dallas	61,630
11/01	W	28–23	@St. Louis	24,586
11/08	W	31–27	Washington	63,609
11/15	L	17–20	NY Giants	66,172
11/22	L	19–31	St. Louis	55,592
11/29	W	34–31ot	@New England	54,198
12/06	L	20–23ot	@NY Giants	65,874
12/13	L	10–28	Miami	63,841
12/20	W	38–27	@NY Jets	30,572
12/27	W	17–7	Buffalo	57,547

Ron Jaworski, who set nearly every Eagles passing record between 1977 and 1986, is released in March after the club decides not to guarantee his contract.

The Eagles split their first two games of the season before the NFL Players Association goes on strike. After all Week 3 games are canceled, the season resumes with teams comprised of replacement players. The Eagles' replacement team loses all three of its games, which count in the standings and contribute to the team missing the playoffs with a 7–8 overall record.

Randall Cunningham leads the offense by throwing 23 touchdown passes. He becomes the first quarterback to lead his team in rushing (505 yards) since the Chicago Bears' Bobby Douglass did it in 1972.

Reggie White is named the NFL's Defensive Player of the Year after setting an NFC record with 21 sacks. White sets the mark in just 12 games due to the strike.

In the first game back after the strike, defensive end Clyde Simmons plays one of the best games of his career in a 37–20 win over Dallas. Simmons has two of the Eagles' five sacks and one of the club's five fumble recoveries, and blocks a field goal attempt.

Cunningham and wide receiver Gregg Garrity team up for the winning touchdowns in the next two Eagles triumphs— 28–23 over St. Louis and 31–27 against Washington. Garrity's nine-yard catch caps a 70-yard drive in the last 1:50 against the Cardinals, and his 40-yard reception with 1:06 left helps beat the Redskins.

The Eagles defeat New England, 34–31, in overtime as Cunningham has the first 300-yard passing game (314) of his career and throws touchdown passes of 61 and 29 yards to Mike Quick. Paul McFadden wins it with a 38-yard field goal.

The team snaps a two-game losing streak by beating the New York Jets, 38–27, and Buffalo, 17–7, to close the season. Cunningham tosses three touchdown passes against the Jets, two of them to Quick. Fullback Anthony Toney scores twice against the Bills.

1988

Record: 10–6, 1st in NFC East
Head Coach: Buddy Ryan

Date	W/L	Score	Opponent	Att.
9/04	W	41–14	@Tampa Bay	43,502
9/11	L	24–28	Cincinnati	43,502
9/19	L	10–17	@Washington	53,920
9/25	L	21–23	@Minnesota	56,012
10/02	W	32–23	Houston	64,692
10/10	W	24–13	NY Giants	63,736
10/16	L	3–19	@Cleveland	78,787
10/23	W	24–23	Dallas	66,309
10/30	L	24–27	Atlanta	60,091
11/06	W	30–24	LA Rams	65,624
11/13	W	27–26	@Pittsburgh	46,026
11/20	W	23–17ot	@NY Giants	43,621
11/27	W	31–21	Phoenix	57,918
12/04	L	19–20	Washington	65,947
12/10	W	23–17	@Phoenix	54,832
12/18	W	23–7	@Dallas	46,131

NFC Divisional Playoff

12/31	L	12–20	@Chicago	65,534

The Eagles record the best mark in the NFL (6–1) in the last seven weeks of the regular season en route to a 10–6 finish and the NFC Eastern Division title. In the playoffs, they lose the infamous "Fog Bowl" to the Chicago Bears, 20–12.

The Eagles lose three of their first four games, only defeating Tampa Bay, 41–14, in their opener by scoring their highest point total since a 52–10 win over St. Louis in 1981. Randall Cunningham throws two touchdown passes and runs for another as the Eagles intercept Vinnie Testaverde five times.

The Eagles beat Houston, 32–23, in Week 5, but lose Mike Quick for eight weeks after he suffers a fractured leg.

In the team's first "Monday Night Football" appearance since 1981, the Eagles put on a spectacular show while beating the New York Giants, 24–13. Cunningham sets season highs with 31 completions, 369 yards, and three touchdowns, one of them an 80-yarder to Cris Carter, who catches five passes for 162 yards.

In addition to a pair of victories over Phoenix, the Eagles nip Pittsburgh, 27–26, as Clyde Simmons blocks Gary Anderson's bid for his fifth field goal of the game, a 57-yard attempt on the final play.

The Eagles beat Dallas twice, battling back from a 20–0 deficit for a 24–23 win in the first game as Cunningham directs a 16-play, 85-yard drive for the winning touchdown, scored on a two-yard pass to Anthony Toney with four seconds left.

The Eagles defeat the Cowboys, 23–7, in the last regular-season game. Moments after the final gun sounds at Texas Stadium, the team learns it has won the division title as the Jets upset the Giants to knock them out of first place.

Cunningham sets a number of Eagles single-season passing records and leads the team in rushing for the second straight year. White leads the NFL in sacks with 18, and rookie tight end Keith Jackson sets an Eagles receiving record with 81 catches.

1989

Record: 11–5, 2nd in NFC East
Head Coach: Buddy Ryan

Date	W/L	Score	Opponent	Att.
9/10	W	31–7	Seattle	64,287
9/17	W	42–37	@Washington	53,493
9/24	L	28–38	San Francisco	66,042
10/02	L	13–27	@Chicago	66,625
10/08	W	21–19	NY Giants	65,688
10/15	W	17–5	@Phoenix	42,620
10/22	W	10–7	LA Raiders	64,019
10/29	W	28–24	@Denver	75,065
11/05	L	17–20	@San Diego	47,019
11/12	L	3–10	Washington	65,443
11/19	W	10–9	Minnesota	65,944
11/23	W	27–0	@Dallas	54,444
12/03	W	24–17	@NY Giants	74,809
12/10	W	20–10	Dallas	59,842
12/18	L	20–30	@New Orleans	59,218
12/24	W	31–14	Phoenix	43,287

NFC Wild Card

Date	W/L	Score	Opponent	Att.
12/31	L	7–21	LA Rams	57,869

Led by an aggressive defense that leads the NFL with 56 take-aways, 30 interceptions, and a club-record 62 quarterback sacks, the Eagles win 11 games. But they finish second to the New York Giants in the NFC East despite beating them twice during the regular season.

Randall Cunningham has another big year, highlighted by a 42–37 win in Washington in which he passes for a team-record 447 yards and five touchdowns, three of them to Keith Jackson, who catches the game winner late in the fourth quarter. Al Harris sets up that score by recovering a Gerald Riggs fumble and lateraling it to Wes Hopkins, who races 77 yards to the Redskins' four-yard line.

The Eagles hand the eventual AFC champion Denver Broncos their only home loss of the season, 28–24. William Frizzell recovers a muffed punt on Denver's 24-yard line late in the fourth quarter. Six plays later, Keith Byars scores his second touchdown for the game winner.

Byron Evans recovers a Herschel Walker fumble late in the game to set up a three-yard pass from Cunningham to Cris Carter, who outjumps a defender and makes a one-handed catch in the end zone to tie Minnesota, 9–9, with 2:32 remaining. Steve DeLine's extra point wins it.

The Eagles beat Dallas twice in three weeks with Carter catching a pair of touchdown passes in each game. The Eagles earn their first ever shutout of the Cowboys, 27–0, on Thanksgiving as ex–Eagle kicker Luis Zendejas claims Buddy Ryan put a bounty on him. Zendejas was flattened by rookie linebacker Jessie Small.

Two weeks later, the teams meet again, with the Eagles winning 20–10 and the Veterans Stadium crowd pelting Jimmy Johnson with snowballs.

In between the two Dallas games, the Eagles beat the New York Giants, 24–17, as Cunningham boots a 91-yard punt, the longest in Eagles history.

The Eagles clinch a Wild Card playoff spot by defeating Phoenix, 31–14, in the last regular-season game. Then hosting a playoff game at the Vet for the first time since 1981, the Eagles lose to the Los Angeles Rams, 21–7, in the Wild Card contest.

1990

Record: 10–6, 2nd in NFC East
Head Coach: Buddy Ryan

Date	W/L	Score	Opponent	Att.
9/09	L	20–27	@NY Giants	76,202
9/16	L	21–23	Phoenix	64,396
9/23	W	27–21	@LA Rams	63,644
9/30	L	23–24	Indianapolis	62,067
10/15	W	32–24	Minnesota	66,296
10/21	L	7–13	@Washington	53,567
10/28	W	21–20	@Dallas	62,605
11/04	W	48–20	New England	65,514
11/12	W	28–14	Washington	65,857
11/18	W	24–23	@Atlanta	53,755
11/25	W	31–13	NY Giants	66,706
12/02	L	23–30	@Buffalo	79,320
12/09	L	20–23ot	@Miami	67,034
12/16	W	31–0	Green Bay	65,627
12/23	W	17–3	Dallas	63,895
12/29	W	23–21	Phoenix	31,796

NFC Wild Card

Date	W/L	Score	Opponent	Att.
1/05	L	6–20	Washington	65,287

The Eagles lead the NFL in rushing (2,556 yards) and time of possession (33:19). They lead the NFC in scoring (396 points) and TD passes (34). The defense leads the NFL in stopping the run, making the Eagles the first team to lead the league in both rushing categories since the Chicago Bears did it in 1985.

Quarterback Randall Cunningham leads the NFC with 30 touchdown passes and leads the team with 942 rushing yards. Running back Keith Byars ties a team record with 81 pass receptions and also throws four touchdown passes.

The Eagles recover from a 1–3 start by defeating Minnesota 32–24 on a Monday night at the Vet. They force five turnovers, and finally go ahead on Anthony Toney's six-yard run in the fourth quarter. Seth Joyner sets it up by sacking Vikings quarterback Rich Gannon, forcing a fumble that is recovered by Clyde Simmons.

In another Monday night game, Heath Sherman runs for 124 yards, ties Steve Van Buren's club record of 35 carries, and scores a touchdown as the Eagles defeat Washington, 28–14. William Frizzell and Simmons score on interception and fumble returns, and six Redskins leave the game with injuries in what becomes known as "the body bag game."

Cunningham throws touchdown passes to Fred Barnett and Calvin Williams and scores, himself, as the Eagles upend the previously unbeaten New York Giants, 31–13. They clinch a wild card spot by blanking Green Bay, 31–0, as Byars scores twice in the club's first home shutout since 1981.

The Eagles finish 10–6 but suffer their third straight opening-round loss in the playoffs, this time to Washington, 20–6, in the Wild Card Game. Three days later, owner Norman Braman fires Buddy Ryan and promotes offensive coordinator Rich Kotite to head coach.

1991

Record: 10–6, 3rd in NFC East
Head Coach: Rich Kotite

Date	W/L	Score	Opponent	Att.
9/01	W	20–3	@Green Bay	58,991
9/08	L	10–26	Phoenix	63,818
9/15	W	24–0	@Dallas	62,656
9/22	W	23–14	Pittsburgh	65,511
9/30	L	0–23	@Washington	55,198
10/06	L	13–14	@Tampa Bay	41,219
10/13	L	6–13	New Orleans	64,224
10/27	L	7–23	San Francisco	65,796
11/04	W	30–7	NY Giants	65,816
11/10	W	32–30	@Cleveland	72,086
11/17	W	17–10	Cincinnati	63,189
11/24	W	34–14	@Phoenix	37,307
12/02	W	13–6	@Houston	62,141
12/08	W	19–14	@NY Giants	76,099
12/15	L	13–25	Dallas	65,854
12/22	W	24–22	Washington	58,988

The Eagles suffer a devastating setback in the opener, a 20–3 triumph at Green Bay, when quarterback Randall Cunningham sustains a knee injury and is lost for the season.

Backup quarterback Jim McMahon comes on and does well before being injured in Game 5, a 23–0 loss at Washington, the start of a four-game losing streak. By midseason, the Eagles have used five quarterbacks as their record falls to 3–5. They rebound to win six straight games, but a 25–13 loss to Dallas in Game 15 knocks them out of the playoff hunt.

However, the Eagles join San Francisco as the only NFL clubs to win ten games in the last four seasons. The defense leads the league in fewest yards allowed overall, against the run, and against the pass, making them the first club to lead in these three categories since the 1975 Minnesota Vikings.

The Eagles blank Dallas, 24–0, shutting down the Cowboys' offense, ranked No. 1 in the NFC, with a team-record 11 sacks. They permit just 90 yards of total offense, the fewest yards allowed by the Eagles in more than 30 years.

The Eagles record the third-best comeback in team history by battling back from a 23–0 deficit to edge the Browns in Cleveland, 32–30. The 1946 and 1959 teams overcame 24-point deficits. McMahon wins it with his third touchdown pass of the day, five yards to Fred Barnett. Eagles cornerback Ben Smith goes out for the season with a knee injury shortly after intercepting a pass that snapped Bernie Kosar's string of 309 throws without a turnover.

The Eagles beat Cincinnati, 17–10, with James Joseph scoring the go-ahead touchdown in the fourth quarter. They defeat Phoenix, 34–14, as the defense forces seven turnovers and scores twice on fumble returns by Seth Joyner and Clyde Simmons.

The Eagles' sixth straight win comes against Houston in a Monday night game, 13–6, with the defense recovering five fumbles. Quarterback Jeff Kemp relieves McMahon and throws a 21-yard touchdown pass to Keith Jackson.

The Eagles close the season by scoring 17 points in the fourth quarter to edge eventual Super Bowl champion Washington, 24–22.

1992

Record: 11–5, 2nd in NFC East
Head Coach: Rich Kotite

Date	W/L	Score	Opponent	Att.
9/06	W	15–13	New Orleans	65,513
9/13	W	31–14	@Phoenix	42,533
9/20	W	30–0	Denver	65,833
10/05	W	31–7	Dallas	66,572
10/11	L	17–24	@Kansas City	76,626
10/18	L	12–16	@Washington	56,380
10/25	W	7–3	Phoenix	64,676
11/01	L	10–20	@Dallas	65,012
11/08	W	31–10	LA Raiders	65,388
11/15	L	24–27	@Green Bay (Milwaukee)	52,689
11/22	W	47–34	@NY Giants	68,153
11/29	L	14–20	@San Francisco	64,374
12/06	W	28–17	Minnesota	65,280
12/13	W	20–17ot	@Seattle	47,492
12/20	W	17–13	Washington	65,841
12/27	W	20–10	NY Giants	64,266

NFC Wild Card

| 1/03 | W | 36–20 | @New Orleans | 68,893 |

NFC Divisional Playoff

| 1/10 | L | 10–34 | @Dallas | 63,721 |

The Eagles suffer a heartbreaking loss before the season when All-Pro defensive tackle Jerome Brown is killed in an automobile accident in his hometown of Brooksville, Florida, on June 25.

With quarterback Randall Cunningham returning from his knee injury and running back Herschel Walker joining the team as a free agent, the Eagles finish 11–5 and return to the playoffs where they defeat New Orleans in a wild card game, 36–20, before losing to Dallas, 34–10, in a divisional playoff.

Walker becomes the first Eagle to go over 1,000 rushing yards since Earnest Jackson did it in 1985.

The Eagles blank Denver's defending AFC West champions, 30–0, as Cunningham throws three touchdown passes. Calvin Williams and Fred Barnett become the first pair of Eagles receivers to go over 100 yards in receptions since Mike Quick and Harold Carmichael did it in 1983. Williams has five catches for 108 yards and two scores. Barnett catches five for 102 yards and one touchdown.

In a battle of unbeaten teams, the Eagles thrash Dallas, 31–7, in a Monday night game. Walker runs for two touchdowns as the Eagles take sole possession of first place in the NFC East.

The Eagles defeat the New York Giants twice. Heath Sherman rushes for 109 yards and Walker scores twice in a 47–34 win, the most points scored against the Giants since 1975. The combined 81 points is the most ever scored by the two teams.

Later, Walker runs for 104 yards as the Eagles close the season by beating the Giants, 20–10, making them the only NFL club with a perfect 8–0 home record. It is also the first time an Eagles team goes unbeaten at home since the 1949 NFL champions went 6–0 at Shibe Park.

Eric Allen preserves a 17–13 victory over Washington, clinching a playoff berth by knocking down a five-yard pass from Mark Rypien to Gary Clark in the end zone as time expires.

1993

Record: 8–8, 3rd in NFC East
Head Coach: Rich Kotite

Date	W/L	Score	Opponent	Att.
9/05	W	23–17	Phoenix	59,831
9/12	W	20–17	@Green Bay	59,061
9/19	W	34–31	Washington	65,435
10/03	W	35–30	@NY Jets	72,593
10/10	L	6–17	Chicago	63,601
10/17	L	10–21	@NY Giants	76,050
10/31	L	10–23	Dallas	61,912
11/07	L	3–16	@Phoenix	46,663
11/14	L	14–19	Miami	64,213
11/21	L	3–7	NY Giants	62,928
11/28	W	17–14	@Washington	46,663
12/06	L	17–23	@Dallas	64,521
12/12	L	7–10	Buffalo	60,769
12/19	W	20–10	@Indianapolis	44,952
12/26	W	37–26	New Orleans	50,085
1/03	W	37–34ot	@San Francisco	61,653

The Eagles lose Reggie White, their all-time sack leader, and tight end Keith Jackson to free agency. After jumping off to a 4–0 start, they suffer season-ending injuries to a number of players including quarterback Randall Cunningham and wide receiver Fred Barnett, lose six straight games, and finish with an 8–8 record.

With quarterback Bubby Brister triggering four wins down the stretch, the team remains in playoff contention until the final week of the season.

Rookie Vaughn Hebron rushes for 66 yards and scores the game-winning touchdown as the Eagles capture their third straight opening game, 23–17, over Phoenix.

The Eagles rally from a 17–7 third-quarter deficit to edge the Packers, in Green Bay, 20–17. Rookie wide receiver Victor Bailey catches the winning 40-yard touchdown pass from Cunningham, climaxing a 91-yard drive, with 4:14 left.

Calvin Williams has a career day with eight receptions for 181 yards and three touchdowns as the Eagles score 17 points in the fourth quarter for a 34–31 win over Washington. Williams tallies the 10-yard game winner with four seconds left.

The 35–30 win over the New York Jets is costly as Cunningham goes down with a fractured leg and Barnett goes out with torn knee ligaments. Brister comes in to throw two touchdown passes as the Eagles overcome a 28–21 deficit in the fourth quarter.

The Eagles snap their longest losing streak since 1983 by edging the Redskins in Washington, 17–14, on a two-yard touchdown pass from Brister to James Joseph.

The other wins come over Indianapolis, 20–10, and New Orleans, 37–26. The Eagles hold the Colts to 31 yards on the ground and beat the Saints when Eric Allen ties an NFL record by returning two interceptions for touchdowns.

1994

Record: 7–9, 4th in NFC East
Head Coach: Rich Kotite

Date	W/L	Score	Opponent	Att.
9/04	L	23–28	@NY Giants	76,130
9/12	W	30–22	Chicago	64,890
9/18	W	13–7	Green Bay	63,922
10/02	W	40–8	@San Francisco	64,843
10/09	W	21–17	Washington	63,947
10/16	L	13–24	@Dallas	64,703
10/24	W	21–6	Houston	65,233
10/30	W	31–29	@Washington	53,530
11/06	W	17–7	Arizona	64,952
11/13	L	7–26	Cleveland	65,233
11/20	L	6–12	@Arizona	62,779
11/27	L	21–28	@Atlanta	60,008
12/04	L	19–31	Dallas	65,974
12/11	L	3–14	@Pittsburgh	55,474
12/18	L	13–16	NY Giants	64,540
12/24	L	30–33	@Cincinnati	39,923

Jeffrey Lurie, a native of Boston and president of a Hollywood-based film production company, purchases the Eagles from Norman Braman. *The Wall Street Journal* reports that the total sale price is $198 million.

The Eagles lose their opener but bounce back to win seven of their next eight games. They drop their last seven contests, however, and miss the playoffs for the second straight year.

Running back Herschel Walker becomes the first player in the 75-year history of the NFL to record a 90-plus-yard run, pass reception, and kickoff return in the same season. Defensive end William Fuller, a free-agent acquisition from Houston, registers at least one sack in seven straight games, a club record.

The Eagles defeat the Chicago Bears, 30–22, in a Monday night game to give Lurie his first win as an owner. Randall Cunningham throws for 311 yards and three touchdowns, two of them to Calvin Williams.

The season highlight is a 40–8 win in San Francisco. It is the 49ers' worst defeat ever in Candlestick Park. Rookie Charlie Garner gains 111 yards on 16 carries and scores two touchdowns. Williams catches nine passes for 122 yards.

Garner rushes for 122 yards, making him the first Eagles rookie ever to go over the 100-yard mark in two straight games, as the Eagles clip Washington, 21–17, with Walker scoring the winning touchdown in the fourth quarter.

After a loss to Dallas, the Eagles bounce back to take three straight games—21–6 over Houston, 31–29 over Washington, and 17–7 over Arizona.

Cunningham highlights the Monday night game against the Oilers by throwing spectacular passes of 53 yards to Fred Barnett and 35 yards to James Joseph.

Eddie Murray's 30-yard field goal with 19 seconds left gives the Eagles their fifth straight win over Washington. It is also the fifth consecutive contest between the Eagles and Redskins that is decided in the final minute of play.

Cunningham and Barnett team up on scoring plays of 50 and 47 yards to defeat the Cardinals, 17–7, and spoil the return to Philadelphia of Arizona coach Buddy Ryan.

Two days after the end of the season, Rich Kotite is dismissed after four years as coach.

1995

Record: 10–6, 2nd in NFC East
Head Coach: Ray Rhodes

Date	W/L	Score	Opponent	Att.
9/03	L	6–21	Tampa Bay	66,266
9/10	W	31–19	@Arizona	45,004
9/17	L	21–27	San Diego	63,081
9/24	L	17–48	@Oakland	48,875
10/01	W	15–10	@New Orleans	43,938
10/08	W	37–34ot	Washington	65,498
10/15	W	17–14	@NY Giants	74,252
10/29	W	20–9	St. Louis	62,172
11/06	L	12–34	@Dallas	64,876
11/12	W	31–13	Denver	60,842
11/19	W	28–19	NY Giants	63,562
11/26	W	14–7	@Washington	50,539
12/03	L	14–26	@Seattle	39,893
12/10	W	20–17	Dallas	66,198
12/17	W	21–20	Arizona	62,076
12/24	L	14–20	@Chicago	52,391

NFC Wild Card

12/30	W	58–37	Detroit	66,492

NFC Divisional Playoff

1/07	L	11–30	@Dallas	64,371

First-year head coach Ray Rhodes overcomes a 1–3 start to lead the Eagles to a 10–6 finish and a return trip to the playoffs.

Running back Ricky Watters, a free-agent acquisition from the San Francisco 49ers, and Charlie Garner combine to give the Eagles a potent rushing attack. Watters finishes sixth in the league in rushing with a career-high 1,273 yards and 11 touchdowns.

Rodney Peete replaces Randall Cunningham as the starting quarterback and leads a 6–1 spurt at midseason.

Watters runs for two touchdowns, and Peete passes for 264 yards and one touchdown and scores another in a 31–13 win over Denver. Watters and Barnett each score twice, and the Eagles have a season-high eight sacks in a 28–19 win over the New York Giants.

The Eagles erase a 14-point deficit to avenge the earlier loss to Dallas, 20–17, and snap a seven-game losing streak against the Cowboys. Dallas coach Barry Switzer makes one of the most controversial calls in NFL history. Facing a fourth and inches at his own 29, Switzer elects to go for the first down instead of punting. The Eagles have to stop Emmitt Smith *twice* running off left guard for no gain because his first attempt is blown dead by the referee for the two-minute warning.

Gary Anderson boots what appears to be the winning 42-yard field goal. That play is waived off because the official has not given the signal for the play to start. Then Anderson nails it perfectly.

The Eagles clinch their first playoff berth since 1992 by overcoming a 17–0 deficit and nipping Arizona, 21–20.

In the Wild Card Game, the Eagles set a postseason scoring record with a 58–37 rout of Detroit. The next week they are beaten by the Cowboys in Dallas, 30–11.

1996

Record: 10–6, 2nd in NFC East
Head Coach: Ray Rhodes

Date	W/L	Score	Opponent	Att.
9/01	W	17–14	@Washington	53,415
9/09	L	13–39	@Green Bay	60,666
9/15	W	24–17	Detroit	66,007
9/22	W	33–18	@Atlanta	40,107
9/30	L	19–23	Dallas	67,201
10/13	W	19–10	@NY Giants	72,729
10/20	W	35–28	Miami	66,240
10/27	W	20–9	Carolina	65,982
11/03	W	31–21	@Dallas	64,952
11/10	L	17–24	Buffalo	66,613
11/17	L	21–26	Washington	66,834
11/24	L	30–36	@Arizona	36,175
12/01	W	24–0	NY Giants	51,468
12/05	L	10–37	@Indianapolis	52,689
12/14	W	21–20	@NY Jets	29,178
12/22	W	29–19	Arizona	63,658

NFC Wild Card

12/29	L	0–14	@San Francisco	56,460

The Eagles finish 10–6 again, and Ray Rhodes becomes the first coach ever to lead the team to the playoffs in each of his first two seasons.

The Eagles lose their starting quarterback to injuries for the third time in six years as Rodney Peete ruptures a tendon in his right knee during a 23–19 loss to Dallas. Ty Detmer takes over and leads the team to four consecutive victories.

Detmer teams up with wide receiver Irving Fryar and running back Ricky Watters to produce the NFC's top offense with 351.7 yards per game. Fryar catches a club-record 88 passes. Watters leads the league with 1,855 total yards from scrimmage.

The Eagles strengthen their secondary by signing veteran free-agent cornerback Troy Vincent from Miami. Defensive end William Fuller again leads the team with 13 sacks.

Detmer throws four touchdown passes to Fryar as the Eagles beat Miami, 35–28. Fryar catches eight passes for 116 yards against his former Dolphin teammates. Watters runs for a career-high 173 yards.

Detmer hits career highs with 38 attempts, 23 completions, and 342 yards in a 20–9 win over Carolina, in the first ever meeting between the two clubs.

The Eagles improve their record to 7–2 and tie Washington for the NFC East lead with a 31–21 win over Dallas. Fryar catches a career-high nine passes for 120 yards and one touchdown. Watters rushes for 116 yards and also scores a touchdown.

The Eagles blank the New York Giants, 24–0, for their first shutout since 1992. Detmer completes 25 of 33 attempts for 284 yards and three touchdowns in a driving rainstorm.

The Eagles win their final two games over the New York Jets, 21–20, and Arizona, 29–19. Gary Anderson kicks five field goals in the win over the Cardinals.

In the Wild Card playoff, the Eagles are blanked by San Francisco, 14–0.

1997

Record: 6–9–1, 3rd in NFC East
Head Coach: Ray Rhodes

Date	W/L	Score	Opponent	Att.
8/31	L	17–31	@NY Giants	70,296
9/07	W	10–9	Green Bay	66,803
9/15	L	20–21	@Dallas	63,942
9/28	L	19–28	@Minnesota	55,149
10/05	W	24–10	Washington	67,008
10/12	L	21–38	@Jacksonville	69,150
10/19	W	13–10ot	Arizona	66,860
10/26	W	13–12	Dallas	67,106
11/02	L	21–31	@Arizona	39,549
11/10	L	12–24	San Francisco	67,133
11/16	T	10–10ot	@Baltimore	63,546
11/23	W	23–20	Pittsburgh	67,166
11/30	W	44–42	Cincinnati	66,623
12/07	L	21–31	NY Giants	67,084
12/14	L	17–20	@Atlanta	42,866
12/21	L	32–35	@Washington	75,939

The Eagles are forced to start a total of 42 different players because of injuries and win only six games. Second-year quarterback Bobby Hoying replaces the previous starters, Ty Detmer and Rodney Peete. Irving Fryar sets a club record with six 100-yard receiving games. Running back Ricky Watters becomes the first Eagle go over the 1,000-yard rushing mark in three consecutive seasons.

The Eagles' best defensive effort of the season comes in the team's first win, 10–9, over Green Bay, when it holds the defending Super Bowl champions without a touchdown, snapping a string of 85 straight games in which the Packers have scored a touchdown.

One of the most devastating losses in franchise history occurs the following week on Monday night when the Eagles botch a seemingly automatic field goal with four seconds left in a 21–20 loss at Dallas. Tom Hutton, the holder, bobbles the snap from center Steve Everitt, and Chris Boniol never gets to attempt the 22-yarder that could have won the game.

The Eagles win back-to-back squeakers against Arizona, 13–10, in overtime, and Dallas, 13–12, as Peete replaces Detmer as the starting quarterback. Boniol wins the game against the Cardinals with a 24-yard field goal in overtime. Peete throws the winning touchdown pass to rookie Chad Lewis with 45 seconds left against Dallas.

Hoying throws two touchdown passes and picks up his first victory, 23–20, over Pittsburgh in his second career start. Boniol kicks three field goals, including the 25-yard game winner in the fourth quarter.

Boniol also kicks the deciding field goal, a 31-yarder on the final play of a wild 44–42 win over Cincinnati. Hoying has the best game of his career, completing 26 of 42 attempts for 313 yards and four touchdowns.

The Eagles drop their final three games, including a 35–32 heartbreaker at Washington, where they fall short despite a 15-point rally in the fourth quarter.

1998

Record: 3–13, 5th in NFC East
Head Coach: Ray Rhodes

Date	W/L	Score	Opponent	Att.
9/06	L	0–38	Seattle	66,418
9/13	L	12–17	@Atlanta	46,456
9/20	L	3–17	@Arizona	36,717
9/27	L	21–24	Kansas City	66,675
10/04	L	16–41	@Denver	73,218
10/11	W	17–12	Washington	66,183
10/18	L	10–13	@San Diego	56,967
11/02	L	0–34	Dallas	67,002
11/08	W	10–9	Detroit	66,785
11/15	L	3–28	@Washington	67,704
11/22	L	0–20	@NY Giants	65,763
11/29	L	16–24	@Green Bay	59,862
12/03	W	17–14	St. Louis	66,155
12/13	L	17–20ot	Arizona	62,176
12/20	L	9–13	@Dallas	62,722
12/27	L	10–20	NY Giants	66,596

A 38–0 loss to Seattle in the opener sets the tone for a 3–13 season. The 13 losses is a single-season record for the Eagles.

There are few highlights. Newly acquired defensive end Hugh Douglas ties a single-game club record with 4½ sacks in a 13–10 loss at San Diego.

Running back Duce Staley becomes the first Eagle draft choice to top the 1,000-yard rushing plateau since Wilbert Montgomery did it in 1981.

The Eagles' only victories come over Washington, 17–12; Detroit, 10–9; and St. Louis, 17–14.

In a battle of 0–5 teams, Peete directs the win over Washington by running 19 yards for one touchdown and passing three yards to Kaseem Sinceno for the other. Chris Boniol adds a 44-yard field goal.

Boniol's 39-yard field goal also provides the margin of victory over the Lions. Charlie Garner rushes for a career-high 129 yards and scores the only touchdown.

Koy Detmer, making only his second professional start, leads the Eagles to the win over St. Louis, spoiling the Philadelphia homecoming of Rams coach Dick Vermeil. Detmer throws two touchdown passes, and Boniol kicks a 50-yard field goal.

In August, Tommy McDonald, who starred for the Eagles as a flanker from 1957 through 1963, is inducted into the Pro Football Hall of Fame.

> *Bobby Hoying finished the 1998 season with zero touchdown passes and nine interceptions. His efficiency rating was 45.6, the lowest among all the NFL starting quarterbacks.*

1999

Record: 5–11, 5th in NFC East
Head Coach: Andy Reid

Date	W/L	Score	Opponent	Att.
9/12	L	24–25	Arizona	64,113
9/19	L	5–19	Tampa Bay	64,285
9/26	L	0–26	@Buffalo	70,872
10/03	L	15–16	@NY Giants	77,959
10/10	W	13–10	Dallas	66,669
10/17	W	20–16	@Chicago	66,944
10/24	L	13–16	@Miami	73,975
10/31	L	17–23ot	NY Giants	66,481
11/07	L	7–33	@Carolina	62,569
11/14	W	35–28	Washington	66,591
11/21	L	17–44	Indianapolis	65,521
11/28	L	17–20ot	@Washington	74,741
12/05	L	17–21	@Arizona	46,550
12/12	L	10–20	@Dallas	64,086
12/19	W	24–9	New England	65,475
1/02	W	38–31	St. Louis	60,700

Andy Reid succeeds Ray Rhodes as head coach. With 14 rookies on the roster, the Eagles finish with a 5–11 record.

Running back Duce Staley enjoys his second consecutive 1,000-yard rushing season and accounts for 41 percent of the team's offense, the best percentage in the NFL.

Defensively, the Eagles lead the NFL with 46 takeaways, including 28 interceptions, with a club-record five being returned for touchdowns. Troy Vincent ties for the league lead with seven interceptions and becomes the first Eagle since Bill Bradley in 1972 to lead the league in this category.

After an 0–5 start, Reid picks up his first win as coach when the Eagles beat Dallas, 13–10, at the Vet. Norm Johnson kicks 48- and 31-yard field goals, and quarterback Doug Pederson throws a 28-yard touchdown pass to wide receiver Charles Johnson to overcome a 10–0 deficit.

The Eagles win the following week in Chicago, defeating the Bears, 20–16, as Duce Staley rushes for 101 yards and Pederson throws touchdown passes to wide receiver Dietrich Jells and tight end Luther Broughton.

Rookie Donovan McNabb makes his first start in Week 10 and defeats Washington, 35–28. McNabb passes and runs for a pair of two-point conversions, scrambles for 49 yards, and completes eight of 21 passes for 60 yards. Allen Rossum returns one kickoff 89 yards for a touchdown and another 86 yards. He finishes the game with 222 yards on five returns, the third-best single-game effort in the club's history.

The Eagles end the season with surprising upset wins over New England, 24–9, and St. Louis, 38–31. McNabb misses the Patriots game with a sprained left knee, but returns for the final game against the Rams and records the first three-touchdown game of his career, throwing scoring passes to Torrance Small, Staley, and tight end Chad Lewis. Defensive end Mike Mamula recovers a fumble and intercepts a Kurt Warner pass, returning it 41 yards for his second career touchdown.

2000

Record: 11–5, 2nd in NFC East
Head Coach: Andy Reid

Date	W/L	Score	Opponent	Att.
9/03	W	41–14	@Dallas	62,872
9/10	L	18–33	NY Giants	65,530
9/17	L	3–6	@Green Bay	59,869
9/24	W	21–7	@New Orleans	64,900
10/01	W	38–10	Atlanta	65,424
10/08	L	14–17	Washington	65,491
10/15	W	33–14	@Arizona	38,293
10/22	W	13–9	Chicago	65,553
10/29	L	7–24	@NY Giants	78,087
11/05	W	16–13ot	Dallas	65,636
11/12	W	26–23ot	@Pittsburgh	56,702
11/19	W	34–9	Arizona	65,356
11/26	W	23–20	@Washington	83,284
12/03	L	13–15	Tennessee	65,639
12/10	W	35–24	@Cleveland	72,318
12/24	W	16–7	Cincinnati	64,902

NFC Wild Card

12/31	W	21–3	Tampa Bay	65,813

NFC Divisional Playoff

1/07	L	10–20	@NY Giants	78,765

Andy Reid receives a number of Coach of the Year awards for leading the Eagles to the greatest turnaround in the club's history. They win 11 of 16 games and finish second in the NFC East. They earn the top Wild Card spot in the NFC and defeat Tampa Bay, 21–3, before losing to the eventual NFC champion New York Giants, 20–10, in the divisional playoff.

Donovan McNabb receives considerable MVP support by accounting for 74.6 percent of the team's total net yards. He breaks the club's single-season records for most passing attempts (569) and completions (330). Chad Lewis leads all NFC tight ends with 69 receptions. Defensive tackle Corey Simon, a first-round draft choice, registers a rookie team record with 9 1/2 sacks.

The Eagles start the season with a perfectly executed onsides kick by David Akers in the 41–14 opening-game win at Dallas. The game-time temperature is 109 degrees and nearly 150 degrees on the Texas Stadium turf. Duce Staley runs for 201 yards and one touchdown, and becomes only the second Eagle in history to surpass the 200-yard rushing mark.

After dropping consecutive games to the New York Giants and Green Bay, the Eagles defeat New Orleans, 21–7, and Atlanta, 38–10. But Staley goes down for the season with a foot injury against the Falcons.

The Eagles thrash Arizona, 34–9, and move into sole possession of first place with an 8–4 record. The Eagles have not been in first place this late in the season since Week 13 of the 1989 campaign. McNabb throws for 217 yards and one touchdown and hits ten different receivers. The defense records eight sacks for the first time since 1996.

McNabb rushes for 125 yards in a 23–20 win over Washington, the most by an NFL quarterback since Chicago's Bobby Douglass ran for 127 yards in 1972. Akers wins the game with a 30-yard field goal.

The Eagles clinch a home wild card game by defeating Cincinnati, 16–7, in the season finale as Akers kicks three field goals to finish with 121 points, breaking the club's single-season record of 116, set by Paul McFadden.

2001

Record: 11–5, 1st in NFC East
Head Coach: Andy Reid

Date	W/L	Score	Opponent	Att.
9/09	L	17–20ot	St. Louis	66,243
9/23	W	27–3	@Seattle	62,826
9/30	W	40–18	Dallas	66,621
10/07	L	20–21	Arizona	66,360
10/22	W	10–9	@NY Giants	78,821
10/28	L	10–20	Oakland	65,342
11/04	W	21–7	@Arizona	33,430
11/11	W	48–17	Minnesota	65,638
11/18	W	36–3	@Dallas	63,204
11/25	L	3–13	Washington	65,666
11/29	W	23–10	@Kansas City	77,087
12/09	W	24–14	San Diego	65,438
12/16	W	20–6	@Washington	84,936
12/22	L	3–13	@San Francisco	68,124
12/30	W	24–21	NY Giants	65,885
1/06	W	17–13	@Tampa Bay	65,541

NFC Wild Card

1/12	W	31–9	Tampa Bay	65,847

NFC Divisional Playoff

1/19	W	33–19	@Chicago	66,944

NFC Championship

1/27	L	24–29	@St. Louis	66,502

The Eagles win eight of their last 10 regular-season games to capture their first NFC Eastern Division title since 1988 and make their first appearance in the NFC Championship Game since the 1980 season.

The team wins the Wild Card Game rematch with Tampa Bay, 31–9. In the divisional playoff, Donovan McNabb makes a successful homecoming to Chicago with a 33–19 win over the Bears. St. Louis then halts a late comeback to defeat the Eagles, 29–24, in the conference final.

The Eagles' 7–1 record on the road is the best in history as they allow a league-low 64 points away from home. David Akers breaks his own club record with 17 consecutive field goals.

McNabb throws for a career-high 25 touchdowns in the regular season and adds five more in the playoffs.

The Eagles take over first place in the NFC East with a 10–9 win over the New York Giants in Week 5. James Thrash scores the winning touchdown on an 18-yard pass from McNabb as the Eagles break a nine-game losing streak against the Giants.

Brian Mitchell returns the opening kickoff 94 yards for a touchdown to spark a 21–7 win at Arizona. It is the first time an Eagle returned an opening kickoff for a TD since Timmy Brown returned one 105 yards in 1961.

Duce Staley racks up 238 total yards from scrimmage, including a 44-yard touchdown run, to help the Eagles defeat Minnesota, 48–21, and record their highest regular-season point total since 1990.

The Eagles make one of their most dramatic finishes in their history to defeat the Giants, 24–21, and clinch their first NFC East title since 1988. Overcoming a 21–14 deficit with 2:43 left, McNabb mounts scoring drives of 67 and 54 yards that result in a seven-yard touchdown pass to Chad Lewis and a 35-yard field goal by Akers with seven seconds left.

2002

Record: 12–4, 1st in NFC East
Head Coach: Andy Reid

Date	W/L	Score	Opponent	Att.
9/08	L	24–27	@Tennessee	68,804
9/16	W	37–7	@Washington	84,982
9/22	W	44–13	Dallas	65,537
9/29	W	35–17	Houston	64,867
10/06	L	25–28	@Jacksonville	65,005
10/20	W	20–10	Tampa Bay	65,523
10/28	W	17–3	NY Giants	65,791
11/03	W	19–13	@Chicago	54,049
11/10	L	13–35	Indianapolis	65,660
11/17	W	38–14	Arizona	64,990
11/25	W	38–17	@San Francisco	67,919
12/01	W	10–3	St. Louis	65,552
12/08	W	27–20	@Seattle	59,862
12/15	W	34–21	Washington	65,615
12/21	W	27–3	@Dallas	63,209
12/28	L	7–10ot	@NYGiants	78,782

NFC Divisional Playoff

1/11	W	20–6	Atlanta	66,452

NFC Championship

1/19	L	10–27	Tampa Bay	66,713

The Eagles celebrate their 31st and final season at Veterans Stadium by setting a team record for points scored (415), tying the club record for regular-season wins (12), and sending an NFL-high 10 players to the Pro Bowl.

The team surprises everyone by winning five of six games without Donovan McNabb after the quarterback suffers a broken ankle during a Week 11 win over Arizona. McNabb returns for the playoffs and engineers a 20–6 win over Atlanta before the Eagles are shocked by Tampa Bay, 27–10, in the NFC title game.

Free safety Brian Dawkins becomes the first player in NFL history to record a sack, an interception, a touchdown catch, and a fumble recovery in the same game in leading the Eagles to a 35–17 victory in their first ever meeting with the Houston Texans.

In a rematch of the 2001 NFC Championship Game, Bobby Taylor returns an intercepted Kurt Warner pass 23 yards for the only touchdown in a 10–3 Eagles win over St. Louis.

A. J. Feeley, who takes over for the injured McNabb and Koy Detmer at quarterback, throws his first two touchdown passes in a 27–20 win in Seattle, with a 20-yarder to Todd Pinkston in the third period being the game winner.

In the final regular-season game ever at the Vet, Feeley throws for 220 yards and a pair of touchdowns as the Eagles defeat Washington, 34–21, and capture their second straight NFC title. Linebacker Carlos Emmons returns a fumble 44 yards for his first career TD.

Feeley wins his fourth game and throws for a career-high 253 yards as the Eagles dominate Dallas again, 27–3, for their 12th victory. Linebacker Shawn Barber returns an interception 80 yards for a touchdown.

The Eagles drop a 10–7 overtime heartbreaker in the regular-season finale to the New York Giants on Matt Bryant's 39-yard field goal, but still clinch home-field advantage in the playoffs after the New York Jets trounce the Green Bay Packers one day later.

2003

Record: 12–4, 1st in NFC East
Head Coach: Andy Reid

Date	W/L	Score	Opponent	Att.
9/08	L	0–17	Tampa Bay	67,772
9/14	L	10–31	New England	67,624
9/28	W	23–13	@Buffalo	73,305
10/05	W	27–25	Washington	67,792
10/12	L	21–23	@Dallas	63,648
10/19	W	14–10	@NY Giants	78,883
10/26	W	24–17	NY Jets	67,853
11/02	W	23–16	@Atlanta	70,064
11/10	W	17–14	@Green Bay	70,291
11/16	W	28–10	NY Giants	67,867
11/23	W	33–20	New Orleans	67,802
11/30	W	25–16	@Carolina	72,977
12/07	W	36–10	Dallas	69,773
12/15	W	34–27	@Miami	73,780
12/21	L	28–31ot	San Francisco	67,866
12/27	W	31–7	@Washington	76,766

NFC Divisional Playoff

1/11	W	20–17ot	Green Bay	67,707

NFC Championship

1/18	L	3–14	Carolina	67,862

The Eagles move to their new home, Lincoln Financial Field, and capture their third consecutive NFC East title and third straight trip to the NFC Championship Game. They defeat Green Bay in an overtime thriller, 20–17, in the divisional play-off, but again fall in the NFC title game, this time to the Carolina Panthers, 14–3.

The Eagles successfully employ a "three-headed" running attack comprised of Correll Buckhalter, Duce Staley, and Brian Westbrook. They combine to record 1,618 yards rushing, 2,465 total yards from scrimmage, and 29 touchdowns. Despite coughing up the ball eight times in their first two games, both home losses, the Eagles establish a club record for fewest turnovers in a season with 22. They also go six games without a giveaway, another franchise record.

The turning point of the season comes in Week 6. Trailing the New York Giants, 10–7, with no timeouts and only 1:34 remaining, Westbrook fields a wobbly, bouncing punt and returns it 84 yards down the sideline for the winning touchdown.

Three weeks later, Donovan McNabb leads a classic two-minute drill to defeat the Green Bay Packers on "Monday Night Football." McNabb leads an eight-play, 65-yard drive and throws the deciding eight-yard touchdown to Todd Pinkston with 32 seconds left.

McNabb and Westbrook team up to virtually knock the New York Giants out of contention, 28–10. McNabb throws for two touchdowns and completes 24 of 30 passing attempts, including his last 12 throws. Westbrook becomes the first Eagle to score three touchdowns since 1998 and piles up 108 total yards from scrimmage.

McNabb throws for a combined 718 yards and six touchdowns in the final three regular-season wins over Dallas, Miami, and Washington. He ties a career high by accounting for all four scores against Washington including a one-yard run.

2004

Record: 13–3, 1st in NFC East
Head Coach: Andy Reid

Date	W/L	Score	Opponent	Att.
9/12	W	31–17	NY Giants	67,532
9/20	W	27–16	Minnesota	67,676
9/26	W	30–13	@Detroit	62,472
10/03	W	19–9	@Chicago	61,894
10/17	W	30–8	Carolina	67,707
10/24	W	34–31	@Cleveland	73,394
10/31	W	15–10	Baltimore	67,715
11/07	L	3–27	@Pittsburgh	64,975
11/15	W	49–21	@Dallas	64,190
11/21	W	28–6	Washington	67,720
11/28	W	27–6	@NY Giants	78,830
12/05	W	47–17	Green Bay	67,723
12/12	W	17–14	@Washington	90,089
12/19	W	12–7	Dallas	67,723
12/27	L	7–20	@St. Louis	66,129
1/02	L	10–38	Cincinnati	67,074

NFC Divisional Playoff

1/16	W	27–14	Minnesota	67,722

NFC Championship

1/23	W	27–10	Atlanta	67,717

Super Bowl XXXIX (at Jacksonville)

2/06	L	21–24	New England	78,125

With Andy Reid surpassing Greasy Neale as the winningest coach in team history, the Eagles set a club record with 13 regular-season victories and finish with the best record in the conference for the third consecutive year.

The Eagles go on to defeat Minnesota and Atlanta in the playoffs for their first NFC Championship in 24 years. They appear in the Super Bowl for the first time since 1981 but lose to the defending champion New England Patriots, 24–21.

Wide receiver Terrell Owens provides the big-play dimension that the team had missed for years. He is tied for the NFL lead with 14 touchdowns when he suffers a severe high-ankle sprain and fractured fibula during a December 19 contest against Dallas. He makes an incredible recovery in time for the Super Bowl where he catches nine passes for 122 yards.

Free-agent addition Jevon Kearse, one of the league's most disruptive pass rushers, helps the defense finish second in the NFL in points allowed (16.3 per game) and sacks (47).

Donovan McNabb has another record-breaking season. He becomes the first player in NFL history to finish with more than 30 touchdown throws and fewer than 10 interceptions. He completes 24 consecutive passes over a span of two games for another NFL mark. He establishes franchise records by completing 64 percent of his passes for 3,875 yards, while throwing for 31 touchdowns and just eight interceptions for a career-high 104.7 QB rating.

Brian Westbrook makes the most of his first year as the Eagles' featured back by piling up 1,515 total yards from scrimmage, scoring nine touchdowns, and leading all NFL running backs with 73 receptions. David Akers sets a league record by booting 17 field goals of 40 yards or longer.

Appendix B

Stats, Records, All-Time Roster, and Draft

EAGLES ALL-TIME ROSTER

Name (Position), College	No.	Yrs. Eagle	Name (Position), College	No.	Yrs. Eagle
Abercrombie, Walter (RB), Baylor	32	1988	Baker, Tony (B), Iowa State	38	1971–72
Absher, Dick (LB), Maryland	53	1972	Baldinger, Brian (G), Duke	62	1992–93
Adams, Gary (DB), Arkansas	6	1969	Ballman, Gary (E), Michigan State	85	1967–72
Adams, Keith (LB), Clemson	57	2002–	Banas, Stephen (B), Notre Dame	NA	1935
Adams, Theo (G), Hawaii	61	1995	Banducci, Bruno (G), Stanford	63	1944–45
Agajanian, Ben (K), New Mexico	89	1945	Banta, Jack (B), Southern Cal	33	1941, 44–45
Akers, David (K), Louisville	2	1999–	Barber, Shawn (LB), Richmond	56	2002
Alexander, David (C), Tulsa	72	1987–94	Barker, Bryan (P), Santa Clara	4	1994
Alexander, Kermit (DB), UCLA	39	1972–73	Barlow, Corey (CB), Auburn	24	1992–94
Allen, Chuck (LB), Washington	54	1972	Barnes, Billy Ray (B), Wake Forest	33	1957–61
Allen, Eric (CB), Arizona State	21	1988–94	Barnes, Larry (FB), Tennessee State	38	1978–79
Allen, Ian (T), Purdue	79	2004	Barnes, Walter (Piggy) (G), LSU	74	1948–51
Allen, Jackie (DB), Baylor	21	1972	Barnett, Fred (WR), Arkansas State	86	1990–95
Allen, Kevin (T), Indiana	72	1985	Barnhardt, Dan (B), Centenary	NA	1934
Allert, Ty (LB), Texas	58	1987–89	Barni, Roy (B), U San Francisco	33	1954–55
Allison, Henry (G), San Diego State	65	1971–72	Barnum, Leonard (B), West Virginia Wesleyan	13	1940–42
Amerson, Glen (B), Texas Tech	46	1961	Barr, Stephen (WR), Pennsylvania	83	1965
Amundson, George (RB), Iowa State	38	1975	Bartholomew, Sam (B), Tennessee	27	1941
Anderson, Gary (K), Syracuse	1	1995–96	Bartlett, Doug (DT), Northern Illinois	95	1988
Andrews, Leroy (B), Pittsburg Teachers (KS)	NA	1934	Bartley, Ephesians (LB), Florida	50	1992
Andrews, Shawn (G), Arkansas	73	2004–	Bartrum, Mike (TE-LS), Marshall	88	2000–
*Angelo, Jim (G), Indiana (PA)	69	1987	Basca, Nick (B), Villanova	47	1941
Antwine, Houston (DT), Southern Illinois	75	1972	Bassi, Dick (G), Santa Clara	35	1940
Archer, Dave (QB), Iowa State	18	1991–92	Bassman, Herman (B), Ursinus	19, 29, 24	1936
Armour, Justin (WR), Stanford	86	1997	*Battaglia, Matt (LB), Louisville	52	1987
Armstrong, Harvey (DT), SMU	96	1982–84	Baughan, Maxie (LB), Georgia Tech	55	1960–65
Armstrong, Neill (E), Oklahoma A&M	80	1947–51	Bauman, Alfred (T), Northwestern	73	1947
Arnold, Jay (B), Texas	34	1937–40	Bausch, Frank (C), Kansas	55	1940–41
Arrington, Rick (QB), Tulsa	11	1970–73	Bavaro, Mark (TE), Notre Dame	84	1993–94
Aschbacher, Darrel (G), Oregon	50	1959	Bawel, Ed (Bibbles) (B), Evansville	20, 81	1952, 55–56
Asher, Jamie (TE), Louisville	84	1999	Baze, Winford (B), Texas Tech	26, 37	1937
Atkins, Steve (FB), Maryland	38	1981	Beach, Pat (TE), Washington State	83	1992
Auer, Howard (T), Michigan	24	1933	Beals, Shawn (WR-KR), Idaho State	81	1988
*Auer, Jim (DE), Georgia	97	1987	Beaver, Jim (G), Florida	65	1962
Autry, Darnell (RB), Northwestern	26, 24	1998, 2000	Beckles, Ian (G), Indiana	62	1997–98
*Ayers, Marvin (DE), Grambling	96	1987	Bednarik, Chuck (C-LB), Pennsylvania	60	1949–62
Bahr, Matt (K), Penn State	11	1993	Beisler, Randy (DE), Indiana	64, 80	1966–68
Bailey, David (DE), Oklahoma State	93	1990	Bell, Eddie (B), Pennsylvania	81	1955–58
*Bailey, Eric (TE), Kansas State	87	1987	Bell, Todd (LB), Ohio State	49, 52	1988–89
Bailey, Howard (T), Tennessee	20	1935	Bellamy, Mike (WR), Illinois	81	1990
Bailey, Tom (B), Florida State	31	1971–74	*Bellamy, Victor (CB), Syracuse	39	1987
Bailey, Victor (WR), Missouri	82	1993–94	*Bendross, Jesse (WR), Alabama	85	1987
Baisi, Albert (G), West Virginia	63	1947	Benson, Henry (G), Western Maryland	30, 39	1935
Baker, Jason (P), Iowa	6	2002	Berger, Mitch (P), Colorado	17	1994
Baker, John (E), North Carolina College	78	1962	Bergey, Bill (LB), Arkansas State	66	1974–80
Baker, Keith (WR), Texas Southern	80	1985	Berry, Dan (B), California	19	1967
Baker, Ron (G), Oklahoma State	63	1980–88	Berzinski, Willie (B), Wisconsin–La Crosse	33	1956
Baker, Sam (K), Oregon State	38	1964–69	Betterson, James (RB), North Carolina	34	1977–78
			Bielski, Dick (B), Maryland	36	1955–59
			Bieniemy, Eric (RB), Colorado	33	1999

*Replacement player during 1987 strike.

Name (Position), College	No.	Yrs. Eagle
Binotto, John (B), Duquesne	30	1942
Bishop, Blaine (SS), Ball State	24	2002
Bjorklund, Robert (C), Minnesota	50	1941
Black, Michael (T-G), Sacramento State	77	1986
Blackmore, Richard (CB), Mississippi State	27	1979–82
Blaine, Ed (G), Missouri	64	1963–66
Blake, Jeff (QB), East Carolina	11	2004
Bleamer, Jeff (T), Penn State	67	1975–76
Bleeker, Mel (B), Southern Cal	49	1944–46
Blue, Luther (WR), Iowa State	80	1980
Blye, Ron (RB), Notre Dame	33	1969
Boatswain, Harry (G-T), New Haven	69	1995, 97
Boedeker, William (B), DePaul	21	1950
Bogren, Vince (E), New Mexico	73	1944
*Bolden, Gary (DT), Southwestern Oklahoma	65	1987
Boniol, Chris (K), Louisiana Tech	18	1997–98
Booty, John (DB), TCU	42	1991–92
Boryla, Mike (QB), Stanford	10	1974–76
Bostic, James (RB), Auburn	27	1998–99
Bostic, Jason (CB), Georgia Tech	32	1999–2000
Bouggess, Lee (B), Louisville	46	1970–73
Bouie, Kevin (RB), Mississippi State	35, 33	1995–96
Bova, Tony (E), St. Francis	85	1943
*Bowman, Kevin (WR), San Jose State	83	1987
Boykin, Deral (S), Louisville	25	1996
Bradley, Bill (FS), Texas	28	1969–76
*Bradley, Carlos (LB), Wake Forest	59	1987
Bradley, Harold (G), Iowa	65	1958
Brady, Rickey (TE), Oklahoma	87	1995
Bredice, John (E), Boston U.	89	1956
Brennan, Leo (T), Holy Cross	70	1942
Brewer, John (B), Louisville	36	1952–53
Brian, William (T), Gonzaga	31	1935–36
Bridges, Jeremy (T-G), Southern Mississippi	74	2003
Brister, Bubby (QB), Northeast Louisiana	6	1993–94
Britt, Rankin (E), Texas A&M	18	1939
Brodnicki, Chuck (T), Temple	30	1934
Brooks, Barrett (T), Kansas State	76	1995–98
Brooks, Clifford (DB), Tennessee State	23	1975–76
Brooks, Tony (RB), Notre Dame	39	1992–93
Brookshier, Tom (B), Colorado	45, 40	1953, 56–61
Broughton, Luther (TE), Furman	49, 86, 88, 84	1997, 99–2000
Brown, Aaron (LB), Ohio State	90	1985
Brown, Bob (T), Nebraska	76	1964–68
Brown, Cedrick (CB), Washington	23	1987
*Brown, David (LB), Miami (OH)	56	1987
Brown, Deauntae (CB), Central State (OH)	35	1997
Brown, Fred (LB), Miami (FL)	55, 87	1967–69
Brown, Greg (DE), Kansas State	98	1981–86
Brown, Jerome (DT), Miami (FL)	99	1987–91
Brown, Na (WR), North Carolina	85	1999–2001
*Brown, Reggie (RB), Oregon	24	1987
Brown, Sheldon (CB), South Carolina	39, 24	2002–
Brown, Thomas (DE), Baylor	97	1980
Brown, Tim (B), Ball State	22	1960–67
Brown, Willie (FL), Southern Cal	23	1966
Brumm, Don (DE), Purdue	80	1970–71
Brunski, Andrew (C), Temple	62	1943
Brutley, Daryon (CB), Northern Iowa	31	2003
Bryant, Bill (CB), Grambling	25	1978
Brzezinski, Doug (G), Boston College	74	1999–2002
Buckhalter, Correll (RB), Nebraska	28	2001–
Budd, Frank (E), Villanova	20	1962
Bukant, Joe (B), Washington U. (St. Louis)	36	1938–40
Bulaich, Norm (RB), TCU	36	1973–74
Bull, Ron (B), Baylor	47	1971
Bunting, John (LB), North Carolina	95	1972–82
Burgess, Derrick (LB-DE), Mississippi	59, 56	2001–04
Burk, Adrian (B), Baylor	10	1951–56
Burke, Mark (DB), West Virginia	29	1976
Burks, Dialleo (WR), Eastern Kentucky	42, 89, 86	1996
Burnette, Tom (B), North Carolina	19	1938
Burnham, Lem (DE), US International	67	1977–80
Burnine, Hank (E), Missouri	84	1956–57

Name (Position), College	No.	Yrs. Eagle
Burroughs, Don (B), Colorado State	45	1960–64
Bushby, Thomas (B), Kansas State	45	1935
Buss, Art (T), Michigan State	45, 12	1936–37
Butler, Bob (G), Kentucky	53	1962
Butler, John (B), Tennessee	27	1943, 45
Byars, Keith (RB), Ohio State	42, 41	1986–92
Byrne, Bill (G), Boston College	66	1963
Cabrelli, Larry (E), Colgate	84	1941–47
Caesar, Ivan (LB), Boston College	53	1993
Caffey, Lee Roy (LB), Texas A&M	52	1963
Cagle, Jim (DT), Georgia	78	1974
Cahill, Dave (DT), Arizona State (Flagstaff)	58	1966
Caldwell, Mike (LB), Middle Tennessee State	56	1998–2001
Calhoun, Don (RB), Kansas State	30	1982
Calicchio, Lonny (K), Mississippi	17	1997
Calloway, Ernie (DT), Texas South	57, 77	1969–72
Campbell, Glenn (E), Emporia Teachers	29	1935
Campbell, Marion (T), Georgia	78	1956–61
Campbell, Stan (G), Iowa State	64	1959–61
Campbell, Tommy (DB), Iowa State	37	1976
Campfield, Billy (RB), Kansas	37	1978–82
Campion, Thomas (T), Southeast Louisiana	72	1947
Canale, Rocco (G), Boston College	73	1943–45
Carmichael, Harold (WR), Southern	17	1971–83
Carollo, Joe (T), Notre Dame	76	1969–70
Carpe, Joe (T), Millikin	NA	1933
Carpenter, Rob (WR), Syracuse	81	1995
Carr, Earl (RB), Florida	32	1979
Carr, Jim (B), Morris Harvey	21	1959–63
Carrioccio, Russ (G), Virginia	64	1955
Carroll, Terrence (S), Oregon State	33	2001
Carson, Carlos (WR), LSU	87	1989
Carter, Cris (WR), Ohio State	80	1987–89
Carter, Joe (E), Austin	31, 17	1933–40
Case, Pete (G), Georgia	67	1962–64
Cassady, Howard (B), Ohio State	41	1962
Castiglia, Jim (B), Georgetown	31	1941, 45–46
*Caterbone, Thomas (CB), Franklin & Marshall	49	1987
Catlin, Tom (LB), Oklahoma	63	1959
Cavanaugh, Matt (QB), Pittsburgh	6	1986–89
Caver, Quinton (LB), Arkansas	55	2001–02
Cemore, Tom (G), Creighton	61	1941
Ceppetelli, Gene (C), Villanova	54	1968–69
Chalenski, Mike (DL), UCLA	71	1993–95
Chapura, Dick (DT), Missouri	97	1990
Cheek, Louis (T), Texas A&M	75	1990
Cherry, Je'Rod (S), California	25	2000
Cherundolo, Chuck (C), Penn State	21	1940
Chesley, Al (LB), Pittsburgh	59	1979–82
Chesson, Wes (WR), Duke	21	1973–74
Christensen, Jeff (QB), Eastern Illinois	11	1984–85
Chuy, Don (G), Clemson	66	1969
Cifelli, Gus (T), Notre Dame	77	1954
Clark, Al (CB), Eastern Michigan	21	1976
Clark, Mike (K), Texas A&M	84	1963
Clark, Myers (B), Ohio State	28	1934
Clark, Willie (CB), Notre Dame	25	1997
Clarke, Ken (DT), Syracuse	71	1978–87
Clayton, Don (T), no college	NA	1936
*Clemons, Topper (RB), Wake Forest	27	1987
Cobb, Garry (LB), Southern Cal	50	1985–87
Cody, Bill (LB), Auburn	66	1972
Colavito, Rocky (LB), Wake Forest	58	1975
Cole, John (B), St. Joseph's	37	1938–40
Coleman, Al (DB), Tennessee State	8	1972
Coleman, Marco (DE), Georgia Tech	93	2003
Collie, Bruce (G), Texas–Arlington	69	1990–91
Colman, Wayne (LB), Temple	49	1968–69
Combs, William (E), Purdue	82	1942
Concannon, Jack (QB), Boston College	3	1964–66
Conjar, Larry (B), Notre Dame	25	1968
*Conlin, Ray (DT), Ohio State	91	1987
Conner, Darion (DE), Jackson State	93	1996–97
Conti, Enio (G), Bucknell	51	1941–45

Name (Position), College	No.	Yrs. Eagle
Conwell, Joe (T), North Carolina	79	1986–87
Cook, Leon (T), Northwestern	72	1942
Cook, Rashard (S), Southern Cal	42	1999–2002
Cooke, Ed (E), Maryland	86	1958
Cooper, Evan (DB-KR), Michigan	21	1984–87
Cooper, Louis (LB), Western Carolina	52	1993
Cooper, Richard (T), Tennessee	77	1996–98
Copeland, Russell (WR), Memphis State	86	1997–98
Cornish, Frank (C), UCLA	68	1995
Coston, Zed (C), Texas A&M	23	1939
Cothren, Paige (K), Mississippi	45	1959
Cowher, Bill (LB), North Carolina State	57	1983–84
Cowhig, Jerry (B), Notre Dame	36	1951
Crabb, Claude (B), Colorado	23	1964–65
Craft, Russ (B), Alabama	33	1946–53
Crafts, Jerry (T-G), Louisville	73, 66	1997–98
Crawford, Charles (RB), Oklahoma State	45	1986–87
Creech, Bob (LB), TCU	58	1971–72
Creswell, Smiley (DE), Michigan State	92	1985
Crews, Terry (LB), Western Michigan	54	1996
Cronin, Bill (E), Boston College	87	1965
Cross, Irv (DB), Northwestern	27	1961–65, 69
Crowe, Larry (RB), Texas Southern	47	1972
Crutchfield, Darrel (CB), Clemson	29	2001
Cuba, Paul (T), Pittsburgh	23, 21	1933–35
Culbreath, Jim (FB), Oklahoma	32	1980
Cullars, Willie (DE), Kansas State	75	1974
*Cumby, George (LB), Kentucky	91	1987
Cunningham, Dick (LB), Arkansas	51	1973
Cunningham, Randall (QB), UNLV	12	1985–95
Cuppoletti, Bree (G), Oregon	37	1939–40
Curcio, Mike (LB), Temple	57	1981–82
Curtis, Scott (LB), New Hampshire	91	1988
D'Agostino, Frank (G), Auburn	66	1956
Darby, Byron (DE), Southern Cal	94	1983–86
Darling, James (LB), Washington State	57	1997–2000
Darwin, Matt (C), Texas A&M	78	1986–90
Davis, Al (B), Tennessee State	43	1971–72
Davis, Antone (T), Tennessee	77, 78	1991–95
Davis, Bob (B), Kentucky	27	1942
Davis, Norm (G), Grambling	64	1970
Davis, Pernell (DT), Alabama–Birmingham	93	1999–2000
Davis, Stan (WB), Memphis State	81	1973
Davis, Sylvester (B), Geneva	16	1933
Davis, Vern (DB), Western Michigan	16	1971
Dawkins, Brian (FS), Clemson	20	1996–
Dawson, Dale (K), Eastern Kentucky	4	1988
Dean, Ted (B), Wichita	35	1960–63
DeLine, Steve (K), Colorado State	2	1989
Dellenbach, Jeff (G-C), Wisconsin	66	1999
DeLucca, Jerry (T), Middle Tennessee State	74	1959
Demas, George (G), Washington & Jefferson	27	1933
Dempsey, Jack (T), Bucknell	27	1934, 37
Dempsey, Tom (K), Palomar JC	19	1971–74
Dennard, Mark (C), Texas A&M	65	1984–85
Dent, Richard (DE), Tennessee State	95	1997
DeSantis, Dan (B), Niagara	49	1941
Detmer, Koy (QB), Colorado	10	1997–
Detmer, Ty (QB), BYU	14	1996–97
DeVaughn, Dennis (DB), Bishop	25	1982–83
Dial, Alan (DB), UCLA	24	1989
Dial, Benjy (B), Eastern New Mexico	4	1967
Diaz-Infante, David (G), San Jose State	63	1999
Dickerson, Kori (TE), Southern Cal	86	2003–
DiFilippo, Dave (G), Villanova	26, 69	1941
Dimmick, Tom (T), Houston	65	1956
Dimry, Charles (CB), UNLV	38	1997
Dingle, Nate (LB), Cincinnati	55	1995
DiRenzo, Danny (P), no college	82	1948
Dirks, Mike (G), Wyoming	62	1968–71
Disend, Leo (T), Albright	73	1943
Ditka, Mike (E), Pittsburgh	89, 98	1967–68
Dixon, Al (TE), Iowa State	86	1983
Dixon, Floyd (WR), Stephen F. Austin	84	1992

Name (Position), College	No.	Yrs. Eagle
Dixon, Ronnie (DT), Cincinnati	90	1995–96
Dixon, Zachary (RB), Temple	25	1980
Dobbins, Herb (T), San Diego State	67	1974
Dogins, Kevin (G-C), Texas A&M–Kingsville	73	2003
Dorow, Al (B), Michigan State	10	1957
Dorsey, Dean (K), Toronto	2	1988
Doss, Noble (B), Texas	45	1947–48
Douglas, Dameane (WR), California	82	1999–2002
Douglas, Hugh (DE), Central State (OH)	53	1998–2002, 04–
Douglas, Merrill (B), Utah	33	1962
Douglas, Otis (T), William & Mary	71	1946–49
Dow, Elwood (B), West Texas State	14	1938–40
Dowda, Harry (B), Wake Forest	44	1954–55
Doyle, Ted (T), Nebraska	72	1943
Drake, Joe (DT), Arizona	99	1985
Drake, Troy (T), Indiana	75	1995–97
Drummond, Robert (RB), Syracuse	36	1989–91
Duckworth, Bobby (WR), Arkansas	80	1986
Dudley, Paul (B), Arkansas	28	1963
Dumbauld, John (DE), Kentucky	93	1987–88
Duncan, Rick (K), Eastern Montana State	32	1968
Dunek, Ken (TE), Memphis State	86	1980
Dunn, Jason (TE), Eastern Kentucky	87	1996–98
Dunstan, Bill (DT), Utah State	61	1973–76
Durko, John (E), Albright	88	1944
Edwards, Anthony (WR), New Mexico Highlands	84	1989–90
Edwards, Herman (DB), San Diego State	46	1977–85
Ehlers, Tom (LB), Kentucky	59	1975–77
Eibner, John (T), Kentucky	76, 77	1941–42, 46
Eiden, Edmund (B), Scranton	71	1944
Elewonibi, Moe (T), BYU	65	1995
Ellis, Drew (T), TCU	35	1938–40
Ellis, Ray (S), Ohio State	24	1981–85
Ellstrom, Marvin (B), Oklahoma City	10	1934
Emanuel, Charles (S), West Virginia	47	1997
Emelianchik, Pete (E), Richmond	39	1967
Emmons, Carlos (LB), Arkansas State	51	2000–03
Emmons, Franklin (B), Oregon	44	1940
Ena, Justin (LB), BYU	95	2002–
Engles, Rick (P), Tulsa	13	1978
Enke, Fred (B), Arizona	17	1952
Ephraim, Alonzo (C), Alabama	50	2003–
Erdlitz, Richard (B), Northwestern	11, 30	1942, 45
Estes, Larry (DE), Alcorn A&M	81	1972
Evans, Byron (LB), Arizona	56	1987–94
Evans, Donald (DE), Winston-Salem State	77	1988
Evans, Mike (C), Boston College	59	1968–73
Everett, Eric (CB), Texas Tech	42	1988–89
Everett, Major (FB), Mississippi College	39	1983–85
Everitt, Steve (C), Michigan	61	1997–99
Fagioli, Carl (G), no college	77	1944
Farmer, Ray (LB), Duke	55	1996–98
Farragut, Ken (C), Mississippi	53	1951–54
*Fazio, Ron (TE), Maryland	87	1987
Feagles, Jeff (P), Miami (FL)	5	1990–93
Feather, E. E. (B), Kansas State	NA	1933
Feehery, Gerry (C-G), Syracuse	67	1983–87
Feeley, A. J. (QB), Oregon	14	2001–03
Felber, Fred (E), No Dakota	32	1933
Feller, Happy (K), Texas	1	1971
Fencl, Richard (E), Northwestern	29	1933
Ferko, John (G), West Chester	11, 19	1937–38
Ferrante, Jack (E), no college	83, 87	1941, 44–50
Ferrara, Frank (DE), Rhode Island	75	2003
Ferris, Neil (B), Loyola (CA)	27	1952
Fiedler, Bill (G), Pennsylvania	38	1938
Fiedler, Jay (QB), Dartmouth	11	1994–95
Field, Richard (G), no college	NA	1939–40
Finn, Mike (T), Arkansas–Pine Bluff	79	1994
Finneran, Brian (WR), Villanova	86	1999
Fitzgerald, Mickey (FB), Virginia Tech	38	1981
Fitzkee, Scott (WR), Penn State	81	1979–80
Flanigan, Jim (DT), Notre Dame	79	2003
Flores, Mike (DT), Louisville	95, 96	1991–94

Name (Position), College	No.	Yrs. Eagle
Floyd, Eric (G), Auburn	61	1992–93
Fogle, DeShawn (LB), Kansas State	54, 52	1997
Folsom, Steve (TE), Utah	86	1981
Fontenot, Chris (TE), McNeese State	85	1998
Ford, Charles (DB), Houston	32	1974
Ford, Fredric (CB), Mississippi Valley State	46	1997
Foules, Elbert (CB), Alcorn State	29	1983–87
Fox, Terry (B), Miami (FL)	36	1941, 45
Frahm, Herald (B), Nebraska	NA	1935
Fraley, Hank (C), Robert Morris	63	2000–
Frank, Joseph (T), Georgetown	61, 70	1941, 43
Franklin, Cleveland (RB), Baylor	30	1977–78
Franklin, Tony (K), Texas A&M	1	1979–83
Franks, Dennis (C), Michigan	53	1976–78
Frazier, Derrick (CB), Texas A&M	23	1993–95
Freeman, Antonio (WR), Virginia Tech	86	2002
Freeman, Bob (B), Auburn	41	1960–61
Frey, Glenn (B), Temple	32	1936–37
Friedlund, Bob (E), Michigan State	85	1946
Friedman, Bob (G), Washington	72	1944
Fritts, George (T), Clemson	71	1945
Fritz, Ralph (G), Michigan	63	1941
Fritzsche, Jim (T-G), Purdue	72	1983
Frizzell, William (S), North Carolina Central	33	1986–90, 92–93
Fryar, Irving (WR), Nebraska	80	1996–98
Fuller, Frank (T), Kentucky	72	1963
Fuller, James (S), Portland State	22	1996
Fuller, William (DE), North Carolina	95	1994–96
Gabbard, Steve (OT), Florida State	67	1989
Gabriel, Roman (B), North Carolina State	5, 18	1973–77
Gambold, Bob (B), Washington State	14	1953
Gaona, Bob (T), Wake Forest	64	1957
Gardner, Barry (LB), Northwestern	52	1999–2002
Garner, Charlie (RB), Tennessee	25, 30	1994–98
Garrity, Gregg (WR), Penn State	86	1984–89
Gary, Russell (DB), Nebraska	24, 38	1986
Gauer, Charles (E), Colgate	32, 85	1943–45
Gay, Blenda (DE), Fayetteville State	68	1975–76
George, Ed (T), Wake Forest	64	1976–78
George, Raymond (T), Southern Cal	23, 42	1940
Gerber, Elwood (G), Alabama	62	1941–42
*Gerhard, Chris (FS), East Stroudsburg	46	1987
Gerhart, Tom (DB), Ohio U.	25	1992
Gersbach, Carl (LB), West Chester	69	1970
Ghecas, Lou (B), Georgetown	11	1941
Giammona, Louie (RB), Utah State	33	1978–82
Giancanelli, Hal (Skippy) (B), Loyola (CA)	27	1953–56
Giannelli, Mario (G), Boston College	64	1948–51
Gibbs, Pat (DB), Lamar	45	1972
Gibron, Abe (G), Purdue	64	1956–57
Giddens, Frank (T), New Mexico	79	1981–82
Giddens, Herschel (T), Louisiana Tech	26	1938
Gilbert, Lewis (TE), Florida	86	1980
Giles, Jimmie (TE), Alcorn State	83	1987–89
Gill, Roger (B), Texas Tech	32	1964–65
Gilmore, Jim (T), Ohio State	75	1986
Ginney, Jerry (G), Santa Clara	31	1940
Glass, Glenn (B), Tennessee	49	1964–65
Gloden, Fred (B), Tulane	37	1941
Glover, Rich (DT), Nebraska	69	1975
Goebel, Brad (QB), Baylor	8	1991
Golden, Tim (LB), Florida	91	1985
Goldston, Ralph (B), Youngstown State	22	1952, 54–55
Golic, Mike (DT), Notre Dame	90	1987–92
Gollomb, Rudy (G), Carroll (WI)	14	1936
Gonya, Robert (T), Northwestern	27	1933–34
Goode, John (TE), Youngstown State	87	1985
Goode, Rob (B), Texas A&M	38	1955
Goodwin, Marvin (FS), UCLA	22	1994
Goodwin, Ron (E), Baylor	31, 81	1963–68
*Gorecki, Chuck (LB), Boston College	51	1987
Gossage, Gene (E), Northwestern	79	1960–62
Gouveia, Kurt (LB), BYU	54	1995
Graham, Dave (T), Virginia	78	1963–69

Name (Position), College	No.	Yrs. Eagle
Graham, Jeff (WR), Ohio State	81	1998
Graham, Lyle (C), Richmond	51	1941
Graham, Tom (G), Temple	NA	1935
Grant, Bud (E), Minnesota	86	1951–52
*Grant, Otis (WR), Michigan State	81	1987
Grasmanis, Paul (DT), Notre Dame	96	2000–
Graves, Ray (C), Tennessee	51, 52	1942–43, 46
Gray, Cecil (G-DT), North Carolina	71	1990–91
Gray, Jim (B), Toledo	28	1967
Gray, Mel (KR-RB), Purdue	28	1997
Green, Donnie (T), Purdue	74	1977
Green, Jamaal (DE), Miami (FL)	65	2003–
Green, John (E), Tulsa	89	1947–51
Green, Roy (WR), Henderson State	81	1991–92
Gregg, Kelly (DT), Oklahoma	94	1999–2000
Gregory, Ken (E), Whittier	80	1962
Griffin, Don (CB), Middle Tennessee State	28	1996
*Griffin, Jeff (CB), Utah	45	1987
Griggs, Anthony (LB), Ohio State	58	1982–85
*Grooms, Elois (DE), Tennessee Tech	98	1987
Gros, Earl (B), LSU	34	1964–66
Grossman, Burt (DE), Pittsburgh	69	1994
Gudd, Leonard (E), Temple	NA	1934
Gude, Henry (G), Vanderbilt	73	1946
Guglielmi, Ralph (QB), Notre Dame	17	1963
Guillory, Tony (LB), Lamar Tech	61	1969
Gunn, Mark (DL), Pittsburgh	96	1995–96
Gunnels, Riley (T), Georgia	74	1960–64
Hackney, Elmer (B), Kansas State	20	1940–41
Haddix, Michael (FB), Mississippi State	26	1983–88
Haden, Nick (G), Penn State	62	1986
Hager, Britt (LB), Texas	54	1989–94
Hairston, Carl (DE), Maryland Eastern Shore	78	1976–83
Hajek, Charles (C), Northwestern	8	1934
Hall, Irving (B), Brown	32	1942
Hall, Rhett (DT), California	97	1995–98
Hallstrom, Ron (G), Iowa	65	1993
Halverson, Bill (T), Oregon State	75	1942
Halverson, Dean (LB), Washington	56	1973–76
Hamilton, Ray (E), Arkansas	18, 42	1940
*Hamilton, Skip (DT), Southern	99	1987
Hamiter, Uhuru (DE), Delaware State	91	2000–01
Hamner, Thomas (RB), Minnesota	33	2000
Hampton, Dave (RB), Wyoming	34	1976
Hampton, William (CB), Murray State	41	2001
Hankton, Karl (WR), Trinity College (IL)	82	1998
Hansen, Roscoe (T), North Carolina	73	1951
Hanson, Homer (C), Kansas State	NA	1935
Hanson, Thomas (Swede) (B), Temple	14, 42	1933–37
*Harding, Greg (DB), Nicholls	28	1987
Harding, Roger (C), California	72	1947
Hardy, Andre (RB), St. Mary's (CA)	47	1984
Hargrove, Marvin (WR), Richmond	80	1990
Harmon, Andy (DT), Kent State	91	1991–97
Harper, Maurice (C), Austin	10	1937–40
Harrington, Perry (RB), Jackson State	35	1980–83
Harris, Al (LB), Arizona State	95	1989–90
Harris, Al (CB), Texas A&M–Kingsville	31	1998–2002
Harris, Jim (B), Oklahoma	20	1957
Harris, Jon (DE), Virginia	90	1997–98
Harris, Leroy (FB), Arkansas State	20	1979–82
Harris, Richard (DE), Grambling	84	1971–73
Harris, Rod (WR), Texas A&M	80	1990–91
Harris, Tim (DE), Memphis State	97	1993
Harrison, Bob (LB), Oklahoma	42	1962–63
Harrison, Dennis (DE), Vanderbilt	68	1978–84
Harrison, Granville (E), Mississippi State	80	1941
Harrison, Tyreo (LB), Notre Dame	54, 55	2002–
Hart, Clinton (S), Central Florida CC	33	2003–
Hart, Dick (G), no college	71	1967–71
Hartman, Fred (T), Rice	73	1948
Harvey, Richard (DB), Jackson State	41	1970
Haskins, Jon (LB), Stanford	52	1998
Hasselbeck, Tim (QB), Boston College	11	2002

Name (Position), College	No.	Yrs. Eagle
Hauck, Tim (SS), Montana	45	1999–2002
Hawkins, Ben (FL), Arizona State	18	1966–73
Hayden, Aaron (RB), Tennessee	33	1998
Hayden, Ken (C), Arkansas	50	1942
Hayes, Ed (DB), Morgan State	47	1970
Hayes, Joe (WR-KR), Central State (OK)	80	1984
Haymond, Alvin (B), Southern Univ	30	1968
Heath, Jo Jo (DB), Pittsburgh	29	1981
Hebron, Vaughn (RB), Virginia Tech	45, 20	1993–95
Heck, Ralph (LB), Colorado	43	1963–65
Hegamin, George (G-T), North Carolina State	69	1998
Heller, Ron (T), Penn State	73	1988–92
Henderson, Jerome (CB), Clemson	26	1995
Henderson, Zac (S), Oklahoma	24	1980
Hendrickson, Steve (LB), California	48	1995
Henry, Maurice (LB), Kansas State	53	1990
Henry, Wally (WR), UCLA	89	1977–82
Henson, Gary (E), Colorado	80	1963
Herrod, Jeff (LB), Mississippi	54	1997
Hershey, Kirk (E), Cornell	80	1941
Hertel, Rob (QB), Southern Cal	16	1980
Hewitt, Bill (E), Michigan	56, 82	1936–39, 43
Hicks, Artis (T), Memphis	77	2002–
Higgins, Tom (T), North Carolina	71	1954–55
Higgs, Mark (RB), Kentucky	22	1989
Hill, Fred (E), Southern Cal	86	1965–71
Hill, King (B), Rice	10	1961–68
Hinkle, Jack (B), Syracuse	43	1941–47
Hix, Billy (E), Arkansas	85	1950
Hoage, Terry (S), Georgia	34	1986–90
Hoague, Joe (B), Colgate	13, 36	1943
Hobbs, Bill (LB), Texas A&M	56	1969–71
Hogan, Mike (FB), Tennessee–Chattanooga	30, 35	1976–78, 80
Holcomb, William (T), Texas Tech	NA	1937
Holly, Bob (QB), Princeton	12	1984
Holmes, Lester (G), Jackson State	73	1993–96
Hood, Roderick (CB), Auburn	29	2003–
Hooks, Alvin (WR), Cal–Northridge	80	1981
Hoover, Mel (WR), Arizona State	85	1982–84
Hopkins, Wes (FS), SMU	48	1983–93
Horan, Mike (P), Long Beach State	2	1984–85
Hord, Roy (G), Duke	64	1962
*Horn, Marty (QB), Lehigh	14	1987
Horrell, Bill (G), Michigan State	62	1952
Hoss, Clark (TE), Oregon	80	1972
Howard, Bob (CB), San Diego State	23	1978–79
Howell, Lane (T), Grambling	79	1965–69
Hoyem, Lynn (G), Long Beach State	63	1964–67
Hoying, Bobby (QB), Ohio State	7	1996–98
Hrabetin, Frank (T), Loyola (CA)	71	1942
Huarte, John (QB), Notre Dame	7	1968
Hudson, Bob (B), Clemson	42, 88	1953–55, 57–58
Hudson, John (G), Auburn	66	1991–95
Hughes, Chuck (FL), Texas–El Paso	13	1967–69
Hughes, William (C), Texas	15, 29	1937–40
Hultz, Don (DT), Southern Mississippi	83	1964–73
Humbert, Dick (E), Richmond	81	1941, 45–49
Humphrey, Claude (DE), Tennessee State	87	1979–81
Hunt, Calvin (C), Baylor	54	1970
Hunter, Herman (RB-KR), Tennessee State	36	1985
Huth, Gerry (G), Wake Forest	54, 65	1959–60
Hutton, Tom (P), Tennessee	4	1995–98
Huxhold, Ken (G), Wisconsin	63	1954–58
Huzvar, John (B), North Carolina State	38	1952
Ignatius, James (G), Holy Cross	NA	1935
Illman, Ed (B), Montana	NA	1933
Ingram, Mark (WR), Michigan State	85	1996
Irvin, Willie (B), Florida A&M	81	1953
Jackson, Al (CB), Georgia	26	1994
Jackson, Bob (B), Alabama	28	1960
Jackson, Don (B), North Carolina	10, 50	1936
Jackson, Earnest (RB), Texas A&M	41	1985–86
Jackson, Greg (FS), LSU	47	1994–95
Jackson, Harold (WR), Jackson State	29	1969–72

Name (Position), College	No.	Yrs. Eagle
Jackson, Jamaal (G-C), Delaware State	67	2003–
Jackson, Johnny (DE), Southern	62	1977
Jackson, Keith (TE), Oklahoma	88	1988–91
Jackson, Kenny (WR), Penn State	81, 83, 84	1984–88, 90–91
Jackson, Randy (RB), Wichita State	33	1974
Jackson, Trenton (FL), Illinois	27	1966
*Jacobs, David (K), Syracuse	4	1987
Jacobs, Proverb (T), California	67	1958
*James, Angelo (CB), Sacramento State	42	1987
James, Ronald (Po) (RB), New Mexico State	27, 33	1972–75
Janet, Ernie (T), Washington	64	1975
Jarmoluk, Mike (T), Temple	78	1949–55
Jarvi, Toimi (B), Northern Illinois State	32	1944
Jasper, Edward (DT), Texas A&M	74	1997–98
Jaworski, Ron (QB), Youngstown State	7	1977–86
Jefferson, Greg (DE), Central Florida	79	1995–2000
Jefferson, William (B), Mississippi State	43	1942
Jelesky, Tom (T), Purdue	77	1985–86
Jells, Dietrich (WR), Pittsburgh	83	1998–99
Jenkins, Izel (CB), North Carolina State	46	1988–92
Jeter, Tommy (DT), Texas	98	1992–95
Jiles, Dwayne (LB), Texas Tech	53	1985–89
Johansson, Ove (K), Abilene Christian	10	1977
Johnson, Albert (B), Kentucky	44	1942
Johnson, Alonzo (LB), Florida	54	1986–87
Johnson, Alvin (B), Hardin-Simmons	27	1948
Johnson, Bill (DT), Michigan State	94	1998–99
Johnson, Charles (WR), Colorado	81	1999–2000
Johnson, Charlie (MG), Colorado	65	1977–81
*Johnson, Chris (DB), Millersville	30	1987
Johnson, Dirk (P), Northern Colorado	8	2003–
Johnson, Don (B), California	40	1953–55
Johnson, Dwight (DE), Baylor	62	2000
Johnson, Eric (DB), Washington State	49	1977–78
Johnson, Gene (B), Cincinnati	27	1959–60
Johnson, Jay (LB), East Texas State	48	1969
Johnson, Jimmie (TE), Howard	88	1995–98
Johnson, Kevin (DT), Texas Southern	94	1995–96
Johnson, Lee (P), BYU	6	2002
Johnson, Maurice (TE), Temple	87	1991–94
Johnson, Norm (K), UCLA	9	1999
Johnson, Reggie (TE), Florida State	80	1995
Johnson, Ron (DE), Shippensburg	62	2003–
Johnson, Ron (WR), Long Beach State	85	1985–89
Johnson, Vaughan (LB), North Carolina State	52	1994
Jonas, Don (B), Penn State	33	1962
Jones, Chris T. (WR), Miami (FL)	82	1995–97
Jones, Dhani (LB), Michigan	55	2004–
Jones, Don (B), Washington	22	1940
Jones, Harry (B), Arkansas	23	1967–71
Jones, Jimmie (DT-DE), Miami (FL)	98	1997
Jones, Joe (DE), Tennessee State	64	1974–75
Jones, Julian (S), Missouri	27	2001–02
Jones, Preston (QB), Georgia	8	1993
Jones, Ray (DB), Southern	21	1970
Jones, Spike (P), Georgia	6	1975–77
Jones, Tyrone (DB), Arkansas State	31	1989
Jordan, Andrew (TE), Western Carolina	49	1998
Jorgenson, Carl (T), St. Mary's	42	1935
Joseph, James (RB), Auburn	32	1991–94
Joyner, Seth (LB), Texas–El Paso	59	1986–93
Jurgensen, Sonny (QB), Duke	9	1957–63
Kab, Vyto (TE), Penn State	84	1982–85
Kalu, N. D. (DE), Rice	53, 94	1997, 2001–
Kane, Carl (B), St Louis	36	1936
Kapele, John (T), BYU	77	1962
Kaplan, Bennie (G), Western Maryland	77	1942
Karnofsky, Sonny (B), Arizona	40	1945
Kasky, Ed (T), Villanova	73	1942
Kaufusi, Steve (DE), BYU	94	1989–90
Kavel, George (B), Carnegie Tech	NA	1934
Kearse, Jevon (DE), Florida	93	2004–
Keeling, Ray (T), Texas	28	1938–39
Keen, Allen (B), Arkansas	24	1937–38

Name (Position), College	No.	Yrs. Eagle
Kekeris, Jim (T), Missouri	77	1947
Keller, Ken (B), North Carolina	23	1956–57
Kelley, Bob (C), West Texas State	50	1955–56
Kelley, Dwight (Ike) (LB), Ohio State	51	1966–72
Kelly, Jim (E), Notre Dame	84	1965–67
Kelly, Joe (LB), Washington	56	1996
Kemp, Jeff (QB), Dartmouth	16	1991
Kenneally, George (E), St. Bonaventure	13	1933–35
Kenney, Steve (G), Clemson	73	1980–85
Kersey, Merritt (P), West Chester State	37	1974–75
Key, Wade (G-T), Southwest Texas State	72	1970–80
Keyes, Leroy (DB), Purdue	20	1969–72
Keys, Howard (T-C), Oklahoma State	61	1960–64
Khayat, Ed (DT), Tulane	73	1958–61, 64–65
Kilroy, Frank (Bucko) (T), Temple	76	1943–55
Kimmel, Jon (LB), Colgate	54	1985
Kinder, Randy (CB), Notre Dame	43	1997
King, Don (T), Kentucky	71	1956
*Kirchbaum, Kelly (LB), Kentucky	54	1987
Kirkland, Levon (LB), Clemson	93	2002
Kirkman, Roger (B), Washington & Jefferson	19, 3	1933–35
Kirksey, Roy (G), Maryland Eastern Shore	65, 66	1973–74
Kish, Ben (B), Pittsburgh	44	1942–49
Klingel, John (DE), Eastern Kentucky	97	1987–88
Klopenburg, Harry (T), Fordham	28	1936
Kmetovic, Pete (B), Stanford	27	1946
Knapper, Joe (B), Ottawa (KS)	11, 24	1934
Knox, Charles (T), St. Edmonds	29	1937
Koeninger, Art (C), Tennessee–Chattanooga	30	1933
Kolberg, Elmer (B), Oregon State	16, 22	1939–40
Koman, Bill (LB), North Carolina	68	1957–58
Konecny, Mark (RB-PR), Alma	35	1988
Konopka, John (B), Temple	15	1936
Kostos, Anthony (E), Bucknell	NA	1933
Kowalczyk, Walt (B), Michigan State	43	1958–59
Kowalkowski, Scott (LB), Notre Dame	57	1991–93
Kramer, Kent (E), Minnesota	87	1971–74
Kraynak, Rich (LB), Pittsburgh	52	1983–86
Krepfle, Keith (TE), Iowa State	84	1975–81
Kresky, Joseph (G), Wisconsin	26, 5	1933–35
Krieger, Robert (E), Dartmouth	82, 89	1941, 46
Kriel, Emmet (G), Baylor	25	1939
Kuczynski, Bert (E), Pennsylvania	80	1946
*Kullman, Mike (SS), Kutztown State	35	1987
Kupcinet, Irv (B), North Dakota	31	1935
Kusko, John (B), Temple	16, 21	1936–38
Laack, Galen (G), College of Pacific	64	1958
Labinjo, Mike (LB), Michigan State	59	2004–
Lachman, Dick (B), no college	24	1933–35
Lainhart, Porter (B), Washington State	18	1933
Landeta, Sean (P), Towson State	7	1999–2002
Landsberg, Mort (B), Cornell	30	1941
Landsee, Bob (G-C), Wisconsin	65	1986–87
Lang, Israel (B), Tennessee State	29	1964–68
Lankas, James (B), St. Mary's (TX)	43	1942
Lansford, Buck (T), Texas	79	1955–57
Lapham, Bill (C), Iowa	54	1960
Larson, Bill (TE), Colorado State	88	1978
Latimer, Al (CB), Clemson	29	1979
Laux, Ted (B), St. Joseph's	15, 27	1942–44
Lavender, Joe (DB), San Diego State	30	1973–75
Lavergne, Damian (T), Louisiana Tech	68	2003–
Lavette, Robert (RB-KR), Georgia Tech	22	1987
Lawrence, Kent (WR), Georgia	12	1969
Lawrence, Reggie (WR), North Carolina State	80	1993
Lazetich, Pete (DT), Stanford	73	1976–77
Leathers, Milton (G), Georgia	27	1933
Le Bel, Harper (TE), Colorado State	87	1990
Lechthaler, Roy (G), Lebanon Valley	34	1933
Ledbetter, Toy (B), Oklahoma A&M	25	1950, 53–55
Lee, Amp (RB), Florida State	28	2000
Lee, Bernie (B), Villanova	11	1938
*Lee, Byron (LB), Ohio State	58	1986–87
*Leggett, Scott (G), Central State (OH)	75	1987

Name (Position), College	No.	Yrs. Eagle
LeJeune, Norman (S), LSU	27	2003
LeMaster, Frank (LB), Kentucky	55	1974–83
Leonard, Jim (B), Notre Dame	19	1934–37
Leshinski, Ron (TE), Army	89	1999
Levanites, Stephen (T), Boston College	72	1942
Levens, Dorsey (RB), Georgia Tech	25	2002, 04
Lewis, Chad (TE), BYU	89	1997–
Lewis, Greg (WR), Illinois	83	2003–
Lewis, Joe (T), Compton	71	1962
Lewis, Michael (S), Colorado	32	2002–
Leyendecker, Charles (T), Vanderbilt	35	1933
Lilly, Sammy (DB), Georgia Tech	37	1989–90
Lince, Dave (E), North Dakota	87	1966–67
Lindskog, Vic (C), Stanford	52	1944–51
Lio, Augie (G), Georgetown	62	1946
Lipski, John (C), Temple	20	1933–34
Liske, Pete (QB), Penn State	14	1971–72
*Liter, Greg (DE), Iowa	99	1987
Little, Dave (TE), Middle Tennessee State	89	1985–89
Lloyd, Dave (LB), Georgia	52	1963–70
Lofton, James (WR), Stanford	80	1993
Logan, Randy (S), Michigan	41	1973–83
*Long, Matt (C), San Diego State	61	1987
Looney, Don (E), TCU	30	1940
Lou, Ron (C), Arizona State	30, 51	1975
Louderback, Tom (LB), San Jose State	61	1958–59
Love, Clarence (CB), Toledo	28	1998
Love, Sean (G), Penn State	64	1997
Lucas, Dick (E), Boston College	87	1960–63
Lueck, Bill (G), Arizona	62	1975
Luft, Don (E), Indiana	89	1954
Luken, Tom (G), Purdue	63	1972–78
Lusk, Herb (RB), Long Beach State	32	1976–78
MacAfee, Ken (E), Alabama	80	1959
MacDowell, Jay (E), Washington	85, 88	1946–51
MacMurdo, Jim (T), Pittsburgh	6, 20	1934–37
Macioszczyk, Art (B), Western Michigan	31	1944–47
Mack, Bill (Red) (FL), Notre Dame	25	1964
Mackey, Kyle (QB), East Texas State	11	1986
Mackrides, Bill (B), Nevada	39	1947–51
Magee, John (G), Rice	67	1948–55
Mahalic, Drew (LB), Notre Dame	54	1976–78
Mahe, Reno (RB-KR), BYU	34	2003–
Mallory, John (B), West Virginia	47	1968
Malone, Art (RB), Arizona State	26	1975–76
Mamula, Mike (DE), Boston College	59	1995–2000
Mandarino, Mike (G), La Salle	62	1944–45
Manning, Roosevelt (DT), N.E. Oklahoma	65	1975
Mansfield, Ray (C), Washington	77	1963
Mansfield, Von (DB), Wisconsin	45	1982
Manske, Ed (E), Northwestern	36, 11	1935–36
Manton, Taldon (B), TCU	33	1940
Manzini, Baptiste (C), St. Vincent's	50, 66	1944–45, 48
Marchi, Basilio (C), NYU	55	1941–42
Marcus, Alex (E), Temple	20	1933
Mark, Greg (DE), Miami (FL)	91	1990
Maronic, Duke (G), no college	61	1944–50
Marshall, Anthony (SS), LSU	35	1998
Marshall, Larry (KR), Maryland	22	1974–77
Marshall, Whit (LB), Georgia	58	1996
Martin, Aaron (DB), North Carolina College	42	1966–67
Martin, Cecil (FB), Wisconsin	38	1999–2002
Martin, Kelvin (WR), Boston College	84	1995
Martin, Steve (DT), Missouri	73, 91	1998–99
Mass, Wayne (T), Clemson	78	1972
Masters, Bob (B), Baylor	30, 31, 33	1937–38, 41–43
Masters, Walt (B), Pennsylvania	53	1936
Matesic, Ed (B), Pittsburgh	12	1934–35
Matson, Ollie (B), San Francisco	33	1964–66
Mavraides, Menil (G), Notre Dame	64, 65	1954, 1957
May, Dean (QB), Louisville	5	1984
Mayberry, Jermane (G-T), Texas A&M–Kingsville	71	1996–2004
Mayes, Rufus (T), Ohio State	77	1979
Maynard, Les (B), Rider	21	1933

Name (Position), College	No.	Yrs. Eagle
Mazzanti, Jerry (DE), Arkansas	62	1963
McAfee, Wesley (B), Duke	40	1941
McAlister, James (RB), UCLA	43	1975–76
McChesney, Bob (E), Hardin-Simmons	86	1950
McClellan, Mike (B), Oklahoma	23	1962–63
McCloskey, Mike (TE), Penn State	84	1987
McCoo, Eric (RB), Penn State	22	2004–
McCrary, Fred (FB), Mississippi State	41	1995
McCullough, Hugh (B), Oklahoma	NA	1943
McCusker, Jim (T), Pittsburgh	75	1959–62
McDonald, Don (E), Oklahoma	81	1944–45
McDonald, Lester (E), Nebraska	76, 26	1940
McDonald, Tommy (FL), Oklahoma	25	1957–63
McDonough, Robert (G), Duke	64	1942–46
McDougle, Jerome (DE), Miami (FL)	95	2003–
McFadden, Paul (K), Youngstown State	8	1984–87
McHale, Tom (G-T), Cornell	68	1993–94
McHugh, Pat (B), Georgia Tech	49	1947–51
McIntyre, Guy (G), Georgia	62	1995–96
McKeever, Marlin (LB), USC	85	1973
McKenzie, Kevin (WR), Washington State	88	1998
McKenzie, Raleigh (C), Tennessee	63	1995–96
McKnight, Dennis (G), Drake	62	1991
McMahon, Jim (QB), BYU	9	1990–92
McMillan, Erik (S), Missouri	43	1993
*McMillen, Dan (DE), Colorado	94	1987
McMillian, Mark (DB), Alabama	29	1992–95
McMullen, Billy (WR), Virginia	81	2003–
McNeill, Tom (P), Stephen F. Austin	12, 36	1971–73
McNabb, Dexter (FB), Florida	38	1995
McNabb, Donovan (QB), Syracuse	5	1999–
McPherson, Don (QB), Syracuse	9	1988–90
McPherson, Forest (T), Nebraska	26, 35	1935–37
McRae, Jerrold (WR), Tennessee State	82	1979
McTyer, Tim (CB), BYU	24	1997–98
Meadows, Ed (E), Duke	66	1958
Medved, Ron (DB), Washington	45	1966–70
Mellekas, John (T), Arizona	65	1963
Mercer, Giradie (DT), Marshall	61	2000
*Merkens, Guido (QB), Sam Houston State	19	1987
Meyer, Fred (E), Stanford	80, 89	1942, 45
Meyers, John (T), Washington	75	1964–67
Miano, Rich (DB), Hawaii	38	1991–94
Michaels, Ed (G), Villanova	60	1943–46
Michel, Mike (P-K), Stanford	2	1978
Michels, John (T), Southern Cal	75	1999
Michels, John (G), Tennessee	61	1953
Middlebrook, Oren (WR), Arkansas State	81	1978
Mike-Mayer, Nick (K), Temple	1	1977–78
Mikell, Quintin (S), Boise State	46	2003–
Millard, Keith (DT), Washington State	77	1993
Miller, Bubba (C-G), Tennessee	65	1996–2001
Miller, Don (B), SMU	46	1954
Miller, Tom (E), Hampden-Sydney	89	1942–44
Milling, Al (G), Richmond	51	1942
Milon, Barnes (G), Austin	30	1934
Milons, Freddie (WR), Alabama	85	2002
Mira, George (QB), Miami (FL)	10	1969
Miraldi, Dean (T), Utah	64	1982–84
Mitcham, Gene (E), Arizona State	80	1958
Mitchell, Brian (RB-KR), S.W. Louisiana	30	2000–02
Mitchell, Freddie (WR), UCLA	84	2001–04
Mitchell, Leonard (DE-T), Houston	74, 99	1981–86
Mitchell, Martin (DB), Tulane	48	1977
*Mitchell, Randall (NT), Tennessee–Chattanooga	90	1987
Molden, Frank (T), Jackson State	74	1968
Monk, Art (WR), Syracuse	85	1995
Monroe, Henry (CB), Mississippi State	24	1979
Montgomery, Monty (CB), Houston	25	2001
Montgomery, Wilbert (RB), Abilene Christian	31	1977–84
*Mooney, Tim (DE), Western Kentucky	74	1987
Moore, Damon (SS), Ohio State	43	1999–2001
Morey, Sean (WR), Brown	19, 85	2001, 03–
Morgan, Dennis (KR), Western Illinois	42	1975

Name (Position), College	No.	Yrs. Eagle
Morgan, Mike (LB), LSU	89	1964–67
Morris, Dwaine (DT), Southwestern Louisiana	69	1985
Morriss, Guy (C), TCU	50, 62	1973–83
Morse, Bobby (RB-KR), Michigan State	36	1987
Mortell, Emmett (B), Wisconsin	31	1937–39
Moseley, Mark (K), Stephen F. Austin	3	1970
Moselle, D. (B), Superior State (WI)	24	1954
Mrkonic, George (T), Kansas	72	1953
Muha, Joe (B), VMI	36	1946–50
Muhlmann, Horst (K), no college	16	1975–77
Mulligan, George (E), Catholic U.	42	1936
Murley, Dick (T), Purdue	68	1956
Murray, Calvin (HB), Ohio State	42	1981–82
Murray, Eddie (K), Tulane	3	1994
Murray, Francis (B), Pennsylvania	11	1939–40
Myers, Brad (B), Bucknell	46	1958
Myers, Jack (B), UCLA	32	1948–50
Nacrelli, Andy (E), Fordham	87	1958
*Nease, Mike (C-T), Tennessee–Chattanooga	78	1987
Nelson, Al (DB), Cincinnati	26	1965–73
Nelson, Dennis (T), Illinois State	68	1976–77
Nettles, Jim (DB), Wisconsin	9	1965–68
Newton, Charles (B), Washington	40	1939–40
Nichols, Gerald (DT), Florida State	74	1993
Niland, John (G), Iowa	74	1975–76
Nipp, Maurice (G), Loyola (CA)	68	1952–53, 56
Nocera, John (LB), Iowa	29	1959–62
Norby, Jack (B), Idaho	26	1934
Nordquist, Mark (G), Pacific	68	1968–74
Norton, Jerry (B), SMU	41	1954–58
Norton, Jim (T), Washington	73	1968
Nowak, Walt (E), Villanova	81	1944
Oakes, Don (T), Virginia Tech	77	1961–62
O'Boyle, Henry (B), Notre Dame	16	1933
O'Brien, Davey (B), TCU	5, 8	1939–40
O'Brien, Ken (QB), California–Davis	7	1993
Obst, Henry (G), Syracuse	22	1933
Oden, Derrick (LB), Alabama	58	1993–95
Olds, Bill (RB), Nebraska	38, 39	1976
Oliver, Greg (RB), Trinity (TX)	48	1973–74
Oliver, Hubie (FB), Arizona	34	1981–85
O'Neal, Brian (FB), Penn State	31	1994
Opperman, Jim (LB), Colorado State	54	1975
O'Quinn, John (E), Wake Forest	81	1951
Ordway, William (B), North Dakota	NA	1939
Oristaglio, Bob (E), Pennsylvania	89	1952
Ormsbe, Elliott (B), Bradley Tech	40	1946
Osborn, Mike (LB), Kansas State	57	1978
Osborne, Richard (TE), Texas A&M	88	1976–78
Outlaw, John (DB), Jackson State	20	1973–78
Overmyer, Bill T (LB), Ashland College	56	1972
Owens, Don (T), Mississippi Southern	70	1958–60
Owens, Terrell (WR), Tennessee–Chattanooga	81	2004–
Pacella, Dave (G-C), Maryland	72	1984
Padlow, Max (E), Ohio State	28	1935
Pagliei, Joe (B), Clemson	32	1959
Palelei, Lonnie (T-G), UNLV	77	1999
Palmer, Leslie (B), North Carolina State	40, 84	1948
Panos, Joe (G), Wisconsin	63, 72	1994–97
Papale, Vince (WR), St. Joseph's	83	1976–78
Pape, Orrin (B), Iowa	19	1933
Parker, Artimus (DB), Southern Cal	24	1974–76
Parker, Rodney (WR), Tennessee State	83	1980–81
Parmer, Jim (B), Oklahoma A&M	43	1948–56
Parry, Josh (FB), San Jose State	49	2004–
Paschka, Gordon (G), Minnesota	61	1943
Pastorini, Dan (QB), Santa Clara	6	1982–83
Pate, Rupert (G), Wake Forest	63	1942
Patton, Cliff (G), TCU	65	1946–50
Patton, Jerry (DT), Nebraska	77	1974
Payne, Ken (WR), Langston	82	1978
Peaks, Clarence (B), Michigan State	26	1957–63
Pederson, Doug (QB), Northeast Louisiana	14	1999
Peete, Rodney (QB), Southern Cal	9	1995–98

Name (Position), College	No.	Yrs. Eagle
Pegg, Harold (C), Bucknell	19	1940
Pellegrini, Bob (LB), Maryland	53	1956, 58–61
Penaranda, Jairo (RB), UCLA	38	1985
Peoples, Woody (G), Grambling	69	1978–80
Perot, Pete (G), Northwestern Louisiana	62	1979–84
*Perrino, Mike (T), Notre Dame	64	1987
Perry, William (DT), Clemson	90	1993–94
Peters, Floyd (T), San Francisco State	72	1964–69
Peters, Scott (C-G), Arizona State	62	2002
Peters, Volney (T), Southern Cal	76	1958
Pettigrew, Gary (DT), Stanford	88	1966–74
Philbin, Gerry (DE), Buffalo	77	1973
*Phillips, Ray (LB), Nebraska	52	1978–81
Phillips, Ray (DE-LB), North Carolina State	93	1987
Piasecky, Albert (E), Duke	NA	1942
Picard, Bob (WR), Washington State	82	1973–76
Pihos, Pete (E), Indiana	35	1947–55
Pilconis, Joe (E), Temple	18, 28, 2, 24	1934, 36–37
Pinder, Cyril (B), Illinois	22	1968–70
Pinkston, Todd (WR), Southern Mississippi	87	2000–
Piro, Henry (E), Syracuse	89	1941
Pisarcik, Joe (QB), New Mexico State	9	1980–84
Pitts, Alabama (B), no college	50	1935
Pitts, Mike (DT-DE), Alabama	74	1987–92
Pivarnick, Joe (G), Notre Dame	29	1936
Poage, Ray (E), Texas	35	1964–65
Pollard, Al (B), West Point	21	1951–53
Polley, Tom (LB), UNLV	57	1985
Pollock, William (B), Pennsylvania Military	44	1943
Porter, Ron (LB), Idaho	50	1969–72
Poth, Phil (G), Gonzaga	NA	1934
Powell, Art (B), San Jose State	87	1959
Powlus, Ron (QB), Notre Dame	11	2000
Preece, Steve (DB), Oregon State	33	1970–72
Prescott, Harold (E), Hardin-Simmons	86	1947–49
President, Andre (TE), Angelo State (TX)	48	1997
Priestly, Robert (E), Brown	81	1942
Prisco, Nick (B), Rutgers	18	1933
Pritchard, Bosh (B), VMI	30	1942, 1946–51
Pritchett, Stanley (RB), South Carolina	36	2000
Puetz, Garry (T), Valparaiso	64	1979
Pylman, Bob (T), South Dakota State	39	1938–39
Pyne, Jim (C-G), Virginia Tech	73	200
Quick, Mike (WR), North Carolina State	82	1982–90
Quinlan, Bill (E), Michigan State	83	1963
Rado, George (E), Duquesne	27	1937–38
Ragazzo, Phil (T), Western Reserve	31, 77	1940–41
Ramsey, Herschel (E), Texas Tech	12, 88	1938–40, 45
Ramsey, Knox (G), William & Mary	62	1952
Ramsey, Nate (DB), Indiana State	24	1963–72
Rash, Lou (CB), Mississippi Valley State	28	1984
Raskowski, Leo (T), Ohio State	45	1935
Ratliff, Don (DE), Maryland	77	1975
Rauch, John (B), Georgia	11	1951
Rayburn, Sam (DT), Tulsa	91	2003–
Raye, Jim (DB), Michigan State	30	1969
Reagan, Frank (B), Pennsylvania	40	1949–51
Reader, Jamie (FB), Akron	34	2001
Reaves, John (QB), Florida	6, 7	1972–75
Recher, Dave (C), Iowa	50, 51	1965–68
Reed, J. R. (S), South Florida	30	2004–
Reed, James (LB), California	57	1977
Reed, Michael (FB), Washington	39	1998
Reed, Taft (B), Jackson State	17	1967
Reese, Henry (C-LB), Temple	25, 20	1935–39
Reese, Ike (LB), Michigan State	58	1998–2004
Reeves, Ken (T), Texas A&M	66	1985–89
Reeves, Marion (DB), Clemson	45	1974
Reichenbach, Mike (LB), East Stroudsburg	55	1984–89
Reichow, Jerry (E), Iowa	17	1960
Reid, Alan (RB), Minnesota	24	1987
Reid, Mike (S), North Carolina State	42	1993–94
Reilly, Kevin (LB), Villanova	52	1973–74
Renfro, Leonard (DT), Colorado	94	1993–94

Name (Position), College	No.	Yrs. Eagle
Renfro, Will (E), Memphis State	66	1961
*Repko, Jay (TE), Ursinus	89	1987
Restic, Joe (E), Villanova	82	1952
Retzlaff, Pete (E), South Dakota State	25, 44	1956–66
Reutt, Ray (E), VMI	81	1943
Ricca, Jim (T), Georgetown	71	1955–56
Richards, Bobby (E), LSU	68	1962–65
Richardson, Paul (WR), UCLA	81	1993
Richardson, Jess (T), Alabama	65, 72	1953–61
Riffle, Dick (B), Albright	45	1938–40
Riley, Lee (B), Detroit	22	1956, 58–59
Rimington, Dave (C), Nebraska	50	1988–89
Ringo, Jim (C), Syracuse	54	1964–67
Rissmiller, Ray (T), Georgia	77	1966
Ritchie, Jon (FB), Stanford	48	2003–
Roberts, John (B), Georgia	12	1933–34
Robinson, Burle (E), BYU	27	1935
*Robinson, Jacque (FB), Washington	22	1987
Robinson, Jerry (LB), UCLA	56	1979–84
Robinson, Wayne (LB), Minnesota	52	1952–56
Robb, Joe (E), TCU	66	1959–60
Roffler, William (B), Washington State	23	1954
Rogalla, John (B), Scranton	32	1945
Rogas, Dan (G), Tulane	65	1952
Romanowski, Bill (LB), Boston College	53	1994–95
Romero, Ray (G), Kansas State	68	1951
Roper, John (LB), Texas A&M	53	1993
Rose, Ken (LB), UNLV	55	1990–94
*Ross, Alvin (FB), Central State (OH)	41	1987
Ross, Oliver (T), Iowa State	73	1999
Rossovich, Tim (DE-LB), Southern Cal	82	1968–71
Rossum, Allen (CB-KR), Notre Dame	25	1998–99
Roton, Herbert (E), Auburn	18, 36	1937
Roussel, Tom (LB), Southern Mississippi	54	1973
Rowan, Everitt (E), Ohio State	32	1933
Rowe, Robert (B), Colgate	37	1935
*Royals, Mark (P), Appalachian State	5	1987
Rucker, Keith (DT), Ohio Wesleyan	96	1996
Rudolph, Joe (G), Wisconsin	64	1995
Runager, Max (P), South Carolina	4	1979–83, 89
Runyan, Jon (T), Michigan	69	2000–
Russell, Booker (FB), Southwest Texas State	32	1981
Russell, James (T), Temple	17, 22	1936–37
Russell, Laf (B), Northwestern	15	1933
Russell, Rusty (T), South Carolina	79	1984
Ruzek, Roger (K), Weber State	7	1989–93
Ryan, Pat (QB), Tennessee	10	1991
Ryan, Rocky (E), Illinois	45	1956–58
*Ryczek, Paul (C), Virginia	73	1987
Rypien, Mark (QB), Washington State	11	1996
Sader, Steve (B), no college	33	1943
Saidock, Tom (T), Michigan State	75	1957
Sampleton, Lawrence (TE), Texas	87	1982–84
Samson, Michael (DT), Grambling	98	1996
Sanders, John (G), SMU	67	1943, 45
Sanders, John (DB), South Dakota	26	1977–79
Sanders, Thomas (RB), Texas A&M	45	1990–91
Sandifer, Dan (B), LSU	31	1950–51
Sapp, Theron (B), Georgia	30	1959–63
Savitsky, George (T), Pennsylvania	75	1948–49
Saxon, James (FB), San Jose State	22	1995
Scarpati, Joe (B), North Carolina State	21	1964–69, 71
Schad, Mike (G), Queen's (Canada)	79	1989–93
Schau, Ryan (T-G), Illinois	67	1999–2001
Schaefer, Don (B), Notre Dame	24	1956
Schmitt, Ted (C), Pittsburgh	41	1938–40
Schnelker, Bob (E), Bowling Green	85	1953
Schneller, Bill (B), Mississippi	24	1940
Schrader, Jim (C), Notre Dame	51	1962–64
Schreiber, Adam (G-C), Texas	76	1986–88
Schuehle, Jake (B), Rice	38	1939
Schultz, Eberle (G), Oregon State	48, 71	1940, 43
Schulz, Jody (LB), East Carolina	53, 95	1983–87
Sciarra, John (DB), UCLA	21	1978–83

Name (Position), College	No.	Yrs. Eagle
Sciullo, Steve (G), Marshall	68	2004–
Scott, Clyde (B), Navy/Arkansas	27	1949–52
Scott, Gari (WR), Michigan State	16, 86	2000–01
Scott, Tom (E), Virginia	82	1953–58
Scotti, Ben (B), Maryland	48	1962–63
Seals, Leon (DT), Jackson State	97	1992
Sears, Vic (T), Oregon State	79	1941–53
Seay, Mark (WR), Long Beach State	81	1996–97
Sebastian, Mike (B), Pittsburgh	34	1935
Selby, Rob (G), Auburn	75	1991–94
Shann, Bob (B), Boston College	25	1965, 67
Sharkey, Ed (T), Duke	66	1954–55
Shaub, Harry (G), Cornell	NA	1935
Shaw, Rickie (T), North Carolina	68	1994
Shaw, Ricky (LB), Oklahoma State	51	1989–90
Sheppard, Lito (CB), Florida	26	2002–
Sherman, Al (B), Brooklyn College	10	1943–47
Sherman, Heath (RB), Texas A&I	23	1989–93
Shires, Marshall (T), Tennessee	72	1945
Shonk, John (E), West Virginia	85	1941
Short, Jason (LB), Eastern Michigan	52	2004–
Shuler, Mickey (TE), Penn State	82, 85	1990–91
*Siano, Mike (WR), Syracuse	86	1987
Sikahema, Vai (RB-KR), BYU	22	1992–93
Simerson, John (C), Purdue	53, 64	1957–58
Simmons, Clyde (DE), Western Carolina	96	1986–93
Simon, Corey (DT), Florida State	90	2000–
Simoneau, Mark (LB), Kansas State	53	2003–
Sinceno, Kaseem (TE), Syracuse	89	1998–99
Sinclair, Michael (DE), Eastern New Mexico	75	2002
Singletary, Reggie (DT-G), N. Carolina State	68, 97	1986–90
Sisemore, Jerry (T), Texas	76	1973–84
Sistrunk, Manny (DT), Arkansas AM&N	79	1976–79
Skaggs, Jim (G), Washington	70	1963–72
Skladany, Leo (E), Pittsburgh	63	1949
Skladany, Tom (P), Ohio State	5	1983
Slater, Mark (C), Minnesota	61	1979–83
Slay, Henry (DT), West Virginia	95	1998
Slechta, Jeremy (DT), Nebraska	79	2002
Small, Jessie (LB), Eastern Kentucky	52	1989–91
Small, Torrance (WR), Alcorn State	80	1999–2000
*Smalls, Fred (LB), West Virginia	53	1987
Smart, Rod (RB), Western Kentucky	24	2001
Smeja, Rudy (E), Michigan	82	1946
Smith, Ben (CB-S), Georgia	26	1990–93
Smith, Charles (WR), Grambling	85	1974–81
Smith, Darrin (LB), Miami (FL)	56	1997
Smith, Daryle (T), Tennessee	63, 75	1990–92
Smith, Ed (TE), no college	89	1999
Smith, J D (T), Rice	76	1959–63
Smith, Jack (T), Florida	83	1945
Smith, Jackie (DB), Troy State	32	1971
Smith, John (C), Stanford	83	1942
Smith, L. J. (TE), Rutgers	82	2003–
Smith, Milton (E), UCLA	30, 82	1945
Smith, Otis (CB), Missouri	30	1991–94
Smith, Phil (WR), San Diego State	83	1986
Smith, Ralph (E), Mississippi	85	1962–64
Smith, Ray (C), Missouri	29	1933
Smith, Rich (C), Ohio State	35	1933
Smith, Robert (B), Nebraska	43	1956
Smith, Ron (WR), San Diego State	81	1981–83
Smith, Steve (T), Michigan	74, 78	1971–74
Smith, Troy (WR), East Carolina	83, 19	1999
Smothers, Howard (G), Bethune-Cookman	77	1995
Smukler, Dave (B), Temple	13	1936–39
Snead, Norman (B), Wake Forest	16	1964–70
Snyder, Lum (T), Georgia Tech	73, 79	1952–55, 58
Sodaski, John (LB), Villanova	96	1972–73
Sokolis, Stan (T), Pennsylvania	NA	1933
Solomon, Freddie (WR), S. Carolina State	17, 84	1995–98
Solt, Ron (G), Maryland	65	1988–91
Somers, George (T), La Salle	19	1939–40
Spagnola, John (TE), Yale	88	1979–87

Name (Position), College	No.	Yrs. Eagle
Spillers, Ray (T), Arkansas	33	1937
Stackpool, John (B), Washington	36	1942
Stacy, Siran (RB), Alabama	27	1992
Stafford, Dick (E), Texas Tech	86	1962–63
Staley, Duce (RB), South Carolina	22	1997–2003
Stasica, Leo (B), Colorado	NA	1941
Steele, Ernie (B), Washington	37	1942–48
Steere, Dick (T), Drake	72	1951
Steinbock, Laurence (T), St. Thomas	34	1933
Steinke, Gil (B), Texas A&I	41	1945–48
Stetz, Bill (G), Boston College	65	1967
Stevens, Don (B), Illinois	20	1952, 54
Stevens, Matt (S), Appalachian State	45	1997–98
Stevens, Pete (C), Temple	20	1936
Stevens, Richard (T), Baylor	73	1970–74
Steward, Dean (B), Ursinus	36	1943
Stewart, Tony (TE), Penn State	81	2001–02
Stickel, Walt (T), Pennsylvania	72	1950–51
Stockton, Herschel (G), McMurry	21	1937–38
Storm, Edward (B), Santa Clara	22	1934–35
Strauthers, Tom (DE), Jackson State	93	1983–86
Stribling, Bill (E), Mississippi	80	1955–57
Striegel, Bill (G), College of Pacific	68	1959
Stringer, Bob (B), Tulsa	44	1952–53
Stuart, Roy (T), Tulsa	NA	1943
Stubbs, Daniel (DE), Miami (FL)	93	1995
Sturgeon, Cecil (T), North Dakota State	71	1941
Sturm, Jerry (C), Illinois	55	1972
Suffridge, Bob (G), Tennessee	60, 65	1941–45
Sugar, Leo (E), Purdue	84	1961
Sullivan, Tom (RB), Miami (FL)	25	1972–77
Supluski, Leonard (E), Dickinson	80	1942
Sutton, Joe (B), Temple	45	1950–52
Sutton, Mitch (DT), Kansas	79	1974–75
Swift, Justin (TE), Kansas State	89	1999
Sydner, Jeff (WR-PR), Hawaii	85	1992–94
Szafaryn, Len (T), North Carolina	74, 76	1957–58
Szymanski, Frank (C), Notre Dame	51	1948
Talcott, Don (T), Nevada	62	1947
Taliaferro, George (B), Indiana	24	1955
Tamburello, Ben (C-G), Auburn	61	1987–90
Tapeh, Thomas (RB), Minnesota	41	2004–
Tarasovic, George (E), LSU	82	1963–65
Tarver, John (RB), Colorado	49	1975
Taseff, Carl (B), John Carroll	23	1961
Tautalatasi, Junior (RB), Washington State	37	1986–88
Tautolo, Terry (LB), UCLA	58	1976–79
Taylor, Bobby (CB), Notre Dame	21	1995–2003
Teltschik, John (P), Texas	10	1986–90
Thacker, Alvin (B), Morris Harvey	60	1941
Thomas, Hollis (DT), Northern Illinois	78	1996–
Thomas, Johnny (CB), Baylor	41	1996
Thomas, Markus (RB), Eastern Kentucky	46	1993
Thomas, Tra (T), Florida State	72	1998–
Thomas, William (LB), Texas A&M	51	1991–99
Thomason, Bobby (B), VMI	11	1952–57
Thomason, J. (Stumpy) (B), Georgia Tech	28, 29	1935–36
Thomason, Jeff (TE), Oregon	83	2000–02, 04
Thompson, Broderick (T), Kansas	76	1993–94
Thompson, Don (E), Richmond	84	1964
Thompson, Russ (T), Nebraska	25	1940
Thompson, Tommy (B), Tulsa	10, 11	1941–42, 45–50
Thoms, Art (DE), Syracuse	80	1977
Thornton, Richard (B), Missouri School of Mines	28	1933
Thrash, James (WR), Missouri Southern	80	2001–03
Thrower, Jim (DB), East Texas State	49	1970–72
Thurbon, Robert (B), Pittsburgh	49	1943
Timpson, Michael (WR), Penn State	83	1997
*Tinsley, Scott (QB), Southern Cal	11	1987
Tom, Mel (DE), San Jose State	58, 99	1967–73
Tomasetti, Lou (B), Bucknell	15	1940–41
Toney, Anthony (FB), Texas A&M	25	1986–90
Torrey, Bob (FB), Penn State	39	1980
Townsend, Greg (DE), TCU	93	1994

Name (Position), College	No.	Yrs. Eagle
Tracey, John (E), Texas A&M	80	1961
Tremble, Greg (DB), Georgia	25	1995
Tripucka, Frank (B), Notre Dame	10	1949
Trost, Milton (T), Marquette	27	1940
Trotter, Jeremiah (LB), Stephen F. Austin	54	1998–2001, 04–
Troup, Bill (QB), South Carolina	12	1975
Tupper, Jeff (DE), Oklahoma	69	1986
Turnbow, Guy (T), Mississippi	33, 28	1933–34
Turner, Kevin (FB), Alabama	34	1995–99
*Turral, Willie (RB), New Mexico	23	1987
Tuten, Rick (P), Florida State	14	1989
Tyrrell, Joe (G), Temple	69	1952
*Ulmer, Michael (DB), Doane College	32	1987
Unutoa, Morris (C), BYU	68	1996–98
Uperesa, Tuufuli (G), Montana	75	1971
Urevig, Claude (B), North Dakota	30	1935
Valentine, Zack (LB), East Carolina	54	1982–83
Van Brocklin, Norm (QB), Oregon	11	1958–60
Van Buren, Ebert (B), LSU	17, 31	1951–53
Van Buren, Steve (B), LSU	15	1944–51
Van Dyke, Alex (WR), Nevada	86	1999–2000
Van Dyke, Bruce (G), Missouri	66	1966
Vasys, Arunas (LB), Notre Dame	61	1966–68
Vick, Roger (RB), Texas A&M	43	1990
Vincent, Troy (CB), Wisconsin	23	1996–2003
Wagner, Steve (S-LB), Wisconsin	42	1980–81
Wainright, Frank (TE), Northern Colorado	87	1995
Walik, Billy (WR), Villanova	9	1970–72
Walker, Adam (FB), Pittsburgh	29	1996
Walker, Corey (RB), Arkansas State	39, 29	1997–98
Walker, Darwin (DT), Tennessee	97	2000–
Walker, Herschel (RB), Georgia	34	1992–94
Wallace, Al (DE-LB), Maryland	96	1997–99
Walston, Bobby (E-K), Georgia	83	1951–62
*Walters, Pete (G), Western Kentucky	68	1987
Walters, Stan (T), Syracuse	75	1975–83
Walton, John (QB), Elizabeth City State	10, 11	1976–79
Ward, Jim (QB), Gettysburg	7	1971–72
Ware, Matt (DB), UCLA	21	2004–
Warren, Buist (B), Tennessee	41	1945
Warren, Chris (RB), Ferrum	35	2000
Waters, Andre (SS), Cheyney	20	1984–93
Waters, Mike (FB), San Diego State	33	1986
Watkins, Foster (B), West Texas State	39, 41	1940–41
Watkins, Larry (B), Alcorn A&M	34	1970–72
Watson, Edwin (RB), Purdue	35	1999
Watson, Tim (SS), Howard	33	1997
Watters, Ricky (RB), Notre Dame	32	1995–97
Wayne, Nate (LB), Mississippi	54	2003–04
Wear, Robert (C), Penn State	51	1942
Weatherall, Jim (T), Oklahoma	77	1955–57
Weaver, Jed (TE), Oregon	87	1999
Weber, Chuck (LB), West Chester	51	1959–61
Weedon, Don (G), Texas	60	1947
Wegert, Ted (B), no college	46	1955–56
Weiner, Albert (B), Muhlenberg	18	1934
Weinstock, Isadore (B), Pittsburgh	10	1935
Welbourn, John (G-T), California	76	1999–2003
Weldon, Casey (QB), Florida State	11	1992
Wells, Billy (B), Michigan State	27	1958
Wells, Harold (LB), Purdue	53	1965–68
Wendlick, Joseph (F), Oregon State	59	1940
*Wenzel, Jeff (T), Tulane	72	1987
West, Ed (TE), Auburn	83	1995–96
West, Hodges (T), Tennessee	72	1941
*West, Troy (SS), Southern Cal	31	1987
Westbrook, Brian (RB), Villanova	36	2002–
Whalen, Jim (E), Boston College	81	1971
Wheeler, Mark (DT), Texas A&M	97	1999
Whire, John (B), Georgia	NA	1933
White, Allison (T), TCU	21	1939
White, Reggie (DE-DT), Tennessee	91, 92	1985–92
Whiting, Brandon (DT-DE), California	98	1998–2003

Name (Position), College	No.	Yrs. Eagle
Whitmore, David (S), Stephen F. Austin	42	1995
Whittingham, Fred (LB), California Poly	53, 56	1966, 71
Wiatrak, John (C), Washington	NA	1939
Wilburn, Barry (FS), Mississippi	45	1995–96
Wilcox, John (T), Oregon	71	1960
Wilkes, Reggie (LB), Georgia Tech	51	1978–85
Wilkins, Jeff (K), Youngstown State	14	1994
Will, Erwin (DT), Dayton	67	1965
Willey, Norman (E), Marshall	44, 63, 86	1950–57
Williams, Ben (DT), Minnesota	90	1999
Williams, Bernard (T), Georgia	74	1994
Williams, Bobbie (G), Arkansas	66	2000–03
Williams, Boyd (C), Syracuse	51	1947
Williams, Byron (WR), Texas–Arlington	80	1983
Williams, Calvin (WR), Purdue	89	1990–96
Williams, Charlie (CB), Jackson State	47	1978
Williams, Clyde (T), Georgia Tech	20	1935
Williams, Henry (WR-KR), East Carolina	81	1989
Williams, Jerry (B), Washington State	49	1953–54
Williams, Joel (LB), Wisconsin–La Crosse	59	1983–85
Williams, Michael (RB), Mississippi College	32	1983–84
Williams, Roger (DB), Grambling	23	1973
Williams, Ted (B), Boston College	31	1942
Williams, Tex (G), Auburn	77	1942
Williams, Tyrone (DE), Wyoming	95	1999–2000
Willis, James (LB), Auburn	50	1995–98
Wilson, Bill (E), Gonzaga	23	1938
Wilson, Brenard (S), Vanderbilt	22	1979–86
Wilson, Harry (B), Nebraska	41	1967–70
Wilson, Jerry (E), Auburn	88	1959–60
Wilson, Osborne (G), Pennsylvania	25, 15	1933–35
Winfield, Vern (G), Minnesota	67	1972–73
Wink, Dean (DT), Yankton	64	1967–68
Wirgowski, Dennis (DE), Purdue	75	1973
Wistert, Al (T), Michigan	70	1943–51
Witherspoon, Derrick (RB), Clemson	31	1995–97
Wittenborn, John (G), Southeast Missouri	62	1960–62
Wojciechowicz, Alex (C), Fordham	53	1946–50
Wolfe, Hugh (B), West Texas Teachers	32	1940
Woltman, Clem (T), Purdue	15	1938–40
Woodard, Marc (LB), Mississippi State	57	1994–96
Woodeshick, Tom (B), West Virginia	37	1963–71
Woodruff, Lee (B), Mississippi	11	1933
Woodruff, Tony (WR), Fresno State	83	1982–84
Woodson, Sean (S), Jackson State	37	1998
Worden, Neil (B), Notre Dame	32	1954, 57
Woulfe, Mike (LB), Colorado	63	1962
Wright, Gordon (G), Delaware State	66	1967
Wright, Sylvester (LB), Kansas	52	1995–96
Wukits, Al (C), Duquesne	50	1943
Wyatt, Antwuan (WR), Bethune-Cookman	85	1997
Wydo, Frank (T), Duquesne/Cornell	74, 75	1952–57
Wyhonic, John (G), Alabama	66	1946–47
Wynn, Dexter (DB), Colorado State	31	2004–
Wynn, Will (DE), Tennessee State	71	1973–76
Young, Adrian (LB), Southern Cal	35	1968–72
Young, Charles (TE), Southern Cal	86	1973–76
Young, Glen (WR), Mississippi State	89	1983
Young, Michael (WR), UCLA	83	1993
Young, Roynell (CB), Alcorn State	43	1980–88
Youngelman, Sid (T), Alabama	73	1956–58
Yovicsin, John (E), Gettysburg	81	1944
Zabel, Steve (E-LB), Oklahoma	89	1970–74
Zandofsky, Mike (G), Washington	66	1997
Zendejas, Luis (K), Arizona State	8	1988–89
Ziegler, Frank (B), Georgia Tech	41	1949–53
Zilly, John (E), Notre Dame	88	1952
Zimmerman, Don (WR), Northeast Louisiana	80	1972–76
Zimmerman, Roy (B), San Jose State	7	1942–46
Zizak, Vince (T), Villanova	23	1934–37
Zomalt, Eric (SS), California	27	1994–96
Zordich, Michael (SS), Penn State	36	1994–98
Zyntell, James (G), Holy Cross	21, 9, 16	1933–35

EAGLES DRAFT HISTORY

Rnd.	Sel. No.	Name (Position), College
1936		
1	1	Jay Berwanger (B), Chicago
2	10	John McCauley (B), Rice
3	19	Wes Muller (C), Stanford
4	28	Bill Wallace (B), Rice
5	37	Harry Shuford (B), Southern Methodist
6	46	Al Barabas (B), Columbia
7	55	Jack Weller (G), Princeton
8	64	Pepper Constable (B), Princeton
9	73	Paul Pauk (B), Princeton
1937		
1	1	Sam Francis (B), Nebraska
2	11	Franny Murray (B), Pennsylvania
3	21	Drew Ellis (T), Texas Christian
4	31	Walt Gilbert (B), Auburn
5	41	Alex Drobnitch (G), Denver
6	51	Bill Guckeyson (B), Maryland
7	61	Herb Barna (E), West Virginia
8	71	Nestor Hennon (E), Carnegie-Mellon
9	81	Paul Fanning (T), Kansas State
10	91	Ray Antil (E), Minnesota
1938		
1	2	Jim McDonald (B), Ohio State
2	12	Dick Riffle (B), Albright
3	17	Joe Bukant (B), Washington (St. Louis)
4	27	John Meek (B), California
5	32	Fred Shirey (T), Nebraska
6	42	Herschel Ramsey (E), Texas Tech
7	52	Bob Lannon (E), Iowa
8	62	Clem Woltman (T), Purdue
9	72	Elber Kolberg (B), Oregon State
10	82	Emmett Kriel (B), Baylor
11	92	Carl Hinkle (C), Vanderbilt
12	102	Johnny Michelosen (B), Pittsburgh
1939		
1	4	Davey O'Brien (QB), Texas Christian
2	14	Charlie Newton (B), Washington
3	19	Joe Mihal (T), Purdue
4	29	Bill Dewell (E), Southern Methodist
5	34	Fred Coston (G), Texas A&M
6	44	Carl Schuehle (B), Rice
7	54	Tony Ippolito (B), Purdue
8	64	George Somers (T), LaSalle
9	74	Rankin Britt (E), Texas A&M
10	84	Bill McKeever (T), Cornell
11	94	Paul Humphrey (C), Purdue
12	104	Jack Kraynick (B), North Carolina
13	114	Thomas (Allie) White (T), Texas Christian
14	124	Joe Aleskus (T), Ohio State
15	134	Forrest Watkins (B), West Texas State Teachers
16	144	Irv Hall (B), Brown
17	154	Bob Riddell (E), South Dakota State
18	164	Charley Gainor (E), North Dakota
19	174	Morris White (B), Tulsa
20	184	Dick Gomley (C), LSU
1940		
1	2	George McAfee (RB), Duke
2	13	Johnny Schiechl (C), Santa Clara
3	17	Dick Favor (B), Oklahoma
4	28	Eberle Schultz (G), Oregon State
5	32	Frank Emmons (B), Oregon
6	43	Saul Singer (T), Arkansas
7	52	Hal (Mike) Pegg (C), Bucknell
8	63	Don Looney (E), Texas Christian
9	72	Don Jones (B), Washington
10	83	Frank Maher (B), Toledo

Rnd.	Sel. No.	Name (Position), College
11	92	Elmer Hackney (B), Kansas
12	103	Durward Hoerner (E), Texas Christian
13	112	Ted Hennis (B), Purdue
14	123	Bill Bunsen (B), Kansas
15	132	Don Crumbaker (E), Kansas State
16	143	J. R. Green (T), Rice
17	152	Jim Molnar (B), Bradley
18	163	Ernie Schwartzer (G), Boston College
19	172	Bill Schneller (B), Mississippi
20	183	Bill Debord (T), Kansas State
1941		
1		choice traded to Chicago Bears
2	11	Art Jones (B), Richmond
3	16	Marion Pugh (B), Texas A&M
4	26	Al Ghesquiere (B), Detroit
5	31	Royal Kahler (T), Nebraska
6	41	Howard (Red) Hickey (E), Arkansas
7	51	Julius (Mush) Battista (G), Florida
8		choice traded to Chicago Bears
9	71	P. K. Rogers (B), East Texas State
10	81	Don Williams (T), Texas
11	91	Marshall Stenstrom (B), Oregon
12	101	John Patrick (B), Penn State
13	111	Joe Hoague (B), Colgate
14	121	Les Dodson (B), Mississippi
15	131	Alex Lukachick (E), Boston College
16	141	Bill Conatser (B), Texas A&M
17	151	John Yauckoes (T), Boston College
18	161	Joe McFadden (B), Georgetown (DC)
19	171	John Shonk (E), West Virginia
20	181	L. B. Russell (B), Hardin-Simmons
21	201	Charley Henke (G), Texas A&M
22	203	Mike Fernella (T), Akron
1942		
1	3	Pete Kmetovic (B), Stanford
2	13	Vic Lindskog (C), Stanford
3	18	Ted Williams (B), Boston College
4	28	Gordon Paschka (G), Minnesota
5	33	Ernie Blandin (T), Tulane
6	43	Earl Younglove (E), Washington
7	53	Billy Sewell (B), Washington State
8	63	Bill Halverson (G), Oregon State
9	73	Ray Graves (C), Tennessee
10	83	Jack Stackpool (B), Washington
11	93	Noble Doss (B), Texas
12	103	Fred Meyer (E), Stanford
13	113	Bob Brenton (T), Missouri
14	123	John Wyhonic (G), Alabama
15	133	O'Dell Griffin (G), Baylor
16	143	Bill Smaltz (B), Penn State
17	153	Arnie Meiners (E), Stanford
18	163	Bill Braun (T), Santa Clara
19	173	Charley Dvoracek (B), Texas Tech
20	183	Marv Tommervik (B), Pacific Lutheran
1943		
1	2	Joe Muha (B), Virginia Military Inst.
2	12	Lamar (Racehorse) Davis (B), Georgia
3	17	Roy (Monk) Gafford (B), Auburn
4	27	Bob Kennedy (B), Washington State
5	32	Al Wistert (T), Michigan
6	42	Bruno Baducci (G), Stanford
7	52	Walt Harrison (C), Washington
8	62	Bruce Alford (E), Texas Christian
9	72	Rocco Canale (G), Boston College
10	82	Bill Conoly (T), Texas
11	92	John Billman (G), Minnesota
12	102	Jack Donaldson (T), Pennsylvania

Rnd.	Sel. No.	Name (Position), College
1943 (continued)		
13	112	Bill Erickson (C), Georgetown (DC)
14	122	George Weeks (E), Alabama
15	132	Russ Craft (B), Alabama
16	142	Paul Darling (B), Iowa State
17	152	Walt Gorinski (B), LSU
18	162	Bob Friedman (T), Washington
19	172	Johnny Bezemes (B), Holy Cross
20	182	Chet Mutryn (B), Xavier
21	192	Baptiste Manzini (C), St. Vincent's
22	202	Bernie Gillespie (E), Scranton
23	212	Jay (Mule) Lawhon (T), Arkansas
24	222	Vince Zachem (C), Morehead State (KY)
25	232	Joe Schwarting (E), Texas
26	242	Bob Neff (T), Notre Dame
27	252	Art Macioszczyk (B), Western Michigan
28	262	Jim Arata (T), Xavier
29	272	Wally Scott (E), Texas
30	282	Stan Jaworowski (T), Georgetown (DC)
1944		
1	5	Steve Van Buren (RB), Louisiana State
2	20	Loren LaPrade (G), Stanford
3	36	Joe Parker (E), Texas
4	52	Hillary Horne (T), Mississippi State
5	58	Vic Kulbitski (B), Minnesota
6	74	George Phillips (B), UCLA
7	80	Paul Sarringhaus (B), Ohio State
8	96	John Perko (G), Minnesota
9	102	Elliott Ormsbee (B), Bradley
10	118	Earle Parsons (B), USC
11	124	Bob Hanzlik (E), Wisconsin
12	140	Jim Talley (C), LSU
13	146	Dom Fusci (T), South Carolina
14	162	Johnny Green (E), Tulsa
15	168	Jackie Freeman (B), William & Mary
16	184	Joe Kane (B), Pennsylvania
17	190	Tony Schiro (G), Santa Clara
18	206	Norm Michael (B), Syracuse
19	212	Eddie Kulakowski (T), West Virginia
20	228	Al Postus (B), Villanova
21	234	Milt Smith (E), UCLA
22	250	Earl Klapstein (T), Pacific
23	256	Bob Frisbee (B), Stanford
24	272	Ed Eiden (B), Scranton
25	278	Barney Burdick (E), Creighton
26	294	Nick Daukas (T), Dartmouth
27	300	Pasquale Darone (G), Boston College
28	316	Bill Clark (T), Colorado College
29	322	Pete Pasko (E), East Stroudsburg
30	328	Myron Majewski (T), American International
1945		
1	9	John Yonaker (E), Notre Dame
2	25	Alvin Dark (B), LSU
3	41	Pete Pihos (E), Indiana
4	52	Chuck Dellago (G), Minnesota
5	63	Gonzalo Morales (B), St. Mary's (CA)
6	74	Sam Robinson (B), Washington
7	85	Forrest Hall (B), San Francisco
8	96	Joe Sadonis (T), Fordham
9	107	Rudy Mobley (B), Hardin-Simmons
10	118	Jim Newmeyer (T), St. Vincent
11	129	Bill Chambers (T), UCLA
12	140	John Duda (B), Virginia
13	151	Bill Montgomery (B), LSU
14	162	Howard Werner (E), Syracuse
15	173	Jim Austin (B), Missouri
16	184	Quentin Klenk (T), USC
17	195	Joe Spencer (T), Oklahoma State
18	206	Leo Pratt (T), Oklahoma State
19	217	Phil Teschner (T), Brown
20	228	Johnny Magee (G), Rice
21	239	Norm (Monk) Mosley (B), Alabama

Rnd.	Sel. No.	Name (Position), College
22	250	Blair Brown (G), Oklahoma State
23	261	Bob Hall (E), Stanford
24	272	Don Talcott (T), Nevada–Reno
25	283	Bill Thompson (T), New Mexico
26	294	Al Fleming (C), Wichita State
27	305	Leo Benjamin (C), West Virginia
28	316	Jim Dougherty (B), Miami (OH)
29	322	Ken Reese (B), Alabama
30	328	Loren Braner (C), Pittsburgh
1946		
1	7	Leo Riggs (B), USC
2	23	Gordon Gray (E), USC
3	37	Walt Slater (B), Tennessee
4	48	Felto Prewitt (C), Tulsa
5	57	George Robotham (E), UCLA
6	68	Jim Lecture (G), Northwestern
7	77	Ernie Lewis (B), Colorado
8	88	Al Vandeweghe (E), William & Mary
9	97	Bill Iancelli (E), Franklin & Marshall
10	108	Pat McHugh (B), Georgia Tech
11	117	John Wingender (B), Washington
12	128	Homer Paine (T), Tulsa
13	137	John Kerns (T), Ohio
14	148	Buddy Hubbard (B), William & Mary
15	157	Allen Smith (B), Tulsa
16	168	Bernie Millham (E), Fordham
17	177	Lawrence Mauss (C), Utah
18	188	Dave Butcher (B), William & Mary
19	197	Don Fabling (B), Colorado
20	208	George Feldman (B), Tufts
21	217	Ed Cameron (G), Miami (OH)
22	228	Charley Steed (B), Arkansas–Monticello
23	237	Ed Grygiel (B), Dartmouth
24	248	Ben Raimondi (B), Indiana
25	257	Sam Bailey (E), Georgia
26	268	Bob Long (B), Tennessee
27	277	Bill Fisher (T), Harvard
28	288	George Slusser (B), Ohio State
29	292	John Itzel (B), Pittsburgh
30	298	Larry Kirkman (B), Boston University
1947		
1	8	Neill Armstrong (E), Oklahoma State
2	19	Bill Mackrides (B), Nevada–Reno
3	30	George Savitsky (T), Pennsylvania
4		choice traded to Chicago Bears
5	51	Tony Yovicsin (E), Miami (FL)
6	61	Alf Satterfield (T), Vanderbilt
7	71	Bob Leonetti (G), Wake Forest
8	80	Ulysses Cornogg (T), Wake Forest
9	91	Alex Sarkisian (C), Northwestern
10	102	Jerry D'Arcy (C), Tulsa
11	110	John Hamberger (T), Southern Methodist
12	121	Alvin Johnson (B), Hardin-Simmons
13	132	Joe Cook (B), Hardin-Simmons
14	140	Jeff Durkota (B), Penn State
15	152	Hubert Shurtz (T), LSU
16	161	Hal Bell (B), Muhlenberg
17	170	Tom Campion (T), Southeastern Louisiana
18	182	Fred Hall (G), LSU
19	191	Jim Clayton (T), Wyoming
20	200	George Blomquist (E), North Carolina State
21	212	Joe Haynes (G), Tulsa
22	221	Stanton Hense (E), Xavier
23	230	Johnny Kelly (B), Rice
24	242	H. J. Roberts (G), Rice
25	251	Phil Cutchin (B), Kentucky
26	261	Charley Wakefield (T), Stanford
27	272	Dick Lagenbeck (T), Cincinnati
28	281	Bernie Winkler (T), Texas Tech
29	288	Bill Stephens (T), Baylor
30	298	Mike Kalash (E), Wisconsin–La Crosse

Rnd.	Sel. No.	Name (Position), College
1948		
1	8	Clyde (Smackover) Scott (B), Arkansas/Navy
2	22	Paul Campbell (QB), Texas
3	33	Jack (Moose) Myers (B), UCLA
4	42	Howard Duncan (C), Ohio State
5	54	Buddy Tinsley (T), Baylor
6	63	Marty Wendell (G), Notre Dame
7	72	Scott Beasley (E), Nevada–Reno
8	84	Ray Richeson (G), Alabama
9	93	Gil Johnson (QB), Southern Methodist
10	102	Bill Wyman (T), Rice
11	114	Jim Waithall (B), West Virginia
12	123	Dick Kempthorn (B), Michigan
13	132	Dick Rifenburg (E), Michigan
14	144	Don Stanton (T), Oregon
15	153	Ralph Kohl (T), Michigan
16	162	Aubrey Fowler (B), Arkansas
17	174	Rudy Krall (B), New Mexico
18	183	Ed Claunch (C), LSU
19	192	Negley Norton (T), Penn State
20	204	Lockwood Frizzell (C), Virginia
21	213	Jack Swaner (B), California
22	222	Art Littleton (E), Pennsylvania
23	234	Jim Parmer (B), Oklahoma State
24	243	Lou Creekmur (T), William & Mary
25	252	Bill Stanton (E), North Carolina State
26	264	Benny Ellender (B), Tulane
27	273	Rex Grossman (B), Indiana
28	282	A. B. Kitchens (T), Tulsa
29	292	Art Statuto (C), Notre Dame
30	298	Tom Novak (C), Nebraska
1949		
1a	1	Chuck Bednarik (C-LB), Pennsylvania (bonus choice)
1b	9	Frank Tripucka (QB), Notre Dame
2	19	Frank Burns (B), Rutgers
3	29	Frank Ziegler (B), Georgia Tech
4	41	Don Panciera (B), San Francisco
5	51	Terry Brennan (B), Notre Dame
6a	58	Warren Huey (E), Michigan State (choice obtained from Washington)
6b		choice traded to Boston
7	71	Frank Gillespie (G), Clemson
8	81	Bob Dean (B), Cornell
9	91	Jonathan Jenkins (T), Dartmouth
10	101	Roy Lester (E), West Virginia
11	111	Bobby Wilson (B), Mississippi
12	121	Dale Armstrong (E), Dartmouth
13	131	Lyle Button (T), Illinois
14	141	Bobby Lund (B), Tennessee
15	151	Carl Copp (T), Vanderbilt
16	161	Frank Reno (E), West Virginia
17	171	Leo Skladany (E), Pittsburgh
18	181	Russ Strait (B), Muhlenberg
19	191	Paul Odom (G), Rollins
20	201	Lloyd Brinkman (B), Missouri
21	211	Lou Futrell (B), USC
22	221	Harvey Kingry (B), Colorado School of Mines
23	231	Hank Kalver (T), Oklahoma City
24	241	Fred Leon (T), Nevada–Reno
25	251	John (Bull) Schweder (G), Pennsylvania
1950		
1	14	Harold (Bud) Grant (E), Minnesota
2		choice traded to Detroit
3	40	Bob Sanders (B), Oregon
4	53	Bob McChesney (E), Hardin-Simmons
5	66	Mike Kaysserian (B), Detroit
6	79	Lloyd McDermott (T), Kentucky
7	92	Mel Olix (B), Miami (OH)
8	105	Dick O'Hanlon (T), Ohio State
9	118	Bobby Wilson (B), Mississippi
10	131	Ernie Johnson (B), UCLA
11	144	Bobby Lantrip (B), Rice

Rnd.	Sel. No.	Name (Position), College
12	157	Frank Mahoney (E), Brown
13	170	Norm (Wildman) Willey (DE), Marshall
14	183	Billy Hix (E), Arkansas
15	196	Herb Carey (B), Dartmouth
16	209	Jim Marck (T), Xavier
17	222	Jerry Taylor (C), Mississippi State
18	235	Ed Tunnicliff (B), Northwestern
19	248	Darrell Robinson (E), Oregon
20	261	Merv Pregulman (G), Michigan
21	274	Marv Cross (B), Washington State
22	287	Jim Hague (E), Ohio State
23	300	Al Lesko (T), St. Bonaventure
24	313	Tom DeSylvia (G), Oregon State
25	326	Jim Eagles (C), North Texas State
26	339	Rod Franz (G), California
27	352	Bill Martin (B), USC
28	365	Don Burson (B), Northwestern
29	378	Wes Curtier (T), Richmond
30	391	Dud Parker (B), Baylor
1951		
1a	7	Ebert Van Buren (B), LSU
1b	8	Chet Mutryn (B), Xavier (choice obtained from Detroit from Baltimore)
2		choice traded to Washington
3	32	Al Bruno (E), Kentucky
4	43	Fran Nagle (B), Nebraska
5	57	Jack Dwyer (B), Loyola (CA)
6	68	Ken Farragut (C), Mississippi
7	79	Frank Boydston (B), Baylor
8	93	Jack Richards (E), Arkansas
9	104	Denny Doyle (G), Tulane
10	116	Louis Schaufele (B), Arkansas
11	130	Bob Pope (T), Kentucky
12	141	Henry Rich (B), Arizona State
13	152	Pete Mastellone (C), Miami (FL)
14	166	Bobby Walston (E-K), Georgia
15	177	Bobby North (B), Georgia Tech
16	188	Hal Hatfield (E), USC
17	202	Hal Waggoner (B), Tulane
18	213	Bill Weeks (B), Iowa State
19	224	Jack Bove (T), West Virginia
20	238	John Glorioso (B), Missouri
21	249	Neal Franklin (T), Southern Methodist
22	260	Jack Rucker (B), Mississippi State
23	274	Jack Bighead (E), Pepperdine
24	285	Tony Kotowski (E), Mississippi State
25	296	Glenn Drahn (B), Iowa
26	310	Billy Stewart (B), Mississippi State
27	321	Bob Winship (T), Rice
28	332	Marv Stendel (E), Arkansas
29	346	Roscoe Hansen (T), North Carolina
30	357	John (Model-T) Ford (QB), Hardin-Simmons
1952		
1	5	Johnny Bright (B), Drake
2	17	Jim Weatherall (T), Oklahoma
3	29	Lum Snyder (T), Georgia Tech
4	41	Chuck Ulrich (T), Illinois
5		choice traded to Texas
6	65	Dick Lemmon (B), California
7	77	John Thomas (E), Oregon State
8	89	Wayne Robinson (LB), Minnesota
9	101	Maury Nipp (G), Loyola (CA)
10	113	Gerry McGinley (G), Pennsylvania
11	125	Ralph Goldston (B), Youngstown State
12	137	Jack Blount (T), Mississippi State
13	149	Ed Hamilton (B), Kentucky
14	161	Bob Stringer (B), Tulsa
15	173	Malcolm Schmidt (E), Iowa State
16	185	Jim Brewer (G), North Texas State
17	197	John Weigle (E), Oklahoma State
18	209	Ed Romanowski (B), Scranton
19	221	Talbott Trammell (E), Washington & Lee

Rnd.	Sel. No.	Name (Position), College
1952 *(continued)*		
20	233	Bobby Blaik (B), Army/Colorado College
21	245	Les Wheeler (G), Abilene Christian
22	257	Johnny Turco (B), Holy Cross
23	269	Maury Schnell (B), Iowa State
24	281	Joe Tyrrell (G), Temple
25	293	Bob Kelley (C), West Texas State
26	305	Bob Albert (B), Bucknell
27	317	Chuck Hill (B), New Mexico
28	329	Johnny Brewer (B), Louisville
29	341	Tony (Zippy) Morocco (B), Georgia
30	353	Don Stevens (B), Illinois
1953		
1		choice traded to Los Angeles Rams
2	20	Al Conway (B), Army/William Jewell
3	34	Don Johnson (B), California
4	45	George Mrkonic (G), Kansas
5a	56	Eddie Bell (E), Pennsylvania
5b	61	Rex Smith (E), Illinois (choice obtained from Detroit)
6		choice traded to Chicago Cardinals
7a	76	Jack Erickson (T), Army/Beloit (choice obtained from Chicago Cardinals)
7b	81	Ray Malavasi (G), Army/Mississippi State
8	92	Jess Richardson (T), Alabama
9	106	Roger French (E), Minnesota
10	117	Tom Brookshier (B), Colorado
11	128	Bob Pollard (B), Penn State
12	142	George Porter (T), San Jose State
13	153	Ray Westort (G), Utah
14	164	Roy Bailey (B), Tulane
15	178	Willie Irvin (E), Florida A&M
16	189	Bud Wallace (B), North Carolina
17	200	Tony Rados (B), Penn State
18	214	Marv Trauth (T), Mississippi
19	225	Pete Bachouros (B), Illinois
20	236	Rollie Arns (C), Iowa State
21	250	Hal Brooks (T), Washington & Lee
22	261	Laurie LeClaire (B), Michigan
23	272	Jeff Knox (E), Georgia Tech
24	286	Eli Romero (B), Wichita State
25	297	Johnny Michels (G), Tennessee
26	308	Harvey Achziger (T), Colorado State
27	322	Earl Hersh (B), West Chester
28	333	Joe Gratson (B), Penn State
29	344	Ralph Paolone (B), Kentucky
30	357	Chuck Hren (B), Northwestern
1954		
1	9	Neil Worden (B), Notre Dame
2	21	Rocky Ryan (E), Illinois
3	33	Ted Connor (T), Nebraska
4	45	Menil (Minnie) Mavraides (G), Notre Dame
5		choice traded to Los Angeles Rams
6	69	Hal Lambert (T), Texas Christian
7	81	Jerry Norton (B), Southern Methodist
8	93	Dan Hunter (T), Florida
9	105	Phil Branch (G), Texas
10		choice traded to Los Angeles Rams
11	129	Dave McLaughlin (E), Dartmouth
12	141	Dick Clasby (B), Harvard
13	153	Joe Mehalick (T), Virginia
14	165	Hal Patterson (B), Kansas
15	177	Ray McKown (B), Texas Christian
16	189	Charlie Grant (C), Utah
17	201	Bob Knowles (T), Baylor
18	213	Sam Mrvos (G), Georgia
19	225	Jerry Clem (G), Southern Methodist
20	237	Tommy Bailes (B), Houston
21	249	Johnny Crouch (E), Texas Christian
22	261	Jim Wojciehowski (E), Purdue
23	273	Harold Lofton (B), Mississippi
24	285	Nate Gressette (T), Clemson
25	297	Ray Zambiasi (B), Detroit

Rnd.	Sel. No.	Name (Position), College
26	309	Charley Smith (B), Baylor
27	321	Ben Addiego (B), Villanova
28	333	John Gerdes (T), Cornell
29	345	Jack Stone (B), West Virginia
30	357	Tommy Woodlee (B), South Carolina
1955		
1	9	Dick Bielski (B), Maryland
2	22	Alex (Buck) Lansford (T), Texas
3	33	Frank Eidom (B), Southern Methodist
4	46	Dean Dugger (E), Ohio State
5	57	Gene Lamone (G), West Virginia
6	70	Billy Quinn (B), Texas
7	81	Bill McKenna (E), Brandeis
8	94	Herman Watson (T), Vanderbilt
9	105	Von Morgan (E), Abilene Christian
10	118	Talmadge (Duke) Washington (B), Washington State
11	129	Bob Hardy (B), Kentucky
12	142	Andy Nacrelli (E), Fordham
13	153	Jerry Krisher (C), Ohio State
14	166	Tommy Bell (B), Army
15	177	Don Brougher (C), Maryland
16	190	Clyde White (G), Clemson
17	201	Nick Maravic (B), Wake Forest
18	214	Duane Nutt (B), Southern Methodist
19	225	Terry Fails (E), Vanderbilt
20	238	Jimmy Wade (B), Tennessee
21	249	John Anderson (E), Kansas
22	262	Ernie Lewis (G), Arizona
23	273	Cecil Ingram (B), Alabama
24	286	Vic (Hootie) Postula (B), Michigan State
25	297	Frank Pavich (G), USC
26	310	George Palachunik (G), Maryland
27	321	Bob Gringrass (B), Wisconsin
28	334	Wingo Avery (C), Clemson
29	345	Ron Lloyd (T), Bucknell
30	357	Dave Finney (B), Texas Christian
1956		
1	4	Bob Pellegrini (LB), Maryland
2	16	Frank D'Agnostino (T), Auburn
3	28	Don Schaffer (B), Notre Dame
4		choice traded to Washington
5	54	Fred (Fuzzy) Thurston (G), Valparaiso
6	65	Tirrel Burton (B), Miami (OH)
7	78	John Waedekin (T), Hardin-Simmons
8	89	Elroy Payne (B), McMurry
9	102	Johnny Bredice (E), Boston University
10	113	Tom Dimmick (C), Houston
11	126	Kenny Keller (B), North Carolina
12	137	Tommy Harkins (E), Vanderbilt
13	150	James Sides (B), Texas Tech
14	161	Frank Relch (C), Penn State
15	174	Don Brant (B), Montana
16	185	Billy Hix (T), Middle Tennessee State
17	198	Joe Mastrogiovanni (B), Wyoming
18	209	Nick Consoles (DB), Wake Forest
19	222	Delano Womack (B), Texas
20	233	Darrell Glover (T), Maryland–Eastern Shore
21	246	Jack Adams (T), San Jose State
22	257	Joe Miller (B), Cincinnati
23	270	Chet Spencer (E), Oklahoma State
24	281	John Parham (B), Wake Forest
25	294	Johnny Grogan (T), Dayton
26	305	Earl Lunsford (B), Oklahoma State
27	318	Al Ellett (T), Alabama
28	329	Bill Strawn (LB), Western Kentucky
29	342	Bob Hughes (B), Southern Mississippi
30	352	Joe Ulm (B), San Jose State
1957		
1	7	Clarence Peaks (B), Michigan State
2	19	Billy Ray Barnes (B), Wake Forest
3	31	Tommy McDonald (WR), Oklahoma

Rnd.	Sel. No.	Name (Position), College
4	43	Sonny Jurgensen (QB), Duke
5	50	Jimmy Harris (QB), Oklahoma
6		choice traded to San Francisco
7	74	Tom Saidock (T), Michigan State
8	86	Hal McElhaney (B), Duke
9	98	Hal Davis (B), Westminster (PA)
10	110	Don Bruhns (C), Drake
11	122	Gil Shoaf (T), Wabash
12	134	Buddy Dike (B), Texas Christian
13	146	Hubert Bobo (B), Ohio State
14	158	Jerry Cashman (T), Syracuse
15	170	Mort Moriarity (E), Texas
16	182	John Nocera (LB), Iowa
17	194	Dan Radakovich (C), Penn State
18	206	Billy Kelley (T), Baylor
19	218	Paul Harasimowicz (T), Vermont
20	230	Leroy Thompson (B), Butler
21	242	Charley Brooks (E), Michigan
22	254	John Simerson (C), Purdue
23	266	Lou Lovely (G), Boston University
24	278	Dennis McGill (B), Yale
25	290	Bob Ratliff (B), West Texas State
26	302	Alvin Richardson (T), Grambling
27	314	Frank Hall (B), USC
28	326	Clem Corona (G), Michigan
29	338	John Niznik (E), Wake Forest
30	350	Larry Hubbard (E), Marquette

1958

1	6	Walt Kowalczyk (FB), Michigan State
2	17	Proverb Jacobs (T), California
3		choice traded to Washington
4	43	Frank Rigney (T), Iowa
5	52	Bobby Mulgado (B), Arizona State
6	64	John Kersey (T), Duke
7	76	Len Mansfield (T), Pittsburg State
8	88	Bill Striegel (LB), Pacific
9		choice traded to Pittsburgh
10	112	Theron Sapp (B), Georgia
11	124	Mel Dillard (B), Purdue
12	136	Jack Crabtree (B), Oregon
13	148	Mickey Trimarki (QB), West Virginia
14	160	Bill Lapham (C), Iowa
15	172	Stan Hinos (T), Mississippi Valley State
16	184	Mike Meatheringham (T), Georgia
17	196	Bill Van Buren (C), Iowa
18	208	John Burroughs (T), Iowa
19	220	Ron Sabal (G), Purdue
20	232	Kent Lovelace (B), Mississippi
21	244	John Madden (T), Cal Poly–San Luis Obispo
22	256	George Sherwood (E), St. Joseph's (IN)
23	268	Billy Templeton (E), Mississippi
24	280	Jim Padget (C), Clemson
25	292	Hal Divine (T), Memphis State
26	304	Neil MacLean (B), Wake Forest
27	316	Hindman Wall (E), Auburn
28	328	Gene Gossage (T), Northwestern
29	340	Don McDonald (B), Houston
30	351	Jim Thompson (E), Temple

1959

1		choice traded to Los Angeles for Norm Van Brocklin
2	15	J. D. Smith (T), Rice
3	26	Wray Carlton (B), Duke
4	39	Jim Grazione (QB), Villanova
5	51	Nick Mumley (T), Purdue
6	62	Al Benecick (G), Syracuse
7		choice traded to Chicago Bears
8	86	Wilmer Fowler (B), Northwestern
9	99	Gene Johnson (B), Cincinnati
10	110	Rollie West (B), Villanova
11	123	Art Powell (WR), San Jose State
12	134	Howard Keys (T), Oklahoma State
13	147	Dick Stillwagon (B), Purdue

Rnd.	Sel. No.	Name (Position), College
14	158	Jack Smith (T), Clemson
15	171	Jim Poteete (C), Mississippi State
16	182	Ken Paduch (T), Auburn
17	195	Bill Craig (T), Villanova
18	206	Jim Benson (B), Georgia Tech
19	219	Alan Miller (B), Boston College
20	230	Jim Payne (G), Clemson
21	243	Bob Salerno (G), Colorado
22	254	Jim Bowie (T), Kentucky
23	267	Dick Williams (E), Southern
24	278	Gerry Benn (T), Oklahoma State
25	291	Dick Jamieson (QB), Bradley
26	302	Jim Burks (T), Virginia Tech
27	315	Lowell Jenkins (T), Wisconsin
28	326	Leo Sexton (E), Auburn
29	339	John Stolte (T), Kansas State
30	350	Angelo Mosca (T), Notre Dame

1960

1	9	Ron Burton (HB), Northwestern
2	20	Maxie Baughan (LB), Georgia Tech
3	31	Curt Merz (E), Iowa
4a	40	Ted Dean (RB), Wichita State (choice obtained from Washington)
4b	45	Jack Cummings (QB), North Carolina
5	56	Don Norton (E), Iowa
6	67	Emmett Wilson (T), Georgia Tech
7	81	John Wilkins (T), USC
8	92	Monte Lee (E), Texas
9		choice traded to Baltimore
10		choice traded to Detroit
11		choice traded to Chicago Bears
12	139	Dave Grosz (QB), Oregon
13	153	Dave Graham (E), Virginia
14	164	Ray Petersen (B), West Virginia
15	175	John Wilcox (T), Oregon
16	189	Larry Lancaster (T), Georgia
17	200	Mike Graney (E), Notre Dame
18	211	Emory Turner (G), Purdue
19	225	Bob Hain (T), Iowa
20	236	Ramon Armstrong (G), Texas Christian

1961

1	14	Art Baker (RB), Syracuse
2	28	Bo Strange (C), LSU
3a	36	Jim Wright (QB), Memphis State (choice obtained from St. Louis for Don Owens)
3b	42	Don Oakes (T), Virginia Tech
4a	53	Dan Ficca (G), USC (choice obtained from New York Giants)
4b		choice traded to Green Bay
5		choice traded to Detroit
6	84	Ben Balme (G), Yale
7	98	Irv Cross (B), Northwestern
8	112	Jim Beaver (G), Florida
9	126	Wayne Fontes (RB), Michigan State
10	140	Luther Hayes (E), USC
11	154	L. E. Hicks (T), Florida
12	168	Billy Majors (B), Tennessee
13	182	Don Jonas (QB), Penn State
14	196	Willie Fleming (RB), Iowa
15	210	Bobby Richards (DE), LSU
16	224	G. W. Clapp (G), Auburn
17	238	Larry Lavery (T), Illinois
18	252	Nick Maravich (T), North Carolina State
19	266	Dick Wilson (C), Penn State
20	280	Jacque MacKinnon (B), Colgate

1962

1		choice traded to St. Louis for King Hill
2	27	Pete Case (T), Georgia
3	40	Pat Holmes (T), Texas Tech
4	55	Bill Byrne (G), Boston College
5		choice traded to Los Angeles Rams

Rnd.	Sel. No.	Name (Position), College
1962 *(continued)*		
6a	77	Gus Gonzales (G), Tulane (choice obtained from Chicago Bears)
6b	83	John McGeever (RB), Auburn
7a	86	Jim Perkins (T), Colorado (choice obtained from Minnesota)
7b	96	Frank Budd (WR), Villanova
8	111	Ralph (Catfish) Smith (E), Mississippi
9	124	Bob Butler (T), Kentucky
10	139	Jim Skaggs (G), Washington
11	152	George Horne (T), Brigham Young
12	167	Larry Thompson (C), Tulane
13	180	George McKinney (B), Arkansas
14	195	Jim Schwab (E), Penn State
15	208	Mike Woulfe (LB), Colorado
16	223	Jerry Mazzanti (DE), Arkansas
17	236	Mike Martin (T), Washington State
18	251	Tom Larscheid (B), Utah State
19	264	Harold Ericksen (G), Georgia Tech
20	279	Ron Turner (E), Wichita State
1963		
1	4	Ed Budde (T), Michigan State
2	18	Ray Mansfield (T), Washington
3a	32	Dave Crossan (G), Maryland
3b	40	Louis Guy (B), Mississippi (choice obtained from Detroit)
4		choice traded to San Francisco for Bob Harrison
5		choice traded to Los Angeles for Roy Hord
6		choice traded to Cleveland for Howard Cassady
7	88	Lee Roy Caffey (LB), Texas A&M
8a	102	Tom Woodeshick (RB), West Virginia
8b	106	Gene Sykes (B), LSU (choice obtained from Washington)
9	116	Dennis Ward (T), Oklahoma
10	130	Pete Liske (QB), Penn State
11	144	Ralph Heck (LB), Colorado
12	158	Roger Gill (B), Texas Tech
13	172	Joe Iacone (B), West Chester
14	186	Nate Ramsey (B), Indiana
15	200	George Heard (E), New Mexico
16	214	Ronnie Goodwin (E), Baylor
17	228	Gordon Rush (B), Tulane
18	242	Rudy Mathews (T), Texas Christian
19	256	Mike Wasdovich (G), Indiana
20	270	Ben Rizzo (B), Miami (FL)
1964		
1	2	Bob Brown (G), Nebraska
2	16	Jack Concannon (QB), Boston College
3		choice traded to Detroit
4a	46	Ray Kubala (C), Texas A&M (choice obtained from Washington)
4b		choice traded to Green Bay
5	58	Mickey Babb (E), Georgia
6	72	Al Denson (E), Florida A&M
7	86	Pete Goimarac (C), West Virginia
8		choice traded to New York Giants
9	114	Larry Smith (B), Mississippi
10	128	Tom Boris (B), Purdue
11	142	Bob Berry (QB), Oregon
12	156	John Sapinsky (T), William & Mary
13	170	Howard Kindig (C), Cal State–Los Angeles
14	184	Ernie Arizzi (B), Maryland
15	198	Bob Burrows (T), East Texas State
16	212	Will Radosevich (T), Wyoming
17	226	Mike Morgan (LB), LSU
18	240	Izzy Lang (RB), Tennessee State
19	254	Dick Bowe (T), Rice
20	268	Tommy Lucas (G), Mississippi
1965		
1		choice traded to Green Bay along with Lee Roy Caffey for Jim Ringo and Earl Gros
2	20	Ray Rissmiller (T), Georgia
3	35	Al Nelson (DB), Cincinnati
4	48	Fred Hill (WR), USC

Rnd.	Sel. No.	Name (Position), College
5	63	John Henderson (E), Michigan
6a	76	John Huarte (QB), Notre Dame
6b	77	Gary Garrison (WR), San Diego State (choice obtained from Washington)
7	91	Erwin Will (T), Dayton
8	104	Al Piraino (T), Wisconsin
9	119	Floyd Hudlow (B), Arizona
10	132	Rick Redman (C), Washington
11	147	Louis James (RB), Texas–El Paso
12	161	John Kuznieski (RB), Purdue
13	175	John Fouse (E), Arizona
14	188	Tom Longo (B), Notre Dame
15	203	Otis Taylor (WR), Prairie View A&M
16	216	Jim Gray (B), Toledo
17	231	Dave Austin (E), Georgia Tech
18	244	Bill Marcordes (E), Bradley
19	259	Charley Englehart (T), John Carroll
20	272	Bobby Shann (RB), Boston College
1966		
1	4	Randy Beisler (DE), Indiana
2	20	Gary Pettigrew (DE), Stanford
3	36	Ben Hawkins (WR), Arizona State
4	52	Frank Emanuel (LB), Tennessee
5	68	Dan Berry (RB), California
6a	84	Bob Sherlag (DB), Memphis State
6b	89	Mel Tom (DE), San Jose State (choice obtained from Detroit)
7	99	David Lince (TE), North Dakota
8	114	John Mason (E), Stanford
9	129	Jim Todd (RB), Ball State
10	144	John Osmond (C), Tulsa
11	159	Welford Walton (DE), Nevada–Reno
12	174	Bruce Van Dyke (G), Missouri
13	189	Jim Bohl (RB), New Mexico State
14	204	Ron Medved (DB), Washington
15	219	Harry Day (T), Memphis State
16	234	Arunas Vasys (LB), Notre Dame
17	249	Ike Kelley (LB), Ohio State
18	264	Bill Moorer (C), Georgia Tech
19	279	Taft Reed (DB), Jackson State
20a	294	Bill Risio (T), Boston College
20b	298	Gerald Circo (K), Cal State–Chico (choice obtained from Minnesota)
1967		
1	19	Harry Jones (RB), Arkansas
2	44	Jon Brooks (G), Kent State
3a	68	Harry Wilson (RB), Nebraska (choice obtained from Los Angeles Rams)
3b		choice traded to Pittsburgh
4	99	Chuck Hughes (WR), Texas–El Paso
5a	114	Bob Van Pelt (C), Indiana (choice obtained from Detroit)
5b	125	Dick Absher (TE), Maryland
6	153	Bob Hughes (DE), Jackson State
7a	174	John Williams (DB), San Diego State (choice obtained from Los Angeles Rams)
7b	178	Bob Crenshaw (G), New Mexico State
8	203	Don Klacking (RB), Wyoming
9	231	Harold Stancell (DB), Tennessee
10	256	Maurice Bates (DE), Northern (SD)
11	281	Omar Parker (G), Washington
12	309	Ben Monroe (QB), New Mexico
13	334	Bill Downes (DT), Louisville
14	358	Dick Kenney (K), Michigan State
15	387	David Poche (T), McNeese
16	412	Lynn Baker (DB), Colorado
17	437	George Catavolos (DB), Purdue
1968		
1	14	Tim Rossovich (DE), USC
2	39	Cyril Pinder (RB), Illinois
3	68	Adrian Young (LB), USC
4	95	Len McNeil (G), Fresno State

Rnd.	Sel. No.	Name (Position), College
5a	122	Mike Dirks (T), Wyoming (choice obtained from Washington)
5b	124	Mark Nordquist (T), Pacific
6a	150	Thurman Randle (T), Texas–El Paso
6b	157	Dave Martin (DB), Notre Dame (choice obtained from Cleveland)
7	178	Joe Przybycki (G), Michigan State
8	204	Al Lavan (DB), Colorado State
9	232	Mike Evans (C), Boston College
10	258	John Mallory (DB), West Virginia
11	286	Len Persin (DE), Boston College
12	312	Thurston Taylor (TE), Florida State
13	340	George Barron (T), Mississippi State
14	366	Dan Williamson (LB), West Virginia
15	394	Joe Graham (G), Tennessee
16	420	Phil Creel (T), Northwestern State (LA)
17a	448	Joe Forzani (LB), Utah State
17b	459	Frank Antonini (RB), Parsons (choice obtained from Los Angeles Rams)

1969

Rnd.	Sel. No.	Name (Position), College
1	3	Leroy Keyes (RB), Purdue
2	28	Ernest Calloway (LB), Texas Southern
3a		choice traded to Cleveland for Larry Conjar
3b	69	Bill Bradley (DB), Texas (choice obtained from Minnesota for King Hill)
4	80	Bob Kuechenberg (G), Notre Dame
5	107	Jim Anderson (G), Missouri
6	132	Richard Barnhorst (TE), Xavier
7	159	Mike Schmeising (RB), St. Olaf
8	184	Bill Hobbs (LB), Texas A&M
9a	211	Kent Lawrence (WR), Georgia
9b	218	Lynn Buss (LB), Wisconsin (choice obtained from Washington for Mike Morgan)
10a	236	Sonny Wade (QB), Emory & Henry
10b	243	Donnie Shanklin (RB), Kansas (choice obtained from Washington for Mike Morgan)
11	263	Jim Marcum (DB), Texas–Arlington
12	288	Gary Adams (DB), Arkansas
13	314	Wade Key (TE), Southwest Texas State
14	340	James Ross (T), Bishop
15	367	Leon Angevine (WR), Penn State
16	392	Tom McClinton (DB), Southern
17	419	Bob Haack (T), Linfield (OR)

1970

Rnd.	Sel. No.	Name (Position), College
1	6	Steve Zabel (TE), Oklahoma
2	34	Raymond Jones (DB), Southern
3	59	Lee Bouggess (RB), Louisville
4		choice traded to Atlanta
5		choice traded to New York Giants for Ronnie Blye
6		choice traded to St. Louis for Curtis Gentry
7	158	Terry Brennan (T), Notre Dame
8	190	Ira Gordon (T), Kansas State
9	215	David King (LB), Stephen F. Austin
10	240	Steve Jaggard (DB), Memphis State
11	268	Billy Walik (KR), Villanova
12	293	Robert Jones (DT), Grambling
13	318	Richard Stevens (T), Baylor
14	346	Mark Moseley (K), Stephen F. Austin
15	371	John Carlos (WR), San Jose State
16	396	Tuufuli Uperesa (T), Montana
17	424	Mike Sizelove (TE), Idaho

1971

Rnd.	Sel. No.	Name (Position), College
1	5	Richard Harris (DE), Grambling
2	50	Henry Allison (G), San Diego State
3		choice traded to San Francisco along with Randy Beisler for George Mira
4	83	Happy Feller (K), Texas
5	108	Tom Shellabarger (T), San Diego State
6a	133	Jack Smith (DB), Troy State
6b	154	Wyck Neely (DB), Mississippi (choice obtained from Minnesota for Norm Snead)
7	161	Harold Carmichael (WR), Southern

Rnd.	Sel. No.	Name (Position), College
8	186	Leonard Gotshalk (C), Humboldt State
9	211	Len Pettigrew (LB), Ashland
10	256	Tom Bailey (RB), Florida State
11	264	Albert Davis (RB), Tennessee State
12	289	Rich Saathoff (DE), Northern Arizona
13	317	Danny Lester (DB), Texas
14	342	Robert Creech (LB), Texas Christian
15	367	Ed Fisher (G), Prairie View A&M
16	395	Bruce James (LB), Arkansas
17	420	John Sage (LB), Louisiana State

1972

Rnd.	Sel. No.	Name (Position), College
1	14	John Reaves (QB), Florida
2	37	Dan Yochum (T), Syracuse
3a		choice traded to Detroit
3b	68	Tom Luken (G), Purdue (choice obtained from Detroit for Bill Cappelman)
3c	76	Bobby Majors (DB), Tennessee (choice obtained from Minnesota for Norm Snead)
4	92	Ron (Po) James (RB), New Mexico State
5		choice traded to Denver for Pete Liske
6	144	Vern Winfield (G), Minnesota
7	170	Will Foster (LB), Eastern Michigan
8	196	Larry Ratcliff (RB), Eastern Michigan
9	222	Pat Gibbs (DB), Lamar University
10	248	John Bunting (LB), North Carolina
11	274	Dennis Sweeney (DE), Western Michigan
12	300	Don Zimmerman (WR), Northeast Louisiana
13	326	Preston Carpenter (DE), Mississippi
14	352	Bill Overmyer (LB), Ashland
15	378	Tom Sullivan (RB), Miami (FL)
16	404	Steve Bielenberg (LB), Oregon State
17	430	Tom Nash (T), Georgia

1973

Rnd.	Sel. No.	Name (Position), College
1a	3	Jerry Sisemore (T), Texas
1b	6	Charles Young (TE), USC (choice obtained from San Diego for Tim Rossovich)
2	28	Guy Morriss (G), Texas Christian
3	55	Randy Logan (DB), Michigan
4		choice traded to Baltimore for Norm Bulaich
5		choice traded to Chicago for Ron Bull
6	132	Bob Picard (WR), Eastern Washington
7	159	Will Wynn (DE), Tennessee State
8	184	Dan Lintner (DB), Indiana
9	211	John Nokes (LB), Northern Illinois
10		choice traded to Minnesota for Bill Cody
11	263	Gary Van Elst (DT), Michigan State
12	288	Joe Lavender (DB), San Diego State
13	315	Stan Davis (WR), Memphis State
14	340	Ralph Sacra (T), Texas A&M
15	367	Ken Schlezes (DB), Notre Dame
16	392	Frank Dowsing (DB), Mississippi State
17	419	Greg Oliver (RB), Trinity

1974

Rnd.	Sel. No.	Name (Position), College
1		choice traded to Los Angeles Rams for Roman Gabriel
2		choice traded to Baltimore for Norm Bulaich
3	63	Mitch Sutton (DT), Kansas
4	89	Frank LeMaster (LB), Kentucky
5a	108	Jim Cagle (DT), Georgia (choice obtained from Chicago)
5b	115	Keith Krepfle (TE), Iowa State
6		choice traded to New England
7	167	Willie Cullars (DE), Kansas State
8	193	Robert Woods (LB), Howard Payne
9	219	Mark Sheridan (WR), Holy Cross
10	245	Phil Polak (RB), Bowling Green
11	271	Bill Brittain (C), Kansas State
12	297	Artimus Parker (DB), USC
13	323	Lars Ditlev (DE), Colorado School of Mines
14	349	Dave Smith (LB), Oklahoma
15	375	Sid Bond (T), Texas Christian
16	401	Jim Smith (LB), Monmouth
17	427	Cliff Brown (RB), Notre Dame

Rnd.	Sel. No.	Name (Position), College
1975		
1		choice traded to Los Angeles Rams for Roman Gabriel
2		choice traded to Buffalo for Jerry Patton
3		choice traded to Los Angeles Rams for Roman Gabriel
4		choice traded to New Orleans for Dick Absher
5		choice traded to New England for John Tarver
6		choice traded to Cincinnati for Mike Boryla
7	167	Bill Capraun (T), Miami (FL)
8	198	Jeff Bleamer (T), Penn State
9		choice traded to San Francisco for Randy Jackson
10	248	Ken Schroy (DB), Maryland
11	273	Keith Rowen (G), Stanford
12	298	Richard Pawlewicz (RB), William & Mary
13	323	Tom Ehlers (LB), Kentucky
14	354	Larry O'Rourke (DT), Ohio State
15	379	Clayton Korver (DE), Northwestern (Iowa)
16	404	Calvin Jones (WR), Texas Tech
17	429	Garry Webb (DE), Temple
1976		
1		choice traded to Cincinnati for Mike Boryla
2		choice traded to Cincinnati along with John Reaves for Stan Walters and Wayne Clark
3		choice traded to Cincinnati for Horst Muhlmann
4a		choice traded to San Francisco for Randy Jackson
4b	111	Mike Smith (DE), Florida (choice obtained from Miami)
4c		choice obtained from New England for Steve Zabel was traded to Cleveland for Clifford Brooks
5	135	Greg Johnson (DT), Florida State
6	165	Kirk Johnson (T), Howard Payne
7	191	Carl Hairston (DE), Maryland–Eastern Shore
8	216	Richard LaFargue (C), Arkansas
9a	247	Mike Hogan (RB), Tennessee–Chattanooga (choice obtained from Chicago for Mark Nordquist)
9b	248	Richard Osborne (TE), Texas A&M
10	273	Herb Lusk (RB), Long Beach State
11	300	Mike Gilbert (DT), San Diego State
12		choice traded to New York Jets
13a	353	Terry Tautolo (LB), UCLA (choice obtained from New York Jets)
13b	358	Steve Ebbecke (DB), Villanova
14	385	Melvin Shy (DB), Tennessee State
15	412	Brett White (P), UCLA
16	439	Steve Campassi (RB), Kentucky
17	470	Anthony Terry (DB), California–Davis
1977		
1		choice traded to Cincinnati for Bill Bergey
2		choice traded to Oakland for James McAlister
3		choice traded to Dallas for John Niland
4		choice traded to Kansas City for Cliff Frazier
5	119	Skip Sharp (DB), Kansas
6a	145	Kevin Russell (DB), Tennessee State
6b	154	Wilbert Montgomery (RB), Abilene Christian (choice obtained from Chicago)
6c	158	Martin Mitchell (DB), Tulane (choice obtained from St. Louis through Washington for Joe Lavender)
7	175	Charles Johnson (DT), Colorado
8	202	Cleveland Franklin (RB), Baylor
9	229	T. J. Humphreys (G), Arkansas State
10	259	John Mastronardo (WR), Villanova
11a	283	Rocco Moore (T), Western Michigan (choice obtained from New York Jets)
11b	286	Mike Cordova (QB), Stanford
12		choice traded to New York Jets
1978		
1		choice traded to Cincinnati
2		choice traded to Cincinnati
3	66	Reggie Wilkes (LB), Georgia Tech
4	92	Dennis Harrison (DT), Vanderbilt
5a		choice traded to Kansas City
5b	130	Norris Banks (RB), Kansas (choice obtained from Washington)

Rnd.	Sel. No.	Name (Position), College
6		choice traded to Buffalo
7a		choice traded to Oakland
7b	186	Greg Marshall (DT), Oregon State (choice obtained from Minnesota)
8		choice traded to New York Jets
9	230	Charles Williams (DB), Jackson State
10		choice traded to Atlanta
11	288	Bill Campfield (RB), Kansas
12	315	Mark Slater (C), Minnesota
1979		
1	21	Jerry Robinson (LB), UCLA
2	48	Petey Perot (G), Northwest Louisiana
3	74	Tony Franklin (K), Texas A&M
4a	94	Ben Cowins (RB), Arkansas (choice obtained from St. Louis through Washington for Joe Lavender)
4b		choice traded to Atlanta
5	126	Scott Fitzkee (WR), Penn State
6		choice traded to New York Giants
7a	178	Don Swafford (T), Florida (choice obtained from Cleveland)
7b	185	Curtis Bunche (DE), Albany State
8a	196	Chuck Correal (C), Penn State (choice obtained from Buffalo)
8b	211	Max Runager (P), South Carolina
9		choice traded to Oakland
10		choice traded to San Diego
11	296	Al Chesley (LB), Pittsburgh
12		choice traded to Pittsburgh
1980		
1	23	Roynell Young (DB), Alcorn State
2	53	Perry Harrington (RB), Jackson State
3		choice forfeited
4		choice traded to Atlanta
5	135	Nate Rivers (WR), South Carolina State
6	161	Greg Murtha (T), Minnesota
7	188	Terrell Ward (DB), San Diego State
8	218	Mike Curcio (LB), Temple
9	245	Bob Harris (T), Bowling Green
10		choice traded to Miami
11a	298	Lee Jukes (WR), North Carolina State (choice obtained from Miami)
11b	302	Thomas Brown (DE), Baylor
12	329	Howard Fields (DB), Baylor
1981		
1	27	Leonard Mitchell (DE), Houston
2	55	Dean Miraldi (G), Utah
3	82	Greg LaFleur (TE), Louisiana State
4	110	Calvin Murray (RB), Ohio State
5		choice traded to Miami
6		choice traded to New York Giants
7a	174	Alan Duncan (K), Tennessee (choice obtained from San Francisco)
7b	192	Doak Field (LB), Baylor
8		choice traded to Baltimore
9	247	Chuck Commiskey (DB), Mississippi
10	275	Hubert Oliver (RB), Arizona
11	303	Gail Davis (DT), Virginia Union
12	331	Ray Ellis (DB), Ohio State
1982		
1	20	Mike Quick (WR), North Carolina State
2	47	Lawrence Sampleton (TE), Texas
3	78	Vyto Kab (TE), Penn State
4	105	Anthony Griggs (LB), Ohio State
5	132	Dennis DeVaughn (DB), Bishop
6	159	Curt Grieve (WR), Yale
7	190	Harvey Armstrong (DT), Southern Methodist
8	217	Jim Fritzche (T), Purdue
9	244	Tony Woodruff (WR), Fresno State
10		choice traded to Miami
11	301	Ron Ingram (WR), Oklahoma State
12	328	Rob Taylor (T), Northwestern

Rnd.	Sel. No.	Name (Position), College
1983		
1	8	Michael Haddix (RB), Mississippi State
2a	35	Wes Hopkins (DB), Southern Methodist
2b	46	Jody Schulz (LB), East Carolina (choice obtained from Minnesota)
3	62	Glen Young (WR), Mississippi State
4	89	Mike Williams (RB), Mississippi College
5	120	Byron Darby (DT), USC
6	147	Victor Oatis (WR), Northwest Louisiana
7a	174	Anthony Edgar (RB), Hawaii
7b	182	Jon Schultheis (G), Princeton (choice obtained from Cleveland)
8	201	Rich Kraynak (LB), Pittsburgh
9	232	Rich Pelzer (T), Rhode Island
10	258	Thomas Strauthers (DT), Jackson State
11	285	Steve Sebahar (C), Washington State
12	312	David Mangrum (QB), Baylor
1984		
1	4	Kenny Jackson (WR), Penn State
2		choice traded to Atlanta
3	60	Rusty Russell (T), South Carolina
4	88	Evan Cooper (DB), Michigan
5	116	Andre Hardy (RB), St. Mary's (CA)
6	144	Scott Raridon (T), Nebraska
7	172	Joe Hayes (RB), Central State (OK)
8	200	Manny Matsakis (K), Capital
9		choice traded to Cleveland
10	256	John Thomas (DB), Texas Christian
11	284	John Robertson (T), East Carolina
12	312	Paul McFadden (K), Youngstown State
1984 Supplemental Draft		
1		Reggie White (DE), Tennessee
2		Daryl Goodlow (LB), Oklahoma
3		Thomas Carter (LB), San Diego State
1985		
1	9	Kevin Allen (T), Indiana
2	37	Randall Cunningham (QB), UNLV
3		choice traded to Miami
4	93	Greg Naron (G), North Carolina
5	121	Dwayne Jiles (LB), Texas Tech
6a		choice traded to Kansas City
6b	156	Ken Reeves (T), Texas A&M (choice obtained from New England)
7		choice traded to Washington
8	205	Tom Polley (LB), UNLV
9a	231	Dave Toub (C), Texas–El Paso (choice obtained from Cleveland)
9b	233	Joe Drake (DT), Arizona
10	261	Mark Kelso (DB), William & Mary
11	289	Herman Hunter (RB), Tennessee State
12	317	Todd Russell (DB), Boston College
1986		
1	10	Keith Byars (RB), Ohio State
2a	37	Anthony Toney (RB), Texas A&M
2b	48	Alonzo Johnson (LB), Florida (choice obtained from Washington through Los Angeles Raiders)
3		choice traded to San Francisco for Matt Cavanaugh
4a		choice traded to San Diego for Earnest Jackson
4b	106	Matt Darwin (C), Texas A&M (choice obtained from Los Angeles Rams)
5a	121	Ray Criswell (P), Florida
5b	128	Dan McMillen (DE), Colorado (choice obtained from Washington through Atlanta)
6	149	Bob Landsee (C), Wisconsin
7a	169	Corn Redick (WR), Cal State–Fullerton (choice obtained from Atlanta)
7b	176	Byron Lee (LB), Ohio State
8a		choice traded to San Francisco for Keith Baker
8b	208	Seth Joyner (LB), Texas–El Paso (choice obtained from Cleveland)

Rnd.	Sel. No.	Name (Position), College
9	233	Clyde Simmons (DE), Western Carolina
10	261	Junior Tautalatasi (RB), Washington State
11	288	Steve Bogdalek (G), Michigan State
12a	315	Reggie Singletary (DE), North Carolina State
12b	325	Bobby Howard (RB), Indiana (choice obtained from New York Giants)
1986 Supplemental Draft		
1		Charles Crawford (RB), Oklahoma State
1987		
1	9	Jerome Brown (DT), Miami (FL)
2		choice traded to San Francisco
3	65	Ben Tamburello (C), Auburn
4	93	Byron Evans (LB), Arizona
5	121	David Alexander (C), Tulsa
6a	149	Ron Moten (LB), Florida
6b	158	Chris Pike (DT), Tulsa (choice obtained from Seattle)
7a	177	Brian Williams (T), Central Michigan
7b		choice exercised in 1986 Supplemental Draft (choice obtained from Los Angeles Rams)
8		choice traded to San Diego
9	232	Ken Lambiotte (QB), William & Mary
10	260	Paul Carberry (DT), Oregon State
11		choice traded to Los Angeles Raiders through San Francisco
12	316	Bobby Morse (RB), Michigan State
1987 Supplemental Draft		
1		Cris Carter (WR), Ohio State
1988		
1	13	Keith Jackson (TE), Oklahoma
2a	30	Eric Allen (DB), Arizona State (choice obtained from Tampa Bay)
2b		choice traded to San Francisco through Tampa Bay
3	64	Matt Patchan (T), Miami (FL)
4		choice exercised in 1987 Supplemental Draft
5	122	Eric Everett (DB), Texas Tech
6a	149	Don McPherson (QB), Syracuse
6b	160	Rob Sterling (DB), Maine (choice obtained from Cleveland)
7	176	Todd White (WR), Fullerton State
8	207	David Smith (RB), Western Kentucky
9		choice traded to Detroit
10	261	Joe Schuster (DT), Iowa
11	288	Izel Jenkins (DB), North Carolina State
12	319	Steve Kaufusi (DE), Brigham Young
1989		
1		choice traded to Indianapolis
2	49	Jessie Small (LB), Eastern Kentucky
3a	76	Robert Drummond (RB), Syracuse
3b	81	Britt Hager (LB), Texas (choice obtained from Chicago)
4		choice traded to Seattle
5		choice traded to Chicago
6	162	Heath Sherman (RB), Texas A&I
7–12		choices traded to Chicago
1990		
1	22	Ben Smith (DB), Georgia
2	50	Mike Bellamy (WR), Illinois
3	77	Fred Barnett (WR), Arkansas State
4		choice traded to Indianapolis
5	133	Calvin Williams (WR), Purdue
6	162	Kevin Thompson (DB), Oklahoma
7	189	Terry Strouf (T), Wisconsin–La Crosse
8	217	Curt Dykes (T), Oregon
9	244	Cecil Gray (DT), North Carolina
10	273	Orlando Adams (DT), Jacksonville State
11a	294	John Hudson (C), Auburn (choice obtained from New Orleans)
11b	300	Tyrone Watson (WR), Tennessee State
12	327	Judd Garrett (RB), Princeton

Rnd.	Sel. No.	Name (Position), College
1991		
1a	8	Antone Davis (T), Tennessee (choice obtained from Green Bay)
1b		choice traded to Green Bay
2	48	Jesse Campbell (DB), North Carolina State
3	75	Rob Selby (T), Auburn
4	104	William Thomas (LB), Texas A&M
5	131	Craig Erickson (QB), Miami (FL)
6a	156	Andy Harmon (DE), Kent State (choice obtained from Houston)
6b		choice traded to New York Jets
7	187	James Joseph (RB), Auburn
8	216	Scott Kowalkowski (LB), Notre Dame
9	242	Chuck Weatherspoon (RB), Houston
10	271	Eric Harmon (G), Clemson
11	298	Mike Flores (DE), Louisville
12	327	Darrell Beavers (DB), Morehead State
1992		
1		choice traded to Dallas through Green Bay and Atlanta
2	48	Siran Stacy (RB), Alabama
3	75	Tommy Jeter (DT), Texas
4a	92	Tony Brooks (RB), Notre Dame (choice obtained from Cleveland)
4b	102	Casey Weldon (QB), Florida State
5	129	Corey Barlow (DB), Auburn
6	160	Jeff Sydner (WR), Hawaii
7	187	William Boatwright (G), Virginia Tech
8	214	Chuck Bullough (LB), Michigan State
9	241	Ephesians Bartley (LB), Florida
10	272	Mark McMillian (DB), Alabama
11	299	Pumpy Tudors (P), Tennessee–Chattanooga
12	326	Brandon Houston (T), Oklahoma
1993		
1a		choice traded to Houston
1b	19	Lester Holmes (G), Jackson State (choice obtained from Houston)
1c	24	Leonard Renfro (DT), Colorado (compensatory choice awarded by the NFL)
2	50	Victor Bailey (WR), Missouri
3a	75	Derrick Frazier (DB), Texas A&M (choice obtained from Houston)
3b	77	Mike Reid (DB), North Carolina State
4		choice traded to Tampa Bay through San Diego
5		choice traded to Buffalo
6	163	Derrick Oden (LB), Alabama
7	190	Joey Mickey (TE), Oklahoma
8	217	Doug Skene (T), Michigan
1994		
1	14	Bernard Williams (T), Georgia
2a	37	Bruce Walker (DT), UCLA (choice obtained from Atlanta)
2b	42	Charlie Garner (RB), Tennessee
3a	77	Joe Panos (G), Wisconsin
3b	103	Eric Zomalt (DB), California (compensatory choice awarded by the NFL)
4		choice traded to Atlanta
5	144	Marvin Goodwin (DB), UCLA
6a	174	Ryan McCoy (LB), Houston
6b	193	Mitch Berger (P), Colorado (compensatory choice awarded by the NFL)
7	206	Mark Montgomery (RB), Wisconsin
1995		
1a	7	Mike Mamula (DE), Boston College (choice obtained from Tampa Bay)
1b		choice traded to Tampa Bay
2a		choice traded to Tampa Bay
2b	50	Bobby Taylor (DB), Notre Dame (choice obtained from Kansas City)

Rnd.	Sel. No.	Name (Position), College
2c	58	Barrett Brooks (T), Kansas State (choice obtained from Cleveland)
2d		compensatory choice awarded by the NFL traded to Dallas through Tampa Bay
3a	72	Greg Jefferson (DE), Central Florida (choice obtained from Tampa Bay)
3b		choice traded to New England
3c	78	Chris T. Jones (WR), Miami (FL) (choice obtained from Denver)
4a		choice traded to New England through Kansas City
4b	119	Dave Barr (QB), California (choice obtained from Kansas City through San Francisco and Cleveland)
5a		choice traded to Cleveland
5b		choice traded to Jacksonville
6a		choice traded to San Diego
6b	208	Fred McCrary (RB), Mississippi State (choice obtained from Jacksonville)
7a	210	Kevin Bouie (RB), Mississippi State (choice obtained from Jacksonville)
7b		choice traded to Jacksonville
7c	248	Howard Smothers (T), Bethune-Cookman (choice obtained from Jacksonville)
1996		
1	25	Jermane Mayberry (G), Texas A&M–Kingsville
2a	54	Jason Dunn (TE), Eastern Kentucky
2b	61	Brian Dawkins (DB), Clemson (compensatory choice awarded by the NFL)
3	85	Bobby Hoying (QB), Ohio State
4	121	Ray Farmer (LB), Duke
5a	147	Whit Marshall (LB), Georgia (choice obtained from Denver)
5b		choice traded to Dallas through Baltimore
6a	194	Steve White (DE), Tennessee
6b	197	Tony Johnson (TE), Alabama (choice obtained from Green Bay)
6c	199	Phillip Riley (WR), Florida State (choice obtained from Kansas City)
7		choice traded to Baltimore
1997		
1a		choice traded to Dallas
1b	25	Jon Harris (DE), Virginia (choice obtained from Dallas)
2a		choice traded to San Francisco
2b	57	James Darling (LB), Washington State (choice obtained from San Francisco)
3a	71	Duce Staley (RB), South Carolina (choice obtained from Arizona)
3b		choice traded to Arizona
4	119	Damien Robinson (DB), Iowa
5a	152	N. D. Kalu (DE), Rice
5b	155	Luther Broughton (TE), Furman (choice obtained from Dallas)
6a		choice traded to Arizona
6b	190	Antwuan Wyatt (WR), Bethune-Cookman (choice obtained from San Francisco)
6c	198	Edward Jasper (DT), Texas A&M (compensatory choice awarded by the NFL)
7a	207	Koy Detmer (QB), Colorado (choice obtained from St. Louis through New York Jets)
7b	225	Byron Capers (DB), Florida State
7c	227	Deauntae Brown (DB), Central State (OH) (choice obtained from San Francisco)
1998		
1	11	Tra Thomas (T), Florida State
2		choice traded to Pittsburgh through New York Jets
3a	72	Jeremiah Trotter (LB), Stephen F. Austin
3b	85	Allen Rossum (DB), Notre Dame (choice obtained from New York Giants)
4a		choice traded to Miami
4b	112	Brandon Whiting (DT), California (choice obtained from Miami)

Rnd.	Sel. No.	Name (Position), College
4c	116	Clarence Love (DB), Toledo (choice obtained from New York Giants)
5a		choice traded to New York Jets
5b	142	Ike Reese (LB), Michigan State (choice obtained from Miami)
6		choice traded to New York Jets
7a		choice traded to Denver
7b	220	Chris Akins (DT), Texas (compensatory choice awarded by the NFL)
7c	240	Melvin Thomas (G), Colorado (compensatory choice awarded by the NFL)

1999

Rnd.	Sel. No.	Name (Position), College
1	2	Donovan McNabb (QB), Syracuse
2	35	Barry Gardner (LB), Northwestern
3	64	Doug Brzezinski (G), Boston College
4a	97	John Welbourn (G), California
4b	128	Damon Moore (DB), Ohio State (compensatory choice awarded by the NFL)
4c	130	Na Brown (WR), North Carolina (compensatory choice awarded by the NFL)
5		choice traded to Detroit
6a	172	Cecil Martin (RB), Wisconsin
6b	201	Troy Smith (WR), East Carolina (choice obtained from Denver)
7a	208	Jed Weaver (TE), Oregon
7b	251	Pernell Davis (DE), Alabama–Birmingham (compensatory choice awarded by the NFL)

2000

Rnd.	Sel. No.	Name (Position), College
1	6	Corey Simon (DT), Florida State
2a	36	Todd Pinkston (WR), Southern Mississippi
2b	61	Bobby Williams (T), Arkansas (choice obtained from Tennessee)
3		choice traded to Tennessee
4a	99	Gari Scott (WR), Michigan State
4b		choice traded to San Diego
5		choice traded to Tennessee
6a	171	Thomas Hamner (RB), Minnesota
6b	178	John Frank (DE), Utah (choice obtained from Oakland)
6c	192	John Romero (C), California (choice obtained from Washington)
7		choice traded to New England for Dietrich Jells in 1998

2001

Rnd.	Sel. No.	Name (Position), College
1	25	Freddie Mitchell (WR), UCLA
2	55	Quinton Caver (LB), Arkansas
3a	63	Derrick Burgess (DE), Mississippi (choice obtained from San Diego)
3b		choice traded to Miami
4	121	Correll Buckhalter (RB), Nebraska
5a	147	Tony Stewart (TE), Penn State (choice obtained from Green Bay)
5b	155	A. J. Feeley (QB), Oregon
6		choice traded to Miami
7		choice traded to Carolina

2002

Rnd.	Sel. No.	Name (Position), College
1	26	Lito Sheppard (DB), Florida
2a	58	Michael Lewis (DB), Colorado
2b	59	Sheldon Brown (DB), South Carolina (choice obtained from Miami)
3	91	Brian Westbrook (RB), Villanova
4	124	Scott Peters (C), Arizona State
5	162	Freddie Milons (WR), Alabama
6	198	Tyreo Harrison (LB), Notre Dame
7	238	Raheem Brock (DE), Temple

2003

Rnd.	Sel. No.	Name (Position), College
1a	15	Jerome McDougle (DE), Miami (FL) (choice obtained from San Diego)
1b		choice traded to San Diego
2	61	L. J. Smith (TE), Rutgers
3	95	Billy McMullen (WR), Virginia
4a		choice traded to Green Bay
4b	131	Jamaal Green (DE), Miami (FL) (compensatory choice awarded by the NFL)
5		choice traded to Green Bay
6a	185	Jeremy Bridges (G), Southern Mississippi (choice obtained from Green Bay)
6b		choice traded to Atlanta
7a	244	Norman Lejeune (DB), Louisiana State (choice obtained from Green Bay)
7b		choice traded to Green Bay

2004

Rnd.	Sel. No.	Name (Position), College
1a	16	Shawn Andrews (T), Arkansas (choice obtained from San Francisco)
1b		choice traded to San Francisco
2		choice traded to San Francisco
3	89	Matt Ware (DB), UCLA
4a		choice traded to Atlanta
4b	129	J. R. Reed (DB), South Florida (compensatory choice awarded by the NFL)
4c	131	Trey Darilek (G), Texas–El Paso (compensatory choice awarded by the NFL)
5a		choice traded to Baltimore
5b	162	Thomas Tapeh (RB), Minnesota (choice obtained from Kansas City)
6a	185	Andy Hall (QB), Delaware (choice obtained from Green Bay)
6b	192	Dexter Wynn (DB), Colorado State
7a	227	Adrien Clarke (G), Ohio State
7b	242	Bruce Perry (RB), Maryland (compensatory choice awarded by the NFL)
7c	243	Dominic Furio (C), Nevada–Las Vegas (compensatory choice awarded by the NFL)

2005

Rnd.	Sel. No.	Name (Position), College
1	31	Mike Patterson (DT), USC
2a	35	Reggie Brown (WR), Georgia (choice obtained from Miami)
2b	63	Matt McCoy (LB), San Diego State
3a	77	Ryan Moats (RB), Louisiana Tech (choice obtained from Kansas City)
3b		choice traded to San Francisco
4a	102	Sean Considine (S), Iowa (choice obtained from San Francisco)
4b	126	Todd Herremans (T), Saginaw Valley State (choice obtained from Denver)
4c		choice traded to Dallas
5a	146	Trent Cole (DE), Cincinnati (choice obtained from Washington)
5b	172	Scott Young (G), Brigham Young (compensatory choice awarded by the NFL)
5c		choice traded to Green Bay
6a		choice traded to Oakland
6b		choice traded to San Francisco
6c	211	Calvin Armstrong (T), Washington State (compensatory choice awarded by the NFL)
7a		choice traded to Green Bay
7b	247	Keyonta Marshall (DT), Grand Valley State (compensatory choice awarded by the NFL)
7c	252	David Bergeron (LB), Stanford (compensatory choice awarded by the NFL)

REGULAR-SEASON INDIVIDUAL RECORDS

SERVICE

Most Seasons

14	Chuck Bednarik (1949–62)
13	Harold Carmichael (1971–83)
13	Frank (Bucko) Kilroy (1943–55)
13	Vic Sears (1941–53)
12	Jerry Sisemore (1973–84)
12	Bobby Walston (1951–62)

Most Games Played

180	Harold Carmichael (1971–83)
169	Chuck Bednarik (1949–62)
159	Randy Logan (1973–83)
157	Guy Morriss (1973–83)
156	Jerry Sisemore (1973–84)

Most Consecutive Games

162	Harold Carmichael (1972–83)
159	Randy Logan (1973–83)
148	Bobby Walston (1951–62)
139	Ken Clarke (1977–87)
135	Herman Edwards (1977–85)
129	Frank LeMaster (1974–82)
127	Jerry Sisemore (1974–82)

SCORING

Most Points, Career

881	Bobby Walston (1951–62)
616	David Akers (1999–2004)
475	Sam Baker (1964–69)
474	Harold Carmichael (1971–83)
464	Steve Van Buren (1944–51)
412	Tony Franklin (1979–83)
402	Tommy McDonald (1957–63)
390	Paul McFadden (1984–87)
382	Roger Ruzek (1989–93)
378	Pete Pihos (1947–55)
372	Timmy Brown (1960–67)
366	Mike Quick (1982–90)

Most Points, Season

133	David Akers (2002)
122	David Akers (2004)
121	David Akers (2000)
116	Paul McFadden (1984)
115	David Akers (2001)
115	Gary Anderson (1996)

Most Points, Game

25	Bobby Walston (10/17/54 at Redskins)
24	*see* Most Touchdowns, Game

Most Touchdowns, Career

79	Harold Carmichael (1971–83)
77	Steve Van Buren (1944–51)
67	Tommy McDonald (1957–63)
63	Pete Pihos (1947–55)
62	Timmy Brown (1960–67)
61	Mike Quick (1982–90)
58	Wilbert Montgomery (1977–84)

Most Touchdowns, Season

18	Steve Van Buren (1945)
14	Terrell Owens (2004)
14	Wilbert Montgomery (1979)
14	Steve Van Buren (1947)
13	6 times; most recently by Brian Westbrook (2003)

Most Touchdowns, Game

4	Irving Fryar (10/20/96 vs. Dolphins)
4	Wilbert Montgomery (10/15/78 at Redskins and 10/7/79 vs. Redskins)
4	Ben Hawkins (9/28/69 vs. Steelers)
4	Tommy McDonald (10/4/59 vs. Giants)
4	Clarence Peaks (11/16/58 vs. Chicago Cardinals)
4	Joe Carter (11/6/34 vs. Cincinnati Reds)
3	Tommy McDonald (5 times); Steve Van Buren and Timmy Brown (3 times); Pete Retzlaff, Terrell Owens, and Brian Westbrook (2 times); Swede Hanson, Joe Carter, Bosh Pritchard, Jack Ferrante, Harold Giancanelli, Pete Pihos, Bobby Walston, Wilbert Montgomery, Mike Quick, Keith Jackson, Calvin Williams, Charlie Garner, Irving Fryar, and Duce Staley (once each)

Most Points After Touchdown, Career

365	Bobby Walston (1951–62)
205	Sam Baker (1964–69)
199	David Akers (1999–2004)
172	Tony Franklin (1979–83)
139	Roger Ruzek (1989–93)
117	Paul McFadden (1984–87)

Most Points After Touchdown, Season

50	Cliff Patton (1948)
48	Roger Ruzek (1990)
48	Tony Franklin (1980)
45	Sam Baker (1967)
45	Bobby Walston (1953)

Most Consecutive Points After Touchdown

153	David Akers (2001–04)
84	Cliff Patton (1947–49)

Most Field Goals, Career

139	David Akers (1999–2004)
91	Paul McFadden (1984–87)
90	Sam Baker (1964–69)
81	Roger Ruzek (1989–93)
80	Tony Franklin (1979–83)
80	Bobby Walston (1951–62)

Most Field Goals, Season

30	David Akers (2002)
30	Paul McFadden (1984)
29	David Akers (2000)
28	Roger Ruzek (1991)
27	David Akers (2004)

Most Field Goals, Game

6	Tom Dempsey (11/12/72 at Houston Oilers; 7 att.)
5	David Akers (11/18/01 at Cowboys; 5 att.)
5	Gary Anderson (12/22/96 vs. Arizona Cardinals; 5 att.)
5	Gary Anderson (10/1/95 at Saints; 5 att.)
4	19 times; most recently by David Akers (12/5/04 vs. Packers; 4 att.)

Longest Field Goals

59	Tony Franklin (11/12/79 at Cowboys)
57	David Akers (9/14/03 vs. Patriots)
54	Tom Dempsey (12/12/71 vs. St. Louis Cardinals)
53	David Akers (10/24/99 at Dolphins)
53	Roger Ruzek (12/9/90 at Dolphins)
52	David Akers (10/5/03 vs. Redskins)
52	Paul McFadden (10/13/85 vs. St. Louis Cardinals and 11/4/84 at Lions)
52	Tony Franklin (11/27/83 at Redskins)
52	Tom Dempsey (12/5/71 at Lions, 11/12/72 at Houston Oilers, and 10/15/72 vs. LA Rams)

Most Consecutive Field Goals Made

17	David Akers (2001)
15	David Akers (2004)
13	David Akers (2003)
13	David Akers (1999–2000) (1 in 1999, 12 in 2000)
12	David Akers (2002)
12	Gary Anderson (1996)
12	Sam Baker (1966–67)

RUSHING

Most Attempts, Career

1,465	Wilbert Montgomery (1977–84)
1,320	Steve Van Buren (1944–51)
1,200	Duce Staley (1997–2003)
975	Ricky Watters (1995–97)
871	Tom Sullivan (1972–77)
850	Timmy Brown (1960–67)

Most Attempts, Season

353	Ricky Watters (1996)
338	Wilbert Montgomery (1979)
337	Ricky Watters (1995)
325	Duce Staley (1999)
286	Wilbert Montgomery (1981)
285	Ricky Watters (1997)

Most Attempts, Game

35	Heath Sherman (10/6/91 at Buccaneers and 11/12/90 vs. Redskins)
35	Steve Van Buren (11/20/49 vs. NY Bulldogs)
34	Earnest Jackson (10/13/85 at St. Louis Cardinals)
33	Ricky Watters (12/10/95 vs. Cowboys)
33	Steve Van Buren (10/3/49 vs. Lions)
32	Tom Sullivan (9/23/73 at Giants)

Longest Run from Scrimmage

91t	Herschel Walker (11/27/94 at Falcons)
90t	Wilbert Montgomery (12/19/82 vs. Oilers)
85t	Brian Mitchell (10/1/00 vs. Falcons)
80	Leroy Harris (11/25/79 at Packers)
77t	Bosh Pritchard (10/23/49 vs. Redskins)
72t	Wilbert Montgomery (9/14/80 at Vikings)
71t	John Brewer (10/4/52 vs. Giants)

Most Yards Gained, Career

6,538	Wilbert Montgomery (1977–84)
5,860	Steve Van Buren (1944–51)
4,807	Duce Staley (1997–2003)
4,482	Randall Cunningham (1985–95)
3,794	Ricky Watters (1995–97)
3,703	Timmy Brown (1960–67)
3,563	Tom Woodeshick (1963–71)
3,135	Tom Sullivan (1972–77)

Most Yards Gained, Season

1,512	Wilbert Montgomery (1979)
1,411	Ricky Watters (1996)
1,402	Wilbert Montgomery (1981)
1,273	Duce Staley (1999)
1,273	Ricky Watters (1995)
1,220	Wilbert Montgomery (1978)
1,146	Steve Van Buren (1949)
1,110	Ricky Watters (1997)
1,070	Herschel Walker (1992)
1,065	Duce Staley (1998)
1,029	Duce Staley (2002)
1,028	Earnest Jackson (1985)
1,008	Steve Van Buren (1947)

Most Yards Gained, Game

205	Steve Van Buren (11/27/49 vs. Steelers)
201	Duce Staley (9/3/00 at Cowboys)
197	Wilbert Montgomery (11/4/79 vs. Browns)
190	Swede Hanson (11/6/34 vs. Cincinnati Reds)
186	Timmy Brown (11/7/65 at Browns)
180	Timmy Brown (11/28/65 at St. Louis Cardinals)
174	Steve Van Buren (11/20/49 vs. NY Bulldogs)
173	Ricky Watters (10/20/96 vs. Dolphins)
171	Steve Van Buren (11/21/48 vs. Redskins)

Most Touchdowns Rushing, Career

69	Steve Van Buren (1944–51)
45	Wilbert Montgomery (1977–84)
32	Randall Cunningham (1985–95)
31	Ricky Watters (1995–97)
29	Timmy Brown (1960–67)
22	Duce Staley (1997–2003)

Most Touchdowns Rushing, Season

15	Steve Van Buren (1945)
13	Ricky Watters (1996)
13	Steve Van Buren (1947)
11	3 times; most recently by Ricky Watters (1995)

Most Touchdowns Rushing, Game

3	Charlie Garner (10/8/95 vs. Redskins)
3	Wilbert Montgomery (12/19/82 vs. Houston Oilers, 10/7/79 vs. Redskins, and 9/10/78 at Redskins)
3	Tom Sullivan (10/13/74 vs. Giants)
3	Clarence Peaks (11/16/58 vs. Chicago Cardinals)
3	Steve Van Buren (12/9/45 vs. Boston Yanks)
3	Swede Hanson (11/6/34 vs. Cincinnati Reds)

Consecutive Games Rushing Touchdowns

8	Steve Van Buren (1947)

ROOKIE RUSHING RECORDS

Most Yards Gained, Game, Rookie

134	Correll Buckhalter (10/7/01 vs. Arizona Cardinals)
129	Steve Van Buren (11/5/44 at Brooklyn Dodgers)
127	Keith Byars (12/7/86 vs. St. Louis Cardinals)
122	Charlie Garner (10/9/94 vs. Redskins)
111	Charlie Garner (10/2/94 at 49ers)
103	Wilbert Montgomery (12/18/77 vs. Jets)

Most Yards Gained, Rookie Season

586	Correll Buckhalter (2001)
577	Keith Byars (1986)

PASSING

Most Passes Attempted, Career

3,918	Ron Jaworski (1977–86)
3,362	Randall Cunningham (1985–95)
2,586	Donovan McNabb (1999–2004)
2,236	Norman Snead (1964–70)
1,396	Tommy Thompson (1941–42, 1945–50)

Most Passes Attempted, Season

569	Donovan McNabb (2000)
560	Randall Cunningham (1988)
532	Randall Cunningham (1989)
493	Donovan McNabb (2001)
490	Randall Cunningham (1994)
484	Ron Jaworski (1985)

Most Passes Attempted, Game

62	Randall Cunningham (10/2/89 at Bears)
60	Davey O'Brien (12/1/40 at Redskins)
57	Sonny Jurgensen (9/23/62 vs. Giants)
55	Donovan McNabb (11/12/00 at Steelers)
55	Roman Gabriel (12/2/73 at 49ers)
53	Randall Cunningham (10/23/88 vs. Cowboys)
51	Randall Cunningham (11/22/87 vs. St. Louis Cardinals)

Most Passes Completed, Career

2,088	Ron Jaworski (1977–86)
1,874	Randall Cunningham (1985–95)
1,507	Donovan McNabb (1999–2004)
1,154	Norman Snead (1964–70)
723	Tommy Thompson (1941–42, 1945–50)

Most Passes Completed, Season

330	Donovan McNabb (2000)
301	Randall Cunningham (1988)
300	Donovan McNabb (2004)
290	Randall Cunningham (1989)
285	Donovan McNabb (2001)
275	Donovan McNabb (2003)
271	Randall Cunningham (1990)
270	Roman Gabriel (1973)

Most Passes Completed, Game

34	Randall Cunningham (9/17/89 at Redskins)
33	Sonny Jurgensen (9/23/62 vs. Giants)
33	Davey O'Brien (12/1/40 at Redskins)

32	Donovan McNabb (12/5/04 vs. Packers)
32	Donovan McNabb (9/9/01 vs. St. Louis Rams)
32	Randall Cunningham (10/2/89 at Bears)
31	Randall Cunningham (10/10/88 vs. Giants)

Most Consecutive Completions

24	Donovan McNabb (first 10 on 11/28/04 at Giants and last 14 on 12/5/04 vs. Packers)
13	Donovan McNabb (first 12 on 11/16/03 vs. Giants and last one on 11/23/03 vs. Saints)
13	Bobby Hoying (11/16/97 at Ravens)
12	Donovan McNabb (11/17/02 vs. Arizona Cardinals)
12	Rodney Peete (10/12/97 at Jaguars)

Most Yards Gained, Career

26,963	Ron Jaworski (1977–86)
22,877	Randall Cunningham (1985–95)
16,926	Donovan McNabb (1999–2004)
15,672	Norman Snead (1964–70)
10,255	Tommy Thompson (1941–42, 1945–50)
9,639	Sonny Jurgensen (1957–63)
8,124	Bobby Thomason (1952–57)

Most Yards Gained, Season

3,875	Donovan McNabb (2004)
3,808	Randall Cunningham (1988)
3,723	Sonny Jurgensen (1961)
3,529	Ron Jaworski (1980)
3,466	Randall Cunningham (1990)
3,450	Ron Jaworski (1985)
3,400	Randall Cunningham (1989)
3,399	Norman Snead (1967)
3,365	Donovan McNabb (2000)

Most Yards Gained, Game

464	Donovan McNabb (12/5/04 vs. Packers)
447	Randall Cunningham (9/17/89 at Redskins)
437	Bobby Thomason (11/8/53 vs. Giants)
436	Sonny Jurgensen (10/28/61 at Redskins)
419	Sonny Jurgensen (12/16/62 at St. Louis Cardinals)
403	Sonny Jurgensen (12/17/61 at Lions)
401	Randall Cunningham (10/2/89 at Bears)
399	Sonny Jurgensen (10/1/61 vs. St. Louis Cardinals)

Most Touchdown Passes, Career

175	Ron Jaworski (1977–86)
150	Randall Cunningham (1985–95)
118	Donovan McNabb (1999–2004)
111	Norman Snead (1964–70)
90	Tommy Thompson (1941–42, 1945–50)
76	Sonny Jurgensen (1957–63)

Most Touchdown Passes, Season

32	Sonny Jurgensen (1961)
31	Donovan McNabb (2004)
30	Randall Cunningham (1990)
29	Norman Snead (1967)
27	Ron Jaworski (1980)
25	Donovan McNabb (2001)
25	Tommy Thompson (1948)

Most Touchdown Passes, Game

7	Adrian Burk (10/17/54 at Redskins)
5	Donovan McNabb (12/5/04 vs. Packers)
5	Randall Cunningham (9/17/89 at Redskins)
5	Norman Snead (9/28/69 vs. Steelers)
5	Sonny Jurgensen (12/16/62 at St. Louis Cardinals and 11/26/61 vs. Cowboys)
5	Adrian Burk (11/28/54 vs. Redskins)

Longest Pass Play

99t	Ron Jaworski to Mike Quick (11/10/85 vs. Falcons)
95t	Randall Cunningham to Fred Barnett (12/2/90 at Bills)
93	Randall Cunningham to Herschel Walker (9/4/94 at Giants)
92t	King Hill to Ben Hawkins (9/22/68 vs. Giants)
91t	Norm Van Brocklin to Tommy McDonald (10/5/58 vs. Giants)
90t	Ron Jaworski to Mike Quick (10/28/84 vs. St. Louis Cardinals)
87t	Norman Snead to Ben Hawkins (10/22/67 at St. Louis Cardinals)
87t	Norman Snead to Timmy Brown (10/4/64 vs. Steelers)

Most Passes Intercepted, Career

151	Ron Jaworski (1977–86)
124	Norm Snead (1964–70)
105	Randall Cunningham (1985–95)
100	Tommy Thompson (1941–42, 1945–50)
80	Bobby Thomason (1952–57)

Most Passes Intercepted, Season

26	Sonny Jurgensen (1962)
24	Norm Snead (1967)
24	Sonny Jurgensen (1961)
23	Norm Snead (1969)
23	Adrian Burk (1951)

Most Passes Intercepted, Game

6	Pete Liske (9/26/71 vs. Cowboys)
6	Bobby Thomason (10/21/56 vs. Chicago Cardinals)

Fewest Passes Intercepted, Season (min. 150 att.)

5	A. J. Feeley (2002; 154 att.)
5	Koy Detmer (1998; 181 att.)
5	Bubby Brister (1993; 309 att.)
6	Donovan McNabb (2002; 361 att.)
6	Ty Detmer (1997; 244 att.)
6	Bobby Hoying (1997; 225 att.)
6	Ron Jaworski (1986; 245 att.)

Lowest Interception Percentage, Season (min. 150 att.)

1.6	Bubby Brister (5–309; 1993)
1.7	Donovan McNabb (8–469; 2004)
1.7	Donovan McNabb (6–361; 2002)
2.3	Donovan McNabb (11–478; 2003)
2.3	Donovan McNabb (13–569; 2000)
2.4	Donovan McNabb (12–493; 2001)
2.4	Ron Jaworski (6–245; 1986)
2.5	Ty Detmer (6–244; 1997)

RECEIVING

Most Passes Caught, Career

589	Harold Carmichael (1971–83)
452	Pete Retzlaff (1956–66)
373	Pete Pihos (1947–55)
371	Keith Byars (1986–92)
363	Mike Quick (1982–90)
311	Bobby Walston (1951–62)
308	Fred Barnett (1990–95)
295	Calvin Williams (1990–96)
287	Tommy McDonald (1957–63)
275	Duce Staley (1997–2003)

Most Passes Caught, Season

88	Irving Fryar (1996)
86	Irving Fryar (1997)
81	Keith Byars (1990)
81	Keith Jackson (1988)
78	Fred Barnett (1994)
77	Terrell Owens (2004)
75	Herschel Walker (1993)
73	Brian Westbrook (2004)
73	Mike Quick (1985)
72	Keith Byars (1988)
70	Chris T. Jones (1996)

Most Passes Caught, Game

14	Don Looney (12/1/40 at Redskins)
12	Keith Byars (9/30/90 vs. Indianapolis Colts)
12	Keith Jackson (11/19/89 vs. Vikings and 9/17/89 at Redskins)
12	John Spagnola (10/6/85 at Saints)
12	Harold Carmichael (10/14/73 at St. Louis Cardinals)
11	11 times; most recently by Brian Westbrook (12/5/04 vs. Packers)

Most Yards Gained Receiving, Career

8,978	Harold Carmichael (1971–83)
7,412	Pete Retzlaff (1956–66)
6,464	Mike Quick (1982–90)
5,619	Pete Pihos (1947–55)
5,499	Tommy McDonald (1957–63)

Most Yards Gained Receiving, Season

1,409	Mike Quick (1983)
1,316	Irving Fryar (1997)
1,265	Ben Hawkins (1967)
1,247	Mike Quick (1985)
1,200	Terrell Owens (2004)
1,195	Irving Fryar (1996)
1,190	Pete Retzlaff (1965)
1,146	Tommy McDonald (1962)
1,144	Tommy McDonald (1961)
1,127	Fred Barnett (1994)
1,116	Harold Carmichael (1973)
1,116	Harold Jackson (1969)
1,083	Fred Barnett (1992)
1,072	Harold Carmichael (1978)
1,049	Pete Pihos (1953)
1,048	Harold Jackson (1972)
1,028	Harold Carmichael (1981)

Most Yards Gained Receiving, Game

237	Tommy McDonald (12/10/61 vs. Giants)
204	Pete Retzlaff (11/14/65 vs. Redskins)
203	Bud Grant (12/7/52 vs. Dallas Texans)
199	Timmy Brown (12/16/62 at St. Louis Cardinals)

197	Ben Hawkins (10/22/67 at St. Louis Cardinals)
194	Harold Jackson (10/11/70 at Giants)
193	Fred Barnett (9/13/92 at Phoenix Cardinals)

100-Yard Receiving Games, Season

7	Terrell Owens (2004)
6	Irving Fryar (1997)
6	Mike Quick (1983)
5	7 times; most recently by Mike Quick (1984)

Consecutive 100-Yard Receiving Games, Same Season

5	Terrell Owens (2004)
4	Mike Quick (1983)
3	8 times; most recently by Irving Fryar (1996)

Consecutive 100-Yard Receiving Games, Two Seasons

5	Harold Jackson (last three games of 1971 and first two games of 1972)

Most Touchdowns Caught, Career

79	Harold Carmichael (1971–83)
66	Tommy McDonald (1957–63)
61	Mike Quick (1982–90)
61	Pete Pihos (1947–55)
47	Pete Retzlaff (1956–66)
46	Bobby Walston (1951–62)

Most Touchdowns Caught, Season

14	Terrell Owens (2004)
13	Mike Quick (1983)
13	Tommy McDonald (1960 and 1961)
11	Irving Fryar (1996)
11	Cris Carter (1989)
11	Mike Quick (1985 and 1987)
11	Harold Carmichael (1979)
11	Bobby Walston (1954)
11	Pete Pihos (1948)

Most Touchdowns Caught, Game

4	Irving Fryar (10/20/96 vs. Dolphins)
4	Ben Hawkins (9/28/69 vs. Steelers)
4	Joe Carter (11/6/34 vs. Cincinnati Reds)
3	19 times; most recently by Brian Westbrook (12/4/05 vs. Packers)

ROOKIE RECEIVING RECORDS

Most Passes Caught, Rookie Season

81	Keith Jackson (1988)
55	Charles Young (1973)
50	Lee Bouggess (1970)
41	Victor Bailey (1993)
41	Junior Tautalatasi (1986)
37	Calvin Williams (1990)
36	Fred Barnett (1990)

Most Touchdown Passes Caught, Rookie Season

9	Calvin Williams (1990)
8	Fred Barnett (1990)
8	Bobby Walston (1951)
7	Pete Pihos (1947)
6	Charles Young (1973)
6	Keith Jackson (1988)

INTERCEPTIONS

Most Interceptions, Career

34	Eric Allen (1988–94)
34	Bill Bradley (1969–76)
33	Herman Edwards (1977–85)
30	Wes Hopkins (1983–93)
29	Don Burroughs (1960–64)
28	Troy Vincent (1996–2003)
25	Brian Dawkins (1996–2004)
24	Joe Scarpati (1964–69, 1971)
23	Roynell Young (1980–88)
23	Randy Logan (1973–83)
22	Ernie Steele (1944–48)
21	Nate Ramsey (1963–72)
20	Chuck Bednarik (1949–62)
20	Tom Brookshier (1953, 1956–61)

Most Interceptions, Season

11	Bill Bradley (1971)
9	Bill Bradley (1972)
9	Don Burroughs (1960)
9	Ed Bawel (1955)
8	7 times; most recently by Eric Allen (1989)

Most Interceptions, Season (by a non-DB)

7	William Thomas (1995)

Most Interception Returns for Touchdown, Career

5	Eric Allen (1988–93)
3	Joe Scarpati (1964–69, 1971)
2	by 11 players; most recently by Lito Sheppard

Most Interception Returns for Touchdown, Season

4	Eric Allen (1993)
2	Lito Sheppard (2004)
2	Seth Joyner (1992)
2	Ed Bawel (1955)

Most Interception Returns for Touchdown, Game

2	Eric Allen (12/26/93 vs. Saints)

Most Interceptions, Game

4	Russ Craft (9/24/50 at Chicago Cardinals)
3	Joe Scarpati (10/23/66 at Giants)
3	Jim Nettles (12/12/65 at Steelers)
3	Nate Ramsey (11/28/65 at St. Louis Cardinals)
3	Don Burroughs (12/3/61 at Steelers)
3	Chuck Weber (9/30/60 at Cowboys)
3	Joe Sutton (9/24/50 at Chicago Cardinals)
3	Gil Steinke (11/10/46 at Giants)
3	Roy Zimmerman (12/10/44 vs. Cleveland Rams)

Longest Interception Return

104t	James Willis intercepted a pass 4 yards deep in the end zone and returned it 14 yards before lateraling to Troy Vincent, who ran 90 yards (11/3/96 at Cowboys; QB Troy Aikman)
101t	Lito Sheppard (11/15/04 at Cowboys; QB Vinny Testeverde)
99t	Jerry Norton (10/5/57 vs. Giants; QB Charlie Conerly, deflected off goal post)

94t	Eric Allen (10/3/93 at Jets; QB Boomer Esiason)
94t	Irv Cross (10/25/64 at Steelers; QB Terry Nofsinger)
91	Jack Hinkle (10/9/43 vs. Giants; QB Tuffy Leemans)
90t	Troy Vincent, after a lateral from James Willis, who made the interception (11/3/96 at Cowboys; QB Troy Aikman)
89t	Frank LeMaster (12/21/75 at Redskins; QB Joe Theismann)
87t	Lee Roy Caffey (11/10/63 at Giants; QB Glynn Griffing)

Most Yards Interceptions Returned, Career

536	Bill Bradley (34 int.; 1969–76)
482	Eric Allen (34 int.; 1988–94)
427	Brian Dawkins (25 int.; 1996–2004)
402	Joe Scarpati (24 int.; 1964–69, 1971)
355	Ernie Steele (22 int.; 1944–48)

Most Yards Interceptions Returned, Season

248	Bill Bradley (11 int.; 1971)
201	Eric Allen (6 int.; 1993)
182	Joe Scarpati (8 int.; 1966)
172	Lito Sheppard (5 int.; 2004)
168	Ed Bawel (9 int.; 1955)

PUNTING

Most Punts, Career

393	Adrian Burk (1951–56)
349	Tom Hutton (1995–98)
345	John Teltschik (1986–89)
342	Sean Landeta (1999–2002)

Most Punts, Season

108	John Teltschik (1986)
107	Sean Landeta (1999)
104	Tom Hutton (1998)
98	John Teltschik (1988)

Most Punts, Game

15	John Teltschik (12/6/87 at Giants; OT)
12	Adrian Burk (12/12/54 vs. Giants and 11/2/52 at Packers)
12	Len Barnum (10/4/42 vs. Redskins)

Best Punting Average, Career

42.9	Joe Muha (179–7,688; 1946–50)

Best Punting Average, Season

47.2	Joe Muha (57 punts; 1948)
43.7	King Hill (55 punts; 1961)
43.6	Len Barnum (41 punts; 1941)

Longest Punt

91	Randall Cunningham (12/3/89 at Giants)
82	Joe Muha (10/10/48 vs. Giants)
80	Randall Cunningham (10/16/94 at Cowboys)
80	King Hill (11/11/62 vs. Packers)
77	Jeff Feagles (9/15/91 at Cowboys)

Most Punts Downed Inside the 20, Career

106	Jeff Feagles (1990–93)
95	Max Runager (1979–83, 1989)
89	Sean Landeta (1999–2002)
77	Tom Hutton (1995–98)

Most Punts Downed Inside the 20, Season

31	Jeff Feagles (1993)
29	Jeff Feagles (1991)
28	John Teltschik (1988)
27	Dirk Johnson (2003)
26	Sean Landeta (2001)
26	Jeff Feagles (1992)

Note: Inside-the-20 became an official stat in 1976.

PUNT AND KICKOFF RETURNS

Most Punt Returns, Career

148	Wally Henry (1977–82)
117	Brian Mitchell (2000–02)
117	John Sciarra (1978–83)
111	Bill Bradley (1969–76)
104	Larry Marshall (1974–77)

Most Punt Returns, Season

54	Wally Henry (1981)
53	Rod Harris (1991)
46	Brian Mitchell (2002)
46	Larry Marshall (1977)
43	Evan Cooper (1985)

Most Punt Returns, Game

9	Larry Marshall (9/18/77 vs. Buccaneers)
8	Vai Sikahema (12/13/92 at Seahawks)
7	Brian Mitchell (9/23/01 at Seahawks)
7	Evan Cooper (12/1/85 vs. Vikings)
7	Russ Craft (9/16/50 vs. Browns)
7	Bosh Pritchard (11/29/42 vs. Packers)

Punt Return Average, Career (min. 20 returns)

14.5	Brian Westbrook (22 ret.; 2002–04)
13.9	Steve Van Buren (34 ret.; 1944–51)
11.7	Brian Mitchell (117 ret.; 2000–02)
10.7	Bosh Pritchard (91 ret.; 1942, 1946–51)
10.7	Vai Sikahema (73 ret.; 1992–93)

Punt Return Average, Season (min. 10 returns)

16.6	Ernie Steele (11 ret.; 1947)
15.3	Brian Westbrook (20 ret.; 2003)
15.3	Steve Van Buren (15 ret.; 1944)

Most Punt-Return Touchdowns, Career

2	Brian Westbrook (2002–04)
2	Brian Mitchell (2000–02)
2	Steve Van Buren (1944–51)

Most Punt-Return Touchdowns, Season

2	Brian Westbrook (2003)

Most Yards on Punt Returns, Career

1,369	Brian Mitchell (2000–02)
1,231	Wally Henry (1977–82)
1,086	Larry Marshall (1974–77)

Most Yards on Punt Returns, Season

567	Brian Mitchell (2002)
503	Vai Sikahema (1992)
489	Larry Marshall (1977)
467	Brian Mitchell (2001)
416	Rod Harris (1991)

Longest Punt Return

87t	Vai Sikahema (11/22/92 at Giants)
84t	Brian Westbrook (10/19/03 at Giants)
81t	Brian Westbrook (12/21/03 vs. 49ers)
81t	Tommy McDonald (10/4/59 vs. Giants)
76t	Brian Mitchell (11/25/02 at 49ers)
76t	Gregg Garrity (11/30/86 at LA Raiders)
72t	Brian Mitchell (9/24/00 at Saints)
70t	Clyde Scott (10/30/49 at Steelers)

Most Kickoff Returns, Career

169	Timmy Brown (1960–67)
131	Brian Mitchell (2000–02)
101	Al Nelson (1965–73)
98	Allen Rossum (1998–99)
88	Larry Marshall (1974–77)

Most Kickoff Returns, Season

54	Allen Rossum (1999)
53	Derrick Witherspoon (1996)
48	Herman Hunter (1985)
47	Brian Mitchell (2000)
47	Duce Staley (1997)

Most Yards on Kickoff Returns, Career

4,483	Timmy Brown (1960–67)
3,311	Brian Mitchell (2000–02)
2,625	Al Nelson (1965–73)
2,427	Allen Rossum (1998–99)
2,075	Larry Marshall (1974–77)
2,030	Steve Van Buren (1944–51)

Most Yards on Kickoff Returns, Season

1,347	Allen Rossum (1999)
1,271	Derrick Witherspoon (1996)
1,162	Brian Mitchell (2002)
1,139	Duce Staley (1997)
1,124	Brian Mitchell (2000)

Kickoff Return Average, Career (min. 20 returns)

26.7	Steve Van Buren (76 ret.; 1944–51)
26.5	Timmy Brown (169 ret.; 1960–67)

Kickoff Return Average, Season (min. 10 returns)

29.1	Al Nelson (25 ret.; 1972)
28.6	Timmy Brown (33 ret.; 1963)

Longest Kickoff Returns

105t	Timmy Brown (9/17/61 vs. Browns)
103t	Russ Craft (10/7/50 vs. Los Angeles Rams)
101t	Dave Smukler (11/6/38 vs. Brooklyn Dodgers)
100t	Timmy Brown (9/22/63 vs. St. Louis Cardinals)

Most Kickoff Returns for Touchdown, Career

5	Timmy Brown (1960–67)
3	Derrick Witherspoon (1995–97)
3	Steve Van Buren (1944–51)
2	Brian Mitchell (2000–02)
1	by 10 players

Most Kickoff Returns for Touchdown, Season

2	Derrick Witherspoon (1996)
2	Timmy Brown (1966)

Most Kickoff Returns for Touchdown, Game

2	Timmy Brown (11/6/66, 93 and 90 yards vs. Cowboys)

MISCELLANEOUS RETURNS

Longest Return of Fumble for TD

96t	Joe Lavender (9/23/74 vs. Cowboys)
87t	Will Wynn (12/1/74 vs. Packers)

Fumbles Returned for Touchdowns, Career

2	Greg Brown (1981–84)
2	Clyde Simmons (1986–90)
2	William Thomas (1991–97)
2	Reggie White (1985–92)
2	Will Wynn (1973–76)
1	by 38 players; most recently by Carlos Emmons (12/15/02)

Blocked Punts Returned for Touchdowns

1	by 7 players; most recently by Ken Rose (11/22/92 at Giants; 3 yards)

Longest Return with Missed Field Goal

101t	Al Nelson (9/26/71 vs. Dallas Cowboys)
100t	Al Nelson (12/11/66 vs. Browns)
99	Timmy Brown (9/16/62 vs. St. Louis Cardinals)

QUARTERBACK SACKS

Most Sacks, Career

124.0	Reggie White, DE (1985–92)
76.5	Clyde Simmons, DE (1986–93)
54.5	Hugh Douglas, DE (1998–2002, 2004)
50.5	Greg Brown, DE (1982–86)
40.0	Andy Harmon, DT (1991–97)
37.5	Seth Joyner, LB (1986–93)
35.5	William Fuller, DE (1994–96)
34.0	Dennis Harrison, DE (1978–84)
33.0	William Thomas, LB (1991–99)
32.0	Corey Simon, DT (2000–04)
31.5	Mike Mamula, DE (1995–2000)
31.0	Ken Clarke, DT (1982–87)

Most Sacks, Season

21.0	Reggie White (1987)
19.0	Clyde Simmons (1992)
18.0	Reggie White (1986 and 1988)
16.0	Greg Brown (1984)
15.5	Clyde Simmons (1989)
15.0	Hugh Douglas (2000)
15.0	Reggie White (1991)
14.0	Reggie White (1990 and 1992)

Most Sacks, Game

4.5	Hugh Douglas (10/18/98 at Chargers)
4.5	Clyde Simmons (9/15/91 at Cowboys)
4.0	Reggie White (9/25/88 at Vikings, 11/30/86 at LA Raiders, and 11/2/86 at St. Louis Cardinals)
4.0	Garry Cobb (10/5/86 at Falcons)
4.0	Greg Brown (12/16/84 at Falcons)

Most Consecutive Games with a Full Sack

7	William Fuller (1994)
6	Clyde Simmons (1992)
6	Reggie White (last three games of 1986 and first three games of 1987)

Most Sacks, Season, Rookie

9.5	Corey Simon, DT (2000)
6.0	Derrick Burgess, DE (2001)
5.5	Mike Mamula, DE (1995)

Note: Includes only figures since 1982, when sacks first became an official NFL statistic.

NFL RECORDS HELD BY EAGLES

Most Touchdown Passes, Game

7	Adrian Burk (10/17/54 at Redskins); tied with Sid Luckman, Bears (1943); Y. A. Tittle, Giants (1962); George Blanda, Oilers (1961); and Joe Kapp, Vikings (1969)

Longest Touchdown Pass

99	Ron Jaworski to Mike Quick (11/10/85 vs. Falcons; OT); tied with eight others

Most Consecutive Completions

24	Donovan McNabb (first 10 on 11/28/04 at Giants and last 14 on 12/5/04 vs. Packers)

Most 40-plus–Yard Field Goals, Season

17	David Akers (2004)

Most Interception Returns for Touchdown, Season

4	Eric Allen, 1993; tied with Jim Kearney, Chiefs (1972); and Ken Houston, Oilers (1971)

Most Interceptions, Game

4	Russ Craft (9/24/50 at Cardinals); tied with 17 others

Most Touchdowns Returning Kickoffs, Game

2	Timmy Brown (11/6/66 vs. Cowboys), 93 and 90 yards; tied with Travis Williams, Packers (1967); Ron Brown, Rams (1985); Tyrone Hughes, Saints (1994); and Chad Morton, Jets (2002)

REGULAR-SEASON TEAM RECORDS

POINTS

Most Scored

415	2002	(16 games)
396	1990	(16 games)
386	2004	(16 games)
384	1980	(16 games)
379	1988	(16 games)
376	1948	(12 games)

Fewest Scored

51	1936	(12 games)
60	1935	(11 games)
77	1933	(9 games)

Most Allowed

409	1967	(14 games)
393	1973	(14 games)
381	1963	(14 games)

Fewest Allowed

85	1934	(11 games)
131	1944	(10 games)
133	1945	(10 games)

TOUCHDOWNS

Most Scored

50	1948	(12 games)
49	1953	(12 games)
48	1990	(16 games)
48	1980	(16 games)
48	1965	(14 games)
48	1949	(12 games)

Fewest Scored

6	1936	(12 games)

Most Allowed

52	1967	(14 games)
47	1987	(15 games)
47	1973	(14 games)
47	1965	(14 games)
47	1963	(14 games)

Fewest Allowed

9	1934	(11 games)
17	1950	(12 games)
17	1949	(12 games)
18	1945	(10 games)

Most by Rushing

30	1949	(12 games)
28	1944	(10 games)
27	1945	(10 games)

Most by Passing

34	1990	(16 games)
34	1961	(14 games)
33	1954	(12 games)
32	2004	(16 games)
30	1967	(14 games)

KICKING

Most Field Goals Made

30	2002	(16 games)
30	1984	(16 games)
29	2000	(16 games)
28	1991	(16 games)
27	2004	(16 games)
26	2001	(16 games)
25	1996	(16 games)
25	1985	(16 games)

Most PATs Made

50	1948	(12 games)
48	1980	(16 games)
47	1949	(12 games)

RUSHING

Most Attempts

587	1978	(16 games)
581	1950	(12 games)
567	1979	(16 games)

Most Yards Gained

2,607	1949	(12 games)
2,556	1990	(16 games)
2,509	1981	(16 games)
2,456	1978	(16 games)

PASSING

Most Attempts

606	1984	(16 games)
587	1997	(16 games)
581	1988	(16 games)
575	2000	(16 games)
567	1985	(16 games)

Most Completions

336	2004	(16 games)
331	2000	(16 games)
331	1984	(16 games)
330	1997	(16 games)
328	1996	(16 games)
328	1993	(16 games)

Most Yards Gained

4,208	2004	(16 games)
4,042	1985	(16 games)
4,009	1997	(16 games)
3,979	1996	(16 games)
3,824	1961	(14 games)
3,771	1980	(16 games)

TOTAL YARDS

Most Yards Gained

5,766	1980	(16 games)
5,758	1981	(16 games)
5,700	1990	(16 games)
5,627	1996	(16 games)

FIRST DOWNS

Most First Downs

332	1981	(16 games)
326	1997	(16 games)
326	1980	(16 games)
325	1990	(16 games)
321	1989	(16 games)

Most by Rushing

157	1981	(16 games)
143	1978	(16 games)
143	1949	(12 games)
142	1950	(12 games)

Most by Passing

203	1997	(16 games)
196	1996	(16 games)
188	2004	(16 games)
188	1985	(16 games)
186	1980	(16 games)
184	1993	(16 games)

Most by Penalty

41	2003	(16 games)
34	1988	(16 games)
32	1998	(16 games)
30	1989	(16 games)

FUMBLES

Most Opponents' Fumbles Recovered

27	1987	(15 games)
26	1989	(16 games)

INTERCEPTIONS

Most Thrown

31	1962	(14 games)
29	1968	(14 games)
29	1951	(12 games)

Most Intercepted

33	1944	(10 games)
32	1988	(16 games)
31	1960	(12 games)
30	1989	(16 games)

PENALTIES

Most Penalties

138	1994	(16 games)
124	2004	(16 games)
120	1990	(16 games)
117	1996	(16 games)
116	1987	(15 games)
115	1988	(16 games)

Most Yards Penalized

1,107	1994	(16 games)
981	1990	(16 games)
980	2000	(16 games)
963	1996	(16 games)
952	2004	(16 games)
938	1989	(16 games)

QUARTERBACK SACKS

Most Sacks Made

62	1989	(16 games)
60	1984	(16 games)
57	1987	(15 games)
56	2002	(16 games)
56	1992	(16 games)
55	1991	(16 games)
53	1986	(16 games)
53	1985	(16 games)

Most Sacks Allowed

104	1986	(16 games)
72	1987	(15 games)
64	1997	(16 games)
64	1992	(16 games)
60	1984	(16 games)
57	1988	(16 games)
57	1983	(16 games)

Fewest Sacks Allowed

22	1981	(16 games)
23	1970	(14 games)
26	1980	(16 games)
26	1971	(14 games)

SINGLE-GAME TEAM RECORDS

POINTS

Most Scored

64	vs. Cincinnati Reds, 11/6/34
56	at Chicago Cardinals, 10/25/53
56	vs. Los Angeles Rams, 10/7/50

Most Allowed

62	at Giants, 11/26/72
56	at Cowboys, 10/9/66
56	at Giants, 10/15/33

Most, Both Teams

87	Eagles 45, Redskins 42 (at Philadelphia), 9/28/47
86	Eagles 44, Bengals 42 (at Philadelphia), 11/30/97

Most, Both Teams—One Quarter

47	Eagles 20, Cardinals 27 (at St. Louis), 12/13/64

Fewest, Both Teams

0	Eagles 0, Brooklyn Dodgers 0 (at Philadelphia), 10/1/39

Most Scored in First Half

35	vs. Packers, 12/5/04
35	vs. Cowboys, 11/15/04
35	vs. Redskins, 10/23/49
34	at Buccaneers, 9/4/88
34	at Steelers, 12/12/65
33	vs. Cowboys, 9/30/01
33	vs. Cincinnati Reds, 11/6/34
31	vs. Vikings, 11/11/01
31	vs. Saints, 11/19/67

Most Scored in First Quarter

27	at Steelers, 12/12/65
26	vs. Cincinnati Reds, 11/6/34
24	at Falcons, 10/8/67

Most Scored in Second Quarter

28	vs. Packers, 12/5/04
28	vs. Cowboys, 11/15/04
28	vs. Saints, 11/19/67
26	vs. Cowboys, 9/30/01
24	5 times; most recently vs. Vikings, 11/11/01

Most Scored in Third Quarter

21	6 times; most recently vs. Redskins, 11/12/90

Most Scored in Fourth Quarter

24	vs. Baltimore Colts, 11/15/53
22	vs. Redskins, 9/27/81
21	6 times; most recently vs. Falcons, 10/1/00

Most Decisive Victory

64	Eagles 64, Cincinnati Reds 0, 11/6/34

Most Decisive Loss

56	Giants 56, Eagles 0, 10/15/33

TOUCHDOWNS

Most Scored

10	vs. Cincinnati Reds, 11/6/34
8	at Chicago Cardinals, 10/25/53
8	vs. Los Angeles Rams, 10/7/50

Most Allowed

8	3 times; most recently at Giants, 11/26/72

Most Scored by Rushing

5	at Cowboys, 10/22/61
5	at Chicago Cardinals, 10/25/53
5	vs. Redskins, 10/23/49
5	at Redskins, 10/17/48
5	vs. Boston Yanks, 12/9/45
5	vs. Cincinnati Reds, 11/6/34

Most Allowed by Rushing

6	Packers, 11/11/62

Most by Passing

7	at Redskins, 10/17/54

Most Allowed by Passing

5	7 times; most recently vs. 49ers, 9/24/89

KICKING

Most Field Goals Made

6	at Houston Oilers, 11/12/72
5	3 times; most recently at Cowboys, 11/18/01

Most Field Goals Allowed

5	6 times; most recently vs. Titans, 12/3/00

RUSHING

Most Attempts

64	at Redskins, 12/2/51
64	at Baltimore Colts, 10/15/50
64	vs. Los Angeles Rams, 11/6/49
64	at Redskins, 11/28/43

Most Attempts Allowed

60	Giants, 11/20/83

Most Yards Gained

376	vs. Redskins, 10/21/48

Fewest Yards Gained

−36	at Bears, 11/19/39
−23	vs. Lions, 11/17/40

Most Yards Allowed

370	at Lions, 9/20/35

Fewest Yards Allowed

−33	vs. Brooklyn Dodgers, 10/2/43
10	vs. Boston Yanks, 10/22/44
14	vs. Redskins, 9/28/47
21	at Bills, 9/28/03
21	at Houston Oilers, 12/2/91

PASSING

Most Attempts

62	at Bears, 10/2/89
60	at Redskins, 12/1/40

Fewest Attempts

3	vs. Steelers, 12/1/46

Most Attempts Allowed

63	at 49ers, 11/25/02
55	vs. Los Angeles Rams, 10/7/50
54	at Los Angeles Rams, 9/23/90

Fewest Attempts Allowed

0	at Browns, 12/3/50
1	at NY Bulldogs, 9/22/49
1	at Chicago Cardinals, 11/8/36

Most Completions

34	at Redskins, 9/17/89
33	vs. Giants, 9/23/62
33	at Redskins, 12/1/40

Fewest Completions

0	at Boston Redskins, 10/18/36

Most Completions Allowed

36	at 49ers, 11/25/02
34	vs. Patriots, 11/29/87
33	at Falcons, 9/22/96
33	at 49ers, 1/3/94

Fewest Completions Allowed

0	at Browns, 12/3/50
0	vs. NY Bulldogs, 9/22/49
0	vs. Cincinnati Reds, 11/6/34
1	4 times; most recently vs. Steelers, 11/10/40

Most Yards Gained (gross)

464	vs. Packers, 12/5/04
460	vs. Giants, 11/8/53

Fewest Yards Gained (gross)

0	at Boston Redskins, 10/18/36

Most Yards Allowed (gross)

447	at Cowboys, 10/9/66

Fewest Yards Allowed (gross)

0	at Browns, 12/3/50
0	at NY Bulldogs, 9/22/49
0	at Chicago Cardinals, 11/8/36
0	vs. Cincinnati Reds, 11/6/34

TOTAL YARDS

Most Yards Gained

582	at Browns, 11/7/65 (352 passing, 230 rushing)
575	vs. Redskins, 11/21/48 (199 passing, 376 rushing)
574	vs. Baltimore Colts, 11/15/81 (339 passing, 235 rushing)

Fewest Yards Gained

23	at Lions, 9/20/35
33	at Bears, 10/25/42

Most Yards Allowed

652   at Cowboys, 10/9/66 (440 passing, 212 rushing)

Fewest Yards Allowed

29   vs. Brooklyn Dodgers, 12/3/44

FIRST DOWNS

Most, Total

34   vs. Baltimore Colts, 11/15/81
33   vs. Vikings, 11/11/01
32   at Redskins, 9/17/89
32   at Redskins, 12/2/51

Most Allowed, Total

37   vs. Packers, 11/11/62

Fewest Allowed, Total

1   at NY Bulldogs, 9/22/49
1   vs. Brooklyn Dodgers, 10/1/39
2   at Browns, 12/3/50
2   vs. Brooklyn Dodgers, 11/11/34

Most by Rushing

25   at Redskins, 12/2/51

Most Allowed by Rushing

21   vs. Packers, 11/11/62
21   vs. Browns, 12/13/59

Fewest Allowed by Rushing

0   6 times; most recently at Indianapolis Colts, 12/19/93

Most by Passing

24   at Redskins, 9/17/89
20   3 times; most recently vs. Bengals, 11/30/97

Most Allowed by Passing

22   at St. Louis Cardinals, 12/13/64
21   at Dolphins, 12/9/90
21   at Patriots, 11/29/87

Fewest Allowed by Passing

0   8 times; most recently at Browns, 12/3/50

Most by Penalty

8   at Bears, 11/3/02
7   at Steelers (OT), 11/12/00
7   vs. Bears, 11/26/44
6   vs. Packers, 12/5/04

Most Allowed by Penalty

6   3 times; most recently at Redskins, 11/26/00

PENALTIES

Most Penalties

19   vs. Houston Oilers, 10/2/88
17   at Seahawks, 12/13/92
16   at Giants, 12/3/89

Fewest Penalties

0   14 times; most recently vs. Giants, 12/27/98

Most Penalties by Opponent

22   Bears (at Philadelphia), 11/26/44

Fewest Penalties by Opponent

0   10 times; most recently at Bears, 12/24/95

Most Yards Penalized

191   at Seahawks, 12/13/92
171   vs. Saints, 11/23/03

Fewest Yards Penalized

0   14 times; most recently vs. Giants, 12/27/98

Most Yards Opponent Penalized

170   vs. Bears, 11/26/44

Fewest Yards Opponent Penalized

0   10 times; most recently at Bears, 12/24/95

Most Penalties, Both Teams

31   Eagles 19, Houston Oilers 12 (at Philadelphia), 10/2/88
27   Eagles 15, Chicago Cardinals 12 (at Chicago), 11/30/52

Fewest Penalties, Both Teams

1   Eagles 1, Brooklyn Dodgers 0 (at Philadelphia), 10/1/39
1   Eagles 1, Chicago Cardinals 0 (at Chicago), 11/10/35
1   Eagles 1, Brooklyn Dodgers 0 (at Philadelphia), 11/11/34

Most Yards Penalized, Both Teams

272   Eagles 171, Saints 101 (at Philadelphia), 11/23/03
262   Eagles 157, Chicago Cardinals 105 (at Chicago), 11/30/52

Fewest Yards Penalized, Both Teams

5   Eagles 5, Brooklyn Dodgers 0 (at Philadelphia), 10/1/39
5   Eagles 5, Chicago Cardinals 0 (at Chicago), 11/10/35
5   Eagles 5, Brooklyn Dodgers 0 (at Philadelphia), 11/11/34

FUMBLES

Most Committed

10   vs. Giants, 10/9/43

Most Lost

6   at Redskins, 11/6/55

Most Committed by Opponent

8   Packers (at Philadelphia), 12/1/74
7   6 times; most recently by Giants (at New York), 12/28/02

Most Fumbles Lost by Opponent

6   Giants (at New York), 11/17/68
6   NY Bulldogs (at Philadelphia), 11/20/49
5   3 times; most recently by Oilers (at Houston), 12/2/91

INTERCEPTIONS

Most Thrown

7   vs. Cowboys, 9/26/71
6   vs. Chicago Cardinals, 10/21/56
6   vs. Packers, 12/5/43

Most Intercepted

9   at Steelers, 12/12/65
8   at Chicago Cardinals, 9/24/50
7   at Redskins, 12/21/75

TOTAL TURNOVERS

Most Committed

9   at Bears, 10/12/47

Most Forced by Defense

12   at Steelers, 12/12/65 (9 int., 3 fumble rec.)
12   at Chicago Cardinals, 9/24/50 (8 int., 4 fumble rec.)

PUNTS

Most Punts

15   at Giants, 12/6/87
12   vs. Giants, 12/12/54
12   at Packers, 11/2/52
12   vs. Redskins, 10/4/42

Fewest Punts

0   4 times; most recently vs. Baltimore Colts, 11/15/81

PUNT RETURNS

Most Punt Returns

10   vs. Buccaneers, 9/18/77

Most Punt Returns by Opponent

9   at Giants, 12/6/87
9   vs. Giants, 11/20/83

Most Yards Punt Returns

148   at Boston Yanks, 12/8/46

Most Yards Punt Returns Allowed

144   at 49ers, 9/27/59

KICKOFF RETURNS

Most Kickoff Returns

9   at Giants, 11/10/46

Most Kickoff Returns Allowed

9   4 times; most recently vs. Vikings, 11/11/01

Most Yards Kickoff Returns

261   vs. Cowboys, 11/6/66
253   at Arizona Cardinals, 11/24/96
235   vs. St. Louis Cardinals, 9/19/65

Most Yards Kickoff Returns by Opponent

249   at St. Louis Cardinals, 11/21/71

QUARTERBACK SACKS

Most Sacks Made

11   at Cowboys, 9/15/91
9   at Falcons, 12/16/84
8   12 times; most recently vs. St. Louis Rams, 12/1/02

Most Sacks Allowed

11   vs. Bears, 10/4/87
11   at Los Angeles Raiders, 11/30/86
11   vs. Lions, 11/16/86
11   at St. Louis Cardinals, 12/18/83

YEAR-BY-YEAR LEADERS

SCORING

Year	Name	TD	PAT	FG	Pts.
2004	David Akers	0	41–42	27–32**	122**
2003	David Akers	0	42–42	24–29	114
2002	David Akers	0	43–43	30–34	133
2001	David Akers	0	37–38	26–31	115
2000	David Akers	0	34–36	29–33	121
1999	Norm Johnson	0	25–25	18–25	79
1998	Chris Boniol	0	15–17	14–21	57
1997	Chris Boniol	0	33–33	22–31	99
1996	Gary Anderson	0	40–40	25–29	115
1995	Gary Anderson	0	32–33	22–30	98
1994	Eddie Murray	0	33–33	21–25	96
1993	Calvin Williams	10	0–0	0–0	60
1992	Roger Ruzek	0	40–44	16–25	88
1991	Roger Ruzek	0	27–29	28–33	111
1990	Roger Ruzek	0	45–48**	21–29	108
1989	Cris Carter	11	0–0	0–0	66
1988	Luis Zendejas	0	30–31	19–24	87
1987	Paul McFadden	0	36–36	16–26	84
1986	Paul McFadden	0	26–27	20–31	86
1985	Paul McFadden	0	29–29	25–30	104
1984	Paul McFadden	0	26–27	30–37*	116
1983	Mike Quick	13	0–0	0–0	78
1982	Wilbert Montgomery	9	0–0	0–0	54
1981	Tony Franklin	0	41–43	20–31	101
1980	Tony Franklin	0	48–48	16–31	96
1979	Tony Franklin	0	36–39	23–31	105
1978	Wilbert Montgomery	10	0–0	0–0	60
1977	Harold Carmichael	7	0–0	0–0	42
1976	Horst Muhlmann	0	18–19	11–11	51
1975	Horst Muhlmann	0	21–24	20–29	81
1974	Tom Sullivan	12	0–0	0–0	72
1973	Tom Dempsey	0	34–34	24–40	106
1972	Tom Dempsey	0	11–12	20–35	71
1971	Tom Dempsey	0	13–14	12–17	49
1970	Mark Moseley	0	25–28	14–25	67
1969	Sam Baker	0	31–31	16–30	79
1968	Sam Baker	0	17–21	19–30	74
1967	Sam Baker	0	45–45	12–19	81
1966	Sam Baker	0	38–39	18–25	92
1965	Sam Baker	0	38–40	9–23	65
1964	Sam Baker	0	36–37	16–26	84
1963	Tim Brown	11	0–0	0–0	66
1962	Tim Brown	13	0–0	0–0	78
1961	Bobby Walston	2	43–46	14–25	97
1960	Bobby Walston	4	39–40	14–20	105
1959	Tommy McDonald	11	0–0	0–0	66
1958	Bobby Walston	3	31–31	6–14	67
1957	Bobby Walston	1	20–21	9–12	53
1956	Bobby Walston	3	17–18	6–13	53
1955	Dick Bielski	1	23–24	9–23	56
1954	Bobby Walston	11	36–39	4–10	114*
1953	Bobby Walston	5	45–48	4–13	87
1952	Bobby Walston	3	31–31	11–20	82
1951	Bobby Walston	8	28–31	6–11	94
1950	Cliff Patton	0	32–33	8–17	56
1949	Steve Van Buren	12	0–0	0–0	72
1948	Cliff Patton	0	50–50	8–12*	74
1947	Steve Van Buren	14*	0–0	0–0	84
1946	Augie Lio	1	27–27	6–11	51
1945	Steve Van Buren	18*	2–2	0–0	110*
1944	Leroy Zimmerman	3	32–34	4–8	62
1943	Ernie Steele	6	0–0	0–0	36
	Bob Thurbon	6	0–0	0–0	36
1942	Bob Davis	3	0–0	0–0	18
1941	Jim Castiglia	4	0–0	0–0	24
1940	Don Looney	5	0–0	0–0	30
	Dick Riffle	5	0–0	0–0	30

Year	Name	TD	PAT	FG	Pts.
1939	Franny Murray	2	8–12	2–4	26
1938	Joe Carter	8	0–0	0–0	48
1937	Bill Hewitt	5	0–0	0–0	30
1936	Hank Reese	0	NA	2–2	9
1935	Ed Manske	4	0–0	0–0	24
1934	Swede Hanson	8	2–2	0–0	50
1933	Swede Hanson	4	0–0	0–0	24

PASSING

Year	Name	Att.	Cmp.	Pct.	Yds.	TD	Int.
2004	Donovan McNabb	469	300	64.0	3,875	31	8
2003	Donovan McNabb	478	275	57.5	3,216	16	11
2002	Donovan McNabb	361	211	58.4	2,289	17	6
2001	Donovan McNabb	493	285	57.8	3,233	25	12
2000	Donovan McNabb	569**	330	58.0	3,365	21	13
1999	Doug Pederson	227	119	52.4	1,276	7	9
1998	Koy Detmer	181	97	53.6	1,011	5	5
1997	Bobby Hoying	225	128	56.9	1,573	11	6
1996	Ty Detmer	401	238	59.4	2,911	15	13
1995	Rodney Peete	375	215	57.3	2,326	8	14
1994	Randall Cunningham	490	265	54.1	3,229	16	13
1993	Bubby Brister	309	181	58.6	1,905	14	5
1992	Randall Cunningham	384	233	60.7	2,775	19	11
1991	Jim McMahon	311	187	60.1	2,239	12	11
1990	Randall Cunningham	465	271	58.3	3,466	30**	13
1989	Randall Cunningham	532	290	54.5	3,400	21	15
1988	Randall Cunningham	560	301	53.8	3,808	24	16
1987	Randall Cunningham	406	223	54.9	2,786	23	12
1986	Ron Jaworski	245	128	52.2	1,405	8	6
1985	Ron Jaworski	484	255	52.7	3,450	17	20
1984	Ron Jaworski	427	234	54.8	2,754	16	14
1983	Ron Jaworski	446	235	52.7	3,315	20	18
1982	Ron Jaworski	286	167	58.4	2,076	12	12
1981	Ron Jaworski	461	250	54.2	3,095	23	20
1980	Ron Jaworski	451	257	57.0	3,529	27	12
1979	Ron Jaworski	374	190	50.8	2,669	18	12
1978	Ron Jaworski	398	206	51.8	2,487	16	16
1977	Ron Jaworski	346	166	48.0	2,183	18	21
1976	Mike Boryla	246	123	50.0	1,247	9	14
1975	Roman Gabriel	292	151	51.7	1,644	13	11
1974	Roman Gabriel	338	193	57.1	1,867	9	12
1973	Roman Gabriel	460*	270*	58.7	3,219*	23*	12
1972	John Reaves	224	108	48.2	1,508	7	12
1971	Pete Liske	269	143	53.2	1,937	11	15
1970	Norm Snead	335	181	54.0	2,323	15	20
1969	Norm Snead	379	190	50.1	2,768	19	23
1968	Norm Snead	291	152	52.2	1,655	11	21
1967	Norm Snead	434	240	55.3	3,399	29	24
1966	Norm Snead	226	103	45.6	1,275	8	11
1965	Norm Snead	288	150	52.1	2,346	15	13
1964	Norm Snead	283	138	48.8	1,906	14	12
1963	Sonny Jurgensen	184	99	53.8	1,413	11	13
1962	Sonny Jurgensen	366	196	53.6	3,261*	22	26
1961	Sonny Jurgensen	416	235*	56.5	3,723*	32*	24
1960	Norm Van Brocklin	284	153	53.9	2,471	24	17
1959	Norm Van Brocklin	340	191	56.2	2,617	16	14
1958	Norm Van Brocklin	374*	198*	52.9	2,409	15	20
1957	Bobby Thomason	92	46	50.0	630	4	10
1956	Bobby Thomason	164	82	50.0	1,119	4	21
1955	Bobby Thomason	171	88	51.5	1,337	10	7
	Adrian Burk	228	110	48.2	1,359	9	17
1954	Adrian Burk	231	123	53.2	1,740	23*	20
1953	Bobby Thomason	304	162	53.3	2,462	21*	17
1952	Bobby Thomason	212	95	44.8	1,334	8	9
1951	Adrian Burk	218	92	42.2	1,329	14	23
1950	Tommy Thompson	239	107	44.8	1,608	11	22
1949	Tommy Thompson	214	116	54.2	1,727	16	11
1948	Tommy Thompson	246	141	57.3	1,965	25*	11
1947	Tommy Thompson	201	106	52.7	1,680	16	15

*Led NFL.   **Led Conference.

Year	Name	Att.	Cmp.	Pct.	Yds.	TD	Int.
1946	Tommy Thompson	103	57	55.3*	745	6	9
1945	Roy Zimmerman	132	67	50.8	991	9	8
1944	Roy Zimmerman	105	39	37.1	785	8	10
1943	Roy Zimmerman	124	43	34.7	846	9	17
1942	Tommy Thompson	203	95	46.8	1,410	8	16
1941	Tommy Thompson	162	86	53.1	974	8	14
1940	Davey O'Brien	277*	124*	44.7	1,290	5	17
1939	Davey O'Brien	201	99	49.7	1,324*	6	17
1938	Dave Smukler	102	42	41.1	524	7	8
1937	Dave Smukler	118	42	35.6	432	6	14
1936	Dave Smukler	68	21	31.0	345	3	6
1935	Ed Storm	44	15	34.1	372	3	NA
1934	Ed Matesic	60	20	33.3	272	3	5
1933	Reds Kirkman	73	22	33.1	354	2	13

RUSHING

Year	Name	No.	Yds.	Avg.	LG	TD
2004	Brian Westbrook	177	812	4.6	50	3
2003	Brian Westbrook	117	613	5.2	62t	7
2002	Duce Staley	269	1,029	3.8	57	5
2001	Duce Staley	166	604	3.6	44t	2
2000	Donovan McNabb (QB)	86	629	7.3*	54	6
1999	Duce Staley	325	1,273	3.9	29	4
1998	Duce Staley	258	1,065	4.1	64t	5
1997	Ricky Watters	285	1,110	3.9	28	7
1996	Ricky Watters	353*	1,411	4.0	56t	13
1995	Ricky Watters	337	1,273	3.8	57	11
1994	Herschel Walker	113	528	4.7	91t	5
1993	Herschel Walker	174	746	4.3	35	1
1992	Herschel Walker	267	1,070	4.0	38	8
1991	James Joseph	135	440	3.3	24	3
1990	Randall Cunningham (QB)	118	942	8.0*	52t	5
1989	Randall Cunningham (QB)	104	621	6.0	51	4
1988	Randall Cunningham (QB)	93	624	6.7	33t	6
1987	Randall Cunningham (QB)	76	505	6.6	45	3
1986	Keith Byars	177	577	3.3	32	1
1985	Earnest Jackson	282	1,028	3.6	59	5
1984	Wilbert Montgomery	201	789	3.9	27	2
1983	Hubie Oliver	121	434	3.6	24	1
1982	Wilbert Montgomery	114	515	4.5	90t	7
1981	Wilbert Montgomery	286	1,402	4.9	41	8
1980	Wilbert Montgomery	193	778	4.0	72t	8
1979	Wilbert Montgomery	338	1,512	4.5	62t	9
1978	Wilbert Montgomery	259	1,220	4.7	47	9
1977	Mike Hogan	155	546	3.5	19	0
1976	Mike Hogan	123	561	4.6	32	0
1975	Tom Sullivan	173	632	3.7	28	0
1974	Tom Sullivan	244	760	3.1	28t	11
1973	Tom Sullivan	217	968	4.5	37	4
1972	Po James	182	565	3.1	22	0
1971	Ron Bull	94	351	3.7	39	0
1970	Cyril Pinder	166	657	3.9	40t	2
1969	Tom Woodeshick	186	831	4.5	21	4
1968	Tom Woodeshick	217	947	4.4	54t	3
1967	Tom Woodeshick	155	670	4.3	41	6
1966	Timmy Brown	161	548	3.4	24	3
1965	Timmy Brown	158	861	5.4*	54t	6
1964	Earl Gros	154	748	4.9	59t	6
1963	Timmy Brown	192	841	4.4	34	6
1962	Timmy Brown	137	545	4.0	61t	5
1961	Clarence Peaks	135	471	3.5	33	5
1960	Clarence Peaks	86	465	5.4	57	3
1959	Billy Barnes	181	687	3.8	61t	7
1958	Billy Barnes	156	551	3.5	70t	7
1957	Billy Barnes	143	529	3.7	41	1
1956	Ken Keller	112	433	3.9	51	4
1955	Harold Giancanelli	97	385	4.9	20	2
1954	Jim Parmer	119	408	3.4	24	0
1953	Don Johnson	83	439	5.3	66	5
1952	John Huzvar	105	349	3.3	26	2
1951	Frank Ziegler	113	418	3.7	34	2
1950	Frank Ziegler	172	733	4.3	52	1
	Steve Van Buren	188*	629	3.3	41	4

Year	Name	No.	Yds.	Avg.	LG	TD
1949	Steve Van Buren	263*	1,146*	4.4	41	11*
1948	Steve Van Buren	201*	945*	4.7	29	10*
1947	Steve Van Buren	217*	1,008*	4.6	45	13*
1946	Steve Van Buren	116	529	4.6	58	5
1945	Steve Van Buren	143*	832*	5.8	69t	15*
1944	Steve Van Buren	80	444	5.5	70t	5
1943	Jack Hinkle	116	571	4.9	56	4
1942	Bob Davis	43	207	4.8	44	2
1941	Jim Castiglia	60	183	3.1	47	4
1940	Dick Riffle	81	238	2.9	NA	4
1939	Dave Smukler	45	218	4.8	NA	0
1938	Dave Smukler	96	313	3.3	NA	1
1937	Emmett Mortell	100	312	3.1	NA	0
1936	Swede Hanson	119	359	3.0	NA	1
1935	Swede Hanson	77	209	2.8	NA	0
1934	Swede Hanson	147*	805	5.5	NA	7
1933	Swede Hanson	133	494	3.7	NA	3

RECEIVING

Year	Name	Att.	Yds.	Avg.	LG	TD
2004	Terrell Owens	77	1,200	15.6	59t	14
2003	James Thrash	49	558	11.4	51	1
2002	Todd Pinkston	60	798	13.3	42t	7
2001	James Thrash	63	833	13.2	64t	8
	Duce Staley (RB)	63	626	9.9	46t	2
2000	Chad Lewis (TE)	69	735	10.7	52	3
1999	Torrance Small	49	655	13.4	84t	4
1998	Duce Staley (RB)	57	432	7.6	33	1
1997	Irving Fryar	86	1,316	15.3	72t	6
1996	Irving Fryar	88	1,195	13.6	42	11**
1995	Calvin Williams	63	768	12.2	37t	2
1994	Fred Barnett	78	1,127	14.4	54	5
1993	Herschel Walker (RB)	75	610	8.1	55	3
1992	Fred Barnett	67	1,083	16.2	71t	6
1991	Fred Barnett	62	948	15.3	75t	4
	Keith Byars (RB)	62	564	9.1	37	3
1990	Keith Byars (RB)	81	819	10.1	54	3
1989	Keith Byars (RB)	68	721	10.6	60	0
1988	Keith Jackson (TE)	81	869	10.7	41	6
1987	Mike Quick	46	790	17.2	61t	11
1986	Mike Quick	60	939	15.7	75t	9
1985	Mike Quick	73	1,247*	17.1	99t*	11**
1984	John Spagnola (TE)	65	701	10.8	34	1
1983	Mike Quick	69	1,409*	20.4	83t	13
1982	Harold Carmichael	35	540	15.4	44t	4
1981	Harold Carmichael	61	1,028	16.9	85t	6
1980	Wilbert Montgomery (RB)	50	407	8.1	46	2
1979	Harold Carmichael	52	872	16.8	50	11**
1978	Harold Carmichael	55	1,072	19.5	56t	8
1977	Harold Carmichael	46	665	14.5	50t	7
1976	Harold Carmichael	42	503	12.0	24	5
1975	Charles Young (TE)	49	659	13.4	47	3
	Harold Carmichael	49	639	13.0	62t	7
1974	Charles Young (TE)	63*	696	11.0	29	3
1973	Harold Carmichael	67*	1,116*	16.6	73	9
1972	Harold Jackson	62*	1,048*	16.9	77t	4
1971	Harold Jackson	47	716	15.2	69t	3
1970	Lee Bouggess (RB)	50	401	8.0	34	2
1969	Harold Jackson	65	1,116*	17.2	65t	9
1968	Ben Hawkins	42	707	16.8	92t	5
1967	Ben Hawkins	59	1,265*	21.4	87t	10
1966	Pete Retzlaff	40	653	16.3	40	6
1965	Pete Retzlaff	66	1,190	18.0	78	10
1964	Pete Retzlaff	51	855	16.8	44	8
1963	Pete Retzlaff	57	895	15.7	46	4
1962	Tommy McDonald	58	1,146	19.8	60t	10
1961	Tommy McDonald	64	1,144*	17.6	66	13*
1960	Pete Retzlaff	46	826	18.0	57	5
	Tommy McDonald	39	801	20.5	64	13
1959	Tommy McDonald	47	846	18.0	71	10
1958	Pete Retzlaff	56*	766	13.7	49	2
1957	Billy Barnes (RB)	19	212	11.2	67t	1
1956	Bobby Walston	39	590	15.1	51	3

Year	Name	Att.	Yds.	Avg.	LG	TD
1955	Pete Pihos	62*	864*	13.9	40	7
1954	Pete Pihos	60*	872	14.5	34	10
1953	Pete Pihos	63*	1,049*	16.7	59	10*
1952	Bud Grant	56	997	17.8	84t	7
1951	Pete Pihos	35	536	15.3	38	5
1950	Pete Pihos	38	447	11.8	43	6
	Jack Ferrante	35	588	17.3	75	3
1949	Jack Ferrante	34	508	14.9	64	5
	Pete Pihos	34	484	14.2	49	4
1948	Pete Pihos	46	766	16.7	48	11
1947	Pete Pihos	23	382	16.6	66	7
1946	Jack Ferrante	28	451	16.1	48	4
1945	Jack Ferrante	21	474	22.5	74	7
1944	Larry Cabrelli	13	152	11.6	30	1
1943	Tony Bova	17	419	24.6*	51	5
1942	Fred Meyer	16	323	20.1	60	1
1941	Dick Humbert	29	332	11.4	33	3
1940	Don Looney	58*	707*	12.2	NA	4
1939	Herschel Ramsey	31	359	11.6	NA	1
1938	Joe Carter	27	386	14.3	NA	7
1937	Bill Hewitt	16	197	12.3	NA	5
1936	Ed Manske	17	325	19.1	NA	0
1935	Joe Carter	11	260	23.6*	NA	2
1934	Joe Carter	16*	238	15.0	NA	4
1933	Swede Hanson (RB)	9	140	15.5	NA	1

SACKS

Year	Name (Position)	Sacks
2004	Jevon Kearse (DE)	7.5
2003	Corey Simon (DT)	7.5
2002	Hugh Douglas (DE)	12.5
2001	Hugh Douglas (DE)	9.5
2000	Hugh Douglas (DE)	15.0
1999	Mike Mamula (DE)	8.5
1998	Hugh Douglas (DE)	12.5
1997	Rhett Hall (DT)	8.0
1996	William Fuller (DE)	13.0
1995	William Fuller (DE)**	13.0
1994	William Fuller (DE)	9.5
1993	Andy Harmon (DT)	11.5
1992	Clyde Simmons (DE)*	19.0
1991	Reggie White (DE)	15.0
1990	Reggie White (DE)	14.0
1989	Clyde Simmons (DE)	15.5
1988	Reggie White (DE)*	18.0
1987	Reggie White (DE)*	21.0
1986	Reggie White (DE)	18.0
1985	Greg Brown (DE) and Reggie White (DE)	13.0
1984	Greg Brown (DE)	14.0
1983	Dennis Harrison (DE)	11.5
1982	Dennis Harrison (DE)	10.5

INDIVIDUAL HIGHLIGHTS

PASSING

Most 400-Yard Passing Games

3	Randall Cunningham
3	Sonny Jurgensen
1	Donovan McNabb
1	Bobby Thomason

Most 300-Yard Passing Games

13	Randall Cunningham
12	Ron Jaworski
11	Donovan McNabb
10	Sonny Jurgensen
8	Norm Snead
4	Bobby Thomason
3	Ty Detmer, Roman Gabriel
2	Bubby Brister
1	Adrian Burk, King Hill, Bobby Hoying, Pete Liske, Jim McMahon, Davey O'Brien, Joe Pisarcik, Scott Tinsley, Norm Van Brocklin

Note: Includes playoff games; includes games over 400 yards.

300-Yard Passing Games

Date	Player, Opponent, and Result	Att.	Cmp.	Yds.	TD	Int.
2/06/05	Donovan McNabb vs. Patriots (L)	51	30	357	3	3
12/05/04	Donovan McNabb vs. Packers (W)	43	32	464	5	0
11/15/04	Donovan McNabb at Cowboys (W)	27	15	345	4	0
10/24/04	Donovan McNabb at Browns (W) OT	43	28	376	4	1
9/26/04	Donovan McNabb at Lions (W)	42	29	356	2	0
9/12/04	Donovan McNabb vs. Giants (W)	36	26	330	4	0
11/16/03	Donovan McNabb vs. Giants (W)	30	24	314	2	0
11/02/03	Donovan McNabb at Falcons (W)	33	21	312	1	0
9/09/01	Donovan McNabb vs. Rams (L)	48	32	312	2	1
12/10/00	Donovan McNabb at Browns (W)	36	23	390	4	0
10/01/00	Donovan McNabb vs. Falcons (W)	44	30	311	2	1

Date	Player, Opponent, and Result	Att.	Cmp.	Yds.	TD	Int.
11/30/97	Bobby Hoying vs. Bengals (W)	42	26	313	4	1
11/24/96	Ty Detmer at Cardinals (L)	38	21	322	0	1
11/10/96	Ty Detmer vs. Bills (L)	44	26	315	2	1
10/27/96	Ty Detmer vs. Panthers (W)	38	23	342	1	1
12/24/94	Bubby Brister at Bengals (L)	37	26	325	1	0
12/04/94	Randall Cunningham vs. Cowboys (L)	46	29	327	2	1
10/24/94	Randall Cunningham vs. Oilers (W)	24	13	310	2	1
9/12/94	Randall Cunningham vs. Bears (W)	36	24	311	3	0
9/04/94	Randall Cunningham at Giants (L)	39	20	344	2	0
1/03/94	Bubby Brister at 49ers (W) OT	43	26	350	3	1
9/19/93	Randall Cunningham vs. Redskins (W)	39	25	360	3	2
12/13/92	Randall Cunningham at Seattle (W) OT	44	27	365	0	1
11/10/91	Jim McMahon at Browns (W)	43	26	341	3	1
12/18/89	Randall Cunningham at Saints (L)	39	19	306	2	2
10/02/89	Randall Cunningham at Bears (L)	62	32	401	1	4
9/17/89	Randall Cunningham at Redskins (W)	46	34	447	5	1
12/31/88	Randall Cunningham at Bears (L)	54	27	407	0	3
11/06/88	Randall Cunningham vs. Rams (W)	39	22	323	3	0
10/10/88	Randall Cunningham vs. Giants (W)	41	31	369	3	0
11/29/87	Randall Cunningham at Patriots (W) OT	31	18	314	2	1
10/11/87	Scott Tinsley at Cowboys (L)	34	24	338	3	0
12/15/85	Ron Jaworski at Chargers (L)	48	29	334	1	3
12/01/85	Ron Jaworski vs. Vikings (L)	42	23	320	2	1
11/03/85	Ron Jaworski at 49ers (L)	48	24	394	1	3
10/20/85	Ron Jaworski vs. Cowboys (W)	35	22	380	1	0
12/16/84	Joe Pisarcik at Falcons (L)	46	24	334	0	1
10/28/84	Ron Jaworski vs. Cardinals (L)	38	22	340	2	3
11/27/83	Ron Jaworski at Redskins (L)	36	19	333	3	1
9/11/83	Ron Jaworski vs. Redskins (L)	37	24	326	1	2
9/19/82	Ron Jaworski at Browns (W)	41	25	334	2	1
9/12/82	Ron Jaworski vs. Redskins (L)	38	27	371	2	0
10/18/81	Ron Jaworski at Vikings (L)	45	30	345	2	2
12/21/80	Ron Jaworski at Cowboys (L)	30	18	331	1	0
11/09/80	Ron Jaworski at Saints (W)	32	21	323	3	1
12/16/73	Roman Gabriel at Redskins (L)	39	22	302	1	1

Date	Player, Opponent, and Result	Att.	Cmp.	Yds.	TD	Int.
12/02/73	Roman Gabriel at 49ers (L)	55	28	322	2	1
10/14/73	Roman Gabriel at Cardinals (W)	45	29	379	3	0
9/19/71	Pete Liske at Bengals (L)	40	20	301	2	3
9/28/69	Norm Snead vs. Steelers (W)	30	22	335	5	1
11/19/67	Norm Snead vs. Saints (W)	27	19	309	4	2
10/22/67	Norm Snead at Cardinals (L)	32	16	321	2	2
9/17/67	Norm Snead vs. Redskins (W)	27	18	301	2	0
12/05/65	Norm Snead vs. Cowboys (L)	43	20	320	0	0
11/14/65	Norm Snead vs. Redskins (W)	28	21	311	0	1
11/07/65	Norm Snead at Browns (L)	36	18	362	3	2
10/17/65	King Hill at Giants (L)	41	23	321	3	4
12/13/64	Norm Snead at Cardinals (L)	31	15	301	3	2
10/13/63	Sonny Jurgensen at Redskins (W)	29	17	315	4	2
9/15/63	Sonny Jurgensen vs. Steelers (T)	26	16	322	3	2
12/16/62	Sonny Jurgensen at Cardinals (L)	34	15	419	5	3
11/25/62	Sonny Jurgensen vs. Cowboys (W)	21	13	342	1	2
9/23/62	Sonny Jurgensen vs. Giants (L)	57	33	396	1	3
12/17/61	Sonny Jurgensen at Lions (W)	42	27	403	3	2
12/10/61	Sonny Jurgensen vs. Giants (L)	31	16	367	3	2
11/26/61	Sonny Jurgensen vs. Cowboys (W)	23	16	351	5	2
10/29/61	Sonny Jurgensen at Redskins (W)	41	27	436	3	2
10/01/61	Sonny Jurgensen vs. Cardinals (L)	36	24	399	3	2
11/16/58	Norm Van Brocklin vs. Cardinals (W)	29	19	318	2	1
10/01/55	Bobby Thomason vs. Redskins (L)	37	25	349	4	0
11/28/54	Adrian Burk vs. Redskins (W)	28	17	345	5	1
12/13/53	Bobby Thomason vs. Browns (W)	35	23	331	3	0
11/15/53	Bobby Thomason vs. Colts (W)	37	18	329	3	5
11/08/53	Bobby Thomason vs. Giants (W)	44	22	437	4	1
12/01/40	Davey O'Brien at Redskins (L)	60	33	316	1	0

RUSHING

Most 100-Yard Rushing Games

26	Wilbert Montgomery
19	Steve Van Buren
13	Duce Staley
12	Ricky Watters
7	Tom Woodeshick
6	Timmy Brown
5	Charlie Garner, Herschel Walker
4	Swede Hanson, Donovan McNabb, Heath Sherman, Tom Sullivan
3	Correll Buckhalter, Randall Cunningham, Earl Gros, Mike Hogan, Earnest Jackson, Frank Ziegler
2	Bill Barnes, Keith Byars, Jack Hinkle, Don Johnson, Bosh Pritchard, Anthony Toney, Brian Westbrook
1	Norm Bulaich, Jack Concannon, Leroy Harris, Izzy Lang, Toy Ledbetter, Herb Lusk, Ollie Matson, Brian Mitchell, Clarence Peaks, Cyril Pinder

Note: Includes playoff games.

100-Yard Rushing Games

Date	Player, Opponent, and Result	Att.	Yds.	LG	TD
10/03/04	Brian Westbrook at Bears (W)	22	119	29	0
9/12/04	Brian Westbrook vs. Giants (W)	17	119	50	0
1/11/04	Donovan McNabb vs. Packers (W)	11	107	41	0
12/07/03	Correll Buckhalter vs. Cowboys (W)	13	115	64t	1
10/26/03	Correll Buckhalter vs. Jets (W)	15	100	21	2
12/08/02	Duce Staley at Seahawks (W)	21	100	21t	1
11/17/02	Duce Staley vs. Cardinals (W)	31	135	13	0
10/28/02	Duce Staley vs. Giants (W)	24	126	23	0
10/28/02	Donovan McNabb vs. Giants (W)	8	107	40t	1
10/20/02	Duce Staley vs. Buccaneers (W)	24	152	57	0
10/06/02	Donovan McNabb at Jaguars (L)	12	100	26	1
11/18/01	Duce Staley at Cowboys (W)	26	102	18	0
11/11/01	Duce Staley vs. Vikings (W)	17	146	44t	1
10/07/01	Correll Buckhalter vs. Cardinals (L)	21	134	37	0
11/26/00	Donovan McNabb at Redskins (W)	11	125	54	1

Date	Player, Opponent, and Result	Att.	Yds.	LG	TD
10/01/00	Brian Mitchell vs. Falcons (W)	2	105	85t	1
9/03/00	Duce Staley at Cowboys (W)	26	201	60	1
11/14/99	Duce Staley vs. Redskins (W)	28	122	20t	1
11/07/99	Duce Staley at Panthers (L)	17	140	29	1
10/17/99	Duce Staley at Bears (W)	23	101	26	0
10/10/99	Duce Staley vs. Cowboys (W)	22	110	19	0
9/12/99	Duce Staley vs. Cardinals (L)	21	111	24t	1
12/13/98	Duce Staley vs. Cardinals (L) OT	30	141	30t	1
11/08/98	Charlie Garner vs. Lions (W)	16	129	40	1
12/21/97	Charlie Garner at Redskins (L)	18	115	26	2
10/05/97	Ricky Watters vs. Redskins (W)	31	104	13	2
9/15/97	Ricky Watters vs. Cowboys (L)	20	106	20	0
12/01/96	Ricky Watters vs. Giants (W)	29	104	11	0
11/03/96	Ricky Watters at Cowboys (W)	24	116	17	1
10/20/96	Ricky Watters vs. Dolphins (W)	25	173	49t	1
10/13/96	Ricky Watters at Giants (W)	27	110	11	0
9/22/96	Ricky Watters at Falcons (W)	26	121	56t	2
9/15/96	Ricky Watters vs. Lions (W)	27	153	52	1
12/10/95	Ricky Watters vs. Cowboys (W)	33	112	15	1
11/26/95	Ricky Watters at Redskins (W)	25	124	25	2
10/15/95	Ricky Watters at Giants (W)	30	122	14	1
10/08/95	Ricky Watters vs. Redskins (W) OT	25	139	24	0
10/08/95	Charlie Garner vs. Redskins (W) OT	9	120	55t	3
10/09/94	Charlie Garner vs. Redskins (W)	28	122	12	0
10/02/94	Charlie Garner at 49ers (W)	16	111	28t	2
1/03/93	Heath Sherman at Saints (W)	21	105	16	1
12/27/92	Herschel Walker vs. Giants (W)	16	104	38	0
12/13/92	Herschel Walker at Seahawks (W) OT	23	111	18	1
12/06/92	Randall Cunningham vs. Vikings (W)	12	121	30	2
11/22/92	Heath Sherman at Giants (W)	17	109	30t	1
10/25/92	Herschel Walker vs. Cardinals (W)	20	112	36	0
9/13/92	Herschel Walker at Cardinals (W)	28	115	20	0
9/06/92	Herschel Walker vs. Saints (W)	26	112	32	0
11/12/90	Heath Sherman vs. Redskins (W)	35	124	22	0
11/04/90	Randall Cunningham vs. Patriots (W)	8	124	52t	1
11/04/90	Heath Sherman vs. Patriots (W)	24	113	17	0
9/23/90	Anthony Toney at Rams (W)	24	103	20	0
12/27/87	Keith Byars vs. Bills (W)	23	102	22	0
11/29/87	Anthony Toney at Patriots (W) OT	24	123	36	1
12/07/86	Keith Byars vs. Cardinals (T) OT	24	127	32	0
11/16/86	Randall Cunningham vs. Lions (L)	14	110	20	0
12/22/85	Earnest Jackson at Vikings (W)	25	106	59	2
11/17/85	Earnest Jackson at Cardinals (W)	34	162	51t	1
10/13/85	Earnest Jackson vs. Cardinals (W)	27	103	13	0
12/09/84	Wilbert Montgomery vs. Patriots (W)	19	100	14	1
12/19/82	Wilbert Montgomery vs. Oilers (W)	17	147	90t	3
12/20/81	Wilbert Montgomery vs. Cardinals (W)	13	108	41	1
12/06/81	Wilbert Montgomery at Redskins (L)	27	116	13	0
11/22/81	Wilbert Montgomery vs. Giants (L)	25	102	24	0
11/15/81	Wilbert Montgomery vs. Colts (W)	22	115	13	2
11/08/81	Wilbert Montgomery at Cardinals (W)	20	118	23	0
10/25/81	Wilbert Montgomery vs. Buccaneers (W)	22	119	12	1
9/17/81	Wilbert Montgomery at Bills (W)	27	125	15	0
9/13/81	Wilbert Montgomery vs. Patriots (W)	18	137	41	0
1/11/81	Wilbert Montgomery vs. Cowboys (W)	26	194	55	1
9/14/80	Wilbert Montgomery at Vikings (W)	20	169	72t	2
12/02/79	Wilbert Montgomery vs. Lions (W)	22	108	20	1
11/25/79	Leroy Harris vs. Packers (W)	9	137	80	0
11/18/79	Wilbert Montgomery vs. Cardinals (W)	26	118	52	0
11/12/79	Wilbert Montgomery at Cowboys (W)	25	127	37t	1
11/04/79	Wilbert Montgomery vs. Browns (L)	30	197	62t	1
10/14/79	Wilbert Montgomery at Cardinals (W)	25	117	13	1
10/07/79	Wilbert Montgomery vs. Redskins (W)	22	127	24	3
9/23/79	Wilbert Montgomery at Giants (W)	29	126	12	1
12/17/78	Wilbert Montgomery vs. Giants (W)	25	130	47	2
12/17/78	Mike Hogan vs. Giants (W)	22	100	18	0
12/03/78	Wilbert Montgomery at Vikings (L)	24	115	36	1
10/15/78	Wilbert Montgomery vs. Redskins (W)	25	125	24	1
10/01/78	Wilbert Montgomery at Colts (W)	25	144	14	1
9/24/78	Wilbert Montgomery vs. Dolphins (W)	25	111	12	0

Date	Player, Opponent, and Result	Att.	Yds.	LG	TD
9/17/78	Wilbert Montgomery at Saints (W)	18	104	19	0
12/18/77	Wilbert Montgomery vs. Jets (W)	22	103	27	2
10/09/77	Herb Lusk at Giants (W)	17	117	70	2
12/12/76	Tom Sullivan vs. Seahawks (W)	23	121	26	2
12/12/76	Mike Hogan vs. Seahawks (W)	19	104	18	0
9/27/76	Mike Hogan vs. Redskins (L) OT	22	100	32	0
11/25/73	Tom Sullivan vs. Giants (W)	32	156	27	1
10/07/73	Tom Sullivan at Bills (L)	26	155	30	0
10/07/73	Norm Bulaich at Bills (L)	13	104	20	0
9/23/73	Tom Sullivan at Giants (T)	18	100	14	1
12/21/69	Cyril Pinder at 49ers (L)	25	128	29	1
12/07/69	Tom Woodeshick vs. Redskins (L)	20	102	21	0
11/16/69	Tom Woodeshick vs. Rams (L)	25	130	21	1
12/08/68	Tom Woodeshick vs. Saints (W)	18	122	30	1
9/22/68	Tom Woodeshick vs. Giants (L)	15	129	54	1
10/29/67	Tom Woodeshick vs. Cowboys (W)	20	101	26	1
10/08/67	Tom Woodeshick at Falcons (W)	20	129	41	1
12/18/66	Tom Woodeshick at Redskins (W)	27	105	21	2
12/04/66	Jack Concannon vs. Steelers (W)	15	129	29	1
10/23/66	Timmy Brown at Giants (W)	21	100	24	0
9/18/66	Izzy Lang vs. Falcons (W)	16	114	39	1
11/28/65	Timmy Brown at Cardinals (W)	18	180	43	1
11/07/65	Timmy Brown at Browns (L)	16	186	54	1
11/22/64	Earl Gros vs. Cardinals (L)	21	103	22	0
11/15/64	Earl Gros at Cowboys (W)	16	118	47	0
10/18/64	Ollie Matson at Giants (W)	19	100	54	2
10/11/64	Timmy Brown at Redskins (L)	14	101	36	2
10/04/64	Timmy Brown vs. Steelers (W)	16	116	33	0
10/04/64	Earl Gros vs. Steelers (W)	19	129	47	0
11/25/62	Timmy Brown vs. Cowboys (W)	17	107	22	2
10/23/60	Clarence Peaks at Browns (W)	13	102	57	0
10/25/59	Bill Barnes vs. Cardinals (W)	23	111	22	2
11/01/59	Bill Barnes vs. Redskins (W)	13	163	61	1
11/29/53	Don Johnson vs. Giants (L)	13	121	63	1
11/15/53	Don Johnson vs. Colts (W)	11	100	66	2
12/02/51	Frank Ziegler at Redskins (W)	20	136	28	0
11/19/50	Frank Ziegler vs. Cardinals (L)	18	113	52	0
11/12/50	Steve Van Buren at Redskins (W)	23	108	23	1
10/15/50	Toy Ledbetter at Colts (W)	23	107	14	1
10/07/50	Frank Ziegler vs. Rams (W)	17	106	38	1
12/18/49	Steve Van Buren at Rams (W)	31	196	49	0
11/27/49	Steve Van Buren vs. Steelers (W)	27	205	41	0
11/20/49	Steve Van Buren vs. NY Bulldogs (W)	35	174	38	2
10/30/49	Steve Van Buren at Steelers (W)	17	103	31	2
10/23/49	Bosh Pritchard vs. Redskins (W)	11	128	77	1
10/03/49	Steve Van Buren at Lions (W)	33	135	12	2
11/21/48	Steve Van Buren vs. Redskins (W)	29	171	21	1
11/14/48	Steve Van Buren vs. Boston Yanks (W)	16	137	28	0
11/07/48	Steve Van Buren at Giants (W)	25	143	20	2
10/31/48	Steve Van Buren at Steelers (W)	22	109	21	1
11/02/47	Steve Van Buren at Redskins (W)	17	138	37	2
10/19/47	Steve Van Buren at Steelers (L)	21	133	45	0
10/05/47	Steve Van Buren vs. Giants (W)	16	105	28	0
11/24/46	Steve Van Buren vs. Redskins (L)	25	130	58	0
12/09/45	Steve Van Buren vs. Boston Yanks (W)	22	100	29	3
12/02/45	Steve Van Buren at Giants (L)	19	100	32	2
11/18/45	Steve Van Buren vs. Steelers (W)	19	107	24	2
11/11/45	Steve Van Buren vs. Giants (W)	19	129	28	2
11/05/44	Steve Van Buren at Dodgers (W)	12	129	70	2
11/28/43	Jack Hinkle at Redskins (W)	26	117	14	1
11/21/43	Jack Hinkle vs. Lions (W)	13	132	56	1
11/15/42	Bosh Pritchard at Dodgers (W)	14	104	26	0
9/13/36	Swede Hanson vs. Giants (W)	15	107	NA	0
11/11/34	Swede Hanson vs. Dodgers (L)	17	118	NA	0
11/06/34	Swede Hanson vs. Reds (W)	18	190	NA	3
9/16/34	Swede Hanson at Packers (L)	13	116	NA	1

RECEIVING

Most 100-Yard Receiving Games

24	Pete Retzlaff
21	Mike Quick
20	Harold Carmichael
17	Tommy McDonald
14	Fred Barnett, Pete Pihos
13	Ben Hawkins, Harold Jackson
10	Irving Fryar, Bobby Walston
8	Timmy Brown, Terrell Owens
6	Keith Byars, Jack Ferrante, Calvin Williams, Charles Young
5	Charles Smith
4	Bud Grant
3	Gary Ballman, Keith Jackson, Don Looney, James Thrash, Todd Pinkston
2	Cris Carter, Joe Carter, Kenny Jackson, Torrance Small, John Spagnola, Herschel Walker, Jerry Williams
1	Bill Barnes, Tony Bova, Kevin Bowman, Norm Bulaich, Howard Cassidy, Antonio Freeman, Otis Grant, Roy Green, Fred Hill, Herman Hunter, Chris T. Jones, James Joseph, Keith Krepfle, Chad Lewis, Red Mack, Lester McDonald, Fred Meyer, Wilbert Montgomery, Don Moselle, Ray Poage, Herschel Ramsey, Clyde Scott, Duce Staley, Bill Stribling, Michael Timpson, Brian Westbrook

Note: Includes playoff games.

150-Yard Receiving Games

Date	Player, Opponent, and Result	Rec.	Yds.	TD
12/05/04	Terrell Owens vs. Packers (W)	8	161	1
12/05/04	Brian Westbrook vs. Packers (W)	11	156	3
9/23/01	James Thrash at Seahawks (W)	10	165	2
11/06/94	Fred Barnett vs. Cardinals (W)	11	173	2
10/24/94	Fred Barnett vs. Oilers (W)	5	187	1
9/19/93	Calvin Williams vs. Redskins (W)	8	181	3
12/13/92	Fred Barnett at Seahawks (W) OT	9	161	0
9/13/92	Fred Barnett at Cardinals (W)	8	193	2
10/10/88	Cris Carter vs. Giants (W)	5	162	1
10/28/84	Mike Quick vs. Cardinals (L)	6	170	1
9/18/83	Mike Quick at Broncos (W)	6	152	1
11/01/81	Harold Carmichael vs. Cowboys (L)	5	151	1
10/14/73	Harold Carmichael at Cardinals (W)	12	187	2
11/26/72	Harold Jackson at Giants (L)	5	152	1
9/17/72	Harold Jackson at Cowboys (L)	9	161	0
10/11/70	Harold Jackson at Giants (L)	7	194	2
12/03/67	Ben Hawkins at Redskins (T)	5	151	2
10/22/67	Ben Hawkins at Cardinals (L)	6	197	1
10/15/67	Ben Hawkins vs. 49ers (L)	6	150	1
10/01/67	Ben Hawkins vs. Steelers (W)	8	187	2
11/14/65	Pete Retzlaff vs. Redskins (W)	7	204	0
11/07/65	Pete Retzlaff at Browns (L)	7	151	3
9/15/63	Tommy McDonald vs. Steelers (T)	7	179	2
12/16/62	Tommy McDonald at Cardinals (L)	4	162	3
12/16/62	Timmy Brown at Cardinals (L)	5	199	2
10/28/62	Timmy Brown at Vikings (L)	5	174	1
9/23/62	Timmy Brown vs. Giants (L)	9	160	1
12/10/61	Tommy McDonald vs. Giants (L)	7	237	0
10/01/61	Tommy McDonald vs. Cardinals (L)	11	187	0
12/06/59	Tommy McDonald at Redskins (W)	9	153	0
11/28/54	Jerry Williams vs. Redskins (W)	6	163	1
10/03/54	Jerry Williams at Cardinals (W)	5	166	1
11/08/53	Bobby Walston vs. Giants (W)	8	176	2
10/25/53	Pete Pihos at Cardinals (W)	8	156	1
12/07/52	Bud Grant vs. Dallas Texans (W)	11	203	2
11/30/52	Bud Grant at Cardinals (L)	8	186	1
12/12/48	Jack Ferrante vs. Lions (W)	7	184	3
12/01/40	Don Looney at Redskins (L)	14	180	0